THOMAS CARLYLE

VOL. I.

THOMAS CARLYLE, 1849.

THOMAS CARLYLE

A HISTORY OF THE FIRST FORTY
YEARS OF HIS LIFE

1795–1835

BY

JAMES ANTHONY FROUDE, M.A.

FORMERLY FELLOW OF EXETER COLLEGE, OXFORD

TWO VOLUMES IN ONE

VOL. I.

MINNESOTA
HISTORICAL SOCIETY

NEW YORK
CHARLES SCRIBNER'S SONS
1882

[*All rights reserved*]

MINNESOTA
HISTORICAL SOCIETY

E45
C28
F9

PREFACE TO THE AMERICAN EDITION.

In submitting to the American people my history of the early life of Thomas Carlyle I attach an extract from Carlyle's diary, which will be read among them with pleasure and perhaps with pride.

"8th February, 1839.

"Yesterday came a letter from Emerson at Concord, New "England, enclosing me a draft for £100, the produce of my "French Revolution there! Already £50 had come; this is "£150 in all; *not a farthing having yet been realized here* "*by our English bibliopoly.* It is very strange, this American "occurrence, very gratifying: nothing more so has oc-"curred in the history of my economics. Thanks to the kind "friends across the salt waters yonder.

"This American cash is so welcome *because* I am so poor. "Had I been rich I could not have had that true pleasure. "Sic de multis; I must own it, bitterly as I often grumble "over my poverty. On the whole I shall rejoice to *have*

"*been* poor if in my old days I be not still persecuted and
" dogged by the spectre of absolute poverty."

The swift recognition which Carlyle obtained
from America, perhaps alone enabled him to go on
with his work at the most critical period of his
career.

The Messrs. Scribner are the authorised American publishers of this book.

J. A. FROUDE.

LONDON, February 28, 1882.

PREFACE.

Mr. Carlyle expressed a desire in his will that of him no biography should be written. I find the same reluctance in his Journal. No one, he said, was likely to understand a history, the secret of which was unknown to his closest friends. He hoped that his wishes would be respected.

Partly to take the place of a biography of himself, and partly for other reasons, he collected the letters of his wife—letters which covered the whole period of his life in London to the date of her death, when his own active work was finished. He prepared them for publication, adding notes and introductory explanations, as the last sacred duty which remained to him in the world. He intended it as a monument to a character of extreme beauty; while it would tell the public as much about himself as it could reasonably expect to learn.

These letters he placed in my hands eleven years ago, with materials for an Introduction which he was himself unable to complete. He could do no more with it, he said. He could not make up his mind to direct positively the publication even of the letters themselves. He wished them to be published, but he left the decision to myself ; and when I was reluctant to undertake the sole responsibility, he said that, if I was in doubt when the time came, I might consult his brother John and his friend Mr. Forster.

Had he rested here, my duty would have been clear. The collection of letters, with the Memoir of Mrs. Carlyle which was to form part of the Introduction, would have been considered among us, and would have been either published or suppressed, as we might jointly determine. Mr. Carlyle's remaining papers would have been sealed up after his death, and by me at least no use would have been made of them.

Two years later, however, soon after he had made his will, Carlyle discovered that, whether he wished it or not, a life, or perhaps various lives, of himself would certainly appear when he was gone. When a man has exercised a large influence on the minds of his contemporaries, the world requires to know whether his own actions have corresponded with his teaching, and whether his moral and personal character entitles him to confidence. This is not idle curiosity ; it is a legitimate demand. In proportion to a man's greatness is the scrutiny to which his conduct is submitted. Byron, Burns, Scott, Shelley, Rousseau,

Voltaire, Goethe, Pope, Swift, are but instances, to which a hundred others might be added, showing that the public will not be satisfied without sifting the history of its men of genius to the last grain of fact which can be ascertained about them. The publicity of their private lives has been, is, and will be, either the reward or the penalty of their intellectual distinction. Carlyle knew that he could not escape. Since a 'Life' of him there would certainly be, he wished it to be as authentic as possible. Besides the Memoir of Mrs. Carlyle, he had written several others, mainly autobiographical, not distinctly to be printed, but with no fixed purpose that they should not be printed. These, with his journals and the whole of his correspondence, he made over to me, with unfettered discretion to use in any way that I might think good.

In the papers thus in my possession, Carlyle's history, external and spiritual, lay out before me as in a map. By recasting the entire material, by selecting chosen passages out of his own and his wife's letters, by exhibiting the fair and beautiful side of the story only, it would have been easy, without suppressing a single material point, to draw a picture of a faultless character. When the Devil's advocate has said his worst against Carlyle, he leaves a figure still of unblemished integrity, purity, loftiness of purpose, and inflexible resolution to do right, as of a man living consciously under his Maker's eye, and with his thoughts fixed on the account which he would have to render of his talents.

Of a person of whom malice must acknowledge so much as this, the prickly aspects might fairly be passed by in silence; and if I had studied my own comfort or the pleasure of my immediate readers, I should have produced a portrait as agreeable, and at least as faithful, as those of the favoured saints in the Catholic calendar. But it would have been a portrait without individuality —an ideal, or, in other words, an 'idol,' to be worshipped one day and thrown away the next. Least of all men could such idealizing be ventured with Carlyle, to whom untruth of any kind was abominable. If he was to be known at all, he chose to be known as he was, with his angulari- ties, his sharp speeches, his special peculiarities, meritorious or unmeritorious, precisely as they had actually been. He has himself laid down the conditions under which a biographer must do his work if he would do it honestly, without the fear of man before him; and in dealing with Carlyle's own memory I have felt myself bound to conform to his own rule. He shall speak for himself. I extract a passage from his review of Lockhart's ' Life of Sir Walter Scott.' [1]

' One thing we hear greatly blamed in Mr. Lockhart, that he has been too communicative, in-

---

[1] *Miscellanies*, vol. v. p. 221 sqq.

discreet, and has recorded much that ought to
have lain suppressed. Persons are mentioned, and
circumstances not always of an ornamental sort.
It would appear that there is far less reticence
than was looked for! Various persons, name and
surname, have "received pain." Nay, the very
hero of the biography is rendered unheroic; unor-
namental facts of him, and of those he had to do
with, being set forth in plain English : hence
"personality," "indiscretion," or worse, "sancti-
ties of private life," &c. How delicate, decent, is
English biography, bless its mealy mouth! A
Damocles' sword of *Respectability* hangs for ever
over the poor English life-writer (as it does over
poor English life in general), and reduces him to
the verge of paralysis. Thus it has been said,
"There are no English lives worth reading, except those of players, who, by the nature of the
case, have bidden respectability good day." The
English biographer has long felt that if in writing
his biography he wrote down anything that could
by possibility offend any man, he had written
wrong. The plain consequence was that, properly
speaking, no biography whatever could be produced. The poor biographer, having the fear *not*
of God before his eyes, was obliged to retire as it
were into vacuum, and write in the most melancholy straitened manner, with only vacuum for a
result. Vain that he wrote, and that we kept
reading volume on volume. There was no biogra-

phy, but some vague ghost of a biography, white,
stainless, without feature or substance ; *vacuum*
as we say, and wind and shadow. . . . Of all the
praises copiously bestowed on Mr. Lockhart's
work there is none in reality so creditable to him
as this same censure which has also been pretty
copious.   It is a censure better than a good many
praises.   He is found guilty of having said this
and that, calculated not to be entirely pleasant to
this man and that ; in other words, calculated to
give him and the thing he worked in a living set
of features, not to leave him vague in the white
beatified ghost condition.   Several men, as we
hear, cry out, "See, there is something written not
entirely pleasant to me !"   Good friend, it is pity ;
but who can help it ?   They that will crowd about
bonfires may sometimes very fairly get their beards
singed ; it is the price they pay for such illumination ; natural twilight is safe and free to all.   For
our part we hope all manner of biographies that
are written in England will henceforth be written
so.   If it is fit that they be written otherwise, then
it is still fitter that they be not written at all.   To
produce not things, but the ghosts of things, can
never be the duty of man. . . . The biographer
has this problem set before him : to delineate a
likeness of the earthly pilgrimage of a man.   He
will compute well what profit is in it, and what
disprofit ; under which latter head this of offend-
ing any of his fellow-creatures will surely not be

forgotten. Nay, this may so swell the disprofit side of his account, that many an enterprise of biography otherwise promising shall require to be renounced. But once taken up, the rule before all rules is to do *it*, not to do the ghost of it. In speaking of the man and men he has to do with, he will of course keep all his charities about him, but all his eyes open. Far be it from him to set down aught *untrue;* nay, not to abstain from, and leave in oblivion, much that is true. But having found a thing or things essential for his subject, and well computed the for and against, he will in very deed set down such thing or things, nothing doubting, *having,* we may say, the fear of God before his eyes, and no other fear whatever. Censure the biographer's prudence; dissent from the computation he made, or agree with it; be all malice of his, be all falsehood, nay be all offensive avoidable inaccuracy condemned and consumed; but know that by this plan only, executed as was possible, could the biographer hope to make a biography; and blame him not that he did what it had been the worst fault not to do. . . . The other censure of Scott being made unheroic springs from the same stem, and is perhaps a still more wonderful flower of it. Your true hero must have no features, but be a white, stainless, impersonal ghost hero! But connected with this, there is an hypothesis now current that Mr. Lockhart at heart has a dislike to Scott, and has done his best in an un-

derhand treacherous manner to dis-hero him!
Such hypothesis is actually current. He that has
ears may hear it now and then—on which astound-
ing hypothesis if a word must be said, it can only
be an apology for silence. If Mr. Lockhart is fairly
chargeable with any radical defect, if on any side
his insight entirely fails him, it seems even to be
in this, that Scott is altogether lovely to him, that
Scott's greatness spreads out before him on all hands
beyond reach of eye, that his very faults become
beautiful, and that of his worth there is no measure.'

I will make no comment on this passage further
than to say that I have considered the principles
here laid down by Carlyle to be strictly obligatory
upon myself in dealing with his own remains.
The free judgments which he passed on men and
things were part of himself, and I have not felt
myself at liberty to suppress them. Remarks
which could injure any man—and very few such
ever fell from Carlyle's lips—I omit, except where
indispensable. Remarks which are merely legitimate expressions of opinion I leave for the most
part as they stand. As an illustration of his own
wishes on this subject, I may mention that I consulted him about a passage in one of Mrs. Carlyle's letters describing an eminent living person.
Her judgment was more just than flattering, and
I doubted the prudence of printing it. Carlyle
merely said, 'It will do him no harm to know
what a sensible woman thought of him.'

As to the biography generally, I found that I could not myself write a formal Life of Carlyle within measurable compass without taking to pieces his own Memoirs and the collection of Mrs. Carlyle's letters; and this I could not think it right to attempt. Mr. Forster and John Carlyle having both died, the responsibility was left entirely to myself. A few weeks before Mrs. Carlyle's death, he asked me what I meant to do. I told him that I proposed to publish the Memoirs as soon as he was gone—those which form the two volumes of the 'Reminiscences.' Afterwards I said that I would publish the letters about which I knew him to be most anxious. He gave his full assent, merely adding that he trusted everything to me. The Memoirs, he thought, had better appear immediately on his departure. He expected that people would then be talking about him, and that it would be well for them to have something authentic to guide them.

These points being determined, the remainder of my task became simplified. Mrs. Carlyle's letters are a better history of the London life of herself and her husband than could be written either by me or by anyone. The connecting narrative is Carlyle's own, and to meddle with his work would be to spoil it. It was thus left to me to supply an account of his early life in Scotland, the greater part of which I had written while he was alive, and which is contained in the present volumes. The publication of the letters will follow at no distant period. Afterwards, if I live to do it, I shall add a brief account of his last years, when I was in constant intercourse with him.

It may be said that I shall have thus produced no 'Life,' but only the materials for a 'Life.' That is true. But I believe that I shall have given, notwithstanding, a real picture as far as it goes; and an adequate estimate of Carlyle's work in this world is not at present possible. He was a teacher and a prophet in the Jewish sense of the word. The prophecies of Isaiah and Jeremiah have become a part of the permanent spiritual inheritance of mankind, because events proved that they had interpreted correctly the signs of their own times, and their prophecies were fulfilled. Carlyle, like them, believed that he had a special message to deliver to the present age. Whether he was correct in that belief, and whether his message was a true message, remains to be seen. He has told us that our most cherished ideas of political liberty, with their kindred corollaries, are mere illusions, and that the progress which has seemed to go along with them is a progress towards anarchy and social dissolution. If he was wrong, he has misused his powers. The principles of his teaching are false. He has offered himself as a guide upon a road of which he had no knowledge; and his own desire for himself would be the speediest oblivion both of his person and his works. If, on the other

hand, he has been right ; if, like his great predecessors, he has read truly the tendencies of this modern age of ours, and his teaching is authenticated
by facts, then Carlyle, too, will take his place among
the inspired seers, and he will shine on, another
fixed star in the intellectual sky.

Time only can show how this will be :

ἀμέραι ἐπίλοιποι μάρτυρες σοφώτατοι.

CONTENTS

OF

THE FIRST VOLUME.

XX   *Contents.*

CONTENTS

OF

THE SECOND VOLUME.

Contents.

LIFE OF

THOMAS CARLYLE.

CHAPTER I.

THE RIVER Annan, rising above Moffat in Hartfell, descends from the mountains through a valley gradually widening and spreading out, as the fells are left behind, into the rich and well-cultivated district known as Annandale. Picturesque and broken in the upper part of its course, the stream, when it reaches the level country, steals slowly among meadows and undulating wooded hills, till at the end of forty miles it falls into the Solway at Annan town. Annandale, famous always for its pasturage, suffered especially before the union of the kingdoms from border forays, the effects of which were long to be traced in a certain wildness of disposition in the inhabitants. Dumfriesshire, to which it belongs, was sternly Cameronian. Stories of the persecutions survived in the farmhouses as their most treasured historical traditions. Cameronian congregations lingered till the beginning of the present century, when they merged in other bodies of seceders from the established religion.

In its hard fight for spiritual freedom Scotch Protestantism lost respect for kings and nobles, and looked to Christ rather than to earthly rulers; but before the Reformation all Scotland was clannish or feudal; and the

Dumfriesshire yeomanry, like the rest, were organised under great noble families, whose pennon they followed, whose name they bore, and the remotest kindred with which, even to a tenth generation, they were proud to claim. Among the families of the western border the Carlyles were not the least distinguished. They were originally English, and were called probably after Carlisle town. They came to Annandale with the Bruces in the time of David the Second. A Sir John Carlyle was created Lord Carlyle of Torthorwald in reward for a beating which he had given the English at Annan. Michael, the fourth lord, signed the Association Bond among the Protestant lords when Queen Mary was sent to Lochleven, being the only one among them, it was observed, who could not write his name. Their work was rough. They were rough men themselves, and with the change of times their importance declined. The title lapsed, the estates were dissipated in lawsuits, and by the middle of the last century nothing remained of the Carlyles but one or two households in the neighbourhood of Burnswark who had inherited the name either through the adoption by their forefathers of the name of their leader, or by some descent of blood which had trickled down through younger sons.[1]

In one of these families, in a house which his father, who was a mason, had built with his own hands, Thomas Carlyle was born on December 4, 1795. Ecclefechan, where his father lived, is a small market town on the east side of Annandale, six miles inland from the Solway, and about sixteen on the great north road from Carlisle.[2] It consists

[1] When Carlyle became famous, a Dumfries antiquary traced his ancestry with apparent success through ten generations to the first Lord Torthorwald. There was much laughter about it in the house in Cheyne Row, but Carlyle was inclined to think on the whole that the descent was real.

[2] The usually received etymology of Ecclefechan is that it is the same as Kirkfechan, Church of St. Fechanus, an Irish saint supposed to have come to Annandale in the seventh century; but Fechan is a not unusual termination in Welsh, and means '*small*,' as in Llanfairfechan.

of a single street, down one side of which, at that time, ran an open brook. The aspect, like that of most Scotch towns, is cold, but clean and orderly, with an air of thrifty comfort. The houses are plain, that in which the Carlyles lived alone having pretensions to originality. In appearance one, it is really double, a central arch dividing it. James Carlyle, Thomas Carlyle's father, occupied one part. His brother, who was his partner in his trade, lived in the other.

Of their ancestors they knew nothing beyond the second generation. Tradition said that they had been long settled as farmers at Burrens, the Roman station at Middlebie (two miles from Ecclefechan). One of them, it was said, had been unjustly hanged on pretext of border cattle-stealing. The case was so cruel that the farm had been given as some compensation to the widow, and the family had continued to possess it till their title was questioned, and they were turned out, by the Duke of Queensberry. Whether this story was true or not, it is certain that James Carlyle's grandmother lived at Middlebie in extreme poverty, and that she died in the early part of the last century, leaving two sons. Thomas, the elder, was a carpenter, worked for some time at Lancaster, came home afterwards, and saw the Highlanders pass through Ecclefechan in 1745 on their way to England. Leaving his trade, he settled at a small farm called Brownknowe, near Burnswark Hill, and, marrying a certain Mary Gillespie, produced four sons and two daughters. Of these sons James Carlyle was the second. The household life was in a high degree disorderly. Old Thomas Carlyle was formed after the border type, more given to fighting and wild adventure than to patient industry. 'He did not drink,' his grandson says, 'but he was a fiery man, irascible, indomitable, of the toughness and springiness of steel. An old market brawl, called Ecclefechan dog-fight, in which he was a principal, survives in tradition to this day.'[1] He was proud, poor, and discontented, leaving his family for the most part to shift for themselves. They were often without food or fuel; his sons were dressed in breeks made mostly of leather.

They had to scramble (Carlyle says), scraffle for their very clothes and food. They knit, they thatched for hire, they hunted. My father tried all these things almost in boyhood. Every dale and burngate and cleugh of that district he had traversed seeking hares and the like. He used to talk of these pilgrimages. Once I remember his gun-flint was tied on with a hatband. He was a real hunter like a wild Indian from necessity. The hare's flesh was food. Hareskins at sixpence each would accumulate into the purchase money of a coat. His hunting years were not useless to him. Misery was early training the rugged boy into a stoic, that one day he might be the assurance of a Scottish man.

'Travelling tinkers,' 'Highland drovers,' and such like were occasional guests at Brownknowe. 'Sandy Macleod, a pensioned soldier who had served under Wolfe, lived in an adjoining cottage, and had stories to tell of his adventures.' Old Thomas Carlyle, notwithstanding his rough, careless ways, was not without cultivation. He studied 'Anson's Voyages,' and in his old age, strange to say, when his sons were growing into young men, he would sit with a neighbour over the fire, reading, much to their scandal, the 'Arabian Nights.' They had become, James Carlyle especially, and his brother through him, serious lads, and they were shocked to see two old men occupied on the edge of the grave with such idle vanities.

Religion had been introduced into the house through another singular figure, John Orr, the schoolmaster of Hoddam, who was also by trade a shoemaker. Schoolmastering in those days fell to persons of clever irregular habits, who took to it from taste partly, and also because

---

[1] This, it should be said, was written fifty years ago.

other forms of business did not answer with them. Orr was a man of strong pious tendencies, but was given to drink. He would disappear for weeks into pothouses, and then come back to his friends shattered and remorseful. He, too, was a friend and visitor at Brownknowe, teaching the boys by day, sleeping in the room with them at night, and discussing arithmetical problems with their father. From him James Carlyle gained such knowledge as he had, part of it a knowledge of the Bible, which became the guiding principle of his life. The effect was soon visible on a remarkable occasion. While he was still a boy, he and three of his companions had met to play cards. There was some disagreement among them, when James Carlyle said that they were fools and worse for quarrelling over a probably sinful amusement. They threw the cards into the fire, and perhaps no one of the four, certainly not James Carlyle, ever touched a card again. Hitherto he and his brother had gleaned a subsistence on the skirts of settled life. They were now to find an entrance into regular occupation. James Carlyle was born in 1757. In 1773, when he was sixteen, a certain William Brown, a mason from Peebles, came into Annandale, became acquainted with the Carlyles, and married Thomas Carlyle's eldest daughter Fanny. He took her brothers as apprentices, and they became known before long as the most skilful and diligent workmen in the neighbourhood. James, though not the eldest, had the strongest character, and guided the rest. 'They were noted for their brotherly affection and coherence.' They all prospered. They were noted also for their hard sayings, and it must be said also, in their early manhood, for 'hard strikings.' They were warmly liked by those near them; 'by those at a distance they were viewed as something dangerous to meddle with, something not to be meddled with.'

James Carlyle never spoke with pleasure of his young

days, regarding them 'as days of folly, perhaps sinful days;' but it was well known that he was strictly temperate, pure, abstemious, prudent, and industrious. Feared he was from his promptness of hand, but never aggressive, and using his strength only to put down rudeness and violence. 'On one occasion,' says Carlyle, 'a huge peasant was rudely insulting and defying the party my father belonged to. The other quailed, and he bore it till he could bear it no longer, but clutched his rough adversary by the two flanks, swung him with ireful force round in the air, hitting his feet against some open door, and hurled him to a distance, supine, lamed, vanquished, and utterly humbled. He would say of such things, "I am wae to think of it "—wae from repentance. Happy he who has nothing worse to repent of!'

The apprenticeship over, the brothers began work on their own account, and with marked success; James Carlyle taking the lead. He built, as has been already said, a house for himself, which still stands in the street of Ecclefechan. His brothers occupied one part of it, he himself the other; and his father, the old Thomas, life now wearing out, came in from Brownknowe to live with them. James, perhaps the others, but James decisively, became an avowedly religious man. He had a maternal uncle, one Robert Brand, whose advice and example influenced him in this matter. Brand was a 'vigorous religionist,' of strict Presbyterian type. From him James Carlyle received a definite faith, and made his profession as a 'Burgher,' a seceding sect which had separated from the Establishment as insufficiently in earnest for them. They had their humble meeting-house, 'thatched with heath;' and for minister a certain John Johnstone, from whom Carlyle himself learned afterwards his first Latin; 'the priestliest man,' he says, 'I ever under any ecclesiastical guise was privileged to look upon.'

This peasant union, this little heath-thatched house, this simple evangelist, together constituted properly the church of that district; they were the blessing and the saving of many; on me too their pious heaven-sent influences still rest and live. There was in those days a 'teacher of the people.' He sleeps not far from my father who built his monument in the Ecclefechan churchyard, the Teacher and the Taught. Blessed, I again say, are the dead that die in the Lord.

In 1791, having then a house of his own, James Carlyle married a distant cousin of the same name, Janet Carlyle. They had one son, John, and then she died of fever. Her long fair hair, which had been cut off in her illness, remained as a memorial of her in a drawer, into which the children afterwards looked with wondering awe. Two years after the husband married again Margaret Aitken, ' a woman,' says Carlyle, ' of to me the fairest descent, that of the pious, the just, and the wise.' Her character will unfold itself as the story goes on. Thomas Carlyle was her first child, born December 4, 1795; she lived to see him at the height of his fame, known and honoured wherever the English language was spoken. To her care 'for body and soul' he never ceased to say that 'he owed endless gratitude.' After Thomas came eight others, three sons and five daughters, one of whom, *Janet*, so called after the first wife, died when she was a few months old.

The family was prosperous, as Ecclefechan working life understood prosperity. In one year, his best, James Carlyle made in his business as much as 100*l*. At worst he earned an artisan's substantial wages, and was thrifty and prudent. The children, as they passed out of infancy, ran about barefoot, but were otherwise cleanly clothed, and fed on oatmeal, milk, and potatoes. Our Carlyle learned to read from his mother too early for distinct remembrance; when he was five his father taught him arithmetic, and sent him with the other village boys to school. Like the Carlyles generally he had a violent temper. John, the son of the first marriage, lived usually with his grand-father, but came occasionally to visit his parents. Carlyle's earliest recollection is of throwing his little brown stool at his brother in a mad passion of rage, when he was scarcely more than two years old, breaking a leg of it, and 'feeling for the first time the united pangs of loss and remorse.' The next impression which most affected him was the small round heap under the sheet upon a bed where his little sister lay dead. Death, too, he made acquaintance with in another memorable form. His father's eldest brother John died. 'The day before his funeral, an ill-behaving ser-vant wench lifted the coverlid from off his pale ghastly befilleted head to show it to some crony of hers, unheeding of the child who was alone with them, and to whom the sight gave a new pang of horror.' The grandfather fol-lowed next, closing finally his Anson and his 'Arabian Nights.' He had a brother whose adventures had been remarkable. Francis Carlyle, so he was called, had been apprenticed to a shoemaker. He, too, when his time was out, had gone to England, to Bristol among other places, where he fell into drink and gambling. He lost all his money; one morning after an orgie he flung himself des-perately out of bed and broke his leg. When he recov-ered he enlisted in a brig of war, distinguished himself by special gallantry in supporting his captain in a mutiny, and was rewarded with the command of a Solway revenue cutter. After many years of rough creditable service he retired on half-pay to his native village of Middlebie. There had been some family quarrel, and the brothers, though living close to one another, had held no intercourse. They were both of them above eighty years of age. The old Thomas being on his death-bed, the sea captain's heart relented. He was a grim, broad, fierce-looking man; 'pro-totype of Smollett's Trunnion.' Being too unwiedly to walk, he was brought into Ecclefechan in a cart, and carried in a chair up the steep stairs to his dying brother's room. There he remained some twenty minutes, and came down again with a face which printed itself in the little Carlyle's memory. They saw him no more, and after a brief interval the old generation had disappeared.

Amidst such scenes our Carlyle struggled through his early boyhood.

It was not a joyful life (he says); what life is? yet a safe and quiet one, above most others, or any other I have witnessed, a wholesome one. We were taciturn rather than talkative, but if little was said that little had generally a meaning.

More remarkable man than my father I have never met in my journey through life; sterling sincerity in thought, word, and deed, most quiet, but capable of blazing into whirlwinds when needful, and such a flash of just insight and brief natural eloquence and emphasis, true to every feature of it as I have never known in any other. Humour of a most grim Scandinavian type he occasionally had; wit rarely or never—too serious for wit—my excellent mother with perhaps the deeper piety in most senses had also the most sport. No man of my day, or hardly any man, can have had better parents.

The Sunday services in Mr. Johnstone's meeting-house were the events of the week. The congregation were 'Dissenters' of a marked type, some of them coming from as far as Carlisle; another party, and among these at times a little eager boy, known afterwards as Edward Irving, appearing regularly from Annan, 'their streaming plaids in wet weather hanging up to drip.'

A man (Carlyle wrote in 1866) who in those days awoke to the belief that he actually had a soul to be saved or lost was apt to be found among the Dissenting people and to have given up attendance at Kirk. All dissent in Scotland is merely stricter adherence to the Church of the Reformation. Very venerable are those old Seceder clergy to me now when I look back. . . . Most figures of them in my time were hoary old men; men so like evangelists in modern vesture and poor scholars and gentlemen of Christ I have nowhere met with among Protestant or Papal clergy in any country in the world. . . . That poor temple of my childhood is more sacred to me than the biggest cathedral then extant could have been; rude, rustic, bare, no temple in the world was more so; but there were sacred lambencies, tongues of authentic flame which kindled what was best in one, what has not yet gone out. Strangely vivid are some twelve or twenty of those old faces whom I used to see every Sunday, whose names, employments or precise dwelling places I never knew, but whose portraits are yet clear to me as in a mirror.

Their heavy-laden, patient, ever attentive faces, fallen solitary most of them, children all away, wife away forever, or, it might be, wife still there and constant like a shadow and grown very like the old man, the thrifty cleanly poverty of these good people, their well saved coarse old clothes, tailed waistcoats down to mid-thigh—all this I occasionally see as with eyes sixty or sixty-five years off, and hear the very voice of my mother upon it, whom sometimes I would be questioning about these persons of the drama and endeavoring to describe and identify them.

Of one of these worshippers in the Ecclefechan meeting-house, 'tall, straight, very clean always, brown as mahogany, with a beard white as snow,' Carlyle tells the following anecdote :—

Old David Hope [that was his name] lived on a little farm close by Solway shore, a mile or two east of Annan—a wet country with late harvests which are sometimes incredibly difficult to save,—ten days continuously pouring, then a day, perhaps two days, of drought, part of them, it may be, of high roaring wind; during which the moments are golden for you, and perhaps you had better work all night as presently there will be deluges again. David's stuff, one such morning, was all standing dry, ready to be saved still if he stood to it, which was very much his intention. Breakfast, wholesome hasty porridge, was soon over, and next in course came family worship, what they call taking the book, *i.e.* taking your Bible, psalm and chapter always part of the service. David was putting on his spectacles when somebody rushed in. 'Such a raging wind risen will drive the stooks (shocks) into the sea if let alone.' 'Wind!' answered David. 'Wind canna get ae straw that has been appointed mine. Sit down and let us worship God.'

CHAPTER II.

EDUCATION is a passion in Scotland. It is the pride of
every honourable peasant, if he has a son of any promise,
to give him a chance of rising as a scholar. As a child
Carlyle could not have failed to show that there was something unusual in him. The schoolmaster in Ecclefechan
gave a good account of his progress in 'figures.' The
minister reported favourably of his Latin. 'I do not
grudge thee thy schooling, Tom,' his father said to him
one day, 'now that thy uncle Frank owns thee a better
arithmetician than himself.' It was decided that he
should go to Annan Grammar School, and thence, if he
prospered, to the University, with final outlook to the
ministry.

He was a shy thoughtful boy, shrinking generally from
rough companions, but with the hot temper of his race.
His mother, naturally anxious for him, and fearing perhaps the family tendency, extracted a promise before parting with him that he would never return a blow, and, as
might be expected, his first experiences of school were
extremely miserable. Boys of genius are never well received by the common flock, and escape persecution only
when they are able to defend themselves.

'Sartor Resartus' is generally mythic, but parts are
historical, and among them the account of the first launch
of Teufelsdröckh into the Hinterschlag Gymnasium.
Hinterschlag (smite behind) is Annan. Thither, leaving

home and his mother's side, Carlyle was taken by his father, being then in his tenth year, and ' fluttering with boundless hopes,' at Whitsuntide, 1805, to the school which was to be his first step into a higher life.

Well do I remember (says Teufelsdröckh) the red sunny Whit-suntide morning when, trotting full of hope by the side of Father Andreas, I entered the main street of the place and saw its steeple clock (then striking eight) and Schuldthurm (jail) and the aproned or disaproned Burghers moving in to breakfast ; a little dog, in mad terror, was rushing past, for some human imps had tied a tin kettle to its tail, fit emblem of much that awaited myself in that mischievous den. Alas ! the kind beech rows of Entepfuhl (Ecclefechan) were hidden in the distance. I was among strangers harshly, at best indifferently, disposed to me ; the young heart felt for the first time quite orphaned and alone. . . . My school-fellows were boys, mostly rude boys, and obeyed the impulse of rude nature which bids the deer-herd fall upon any stricken hart, the duck-flock put to death any broken-winged brother or sister, and on all hands the strong tyrannise over the weak.

Carlyle retained to the end of his days a painful and indeed resentful recollection of these school experiences of his. ' This,' he said of the passage just quoted from ' Sartor,' ' is true, and not half the truth.'

He had obeyed his mother's injunctions. He had courage in plenty to resent ill usage, but his promise was sacred. He was passionate, and often, probably, violent, but fight he would not, and everyone who knows English and Scotch life will understand what his fate must have been. One consequence was a near escape from drowning. The boys had all gone to bathe; the lonely child had stolen apart from the rest, where he could escape from being tormented. He found himself in a deep pool which had been dug out for a dock and had been filled with the tide. The mere accident of someone passing at the time saved him. At length he could bear his condition no longer; he turned on the biggest bully in the school and furiously kicked him; a battle followed in which he was beaten; but he left marks of his fists upon his adversary, which were not forgotten. He taught his companions to fear him, if only like Brasidas's mouse. He was persecuted no longer, but he carried away bitter and resentful recollections of what he had borne, which were never entirely obliterated.

The teaching which Carlyle received at Annan, he says, ' was limited, and of its kind only moderately good. Latin and French I did get to read with fluency. Latin quantity was left a frightful chaos, and I had to learn it afterwards; some geometry. Algebra, arithmetic tolerably well. Vague outlines of geography I learnt; all the books I could get were also devoured. Greek consisted of the alphabet merely.'

Elsewhere in a note I find the following account of his first teaching and school experience :—

My mother (writes Carlyle, in a series of brief notes upon his early life) had taught me reading. I never remember when. Tom Donaldson's school at Ecclefechan—a severely-correct kind of man Tom . . . from Edinburgh—went afterwards to Manchester; I never saw his face again, though I still remember it well as always merry and kind to me, though to the undeserving severe. The school then stood at Hoddam Kirk. Sandie Beattie, subsequently a Burgher minister at Glasgow, I well remember examining me. He reported me complete in English, age then about seven . . . that I must go to Latin or waste my time. Latin accordingly, with what enthusiasm! But the schoolmaster did not himself know Latin. I gradually got altogether swamped and bewildered under him. Reverend Mr. Johnstone, of Ecclefechan, or rather first his son, home from college, and already teaching a nephew or a cousin, had to take me in hand, and once pulled afloat I made rapid and sure way.

In my tenth year I was sent to the grammar school at Annan. May 26, a bright sunny morning—Whit-Monday—which I still vividly remember, I trotting at my father's side in the way alluded

to in 'Sartor.' It was a bright morning, and to me full of moment—of fluttering, boundless hopes, saddened by parting with
mother, with home, and which afterwards were cruelly disappointed.

'Sartor' is not to be trusted in details. Greek consisted of the
Alphabet mainly. Hebrew is a German entity.[1] Nobody in that
region except old Mr. Johnstone could have read a sentence of it
to save his life. I did get to read Latin and French with fluency
—Latin quantity was left a frightful chaos, and I had to learn it
afterwards. Some geometry, algebra, arithmetic thoroughly well,
vague outlines of geography, I did learn; all the books I could
get were also devoured. Mythically true is what 'Sartor' says of
my schoolfellows, and not half the truth. Unspeakable is the
damage and defilement I got out of those coarse unguided
tyrannous cubs, especially till I revolted against them and gave
stroke for stroke, as my pious mother, in her great love of peace
and of my best interests, spiritually chiefly, had imprudently forbidden me to do. One way and another I had never been so
wretched as here in that school, and the first two years of my
time in it still count among the miserable of my life. Academia!
High School Instructors of Youth! Oh, ye unspeakable!

Of holidays we hear nothing, though holidays there
must have been at Christmas and Midsummer; little also
of school friendships or amusements. For the last, in
such shape as could have been found in boys of his class
in Annan, Carlyle could have had little interest. He
speaks warmly of his mathematical teacher, a certain Mr.
Morley, from Cumberland, 'whom he loved much, and
who taught him well.' He had formed a comradeship
with one or two boys of his own age, who were not entirely uncongenial to him; but only one incident is preserved which was of real moment. In his third school
year Carlyle first consciously saw Edward Irving. Irving's family lived in Annan. He had himself been at
the school, and had gone thence to the University of Edin-

---

[1] Alluding to a German biography in which he was said to have learnt
Hebrew.

burgh. He had distinguished himself there, gained prizes, and was otherwise honourably spoken of. Annan, both town and school, was proud of the brilliant lad that they had produced. And Irving one day looked in upon the class room, the masters out of compliment attending him. ' He was scrupulously dressed, black coat, tight pantaloons, in the fashion of the day, and looked very neat, self-possessed, and amiable; a flourishing slip of a youth with coal-black hair, swarthy clear complexion, very straight on his feet, and, except for the glaring squint, decidedly handsome.' The boys listened eagerly as he talked in a free airy way about Edinburgh and its professors. A University man who has made a name for himself is infinitely admirable to younger ones ; he is not too far above them to be comprehensible. They know what he has done, and they hope distantly that they too one day may do the like. Of course Irving did not distinguish Carlyle. He walked through the rooms and disappeared.

The Hinterschlag Gymnasium was over soon after, and Carlyle's future career was now to be decided on. The Ecclefechan family life was not favourable to displays of precocious genius. Vanity was the last quality that such a man as James Carlyle would encourage, and there was a severity in his manner which effectively repressed any disposition to it.

We had all to complain (Carlyle says) that we dared not freely love our father. His heart seemed as if walled in. My mother has owned to me that she could never understand him, and that her affection and admiration of him were obstructed. It seemed as if an atmosphere of fear repelled us from him, me especially. My heart and tongue played freely with my mother. He had an air of deepest gravity and even sternness. He had the most entire and open contempt for idle tattle—what he called clatter. Any talk that had meaning in it he could listen to ; what had no meaning in it, above all what seemed false, he absolutely could not and would not hear, but abruptly turned from it. Long may we remember his 'I don't believe thee;' his tongue-paralysing cold in-different 'Hah.'

Besides fear, Carlyle, as he grew older, began to experi-ence a certain awe of his father as of a person of alto-gether superior qualities.

None of us (he writes) will ever forget that bold glowing style of his, flowing free from the untutored soul, full of metaphor, though he knew not what metaphor was, with all manner of potent words which he appropriated and applied with surprising accuracy— brief, energetic, conveying the most perfect picture, definite, clear, not in ambitious colours, but in full white sunlight. Emphatic I have heard him beyond all men. In anger he had no need of oaths; his words were like sharp arrows that smote into the very heart.

Such a father may easily have been alarming and slow to gain his children's confidence. He had silently observed his little Tom, however. The reports from the Annan masters were all favourable, and when the question rose what was to be done with him, he inclined to venture the University. The wise men of Ecclefechan shook their heads. 'Educate a boy,' said one of them, ' and he grows up to despise his ignorant parents.' Others said it was a risk, it was waste of money, there was a large family to be provided for, too much must not be spent upon one, &c. James Carlyle had seen something in his boy's character which showed him that the risk, if risk there was, must be encountered; and to Edinburgh it was decided that Tom should go and be made a scholar of.

To English ears university life suggests splendid build-ings, luxurious rooms, rich endowments as the reward of successful industry; as students, young men between nine-teen and twenty-three with handsome allowances, spend-ing each of them on an average double the largest income which James Carlyle had earned in any year of his life.

Universities north of the Tweed had in those days no money prizes to offer, no fellowships and scholarships, nothing at all but an education, and a discipline in poverty and self-denial. The lads who went to them were the children, most of them, of parents as poor as Carlyle's father. They knew at what a cost the expense of sending them to college, relatively small as it was, could be afforded; and they went with the fixed purpose of making the very utmost of their time. Five months only of each year they could remain in their classes; for the rest of it they taught pupils themselves, or worked on the farm at home to pay for their own learning.

Each student, as a rule, was the most promising member of the family to which he belonged, and extraordinary confidence was placed in them. They were sent to Edinburgh, Glasgow, or wherever it might be, when they were mere boys of fourteen. They had no one to look after them either on their journey or when they came to the end. They walked from their homes, being unable to pay for coach-hire. They entered their own names at the college. They found their own humble lodgings, and were left entirely to their own capacity for self-conduct. The carriers brought them oatmeal, potatoes, and salt butter from the home farm, with a few eggs occasionally as a luxury. With their thrifty habits they required no other food. In the return cart their linen went back to their mothers to be washed and mended. Poverty protected them from temptations to vicious amusements. They formed their economical friendships; they shared their breakfasts and their thoughts, and had their clubs for conversation or discussion. When term was over they walked home in parties, each district having its little knot belonging to it; and known along the roads as University scholars, they were assured of entertainment on the way.

As a training in self-dependence no better education

could have been found in these islands. If the teaching had been as good as the discipline of character, the Scotch universities might have competed with the world. The teaching was the weak part. There were no funds, either in the colleges or with the students, to provide personal instruction as at Oxford and Cambridge. The professors were individually excellent, but they had to teach large classes, and had no leisure to attend particularly to this or that promising pupil. The universities were opportunities to boys who were able to take advantage of them, and that was all.

Such was the life on which Carlyle was now to enter, and such were the circumstances of it. It was the November term 1809. He was to be fourteen on the fourth of the approaching December. Edinburgh is nearly one hundred miles from Ecclefechan. He was to go on foot like the rest, under the guardianship of a boy named 'Tom Smail,' two or three years his senior, who had already been at college, and was held, therefore, to be a sufficient protector.

How strangely vivid (he says in 1866), how remote and wonderful, tinged with the hues of far-off love and sadness, is that journey to me now after fifty-seven years of time! My mother and father walking with me in the dark frosty November morning through the village to set us on our way; my dear and loving mother, her tremulous affection, my &c.

'Tom Smail' was a poor companion, very innocent, very conceited, an indifferent scholar. Carlyle in his own mind had a small opinion of him. The journey over the moors was a weary one, the elder lad stalking on generally ahead, whistling an Irish tune; the younger 'given up to his bits of reflections in the silence of the hills.' Twenty miles a day the boys walked, by Moffat and over Airock Stane. They reached Edinburgh early one afternoon, got

a lodging in Simon Square, got dinner, and sallied out
again that 'Palinurus Tom' might give the novice a
glance of the great city. The scene so entirely new to
him left an impression on Carlyle which remained distinct
after more than half a century.

The novice mind (he says) was not excessively astonished all at
once, but kept its eyes open and said nothing. What streets we
went through I don't the least recollect, but have some faint
image of St. Giles's High Kirk, and of the Lucken booths there
with their strange little ins and outs and eager old women in
miniature shops, of combs, shoe-laces, and trifles; still fainter
image, if any, of the sublime horse statue in Parliament Square
hard by; directly after which Smail, audaciously, so I thought,
pushed open a door free to all the world and dragged me in with
him to a scene which I have never forgotten. An immense hall
dimly lighted from the top of the walls, and perhaps with candles
burning in it here and there, all in strange chiaroscuro, and filled
with what I thought exaggeratively a thousand or two of human
creatures, all astir in a boundless buzz of talk, and simmering
about in every direction—some solitary, some in groups. By degrees I noticed that some were in wig and black gown, some not,
but in common clothes, all well-dressed; that here and there on
the sides of the hall were little thrones with enclosures and steps
leading up, red velvet figures sitting in said thrones, and the
black-gowned eagerly speaking to them; advocates pleading to
judges as I easily understood. How they could be heard in such
a grinding din was somewhat a mystery. Higher up on the walls,
stuck there like swallows in their nests, sate other humbler figures; these I found were the sources of certain wildly plangent
lamentable kinds of sounds, or echoes, which from time to time
pierced the universal noise of feet and voices, and rose unintelli-
gibly above it as in the bitterness of incurable woe : criers of the
court I gradually came to understand. And this was Themis in
her 'outer house;' such a scene of chaotic din and hurly-burly as
I had never figured before. It seems to me that there were four
times or ten times as many people in that 'outer house' as there
now usually are; and doubtless there is something of fact in this,
such have been the curtailments and abatements of law practice
in the head courts since then, and transference of it to county

jurisdiction. Last time I was in that outer house (some six or seven years ago in broad daylight) it seemed like a place fallen asleep, fallen almost dead.

Notable figures, now all vanished utterly, were doubtless wandering about as part of that continual hurly-burly when I first set foot in it fifty-seven years ago; great law lords this and that, great advocates *alors célèbres*, as Thiers has it. Cranstoun, Cockburn, Jeffrey, Walter Scott, John Clark. To me at that time they were not even names; but I have since occasionally thought of that night and place where probably they were living substances— some of them in a kind of relation to me afterwards. Time with his *tenses*—what a wonderful entity is he always! The only figure I distinctly recollect and got printed on my brain that night was John Clark, there veritably hitching about, whose grim strong countenance with its black far-projecting brows, and look of great sagacity, fixed him in my memory.

This scene alone remains recorded of Carlyle's early Edinburgh experience. Of the University he says that he learned little there. In the Latin class he was under Professor Christieson, who 'never noticed him nor could distinguish him from another Mr. Irving Carlyle, an older, bigger boy, with red hair, wild buck teeth, and scorched complexion, and the worst Latinist of his acquaintance.'

In the classical field (he writes elsewhere) I am truly as nothing. Homer I learnt to read in the original with difficulty, after Wolf's broad flash of light thrown into it; Æschylus and Sophocles mainly in translations. Tacitus and Virgil became really interesting to me; Homer and Æschylus above all; Horace egoistical, *leichtfertig*, in sad fact I never cared for; Cicero, after long and various trials, always proved a windy person and a weariness to me, extinguished altogether by Middleton's excellent though misjudging life of him.

It was not much better with philosophy. Dugald Stewart had gone away two years before Carlyle entered. Brown was the new professor, 'an eloquent acute little gentleman, full of enthusiasm about simple suggestions,

relative, &c.,' unprofitable utterly to Carlyle, and bewilder-
ing and dispiriting, as the autumn winds among withered
leaves.

In mathematics only he made real progress. His temperament was impatient of uncertainties. He threw himself with delight into a form of knowledge in which the
conclusions were indisputable, where at each step he could
plant his foot with confidence. Professor Leslie (Sir John
Leslie afterwards) discovered his talent and exerted himself to help him with a zeal of which Carlyle never afterwards ceased to speak with gratitude. That he made
progress in mathematics was 'perhaps,' as he says,

due mainly to the accident that Leslie alone of my Professors had
some genius in his business, and awoke a certain enthusiasm in
me. For several years geometry shone before me as the noblest
of all sciences, and I prosecuted it in all my best hours and
moods. But far more pregnant inquiries were rising in me, and
gradually engrossing me, heart as well as head, so that about 1820
or 1821 I had entirely thrown mathematics aside, and except in
one or two brief spurts, more or less of a morbid nature, have
never in the least regarded it further.

Yet even in mathematics, on ground with which he was
familiar, his shy nature was unfitted for display. He carried off no prizes. He tried only once, and though he
was notoriously superior to all his competitors the crowd
and noise of the class room prevented him from even attempting to distinguish himself. I have heard him say
late in life that his thoughts never came to him in proper
form except when he was alone.

'Sartor Resartus,' I have already said, must not be followed too literally as a biographical authority. It is
mythic, not historical. Nevertheless, as mythic it may be
trusted for the general outlines.

The university where I was educated (says Teufelsdröckh) still
stands vivid enough in my remembrance, and I know its name

well, which name, however, I from tenderness to existing interests
shall in no wise divulge.   It is my painful duty to say that out of
England and Spain ours was the worst of all hitherto discovered
universities.   This is indeed a time when right education is, as
nearly as may be, impossible; however in degrees of wrongness
there is no limit; nay, I can conceive a worse system than that of
the Nameless itself, as poisoned victual may be worse than absolute hunger.

It is written, when the blind lead the blind, both shall fall into
the ditch.   Wherefore in such circumstances may it not sometimes be safer if both leader and led simply—sit still ?   Had you
anywhere in Crim Tartary walled in a square enclosure, furnished it
with a small ill-chosen library, and then turned loose into it eleven
hundred Christian striplings, to tumble about as they listed from
three to seven years ; certain persons under the title of professors
being stationed at the gates to declare aloud that it was a university and exact considerable admission fees, you had, not indeed
in mechanical structure, yet in spirit and result, some imperfect
substance of our High Seminary. . . .   The professors in the
Nameless lived with ease, with safety, by a mere reputation constructed in past times—and then, too, with no great effort—by
quite another class of persons; which reputation, like a strong
brisk-going undershot wheel sunk into the general current, bade
fair, with only a little annual repainting on their part, to hold long
together, and of its own accord assiduously grind for them.
Happy that it was so for the millers !   They themselves needed
not to work.   Their attempts at working, what they called educat-
ing, now when I look back on it fill me with a certain mute admiration. . . .

Besides all this we boasted ourselves a rational university, in
the highest degree hostile to mysticism.   Thus was the young
vacant mind furnished with much talk about progress of the
species, dark ages, prejudice and the like, so that all were quickly
blown out into a state of windy argumentativeness, whereby the
better sort had soon to end in sick impotent scepticism ; the
worser sort explode in finished self-conceit, and to all spiritual
interests become dead. . . .   The hungry young looked up to
their spiritual nurses, and for food were bidden eat the east wind.
What vain jargon of controversial metaphysics, etymology, and
mechanical manipulation falsely named Science was current there,
I indeed learnt better than perhaps the most.   Among eleven

hundred Christian youths there will not be wanting some eleven eager to learn. By collision with such, a certain warmth, a certain polish was communicated; by instinct and by happy accident I took less to rioting than to thinking and reading, which latter also I was free to do. Nay, from the Chaos of that library I succeeded in fishing up more books than had been known to the keeper thereof. The foundation of a literary life was hereby laid. I learned on my own strength to read fluently in almost all cultivated languages, on almost all subjects and sciences. A certain ground-plan of human nature and life began to fashion itself in me, by additional experiments to be corrected and indefinitely extended.[1]

The teaching at a university is but half what is learned there; the other half, and the most important, is what young men learn from one another. Carlyle's friends at Edinburgh, the eleven out of the eleven hundred, were of his own rank of life, sons of peasants who had their own way to make in life. From their letters, many of which have been preserved, it is clear that they were clever good lads, distinctly superior to ordinary boys of their age, Carlyle himself holding the first place in their narrow circle. Their lives were pure and simple. Nowhere in these letters is there any jesting with vice, or light allusions to it. The boys wrote to one another on the last novel of Scott or poem of Byron, on the 'Edinburgh Review,' on the war, on the fall of Napoleon, occasionally on geometrical problems, sermons, college exercises, and divinity lectures, and again on innocent trifles, with sketches, now and then humorous and bright, of Annandale life as it was seventy years ago. They looked to Carlyle to direct their judgment and advise them in difficulties. He was the prudent one of the party, able, if money matters went wrong, to help them out of his humble savings. He was already noted, too, for power of effective speech—'far too sarcastic for so young a man' was what elder people said of him.

---

[1] *Sartor Resartus*, book ii. chap. iii.

One of his correspondents addressed him always as 'Jonathan,' or 'Dean,' or 'Doctor,' as if he was to be a second Swift. Others called him Parson, perhaps from his intended profession. All foretold future greatness to him of one kind or another. They recognised that he was not like other young men, that he was superior to other young men, in character as well as intellect. ' Knowing how you abhor all affectation ' is an expression used to him when he was still a mere boy.

His destination was ' the ministry,' and for this, knowing how much his father and mother wished it, he tried to prepare himself. He was already conscious, however, 'that he had not the least enthusiasm for that business, that even grave prohibitory doubts were gradually rising ahead. Formalism was not the pinching point, had there been the preliminary of belief forthcoming.' 'No church or speaking entity whatever,' he admitted, 'can do without formulas, but it must *believe* them first if it would be honest.'

Two letters to Carlyle from one of these early friends may be given here as specimens of the rest. They bring back the Annandale of 1814, and show a faint kind of image of Carlyle himself reflected on the writer's mind. His name was Hill. He was about Carlyle's age, and subscribes himself Peter Pindar.

To Thomas Carlyle.

Castlebank : January 1, 1814.
Wind SW. Weather hazy.

What is the life of man? Is it not to shift from trouble to trouble and from side to side? to button up one cause of vexation and unbutton another? So wrote the celebrated Sterne, so quoted the no less celebrated Jonathan, and so may the poor devil Pindar apply it to himself. You mention some two or three disappointments you have met with lately. For shame, Sir, to be so peevish and splenetic! Your disappointments are 'trifles light as air' when compared with the vexations and disappointments I have

experienced. I was vexed and grieved to the very soul and beyond the soul, to go to Galloway and be deprived of the pleasure
of—something you know nothing about. I was disappointed on
my return at finding *her* in a devil of a bad shy humour. I was—
but why do I talk to *you* about such things? There are joys and
sorrows, pleasures and pains, with which a Stoic Platonic hum-
drum bookworm sort of fellow like you, Sir, intermeddleth not, and
consequently can have no idea of. I was disappointed in Bona-
parte's escaping to Paris when he ought to have been taken prisoner by the allies at Leipsic. I was disappointed at your not men-
tioning anything about our old acquaintances at Edinburgh. Last
night there was a flag on the mail, and to-night when I expected
a Gazette announcing some great victory, the taking of Bayonne
or the marching of Wellington to Bordeaux, I was disappointed
that the cause of all the rejoicing was an engagement with the
French under the walls of Bayonne, in which we lost upwards of
500 men killed and 3,000 wounded, and drew off the remainder of
our army safe from the destroying weapons of the enemy. I was
disappointed last Sunday, after I had got my stockings on, to find
that there was a hole in the heel of one of them. I read a great
many books at Kirkton, and was disappointed at finding faults in
almost every one of them. I will be disappointed; but what sig-
nifies going on at this rate? Unmixed happiness is not the lot
of man—

> Of chance and change, oh! let not man complain,
> Else never, never, will he cease to wail.

The weather is dull; I am melancholy. Good night.

P.S.—My dearest Dean,—The weather is quite altered. The
wind has veered about to the north. I am in good spirits, am
happy.

From the Same.

Castlebank : May 9.

Dear Doctor,—I received yours last night, and a scurrilous,
blackguarding, flattering, vexing, pernicked, humorous, witty,
daft letter it is. Shall I answer it piecemeal as a certain Honourable House does a speech from its Sovereign, by echoing back
each syllable? No. This won't do. Oh! how I envy you, Dean,
that you can run on in such an offhand way, ever varying the
scene with wit and mirth, while honest Peter must hold on in one
numskull track to all eternity pursuing the even tenour of his
way, so that one of Peter's letters is as good as a thousand.

You seem to take a friendly concern in my *affaires de cœur*. By the bye, now, Jonathan, without telling you any particulars of my situation in these matters, which is scarcely known to myself, can't I advise *you* to fall in love? Granting as I do that it is attended with sorrows, still, Doctor, these are amply compensated by the tendency that this tender passion has to ameliorate the heart, 'provided always, and be it further enacted,' that, chaste as Don Quixote or Don Quixote's horse, your heart never breathes a wish that angels may not register. Only have care of this, Dean, and fall in love as soon as you can—you will be the better for it.

Pages follow of excellent criticism from Peter on Leyden's poems, on the Duke of Wellington, Miss Porter, &c. Carlyle has told him that he was looking for a subject for an epic poem. Peter gives him a tragi-comic description of a wedding at Middlebie, with the return home in a tempest, which he thinks will answer ; and concludes :—

Your reflections on the fall of Napoleon bring to my mind an observation of a friend of mine the other day. I was repeating these lines in Shakespeare and applying them to Bony—

> But yesterday the word of Cæsar might
> Have stood against the world ; now lies he there,
> And none so poor to do him reverence.

'Ay, very true,' quoth he ; 'the fallow could na be content wi' maist all Europe, and now he's glad o' Elba room.'

Now, Doctor, let me repeat my instructions to you in a few words. Write immediately a very long letter ; write an epic poem as soon as may be. Send me some more 'remarks.' Tell me how you are, how you are spending your time in Edinburgh. Fall in love as soon as you can meet with a proper object. Ever be a friend to Pindar, and thou shalt always find one in the heart subdued, not subduing.

PETER.

In default of writings of his own, none of which survive out of this early period, such lineaments of Carlyle as appear through these letters are not without instructiveness.

CHAPTER III.

HAVING finished his college course, Carlyle looked out for
pupils to maintain himself. The ministry was still his
formal destination, but several years had still to elapse
before a final resolution would be necessary—four years if
he remained in Edinburgh attending lectures in the Divinity Hall; six if he preferred to be a rural Divinity student, presenting himself once in every twelve months at
the University and reading a discourse. He did not wish
to hasten matters, and, the pupil business being precarious
and the mathematical tutorship at Annan falling vacant,
Carlyle offered for it and was elected by competition in
1814. He never liked teaching. The recommendation of
the place was the sixty or seventy pounds a year of salary,
which relieved his father of further expense upon him,
and enabled him to put by a little money every year, to
be of use in future either to himself or his family. In
other respects the life at Annan was only disagreeable to
him. His tutor's work he did scrupulously well, but the
society of a country town had no interest for him. He
would not visit. He lived alone, shutting himself up with
his books, disliked the business more and more, and came
finally to hate it. Annan, associated as it was with the
odious memories of his schooldays, had indeed but one
merit—that he was within reach of his family, especially
of his mother, to whom he was attached with a real
passion.

His father had by this time given up business at Ecclefechan, and had taken a farm in the neighbourhood. The great north road which runs through the village rises gradually into an upland treeless grass country. About two miles distant on the left-hand side as you go towards Lockerby, there stands, about three hundred yards in from the road, a solitary low whitewashed cottage, with a few poor outbuildings attached to it. This is Mainhill, which was now for many years to be Carlyle's *home*, where he first learned German, studied 'Faust' in a dry ditch, and completed his translation of 'Wilhelm Meister.' The house itself is, or was when the Carlyles occupied it, of one story, and consisted of three rooms, a kitchen, a small bedroom, and a large one connected by a passage. The door opens into a square farmyard, on one side of which are stables, on the other side opposite the door the cow byres, on the third a washhouse and dairy. The situation is high, utterly bleak and swept by all the winds. Not a tree shelters the premises; the fences are low, the wind permitting nothing to grow but stunted thorn. The view alone redeems the dreariness of the situation. On the left is the great hill of Burnswark. Broad Annandale stretches in front down to the Solway, which shines like a long silver riband; on the right is Hoddam Hill with the Tower of Repentance on its crest, and the wooded slopes which mark the line of the river. Beyond towers up Criffel, and in the far distance Skiddaw, and Saddleback, and Helvellyn, and the high Cumberland ridges on the track of the Roman wall. Here lived Carlyle's father and mother with their eight children, Carlyle himself spending his holidays with them; the old man and his younger sons cultivating the sour soil and winning a hard-earned living out of their toil, the mother and daughters doing the household work and minding cows and poultry, and taking their turn in the field with the rest in harvest time.

So two years passed away; Carlyle remaining at Annan.

Of his own writing during this period there is little preserved, but his correspondence continued, and from his friends' letters glimpses can be gathered of his temper and occupations. He was mainly busy with mathematics, but he was reading incessantly, Hume's Essays among other books. He was looking out into the world, meditating on the fall of Napoleon, on the French Revolution, and thinking much of the suffering in Scotland which followed the close of the war. There were sarcastic sketches, too, of the families with which he was thrown in Annan. Robert Mitchell (an Edinburgh student who had become master of a school at Ruthwell) rallies him on 'having reduced the fair and fat academicians into scorched, singed, and shrivelled hags;' and hinting a warning 'against the temper with respect to this world which we are sometimes apt to entertain,' he suggests that young men like him and his correspondent 'ought to think how many are worse off than they,' 'should be thankful for what they had, and not allow imagination to create unreal distress.'

To another friend, Thomas Murray, author afterwards of a history of Galloway, Carlyle had complained of his fate in a light and less bitter spirit. To an epistle written in this tone Murray replied with a description of Carlyle's style, which deserves a place if but for the fulfilment of the prophecy which it contains.

I have had the pleasure of receiving, my dear Carlyle, your very humorous and friendly letter, a letter remarkable for vivacity, a Shandean turn of expression, and an affectionate pathos, which indicate a peculiar turn of mind, make sincerity doubly striking and wit doubly poignant. You flatter me with saying my letter was good; but allow me to observe that among all my elegant and respectable correspondents there is none whose manner of letter-writing I so much envy as yours. A happy flow of language either for pathos, description, or humour, and an easy, graceful current of ideas appropriate to every subject, characterise your style. This is not adulation; I speak what I think. Your letters will always be a feast to me, a varied and exquisite repast; and the time, I hope, will come, but I trust is far distant, when these our juvenile epistles will be read and probably applauded by a generation unborn, and that the name of Carlyle, at least, will be inseparably connected with the literary history of the nineteenth century. Generous ambition and perseverance will overcome every difficulty, and our great Johnson says, 'Where much is attempted something is performed.' You will, perhaps, recollect that when I conveyed you out of town in April, 1814, we were very sentimental: we said that few knew us, and still fewer took an interest in us, and that we would slip through the world inglorious and unknown. But the prospect is altered. We are probably as well known, and have made as great a figure, as any of the same standing at college, and we do not know, but will hope, what twenty years may bring forth.

A letter from you every fortnight shall be answered faithfully, and will be highly delightful; and if we live to be seniors, the letters of the companions of our youth will call to mind our college scenes, endeared to us by many tender associations, and will make us forget that we are poor and old. . . . That you may be always successful and enjoy every happiness that this evanescent world can afford, and that we may meet soon, is, my dear Carlyle, the sincere wish of

Yours most faithfully,
THOMAS MURRAY.

5 Carnegie Street: July 27, 1814.

Murray kept Carlyle's answer to this far-seeing letter.

Thomas Carlyle to Thomas Murray.

August, 1814.

Oh, Tom, what a foolish flattering creature thou art! To talk of future eminence in connection with the literary history of the nineteenth century to such a one as me! Alas! my good lad, when I and all my fancies and reveries and speculations shall have been swept over with the besom of oblivion, the literary history of no century will feel itself the worse. Yet think not, because I talk thus, I am careless of literary fame. No; Heaven knows that ever since I have been able to form a wish, the wish of being known has been the foremost.

Oh, Fortune! thou that givest unto each his portion in this

dirty planet, bestow (if it shall please thee) coronets, and crowns, and principalities, and purses, and pudding, and powers upon the great and noble and fat ones of the earth. Grant me that, with a heart of independence unyielding to thy favours and unbending to thy frowns, I may attain to literary fame; and though starvation be my lot, I will smile that I have not been born a king.

But alas! my dear Murray, what am I, or what are you, or what is any other poor unfriended stripling in the ranks of learning?

These college companions were worthy and innocent young men; none of them, however, came to any high position, and Carlyle's career was now about to intersect with the life of a far more famous contemporary who flamed up a few years later into meridian splendour and then disappeared in delirium. Edward Irving was the son of a well-to-do burgess of Annan, by profession a tanner. Irving was five years older than Carlyle; he had preceded him at Annan School; he had gone thence to Edinburgh University, where he had specially distinguished himself, and had been selected afterwards to manage a school at Haddington, where his success as a teacher had been again conspicuous. Among his pupils at Haddington there was one gifted little girl who will be hereafter much heard of in these pages, Jane Baillie Welsh, daughter of a Dr. Welsh whose surgical fame was then great in that part of Scotland, a remarkable man who liked Irving and trusted his only child in his hands. The Haddington adventure had answered so well that Irving, after a year or two, was removed to a larger school at Kirkcaldy, where, though no fault was found with his teaching, he gave less complete satisfaction. A party among his patrons there thought him too severe with the boys, thought him proud, thought him this or that which they did not like. The dissentients resolved at last to have a second school of their own, to be managed in a different style, and they applied to the classical and mathematical professors at Edinburgh to recommend them a master. Professor Christieson and Professor Leslie, who had noticed Carlyle more than he was aware of, had decided that he was the fittest person that they knew of; and in the summer of 1816 notice of the offered preferment was sent down to him at Annan.

He had seen Irving's face occasionally in Ecclefechan church, and once afterwards, as has been said, when Irving, fresh from his college distinctions, had looked in at Annan school; but they had no personal acquaintance, nor did Carlyle, while he was a master there, ever visit the Irving family. Of course, however, he was no stranger to the reputation of their brilliant son, with whose fame all Annandale was ringing, and with whom kind friends had compared him to his own disadvantage.

I (he says) had heard much of Irving all along, how distinguished in studies, how splendidly successful as a teacher, how two professors had sent him out to Haddington, and how his new academy and new methods were illuminating and astonishing everything there. I don't remember any malicious envy towards this great Irving of the distance for his greatness in study and learning. I certainly might have had a tendency hadn't I struggled against it, and tried to make it emulation. 'Do the like, do the like under difficulties.'

In the winter of 1815 Carlyle for the first time personally met Irving, and the beginning of the acquaintance was not promising. He was still pursuing his Divinity course. Candidates who could not attend the regular lectures at the University came up once a year and delivered an address of some kind in the Divinity Hall. One already he had given the first year of his Annan mastership—an English sermon on the text 'Before I was afflicted I went astray,' &c. He calls it ' a weak flowery sentimental piece,' for which, however, he had been complimented ' by comrades and professors.' His next was a discourse in Latin on the question whether there was or was not such a thing as 'Natural Religion.' This, too, he says was 'weak enough.' It is lost, and nothing is left to show the view which he took about the matter. But here also he gave satisfaction, and was innocently pleased with himself. It was on this occasion that he fell in accidentally with Irving at a friend's room in Edinburgh, and there was a trifling skirmish of tongue between them, where Irving found the laugh turned against him.

A few months after came Carlyle's appointment to Kirkcaldy as Irving's *quasi* rival, and perhaps he felt a little uneasy as to the terms on which they might stand towards each other. His alarms, however, were pleasantly dispelled. He was to go to Kirkcaldy in the summer holidays of 1816 to see the people there and be seen by them before coming to a final arrangement with them. Adam Hope, one of the masters in Annan School, to whom Carlyle was much attached, and whose portrait he has painted, had just lost his wife. Carlyle had gone to sit with the old man in his sorrows, and unexpectedly fell in with Irving there, who had come on the same errand.

If (he says) I had been in doubts about his reception of me, he quickly and for ever ended them by a friendliness which on wider scenes might have been called chivalrous. At first sight he heartily shook my hand, welcomed me as if I had been a valued old acquaintance, almost a brother, and before my leaving came up to me again and with the frankest tone said, 'You are coming to Kirkcaldy to look about you in a month or two. You know I am there; my house and all that I can do for you is yours; two Annandale people must not be strangers in Fife.' The doubting Thomas durst not quite believe all this, so chivalrous was it, but felt pleased and relieved by the fine and sincere tone of it, and thought to himself, 'Well, it would be pretty.'

To Kirkcaldy, then, Carlyle went with hopes so far improved. How Irving kept his word; how warmly he received him; how he opened his house, his library, his heart to him; how they walked and talked together on Kirkcaldy Sands on the summer nights, and toured together in holiday time through the Highlands; how Carlyle found in him a most precious and affectionate companion at the most critical period of his life—all this he has himself described. The reader will find it for himself in the Reminiscences which he has left of the time.

Irving (he says) was four years my senior, the *facile princeps* for success and reputation among the Edinburgh students, famed mathematician, famed teacher, first at Haddington, then here, a flourishing man whom cross fortune was beginning to nibble at. He received me with open arms, and was a brother to me and a friend there and elsewhere afterwards—such friend as I never had again or before in this world, at heart constant till he died.

I am tempted to fill many pages with extracted pictures of the Kirkcaldy life as Carlyle has drawn them. But they can be read in their place, and there is much else to tell; my business is to supply what is left untold, rather than give over again what has been told already.

CHAPTER IV.

CORRESPONDENCE with his family had commenced and was regularly continued from the day when Carlyle went first to college. The letters, however, which are preserved begin with his settlement at Kirkcaldy. From this time they are constant, regular, and, from the care with which they have been kept on both sides, are to be numbered in thousands. Father, mother, brothers, sisters, all wrote in their various styles, and all received answers. They were 'a clannish folk' holding tight together, and Carlyle was looked up to as the scholar among them. Of these letters I can give but a few here and there, but they will bring before the eyes the Mainhill farm, and all that was going on there in a sturdy, pious, and honourable Annandale peasant's household. Carlyle had spent his Christmas holidays 1816–17 at home as usual, and had returned to work.

James Carlyle to Thomas Carlyle.

Mainhill : February 12, 1817.

Dear Son,—I embrace this opportunity of writing you a few lines with the carrier, as I had nothing to say that was worth postage, having written to you largely the last time. But only I have reason to be thankful that I can still tell you that we are all in good health, blessed be God for all his mercies towards us. Your mother has got your stockings ready now, and I think there are a few pairs of very good ones. Times is very bad here for labourers—work is no brisker and living is high. There have been meetings held by the lairds and farmers to assist them in getting meal. They propose to take all the meal that can be sold in the parish to Ecclefechan, for which they shall have full price, and there they sign another paper telling how much money they will give to reduce the price. The charge is given to James Bell, Mr. Miller, and William Graham to sell it.

Mr. Lawson, our priest, is doing very well, and has given us no more paraphrases; but seems to please every person that hears him, and indeed he is well attended every day. The sacrament is to be the first Sabbath of March, and he is visiting his people, but has not reached Mainhill. Your mother was very anxious to have the house done before he came, or else she said she would run over the hill and hide herself. Sandy[1] and I got to work soon after you went away, built partitions, and ceiled—a good floor laid —and indeed it is very dry and comfortable at this time, and we are very snug and have no want of the necessaries of life. Our crop is as good as I expected, and our sheep and all our cattle living and doing very well. Your mother thought to have written to you; but the carrier stopped only two days at home, and she being a very slow writer could not get it done, but she will write next opportunity. I add no more but your mother's compliments, and she sends you half the cheese that she was telling you about. Say in your next how your butter is coming on, and tell us when it is done and we will send you more. Write soon after you receive this, and tell us all your news and how you are coming on. I say no more, but remain,

Dear son, your loving father,
JAMES CARLYLE.

Thomas Carlyle to Mrs. Carlyle (Mainhill).

Kirkcaldy : March 17, 1817.

My dear Mother,—I have been long intending to write you a line or two in order to let you know my state and condition, but having nothing worth writing to communicate I have put it off from time to time. There was little enjoyment for any person at Mainhill when I was there last, but I look forward to the ensuing autumn, when I hope to have the happiness of discussing matters with you as we were wont to do of old. It gives me pleasure to hear that the bairns are at school. There are few things in this world more valuable than knowledge, and youth is the period for acquiring it. With the exception of the religious and moral instruction which I had the happiness of receiving from my parents,

---

[1] Alexander Carlyle, the second son.

and which I humbly trust will not be entirely lost upon me, there is nothing for which I feel more grateful than for the education which they have bestowed upon me. Sandy was getting fond of reading when he went away. I hope he and Aitken [1] will continue their operations now that he is at home. There cannot be imagined a more honest way of employing spare hours.

My way of life in this place is much the same as formerly. The school is doing pretty well, and my health through the winter has been uniformly good. I have little intercourse with the natives here; yet there is no dryness between us. We are always happy to meet and happy to part; but their society is not very valuable to me, and my books are friends that never fail me. Sometimes I see the minister and some others of them, with whom I am very well satisfied, and Irving and I are very friendly; so I am never wearied or at a loss to pass the time.

I had designed this night to write to Aitken about his books and studies, but I will scarcely have time to say anything. There is a book for him in the box, and I would have sent him the geometry, but it was not to be had in the town. I have sent you a scarf as near the kind as Aitken's very scanty description would allow me to come. I hope it will please you. It is as good as any that the merchant had. A shawl of the same materials would have been warmer, but I had no authority to get it. Perhaps you would like to have a shawl also. If you will tell me what colour you prefer, I will send it you with all the pleasure in the world. I expect to hear from you as soon as you can find leisure. You must be very minute in your account of your domestic affairs. My father once spoke of a threshing machine. If twenty pounds or so will help him, they are quite ready at his service.

I remain, dear mother, your affectionate son,
THOMAS CARLYLE.

Mrs. Carlyle could barely write at this time. She taught herself later in life for the pleasure of communicating with her son, between whom and herself there existed a special and passionate attachment of a quite peculiar kind. She was a severe Calvinist, and watched with the most affectionate anxiety over her children's spiritual welfare, her eldest boy's above all. The hope of her

[1] John Aitken Carlyle, the third son, afterwards known as John.

life was to see him a minister—a 'priest' she would have called it—and she was already alarmed to know that he had no inclination that way.

Mrs. Carlyle to Thomas Carlyle.

Mainhill: June 10, 1817.

Dear Son,—I take this opportunity of writing you a few lines, as you will get it free. I long to have a craik,[1] and look forward to August, trusting to see thee once more, but in hope the meantime. Oh, Tom, mind the golden season of youth, and remember your Creator in the days of your youth. Seek God while He may be found. Call upon Him while He is near. We hear that the world by wisdom knew not God. Pray for His presence with you, and His counsel to guide you. Have you got through the Bible yet? If you have, read it again. I hope you will not weary, and may the Lord open your understanding.

I have no news to tell you, but thank God we are all in an ordinary way. I hope you are well. I thought you would have written before now. I received your present and was very proud of it. I called it 'my son's venison.' Do write as soon as this comes to hand and tell us all your news. I am glad you are so contented in your place. We ought all to be thankful for our places in these distressing times, for I dare say they are felt keenly. We send you a small piece of ham and a minding of butter, as I am sure yours is done before now. Tell us about it in your next, and if anything is wanting.

Good night, Tom, for it is a very stormy night, and I must away to the byre to milk.

Now, Tom, be sure to tell me about your chapters. No more from

Your old
MINNIE.

The letters from the other members of the family were sent equally regularly whenever there was an opportunity, and give between them a perfect picture of healthy rustic life at the Mainhill farm—the brothers and sisters down to the lowest all hard at work, the little ones at school, the elders ploughing, reaping, tending cattle, or minding the

[1] Familiar talk.

dairy, and in the intervals reading history, reading Scott's novels, or even trying at geometry, which was then Carlyle's own favourite study. In the summer of 1817 the mother had a severe illness, by which her mind was affected. It was necessary to place her for a few weeks under restraint away from home—a step no doubt just and necessary, but which she never wholly forgave, but resented in her own humorous way to the end of her life. The disorder soon passed off, however, and never returned.

Meanwhile Carlyle was less completely contented with his position at Kirkcaldy than he had let his mother suppose. For one thing he hated schoolmastering, and would, or thought he would, have preferred to work with his hands, while except Irving he had scarcely a friend in the place for whom he cared. His occupation shut him out from the best kind of society, which there, as elsewhere, had its exclusive rules. He was received, for Irving's sake, in the family of Mr. Martin, the minister; and was in some degree of intimacy there, liking Martin himself, and to some extent, but not much, his wife and daughters, to one of whom Irving had, perhaps too precipitately, become engaged. There were others also—Mr. Swan, a Kirkcaldy merchant, particularly—for whom he had a grateful remembrance; but it is clear, both from Irving's letters to him and from his own confession, that he was not popular either there or anywhere. Shy and reserved at one moment, at another sarcastically self-asserting, with forces working in him which he did not himself understand, and which still less could be understood by others, he could neither properly accommodate himself to the tone of Scotch provincial drawing-rooms, nor even to the business which he had especially to do. A man of genius can do the lowest work as well as the highest; but genius in the process of developing, combined with an irritable nervous system and a fiercely impatient temperament, was not happily occupied in teaching stupid lads the elements of Latin and arithmetic. Nor were matters mended when the Town Corporation, who were his masters, took upon them, as sometimes happened, to instruct or rebuke him.

Life, however, even under these hard circumstances, was not without its romance. I borrow a passage from the 'Reminiscences':—

The Kirkcaldy people were a pleasant, solid, honest kind of fellow mortals, something of quietly fruitful, of good old Scotch in their works and ways, more vernacular, peaceably fixed and almost genial in their mode of life, than I had been used to in the border home land. Fife generally we liked. Those ancient little burghs and sea villages, with their poor little havens, salt-pans and weather-beaten bits of Cyclopean breakwaters, and rude innocent machineries, are still kindly to me to think of. Kirkcaldy itself had many looms, had Baltic trade, whale fishery, &c., and was a solidly diligent and yet by no means a panting, puffing, or in any way gambling 'Lang Town.' Its flax-mill machinery, I remember, was turned mainly by wind; and curious blue-painted wheels with oblique vans rose from many roofs for that end. We all, I in particular, always rather liked the people, though from the distance chiefly, chagrined and discouraged by the sad trade one had. Some hospitable human friends I found, and these were at intervals a fine little element; but in general we were but onlookers, the one real society our books and our few selves. Not even with the bright young ladies (which was a sad feature) were we generally on speaking terms. By far the brightest and cleverest, however, an ex-pupil of Irving's, and genealogically and otherwise, being poorish and well-bred, rather an alien in Kirkcaldy, I did at last make some acquaintance with—at Irving's first, I think, though she rarely came thither—and it might easily have been more, had she and her aunt and our economies and other circumstances liked. She was of the fair-complexioned, softly elegant, softly grave, witty and comely type, and had a good deal of gracefulness, intelligence, and other talent. Irving, too, it was sometimes thought, found her very interesting, could the Miss Martin bonds have allowed, which they never would. To me, who had only known her for a few months, and who within a twelve or fifteen months saw the last of her, she continued, for perhaps three years, a figure hanging more or less in my fancy, on the usual romantic, or latterly quite elegiac and silent terms, and to this day there is in me a good will to her, a candid and gentle pity, if needed at all. She was of the Aberdeenshire Gordons. Margaret Gordon, born I think in New Brunswick, where her father, probably in some official post, had died young and poor ; but her accent was prettily English, and her voice very fine.

An aunt (widow in Fife, childless with limited resources, but of frugal cultivated turn ; a lean proud elderly dame, once a Miss Gordon herself ; sang Scotch songs beautifully, and talked shrewd Aberdeenish in accent and otherwise) had adopted her and brought her hither over seas ; and here, as Irving's ex-pupil, she now, cheery though with dim outlooks, was. Irving saw her again in Glasgow one summer's touring, &c.; he himself accompanying joyfully—not joining, so I understood, in the retinue of suitors or potential suitors ; rather perhaps indicating gently 'No, I must not.' A year or so after we heard the fair Margaret had married some rich Mr. Something, who afterwards got into Parliament, thence out to 'Nova Scotia' (or so) as governor, and I heard of her no more, except that lately she was still living childless as the 'dowager lady,' her Mr. Something having got knighted before dying. Poor Margaret ! I saw her recognisable to me here in her London time, 1840 or so, twice ; once with her maid in Piccadilly promenading—little altered ; a second time that same year, or next, on horseback both of us, and meeting in the gate of Hyde Park, when her eyes (but that was all) said to me almost touchingly, yes, yes, that is you.

Margaret Gordon was the original, so far as there was an original, of Blumine in ' Sartor Resartus.' Two letters from her remain among Carlyle's papers, which show that on both sides their regard for each other had found expression. Circumstances, however, and the unpromising appearance of Carlyle's situation and prospects, forbade an engagement between them, and acquit the aunt of needless harshness in peremptorily putting an end to their acquaintance. Miss Gordon took leave of him as a ' sister ' in language of affectionate advice. A single passage may be quoted to show how the young unknown Kirkcaldy schoolmaster appeared in the eyes of the young high-born lady who had thus for a moment crossed his path.

And now, my dear friend, a long long adieu; one advice, and as a parting one consider, value it. Cultivate the milder dispositions of your heart. Subdue the more extravagant visions of the brain. In time your abilities must be known. Among your acquaintance they are already beheld with wonder and delight. By those whose opinion will be valuable, they hereafter will be appreciated. Genius will render you great. May virtue render you beloved! Remove the awful distance between you and ordinary men by kind and gentle manners. Deal gently with their inferiority, and be convinced they will respect you as much and like you more. Why conceal the real goodness that flows in your heart? I have ventured this counsel from an anxiety for your future welfare, and I would enforce it with all the earnestness of the most sincere friendship. Let your light shine before men, and think them not unworthy the trouble. This exercise will prove its own reward. It must be a pleasing thing to live in the affections of others. Again adieu. Pardon the freedom I have used, and when you think of me be it as a kind sister, to whom your happiness will always yield delight, and your griefs sorrow.

Yours, with esteem and regard,

M.

I give you not my address because I dare not promise to see you.

CHAPTER V.

A.D. 1818. ÆT. 23.

CARLYLE had by this time abandoned the thought of the 'ministry' as his possible future profession—not without a struggle, for both his father's and his mother's hearts had been set upon it; but the 'grave prohibitive doubts' which had risen in him of their own accord had been strengthened by Gibbon, whom he had found in Irving's library and eagerly devoured. Never at any time had he 'the least inclination' for such an office, and his father, though deeply disappointed, was too genuine a man to offer the least remonstrance.[1] The 'schoolmastering' too, after two years' experience of it, became intolerable. His disposition, at once shy and defiantly proud, had perplexed and displeased the Kirkcaldy burghers. Both he and Irving also fell into unpleasant collisions with them, and neither of the two was sufficiently docile to submit

---

[1] 'With me,' he says in a private note, 'it was never much in favour, though my parents silently much wished it, as I knew well. Finding I had objections, my father, with a magnanimity which I admired and admire, left me frankly to my own guidance in that matter, as did my mother, perhaps still more lovingly, though not so silently ; and the theological course which could be prosecuted or kept open by appearing annually, putting down your name, but with some trifling fee, in the register, and then going your way, was, after perhaps two years of this languid form, allowed to close itself for good. I remember yet being on the street in Argyll Square, Edinburgh, probably in 1817, and come over from Kirkcaldy with some intent, the languidest possible, still to put down my name and fee. The official person, when I rung, was not at home, and my instant feeling was, "Very good, then, very good ; let this be Finis in the matter," and it really was.'

tamely to reproof.[1] An opposition school had been set
up which drew off the pupils, and finally they both concluded that they had had enough of it—'better die than be
a schoolmaster for one's living'—and would seek some
other means of supporting themselves. Carlyle had
passed his summer holidays as usual at Mainhill (1818),
where he had perhaps talked over his prospects with his
family. On his return to Kirkcaldy in September he
wrote to his father explaining his situation. He had saved
about 90*l.*, on which, with his thrifty habits, he said that
he could support himself in Edinburgh till he could 'fall
into some other way of doing.' He could perhaps get a
few mathematical pupils, and meantime could study for
the *bar.* He waited only for his father's approval to send
in his resignation. The letter was accompanied by one
of his constant presents to his mother, who was again at
home, though not yet fully recovered.

John Carlyle to Thomas Carlyle.

Mainhill : September 16, 1818.

Dear Brother,—We received yours, and it told us of your safe
arrival at Kirkcaldy. Our mother has grown better every day

---

[1] Carlyle says in the *Reminiscences* that Irving was accused of harshness to
the boys. Kirkcaldy tradition has preserved instances of it, which sound
comical enough at a distance, but were no matter of laughter to the sufferers.
A correspondent writes to me:—'Irving has the reputation to this day of
being a very hard master. He thrashed the boys frequently and unmercifully.
A story in illustration was told me. A carpenter, a bit of a character, whose
shop was directly opposite Irving's school, hearing a fearful howling one day,
rushed across, axe in hand, drove up the door, and to Irving's query what he
did there, replied, "I thocht ye were killin' the lad, and cam' over tae see if
ye were needin' help." Carlyle, on the contrary, I was assured, never lifted
his hand to a scholar. Still he had perfect command over them. A look or a
word was sufficient to command attention and obedience. Nor have I ever
heard that this command was attributable to fear. So far as I can learn, it
was entirely due to the respect which he seems to have obtained from the
first.' There is *some* truth in these legends of Irving's severity, for Carlyle
himself admits it. But tradition always tends to shape stories and characters into an artistic completeness which had no real existence. The
authentic evidence of Irving's essential kindness and affectionate gentleness
makes it impossible to believe that he was ever wantonly or carelessly cruel.

since you left us. She is as steady as ever she was, has been upon haystacks three or four times, and has been at church every Sabbath since she came home, behaving always very decently. Also she has given over talking and singing, and spends some of her time consulting Ralph Erskine. She sleeps every night, and hinders no person to sleep, but can do with less than the generality of people. In fact we may conclude that she is as wise as could be expected. She has none of the hypocritical mask with which some people clothe their sentiments. One day, having met Agg Byers, she says : 'Weel, Agg, lass, I've never spoken t'ye sin ye stole our coals. I'll gie ye an advice : never steal nae more.'

Alexander Carlyle to Thomas Carlyle.

September 18, 1818.

My dear Brother,—We were glad to hear of your having arrived in safety, though your prospects were not brilliant. My father is at Ecclefechan to-day at a market, but before he went he told me to mention that with regard to his advising you, he was unable to give you any advice. He thought it might be necessary to consult Leslie before you gave up, but you might do what seemed to you good. Had my advice any weight, I would advise you to try the law. You may think you have not money enough to try that, but with what assistance we could make, and your own industry, I think there would be no fear but you would succeed. The box which contained my mother's bonnet came a day or two ago. She is very well pleased with it, though my father thought it too gaudy ; but she proposes writing to you herself.

The end was, that when December came Carlyle and Irving 'kicked the schoolmaster functions over,' removed to Edinburgh, and were adrift on the world. Irving had little to fear ; he had money, friends, reputation ; he had a profession, and was waiting only for 'a call' to enter on his full privileges. Carlyle was far more unfavourably situated. He was poor, unpopular, comparatively unknown, or, if known, known only to be feared and even shunned. In Edinburgh 'from my fellow-creatures,' he says, 'little or nothing but vinegar was my reception when we happened to meet or pass near each other—my own blame mainly, so proud, shy, poor, at once so insignificant-looking and so grim and sorrowful. That in 'Sartor' of the worm trodden on and proving a torpedo is not wholly a fable, but did actually befall once or twice, as I still with a kind of small, not ungenial, malice can remember.' He had, however, as was said, nearly a hundred pounds, which he had saved out of his earnings; he had a consciousness of integrity worth more than gold to him. He had thrifty self-denying habits which made him content with the barest necessaries, and he resolutely faced his position. His family, though silently disapproving the step which he had taken and necessarily anxious about him, rendered what help they could. Once more the Ecclefechan carrier brought up the weekly or monthly supplies of oatmeal, cakes, butter, and, when needed, under-garments, returning with the dirty linen for the mother to wash and mend, and occasionally presents which were never forgotten; while Carlyle, after a thought of civil engineering, for which his mathematical training gave him a passing inclination, sate down seriously, if not very assiduously, to study law. Letters to and from Ecclefechan were constant, the carrier acting as postman. Selections from them bring the scene and characters before the reader's eyes.

Sister Mary, then twelve years old, writes:—

I take this opportunity of sending you this scrawl. I got the hat you sent with Sandy [brother Alexander], and it fits very well. It was far too good; a worse would have done very well. Boys and I are employed this winter in waiting on the cattle, and are going on very well at present. I generally write a copy every night, and read a little in the 'Cottagers of Glenburnie,' or some such like; and it shall be my earnest desire never to imitate the abominable slutteries of Mrs. Maclarty. The remarks of the author, Mrs. Hamilton, often bring your neat ways in my mind, and I hope to be benefited by them. In the mean time, I shall endeavour to be a good girl, to be kind and obedient to my parents, and obliging to my brothers and sisters. You will write me a long letter when the carrier comes back.

The mother was unwearied in her affectionate solicitude —solicitude for the eternal as well as temporal interests of her darling child.

Mrs. Carlyle to Thomas Carlyle.

Mainhill: January 3, 1819.

Dear Son,—I received yours in due time, and was glad to hear you were well. I hope you will be healthier, moving about in the city, than in your former way. Health is a valuable privilege; try to improve it, then. The time is short. Another year has commenced. Time is on the wing, and flies swiftly. Seek God with all your heart; and oh, my dear son, cease not to pray for His counsel in all your ways. Fear not the world; you will be provided for as He sees meet for you.

As a sincere friend, whom you are always dear to, I beg you do not neglect reading a part of your Bible daily, and may the Lord open your eyes to see wondrous things out of His law! But it is now two o'clock in the morning, and a bad pen, bad ink, and I as bad at writing. I will drop it, and add no more, but remain

Your loving mother,

PEGGIE CARLYLE.

Carlyle had written a sermon on the salutary effects of 'affliction,' as his first exercise in the Divinity School. He was beginning now, in addition to the problem of living which he had to solve, to learn what affliction meant. He was attacked with dyspepsia, which never wholly left him, and in these early years soon assumed its most torturing form, like 'a rat gnawing at the pit of his stomach.' His disorder working on his natural irritability found escape in expressions which showed, at any rate, that he was attaining a mastery of language. The pain made him furious; and in such a humour the commonest calamities of life became unbearable horrors.

I find living here very high (he wrote soon after he was settled in his lodgings). An hour ago I paid my week's bill, which, though 15s. 2d., was the smallest of the three I have yet discharged. This is an unreasonable sum when I consider the slender accommodation and the paltry, ill-cooked morsel which is my daily pittance. There is also a schoolmaster right overhead, whose noisy brats give me at times no small annoyance. On a given night of the week he also assembles a select number of vocal performers, whose music, as they charitably name it, is now and then so clamorous that I almost wished the throats of these sweet singers full of molten lead, or any other substance that would stop their braying.

But he was not losing heart, and liked, so far as he had seen into it, his new profession.

The law (he told his mother) is what I sometimes think I was intended for naturally. I am afraid it takes several hundreds to become an advocate; but for this I should commence the study of it with great hopes of success. We shall see whether it is possible. One of the first advocates of the day raised himself from being a disconsolate preacher to his present eminence. Therefore I entreat you not to be uneasy about me. I see none of my fellows with whom I am very anxious to change places. Tell the boys not to let their hearts be troubled for me. I am a stubborn dog, and evil fortune shall not break my heart or bend it either, as I hope. I know not how to speak about the washing which you offer so kindly. Surely you thought, five years ago, that this troublesome washing and baking was all over; and now to recommence! I can scarcely think of troubling you; yet the clothes are ill-washed here; and if the box be going and coming any way, perhaps you can manage it.

While law lectures were being attended, the difficulty was to live. Pupils were a not very effective resource, and of his adventures in this department Carlyle gave ridiculous accounts. In February, 1819, he wrote to his brother John :—

About a week ago I briefly dismissed an hour of private teaching. A man in the New Town applied to one Nichol, public teacher of mathematics here, for a person to give instruction in arithmetic, or something of that sort. Nichol spoke of me, and I was in consequence directed to call on the man next morning. I went at the appointed hour, and after waiting for a few minutes was met by a stout, impudent-looking man with red whiskers, having much the air of an attorney, or some such creature of that sort. As our conversation may give you some insight into these matters, I report the substance of it. 'I am here,' I said, after making a slight bow, which was just perceptibly returned, 'by the request of Mr. Nichol, to speak with you, sir, about a mathematical teacher whom he tells me you want.' 'Aye. What are your terms?' 'Two guineas a month for each hour.' 'Two guineas a month! that is perfectly extravagant.' 'I believe it to be the rate at which every teacher of respectability in Edinburgh officiates, and I *know* it to be the rate below which I never officiate.' 'That will not do for my friend.' 'I am sorry that nothing else will do for me;' and I retired with considerable deliberation.

Other attempts were not so unsuccessful; one, sometimes two, pupils were found willing to pay at the rate required. Dr. Brewster, afterwards Sir David, discovered Carlyle and gave him occasional employment on his Encyclopædia. He was thus able to earn, as long as the session lasted, about two pounds a week, and on this he contrived to live without trenching on his capital. His chief pleasure was his correspondence with his mother, which never slackened. She had written to tell him of the death of her sister Mary. He replies:—

Edinburgh: Monday, March 29, 1819.

My dear Mother,—I am so much obliged to you for the affectionate concern which you express for me in that long letter that I cannot delay to send you a few brief words by way of reply. I was affected by the short notice you give me of Aunt Mary's death, and the short reflections with which you close it. It is true, my dear mother, 'that we must all soon follow her,' such is the unalterable and not unpleasing doom of men. Then it is well for those who, at that awful moment which is before every one, shall be able to look back with calmness and forward with hope. But I need not dwell upon this solemn subject. It is familiar to the thoughts of every one who has any thought.

I am rather afraid I have not been quite regular in reading that best of books which you recommended to me. However, last night I was reading upon my favourite Job, and I hope to do better in time to come. I entreat you to believe that I am sincerely desirous of being a good man; and though we may differ in some

MINNESOTA HISTORICAL SOCIETY

few unimportant particulars, yet I firmly trust that the same power which created us with imperfect faculties will pardon the errors of every one (and none are without them) who seeks truth and righteousness with a simple heart.

You need not fear my studying too much. In fact, my prospects are so unsettled that I do not often sit down to books with all the zeal I am capable of. You are not to think I am fretful. I have long accustomed my mind to look upon the future with a sedate aspect, and at any rate my hopes have never yet failed me. A French author, d'Alembert (one of the few persons who deserve the honourable epithet of honest men), whom I was lately reading, remarks that one who devoted his life to learning ought to carry for his motto, 'Liberty, Truth, Poverty,' for he that fears the latter can never have the former. This should not prevent one from using every honest effort to attain a comfortable situation in life; it says only that the best is dearly bought by base conduct, and the worst is not worth mourning over. We shall speak of all these matters more fully in summer, for I am meditating just now to come down to stay a while with you, accompanied with a cargo of books, Italian, German, and others. You will give me yonder little room, and you will waken me every morning about five or six o'clock. Then *such* study. I shall delve in the garden, too, and, in a word, become not only the wisest but the strongest man in those regions. This is all *claver*, but it pleases one.

My dear mother, yours most affectionately,

THOMAS CARLYLE.

D'Alembert's name had probably never reached Annandale, and Mrs. Carlyle could not gather from it into what perilous regions her son was travelling—but her quick ear caught something in the tone which frightened her.

Oh, my dear, dear son (she answered at once and eagerly), I would pray for a blessing on your learning. I beg you with all the feeling of an affectionate mother that you would study the Word of God, which He has graciously put in our hands, that it may powerfully reach our hearts, that we may discern it in its true light. God made man after His own image, therefore he behoved to be without any imperfect faculties. Beware, my dear son, of such thoughts; let them not dwell on your mind. God forbid! But I dare say you will not care to read this scrawl.

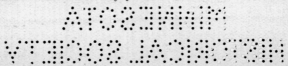

MINNESOTA HISTORICAL SOCIETY

Do make religion your great study, Tom; if you repent it, I will bear the blame for ever.

Carlyle was thinking as much as his mother of religion, but the form in which his thoughts were running was not hers. He was painfully seeing that all things were not wholly as he had been taught to think them; the doubts which had stopped his divinity career were blackening into thunder clouds; and all his reflections were coloured by dyspepsia. 'I was entirely unknown in Edinburgh circles,' he says, 'solitary, eating my own heart, fast losing my health too, a prey to nameless struggles and miseries, which have yet a kind of horror in them to my thoughts, three weeks without any kind of sleep from impossibility to be free of noise.' In fact he was entering on what he called 'the three most miserable years of my life.' He would have been saved from much could he have resolutely thrown himself into his intended profession; but he soon came to hate it, as just then, perhaps, he would have hated anything.

I had thought (he writes in a note somewhere) of attempting to become an advocate. It seemed glorious to me for its independency, and I did read some law books, attend Hume's lectures on Scotch law, and converse with and question various dull people of the practical sort. But it and they and the admired lecturing Hume himself appeared to me mere denizens of the kingdom of dulness, pointing towards nothing but money as wages for all that bogpool of disgust. Hume's lectures once done with, I flung the thing away for ever.

Men who are out of humour with themselves often see their own condition reflected in the world outside them, and everything seems amiss because it is not well with themselves. But the state of Scotland and England also was well fitted to feed his discontent. The great war had been followed by a collapse. Wages were low, food at famine prices. Tens of thousands of artisans were out of

work, their families were starving, and they themselves
were growing mutinous. Even at home from his own
sternly patient father, who never meddled with politics,
he heard things not calculated to reconcile him to existing
arrangements.

I have heard my father say (he mentions), with an impressiveness which all his perceptions carried with them, that the lot of a
poor man was growing worse, that the world would not, and could
not, last as it was, but mighty changes, of which none saw the
end, were on the way. In the dear years when the oatmeal was as
high as ten shillings a stone, he had noticed the labourers, I have
heard him tell, retire each separately to a brook and there drink
instead of dining, anxious only to hide it.[1]

These early impressions can be traced through the whole
of Carlyle's writings ; the conviction was forced upon him
that there was something vicious to the bottom in English
and Scotch society, and that revolution in some form or
other lay visibly ahead. So long as Irving remained in
Edinburgh 'the condition of the people' question was the
constant subject of talk between him and Carlyle. They
were both of them ardent, radical, indignant at the injustice which they witnessed, and as yet unconscious of the
difficulty of mending it. Irving, however, he had seen
little of since they had moved to Edinburgh, and he was
left, for the most part, alone with his own thoughts.
There had come upon him the trial which in these days
awaits every man of high intellectual gifts and noble
nature on their first actual acquaintance with human
things—the question, far deeper than any mere political
one, What is this world then, what is this human life, over
which a just God is said to preside, but of whose presence
or whose providence so few signs are visible ? In happier
ages religion silences scepticism if it cannot reply to its
difficulties, and postpones the solution of the mystery to

[1] *Reminiscences,* p. 48.

another stage of existence. Brought up in a pious family
where religion was not talked about or emotionalised, but
was accepted as the rule of thought and conduct, himself
too instinctively upright, pure of heart, and reverent, Carlyle, like his parents, had accepted the Bible as a direct
communication from Heaven. It made known the will of
God, and the relation in which man stood to his Maker,
as present facts like a law of nature, the truth of it, like the
truth of gravitation, which man must act upon or immediately suffer the consequences. But religion, as revealed
in the Bible, passes beyond present conduct, penetrates all
forms of thought, and takes possession wherever it goes.
It claims to control the intellect, to explain the past, and
foretell the future. It has entered into poetry and art,
and has been the interpreter of history. And thus there
had grown round it a body of opinion, on all varieties
of subjects, assumed to be authoritative ; dogmas which
science was contradicting ; a history of events which it
called infallible, yet which the canons of evidence, by
which other histories are tried and tested successfully,
declared not to be infallible at all. To the Mainhill household the Westminster Confession was a full and complete
account of the position of mankind and of the Being to
whom they owed their existence. The Old and New Testament not only contained all spiritual truth necessary for
guidance in word and deed, but every fact related in them
was literally true. To doubt was not to mistake, but was
to commit a sin of the deepest dye, and was a sure sign of
a corrupted heart. Carlyle's wide study of modern literature had shown him that much of this had appeared to
many of the strongest minds in Europe to be doubtful or
even plainly incredible. Young men of genius are the
first to feel the growing influences of their time, and on
Carlyle they fell in their most painful form. Notwithstanding his pride, he was most modest and self-distrust-

ful. He had been taught that want of faith was sin, yet, like a true Scot, he knew that he would peril his soul if he pretended to believe what his intellect told him was false. If any part of what was called Revelation was mistaken, how could he be assured of the rest? How could he tell that the moral part of it, to which the phenomena which he saw round him were in plain contradiction, was more than a 'devout imagination'? Thus to poverty and dyspepsia there had been added the struggle which is always hardest in the noblest minds, which Job had known, and David, and Solomon, and Æschylus, and Shakespeare, and Goethe. Where are the tokens of His presence? where are the signs of His coming? Is there, in this universe of things, any moral Providence at all? or is it the product of some force of the nature of which we can know nothing save only that 'one event comes alike to all, to the good and to the evil, and that there is no difference'?

Commonplace persons, if assailed by such misgivings, thrust them aside, throw themselves into occupation, and leave doubt to settle itself. Carlyle could not. The importunacy of the overwhelming problem forbade him to settle himself either to law or any other business till he had wrestled down the misgivings which had grappled with him. The greatest of us have our weaknesses, and the Margaret Gordon business had perhaps intertwined itself with the spiritual torment. The result of it was that Carlyle was extremely miserable, 'tortured,' as he says, 'by the freaks of an imagination of extraordinary and wild activity.'

He went home, as he had proposed, after the session, but Mainhill was never a less happy home to him than it proved this summer. He could not conceal, perhaps he did not try to conceal, the condition of his mind; and to his family, to whom the truth of their creed was no more a matter of doubt than the presence of the sun in the sky,

he must have seemed as if 'possessed.' He could not
read; he wandered about the moors like a restless spirit.
His mother was in agony about him. He was her darling,
her pride, the apple of her eye, and she could not restrain
her lamentations and remonstrances. His father, with
supreme good judgment, left him to himself.

His tolerance for me, his trust in me (Carlyle says), was great.
When I declined going forward into the Church, though his heart
was set upon it, he respected my scruples, and patiently let me
have my way. When I had peremptorily ceased from being a
schoolmaster, though he inwardly disapproved of the step as imprudent and saw me in successive summers lingering beside him
in sickness of body and mind, without outlook towards any good,
he had the forbearance to say at worst nothing, never once to
whisper discontent with me.

A letter from Irving, to whom he had written complaining of his condition and of his friend's silence, was welcome at this dreary period.

Edward Irving to Thomas Carlyle.

Edinburgh : June 4, 1819.
Dear Sir,—My apology for neglecting you so long is that I have
been equally negligent of myself. By what fatality I know not,
I have been so entirely devoted to idleness or to insignificant employments since you left me, that German, Italian, and every other
study, useful or serious, has been relinquished. Perhaps this re-
newal of our intercourse may be the date of my awakening from
my slumber, as the breaking up of our intercourse was the date of
its commencement. To speak of myself, that most grateful of
topics, is therefore out of the question; as it would only be to
expose the day dreams of this my lethargy to one whose active
mind has no sympathy with listlessness and drowsiness, and this
subject being excluded, where shall I find materials for this letter?
I could detail to you the mineralogy of the Campsey hills, and
tell you of the overlying formation of porphyry above the green
stone, and of the nearly horizontal bed of limestone on the green

stone which supplies the greater part of Stirling, Dumbarton, and Strathearn, and of a curious quarry of stone which is carried far and near for building stoves and setting grates, with an account of its singular virtue of resisting heat; but well I know you are weary unto death of such jargon. And I could relate to you one most sentimental incident that did befall me on that journey, whereby hangs a tale which might furnish matter for a novel or even a modern tragedy : but then I suspect you have already put me down for an adventure hunter, which is too near a stage to a story-teller to fall in with my fancy.

Now the truth is, to throw in a word of self-defence, if I have a turn for the romantic, it is not for the vanity of being the actor of a strange part, or the spouter of a strange tale, in the various scenes of the great drama of this mortal state ; but rather to be a spectator of those who are so, more especially if they be unfortunate withal; and occasionally I confess to have the privilege of the ancient chorus, of moralising a little, or rather not a little, upon the passing events; and occasionally to reach an admonition or a consolation to the suffering hero or heroine of the piece. But see, I am letting you into some of the vagaries which came and went across my fancy during the interval of apathy which has passed away since I was separated from your conversation for which I have not yet found a substitute.

And I could dwell upon the rich harvest of insight into character, which I gathered from the debates of the General Assembly; and of the lack of genius and honesty which took from its value, and of the rankness and superfluity of vulgarity and bad temper and party zeal, which were as the thistles and ragworts and tares of the crop, but that I know your mind is incurious of these things, engaged as it is with much higher contemplations.

Of the men of Edinburgh and their employments I know as little as of those of Canton in China ; save that Christieson rather inclines to fall in with Lord Lauderdale's views of the Bullion question, than the Committee's, and that he is as sure as ever that all men have mistaken the meaning of Aristotle—which, it seems, is wonderfully wrapped up in the power of the particle $\mathring{a}\nu$—and that Galloway is as ill-bred, and stares as full, and wears his hair hanging over the ample circumference of his globular skull, as usual ; like the thatch of those round rustic Chinese-roofed cottages which gentlemen sometimes plant at the outer gates of their grounds. As to Dickson, he plays quoits with Chartres, and at times with me, and has got his mouth always filled with wit at me for admiring those beautiful lines of Milton's Hymn on the Nativity :—

> It was no season then for her [nature]
> To wanton with the Sun, her lusty paramour.

I need not tell you where the wit lies; and you know when he is primed anything will do for a match. He is just in the predicament of a spring-gun in a garden which has ropes in every direction—you cannot stir a foot, but twitch goes one of its ropes; round it turns full-mouthed upon you, and, hit or miss, off it goes.

' Weary not then, my dear Carlyle, of the country. I am here in the midst of the busy world, and its business only interrupts me and would vex me if I would let it. Fill up with the softness of rural beauty, and the sincerity of rural manners, and the contentment of rural life, those strong impressions of nature and of men which are already in your mind; till the pictures become more mellow and joyous, and yield to yourself more delight in forming, and to others more pleasure in viewing them.

I would I were along with you to charm the melancholy of solitude, and in your company to carry my eye into those marks of beneficence and love which every part of nature exhibits, and win from the contemplation of them a portion of that beneficence; so that the restless and evil passions of my heart might be charmed if not shamed into repose, and I might go forth again into the world of busy speech resolved to mar the enjoyment of no one, but in my little sphere to do all the good it would allow, to wish for a wider sphere, and to live in hope of that wider and better existence, which, when it is revealed, I pray that you and I and all we love and should love may be prepared for.

Don't be so tardy in writing to me as I have been in writing to you. Arrange the plan of a correspondence which may be useful to us both. You proposed it first, and now I reckon myself entitled to press it. Remember me kindly to your father and mother, and to Sandy and the rest.

Your faithful friend,

EDWARD IRVING.

CHAPTER VI.

A.D. 1819. ÆT. 24.

IN November Carlyle was back at Edinburgh again, with his pupils and his law lectures, which he had not yet deserted, and still persuaded himself that he would persevere with. He did not find his friend; Irving had gone to Glasgow to be assistant to Dr. Chalmers; and the state of things which he found in the metropolis was not of a sort to improve his humour.

1819 (he says) was the year of the great Radical rising in Glasgow, and the kind of (altogether imaginary) rising they attempted on Bonnymuir against the yeomanry—a time of great rage and absurd terrors and expectations; a very fierce Radical and anti-Radical time; Edinburgh suddenly agitated by it all round me, not to mention Glasgow in the distance; gentry people full of zeal and foolish terror and fury, and looking disgustingly busy and important. Courier hussars would come in from the Glasgow region, covered with mud, breathless from headquarters, as you took your walk in Princes Street; and you would hear old powdered gentlemen in silver spectacles talking in low-toned but exultant voice about 'Cordon of troops, sir,' as you went along. The mass of the people, not the populace alone, had a quite different feeling, as if the danger was small or imaginary and the grievances dreadfully real, which was, with emphasis, my own poor private notion of it. One bleared Sunday morning I had gone out, perhaps seven or eight A.M., for my walk. At the riding-house in Nicholson Street was a kind of straggly group or small crowd, with red-coats interspersed. Coming up, I perceived it was the Lothian yeomanry (Mid or East I know not), just getting under way for Glasgow, to be part of 'the cordon.' I halting a moment, they took the road, very ill ranked, not numerous, or any way dangerous-looking men of war; but there rose from the little crowd, by way of farewell cheer to them, the strangest shout I have heard human throats utter; not very loud, or loud even for the small numbers; but it said, as plain as words, and with infinitely more emphasis of sincerity: 'May the devil go with you, ye peculiarly contemptible and dead to the distresses of your fellow-creatures.' Another morning, months after, spring and sun now come, and the 'cordon,' &c., all over, I met a gentleman, an advocate, slightly of my acquaintance, hurrying along, musket in hand, towards 'the Links,' there to be drilled as an item of the 'gentlemen volunteers' now afoot. 'You should have the like of this,' said he, cheerily patting his musket. 'H'm, yes; but I haven't yet quite settled on which side!' which, probably, he hoped was quiz, though it really expressed my feeling. Irving, too, and all of us juniors, had the same feeling in different intensities, and spoken of only to one another: a sense that revolt against such a load of unveracities, impostures, and quietly inane formalities would one day become indispensable—sense which had a kind of rash, false, and quasi-insolent joy in it; mutiny, revolt, being a light matter to the young.[1]

The law lectures went on, and Carlyle wrote to his mother about his progress with them. 'The law,' he said, 'I find to be a most complicated subject, yet I like it pretty well, and feel that I shall like it better as I proceed. Its great charm in my eyes is that no mean compliances are requisite for prospering in it.' To Irving he had written a fuller, not yet completely full, account of himself, complaining perhaps of his obstructions and difficulties. Irving's advice is not what would have been given by a cautious attorney. He admired his friend, and only wished his great capabilities to be known as soon as possible.

Edward Irving to Thomas Carlyle.

34, Kent Street, Glasgow : December 28, 1819.

Dear Carlyle,—I pray that you may prosper in your legal studies, provided only you will give your mind to take in all the

[1] *Reminiscences*, p. 120.

elements which enter into the question of the obstacles. But remember, it is not want of knowledge alone that impedes, but want of instruments for making that knowledge available. This you know better than I. Now my view of the matter is that your knowledge, likely very soon to surpass in extent and accuracy that of most of your compeers, is to be made saleable, not by the usual way of adding friend to friend, which neither you nor I are enough patient of, but by a way of your own. Known you must be before you can be employed. Known you will not be for a winning, attaching, accommodating man, but for an original, commanding, and rather self-willed man. Now establish this last character, and you take a far higher grade than any other. How are you to establish it? Just by bringing yourself before the public as you are. First find vent for your notions. Get them tongue; upon every subject get them tongue, not upon law alone. You cannot at present get them either utterance or audience by ordinary converse. Your utterance is not the most favourable. It convinces, but does not persuade; and it is only a very few (I can claim place for myself) that it fascinates. Your audience is worse. They are generally (I exclude myself) unphilosophical, unthinking drivellers who lay in wait to catch you in your words, and who give you little justice in the recital, because you give their vanity or self-esteem little justice, or even mercy, in the rencounter. Therefore, my dear friend, *some other way is to be sought for.* Now pause, if you be not convinced of this conclusion. If you be, we shall proceed. If you be not, read again, and you will see it just, and as such admit it. Now what way is to be sought for? I know no other than the press. You have not the pulpit as I have, and where perhaps I have the advantage. You have not good and influential society. I know nothing but the press for your purpose. None are so good as these two, the 'Edinburgh Review' and 'Blackwood's Magazine.' Do not steal away and say, The one I am not fit for, the other I am not willing for. Both pleas I refuse. The 'Edinburgh Review' you are perfectly fit for; not yet upon law, but upon any work of mathematics, physics, general literature, history, and politics, you are as ripe as the average of their writers. 'Blackwood's Magazine' presents bad company, I confess; but it also furnishes a good field for fugitive writing, and good introductions to society on one side of the question. This last advice, I confess, is against my conscience, and I am inclined to blot it out; for did I not rest satisfied that you were to use your pen for your conscience I would never ask you to use it for your living. Writers in the encyclopædias, except of leading articles, do not get out from the crowd; but writers in the Review come out at once, and obtain the very opinion you want, opinion among the intelligent and active men in every rank, not among the sluggish *savants* alone.

It is easy for me to advise what many perhaps are as ready to advise. But I know I have influence, and I am willing to use it. Therefore, again let me entreat you to begin a new year by an effort continuous, not for getting knowledge, but for communicating it, that you may gain favour, and money, and opinion. Do not disembark all your capital of thought, and time, and exertion into this concern, but disembark a portion equal to its urgency, and make the experiment upon a proper scale. If it succeed, the spirit of adventure will follow, and you will be ready to embark more; if it fail, no great venture was made; no great venture is lost: the time is not yet come. But you will have got a more precise view by the failure of the obstacles to be surmounted, and time and energy will give you what you lacked. Therefore I advise you as a very sincere friend, that forthwith you choose a topic, not that you are best informed on, but that you are most likely to find admittance for, and set apart some portion of each day or week to this object and this alone, leaving the rest free for objects professional and pleasant. This is nothing more than what I urged at our last meeting, but I have nothing to write I reckon so important. Therefore do take it to thought. Depend upon it, you will be delivered by such present adventure from those harpies of your peace you are too much tormented with. You will get a class with whom society will be as pleasant as we have found it together, and you will open up ultimate prospects which I trust no man shall be able to close.

I think our town is safe for every leal-hearted man to his Maker and to his fellow-men to traverse without fear of scaith. Such traversing is the wine and milk of my present existence. I do not warrant against a Radical rising, though I think it vastly improbable. But continue these times a year or two, and unless you unmake our present generation, and unman them of human feeling and of Scottish intelligence, you will have commotion. It is impossible for them to die of starvation, and they are making no provision to have them removed. And what on earth is for them? God and my Saviour enable me to lift their hearts above a world that has deserted them, though they live in its plenty and labour in its toiling service, and fix them upon a world which, my dear Carlyle, I wish you and I had the inheritance in; which we may have if we will. But I am not going to preach, else I would plunge into another subject which I rate above all subjects. Yet this should not be excluded from our communion either.

I am getting on quietly enough, and, if I be defended from the errors of my heart, may do pretty well. The Doctor (Chalmers) is full of acknowledgments, and I ought to be full—to a higher source.

Yours affectionately,

EDWARD IRVING.

Carlyle was less eager to give his thoughts 'tongue' than Irving supposed. He had not yet, as he expressed it, 'taken the Devil by the horns.' He did not mean to trouble the world with his doubts, and as yet he had not much else to trouble it with. But he was more and more restless. Reticence about his personal sufferings was at no time one of his virtues. Dyspepsia had him by the throat. Even the minor ailments to which our flesh is heir, and which most of us bear in silence, the eloquence of his imagination flung into forms like the temptations of a saint. His mother had early described him as 'gey ill to live wi',' and while in great things he was the most considerate and generous of men, in trifles he was intolerably irritable. Dyspepsia accounts for most of it. He did not know what was the matter with him, and when the fit was severe he drew pictures of his condition which frightened everyone belonging to him. He had sent his family in the middle of the winter a report of himself which made them think that he was seriously ill. His brother John, who had now succeeded him as a teacher in Annan School, was sent for in haste to Mainhill to a consultation, and the result was a letter which shows the touching affection with which the Carlyles clung to one another.

John A. Carlyle to Thomas Carlyle.

Mainhill: February 1820.

I have just arrived from Annan, and we are all so uneasy on your account that at the request of my father in particular, and of all the rest, I am determined to write to call on you for a speedy answer. Your father and mother, and all of us, are extremely anxious that you should come home directly if possible, if you think you can come without danger. And we trust that, notwithstanding the bitterness of last summer, you will still find it emphatically a home. My mother bids me call upon you to do so by every tie of affection, and by all that is sacred. She esteems seeing you again and administering comfort to you as her highest felicity. Your father, also, is extremely anxious to see you again at home. The room is much more comfortable than it was last season. The roads are repaired, and all things more convenient; and we all trust that you will yet recover, after you shall have inhaled your native breezes and escaped once more from the unwholesome city of Edinburgh, and its selfish and unfeeling inhabitants. In the name of all, then, I call upon you not to neglect or refuse our earnest wishes; to come home and experience the comforts of parental and brotherly affection, which, though rude and without polish, is yet sincere and honest.

The father adds a postscript:—

My dear Tom,—I have been very uneasy about you ever since we received your moving letter, and I thought to have written to you myself this day and told you all my thoughts about your health, which is the foundation and copestone of all our earthly comfort. But, being particularly engaged this day, I caused John to write. Come home as soon as possible, and forever oblige

Dear son, your loving father,

JAMES CARLYLE.

The fright had been unnecessary. Dyspepsia, while it tortures body and mind, does little serious injury. The attack had passed off. A letter from Carlyle was already on the way, in which the illness was scarcely noticed; it contained little but directions for his brother's studies, and an offer of ten pounds out of his scantily filled purse to assist 'Sandy' on the farm. With his family it was impossible for him to talk freely, and through this gloomy time he had but one friend, though this one was of priceless value. To Irving he had written out his discontent. He was now disgusted with law, and meant to abandon it. Irving, pressed as he was with work, could always afford Carlyle the best of his time and judgment.

Edward Irving to Thomas Carlyle.

Glasgow: March 14, 1820.

Since I received your last epistle, which reminded me of some of those gloomy scenes of nature I have often had the greatest pleasure in contemplating, I have been wrought almost to death, having had three sermons to write, and one of them a charity sermon; but I shall make many sacrifices before I shall resign the entertainment and benefit I derive from our correspondence.

Your mind is of too penetrating a cast to rest satisfied with the frail disguise which the happiness of ordinary life has thrown on to hide its nakedness, and I do never augur that your nature is to be satisfied with its sympathies. Indeed, I am convinced that were you translated into the most elegant and informed circle of this city, you would find it please only by its novelty, and perhaps refresh by its variety; but you would be constrained to seek the solid employment and the lasting gratification of your mind elsewhere. The truth is, life is a thing formed for the average of men, and it is only in those parts of our nature which are of average possession that it can gratify. The higher parts of our nature find their entertainment in sympathising with the highest efforts of our species, which are, and will continue, confined to the closet of the sage, and can never find their station in the drawing-rooms of the talking world. Indeed, I will go higher and say that the highest parts of our nature can never have their proper food till they turn to contemplate the excellencies of our Creator, and not only to contemplate but to imitate them. Therefore it is, my dear Carlyle, that I exhort you to call in the finer parts of your mind, and to try to present the society about you with those more ordinary displays which they can enjoy. The indifference with which they receive them,[1] and the ignorance with which they treat them, operate on the mind like gall and wormwood. I would entreat you to be comforted in the possession of your treasures, and to

[1] *I.e.*, the talk to which you usually treat your friends.

study more the times and persons to which you bring them forth. When I say your treasures, I mean not your information so much, which they will bear the display of for the reward and value of it, but of your feelings and affections, which, being of finer tone than theirs, and consequently seeking a keener expression, they are apt to mistake for a rebuke of their own tameness, or for intolerance of ordinary things, and too many of them, I fear, for asperity of mind.

There is just another panacea for your griefs (which are not imaginary, but for which I see a real ground in the too penetrating and, at times perhaps, too severe turn of your mind); but though I judge it better and more worthy than reserve, it is perhaps more difficult of practice. I mean the habit of using our superiority for the information and improvement of others. This I reckon both the most dignified and the most kindly course that one can take, founded upon the great principles of human improvement, and founded upon what I am wont, or at least would wish, to make my pattern, the example of the Saviour of men, who endured, in His errand of salvation, the contradiction of men. But I confess, on the other hand, one meets with so few that are apt disciples, or willing to allow superiority, that will be constantly fighting with you upon the threshold, that it is very heartless, and forces one to reserve. And besides, one is so apt to fancy a superiority where there is none, that it is likely to produce overmuch self-complacency. But I see I am beginning to prose, and therefore shall change the subject—with only one remark, that your tone of mind reminds me more than anything of my own when under the sense of great religious imperfection, and anxiously pursuing after higher Christian attainments. . . .

I have read your letter again, and, at the risk of further prosing, I shall have another hit at its contents. You talk of renouncing the law, and you speak mysteriously of hope springing up from another quarter. I pray that it may soon be turned into enjoyment. But I would not have you renounce the law unless you coolly think that this new view contains those fields of happiness, from the want of which the prospect of law has become so dreary. Law has within it scope ample enough for any mind. The reformation which it needs, and which with so much humour and feeling you describe,[1] is the very evidence of what I say. Did Adam Smith find the commercial system less encumbered? (I know he

---

[1] Carlyle's letters to Irving are all unfortunately lost.

did not find it more); and see what order the mind of one man has made there. Such a reformation must be wrought in law, and the spirit of the age is manifestly bending that way. I know none who, from his capacity of remembering and digesting facts, and of arranging them into general results, is so well fitted as yourself.

With regard to my own affairs, I am becoming too much of a man of business, and too little a man of contemplation. I meet with few minds to excite me, many to drain me off, and, by the habits of discharging and receiving nothing in return, I am run off to the very lees, as you may easily discern. I have a German master and a class in college. I have seen neither for a week; such is the state of my engagements—engagements with I know not what; with preaching in St. John's once a week, and employing the rest of the week in visiting objects in which I can learn nothing, unless I am collecting for a new series of Tales of my Landlord, which should range among Radicals and smugglers.

Dr. Chalmers, though a most entire original by himself, is surrounded with a very prosaical sort of persons, who please me something by their zeal to carry into effect his philosophical schemes, and vex me much by their idolatry of him. My comforts are in hearing the distresses of the people, and doing my mite to alleviate them. They are not in the higher walks (I mean as to wealth) in which I am permitted to move, nor yet in the greater publicity and notoriety I enjoy. Every minister in Glasgow is an oracle to a certain class of devotees. I would not give one day in solitude or in meditation with a friend as I have enjoyed it often along the sands of Kirkcaldy for ages in this way. . . .

Yours most truly,

EDWARD IRVING.

It does not appear what the 'other quarter' may have been on which the prospect was brightening. Carlyle was not more explicit to his mother, to whom he wrote at this time a letter unusually gentle and melancholy.

Thomas Carlyle to Mrs. Carlyle.

Edinburgh : March 29, 1820.

To you, my dear mother, I can never be sufficiently grateful, not only for the common kindness of a mother, but for the unceasing watchfulness with which you strove to instil virtuous principles into my young mind ; and though we are separated at present, and may be still more widely separated, I hope the lessons which you taught will never be effaced from my memory. I cannot say how I have fallen into this train of thought, but the days of childhood arise with so many pleasing recollections, and shine so brightly across the tempests and inquietudes of succeeding times, that I felt unable to resist the impulse.

You already know that I am pretty well as to health, and also that I design to visit you again before many months have elapsed. I cannot say that my prospects have got much brighter since I left you ; the aspect of the future is still as unsettled as ever it was ; but some degree of patience is behind, and hope, the charmer, that 'springs eternal in the human breast,' is yet here likewise. I am not of a humour to care very much for good or evil fortune, so far as concerns myself ; the thought that my somewhat uncertain condition gives you uneasiness chiefly grieves me. Yet I would not have you despair of your *ribe* of a boy. He *will* do something yet. He is a shy stingy soul, and very likely has a higher notion of his parts than others have. But, on the other hand, he is not incapable of diligence. He is harmless, and possesses the virtue of his country—thrift ; so that, after all, things will yet be right in the end. My love to all the little ones.

Your affectionate son,

T. CARLYLE.

The University term ends early in Scotland. The expenses of the six months which the students spend at college are paid for in many instances by the bodily labours of the other six. The end of April sees them all dispersed, the class rooms closed, the pupils no longer obtainable ; and the law studies being finally abandoned, Carlyle had nothing more to do at Edinburgh, and migrated with the rest. He was going home ; he offered himself for a visit to Irving at Glasgow on the way, and the proposal was warmly accepted. The Irving correspondence was not long continued ; and I make the most of the letters of so remarkable a man which were written while he was still himself, before his intellect was clouded.

34 Kent Street, Glasgow: April 15, 1820.

My dear Carlyle,—Right happy shall I be to have your company and conversation for ever so short a time, and the longer the better; and if you could contrive to make your visit so that the beginning of the week should be the time of your departure, I could bear you company on your road a day's journey. I have just finished my sermon—Saturday at six o'clock—at which I have been sitting without interruption since ten; but I resolved that you should have my letter to-morrow, that nothing might prevent your promised visit, to which I hold you now altogether bound.

It is very dangerous to speak one's mind here about the state of the country. I reckon, however, the Radicals have in a manner expatriated themselves from the political co-operation of the better classes; and, at the same time, I believe there was sympathy enough in the middle and well-informed people to have caused a melioration of our political evils, had they taken time and legal measures. I am very sorry for the poor; they are losing their religion, their domestic comfort, their pride of independence, their everything; and if timeous remedies come not soon, they will sink, I fear, into the degradation of the Irish peasantry; and if that class goes down, then along with it sinks the morality of every other class. We are at a complete stand here; a sort of military glow has taken all ranks. They can see the houses of the poor ransacked for arms without uttering an interjection of grief on the fallen greatness of those who brought in our Reformation and our civil liberty, and they will hardly suffer a sympathising word from anyone. Dr. Chalmers takes a safe course in all these difficulties. The truth is, he does not side with any party. He has a few political nostrums so peculiar that they serve to detach his ideal mind both from Whigs and Tories and Radicals—that Britain would have been as flourishing and full of capital though there had been round the island a brazen wall a thousand cubits high; that the national debt does us neither good nor ill, amounting to nothing more or less than a mortgage upon property, &c. The Whigs dare not speak. The philanthropists are so much taken up each with his own locality as to take little charge of the general concern; and so the Tories have room to rage and talk big about armaments and pikes and battles. They had London well fortified yesterday by the Radicals, and so forth.

Now it will be like the unimprisoning of a bird to come and let me have free talk. Not that I have anything to say in favour of Radicalism, for it is the very destitution of philosophy and religion and political economy; but that we may lose ourselves so delightfully in reveries upon the emendation of the State, to which, in fact, you and I can bring as little help as we could have done against the late inundation of the Vallois.

I like the tone of your last letter; for, remember, I read your very tones and gestures, at this distance of place, through your letter, though it be not the most diaphanous of bodies. I have no more fear of your final success than Noah had of the Deluge ceasing; and though the first dove returned, as you say you are to return to your father's shelter, without even a leaf, yet the next time, believe me, you shall return with a leaf; and yet another time, and you shall take a flight who knows where? But of this and other things I delay further parley.

Yours affectionately,

EDWARD IRVING.

Carlyle went to Glasgow, spent several days there, and noted, according to his habit, the outward signs of men and things. He saw the Glasgow merchants in the Tontine, he observed them, fine, clean, opulent, with their shining bald crowns and serene white heads, sauntering about or reading their newspapers. He criticised the dresses of the young ladies, for whom he had always an eye, remarking that with all their charms they had less taste in their adornments than were to be seen in Edinburgh drawing-rooms. He saw Chalmers too, and heard him preach. 'Never preacher went so into one's heart.' Some private talk, too, there was with Chalmers, 'the Doctor' explaining to him 'some new scheme for proving the truth of Christianity,' 'all written in us already *in sympathetic ink;* Bible awakens it, and you can read.'

But the chief interest in the Glasgow visit lies less in itself than in what followed it—a conversation between two young men, then unknown men, strolling alone together over a Scotch moor, seemingly the most trifling of incidents, a mere feather floating before the wind, yet, like the feather, marking the direction of the invisible tendency of human thought. Carlyle was to walk home to Ecclefechan. Irving had agreed to accompany him fifteen miles of his road, and then leave him and return. They started early, and breakfasted on the way at the manse of a Mr. French. Carlyle himself tells the rest.[1]

Drumclog Moss is the next object that survives, and Irving and I sitting by ourselves under the silent bright skies among the 'peat hags' of Drumclog with a world all silent round us. These peat hags are still pictured in me; brown bog all pitted and broken with heathy remnants and bare abrupt wide holes, four or five feet deep, mostly dry at present; a flat wilderness of broken bog, of quagmire not to be trusted (probably wetter in old days then, and wet still in rainy seasons). Clearly a good place for Cameronian preaching, and dangerously difficult for Claverse and horse soldiery if the suffering remnant had a few old muskets among them! Scott's novels had given the Claverse skirmish here, which all Scotland knew of already, a double interest in those days. I know not that we talked much of this; but we did of many things, perhaps more confidentially than ever before; a colloquy the sum of which is still mournfully beautiful to me though the details are gone. I remember us sitting on the brow of a peat hag, the sun shining, our own voices the one sound. Far far away to the westward over our brown horizon, towered up, white and visible at the many miles of distance, a high irregular pyramid. 'Ailsa Craig' we at once guessed, and thought of the seas and oceans over yonder. But we did not long dwell on that—we seem to have seen no human creature, after French, to have had no bother and no need of human assistance or society, not even of refection, French's breakfast perfectly sufficing us. The talk had grown ever friendlier, more interesting. At length the declining sun said plainly, you must part. We sauntered slowly into the Glasgow Muirkirk highway. Masons were building at a wayside cottage near by, or were packing up on ceasing for the day. We leant our backs to a dry stone fence, and looking into the western radiance continued in talk yet a while, loth both of us to

[1] *Reminiscences*, p. 140.

go. It was just here as the sun was sinking, Irving actually drew from me by degrees, in the softest manner, the confession that I did not think as he of the Christian religion, and that it was vain for me to expect I ever could or should. This, if this was so, he had pre-engaged to take well from me like an elder brother, if I would be frank with him, and right loyally he did so, and to the end of his life we needed no concealments on that head, which was really a step gained.

The sun was about setting when we turned away each on his own path. Irving would have had a good space further to go than I, perhaps fifteen or seventeen miles, and would not be in Kent Street till towards midnight. But he feared no amount of walking, enjoyed it rather, as did I in those young years. I felt sad, but affectionate and good, in my clean, utterly quiet little inn at Muirkirk, which and my feelings in it I still well remember. An innocent little Glasgow youth (young bagman on his first journey, I supposed) had talked awhile with me in the otherwise solitary little sitting room. At parting he shook hands, and with something of sorrow in his tone said, ' Good night. I shall not see *you* again.' I was off next morning at four o'clock.

CHAPTER VII.

NOTHING further has to be recorded of Carlyle's history for some months. He remained quietly through the spring and summer at Mainhill, occupied chiefly in reading. He was beginning his acquaintance with German literature, his friend Mr. Swan, of Kirkcaldy, who had correspondents at Hamburg, providing him with books. He was still writing small articles, too, for 'Brewster's Encyclopædia,' unsatisfactory work, though better than none.

I was timorously aiming towards literature (he says, perhaps in consequence of Irving's urgency). I thought in audacious moments I might perhaps earn some wages that way by honest labour, somehow to help my finances; but in that too I was painfully sceptical (talent and opportunity alike doubtful, alike incredible to me, poor downtrodden soul), and in fact there came little enough of produce and finance to me from that source, and for the first years absolutely none, in spite of my diligent and desperate efforts, which are sad to me to think of even now. *Acti labores.* Yes, but of such a futile, dismal, lonely, dim, and chaotic kind, in a sense all ghastly chaos to me. Sad, dim, and ugly as the shore of Styx and Phlegethon, as a nightmare dream become real. No more of that; it did not conquer me, or quite kill me, thank God.[1]

August brought Irving to Annan for his summer holidays, which opened possibilities of companionship again. Mainhill was but seven miles off, and the friends met and

[1] *Reminiscences*, p. 113.

wandered together in the Mount Annan woods, Irving
steadily cheering Carlyle with confident promises of ultimate success. In September came an offer of a tutorship
in a 'statesman's' [1] family, which Irving urged him to
accept.

You live too much in an ideal world (Irving said), and you are
likely to be punished for it by an unfitness for practical life. It
is not your fault but the misfortune of your circumstances, as it
has been in a less degree of my own. This situation will be more
a remedy for that than if you were to go back to Edinburgh. Try
your hand with the respectable illiterate men of middle life, as I
am doing at present, and perhaps in their honesty and hearty
kindness you may be taught to forget, and perhaps to undervalue
the splendours, and envies, and competitions of men of literature.
I think you have within you the ability to rear the pillars of your
own immortality, and, what is more, of your own happiness, from
the basis of any level in life, and I would always have any man
destined to influence the interests of men, to have read these
interests as they are disclosed in the mass of men, and not in the
few who are lifted upon the eminence of life, and when there too
often forget the man to ape the ruler or the monarch. All that is
valuable of the literary caste you have in their writings. Their
conversations, I am told, are full of jealousy and reserve, or, perhaps to cover that reserve, of trifling.

Irving's judgment was perhaps at fault in this advice.
Carlyle, proud, irritable, and impatient as he he was, could
not have remained a week in such a household. His ambition (downtrodden as he might call himself) was greater
than he knew. He may have felt like Halbert Glendin-
ning when the hope was held out to him of becoming the
Abbot's head keeper—'a body servant, and to a lazy
priest!' At any rate the proposal came to nothing, and
with the winter he was back once more at his lodgings in
Edinburgh, determined to fight his way somehow, though
in what direction he could not yet decide or see.

[1] 'Statesman,' or small freeholder farming his own land, common still in
Cumberland, then spread over the northern counties.

Thomas Carlyle to Alexander Carlyle.

Edinburgh : December 5, 1820.

I sit down with the greatest pleasure to answer your most acceptable letter. The warm affection, the generous sympathy displayed in it go near the heart, and shed over me a meek and kindly dew of brotherly love more refreshing than any but a wandering forlorn mortal can well imagine. Some of your expressions affect me almost to weakness, I might say with pain, if I did not hope the course of events will change our feelings from anxiety to congratulation, from soothing adversity to adorning prosperity. I marked your disconsolate look. It has often since been painted in the mind's eye ; but believe me, my boy, these days will pass over. We shall all get to rights in good time, and long after, cheer many a winter evening by recalling such pensive, but yet amiable and manly thoughts to our minds. And in the meanwhile let me utterly sweep away the vain fear of our forgetting one another. There is less danger of this than of anything. We Carlyles are a clannish people because we have all something original in our formation, and find therefore less than common sympathy with others ; so that we are constrained, as it were, to draw to one another, and to seek that friendship in our own blood which we do not find so readily elsewhere. Jack and I and you will respect one another to the end of our lives, because I predict that our conduct will be worthy of respect, and we will love one another, because the feelings of our young days—feelings impressed most deeply on the young heart—are all intertwined and united by the tenderest yet strongest ties of our nature. But independently of this your fear is vain. Continue to cultivate your abilities, and to behave steadily and quietly as you have done, and neither of the two literati [1] are likely to find many persons more qualified to appreciate their feelings than the farmer their brother. Greek words and Latin are fine things, but they cannot hide the emptiness and lowness of many who employ them.

Brewster has printed my article. He is a pushing man and speaks encouragingly to me. Tait, the bookseller, is loud in his kind anticipations of the grand things that are in store for me. But in fact I do not lend much ear to those gentlemen. I feel quite sick of this drivelling state of painful idleness. I am going to be patient no longer, but quitting study or leaving it in a secondary place I feel *determined*, as it were, to find something sta-

[1] His brother John and himself.

tionary, some local habitation and some name for myself, ere it be long. I shall turn and try all things, be diligent, be assiduous in season and out of season to effect this prudent purpose ; and if health stay with me I still trust I shall succeed. At worst it is but narrowing my views to suit my means. I shall enter the writing life, the mercantile, the lecturing, any life in short but that of country schoolmaster ; and even that sad refuge from the storms of fate rather than stand here in frigid impotence, the powers of my mind all festering and corroding each other in the miserable strife of inward will against outward necessity.

I lay out my heart before you, my boy, because it is solacing for me to do so ; but I would not have you think me depressed. Bad health does indeed depress and undermine one more than all other calamities put together ; but with care, which I have the best of all reasons for taking, I know this will in time get out of danger. Steady then, steady ! as the drill-sergeants say. Let us be steady unto the end. In due time we shall reap if we faint not. Long may you continue to cherish the manly feelings which you express in conclusion. They lead to respectability at least from the world, and, what is far better, to sunshine within which nothing can destroy or eclipse.

In the same packet Carlyle encloses a letter to his mother.

I know well and feel deeply that you entertain the most solici-tous anxiety about my temporal, and still more about my eternal welfare ; as to the former of which, I have still hopes that all your tenderness will yet be repaid ; and as to the latter, though it be-comes not the human worm to boast, I would fain persuade you not to entertain so many doubts. Your character and mine are far more similar than you imagine ; and our opinions too, though clothed in different garbs, are, I well know, still analogous at bottom. I respect your religious sentiments and honour you for feeling them more than if you were the highest woman in the world without them. Be easy, I entreat you, on my account ; the world will use me better than before ; and if it should not, let us hope to meet in that upper country, when the vain fever of life is gone by, in the country where all darkness shall be light, and where the exercise of our affections will not be thwarted by the infirmities of human nature any more. Brewster will give me articles enough. Meanwhile my living here is not to cost me anything, at least for a season more or less. I have two hours of teaching, which both gives me a call to walk and brings in four guineas a month.

Again, a few weeks later :—

Thomas Carlyle to Mrs. Carlyle.

January 30, 1821.

My employment, you are aware, is still very fluctuating, but this I trust will improve. I am advancing, I think, though leisurely, and at last I feel no insuperable doubts of getting honest bread, which is all I want. For as to fame and all that, I see it already to be nothing better than a meteor, a will-o'-the-wisp which leads one on through quagmires and pitfalls to catch an object which, when we have caught it, turns out to be nothing. I am happy to think in the meantime that you do not feel uneasy about my future destiny. Providence, as you will observe, will order it better or worse, and with His award, so nothing mean or wicked lie before me, I shall study to rest satisfied.

It is a striking thing, and an alarming to those who are at ease in the world, to think how many living beings that had breath and hope within them when I left Ecclefechan are now numbered with the clods of the valley! Surely there is something obstinately stupid in the heart of man, or the flight of threescore years, and the poor joys or poorer cares of this our pilgrimage would never move as they do. Why do we fret and murmur, and toil, and consume ourselves for objects so transient and frail? Is it that the soul living here as in her prison-house strives after something boundless like herself, and finding it nowhere still renews the search? Surely we are fearfully and wonderfully made. But I must not pursue these speculations, though they force themselves upon us sometimes even without our asking.

To his family Carlyle made the best of his situation ; and indeed, so far as outward circumstances were concerned, there was no special cause for anxiety. His farm-house training had made him indifferent to luxuries, and he was earning as much money as he required. It was not here that the pinch lay ; it was in the still uncompleted 'temptations in the wilderness,' in the mental uncertainties which gave him neither peace nor respite. He had no friend in Edinburgh with whom he could exchange thoughts, and no society to amuse or distract him. And those who knew his condition best, the faithful Irving especially, became seriously alarmed for him. So keenly Irving felt the danger, that in December he even invited Carlyle to give up Edinburgh and be his own guest for an indefinite time at Glasgow.

You make me too proud of myself (he wrote) when you connect me so much with your happiness. Would that I could contribute to it as I most fondly wish, and one of the richest and most powerful minds I know should not now be struggling with obscurity and a thousand obstacles. And yet if I had the power I do not see by what means I should cause it to be known; your mind, unfortunately for its present peace, has taken in so wide a range of study as to be almost incapable of professional trammels; and it has nourished so uncommon and so unyielding a character, as first unfits you for, and then disgusts you with, any accommodations which would procure favour and patronage. The race which you have run these last years pains me even to think upon it, and if it should be continued a little longer, I pray God to give you strength to endure it. We calculate upon seeing you at Christmas, and till then you can think of what I now propose—that instead of wearying yourself with endless vexations which are more than you can bear, you will consent to spend not a few weeks, but a few months, here under my roof, where enjoying at least wholesome conversation and the sight of real friends, you may undertake some literary employment which may present you in a fairer aspect to the public than any you have hitherto taken before them. Now I know it is quite Scottish for you to refuse this upon the score of troubling me: but trouble to me it is none; and if it were a thousand times more, would I not esteem it well bestowed upon you and most highly rewarded by your company and conversation? I should esteem it an honour that your first sally in arms went forth from my habitation.

Well might Carlyle cherish Irving's memory. Never had he or any man a truer-hearted, more generous friend. The offer could not be accepted. Carlyle was determined before all things to earn his own bread, and he would not abandon his pupil work. Christmas he did spend at Glasgow, but he was soon back again. He was corresponding now with London booksellers, offering a complete translation of Schiller for one thing, to which the answer had been an abrupt No. Captain Basil Hall, on the other hand, having heard of Carlyle, tried to attach him to himself, as a sort of scientific companion on easy terms—Carlyle to do observations which Captain Hall was to send to the Admiralty as his own, and to have in return the advantage of philosophical society, &c., to which his answer had in like manner been negative. His letters show him still suffering from mental fever, though with glimpses of purer light.

Thomas Carlyle to John Carlyle.

Edinburgh : March 9, 1821.

It is a shame and misery to me at this age to be gliding about in strenuous idleness, with no hand in the game of life where I have yet so much to win, no outlet for the restless faculties which are there up in mutiny and slaying one another for lack of fair enemies. I must do or die then, as the song goes. Edinburgh, with all its drawbacks, is the only scene for me. In the country I am like an alien, a stranger and pilgrim from a far-distant land. I must endeavor most sternly, for this state of things cannot last, and if health do but revisit me as I know she will, it shall ere long give place to a better. If I grow seriously ill, indeed, it will be different ; but when once the weather is settled and dry, exercise and care will restore me completely. I am considerably clearer than I was, and I should have been still more so had not this afternoon been wet, and so prevented me from breathing the air of Arthur's Seat, a mountain close beside us, where the atmosphere is pure as a diamond, and the prospect grander than any you ever saw. The blue majestic everlasting ocean, with the Fife hills swelling gradually into the Grampians behind ; rough crags and rude precipices at our feet (where not a hillock rears its head unsung), with Edinburgh at their base clustering proudly over her rugged foundations, and covering with a vapoury mantle the jagged black venerable masses of stonework that stretch far and wide and show like a city of Fairy-land. . . . I saw it all last evening when the sun was going down, and the moon's fine crescent, like a pretty silver creature as it is, was riding quietly above me. Such a sight does one good. But I am leading you astray after my fantasies when I should be inditing plain prose.

The gloomy period of Carlyle's life—a period on which he said that he ever looked back with a kind of horror— was drawing to its close, this letter among other symptoms showing that the natural strength of his intellect was asserting itself. Better prospects were opening; more regular literary employment; an offer, if he chose to accept it, from his friend Mr. Swan, of a tutorship at least more satisfactory than the Yorkshire one. His mother's affection was more precious to him, however simply expressed, than any other form of earthly consolation.

Mrs. Carlyle to Thomas Carlyle.

Mainhill: March 21, 1821.

Son Tom,—I received your kind and pleasant letter. Nothing is more satisfying to me than to hear of your welfare. Keep up your heart, my brave boy. You ask kindly after my health. I complain as little as possible. When the day is cheerier, it has a great effect on me. But upon the whole I am as well as I can expect, thank God. I have sent a little butter and a few cakes with a box to bring home your clothes. Send them all home that I may wash and sort them once more. Oh, man, could I but write! I'll tell ye a' when we meet, but I must in the meantime content myself. Do send me a long letter; it revives me greatly: and tell me honestly if you read your chapter e'en and morn, lad. You mind I hod if not your hand, I hod your foot of it. Tell me if there is anything you want in particular. I must run to pack the box, so I am

Your affectionate mother,

MARGARET CARLYLE.

Irving was still anxious. To him Carlyle laid himself bare in all his shifting moods, now complaining, now railing at himself for want of manliness. Irving soothed him as he could, always avoiding preachment.

I see (he wrote)[1] you have much to bear, and perhaps it may be a time before you clear yourself of that sickness of the heart which afflicts you; but strongly I feel assured it will not master you, that you will rise strongly above it and reach the place your genius destines you to. Most falsely do you judge yourself when you seek such degrading similitudes to represent what you call your 'whining.' And I pray you may not again talk of your distresses in so desperate, and to me disagreeable, manner. My dear Sir, is it to be doubted that you are suffering grievously the want of spiritual communion, the bread and water of the soul? and why, then, do you, as it were, mock at your calamity or treat it jestingly? I declare this is a sore offence. You altogether mistake at least *my* feeling if you think I have anything but the kindest sympathy in your case, in which sympathy I am sure there is nothing degrading, either to you or to me. Else were I degraded every time I visit a sick bed in endeavouring to draw forth the case of a sufferer from his own lips that I may if possible administer some spiritual consolation. But oh! I would be angry, or rather I should have a shudder of unnatural feeling, if the sick man were to make a mockery to me of his case or to deride himself for making it known to any physician of body or mind. Excuse my freedom, Carlyle. I do this in justification of my own state of mind towards your distress. I feel for your condition as a brother would feel, and to see you silent about it were the greatest access of painful emotion which you could cause me. I hope soon to look back with you over this scene of trials as the soldier does over a hard campaign, or the restored captives do over their days of imprisonment.

Again, on the receipt of some better account of his friend's condition, Irving wrote on April 26:—

I am beginning to see the dawn of the day when you shall be plucked by the literary world from my solitary, and therefore more clear, admiration; and when from almost a monopoly I shall have nothing but a mere shred of your praise. They will unearth you, and for your sake I will rejoice, though for my own I may regret. But I shall always have the pleasant superiority that I was your friend and admirer, through good and through bad report, to continue, so I hope, unto the end. Yet our honest

[1] March 15, 1821.

Demosthenes,[1] or shall I call him Chrysostom (Boanerges would fit him better), seems to have caught some glimpse of your inner man, though he had few opportunities ; for he never ceases to be inquiring after you. You will soon shift your quarters, though for the present I think your motto should be, 'Better a wee push than na bield.' If you are going to revert to teaching again, which I heartily deprecate, I know nothing better than Swan's conception, although success in it depends mainly upon offset and address, and the studying of humours, which, though it be a good enough way of its kind, is not the way to which I think you should yet condescend.

Friends and family might console and advise, but Carlyle himself could alone conquer the spiritual maladies which were the real cause of his distraction. In June of this year 1821 was transacted what in 'Sartor Resartus' he describes as his 'conversion,' or 'new birth,' when he 'authentically took the Devil by the nose,' when he began to achieve the convictions, positive and negative, by which the whole of his later life was governed.

Nothing in 'Sartor Resartus' (he says) is fact; symbolical myth all, except that of the incident in the Rue St. Thomas de l'Enfer, which occurred quite literally to myself in Leith Walk, during three weeks of total sleeplessness, in which almost my one solace was that of a daily bathe on the sands between Leith and Portobello. Incident was as I went down ; coming up I generally felt refreshed for the hour. I remember it well, and could go straight to about the place.

As the incident is thus authenticated, I may borrow the words in which it is described, opening, as it does, a window into Carlyle's inmost heart.

Shut out from hope in a deeper sense than we yet dream of (for as the professor wanders wearisomely through this world, he has lost all tidings of another and a higher), full of religion, or at least of religiosity, as our friend has since exhibited himself, he hides not that in those days he was totally irreligious. 'Doubt had darkened into unbelief,' says he : 'shade after shade goes grimly

[1] Dr. Chalmers.

over your soul, till you have the fixed starless Tartarean black.' To such readers as have reflected (what can be called reflecting) on man's life, and happily discovered, in contradiction to much profit and less philosophy, that soul is not synonymous with stomach, who understand, therefore, in our friend's words, 'that for man's well-being faith is properly the one thing needful, how with it martyrs, otherwise weak, can cheerfully endure the shame and the cross, and without it worldlings puke up their sick exist-ence by suicide in the midst of luxury;' to such it will be clear that for a pure moral nature the loss of his religious belief was the loss of everything. Unhappy young man! All wounds, the crush of long-continued destitution, the stab of false friendship and of false love, all wounds in thy so genial heart, would have healed again, had not its life-warmth been withdrawn. Well might he exclaim in his wild way: 'Is there no God then? but, at best, an absentee God sitting idle ever since the first Sabbath, at the out-side of his universe, and seeing it go? Has the word "duty" no meaning? Is what we call Duty no divine messenger and guide, but a false earthly fantasm, made up of desire and fear, of emana-tions from the gallows and Dr. Graham's celestial bed? Happi-ness of an approving conscience! Did not Paul of Tarsus, whom admiring men have since named saint, feel that *he* was the chief of sinners; and Nero of Rome, jocund in spirit, spend much of his time in fiddling? Foolish wordmonger and motive grinder, who in thy logic mill hast an earthly mechanism for the godlike itself, and wouldst fain grind me out virtue from the husks of pleasure. I tell thee Nay! To the unregenerate Prometheus Vinctus of a man, it is ever the bitterest aggravation of his wretchedness that he is conscious of virtue, that he feels himself the victim not of suffering only, but of injustice. What then? Is the heroic in-spiration we name Virtue but some passion, some bubble of the blood bubbling in the direction others profit by? I know not; only this I know. If what thou namest Happiness is our true aim, then are we all astray. With stupidity and sound digestion man may front much. But what in these dull imaginative days are the terrors of conscience to the diseases of the liver! Not on morality but on cookery let us build our stronghold. Then brandishing our frying-pan as censer, let us offer sweet incense to the Devil, and live at ease on the fat things *he* has provided for his elect!'

Thus has the bewildered wanderer to stand, as so many have

done, shouting question after question into the Sibyl cave of destiny, and receive no answer but an echo. . . . No pillar of cloud by day and no pillar of fire by night any longer guides the pilgrim. To such length has the spirit of inquiry carried him. 'But what boots it?' cries he; 'it is but the common lot in this era. Not having come to spiritual majority prior to the 'Siècle de Louis Quinze,' and not being born purely a loghead, thou hadst no other outlook. The whole world is like thee sold to unbelief. Their old temples of the godhead, which for long have not been rain-proof, crumble down; and men ask now, where is the godhead; our eyes never saw him.'

Pitiful enough were it for all these wild utterances to call our Diogenes wicked. Unprofitable servants as we all are, perhaps at no era of his life was he more decisively the servant of goodness, the servant of God, than even now when doubting God's existence. 'One circumstance I note,' says he; 'after all the nameless woe that Inquiry, which for me, what it is not always, was genuine love of truth, had wrought me, I nevertheless still loved Truth, and would bate no jot of my allegiance to her.' 'Truth!' I cried, 'though the heavens crush me for following her: no Falsehood! though a whole celestial Lubberland were the price of apostasy.' In conduct it was the same. Had a divine messenger from the clouds, or miraculous handwriting on the wall, convincingly proclaimed to me *This thou shalt do*, with what passionate readiness, as I often thought, would I have done it, had it been leaping into the infernal fire. Thus in spite of all motive grinders and mechanical profit and loss philosophies, with the sick ophthalmia and hallucination they had brought on, was the infinite nature of duty still dimly present to me: living without God in the world, of God's light I was not utterly bereft. If my as yet sealed eyes with their unspeakable longing could nowhere see Him, nevertheless in my heart He was present, and his Heaven-written law still stood legible and sacred there.'

Meanwhile, under all these tribulations and temporal and spiritual destitutions, what must the wanderer in his silent soul have endured!

The painfullest feeling (writes he), is that of your own feebleness; even as the English Milton says, 'to be weak is the true misery.' And yet of your strength there is and can be no clear feeling, save by what you have prospered in, by what you have done. Between vague wavering capability and fixed indubitable performance, what a difference! A certain inarticulate self-consciousness dwells dimly in us, which only our works can render articulate and decisively discernible. Our works are the mirror wherein the spirit first sees its natural lineaments. Hence, too, the folly of that impossible precept, *Know thyself*, till it be translated into this partially possible one, *Know what thou canst work at.*

But for me, so strangely unprosperous had I been, the net result of my workings amounted as yet simply to—nothing. How, then, could I believe in my strength when there was as yet no mirror to see it in? Ever did this agitating, yet, as I now perceive, quite frivolous question remain to me insoluble: Hast thou a certain faculty, a certain worth, such as even the most have not; or art thou the completest dullard of these modern times? Alas, the fearful unbelief is unbelief in yourself; and how could I believe? Had not my first last faith in myself, when even to me the Heavens seemed laid open, and I dared to love, been all too cruelly belied? The speculative mystery of life grew ever more mysterious to me: neither in the practical mystery had I made the slightest progress, but been everywhere buffeted, foiled, and contemptuously cast out. A feeble unit in the middle of a threatening infinitude, I seemed to have nothing given me but eyes whereby to discern my own wretchedness. Invisible yet impenetrable walls, as of enchantment, divided me from all living. Now when I looked back it was a strange isolation I then lived in. The men and women round me, even speaking with me, were but figures; I had practically forgotten that they were alive, that they were not merely automatic. In the midst of their crowded streets and assemblages, I walked solitary, and (except as it was my own heart, not another's, that I kept devouring), savage also as the tiger in his jungle. Some comfort it would have been could I, like Faust, have fancied myself tempted and tormented of the devil; for a hell as I imagine, without life, though only diabolic life, were more frightful: but in our age of downpulling and disbelief, the very devil has been pulled down, you cannot so much as believe in a devil. To me the universe was all void of life, of purpose, of volition, even of hostility: it was one huge, dead, immeasurable steam-engine, rolling on in its dead indifference, to grind me limb from limb. Oh, the vast, gloomy, solitary Golgotha and mill of death! Why was the living banished thither companionless, conscious? Why, if there is no devil, nay, unless the devil is your god? . . . From suicide a certain aftershine (Nachschein) of Christianity withheld me, perhaps also a certain indolence of character; for was not that a remedy I had at any time within reach? Often, however, there was a question present to me: should someone now at the turning of that corner blow thee suddenly out of space into the other world or other no-world by pistol-shot, how were it? . . .

So had it lasted, as in bitter protracted death-agony through long years. The heart within me, unvisited by any heavenly dew-drop, was smouldering in sulphurous slow-consuming fire. Almost since earliest memory I had shed no tear; or once only when I, murmuring half audibly, recited Faust's death-song, that wild 'Selig der, den er im Siegesglanze findet.' Happy whom *he* finds in battle's splendour, and thought that of this last friend even I was not forsaken, that destiny itself could not doom me not to die. Having no hope, neither had I any definite fear, were it of man or devil; nay, I often felt as if it might be solacing could the arch-devil himself, though in Tartarean terrors, but rise to me, that I might tell him a little of my mind. And yet, strangely enough, I lived in a continual indefinite pining fear; tremulous, pusillani-mous apprehension of I knew not what. It seemed as if all things in the heavens above and the earth beneath would hurt me; as if the heavens and the earth were but boundless jaws of a devouring monster, wherein I palpitating waited to be devoured.

Full of such humour was I one sultry dogday after much per-ambulation toiling along the dirty little Rue St. Thomas de l'Enfer in a close atmosphere and over pavements hot as Nebu-chadnezzar's furnace; whereby doubtless my spirits were little cheered; when all at once there rose a thought in me, and I asked myself: 'What *art* thou afraid of? wherefore, like a coward, dost thou for ever pip and whimper, and go cowering and trembling? Despicable biped! what is the sum total of the worst that lies before thee? Death? Well, death; and say the pangs of Tophet too, and all that the devil and man may, will, or can do against thee! Hast thou not a heart? canst thou not suffer whatsoever it be; and as a child of freedom, though outcast, trample Tophet itself under thy feet, while it consumes thee? Let it come, then, and I will meet it and defy it.' And as I so thought, there rushed like a stream of fire over my whole soul, and I shook base fear away from me for ever. I was strong; of unknown strength; a spirit; almost a god. Ever from that time, the temper of my misery was changed; not fear or whining sorrow was it, but in-dignation and grim fire-eyed defiance.

Thus had the everlasting No ('das ewige Nein') pealed authoritatively through all the recesses of my being, of my ME; and then it was that my whole ME stood up in native God-created majesty, and with emphasis recorded its protest. Such a protest, the most important transaction in my life, may that same indignation and defiance, in a psychological point of view, be fitly called. The everlasting No had said : Behold, thou art fatherless, outcast, and the universe is mine (the devil's); to which my whole ME now made answer : *I* am not thine but free, and for ever hate thee.

It is from this hour I incline to date my spiritual new birth; perhaps I directly thereupon began to be a man.[1]

[1] *Sartor*, p. 156, *et seq.*

CHAPTER VIII.

A.D. 1821. ÆT. 26.

CRAIGENPUTTOCK, craig, or whinstone hill of the puttocks,[1]
is a high moorland farm on the watershed between Dumfriesshire and Galloway, sixteen miles from the town of
Dumfries. The manor house, solid and gaunt, and built
to stand for centuries, lies on a slope protected by a planta-
tion of pines, and surrounded by a few acres of reclaimed
grass land—a green island in the midst of heathery hills,
sheep-walks, and undrained peat-bogs. A sterner spot is
hardly to be found in Scotland. Here for many generations had resided a family of Welshes, holding the rank of
small gentry. The eldest son bore always the same name
—John Welsh had succeeded John Welsh as far back as
tradition could record; the earliest John of whom authentic memory remained being the famous Welsh, the minister of Ayr, who married the daughter of John Knox.
This lady it was who, when her husband was banished,
and when she was told by King James that he might return to Scotland if he would acknowledge the authority of
bishops, raised her apron and said, 'Please your Majesty
I'd rather kep his head there.' The king asked her
who she was. 'Knox and Welsh,' he exclaimed, when
she told him her parentage, 'Knox and Welsh! The devil
never made such a match as that.' 'It's right like, sir,'
said she, 'for we never speered his advice.'

[1] Small hawks, so named still in Galloway, and once throughout England.
'Who finds the partridge in the puttock's nest,
But may imagine how the bird was dead.'
—*Shakespeare.*

A family with such an ancestry naturally showed remarkable qualities. 'Several blackguards among them,
but not one blockhead that I ever heard of,' was the account of her kinsfolk given to Jane Welsh [1] by her grandfather.

In the rebellion of 1745 the laird of Craigenputtock had
been among the sympathisers, though he escaped committing himself. Some of his friends who had been more
deeply implicated, had taken shelter with him when they
were inquired for after Culloden. Informers betrayed
their hiding-place, and a party of dragoons were sent up
from Dumfries to arrest them. The alarm was given;
before the dragoons arrived the objects of their pursuit
were away across the hills in Galloway. 'Such and such
men with you, aren't they?' said the officer to the laird,
as he rode to the door. 'Truly they were three hours ago,'
the laird answered; 'and they were rebels, say you? Fie,
the villains! had I but known! But come, let us chase
immediately. Once across the Orr yonder, and the swamps'
(which looked green enough from the house), 'you will
find firm road, and will soon catch the dogs.' Welsh
mounted, and volunteered to guide; guided the dragoons
into a spot where he and his pony, who knew the road,
could pass, and the heavy dragoon horses sank to their
girths. Having provided them with work which would
last till dark, he professed profound regrets, rode off, and
left them.

The son of this laird died young, leaving a widow at
Craigenputtock with a single child, another John, who was
born in 1757. The mother, desiring to give the boy a better education than was to be had on the moors, sent him
down to a tutor in Nithsdale. There he fell in love with
a Miss Hunter, daughter of a neighbouring grazier, and
married her, he being seventeen and the lady a year

[1] Afterwards Mrs. Carlyle.

younger. They returned to the Craig together, and produced one after the other fourteen children. The large
family brought expenses. The income was small. The
laird drifted into difficulties, sold part of the Craigenputtock property, and being unable to make a living out of
the rest, left it and took a farm by the riverside in Nith
valley, above Dumfries. Here he was fairly successful, as
indeed he deserved to be.

A valiant sensible man (says Carlyle), solidly devout, truth's own
self in what he said and did ; had dignity of manners too, in fact a
really brave, sincere, and honourable soul ; reverent of talent, honesty, and sound sense beyond all things ; was silently respected
and honestly esteemed in the district where he lived.

' Not however without a grin here and there,' for he had
his peculiarities. He was a tall man himself ; he had a
fixed notion that size of body and size of mind went together, and he would never admit a new friend till he had
measured him. This old John Welsh (or Penfillan, as he
was called from the name of his farm) did not die till 1823,
outliving his distinguished son who was the father of Carlyle's wife.

This next John Welsh was the eldest of the fourteen.
He was born at Craigenputtock in 1776, and spent his
childish years there. Scotch lads learn early to take care
of themselves. He was sent to Edinburgh University when
a mere lad to study medicine. While attending the classes
he drew attention to himself by his intelligence, and was
taken as an apprentice by one of the celebrated brothers
John or Charles Bell.[1] Dr. Bell saw his extraordinary
merit, and in 1796, when he was but twenty, recommended
him for a commission as regimental surgeon to the Perthshire Fencibles. This post he held for two years, and afterwards, in 1798, he succeeded either by purchase or oth-

---

[1] Probably John, as Sir Charles Bell was only two years John Welsh's
senior.

erwise to the local practice of the town and neighbourhood of Haddington. His reputation rose rapidly, and along with it he made a rapid fortune. To help his brothers and sisters he purchased Craigenputtock from his father, without waiting till it came to him by inheritance. He paid off the incumbrances, and he intended eventually to retire thither when he should give up business.

In 1800 Dr. Welsh married, the wife whom he chose being a Welsh also, though of another family entirely unrelated to his own. She, too, if tradition might be trusted, came of famous blood. John Welsh was descended from Knox. Grace or Grizzie Welsh traced her pedigree through her mother, who was a Baillie, to Wallace. Her father was a well-to-do stock farmer, then living at Caplegill on Moffat Water. Walter Welsh (this was his name), when his daughter left him to go to Haddington, moved himself into Nithsdale, and took a farm then known as Templand, near Penfillan. Thus Jane Welsh's two grandfathers, old Walter and old John, Welshes both of them, though connected only through their children's marriage, became close neighbours and friends. Walter of Templand lived to a great age, and Carlyle after his marriage knew him well. He took to Carlyle, indeed, from the first, having but two faults to find with him, that he smoked tobacco and would not drink whisky punch; not that old Walter drank to excess himself, or at all cared for drinking, but he thought that total abstinence in a young man was a sign of conceit or affectation.

He was a man (Carlyle writes) [1] of much singularity and intellect too, a microcosm of old Scottish life as it *had* been. Hot, impatient temper, breaking out into flashes of lightning if you touched him the wrong way; but they were flashes only, never bolts. Face uncommonly fine, serious yet laughing eyes as if inviting you in, bushy eyebrows picturesquely shaggy, abundant gray hair, beard

[1] *Reminiscences*, p. 368 (abridged).

imperfectly shaved, features massive yet soft, honesty, quick ingenuity, kindliness and frank manhood as the general expression, a
most simple man of stunted utterance, burred with his rr's, had a
chewing kind of way with his words which rapid or few were not
extremely distinct till you attended a little, and then aided by the
face they were distinct and memorable. Clever things Walter
never said or attempted to say, nor wise things either in any shape
beyond that of sincerely accepted commonplace; but he well knew
when such were said by others, and had a bright dimpling chuckle
—smudge of laughter the Scotch call it, one of the prettiest words
and ditto things, and on the whole hated no kind of talk but the
unwise kind. He was serious, pensive, not mournful or sad in
those old times. He had the prettiest laugh that I can remember,
not the loudest. My own father's still rarer laugh was louder far,
though not perhaps more complete. But his was all of artillery
thunder—*feu de joie* from all guns as the main element; while in
Walter there was audible something as of infinite flutes and harps,
as if the vanquished themselves were invited or compelled to par-
take of the triumph. 'Radiant ever young Apollo,' &c. &c. of
Teufelsdröckh's laugh is a reminiscence of that. He had an immense fund of articulate gaiety in his composition, a truly fine
sense of the ridiculous; excellent sense in a man, especially if he
never cultivate it or be conscious of it, as was Walter's case. It
must have been from him that my Jane derived that beautiful
light humour, never going into folly, yet full of tacit fires which
spontaneously illuminated all her best hours. Thanks to Walter!
. . . she was like him in this respect. My father's laugh is mainly
mine: a grimmer and inferior kind. Of my mother's beautifully
sportive vein (which was a third kind, also hereditary I am told)
I seem to have inherited less, though not nothing either, nay, perhaps at bottom not even less, had my life chanced to be easier
and joyfuller. 'Sense of the ridiculous'—worth calling such—i.e.
brotherly sympathy with the downward side, is very indispensable
to a man. Hebrews have it not, hardly any Jew creature—not
even a blackguard Heine to any real length; hence various mis-
qualities of theirs, perhaps most of their qualities too which have
become historical. This is an old remark of mine, though not yet
written anywhere.

The beautiful Miss Baillie, Walter's wife, who came of
Wallace, died early. Their son, called also John (the

many John Welshes may cause some confusion in this biography unless the reader can remember the distinctions), went into business at Liverpool, and was prospering as a merchant there, when a partner who was to have been his brother-in-law proved dishonest, ran off with all the property that he could lay hands on, and left John Welsh to bankruptcy and a debt of 12,000*l*. The creditors were lenient, knowing how the catastrophe had been brought about. John Welsh exerted himself, remade his fortune, and after eight years invited them all to dinner, where each found under his cover a cheque for the full amount of his claim. He was still living at Liverpool long after Carlyle settled in London with his niece, and will be heard of often in her correspondence.

His sister Grace, or Grizzie, was the wife of Dr. Welsh at Haddington. In appearance she was like her mother, tall, aquiline, and commanding.

She had a goodish, well-tending intellect (says Carlyle), with something of real drollery in it, which her daughter inherited. Your mother, my dear, I once said, has narrowly missed being a woman of genius. But she was sensitive, fanciful, capricious. Old Penfillan, who was on a visit at Haddington once after his son's marriage, reported that he had seen her one evening in fifteen different humours. She was not easy to live with for one wiser than herself, though very easy for one more foolish, especially if a touch of hypocrisy and perfect admiration was superadded. The married life at Haddington was loyal and happy, but because the husband took the command and knew how to keep it; he had much loved his wife, but none could less love what of follies she had. She was unusually beautiful, but strangely sad. Eyes bright as if with many tears behind them.

Dr. Welsh himself did not live to know Carlyle. He died in 1819, while still only forty-three, of a fever caught from a patient, three years before Carlyle's acquaintance with the family began. His daughter was so passionately attached to him, that she rarely mentioned his name even to her husband. From others, however, Carlyle gathered a general account of his character.

Dr. Welsh's success (he writes)[1] appears to have been swift and constant, till before long the whole sphere or section of life he was placed in had in all senses, pecuniary and other, become his own, and there remained nothing more to conquer in it : only very much to retain by the methods that had acquired it, and to be extremely thankful for as an allotment in this world, a truly superior man according to all the evidence I from all quarters have— a very valiant man Edward Irving once called him in my hearing. He was of noble and distinguished presence, tall, highly graceful, self-possessed, spontaneously dignified, so that people, if he entered a theatre or the like, asked Who is it? black hair, bright hazel eyes, bright, lively, steadily expressive features. His medical sagacity was reckoned at a higher and higher rate, medical and other honesty as well ; for it was by no means as a wise physician only, but as an honourable, exact, and quietly-dignified man, punctual, faithful in all points, that he was esteemed in the county. It was three years after his death when I first came into the circle which had been his, and nowhere have I met with a posthumous reputation that seemed to be more unanimous or higher among all ranks of men. The brave man himself I never saw ; but my poor Jeannie in her best moments often said to me about this or that, 'Yes, he would have done it so!' 'Ah, he would have liked you!' as her highest praise. Punctuality, Irving described as a thing he much insisted on. Gravely inflexible where right was concerned, and very independent when men of rank attempted to avail upon him. One anecdote I always remember. Riding along one day on his multifarious business, he noticed a poor wounded partridge fluttering and struggling about, wing or leg, or both, broken by some sportsman's lead. He alighted in his haste, gathered up the poor partridge, looped it gently in his handkerchief, brought it home, and by careful splints and other treatment had it soon on wing and sent it forth healed. This in so grave and practical a man had always in it a fine expressiveness to me.

Such was the genealogy of the young lady to whom Carlyle was now about to be introduced by Irving, and who was afterwards to be his wife. Tradition traced her

[1] *Reminiscences*, p. 360.

lineage to Knox and Wallace. Authentic history connected her with parents and kindred of singular, original, and strikingly superior quality. Jane Baillie Welsh was an only child, and was born in 1801. In her earliest years she showed that she was a girl of no common quality. She had black hair, large black eyes shining with soft mockery, pale complexion, broad forehead, nose not regularly formed, but mocking also like the eyes, figure slight, airy, and perfectly graceful. She was called beautiful, and beautiful she was even to the end of her life, if a face be beautiful which to look at is to admire. But beauty was only the second thought which her appearance suggested; the first was intellectual vivacity. Precious as she was to parents who had no other child, she was brought up with exceptional care. Strict obedience in essentials was the rule of the Haddington household. But the stories of her young days show that there was no harsh interference with her natural playfulness. Occasional visits were allowed to Templand, to her grandfather Walter, who was especially fond of her. In that house she was called *Pen* (short for Penfillan) to distinguish her from a second Jane Welsh of the other family. On one of these occasions, when she was six years old, her grandfather took her out for a ride on a quiet little pony. When they had gone as far as was desirable, Walter burring his rr's and intoning his vowels as usual said, 'Now we will go back by so and so, to *vahery the shane.*' 'Where did you ride to, Pen?' the company asked at dinner. 'We rode to *so* and then to *so*,' answered she punctually, 'and then from *so* returned by *so* to *vahery the shane*,' at which, says Carlyle, the old man burst into his cheeriest laugh at the mimicry of tiny little Pen.

She was a collected little lady, with a fine readiness in difficulties. The Welshes were the leading family at Haddington, and were prominent in the social entertainments there. When she was about the same age there was to be a childs' ball at the dancing-school.

Of this (Carlyle writes)[1] I often heard in the daintiest style, how the evening was so great, all the higher public, especially the maternal and paternal sections of it, collected to see the children dance: how Jeannie Welsh, then about six, had been selected to perform some pas-seul, beautiful and difficult, the jewel of the evening, and was privately anxious in her little heart to do it well: how she was dressed to perfection with elegance, with simplicity, and at the due hour was carried over in a clothes-basket (streets being muddy and no carriage), and landed safe, pretty silks and pumps uninjured. Through the ball everything went well and smoothly, nothing to be noted till the pas-seul came. My little woman, with a look that I can still fancy, appeared upon the scene, stood waiting for the music. Music began, but, alas! it was the wrong music. Impossible to dance that pas-seul to it. She shook her little head, looked or made some sign of distress; music ceased, took counsel, scraped, began again: again wrong hopelessly; the pas-seul flatly impossible. Beautiful little Jane alone against the world, forsaken by the music, but not by her presence of mind, plucked up her little skirt, flung it over her head, and, curtseying in that veiled manner, withdrew from the adventure, amidst general applause.

She learned rapidly the usual young lady's accomplishments—music, drawing, modern languages; and she had an appetite for knowledge not easily to be satisfied. A girl's education was not enough. She demanded 'to learn Latin like a boy.' Her mother was against it. Her father, who thought well of her talents, inclined to let her have her way. The question was settled at last in a characteristic fashion by herself. She found some lad in Haddington who introduced her to the mysteries of nouns of the first declension. Having mastered her lesson, one night when she was thought to be in bed, she had hidden herself under the drawing-room table. When an opportunity offered, the small voice was heard from below the cover,

[1] *Reminiscences*, p. 348.

'*Penna*, a pen ; *pennœ*, of a pen,' &c. &c. She crept out amidst the general amusement, ran to her father, and said, 'I want to learn Latin ; please let me be a boy.'

Haddington school was a furlong's distance from her father's house. Boys and girls were taught together there ; and to this accordingly she was sent.

Thither daily at an early hour (records Carlyle again) might be seen my little Jeannie tripping nimbly and daintily along, satchel in hand, dressed by her mother, who had a great talent that way, in tasteful simplicity, neat bit of pelisse (light blue sometimes), fastened with black belt, dainty little cap, perhaps little beaverkin, with flap turned up, and I think one at least with modest little plume in it. Fill that little figure with elastic intellect, love, and generous vivacity of all kinds, and where in nature will you find a prettier? At home was opulence without waste, elegance, good sense, silent, practical affection, and manly wisdom. From threshold to roof tree no paltriness or unveracity admitted into it. I often told her how very beautiful her childhood was to me. So authentic, too, in her charming naïve and humorous way of telling, and that she must have been the prettiest little Jenny Spinner [1] that was dancing on the summer rays in her time.

A fiery temper there was in her too. Boys and girls were kept for the most part in separate rooms at the school, but arithmetic and algebra, in which she was especially proficient, they learnt together,—or perhaps she in her zeal for knowledge was made an exception. The boys were generally devoted to her, but differences rose now and then. A lad one day was impertinent. She doubled her little fist, struck him on the nose, and made it bleed. Fighting in school was punished by flogging. The master came in at the instant, saw the marks of the fray and asked who was the delinquent. All were silent. No one would betray a girl. The master threatened to *tawse* the whole school, and being a man of his word

[1] Scotch name for a long-winged, long-legged, extremely bright and airy insect.—T. C.

would have done it, when the small Jeannie looked up
and said, 'Please it was I.' The master tried to look
grave, failed entirely, and burst out laughing. He told
her she was 'a little deevil,' and had no business there,
and bade her 'go her ways' to the girls' room.

Soon after this there was a change in the school management. Edward Irving, then fresh from college honours, came as master, and, along with the school, was
trusted with the private education of Jane Welsh. Dr.
Welsh had recognised his fine qualities, and took him into
the intimacy of his household, where he was treated as an
elder son. He watched over the little lady's studies, took
her out with him on bright nights to show her the stars
and teach her the movements of them. Irving was then
a young man, and his pupil was a child. A few years
were to make a difference. She worked with feverish
eagerness, getting up at five in the morning and busy
with her books at all hours. She was soon *dux* in mathematics. Her tutor introduced her to 'Virgil,' and the
effect of 'Virgil' and of her other Latin studies was 'to
change her religion and make her into a sort of Pagan.'
In one of her old note-books I find an allusion to this.

It is strictly true (she says), and it was not my religion alone
that these studies influenced, but my whole being was imbued with
them. Would I prevent myself from doing a selfish or cowardly
thing, I didn't say to myself, 'You mustn't, or if you do you will
go to hell hereafter.' Nor yet, 'If you do you will be whipt here;'
but I said to myself simply and grandly, 'A Roman would not
have done it,' and that sufficed under ordinary temptations.
Again, when I had done something heroic—when, for instance, I
had caught a gander which hissed at me by the neck and flung
him to the right about, it was not a good child that I thought
myself, for whom the half-crown bestowed on me was fit reward—
in my own mind I had deserved well of the Republic, and aspired
to a 'civic crown.' But the classical world in which I lived and
moved was best indicated in the tragedy of my doll. It had been
intimated to me by one whose wishes were law, that a young lady

in 'Virgil' should for consistency's sake drop her doll. So the doll being judged, must be made an end of; and I, 'doing what I would with my own,' like the Duke of Newcastle, quickly decided how. She should end as Dido ended, that doll! as the doll of a young lady in 'Virgil' should end! With her dresses, which were many and sumptuous, her four-posted bed, a faggot or two of cedar allumettes, a few sticks of cinnamon, a few cloves and a —nutmeg! I *non ignara futuri* constructed her funeral pyre—*sub auras*, of course; and the new Dido, having placed herself in the bed, with help, spoke through my lips the last sad words of Dido the first, which I had then all by heart as pat as A B C, and have now forgotten all but two lines—

> Vixi et quem dederat cursum fortuna peregi ;
> Et nunc magna mei sub terras ibit imago.

And half a line more—

> Sic, sic juvat ire sub umbras.

The doll having thus spoken, *pallida morte futurâ*, kindled the pile and stabbed herself with a penknife by way of Tyrian sword. Then, however, in the moment of seeing my poor doll blaze up— for being stuffed with bran she took fire and was all over in no time—in that supreme moment my affection for her blazed up also, and I shrieked and would have saved her and could not, and went on shrieking till everybody within hearing flew to me, and bore me off in a plunge of tears—an epitome of most of one's 'heroic sacrifices' it strikes me, magnanimously resolved on, ostentatiously gone about, repented of at the last moment, and bewailed with an outcry. Thus was my inner world at that period three-fourths old Roman and one-fourth old Fairy.

In the same notebook there is a long story of her first child love, told with the same grace, which need not be extracted here. When she was fourteen she wrote a tragedy, rather inflated, but extraordinary for her age. She never repeated the experiment, but for many years she continued to write poetry. She had inherited from her mother the gift of verse-making. Mrs. Welsh's lyrics were soft, sweet, passionate, musical, and nothing besides. Her daughter had less sweetness, but touched intellectual chords which her mother never reached.

The person 'whose wishes were law,' and whose suggestion occasioned the sacrifice of the doll, if it was not Irving, was probably her father.

Of him (says her friend Miss Jewsbury) she always spoke with reverence. He was the only person who had any real influence over her. However wilful she might be, obedience to her parents unquestioning and absolute lay at the foundation of her life. She used to say that this habit was her salvation, and that she owed to it all that was of value in her character. She always spoke of any praise her father gave her as a precious possession. She loved him passionately, and never spoke of him except to friends whom she valued. It was the highest token of her regard when she told anyone about her father.

She lost him, as has been said, at an age when she most needed his guiding hand. Had Dr. Welsh lived, her life would have been happier, whether more useful it is unprofitable to conjecture. The patient from whom he caught the fever which killed him was at some distance from Haddington. She being then eighteen had accompanied him in the carriage in this his last drive, and it was for ever memorable to her. Carlyle writes [1] :—

The usually tacit man, tacit especially about his bright daughter's gifts and merits, took to talking with her that day in a style quite new, told her she was a good girl, capable of being useful and precious to him, and to the circle she would live in; that she must summon her utmost judgment and seriousness to choose her path and be what he expected of her; that he did not think he had ever seen the life partner that would be worthy of her; in short, that he expected her to be wise as well as good-looking and good—all this in a tone and manner which filled her poor little heart with surprise and a kind of sacred joy coming from the man she of all men revered. Often she told me about this, for it was her last talk with him ; on the morrow, perhaps that evening, certainly within a day or two, he caught from some poor old woman patient a typhus fever, which under injudicious treatment killed him in three or four days, and drowned the world for her in the very blackness of darkness. In effect it was her first sorrow, and her greatest of all. It broke her health permanently, and in a sense almost broke her heart. A father so loved and mourned I have never seen. To the end of her life, his title even to me was '*He*' and '*Him*.' Not above twice or thrice, quite in later years, did she ever mention, and then in a quiet, slow tone—my father.

Dr. Welsh's illness being of so deadly a kind, he gave orders that she should not be allowed to enter his room. Persons who were in the house at the time have said that Miss Welsh's agitation was convulsive in its violence. 'I will see him,' she cried. 'I will see my father.' She forced her way to his bedside. He sent her out, and she lay all night on the stairs outside the door, refusing to be moved. Dr. Welsh's end was hastened on, perhaps caused, by the unskilfulness of his brother, a medical man like himself, who bled him too profusely. The first letter of Jane Welsh which has been preserved, is one which she wrote a fortnight later to her Penfillan grandmother, her father's mother. She had spoken laughingly of her paganism; her nature at the bottom was of a seriousness too deep for words, and her real character only showed itself when she was passionately moved.

To Mrs. Welsh, Penfillan.

Haddington: October 5, 1819.

My dear Grandmother,—I cannot allow my uncle to return to you without writing to assure you that the example of resignation to the will of God which you have given has not been totally lost upon us. It has been a great consolation to me under this dreadful trial to see my poor mother support it so well. From the very delicate state of her health for some time past, from the great fatigue she underwent during my dear father's illness, and above all from the acuteness of her feelings on the most ordinary occasions, I had little reason to expect so much fortitude. I will ever be grateful to her for the exertion which she has made (I am convinced in a great measure on my account), and still more grateful to Him who has enabled her to make them.

This has indeed been an unexpected and overwhelming blow. My father's death was a calamity I almost never thought of. If on any occasion the idea did present itself to me, it was immediately repelled as being too dreadful to be realised for many many years, and too painful to occupy any present place in my thoughts. Until this misfortune fell upon me I never knew what it was to be really unhappy. The greatest error and misfortune of my life hitherto has been not being sufficiently grateful for the happiness I enjoyed.

You, my dear grandmother, have had many trials; but if I mistake not, you will still remember the bitterness of the *first* above all others; you will still be able to recall the feeling of disappointment and despair which you experienced when calamity awoke you from your dream of security, and dispelled the infatuation which led you to expect that you alone were to be exempted from this world's misery. But you are good, and I am judging of your feelings by my own; when young as I am perhaps you were not as I was, thoughtless and unprepared for the chastisement of the Divine Power. The ways of the Almighty are mysterious; but in this instance, *though* He has left thousands in the world whose existence is a burden to themselves and to those around them, *though* He has cut off one who was the glory of his family, a most useful member of society, one who was respected and beloved by all who knew him, and *though* He has afflicted those who we thought deserved to be happy, yet His intention appears to me clear and intelligible. Could the annihilation of a thousand useless and contemptible beings have sent such terror and submission to the hearts of the survivors, as the sudden death of one whom their love would, if possible, have gifted with immortality? Oh, no! Hard it is, but we must acknowledge the wisdom of his sentence, even while we are suffering under it—we must kiss the rod even while we are writhing under the tortures which it inflicts.

We shall be in Dumfriesshire in a month or three weeks. My mother will answer your kind letter as soon as she feels able for it. With kind love to my grandfather and my aunts, and with every wish for your health, and the restoration of your peace of mind,

I remain, my dear Grandmother,
Your very affectionate child,
JANE BAILLIE WELSH.

After her father's death, Miss Welsh continued with her mother at Haddington. With the exception of some small annuity for his widow, Dr. Welsh had left everything belonging to him to his daughter. Craigenputtock became hers; other money investments became hers; and though the property altogether was not large according to modern estimates of such things, it was sufficient as long as mother and child remained together to enable them to live with comfort and even elegance. Miss Welsh was now an heiress. Her wit and beauty added to her distinctions, and she was called the flower of Haddington. Her hand became an object of speculation. She had as many suitors as Penelope. They were eligible, many of them, in point of worldly station. Some afterwards distinguished themselves. She amused herself with them, but listened favourably to none, being protected perhaps by a secret attachment, which had grown up unconsciously between herself and her tutor. There were difficulties in the way which prevented them from acknowledging to one another, or even to themselves, the condition of their feelings. Edward Irving had been removed from Haddington to Kirkcaldy, where he had entered while Jane Welsh was still a child into a half-formed engagement with the daughter of the Kirkcaldy minister, Miss Isabella Martin. In England young people often fancy themselves in love. They exchange vows which as they grow older are repented of, and are broken without harm to either party. In Scotland, perhaps as a remains of the ecclesiastical pre-contract which had legal validity, these connections had a more binding character. They could be dissolved by mutual consent; but if the consent of both was wanting, there was a moral stain on the person escaping from the bond. Irving had long been conscious that he had been too hasty, and was longing for release. But there was no encouragement on the side of the Martins. Marriage was out of the question till he had made a position for himself, and he had allowed the matter to drift on, since immediate decision

was unnecessary. Jane Welsh meanwhile had grown into
a woman. Irving, who was a constant visitor at Haddington, discovered when he looked into his heart that his real
love was for his old pupil, and the feeling on her part was
—the word is her own—'passionately' returned. The
mischief was done before they became aware of their danger. Irving's situation being explained, Miss Welsh refused to listen to any language but that of friendship from
him until Miss Martin had set him free. Irving, too, was
equally high principled, and was resolved to keep his word.
But there was an unexpressed hope on both sides that he
would not be held to it, and on these dangerous terms
Irving continued to visit at Haddington, when he could be
spared from his duties. Miss Welsh was working eagerly
at literature, with an ambition of becoming an authoress,
and winning name and fame. Unable or too much occupied himself to be of use to her, Irving thought of his
friend Carlyle, who was living in obscurity and poverty at
Edinburgh, as a fit person to assist and advise her. The
acquaintance, he considered, would be mutually agreeable.
He obtained leave from Mrs. Welsh to bring him over and
introduce him. The introduction was effected a little before Carlyle had 'taken the Devil by the nose,' as he
describes in 'Sartor Resartus;' and perhaps the first visit
to Haddington had contributed to bringing him off victorious from that critical encounter.

In June, 1821 (says Carlyle, but it was rather in the last week of
May), Edward Irving, who was visiting and recruiting about Edinburgh, on one of his occasional holiday sallies from Glasgow,
took me out to Haddington. We walked cheerily together, not
always by the highway, but meandering at our will pleasantly
and multifariously talking, as has been explained elsewhere,[1] and
about sunset of that same day I first saw her who was to be so
important to me thenceforth. A red, dusky evening, the sky
hanging huge and high, but dim as with dust or drought over

[1] *Reminiscences*, p. 137.

Irving and me, as we walked home to our lodging at the George Inn.

The visit lasted three or four days, and included Gilbert Burns and other figures, besides the one fair figure most of all important to me. We were often in her mother's house; sat talking with the two for hours almost every evening. The beautiful bright and earnest young lady was intent on literature as the highest aim in life, and felt imprisoned in the dull element which yielded her no commerce in that kind, and would not even yield her books to read. I obtained permission to send at least books from Edinburgh. Book parcels naturally included bits of writing to and from, and thus an acquaintance and correspondence was begun which had hardly any interruption, and no break at all while life lasted. She was often in Edinburgh on visit with her mother to 'Uncle Robert,' in Northumberland Street, to 'old Mrs. Bradfute, in George's Square,' and I had leave to call on these occasions, which I zealously enough, if not too zealously sometimes, in my awkward way took advantage of. I was not her declared lover, nor could she admit me as such in my waste and uncertain posture of affairs and prospects ; but we were becoming thoroughly acquainted with each other ; and her tacit, hidden, but to me visible friendship for me, was the happy island in my otherwise dreary, vacant, and forlorn existence in those years.

Eager as the interest which Carlyle was taking in his new acquaintance, he did not allow it to affect the regulation of his life, or to drive him into the beaten roads of the established professions on which he could arrive at fortune. His zeal for mathematics had by this time cooled. He had travelled, as he said, into more 'pregnant inquiries.' Inquiry had led to doubt, and doubt had enfeebled and dispirited him till he had grappled with it and conquered it. Traditionary interpretations of things having finally broken down with him, he was now searching for some answer which he could believe to the great central question, What this world is, and what is man's business in it ? Of classical literature he knew little, and that little had not attracted him. He was not living in ancient Greece or Rome, but in modern Europe, modern

Scotland, with the added experiences and discoveries of eighteen centuries ; and light, if light there was, could be looked for only in the writers of his own era. English literature was already widely familiar to him. He had read every book in Irving's library at Kirkcaldy, and his memory had the tenacity of steel. He had studied Italian and Spanish. He had worked at D'Alembert and Diderot, Rousseau and Voltaire. Still unsatisfied, he had now fastened himself upon German, and was devouring Schiller and Goethe. Having abandoned the law, he was becoming conscious that literature must be the profession of his life. He did not suppose that he had any special gift for it. He told me long after, when at the height of his fame, that he had perhaps less capability for literature than for any other occupation. But he was ambitious to use his time to honourable purposes. He was impatient of the trodden ways which led only to money or to worldly fame, and literature was the single avenue which offered an opening into higher regions. The fate of those who had gone before him was not encouraging. ' The biographies of English men of letters,' he says somewhere, ' are the wretchedest chapters in our history, except the Newgate Calendar.' Germany, however, and especially modern Germany, could furnish brighter examples. Schiller first took hold of him : pure, innocent, consistent, clear as the sunlight, with a character in which calumny could detect neither spot nor stain. The situation of Schiller was not unlike his own. A youth of poverty, surrounded by obstructions ; long difficulty in finding a road on which he could travel ; bad health besides, and despondent fits, with which Carlyle himself was but too familiar. Yet with all this Schiller had conquered adversity. He had raised himself to the second, if not to the highest place, in the admiration of his countrymen ; and there was not a single act in his whole career which his

5*

biographer would regret to record. Schiller had found
his inherited beliefs break down under him, and had
been left floating in uncertainties. But he had formed
moral convictions of his own, independent of creeds and
churches, and ˙ had governed his thought and conduct
nobly by them. Nothing that he did required forgiveness,
or even apology. No line ever fell from his pen which
he could have wished unwritten when life was closing
round him. Schiller's was thus an inspiriting figure to a
young man tremulously launching himself on the same
waters. His work was high and serene, clear and healthy
to the last fibre, noble thought and noble feeling rendered into words with true artistic skill.

Nevertheless, the passionate questionings which were
rising in Carlyle's mind could find no answer which would
satisfy him in Schiller's prose or consolation in Schiller's
lyrics. Schiller's nature was direct and simple rather than
profound and many-sided. Kant had spoken the last word
in philosophy to him. His emotions were generous, but
seldom subtle or penetrating. He had never looked with
a determined eye into the intellectual problems of humanity. He worked as an artist with composed vigour on subjects which suited his genius, and while his sentiments are
lofty and his passion hearty and true, his speculative insight is limited. Thus Schiller is great, but not the greatest ; and those who have gone to him for help in the enig-
mas social and spiritual which distract modern Europe,
have found generally that they must look elsewhere. From
Schiller Carlyle had turned to Goethe, and Goethe had
opened a new world to him. Schiller believed in the principles for which Liberals had been fighting for three centuries. To him the enemy of human welfare was spiritual
and political tyranny, and Don Carlos, William Tell, the
revolt of the Netherlands, or the Thirty Years' War, were
ready-made materials for his workshop. He was no vulgar

politician. He soared far above the commonplaces of popular orators and controversialists. He was a poet, with a
poet's sympathies. He could admire greatness of soul in
a Duke of Friedland; he could feel for suffering if the
sufferer was a Mary Stuart. But the broad articles of
faith professed by the believers in liberal progress were
Schiller's also, and he never doubted their efficacy for
man's salvation. Goethe had no such beliefs—no beliefs
of any kind which could be reduced to formulas. If he
distrusted priests, he distrusted still more the Freiheit's
Apostel and the philosophic critics. He had studied his
age on all its sides. He had shared its misgivings; he had
suffered from its diseases; he had measured its possibilities; he had severed himself from all illusions; and held
fast to nothing but what he could definitely recognise as
truth. In 'Werter,' in 'Faust,' in 'Prometheus,' Carlyle
found that another as well as he had experienced the
same emotions with which he was himself so familiar. In
'Wilhelm Meister,' that menagerie of tame creatures, as
Niebuhr called it, he saw a picture of society, accurate
precisely because it was so tame, as it existed in middle-
class European communities; the ardent, well-disposed
youth launched into the middle of it, beginning his apprenticeship in the false charms of the provincial theatre,
and led at last into a recognition of the divine meaning of
Christianity. Goethe had trod the thorny path before
Carlyle. He had not rushed into atheism. He had not
sunk into superstition. He remained true to all that intellect could teach him, and after facing all the spiritual
dragons he seemed to have risen victorious into an atmosphere of tranquil wisdom. On finishing his first perusal
of 'Meister,' and walking out at midnight into the streets
of Edinburgh to think about it, Carlyle said to himself,
'with a very mixed feeling in other respects, that here lay
more insight into the elements of human nature, and a

more poetically perfect combining of them, than in all the other fictitious literature of our generation.'

Having been charged by Irving with the direction of Miss Welsh's studies, he at once introduced her to his German friends. Irving, of the nature of whose interest in her welfare Carlyle had no suspicion, was alarmed at, what he had done. His own religious convictions were profound and sincere. He had occasioned unexpected mischief already with his 'Virgil.' He had laboured afterwards with all his energies to lead his pupil to think about Christianity as he thought himself, and when he heard of the books which she was set to read, he felt that he had been imprudent. Two months after the introduction at Haddington he wrote to Carlyle to confess his uneasiness.

Edward Irving to Thomas Carlyle.

July 24, 1821.

I did not follow your injunctions in transmitting to our fair acquaintance my German grammar and dictionary, her own being as much to the purpose. But I did not fail to instruct her to make all progress through the preliminaries to an easy perusal of the German poets. I am not competent to judge of their value towards the development of thought and character. You are—and therefore I should be silent. But if they should tend to cut our young friend off from any of the wholesome intercourse of those amongst whom she is cast without being able to raise her to a better, I should be very sorry, as it seems to me she is already unhinged from many of the enjoyments her condition might afford her. She contemplates the inferiority of others rather from the point of ridicule and contempt than from that of commiseration and relief; and by so doing she not only leaves objects in distress and loses the luxury of doing good, but she contracts in her own mind a degree of coldness and bitterness which suits ill with my conception of female character and a female's position in society. But I am speaking perhaps away from the truth. The books may not be what they are reported of. At the same time I am daily becoming more convinced that in all the literature of our own which, it is said, holds of the German school, there is something most poisonous to all that in this country has been named virtue, and still more to the distinctions of conduct which religion makes. It seems to me there is a jumble or confusion of former distinctions as if they were preparing for some new ones. They have the language of the highest purity, even of the most sacred religion, in communion with the blackest crimes; and the presence of the former is thought somehow or other to compensate for the latter. There is an attempt, too, I think, at two standards of moral judgment—one for the man of genius and literature, the other for the vulgar. But I dare say these are rather the extravagances of imitators than the errors of the masters.

Another letter is to the same purpose, while it throws interesting light on Irving's opinion of Carlyle.

There is too much of that furniture about the elegant drawing-room of Jane Welsh. I could like to see her surrounded with a more sober set of companions than Rousseau (your friend), and Byron, and such like. They will never make different characters than they were themselves, so deeply are they the prototypes of their own conceptions of character. And I don't think it will much mend the matter when you get her introduced to Von Schiller and Von Goethe and your other nobles of German literature. I fear Jane has already dipped too deep into that spring already, so that unless some more solid food be afforded I fear she will escape altogether out of the region of my sympathies and the sympathies of honest, home-bred men. In these feelings I know you will join me; and in giving to her character a useful and elegant turn you will aid me as you have opportunity.

I have been analysing, as I could, the origin of my esteem and affection for you. You are no more a general favourite than I am, and in the strong points of character we are not alike, nor yet alike in the turn of our general thoughts; and we are both too intrepid to seek in each other pity or consolation, and too independent to let anything sinister or selfish enter into our attachments. How comes it to pass then, that we have so much pleasant communion? I'll tell you one thing. High literature is exiled from my sphere, and simple principle is very much exiled from yours. Thus we feel a blank on both sides, which is supplied in some measure when we meet. I'll tell you another thing. Severed from the ordinary stays of men, influence, place, fortune, each in his way has been obliged to hang his hopes upon something higher; and though we have not chosen the same thing, in both cases it is pure and unearthly, and next to his own the thing which the other admires most. I can easily see that in the progress of our thoughts and characters there will be ample room for toleration and charity, which will form the touchstone of our esteem.

Irving identified 'principle' with belief in the formulas of the Church, and therefore supposed Carlyle to be without it. He considered his friend no doubt to be playing with dangerous weapons, and likely to injure others with them besides himself. But Carlyle's principles when applied to the common duties of life were as rigid as Irving's. He had been struck by his new acquaintance at Haddington, but he was too wise to indulge in dreams of a nearer relation—which their respective positions seemed to put out of the question—and he was too much in earnest to allow himself to be disturbed in the course of life which he had adopted, or forget the dearer friends at Mainhill to whom he was so passionately attached. He had remained this summer in Edinburgh longer than usual, and he and Irving had meditated a small walking tour together at the end of it. Irving, however, was unable to take a holiday. Carlyle went home alone, walking as he always did, and sending his box by the carrier. For him, as for so many of his student countrymen, coaches were rarely tasted luxuries. They tramped over moor and road with their bundles on their shoulder, sleeping by the way at herdsmen's cottages; and journeys which to the rich would be a delightful adventure, were not less pleasing to the sons of Scottish peasants because forced on them by honest poverty. Mainhill had become again by this time the happiest of shelters to him, and between his family and himself the old clear affection and mutual trust had completely re-established themselves. The passing cloud had risen only out of affectionate anxiety for his eternal well-being. Satisfied of the essential piety of his nature, his mother had been contented to believe that the

differences between herself and her son were differences of
expression merely, not of radical conviction. His father
was beginning to be proud of him, and was sensible enough
to leave him to his own guidance. Three quiet months
were spent with his brothers and sisters while he was
writing articles for Brewster's Encyclopædia. In November he was in Edinburgh again with improving prospects.

Things look as if they would go smoothly with me this winter
(he wrote on November 17 to his father). I saw Brewster the
other day, who received me kindly, and spread out his bank draft
for fifteen guineas like a man. He told me further that a translation was *for certain* to be set about, and that I as certainly should
have the first offer of it. The work is a French one, Legendre's
'Elements of Geometry,' which Jack knows well and has in his
possession. It is a thing I can work at, if the '*gea of life*' be in
me at all, and for that cause alone I purpose to accept it. There
is plenty of Encyclopædia work besides, and the worthy Review
men seem to be full as desirous that I should write for them, as I
am willing to write for anything in honour that will pay me well.
That poor article which you saw [1] has done me some good I find
already, and though I respect neither them nor their cause among
the highest, I have thoughts of complying for a time. From the
whole of this you will be happy to conclude that I am free of danger
if I keep a sound body, which I shall surely do to a certain extent.

The first use which Carlyle made of his improved
finance was to send his father a pair of spectacles, and his
mother 'a little sovereign to keep the fiend out of her
hussif.'

You will tell me I am poor (he said to her in a note which went
with his present), and have so few myself of these coins; but I am
going to have plenty by and by; and if I had but one I cannot
see how I could purchase more enjoyment with it than if I shared
it with you. Be not in want of anything, I entreat you, that I can
possibly get for you. It would be hard indeed if in the autumn
of a life—the spring and summer of which you have spent well in

[1] Perhaps one of the short biographies which Carlyle was writing for Brewster. He never republished these sketches, which are little more than exercises.

taking care of us—we should know what would add to your frugal enjoyments and not procure it. The stockings and other things you have sent me are of additional value in my eyes, as proofs of the unwearied care with which you continue to watch over me. I still hope to see the day when I may acknowledge all this more effectually. I think you wanted a bonnet when I was at home. Do not buy any till after the box returns.

His father and mother were not Carlyle's only thought. His brother John was working hard at school, hoping that means might offer to enable him to attend the medical classes at Edinburgh. Power rather than will was alone wanting for Carlyle to take the expense upon himself. He was watching for an opportunity, and meanwhile he encouraged John to persevere with all his energy.

Thomas Carlyle to John Carlyle.

Edinburgh : December 21, 1821.

I send many a thought southward to you; often in the mind's eye you appear seated at your mahogany tippet with the various accoutrements of a solitary student, labouring in secret at the task which—fear it not, my boy—will yet be rewarded openly. Few such quiet things in nature have so much of the sublime in them as the spectacle of a poor but honourable-minded youth, with discouragement all around him, but never-dying hope within his heart ; forging, as it were, the armour with which he is destined to resist and overcome the hydras of this world, and conquer for himself in due time a habitation among the sunny fields of life. Like every other virtue this effort may be called its own reward, even though success should never crown it. How poor, how beggar poor compared with this, is the vulgar rioting, punch-drinking, oyster-eating existence often led by your borough procurator or embryo provost. Truly, Jack, you have chosen the better part, and as your brother I rejoice to see you persevere in it. I perused with deep interest and pleasure your graphic account of the style in which our father received the spectacles. It is a cheap way of purchasing pleasure to make those that love us happy at so small an expense.

Your affectionate brother,

T. CARLYLE.

CHAPTER IX.

A.D. 1822. ÆT. 27.

An important change was now to take place in Carlyle's circumstances, which not only raised him above the need of writing articles for bread or hunting after pupils, but enabled him to give his brother the lift into the University which he had so ardently desired to give him. It came about in this way, through the instrumentality of his constant friend, Edward Irving. Irving's position at Glasgow, Carlyle says, was not an easy one. Theological Scotland was jealous of originality, and Irving was always inclined to take a road of his own. He said himself that 'from the Westland Whigs he had but toleration: when praised it was with reservation, often with cold and unprofitable admonition.' Even Chalmers sometimes, in retailing the general opinion of him, 'made him feel all black in his prospects.' He was growing dispirited about himself, when, just at that time, he received an invitation to go to London on experimental trial. The Caledonian Chapel in Hatton Garden was in need of a minister. 'Certain Glasgow people,' who thought more favourably of Chalmers's assistant than their neighbours thought, or than Chalmers himself, named him to the trustees, and Irving was sent for that his 'gifts' might be ascertained. The gifts proved to be what London wanted. He was brilliantly successful. There was no jealousy of originality in Hatton Garden, but ardent welcome rather to a man who had something new to say on so worn a subject as the Christian religion.

I have preached (he reported to Carlyle after three weeks' experience), but I shall not repeat the compliments which burst upon me. It is so new a thing to me to be praised in my preaching, I know not how to look. I have been hailed with the warmest reception. They anticipate great things. The Duke of York was present at a Charity sermon Sunday week; and much more which it is needless to repeat. One thing would have made your heart feel. My audience was almost entirely young Scotchmen. No fathers, no mothers, no sisters; seats full of youth—and how grave! how attentive!

Not the Duke of York only, but great persons of all kinds were brought to the Caledonian Chapel by the report of a new man of genius who really believed in Christianity. It happened that among the rest there came Mrs. Strachey, wife of a distinguished East Indian director, and her sister, Mrs. Charles Buller. Mr. Buller was also a retired Anglo-Indian of eminence. Mrs. Strachey was devout and evangelical, and had been led to Hatton Garden by genuine interest; Mrs. Buller had accompanied her in languid curiosity; she was struck, like the rest of the world, by Irving's evident ability, and she allowed herself to be afterwards introduced to him. She had three sons—one the Charles Buller who won so brilliant a place for himself in Parliament, and died as he was beginning to show to what a height he might have risen; another, Arthur, the Sir Arthur of coming years, an Indian judge; and a third, Reginald, who became a clergyman. Charles was then fifteen, having just left Harrow, and was intended perhaps for Cambridge; Arthur was a year or two younger, and Reginald was a child. The Bullers were uncertain about the immediate education of the two elder boys. Mrs. Buller consulted Irving, and Irving recommended the University of Edinburgh, adding that he had a friend of remarkable quality there who would prove an excellent tutor for them. Mrs. Buller was prompt in her decisions, if not always stable in adhering to them. A negotiation was opened and was readily concluded. Carlyle's consent having been obtained, he was instructed to expect the arrival of his pupils as soon as arrangements could be made for their board. The family intended to follow, and reside themselves for a time in Scotland. Those who remember Charles Buller will read with revived interest Irving's first impressions of him.

Edward Irving to Thomas Carlyle.

London : January 4, 1822.

. . . My opinion is that in the mother you will meet a most pleasant, elegant, and sensible woman. In the eldest boy, whom I have conversed with, you will meet a rather difficult subject : clever and acute, and not ill-informed for his age ; but his tastes are all given to Boxiana, Bond Street, and pleasure gathered out of the speculations and ambitions of Harrow School. But while he argued for that style of life against his mother and me, he displayed a soul far above it, and sporting with it, and easily to be dislodged from it ; and he confessed, when his mother was gone, that he could apply himself with great good will for several years to study, and would delight to travel. I told him and his mother that I should like myself to be his tutor, and I spoke *bonâ fide*, for nothing I perceive is wanting but a superior mind to give him higher tastes and to breed admiration of excellence. You could soon master him and easily direct him, though at the outset it might be a trial of your patience. But I think you ought to submit to such a trial. You would be no worse by it. You labour upon a good subject, for a most accomplished, quite a gallant and noble woman, and gracious withal, and willing to recompense your labours.

The salary was to be 200*l*. a year. The offer, so desirable in many ways, came opportunely, and at Mainhill was warmly welcomed. The times were hard ; the farm was yielding short returns. For once it was Carlyle who was to raise the spirits of the family.

Edinburgh : January 12, 1822.

. . . As to the times, it is an evil which must be promptly and effectually met, and many will fail for want of a remedy ; perhaps ninety-nine hundredths of the British farmers before *you* need fear greatly. And if the issue prove unfortunate, what then ? You can stand it better than many—many whom it would leave without resources. The worst is over ; we are all past childhood, and with so many brave sons to stand between you and danger, why should you be afraid ? For myself, the eldest and least profitable of them, I do sometimes think that Fate is about to lift its heavy hand off me, and that I shall yet have it in my power to be useful to you all. My health is considerably better than it was last winter. It will return completely, I trust, and my hopes are infinitely more extensive and better founded than they were at that period. I have abundance of employment, and the expectation of more, and more lucrative in process of time. There is a plan in particular about which Irving wrote to me the other day, that promises exceedingly well. It is a tutorship in a London family, who have two sons intended to reside with their parents in Edinburgh till their education is completed. The mother, Irving says, is an excellent person ; the sons likely to be more troublesome ; but the yearly salary is 200*l.*, a round solid sum for which a man would submit to much. Accordingly I have engaged to attend the youths when they arrive, which they are to do shortly, in quality of ' teacher for the interim,' for three months, till their parents arrive, with the understanding that if I like them, and they me, I am to undertake the office permanently.

To his mother Carlyle wrote at the same date :—

The woman, Irving says, is a gallant, accomplished person, and will respect me well. He warned her that I had seen little of life, and was disposed to be rather high in the humour if not well used. The plan, if I like it and be fit for it, will be advantageous for me in many aspects. I shall have time for study and convenience for it, and plenty of cash. At the same time, as it is uncertain, I do not make it my bower anchor by any means. If it go to nothing altogether I shall snap my finger and thumb in the face of all the Indian judges of the earth, and return to my poor desk and quill with as hard a heart as ever.

John Carlyle replies from Mainhill :—

We were all glad to hear from you. The 200*l.* figures largely in the eyes of our father, but not so largely and exclusively, perhaps, as you would be supposed to think, considering all the bearings of his character. He seems to entertain a very great deal more of respect towards you of late than he was wont to cherish when you were strolling about the moors. You can excuse him for doing so. He is one of the most wonderful persons in these parts, considering the manner in which he was brought up.

The young Bullers arrived at Edinburgh early in the spring. They lodged with a Dr. Fleming in George Square, Carlyle being in daily attendance.

From the first (he says), I found my Charles a most manageable, intelligent, cheery, and altogether welcome and agreeable phenomenon—quite a bit of sunshine in my dreary Edinburgh element. I was in waiting for his brother and him when they landed at Fleming's. We set instantly out on a walk round by the foot of Salisbury Crags, up from Holyrood by the Castle and Law Courts, home again to George Square ; and really I recollect few more pleasant walks in my life—so all-intelligent, seizing everything you said to him with such a prompt recognition, so loyal hearted, chivalrous, guileless, so delighted evidently with me as I was with him. Arthur, two years younger, kept mainly silent, being slightly deaf too. But I could perceive that he also was a fine little fellow, honest, intelligent, and kind, and that apparently I had been much in luck in this didactic adventure, which proved abundantly the fact. The two youths took to me with unhesitating liking, and I to them, and we never had anything of quarrel, or even of weariness and dreariness between us—such teaching as I never had in any sphere before or since. Charles, by his qualities, his ingenuous curiosities, his brilliancy of faculty and character, was actually an entertainment to me rather than a labour. If we walked together, which I remember sometimes happening, he was the best company which I could find in Edinburgh. I had entered him in Dunbar's third Greek class at College. In Greek and Latin, in the former in every respect, he was far my superior, and I had to prepare my lessons by way of keeping him to his work at Dunbar's. Keeping him to work was my one difficulty, if there was one, and my essential function. I tried to guide him into reading, into solid inquiry and reflection. He got some mathematics from me, and might have had more. He got, in brief, what expansion into wider fields of intellect and more manful modes of thinking and working my poor possibilities could yield him, and was always generously grateful to me afterwards. Friends of mine in a fine frank way, beyond what I could be thought to merit, he, Arthur, and all the family remained, till death parted us.[1]

Carlyle was now at ease in his circumstances. He could help his brother; he had no more money anxieties. He was living independently in his own rooms in Moray Street. His evenings were his own, and he had leisure to do what he pleased. Yet it was not his nature to be contented. He was full of thoughts which were struggling for expression, and he was beginning that process of ineffectual labour so familiar to every man who has risen to any height in literature, of trying to write something before he knew what the something was to be; of craving to give form to his ideas before those ideas had taken an organic shape. The result was necessarily failure, and along with it self-exasperation. He translated his Legendre easily enough, and made a successful book out of it; but he was aspiring to the production of an original work, and what it should be he could not decide. Now it was an essay on Faust, now a history of the English Commonwealth, now a novel to be written in concert with Miss Welsh. An article on Faust was finished, but it was crude and unsatisfactory. The other schemes were commenced and thrown aside. The workings of his mind appear in his letters to his brother.

Thomas Carlyle to John Carlyle.

Edinburgh : March 15, 1822.

Your two letters came to hand about a fortnight ago. I read them with the pleasure that all your letters give me. They exhibit the same picture of young, arduous, honest affection and

---

[1] *Reminiscences,* p. 154.

inflexible perseverance, in worthy though difficult pursuits, for which I have always loved you. The last quality, perseverance, I particularly respect; it is the very hinge of all virtues. On looking over the world the cause of nine parts in ten of the lamentable failures which occur in men's undertakings, and darken and degrade so much of their history, lies not in the want of talents or the will to use them, but in the vacillating and desultory mode of using them, in flying from object to object, in starting away at each little disgust, and thus applying the force which might conquer any one difficulty to a series of difficulties so large that no human force can conquer them. The smallest brook on earth by continuing to run has hollowed out for itself a considerable valley to flow in. The wildest tempest overturns a few cottages, uproots a few trees, and leaves after a short space no mark behind it. Commend me, therefore, to the Dutch virtue of perseverance. Without it all the rest are little better than fairy gold, which glitters in your purse, but when taken to market proves to be slate or cinders.

This preaching, my beloved Jack, is directed against myself, who have need of it—not against you, who have none. 'Improve the passing hour, for it will never, never return,' is a precept which you not only assent to but practise. In myself study has in a measure ceased to be a thing of which I am capable. At no period of my life did I spend my time more unprofitably than at present. Science and arts and book-learning no longer inspire me with any suitable interest, and my ignorance, my indecision, my weakness of all kinds, prevent me from fixing my heart on any one object of my own inventing. Well did old Crispus say, 'Truly that man lives and enjoys existence who is intent on some undertaking and aims at some excellent attainment.' It is a fact certain that I must write a *book*. Would to Heaven that I had a subject which I could discuss, and at the same time loved to discuss. I cannot say for certain whether I have the smallest genius; but I know I have unrest enough to serve a parish. Pity me, but I hope I shall not always be so pitiful a thing. As for my employment, it goes on pretty fairly. The Bullers are boys of many good qualities and many faults. I am too little beside them at present to grapple on fair terms with their inattentions and frequent peccadillos. However, in the main they are very superior boys, both in head and heart, and I think the undertaking will succeed ultimately.

Again, a few days later, *à propos* of the translation of Legendre :—

I am anxious to get all these mechanical things off my hand, so that I may be able to embark fairly in some more honourable enterprise. I have had a faint purpose for some weeks of writing some essay on the Genius and Character of Milton, if I could. It is not quite the subject I should like, but better than none, so that I am still thinking of it, and determined at least to read the works that relate to it. I am already through Clarendon's 'History of the Rebellion.' To-morrow I shall try to get hold of Ludlow's Memoirs, or some other of them. My condition is rather strange at present. I feel as if I were impelled to write ; as if I had also very little power to do it ; but at the same time as if I had altogether lost the faculty of exerting that power. It is these 'coorsed nervous disorders.' If I had but strong health ! But what is the use of talking ? If I had a super-eminent genius, the end would be still better attained, and the wish is perhaps just about as reasonable. Should I never be healthy again, it will not aid me to complain, to sit and whine, ' put finger in the eye and sob,' because my longings are not gratified. Better to do what I can while it is called to-day ; and if the edifice I create be but a dog-hutch, it is more honourable to have built a dog-hutch than to have dreamed of building a palace. Therefore, Jack, I mean to try if I can bestir myself. Art is long and life is short ; and of the three score and ten years allotted to the liver, how small a portion is spent in anything but vanity and vice, if not in wretchedness, and worse than unprofitable struggling with the adamantine laws of fate ! I am wae when I think of all this, but it cannot be helped.

CHAPTER X.

A.D. 1822.   ÆT. 27.

THE correspondence with Haddington meanwhile grew more intimate. The relations between tutor and pupil developed, or promised to develop, into literary partnership. Miss Welsh sent Carlyle her verses to examine and correct. Carlyle discussed his plans and views with her, and they proposed to write books in concert. But the friendship, at least on her part, was literary only. Carlyle, in one of his earliest letters to her, did indeed adopt something of the ordinary language of gallantry natural in a young man when addressing a beautiful young lady. But she gave him to understand immediately that such a tone was disagreeable to her, and that their intimacy could only continue on fraternal and sisterlv terms. Carlyle obeyed without suspecting the reason. He had known that Irving was engaged to Miss Martin. It never occurred to him as possible that he could be thinking of anyone else, or anyone else of him.

As for Irving himself, the reception which he had met with in London was all that he could desire. A brilliant career appeared to be opening before him, and ardent and enthusiastic as he was, he had allowed his future in all points to be coloured by his wishes. There could be no doubt that the Hatton Garden committee would confirm his London appointment. He would then be able to marry, and his fate would have to be immediately decided. He was to return to Scotland in the spring to be ordained—he was as yet only in his noviciate ; meanwhile he was in high spirits, and his letters were of the rosiest colour.

Edward Irving to Thomas Carlyle.

February 22, 1822.

I have taken new wing by my visit to London. I see my way distinctly. My intellect is putting out new powers, at least I fancy so ; and if God endow me with His grace, I foresee service to His Church. My ambition—a sanctified one, I trust—is taking another direction : no less than an endeavour to bring the spirit and powers of the ancient eloquence into the pulpit, which appears to me the only place in modern manners for its revival. I would like to hear your thoughts upon this subject, both as to the correctness of the idea and its proper execution.

It is for an audience chiefly I am so fond of London ; perhaps as much for a school to learn in by conversation and observation, for which I think nature has fitted me more than by books. I have a wonderful aptitude to sympathise with men. Their manner of feeling, of thinking also, is clear to me, and, even when false, is interesting from a desire to set them right. Jane Welsh accuses me of intolerance, but I think she is wrong, although I think I have some little skirmishes for approbation. But this is not deep, and will yield according as I receive the share which is my due.

And so will yours, my dear Carlyle ; you have within you powers of good the world is not alive to, and which shall yet shine out to the confusion of many who discredit them. Your natural power of devotion will yet have utterance ; and your deep-seated reverence of religion—the largest expansion and highest attainment of the soul, which makes your mother so superior to those around her—will yet make her son superior among the rich and literary men that are hereafter to company with him.

In March the trial period had ended. The trustees were satisfied ; Irving was to be minister of the Hatton Garden chapel. He returned to Glasgow in March to prepare for his ordination. On April 29 he wrote to Carlyle again :—

It is now at length determined that I go to London. I have received the call, most respectably signed ; and, what with subscriptions and the first of the seat-rents, the security of 500*l.* a year. I go to Annan this day three weeks, where I am to abide during the month of June and obtain ordination, then to London, without seeing Edinburgh ; and yet I would like to see you could you come through at the time of the sacrament. Many things oppress my spirit at the present moment, nothing more than parting with these most worthy and kind-hearted people. Some other things also which I cannot render into language unto my own mind. There is an independence about my character, a want of resemblance especially with others of my profession, that will cause me to be apprehended ill of. I hope to come through honestly and creditably. God grant it!

I am not writing Irving's history, save so far as it intersects with that of Carlyle, and I must hasten to the catastrophe of their unconscious rivalry. The 'other things' which he could not render into language, the 'independence of character which might cause him to be apprehended ill of,' referred to his engagement, and to his intentions with respect to it. Miss Martin had been true to him through many years of tedious betrothal, and he was bound to her by the strictest obligations of honour and conscience. But it is only in novels that a hero can behave with entire propriety. Folded among Irving's letters to Miss Welsh is a passionate sonnet addressed to her, and on the other side of it (she had preserved his verses and so much of the accompanying letter as was written on the opposite page of the paper) a fragment, written evidently at this period, in which he told her that he was about to inform Miss Martin and her father of the condition of his feelings. It seems that he did so, and that the answer was unfavourable to his hopes. The Martins stood by their contract, as justice and Scotch custom entirely entitled them to do. Miss Welsh had refused to listen to his addresses until he was free ; and Irving, though he confessed afterwards (I use his own words) that the struggle had almost 'made his faith and principles to totter,' submitted to the inevitable. He must have carried the news to Haddington in person ; what had passed there may be gathered from a letter which he wrote to her from Carlyle's lodgings in Edinburgh, to which he had gone after all.

Edward Irving to Miss Welsh.

My well-beloved Friend and Pupil,—When I think of you my mind is overspread with the most affectionate and tender regard, which I neither know to name nor to describe. One thing I know, it would long ago have taken the form of the most devoted attachment but for an intervening circumstance, and showed itself and pleaded itself before your heart by a thousand actions from which I must now restrain myself. Heaven grant me its grace to restrain myself; and, forgetting my own enjoyments, may I be enabled to combine into your single self all that duty and plighted faith leave at my disposal. When I am in your company my whole soul would rush to serve you, and my tongue trembles to speak my heart's fulness. But I am enabled to forbear, and have to find other avenues than the natural ones for the overflowing of an affection which would hardly have been able to confine itself within the avenues of nature if they had all been opened. But I feel within me the power to prevail, and at once to satisfy duty to another and affection to you. I stand truly upon ground which seems to shake and give way beneath me, but my help is in Heaven. Bear with thus much, my early charge and my present friend, from one who loves to help and defend you, who would rather die than wrong you or see you wronged. Say that I shall speak no more of the painful struggle that I am undergoing, and I shall be silent. If you allow me to speak, then I shall reveal to you the features of a virtuous contention, to be crowned, I pray and trust, with a Christian triumph. It is very extraordinary that this weak nature of mine can bear two affections, both of so intense a kind, and yet I feel it can. It shall feed the one with faith, and duty, and chaste affection; the other with paternal and friendly love, no less pure, no less assiduous, no less constant—in return seeking nothing but permission and indulgence.

I was little comforted by Rousseau's letters, though holding out a most admirable moral; but much comforted and confirmed by the few words which your noble heart dictated the moment before I left you. Oh, persevere, my admirable pupil, in the noble admirations you have taken up. Let affectionateness and manly firmness be the qualities to which you yield your love, and your life shall be honourable; advance your admiration somewhat higher, and it shall be everlastingly happy. Oh, do not forbid me from rising in my communications with one so capable of the loftiest conceptions. Forbid me not to draw you upwards to the love and study of your Creator, which is the beginning of wisdom. I have returned Rousseau. Count for ever, my dear Jane, upon my last efforts to minister to your happiness, present and everlasting.

From your faithful friend and servant,

EDWARD IRVING.

I should not unveil a story so sacred in itself, and in which the public have no concern, merely to amuse their curiosity; but Mrs. Carlyle's character was profoundly affected by this early disappointment, and cannot be understood without a knowledge of it. Carlyle himself, though acquainted generally with the circumstances, never realised completely the intensity of the feeling which had been crushed. Irving's marriage was not to take place for a year, and it was still possible that something might happen in the interval. He went back to his place in London, flung himself into religious excitement as grosser natures go into drink, and took popularity by storm. The fashionable world rushed after him. The streets about Hatton Garden were blocked with carriages. His chapel was like a theatre, to which the admission was by tickets. Great statesmen went with the stream. Brougham, Canning, Mackintosh bespoke their seats, that they might hear the new actor on the theological stage. Irving concluded that he had a divine mission to re-establish practical Christianity. He felt himself honoured above all men, yet he bore his honours humbly, and in his quiet intervals his thoughts still flowed towards Haddington. Miss Welsh's husband he could not be; but he could still be her guide, her spiritual father—some link might remain which would give him an excuse for writing to her. As long as he was actually unmarried there was still hope, but he tried to avoid hinting at so remote a possibility.

Edward Irving to Miss Welsh.

London : September 9, 1822.

My dearest Friend,—I said in the last walk which we enjoyed together on a Sabbath evening—when by the solemn stillness of the scene, no less than the pathetic character of our discourse, my mind was in that solemn frame which is my delight—that in future I was to take upon me in my letters the subject of your religious and moral improvement, leaving to other correspondents matters of literature, taste, and entertainment. But I have not forgot that you discharged me from preaching to you in my letters, and I fear that what you humorously call preaching is the very thing which I shall have to do if I fulfil my resolution. Now I can chat, though somewhat awkwardly I confess; and ten years agone I had a little humour, which has now nearly deceased from neglect. My mind was then light and airy, and loved to utter its conceptions, and to look at them and laugh at them when uttered. Then I could have written letters trippingly, and poured out whatever was uppermost in my mind ; but I can do that no longer. I am aiming from morning till night to be a serious and wise man, though God knows how little I succeed. The shortness of life is evermore in my eye, the wasting of it before my conscience ; the responsibility of it overwhelms me, and the vanity of it ashames me. I cannot make a mock heroic of these things, or laugh them away. I was never so far lost to good sense and good feeling as to try. So they hang over me, and I must either sink down into a melancholy forlorn creature, weeping and sighing and talking over the difficulties of living well, or I must rise up in the strength of Him who made me, and endeavour to work my passage through the best and surest way I can. This last I have chosen, like the wise men who have gone before me, and by God's help I will fulfil it.

Now, my dear friend, bear with me if I violate the law of letter-writing you imposed on me by daring to be serious, and to speak to you whom I love of those things and that strain which most I love. The fine promise of your mind has been to me the theme of much conversation and of far more delightful thought. It is not a part of my character to withhold my admiration from others, or even from those I admire, and you yourself have often charged me with exaggerating your gifts. Your industry to get knowledge, and to accomplish your mind with elegant learning, no one can exaggerate. Your enthusiasm towards the excellent and rare specimens of human genius is beyond that of any other I know ; and your desire to be distinguished by achievements of mind is equalled only by your contempt of all other distinctions. Now there is in these qualities of character not only promise but assurance of the highest excellence, if God give time for all to ripen, and you give ear to his directions for bringing the human character to perfection. Now it does give me great hope that God will yet be pleased to open your mind to the highest of all knowledge, the knowledge of his Blessed Son, and gain therewith the highest of all delights, of being like his Son in character and in destiny, when I see you not alienated from men of genius by their being men of religion, but attracted to them I think rather the more.

I could wish, indeed—and forgive me when I make free to suggest it—that your mind were less anxious for the distinction of being enrolled amidst those whom this world hath crowned with their admiration, than among those whom God hath crowned with his approval. There are two things to be kept in view in judging of the worth of men—first what powers they had, and then what uses they turned them to. You and I agree always when we meet with a person of power, but you do not go so far as I in exacting from them a good use of it. I do not wish it turned to arts of cruelty, which satire and ridicule and scorn are. I can endure this no more than I can endure the tyranny of a despot or the wilfulness of a man of power. They prey upon the physical rights and comforts of their underlings ; the others prey upon the feelings, by far the tenderer and nobler part. I do not wish it turned to the aggrandisement and adulation of its possessor ; for he doth not possess it by virtue of himself, but by his Maker and his Preserver. Keep away these two things, the cruel treatment of another, and the deification of energy, and I will not be offended with the exercise of mental powers ; but to satisfy me I seek for much besides : I must have it husbanded and not wasted in indolence, for that is as bad almost as the indulgence of superiority. Then I must have it turned to the discovery of truth, and to the undeceiving of men, then to lead them into the way of their wellbeing. Then finally, which should have been first, or rather which should be the moving principle of the whole, to do honour unto God who has made us masters of our powers. Find people of this kind from the annals of the world ; admire them, love them, be like them, and God enrol you among them. Oh, how few I find, my dear Jane, hardly have I found a single one, who can stand the intoxication of high talents, or resist presuming to lord it over others. They cry out against kings for their arbitrary tempers. I think men of talents are more so. Nothing can overcome it but the power and wisdom of God, which is in the gospel of his dear Son, your Saviour and mine, and the Saviour of all who believe ; who though the brightness of his Father's glory and the express image of his person, and speaking as no man spoke, took upon Him the form of a servant, and submitted to the death of the cross. Therefore God highly exalted Him, and hath given Him a name above every name. So also will He exalt all others who like Him use those their high gifts and appointments to the service of God and their fellows.

Enough of this, for I have much more to speak of. Of my own condition I can speak with great satisfaction, in as far as favour and friendship are concerned, and the outward popularity of my calling. I have no evidence to judge by farther than that my Chapel is filled, and that their patient hearing of discourses, each an hour and a quarter long, testifies they are not dissatisfied with the stuff they are made of. In another respect I have reason to be thankful that God has revealed to me of late the largeness of my own vanity and the worthlessness of my own services, which, if He follows up with further light upon the best way for me to act in future, and with strength to act as He teaches me, then I have no doubt of a great increase both of happiness and fruit.

I have made no acquaintance in London of any literary eminence, but I shall, I doubt not, in good time. I derive little advantage from my acquaintances, my course is so different from theirs. The next moment I have unemployed I devote to my friend Carlyle, to whom I have not yet found time to write. Oh that God would give rest to his mind, and instruct him in his truth. I meditate a work upon the alienation of clever men from their Maker. But this shall not hinder me from taking up the life of St. Paul, which deserves certainly the highest strain of poetry, but I am utterly unable for such a task.

My love to your mother. Oh, how I would like to see you both, to live with you in the quietness and love which I have so often ——.[1] The next time I come to live with you I hope I shall be

---

[1] Word omitted.

more worthy of your kindness, being more satisfied with myself, and standing firmer in the favour of my God, whom that my dear Jane may always set before her is the first and last prayer of her most true and faithful friend,

EDWARD IRVING.

This letter is one of Irving's best, simple, true, and from his heart, while it is kept firmly within the lines which he had prescribed for himself. Others were less collected, and perhaps less resigned. He would lie on his sofa in the December midnight, listening to the music of the streets, and then pour out his emotions to Mrs. Welsh, telling her how Haddington had been a haven of peace to him; how the happiest days of his life had been spent under her roof; how 'nowhere had thoughts of piety and virtue come to him so little sought as with her and his dear pupil.' Every day in his walk he passed a window where there was a portrait of Miss Kelly as Juliet. 'It had the cast of Miss Welsh's eye,' he said, 'in one of its most piercing moods which he could never stand to meet, the roundness of her forehead, and somewhat of the archness of her smile.' He was very miserable at times, but he struggled with his weakness. His duty was plain and peremptory, and should be done, let the cost be what it might.

Though he seldom found time to write to Carlyle, he had not forgotten him. He was eager to see him in the position which of right belonged to him; especially to see him settled in London. 'Scotland breeds men,' he said, 'but England rears them.' He celebrated his friend's praises in London circles. He had spoken of him to Mr. Taylor, the proprietor of the 'London Magazine.' Carlyle had meditated a series of 'portraits of men of genius and character.' Taylor, on Irving's recommendation, undertook to publish these sketches in monthly numbers, paying Carlyle sixteen guineas a sheet. Carlyle closed with the proposal, and a 'Life of Schiller' was to be the first to appear.

Irving's unwearied kindness unfortunately did not help him out of his own entanglements. The year passed, and then he married, and from that time the old, simple, unconscious Irving ceased to exist. His letters, once so genial and transparent, became verbose and stilted. Though 'faith and principle' escaped unscathed, his intellect was shattered. He plunged deeper and deeper into the great ocean of unrealities. When his illusions failed him his health gave way, and after flaming for a few years as a world's wonder, he died, still young in age, worn out and broken-hearted. 'There would have been no tongues,' Mrs. Carlyle once said, 'had Irving married me.'

Carlyle, meanwhile, was working with his pupils, and so far as circumstances went, had nothing to complain of. The boys gave him little trouble. He was no longer obliged to write articles for Brewster to support himself. The Legendre was well done—so well that he was himself pleased with it.

I still remember (he says) a happy forenoon (Sunday, I fear) in which I did a Fifth book (or complete Doctrine of Proportion) for that work. Complete really and lucid, and yet one of the briefest ever known. It was begun and done that forenoon, and I have, except correcting the press next week, never seen it since; but still feel as if it was right enough and felicitous in its kind. I got only 50*l.* for my entire trouble in that Legendre, and had already ceased to be the least proud of mathematical prowess; but it was an honest job of work honestly done, though perhaps for bread-and-water wages, and that was such an improvement upon wages producing, in Jean Paul's phrase, 'only water without the bread.'

He ought to have been contented; but content was not in him. Small discomforts were exaggerated by his imagination till they actually became the monsters which his fancy represented. He was conscious of exceptional power of some kind, and was longing to make use of it, yet was unable as yet to find out what sort of power it was, or what to do with it.

If I fail (he wrote to Miss Welsh at the beginning of the Buller engagement) to effect anything in my day and generation, anything to justify Providence for having called me into His universe, the weakness of my ability, not of my will, shall be to blame. I have much to strive with, much to do. The few conceptions that actually exist within me are scattered in a thousand directions, distracted, dismembered, without form and void; and I have yet gained no right mastery of my pen, no right familiarity with the public, to express them even if worth expressing. Nevertheless I must persevere. What motives have I not which man can have? The brightest hopes and the darkest fears. On the one side obscurity and isolation, the want of all that can render life endurable, and death, ' sad refuge from the storms of fate,' without even an approving conscience to disarm it of its sting. On the other is ——. I tell you, my friend, to be in no pain for me. Either I shall escape from this obscure sojourn, or persist as I ought in trying it. The game is deep, but I must play it out. I can no other, so away with fear.

Meanwhile I am not unhappy. It is true I have none to love me *here*, none that I can love. But I have long been studying the painful lesson to live alone, and the task is easier than it was. I enjoy quiet and free air and returning health. I have business in abundance for the present, and the future lies before me vaguely, but with some glimpses of a solemn beauty irradiating all its gloom. When I compare the aspect of the world to me now with what it was twelve months ago, I am far from desponding or complaining.

If he could not express himself to his satisfaction when trying to write for the public, he could describe well enough anything which happened to him, when telling it in a private letter. To his mother he was the best of correspondents. Here is a little incident characteristic both in manner and matter.

Thomas Carlyle to Mrs. Carlyle, Mainhill.

3, Moray Street, Edinburgh : June 2, 1822.

It will give you pleasure to know that I continue improving in that most important of qualities, good health. The bathing does me great good, and you need be under no apprehension of my drowning. Unfortunately my mode of sleeping is too irregular to admit of my bathing constantly before breakfast. Small noises disturb me and keep me awake, though I always get to sleep at last, and happily such disturbances occur but rarely. Some two weeks ago I had a little adventure with an ugly *messan,* which a crazy half-pay captain had thought proper to chain in his garden, or, rather, grass-plot, about twenty yards from my window. The pug felt unhappy in its new situation, began repining very pitifully in its own way ; at one time snarling, grinning, yelping, as if it cared not whether it were hanged then or to-morrow ; at another, whining, howling, screaming, as if it meant to excite the compassion of the earth at large—this, at intervals, for the whole night. By five o'clock in the morning I would have given a guinea of gold for its hind legs firm in my right hand by the side of a stone wall.[1] Next day the crazy captain removed it, being threatened by the street at large with prosecution if he did not. But on the evening of the second day, being tired of keeping the cur in his kitchen, he again let it out, and just as I was falling asleep, about one o'clock, the same musical, 'most musical, most melancholy' serenade aroused me from my vague dreamings. I listened about half an hour, then rose indignantly, put on my clothes, went out, and charged the watchman to put an instant stop to the accursed thing. The watchman *could* not for the world interfere with a gentleman's rest at that hour, but next morning he would certainly, &c. &c. I asked to be shown the door, and pulling the crazy captain's bell about six times, his servant at length awoke, and inquired with a tremulous voice, *what was it ?* I alluded to the dog and demanded the instant, the total, the everlasting removal of it, or to-morrow I would see whether justice was in Edinburgh, or the shadow of British law in force. 'Do you hear that ?' said the Irish knight of the rattle and lanthorn. She heard it and obeyed, and no wretched *messan* has since disturbed my slumbers.

You ask about my home coming (he continues, the dog being

[1] Carlyle's mode of speech : he was exceptionally tender to animals.

disposed of); but this must be a very uncertain story for a while. I cannot count on any such thing till the Buller people[1] are arrived, and in the event of my further engaging with them, my period of absence must of course be short. However, there is good and cheap conveyance to Dumfries daily, and it shall go hard if I do not steal a week or so to spend at home. It is the dearest blessing of my life that I have you to write to and to care for me.

I am in very fair health considering everything : about a hundred times as well as I was last year, and as happy as you ever saw me. In fact I want nothing but steady health of body (which I shall get in time) to be one of the comfortablest persons of my acquaintance. I have also books to write and things to say and do in this world which few wot of. This has the air of vanity, but it is not altogether so. I consider that my Almighty Author has given me some glimmerings of superior understanding and mental gifts ; and I should reckon it the worst treason against Him to neglect improving and using to the very utmost of my power these his bountiful mercies. At some future day it shall go hard but I will stand above these mean men whom I have never yet stood *with*. But we need not prate of this. I am very much satisfied with my teaching. In fact, it is a pleasure rather than a task. The Bullers are quite another sort of boys than I have been used to, and treat me in another sort of manner than tutors are used to. When I think of General Dixon's brats,[2] and how they used to vex me, I often wonder I had not broken their backs at once, and left them. This would not have done, to be sure ; but the temptation was considerable. The eldest Buller is one of the cleverest boys I have ever seen. He delights to inquire and argue and be demolished. He follows me almost nigh home every night. Very likely I may bargain finally with the people, but I have no certain intimation on the subject ; and, in fact, I do not care immensely whether or not. There is bread for the diligent to be gained in a thousand ways.

In July the London season ended, and the parent Bullers arrived in Edinburgh with their youngest boy. They took a large house and settled for the autumn and winter. They made acquaintance with Carlyle, and there was imme-

---

[1] Mr. and Mrs. C. Buller.
[2] Past pupils, of whom I find no other notice.

diate and agreeable recognition of one another's qualities, both on his side and theirs. Mrs. Buller was clever and cultivated. [1] In her creed she was a Manichæan. In her youth she had been a beauty, and was still handsome, and was in London the centre of an admiring circle of intellectual politicians and unbelieving Radicals. She was first amused, then charmed and really interested in a person so distinctly original and remarkable as her son's tutor. Her husband, though of different quality, liked him equally well. Mr. Buller was practical and hard-headed; a Benthamite in theory, in theology negative and contemptuous. He had not much sympathy with literature, but he had a keen understanding; he could see faculty, and appreciate it whenever it was genuine, and he forgave Carlyle's imagination for the keenness of his sarcasms. Thus it was not only settled that he was to continue to be the tutor, but he was admitted into the family as a friend, and his presence was expected in the drawing-room in the evenings more often than he liked. The style of society was

---

[1] Mrs. Buller had been a celebrated beauty in her youth. Among Carlyle's papers I find the following beautiful lines by John Leyden, which have never, I believe, before been printed :—

Verses to Mrs. Buller on seeing her in a Highland dress, by Doctor John Leyden.

(From a copy in Mrs. Buller's handwriting, January 1824.)

That bonnet's pride, that tartan's flow,
　My soul with wild emotion fills ;
Methinks I see in Fancy's glow
　A princess from the land of hills.

Oh for a fairy's hand to trace
　The rainbow tints that rise to view,
That slender form of sweeter grace
　Than e'er Malvina's poet drew !

Her brilliant eye, her streaming hair,
　Her skin's soft splendours do display ;
The finest pencil must despair
　Till it can paint the solar ray.

Calcutta, 1811.

new to him, and he could not feel himself at ease. The habits of life were expensive, and the luxuries were not to his taste.

Tea (he wrote) I now consume with urns and china and splendid apparatus all around me, yet I often turn from these grandeurs to the little ' down the house ' at Mainhill, where kind affection makes amends for all deficiencies. Often, often, my dear mother, in coming years, we shall yet drink tea there, enjoy our pipes and friendly chat together, and pity all the empty gorgeousness of the earth.

On the other hand, he found Mrs. Buller, naturally enough, 'one of the most fascinating, refined women he had ever seen.' The 'goodman' he did not take to quite so readily, but he thought him at least ' an honest, worthy, straightforward English gentleman.' His comfort was considered in every way. They would have liked to have him reside in their house, but he wished to keep his lodgings in Moray Street, and no difficulty was made. Even his humours, which were not always under restraint, were endured without resentment.

The people treat me (he wrote to his brother John in September) with a degree of respect which I do not deserve. They have submitted implicitly to all my ideas about a lodging place. They have delivered me, without even a hint on my part, from the drudgery of teaching their youngest boy,[1] and our arrangements for the other two have been formed with a view to my convenience as much as to that of any other. The boys, too, behave well ; and though I clearly perceive that the management of my duties will require the whole of my slender stock of prudence and discretion, yet this stock, I expect, will suffice to carry me through without discredit.

Again, a little later :—

I am well and comfortable as I could wish. Buller's house is becoming more and more a kind of home to me. The elders treat me almost like a son in many respects, the younger members almost like a brother. Our studies are going on moderately well.

---

[1] Reginald, then ten years old.

There is nothing but good agreement as yet, and I think the thing will do.

Not the least of the advantages of this tutorship was the power which it gave Carlyle of being useful to his family. John Carlyle came in the autumn to live with him in Moray Street and attend the University lectures, Carlyle taking upon himself the expenses. With himself, too, all was going well. He had paid a hasty visit to Mainhill in October; where, perhaps, as was likely enough, in some of their midnight smokes together, he had revived the anxieties of his mother about his spiritual state. His constant effort was to throw his own thoughts into her language, and prevent her from distressing herself about him.

Thomas Carlyle to Mrs. Carlyle, Mainhill.

Edinburgh : November 14, 1822.

You have not sent me a line since I went away. I am not surprised at this, knowing how you are circumstanced, but it keeps me very much in the dark with regard to your situation. I can only hope you are in your usual state of health and spirits, fighting as formerly against the inconveniences of your present life, and brightening all its dreariness by the hopes of a better. There is nothing else that can keep the happiest of us in a state of peace, worth calling by the name of peace ; and ' with this anchor of the soul both sure and steadfast ' the unhappiest man alive is to be envied. You think I am a very thoughtless character, careless of eternity, and taken up with the vain concerns of time alone. Depend upon it, my dear mother, you misjudge me. These thoughts are rooted in every reflecting mind, in mine perhaps more deeply than in many that make more noise about them ; and of all the qualities that I love in you, there is none I so much love as that heroic feeling of devotion which elevates you so much above the meanness of ordinary persons in your situation, which gives to the humble circumstances of your lot a dignity unborrowed of earthly grandeur as well as far superior to the highest state of it ; and which ornaments a mind untrained in worldly education and accomplishments with sentiments after which mere literature and philosophy with all their pretensions would for ever strive in vain. The dress of our opinions, as I have often told you, may be different, because our modes of life have been different; but fundamentally our sentiments are completely the same. We should tolerate each other, therefore, in this world, where all is weak and obscure, trusting meanwhile that we shall comprehend all things more perfectly in that clearer land where faith is changed into vision; where the dim though fervent longings of our minds from this their dark prison-house are changed for a richness of actual grandeur, beyond what the most ardent imagination has ventured to conceive. Long may these hopes be yours, my dearest mother. Whoever entertains them is richer than kings.

The young Bullers are gone to college [1] a few days ago, and I do not go near them till two o'clock in the afternoon. By this means I not only secure a competent space of time for my own studies, but find also that my stomach troubles me a good deal less after breakfast than it used to do when I had a long hurried walk to take before it.

My duties are of an easy and brief sort. I dine at half-past three with a small and very civil youth, little Reginald, contracted into Reggy, and I have generally done with the whole against six. I find Jack immersed in study when I return. He cooks the tea for us, and we afterwards devote ourselves to business till between eleven and twelve. My brotherly love to all the younkers about home, to each by name. Why do they never write? Will you not write?

> I am, ever affectionately your son—thy son!!
> > T. CARLYLE.

Once more before the year closed:—

To the Same.

December 4.

It is already past twelve o'clock, and I am tired and sleepy, but I cannot go to rest without answering the kind little note which you sent me, and acknowledging these new instances of your unwearied attention to my interests and comfort. I am almost vexed at these shirts and stockings. My dear mother, why will you expend on superfluities the pittance I intended for very different ends? I again assure you, and would swear it if needful, that you cannot get me such enjoyment with it in any way as by convincing me that it is adding to your own. Do not therefore frustrate my purposes. I send you a small screed of verses which I made some

---

[1] The University Term having begun.

time ago. I fear you will not care a doit for them, though the
subject is good—the deliverance of Switzerland from tyranny by
the hardy mountaineers at the battle of Morgarten above five hundred years ago.

This is my birthday. I am now seven and twenty years of age.
What an unprofitable lout I am! What have I done in this world
to make good my place in it, or reward those that had the trouble
of my upbringing? Great part of an ordinary lifetime is gone by,
and here am I, poor trifler, still sojourning in Meshech, still doing
nothing in the tents of Kedar. May the great Father of all give
me strength to do better in time remaining, to be of service in the
good cause in my day and generation; and, having finished the
work which was given me to do, to lie down and sleep in peace and
purity in the hope of a happy rising.

The ' screed of verses,' was not thought worthy of a
place among the few fragments of his poetry which Carlyle afterwards published, though they are as good as any
of the rest. Long and patiently he had toiled at verse-
making. Infinite loose sheets of paper remain covered
with the memorials of his efforts. It was the received
opinion that in verse alone fine emotion and spiritual
thought could be clothed in adequate form. The poets,
so far as Carlyle could see, had been the wisest men. Inspiration meant poetry, and poetry inspiration, and if he
had any genius in him worth considering, he thought it
his duty to master the mechanical difficulties of the art.
He never entirely succeeded. Rhyme and metre were to
Carlyle like Saul's armour to David, and the intended
vase turned out usually no better than an earthen pitcher.
The ' screed' is good as an echo of Campbell or Byron, or
of both combined, but there is no trace in it of original
native power.

> Proud Hapsburgh came forth in the gloom of his wrath,
>   With his banners of pomp and his Ritters in mail,
> For the herdsmen of Uri have fronted his path,
>   And the standard of freedom is raised in the vale.

All scornful advancing, he thought as he came
  How the peasants would shrink at the glance of his eye;
How their heath-covered chalets in ruin must flame,
  And the hope of the nation must wither and die.

But marked he the moment when thundering and vast
  The voice of the Switzers in echoes arose,
When the rocks of the glen from the hill summits cast,
  Carried vengeance and death on the heads of their foes.

Now charge in your fury, ye sons of the Fell,
  Now plunge ye your blades in the hearts of his men;
If ye conquer, all time of your glory shall tell,
  And conquered ye ne'er shall arouse ye again.

'Tis done, and the spoilers are crushed and o'erthrown,
  And terror has struck through the souls of the proud,
For the Despot of Austria stoops from his throne,
  And the war-cry of Uri is wrathful and loud.

In speed they came on, but still faster they go,
  While ruin and horrour around them are hurled,
And the field of Morgarten in splendour shall grow,
  Like Marathon's field, to the end of the world.

Once only Carlyle did better than this, when love came to assist his inspiration. Miss Welsh's injunctions, though they subdued the tone of his letters, could not prevent a confidential intercourse with a young, fascinating woman from producing its natural effect. Perhaps, after Irving was lost to her, though she gave Carlyle no encouragement, she was less peremptorily cold. He on his part regarded her as the most perfect of women, beyond his practical hopes, but not beyond his adoration, and he indulged in the usual flights of musical imagining:—

They chide thee, fair and fervid one,
  At Glory's goal for aiming,
Does not Jove's bird, its flight begun,
Soar up against the beaming sun,
  Undazed in splendour flaming.

Young brilliant creature, even so
  A lofty instinct draws thee,
Heaven's fires within thy bosom glow,
Could earth's vain fading vulgar show
  One hour's contentment cause thee?

The gay saloon 'twas thine to tread,
  Its stateliest scenes adorning,
Thine be, by nobler wishes led,
With bays to crown thy lofty head,
  All meaner homage scorning.

Bright maid, thy destiny as I view,
  Unuttered thoughts come o'er me;
Enrolled among earth's chosen few,
Lovely as morning, pure as dew,
  Thy image stands before me.

Oh, that on Fame's far shining peak,
  With great and mighty numbered,
Unfading laurels I could seek;
This longing spirit then might speak
  The thoughts within that slumbered.

Oh, in the battle's wildest swell,
  By hero's deeds to win thee,
To meet the charge, the stormy yell,
The artillery's flash, its thundering knell,
  And thine the light within me.

What man in Fate's dark day of power,
  While thoughts of thee upbore him,
Would shrink at danger's blackest lour,
Or faint in Life's last ebbing hour,
  If tears of thine fell o'er him?

These lines are noteworthy for the emotion which they express, but they have not the ring of genuine gold. The feeling did not seek the metre because it could not otherwise find fit expression. The metre was rather laboriously adapted to the feeling, because the metrical form was assumed to be the right and appropriate one. Had Carlyle struggled on upon the false track, he might have written good artificial verses, showing from time to time a mind impatient of its fetters, but he would scarcely have risen to true greatness. Happily he was himself under no illusions. His object was to write out the truth that was in him : he saw his mistake, and he left his ideas to take the shape that was most natural to him. Taylor's offer for the 'London Magazine' came to the help of his resolution, and he began his Life of Schiller as the commencement of the intended series. Goethe was designed to follow. But the biography of Goethe was soon exchanged for a translation of ' Wilhelm Meister.'

Thus opened the year 1823. The Buller connection continued to be agreeable. John Carlyle's companionship relieved the loneliness of the Edinburgh lodgings, while spare moments were occupied with writing letters to Miss Welsh or correcting his exercises.

We lead a quiet life at present (he wrote to his brother Alexander). No incident breaks the smooth current of our history. None meddles with us, we meddle with none. Jack is studying bones, and the like. I write nonsense all the morning, then go and teach from two till six, then come home and read till half-past eleven, and so the day is done. I am happy while I can keep myself busy, which, alas! is not by any means always. The other day I went with Murray to call upon Macculloch, the *Scotsman.* He was sitting like a great Polar bear, chewing, and vainly trying to digest, the doctrines of Adam Smith and Ricardo, which he means to vomit forth again next spring in the shape of lectures to 'the thinking public' of this city. He eyed me with suspicion and distrust; would not come forth into open parley at all. What ailed the great Macculloch I could not tell. Did he ever feel fear? or might I be come to spy out the nakedness of his land?— I would not give a rush to know.

Communications more interesting than political economy came in weekly by the carrier from Mainhill. His father wrote to him on the 1st of January.

Mainhill : Jan. 1, 1823.

I take the pen in hand once more to write to you, though you may look for nothing but a few ill-arranged thoughts. But however that may be, I can tell you that I am in as good health as any of my age can expect to enjoy. In spite of bad times we are fighting away, and by feeding cattle, selling our barley, and one thing and another, we think we can meet our landlord at Candlemas this year as formerly; and when we can do that, you know we may go on so long as we are in any measure of health. How long that may be we cannot say. He who knows all things only knows what is before us; but we may know, both by Scripture and by our own observation, that before long we must leave the place we now occupy for a place in eternity, and only one of two places can we look for, as there is not a third; and the Apostle tells us that, as we spend our time here, so will our eternal state be. May the Lord make us all wise to consider these things, and to think on our latter end.

I forgot the last time I wrote to tell you that I had got the book of sermons safe which you sent me, and I like them very well. When I was reading Balmer's sermon on the Resurrection, it brought into my mind a sermon preached by Mr. William Glen nearly on the same subject. He said many things about the eternity of the body that would rise at the day of judgment, and the subject was disputed about by Robert Scott and George MacIvin. Robert Scott was for the same body rising again. The arguments were talked over one morning at the meeting house door. I was present, and was rather involved in the dispute. I observed that I thought a stinking clogg of a body like Robert Scott the weaver's would be very unfit to inhabit those places.

Your mother wishes you a happy new year, and she wishes it may be the best you ever have seen, and the worst you ever may see. I am, dear Son,

Your loving father,

JAMES CARLYLE.

The family, young and old, often contributed their scraps to the carrier's budget on these occasions. The youngest child of all, Jane, called the Craw, or Crow, from her black hair, and not yet able even to write, was heard composing in bed in the morning, to be enclosed in her father's letter, 'a scrap of doggerel from his affectionate sister Jane Carlyle.'

Of Carlyle's brothers, Alexander had the most natural genius. Of his sisters, the eldest, Margaret, had a tenderness, grace, and dignity of character which, if health and circumstances had been more kind, would have made her into a distinguished woman. But Jane was peculiar and original. She, when the day's work was over, and the young men wandered out in the summer gloaming, would cling to 'Tom's' hand and trot at his side, catching the jewelled sentences which dropped from his lips. She now, when he was far away, sent, among the rest, her little thoughts to him, composing the 'meanest of the letter kind' instinctively in rhyme and metre; her sister Mary, who had better luck in having been at school, writing down the words for her.

'Surely a very singular little crow,' was Carlyle's observation on reading her characteristic lines. 'Meanest of the letter kind' became a family phrase, to be met with for many years when an indifferent composition seemed to require an apology. Carlyle, in return, thought always first of his mother. He must send her a present. She must tell him what she needed most. 'Dearn bairn,' she might answer, 'I want for nothing.' But it was not allowed to serve. 'She must understand that she could not gratify him so much as by enabling him to promote her comfort.'

Life (he wrote to her) is still in prospect to Jack and me. We are not yet what we hope to be. Jack is going to become a large gawsie broad-faced practiser of physic, to ride his horse in time, to give aloes by the rule, to make money and be a large man; while I, in spite of all my dyspepsias and nervousness and hypochondrias, am still bent on being a very meritorious sort of character, rather noted in the world of letters, if it so please Providence, and useful, I hope, whithersoever I go, in the *good old cause*, for which I beg you to believe that I cordially agree with you in feeling my chief interest, however we may differ in our modes of expressing it.

CHAPTER XI.

A.D. 1823. ÆT. 28.

THE BULLERS after a winter's experience grew tired of Edinburgh, and in the spring of 1823 took Kinnaird House, a large handsome residence in Perthshire. Carlyle during the removal was allowed a holiday. He had been complaining of his health again. He had been working hard on Schiller, and was beginning his translation of 'Meister.' His brother had gone home when the University session was over, and describes the anxiety of the family with a degree of humour unusual with him.

John Carlyle to Thomas Carlyle.

May 5, 1823.

I found all the Mainhill people well in body and mind, all very cheerful, and all disposed to give me a hearty welcome and receive me in their 'choicest mood.'[1] They all inquired after you. Question followed question anxiously. 'Thou'se a vast deal leaner, lad, sin' thou gaed away!' 'Is Tom got better? Does he sleep well yet? It gaed to my heart when he told me in the last letter that he couldna sleep without his finger in his ear. Poor fellow, he has had a terrible time o' t. I see by thee thou'se no telling me the worst'—before I could get a word said. She thanks you for the large quantity of tea you sent her. It was the best she had had for a long while. Our father is cheerful and vigorous, and in the very best health. He has got every ounce weight of his corn sown, his potatoes set and covered, and has wherewith to meet his landlord with an 'impudent face.' I gave him Paley's 'Horæ Paulinæ,' with which he was considerably pleased. He told me he had often heard of it, but never could get it. He read a little of it yesterday, and was much pleased.

[1] A phrase of Edward Irving's.

Jane's muse has not visited her frequently of late. The 'letter poetic' which she sent you was entirely her own production. She made it in her bed one night exactly in the form in which you got it.

Kinnaird House is a beautiful place in the midst of woods near Dunkeld on the Tay. Carlyle spent a week in Annandale, and rejoined the Bullers there at the end of May.

I spent a joyful week in Annandale (he reported to Miss Welsh) amidst scenes in themselves unattractive or repulsive, but hallowed in my thoughts by the rude but genuine worth and true affection of those who people them. I think I am going to be comfortable enough in my new quarters. The Bullers are good people ; and, what is better, the first hour when they treat me uncivilly shall likewise be the last. So we live together in that easy style of cheerful indifference which seems to be the fit relation between us. For the rest, I have balmy air to breathe, fine scenery to look at, and stillness deeper than I have ever before enjoyed. My apartments are in a house detached from the larger building, which, except at meals and times of business, I intend to frequent but seldom. My window opens into a smooth bowling green, surrounded with goodly trees, and the thrushes have been singing amongst them, though it has rained every moment since I came. Here I purpose to spend my leisure and to think sweetly of friends that are far away.

Of these friends, Miss Welsh was naturally the most frequently in his mind. Her relations with him were drifting gradually in the direction in which friendships between young men and young women usually do drift. She had no thought of marrying him, but she was flattered by his attachment. It amused her to see the most remarkable person that she had ever met with at her feet. His birth and position seemed to secure her against the possibility of any closer connection between them. Thus he had a trying time of it. In serious moments she would tell him that their meeting had made an epoch in her history, and had influenced her character and life. When the humour changed, she would ridicule his Annandale accent, turned his passionate expressions to scorn, and when she had toned him down again she would smile once more, and enchant him back into illusions. She played with him, frightened him away, drew him back, quarrelled with him, received him again into favour as the fancy took her, till at last the poor man said, 'My private idea is that you are a witch like Sapphira in the New Testament, concerning whom Dr. Nimmo once preached in my hearing: "It seems probable, my friends, that Ananias was tempted into this by some spirit more wicked than his wife."' At last, in the summer of 1823, just after he was settled at Kinnaird, she was staying in some house which she particularly disliked, and on this occasion, in a fit of impatience with her surroundings—for she dated a letter which she wrote to him thence, very characteristically, as from 'Hell'—she expressed a gratitude for Carlyle's affection for her, more warm than she had ever expressed before. He believed her serious, and supposed that she had promised to be his wife. She hastened to tell him, as explicitly as she could, that he had entirely mistaken her.

My friend (she said), I love you. I repeat it, though I find the expression a rash one. All the best feelings of my nature are concerned in loving you. But were you my brother I should love you the same. No. Your friend I will be, your truest, most devoted friend, while I breathe the breath of life. But your wife, never. Never, not though you were as rich as Crœsus, as honoured and renowned as you yet shall be.

Carlyle took his rebuke manfully. 'My heart,' he said, 'is too old by almost half a score of years, and is made of sterner stuff than to break in junctures of this kind. I have no idea of dying in the Arcadian shepherd's style for the disappointment of hopes which I never seriously entertained, or had no right to entertain seriously.' Could they have left matters thus, it had been better for both of them. Two diamonds do not easily form cup and socket. But Irving was gone. Miss Welsh was romantic; and to assist and further the advance of a man of extraordinary genius, who was kept back from rising by outward circumstances, was not without attraction to her. Among her papers there is a curious correspondence which passed about this time between herself and the family solicitor. Her mother had been left entirely dependent on her. Her marriage, she said, was possible, though not probable; and 'she did not choose that her husband, if he was ever to be so disposed, should have it in his power to lessen her mother's income.' She executed an instrument, therefore, by which she transferred the whole of her property to her mother during Mrs. Welsh's life. By another she left it to Carlyle after her own and her mother's death. It was a generous act, which showed how far she had seen into his character and the future which lay before him, if he could have leisure to do justice to his talents. But it would have been happier for her and for him if she could have seen a little further, and had persevered in her refusal to add her person to her fortune.

Men of genius are 'kittle folk,' as the Scotch say. Carlyle had a strange temper, and from a child was 'gey ill to live with.' When dyspepsia was upon him he spared no one, least of all those who were nearest and dearest to him. Dearly as he loved his brother John, yet he had spoken to him while they were lodging together in language which he was ashamed to remember. 'Often in winter,' he acknowledged ruefully to the poor John, 'when Satanas in the shape of bile was heavy upon me, I have said cruel things to thee, and bitterly, though vainly, do I recollect them; but at bottom I hope you never doubted that I loved you.' Penitence, however, sincere as it might be, was never followed by amendment, even to the very end of his life.

But enough will be heard hereafter on this sad subject. The life at Kinnaird went on smoothly. The translation of ' Meister' prospered. An Edinburgh publisher undertook to publish it and pay well for it. There is a letter from Carlyle to his mother, dated June 10 of this year. Half a page is cut off, and contained evidently a cheque for a small sum of money.

Thomas Carlyle to Mrs. Carlyle, Mainhill.

Kinnaird House: June 10, 1823.

This letter may operate as a spur on the diligence of my beloved and valuable correspondents at Mainhill. There is a small blank made in the sheet for a purpose which you will notice. I beg you to accept the little picture which fills it without any murmuring. It is a poor testimonial of the grateful love I should ever bear you. If I hope to get a moderate command of money in the course of my life's operations, I long for it chiefly that I may testify to those dear to me what affection I entertain for them. In the meantime we ought to be thankful that we have never known what it was to be in fear of want, but have always had wherewith to gratify one another by these little acts of kindness, which are worth more than millions unblest by a true feeling between the giver and receiver. You must buy yourself any little odd things you want, and think I enjoy it along with you, if it add to your comfort. I do indeed enjoy it with you. I should be a dog if I did not. I am grateful to you for kindness and true affection such as no other heart will ever feel for me. I am proud of my mother, though she is neither rich nor learned. If I ever forget to love and reverence her, I must cease to be a creature myself worth remembering. Often, my dear mother, in solitary pensive moments does it come across me like the cold shadow of death that we too must part in the course of time. I shudder at the thought, and find no refuge except in humbly trusting that the great God will surely appoint us a meeting in that far country to which we are tending. May He bless you forever, my good mother, and keep up in your heart those sublime hopes which at present serve as a pillar of cloud by day and a pillar of fire by night to guide your footsteps through the wilderness of life. We are in his hands. He will not utterly forsake us. Let us trust in Him.

I have no news of myself to send you except what are good.

The boys are going on very fairly with me. They are excellent creatures in the main. With the rest of the family I am on the best footing. We talk together cheerfully whenever we meet. They show themselves anxious to promote my comfort by every rational arrangement. When with them I forget that there is any difference in worldly rank. They have their wealth, and birth, and connections and accomplishments to brag of. I too have my little stock of vanities within myself. My health was scarcely so good as you saw it for some days after I arrived. The air is pure as may be, and I am quiet as when at home ; but I did not sleep well for some nights, and began to fear that I was again going down hill. On considering what the matter might be, it struck me it was, perhaps, my dining so late, at five o'clock, and fasting so long before dinner. A new regulation took place instantly, and now, except on Sabbath days, when from choice I eat with the family, my meals are served up in a very comfortable manner at the hours I myself selected. The boys and I are up at breakfast a little before nine. We begin work half an hour after it, continuing till one. Then I go out and walk, or smoke, or amuse myself till half-past two, when dinner is waiting for me in the parlour, after which teaching recommences till near five, and then I am free as air for the night. I go into my own room and do whatsoever seemeth me good. I go out of it and walk and sometimes ride, and Donovan, the smart, whisking, and very trustworthy butler, has a dish of tea standing ready for me at seven. By this means I have brought myself round again. I like the arrangement also because I have more time to myself, and am less restricted in my movements. I have begun translating the German book which Jack knows of. I am busy, I shall be healthy, and in the meantime I am as comfortable as I could hope to be.

To John Carlyle.

Kinnaird : June 24.

Tell our mother I have a fire every night, and that all things I want are supplied to me abundantly. We have no incidents in our menage. Buller fishes and rides, and eschews heart(ache).[1] The lady saunters about on the back of a grey stalking pony, and fights against *ennui* as fiercely as she can. Both are uniformly civil and even kind to me. We have got two visitors from the south with us at present, Anna Pole and Reginald Pole her brother ; but they produce no change in our mode of life. The

[1] Paper torn.

lady is fully arrived at the years of discretion, at least if these are under thirty. She is good-humoured, understands all cookery from the mixture of water-gruel up to the composition of the choicest curry. She has a cornelian necklace, and kind blue eyes, and a bit *nimble-gaun* tongue. Reginald has been at Oxford studying the nature of horses. Philosophy is all a hum ; but the short back, and the shoulder, and the hands of height, and the price, and the speed—these are the points for a future parson of the English Church. My own boys in general behave admirably well to me and *very* ill to themselves. . . . Under this fine climate and among these beautiful scenes I am at no loss to pass my time with profit to my body, if not my mind. I wander by the copses on the shores of the Tay, or stroll over these black, interminable, solitary moors, and meditate on many foolish things.

Later in the season, when London began to empty itself, other guests appeared at Kinnaird. The first glimpse into the great world did not please Carlyle.

I see something of fashionable people here (he wrote to Miss Welsh), and truly to my plebeian conception there is not a more futile class of persons on the face of the earth. If I were doomed to exist as a man of fashion, I do honestly believe I should swallow ratsbane, or apply to hemp or steel before three months were over. From day to day and year to year the problem is, not how to use time, but how to waste it least painfully. They have their dinners and their routs. They move heaven and earth to get everything arranged and enacted properly ; and when the whole is done what is it ? Had the parties all wrapped themselves in warm blankets and kept their beds, much peace had been among several hundreds of his Majesty's subjects, and the same result, the uneasy destruction of half a dozen hours, had been quite as well attained. No wonder poor women take to opium and scandal. The wonder is rather that these queens of the land do not some morning, struck by the hopelessness of their condition, make a general finish by simultaneous consent, and exhibit to coroners and juries the spectacle of the whole world of *ton* suspended by their garters, and freed at last from *ennui* in the most cheap and complete of all possible modes. There is something in the life of a sturdy peasant toiling from sun to sun for a plump wife and six eating children ; but as for the Lady Jerseys and the Lord Petershams, peace be with them.

There was a glimpse, too, of modern sporting, which was as little admirable as the fine ladies and gentlemen.

To John Carlyle.

Kinnaird : September 28.

I got your letter last Friday on returning from a roe hunt, which we had all been assisting at in the wood on the hill beside us. A sorrier piece of entertainment, I may observe, is not to be met with in this kingdom. They went hallooing and beating the bushes, and talking Gaelic, the gun-men standing at certain determined points with their pieces ready, and I driving on Mrs. Buller and a wretched old clout of a white pony she was riding on, or doing my best to keep her in talk while we sat for hours in open places among the heath. In the course of the day they got two fawns about as large as your long-eared warlock, in value somewhere about sixpence a piece, and thought it royal sport. Reginald de la Pole shot them both, and never was victor at the Olympic games more charmed with his laurels. Richard Buller,[1] the other Oxford scholar, declared on the first occasion ' he would have given a sovereign for that shot.' After the second he became chop-fallen, and spoke little more for four and twenty hours. *Sic itur ad astra.*

Sporting was not the only amusement at Kinnaird. There was literature also and literary discussion. Irving's popularity had taken fire, as Carlyle called it, and he had become the rage of fashionable London. He had published an argument for judgment to come, written in great excitement and under some imagined quasi inspiration.

Irving's book (Carlyle wrote) is come three days ago. Mrs. Buller bought it. I fear it will hardly do. There is a fierce and very spiteful review of it and him in the last ' Blackwood.' There is strong talent in it, true eloquence and vigorous thought, but the foundation is rotten, and the building itself a kind of monster in architecture, beautiful in parts, vast in dimensions, but on the whole decidedly a monster. Buller has stuck in the middle of it, ' Can't fall in with your friend at all, Mr. C.' Mrs. Buller is very near sticking ; sometimes I burst right out laughing when reading it. At other times I admired it sincerely.

[1] Nephew of Mr. Buller, on a visit at Kinnaird.

I am sorry (he wrote a little later to Miss Welsh) that Irving's preaching has taken such a turn; he had been much better if, without the pleasure of being a newspaper lion and a season's wonder, he had gradually become what he must ultimately pass for—a preacher of first-rate abilities, of great eloquence, with a head fertile above all others in sense and nonsense, and a heart of the most honest and kindly sort. As it is, our friend incurs the risk of many vagaries and disasters, and at best the certainty of much disquietude. His path is steadfast and manly only when he has to encounter opposition and misfortune. When fed with flatteries and prosperity his progress soon changes into 'ground and lofty tumbling,' accompanied with all the hazards and confusion that usually attend this species of condiment. With three newspapers to praise him and three to blame, with about six peers and six dozen right honourables introduced to him every Sunday, tickets issuing for his church as if it were a theatre, and all the devout old women in the capital treating him with comfits and adulation, I know that ere now he is striking the stars with his sublime head—well if he do not break his shins among the rough places of the ground. I wish we saw him safely down again, and walking as other men walk. . . . I have meant to write to him very frequently for almost three months, but I know not well how to effect it. He will be talking about 'the Lord,' and twenty other things which he himself only wishes to believe, and which to one that knows and loves him are truly painful to hear. . . . Happy Irving, after all, that is fitted with a task which he loves and is equal to. He entertains no doubt that he is battering to its base the fortress of the alien, and he lies down every night to dream of planting the old true blue Presbyterian flag upon the summit of the ruins.

'Happy Irving, that is fitted with a task that he loves.' Without any tinge of envy Carlyle could not but contrast his friend's lot with his own; and the sense of this was perhaps the more painful, because his friend was winning fame and name on a course which he knew to be a wrong one. But a few years since they were poor schoolmasters together at Kirkcaldy, and now Irving was the theological lion of the age, the passing wonder of lawyers, statesmen, and men of the world, who, having set religion aside as no longer worthy of serious consideration, were awakened by him to a languid belief that there might be something in it after all. Carlyle saw the hollowness of the success; yet for all that his friend had been lifted into a blaze of distinction, while he was still unnoticed, was still in his own conscience undeserving of notice, and unable to turn to account the talents which he knew that he possessed. He would have been more than mortal if he had not at times repined at the inequalities of Fate.

Poor Irving! Little Carlyle knew or could measure his friend's real condition. So far from 'standing on tiptoe on Fortune's wheel,' he was just then getting married, and trying to forget Haddington. Carlyle saw him on his wedding tour in the Highlands. He has given an account of their meeting in his 'Reminiscences' which need not be repeated here. It had been intended that Miss Welsh should pay Irving and his wife a visit in London as soon as they were settled. But Irving could not face the trial; he only hoped that a time might come when he might be able to face it.

My dear Isabella (he wrote to her) has succeeded in healing the wounds of my heart by her unexampled affection and tenderness; but am I hardly yet in a condition to expose them. My former calmness and piety are returning. I feel growing in grace and holiness; and before another year I shall be worthy in the eye of my own conscience to receive you into my house and under my care, which till then I should hardly be.

Carlyle's lot was happy compared to Irving's, and yet he was already quarrelling with it. The Bullers, as he admitted, were most kind and considerate; yet he must have tried their patience. He was uneasy, restless, with dyspepsia and intellectual fever. He laid the blame on his position, and was already meditating to throw up his engagement.

To John Carlyle.

September 2.

I sleep irregularly here, and feel a little, very little, more than my usual share of torture every day. What the cause is would puzzle me to explain within the limits I could here assign it. I take exercise sufficient daily; I attend with vigorous minuteness to the quality of my food; I take all the precautions that I can, yet still the disease abates not. I should be an unreasonable blockhead did I complain of the conduct of Mr. and Mrs. Buller towards me. Any arrangement that I could suggest would, I have not a doubt, be most cheerfully complied with. Much trouble they have already had with me. But their good resolutions and enactments require to be executed by a pack of lazy, careless, and irregular waiting men and women, and often in this wasteful transmission their good will comes my length almost void. It is the hundred petty omissions and commissions of this *canaille,* coupled with the small inquietudes and vexations, small but often returning, of my official employments that chiefly act against me, and render this Kinnaird a worse place for me than Mainhill. Pity that it were so. I might else be very happy. Here am I sitting in this far highland glen, under a fair autumn night, with my clear fire of oak sticks blazing near me, my books and my tackle all around me, and no sound at all but now and then the twang of honest James Gow's fiddle, who is solacing his labours by this not usual gratification; partly, I suppose, because he sees the sky beautiful and mild and kind, and feels in spirits, he knows not why. The boys and old people and all seem to grow in their esteem for me. It is very hard. But what avails its hardness or softness either? Let us have done with whining and consider what steps can be taken to remedy it. Often and long have I meditated that point since I came hither. I have cudgelled my brains till they are sore to seek deliverance; for, like Joseph of Austria, *par ma tête seule* must I get help if I get help at all. This, then, Jack, I have in view at present. The Bullers—I mean the old gentry, with Miss Pole—are gone to Aberdeen to some Caledonian hunt or other, and will not be back for ten days. At their return, if I am not better than I have been lately, I shall say to them, 'My very noble and approved good masters, allow me to ask you what you purpose doing through the winter with your boys? If to go to Edinburgh, can I be any way accommodated there, so that I shall have the entire command of my eating and drinking, sleeping, waking, and general regimen? If so, then I shall be very glad to serve you. To stay here as you once proposed? This plan I doubt not may be attended with a thousand benefits; but for my poor share of it, I have distinctly ascertained that my *ker-kage* cannot stand it without manifest and permanent injury, and therefore, with the most profound dorsoflexions, I beg to wish you all good-morning as soon as may be.'

So here, you see, the matter rests. I care not the tossing of a halfpenny whether I go or stay. If I go, I have money enough to keep me for a year or two. I can obtain plenty of literary tasks, and get them done about five times as effectually as now. If I stay I shall gather a hundred or two additional pounds, and have the privilege of living for the winter in Edinburgh, where my en-gagements call me to be, at any rate. I shall leave it in spring with books and pens and fresh undertakings. We shall get some accommodation furbished up at Mainhill (the old peel-house or some hole), where, by the aid of Bardolph [1] and my faithful mother, I am nearly certain I can recover my health. I shall be very busy, and we can all live together as merry as maltmen; so I cast my cap into the air in defiance of all things yet; for the spirit that is in me is still unbroken as the spirit of that old lame duck you have at home, who trusts, though at present winged and mashed in both her limbs, that she shall yet by the blessing of Providence lay above five shillings worth of eggs, and be useful in her day and generation.

In better moments Carlyle recognised that the mischief was in himself, and that the spot did not exist upon earth where so sensitive a skin would not be irritated. He wrote three weeks after:—

I find the Bullers are determined to stay here with us all the winter. If I had any quiet place to retire to I believe I should be tempted to throw up my commission to-morrow, and set forth to try the voyage on another tack, as I must ere long do at any rate. But there is none. Mainhill must be full of bustle and confusion at this time,[2] unfit for purposes of literary labour. Of Edinburgh, of living in lodgings with Mantie,[3] and stenches and horrors more

---

[1] A horse bought for Carlyle by his brother Alexander, and with him at Kinnaird.

[2] Harvest.

[3] Mantie was the name of his least-loved landlady.

than tongue can tell to drive me to despair, I cannot think without a cold shudder which scarcely the prospect of the gallows could bring over me. Many a man, I am sure, has been tried by fifteen of his peers, and fairly doomed and hanged, and quartered by the doctors, with less torment than I have suffered in that fatal city for no cause at all. What then shall I do ? In days when wrecked with want of sleep and all its infernal *et cœteras*, I am sometimes within an inch of writing to Buller to signify my resolution of departing; but their kindness to me and the reflection of my inability to mend the matter certainly, and the risk I run of making it considerably worse, always shuts my mouth. Next day, perhaps, I shall sleep better and become as lively as a hawk, and think I might exist here long enough very comfortably. Thus I vary and vacillate. Most probably it will long be so. It seems likely I shall just *thring on* here till I get desperate, and then cut and run.

Meanwhile I make a point of going on with Goethe.[1] Ten pages I find more than I can almost ever execute, for it is very hard, and I scarcely get fairly into the spirit of it till I must leave off. Nevertheless, I *gar my elf* (as our father would do) go on with this thing. I am now more than half through the first volume. It will all be ready long ere spring. You and I could do it in four weeks if we had quiet quarters, and the fiend would give me any respite. I am sometimes tempted to sally off and get it done and then have it printed in winter; then take something different and better down to Mainhill, to work and toil as if I were a brownie, not a man, till I have conquered all these mean impediments that hem in the free-born, heaven-tending soul. I say, Jack, thou and I must never falter. Work, my boy, work unweariedly. I swear that all the thousand miseries of this hard fight, and ill health, the most terrific of them all, shall never chain us down. By the river Styx it shall not. Two fellows from a nameless spot in Annandale shall yet show the world the pluck that is in Carlyles.

Mrs. Buller must have been a most forbearing and discerning woman. She must have suffered, like everyone who came in contact with Carlyle, from his strange humours, but she had mind enough to see what he was, and was willing to endure much to keep such a man at her sons' side.

---

[1] The translation of *Meister.*

CHAPTER XII.

IF Carlyle complained, his complaints were the impatience of a man who was working with all his might. If
his dyspepsia did him no serious harm, it obstructed his
efforts and made him miserable with pain. He had written
the first part of Schiller, which was now coming out in
the 'London Magazine.' He was translating 'Meister,'
and his translation, though the production of a man who
had taught himself with grammar and dictionary, and had
never spoken a word of German, is yet one of the very
best which has ever been made from one language into
another. In everything which he undertook he never
spared labour or slurred over a difficulty, but endeavoured
with all his might to do his work faithfully. A journal
which he kept intermittently at Kinnaird throws light into the inner regions of his mind, while it shows also how
much he really suffered. Deeply as he admired his German friends, his stern Scotch Calvinism found much in
them that offended him. Goethe and even Schiller appeared to think that the hope of improvement for mankind lay in culture rather than morality—in æsthetics, in
arts, in poetry, in the drama, rather than in obedience to
the old rugged rules of right and wrong; and this perplexed and displeased him.

Schiller (he writes) was a very worthy character, possessed of
great talents, and fortunate in always finding means to employ
them in the attainment of worthy ends. The pursuit of the

Beautiful, the representing it in suitable forms, and the diffusion of the feelings arising from it, operated as a kind of religion in his soul. He talks in some of his essays about the æsthetic being a necessary means of improvement among political societies. His efforts in this cause accordingly not only satisfied the restless activity, the desire of creating and working upon others which forms the great want of an elevated mind, but yielded a sort of balsam to his conscience. He viewed himself as an apostle of the Sublime. Pity that he had no better way of satisfying it. A playhouse shows but indifferently as an arena for the moralist. It is even inferior to the synod of the theologian. One is tired to death with his and Goethe's *palabra* about the nature of the fine arts. Did Shakespeare know anything of the æsthetic? Did Homer? Kant's philosophy has a gigantic appearance at a distance, enveloped in clouds and darkness, shadowed forth in types and symbols of unknown and fantastic derivation. There is an apparatus, and a flourishing of drums and trumpets, and a tumultuous *Marktschreyerei*, as if all the earth were going to renew its youth; and the *Esoterics* are equally allured by all this pomp and circumstance, and repelled by the hollowness and airy nothingness of the ware which is presented to them. Any of the results which have been made intelligible to us turn out to be— like Dryden in the 'Battle of the Books'—a helmet of rusty iron large as a kitchen pot, and within it a head little bigger than a nut. What is Schlegel's great solution of the mystery of life?— 'the strife of necessity against the will.' Nothing earthly but the old old story that all men find it difficult to get on in the world, and that one never can get all his humours out. They pretend that Nature gives people true intimations of true beauty and just principles in Art; but the *bildende Künstler* and the *richtende* ought to investigate the true foundation of these obscure intimations, and set them fast on the basis of reason. Stuff and nonsense I fear it is. People made finer pieces of workmanship when there was not a critic among them, just as people did finer actions when there was no theory of the moral sentiments among them. Nature is the sure guide in all cases; and perhaps the only requisite is that we have judgment enough to apply the sentiment implanted in us without an effort to the more complex circumstances that will meet us more frequeutly as we advance in culture or move in a society more artificial. Poor silly sons of Adam! you have been prating on these things for two or three thousand years, and you have not advanced a hair's breadth toward the conclusion. Poor fellows, and poorer me, that take the trouble to repeat such insipidities and truisms.

Here, on the same page, Carlyle sketched the emblem of the wasting candle, with the motto written on it, '*Terar dum prosim*' 'May I be wasted, so that I be of use.' He goes on :—

But what if I do not *prosum?* Why then *terar* still, so I cannot help it. This is the end and beginning of all philosophy, known even to Singleton the blacksmith ; we must just do the best we can. Oh, most lame and impotent conclusion ! I wish I fully understood the philosophy of Kant. Is it a chapter in the history of human folly ? or the brightest in the history of human wisdom ? or both mixed ? and in what degree ?

This was written on May 23. The next entry begins—

It is now November; six weary months have passed away, another portion from my span of being; and here am I, in a wet, dreary night at Kinnaird, with no recollections or acquisitions to fill up that span with ; but the recollection of agonised days and nights, and the acquisition of a state of health worse than ever it was. My time ! my time ! my peace and activity ! where are they ? I could read the curse of Ernulphus, or something twenty times as fierce, upon myself and all things earthly. What will become of me ? Happiness ! Tophet must be happier than this ; or they —— but, *basta !* it is no use talking. Let me get on with Schiller, then with Goethe. 'They that meaned at a gowden gown gat aye the sleeve.' I shall not get even the listing. Schiller is in the wrong vein—laborious, partly affected, meagre, bombastic. Too often it strives by lofty words to hide littleness of thought. Would I were done with it ! Oh, Carlyle ! if thou ever become happy, think on these days of pain and darkness, and thou wilt join trembling with thy mirth.

There is something in reading a weak or dull book very nauseous to me. Reading is a weariness of the flesh. After reading and studying about two scores of good books there is no new thing whatever to be met with in the generality of libraries; repetitions a thousand times repeated of the same general idea. Feelings, opinions, and events, all is what we might anticipate. No man without Themistocles' gift of forgetting can possibly spend his days in reading. Generally about the age of five and twenty he should begin to put the little knowledge he has acquired (it can be but little) from books to some practical use. If I could *write*, that were my practical use. But, alas! alas! Oh Schiller! what secret hadst thou for creating such things as Max and Thekla when thy body was wasting with disease? I am well nigh *done*, I think. To die is hard enough at this age. To die by inches is very hard. But I *will* not. Though all things human and divine are against me, I will not.

December 14.—Schiller, part ii. is off to London three weeks ago. It was very bad. Part iii. I am swithering to begin; would it were finished!

I spent ten days wretchedly in Edinburgh and Haddington. I was consulting doctors, who made me give up my dear nicotium and take to mercury. I am to write letters, and then begin Schiller. May God bless all my friends! my poor mother at the head of them. It sometimes comes on me like the shadow of death that we *are* all parting from one another—each moving his several, his inevitable way; fate driving us on—inexorable, dread relentless fate. No deliverance! (*Mit dem Fusse stampfend.*) No help? Alas, poor sons of Adam!

December 31.—The year is closing. This time eight and twenty years I was a child of three weeks old, sleeping in my mother's bosom.

> Oh! little did my mither think
> That day she cradled me,
> The lands that I should travel in,
> The death I was to dee.

Another hour and 1823 is with the years beyond the flood. What have I done to mark the course of it? Suffered the pangs of Tophet almost daily; grown sicker and sicker; alienated by my misery certain of my friends, and worn out from my own mind a few remaining capabilities of enjoyment; reduced my world a *little* nearer the condition of a bare, rugged desert, where peace and rest for me is none. Hopeful youth, Mr. C.! Another year or two and it will do. Another year or two and thou wilt wholly *be*

—this *caput mortuum* of thy former self; a creature ignorant, stupid, peevish, disappointed, broken-hearted, the veriest wretch upon the surface of the globe. My curse seems deeper and blacker than that of any man : to be immured in a rotten carcase, every avenue of which is changed into an inlet of pain, till my intellect is obscured and weakened, and my head and heart are alike desolate and dark. How have I deserved this? Or is it mere fate that orders these things, caring no jot for merit or demerit, crushing our poor mortal interests among its ponderous machinery, and grinding us and them to dust relentlessly? I know not. Shall I ever know? Then why don't you kill yourself, sir? Is there not arsenic? is there not ratsbane of various kinds? and hemp? and steel? Most true, Sathanas, all these things *are;* but it will be time enough to use them when I have *lost* the game which I am as yet but *losing*. You observe, sir, I have still a glimmering of hope; and while my friends, my mother, father, brothers, sisters live, the duty of not breaking their hearts would still remain to be performed when hope had utterly fled. For which reason— even if there were no others, which, however, I believe there are —the benevolent Sathanas will excuse me. I do not design to be a suicide. God in heaven forbid! That way I was never tempted. But where is the use of going on with this? I am not writing like a reasonable man. If I am miserable the more reason there is to gather my faculties together, and see what can be done to help myself. I want health, health, health! On this subject I am becoming quite furious ; my torments are greater than I am able to bear. If I do not soon recover, I am miserable for ever and ever. They talk of the benefit of ill health in a moral point of view. I declare solemnly, without exaggeration, that I impute nine-tenths of my present wretchedness, and rather more than nine-tenths of all my faults, to this infernal disorder in the stomach.

But if it were once away, I think I could snap my fingers in the face of all the world. The only good of it is the friends it tries for us and endears to us. Oh, there is a charm in true affection that suffering cannot weary, that abides by us in the day of fretfulness and dark calamity, a charm which almost makes amends for misery. Love to friends—alas! I may almost say relatives— is now almost the sole religion of my mind.

I have hopes of 'Meister,' though they are still very faint. Schiller, part iii. I began just three nights ago. I absolutely could not sooner. These drugs leave me scarcely the consciousness of existence. I am scribbling, not writing, Schiller. My mind will not catch hold of it. I skim it, do it as I will, and I am as anxious as possible to get it off my hands. It will not do for publishing separately. It is not in my natural vein. I wrote a very little of it to-night, and then went and talked ineptitudes at the house. Alas! there is mercurial powder in me, and a gnawing pain over all the organs of digestion, especially in the pit and left side of the stomach. Let this excuse the wild absurdity above.

Half-past eleven.—The silly Donovan is coming down (at least so I interpreted his threat) with punch or 'wishes,' which curtails the few reflections that mercury might still leave it in my power to make. To make none at all will perhaps be as well. It exhibits not an interesting, but a true picture of my present mood— stupid, unhappy, by fits wretched, but also dull—dull and very weak.

> Now fare thee well, old twenty-three,
>   No powers, no arts can thee retain;
> Eternity will roll away,
>   And thou wilt never come again.
>
> And welcome thou, young twenty-four,
>   Thou bringest to men of joy and grief;
> Whatever thou bringest in sufferings sour,
>   The heart in faith will hope relief.

Here thou art, by Jove. Donny is not come. Good-night—to whom?

January 7.—Last Sunday came the 'Times' newspaper with the commencement of Schiller, part ii. extracted. So Walter thought it on this side zero. I believe this is about the first compliment (most slender as it is) that ever was paid me by a person who could have no interest in hoodwinking me. I am very weak. It kept me cheerful for an hour. Even yet I sometimes feel it. Certainly no one ever wrote with such tremendous difficulty as I do. Shall I ever learn to write with ease?

There can be no doubt that Carlyle suffered and perhaps suffered excessively. It is equally certain that his sufferings were immensely aggravated by the treatment to which he was submitted. 'A long hairy-eared jackass,' as he called some eminent Edinburgh physician, had ordered him to give up tobacco, but he had ordered him to take mercury, as well; and he told me that along with the mercury he must have swallowed whole hogsheads of castor oil. Much of his pain would be so accounted for; but of all the men whom I have ever seen, Carlyle was the least patient of the common woes of humanity. Nature had, in fact, given him a constitution of unusual strength. He saw his ailments through the lens of his imagination, so magnified by the metaphors in which he described them as to seem to him to be something supernatural; and if he was a torment to himself, he distracted every one with whom he came in contact. He had been to Edinburgh about the printing of 'Meister,' and had slept in the lodgings which he had longed for at Kinnaird. 'There was one of those public guardians there,'[1] he says in a letter, 'whose throat I could have cut that night; his voice was loud, hideous, and ear and soul piercing, resembling the voices of ten thousand gib-cats all molten into one terrific peal.' He had been given rooms in a separate house at Kinnaird for the sake of quiet. This did not content him either. When the winter came he complained of the cold.

My bower (he said) is the most polite of bowers, refusing admittance to no wind that blows from any quarter of the shipmate's card. It is scarcely larger than your room at Mainhill; yet has three windows, and, of course, a door, all shrunk and crazy. The walls, too, are pierced with many crevices, for the mansion has been built by Highland masons, apparently in a remote century. I put on my gray duffle sitting jupe. I bullyrag the sluttish harlots of the place, and cause them to make fires that would melt a stithy. . . .

Poor Mrs. Buller's household management pleased him as little.

This blessed stomach I have lost all patience with (he wrote to his brother Alexander). The want of health threatens to be the

[1] A watchman.

downdraught of all my lofty schemes. My heart is burnt with fury and indignation when I think of being cramped and shackled and tormented as never man till me was. 'There is too much fire in my belly,' as Ram Dass said, to permit my dwindling into a paltry valetudinarian. I must and will be free of these despicable fetters, whatever may betide. . . . I could almost set my house in order, and go and hang myself like Judas. If I take any of their swine-meat porridge, I sleep; but a double portion of stupidity overwhelms me, and I awake very early in the morning with the sweet consciousness that another day of my precious, precious time is gone irrevocably, that I have been very miserable yesterday, and shall be very miserable to-day. It is clear to me that I can never recover or retain my health under the economy of Mrs. Buller. Nothing, therefore, remains for me but to leave it. This kind of life is next to absolute starvation, only slower in its agony. And if I had my health even moderately restored, I could earn as much by my own exertions.

So it would be one day. The next, the pain would be gone, the sun would be shining again, and nothing would remain but a twinge of remorse for the anxiety which his clamours might have caused. He apologised in a letter to his father with characteristic coolness.

I often grieve for the uneasiness my complaining costs you and my dear mother, who is of feebler texture in that respect than you. But by this time she must be beginning to understand me; to know that when I shout 'murder,' I am not always being killed. The truth is, complaint is the natural resource of uneasiness, and I have none that I care to complain to, but you. After all, however, I am not so miserable as you would think. My health is better than it was last year, but I have lost all patience with it; and whenever any retrograde movement comes in view, I get quite desperate in the matter; being determined that I must get well—cost what it will. On days when moderately well, I feel as happy as others; happier perhaps, for sweet is pleasure after pain.

I have dwelt more fully on these aspects of Carlyle's character than in themselves they deserve, because the irritability which he could not or would not try to control followed him through the greater part of his life. It was no light matter to take charge of such a person, as Miss Welsh was beginning to contemplate the possibility of doing. Nor can we blame the anxiety with which her mother was now regarding the closeness of the correspondence between Carlyle and her daughter. Extreme as was the undesirableness of such a marriage in a worldly point of view, it is to Mrs. Welsh's credit that inequality of social position was not the cause of her alarm, so much as the violence of temper which Carlyle could not restrain even before her. The fault, however, was of the surface merely, and Miss Welsh was not the only person who could see the essential quality of the nature which lay below. Mrs. Buller had suffered from Carlyle's humours as keenly as anyone, except, perhaps, her poor 'sluttish harlots;' yet she was most anxious that he should remain with the family and have the exclusive training of her sons. They had been long enough at Kinnaird; their future plans were unsettled. They thought of a house in Cornwall, of a house in London, of travelling abroad, in all of which arrangements they desired to include Carlyle. At length it was settled—so far as Mrs. Buller could settle anything —that they were to stay where they were till the end of January, and then go for the season to London. Carlyle was to remain behind in Scotland till he had carried 'Meister' through the press. Irving had invited him to be his guest at any time in the spring which might suit him, and further plans could then be arranged. For the moment his mind was taken off from his own sorrows by the need of helping his brothers. His brother Alick was starting in business as a farmer. Carlyle found him in money, and refused to be thanked for it. 'What any brethren of our father's house possess,' he said, 'I look on as common stock, from which all are entitled to draw whenever their convenience requires it. Feelings far nobler than pride are my guides in such matters.'

He was already supporting John Carlyle at college, and not supporting only, but directing and advising. His counsels were always wise. As a son and brother his conduct in all essentials was faultlessly admirable. Here is a letter on the value of a profession. John, it seems, was shrinking from drudgery, and inclining to follow the siren of literature.

Thomas Carlyle to John Carlyle.

Kinnaird: Jan. 1, 1824.

I am glad to hear that your repugnance to medicine is gradually wearing away. Persist honestly in the study, and you will like it more and more. Like all practical sciences, medicine is begirt with a tangled border of minute, technical, uninteresting, or, it may be, disgusting details, the whole of which must be mastered before you penetrate into the philosophy of the business, and get the better powers of your understanding at all fastened on the subject. You are now, I suppose, getting across these brambly thickets into the green fields of the science. Go on and prosper, my dear Jack! Let not the difficulties repulse you, nor the little contentions of natural taste abate your ardour. To conquer our inclinations of whatever sort is a lesson which all men have to learn, and the man who learns it soonest will learn it easiest. This medicine your judgment says is to be useful to you. Do you assail it and get the better of it, in spite of all other considerations. It is a noble thing to have a profession by the end: it makes a man independent of all mortals. He is richer than a lord, for no *external* change can destroy the possession which he has acquired for himself. Nor is there any weight in the fears you labour under about failing in more interesting acquisitions by your diligence in following after this. It appears to me that a man who is not born to some independency, if he means to devote himself to literature properly so called, even ought to study some profession which as a first preliminary will enable him to live. It is galling and heartburning to live on the precarious windfalls of literature; and the idea that one has not time for practising an honest calling is stark delusion. I could have studied three professions in the time I have been forced, for want of one, to spend in strenuous idleness. I could practise the most laborious doctor's occupation at this moment in less time than I am constrained to devote to toiling in that which cannot permanently profit, and serves only to make a scanty provision for the day that is passing over me : but I will preach no more, for you are a reasonable youth, Jack, and are already bent on persevering.

The life at Kinnaird was running out. The last roes were shot on the mountains, and the last visitors were drifting away. Carlyle too was longing to be gone, but the move was continually postponed.

He wad need to have a lang ladle that sups with the Deil (he said), and he wad need to have a long head that predicts the movements of aught depending on Mrs. Buller. . . . This accursed Schiller is not finished yet. Patience, patience ; or, rather, fortitude and action, for patience will not do. . . . It is impossible for anything to be more stagnant and monotonous than our life here is. We are all very agreeable together, but there is no new topic among us ; and now, grouse shooting having failed, the good people are weary of their abode here. Two or three squires of the neighbourhood have looked in upon us of late, but their minds are what Pump Sandy calls a 'vaaccum.' *Naiter and airt working together* have rendered them dull. We had the other night a Sir John something—I forget what—perhaps Ogilvie,— 'one of the numerous baronets of the age,' as Arthur Buller described him. Thurtell being hanged last week, we grew duller than ever, till yesterday Mrs. Buller turned off all the servants except two at one swoop. This keeps up our hearts for the time. On the whole, however, I have been happier than I usually was throughout the summer and autumn. My health, I think, is little worse or better than it was ; but I have the prospect of speedy deliverance, and my mind has been full, disagreeably so often, of this miserable Schiller.

He was looking forward to London, though far from sharing the enthusiastic expectations which Irving had formed for him. Irving, it seems, had imagined that his friend had but to present himself before the great world to carry it by storm as he had himself done, and when they met in the autumn had told him so. Carlyle was under no such illusion.

We spoke about this project of his and my share in it (he wrote), but could come to no conclusion. He figured out purposes of unspeakable profit to me. He seemed to think that, if set down in London streets, some strange development of genius would take place in me; that by conversing with Coleridge and the Opium-eater I should find out new channels of speculation and soon learn to speak with tongues. There is but a very small degree of truth in all this. Of genius (bless the mark!) I never imagined in the most lofty humours that I possessed beyond the smallest possible fraction ; and this fraction, be it little or less, can only be turned to account by rigid and stern perseverance through long years of labour, in London as any other spot in the universe. Unrelenting perseverance, stubborn effort, is the remedy. Help cometh not from the hills or valleys. My own poor arm, weak and shackled as it is, must work out my deliverance, or I am forever captive and in bonds. Irving said I had none to love or reverence in Scotland. Kind, simple Irving. I did not tell him of the hearts in Scotland I will love till my own has ceased to feel, whose warm, pure and generous affection I would not exchange for the maudlin sympathy of all the peers and peeresses and prim saints and hypochondriacal old women of either sex in the creation. I told him that love concentered on a few objects, or a single one, was like a river flowing within its appointed banks, calm, clear, rejoicing in its course. Diffused over many, it was like that river spread abroad upon a province, stagnant, shallow, cold and profitless. He puckered up his face into various furrowy peaks at this remark, and talked about the Devil and universal benevolence, reproving me withal because I ventured to laugh at the pretensions of the Devil.

The Bullers went at last. Carlyle returned to his lodgings at Edinburgh, finished his Schiller, and was busy translating the last chapters of ' Meister' while the first were being printed. Miss Welsh came into the city to stay with a friend. They met and quarrelled. She tormented her lover till he flung out of the room, banging the door behind him. A note of penitence followed. 'I declare,' she said, ' I am very much of Mr. Kemp's way of thinking, that certain persons are possessed of devils at the present time. Nothing short of a devil could have tempted me to torment you and myself as I did on that unblessed day.' There was no engagement between them, and under existing circumstances there was to be none; but she shared Irving's conviction that Carlyle had but to be known to spring to fame and fortune; and his fortune, as soon as it was made, she was willing to promise to share with him. Strict secrecy was of course desired. Her mother and his mother were alone admitted to the great mystery; but the 'sorrows of Teufelsdröckh,' bodily and mental, were forgotten for at least three months.

To James Carlyle, Mainhill.

3 Moray Street: April 2, 1824.

My dear Father,—I feel thankful to learn that you are still in moderate health, having little to complain of except the weariness of increasing years, and being supported under the feeling of this by such comforts as it has been your care in life to lay up. To all men journeying through the wilderness of the world religion is an inexhaustible spring of nourishment and consolation; the thorns and flinty places of our path become soft when we view them as leading to an everlasting city, where sorrow and sin shall be alike excluded. To a religious man, and to a mere worldling, the frailties of age speak in very different tones: to the last they are the judgment voice that warns him to an awful reckoning, a dark and dreary change; to the first they are kind assurances of a father, that a place of rest is made ready where the weary shall find refreshment after all their toils.

Judging from your years and past and present health, I expect that we shall yet be all spared together for a long, long season, shall live and see good here below. But it gives me real pleasure to know that you have such approved resources against the worst that can befall. I often think of death, as all reasonable creatures must; but with such prospects there is little in it to be feared. I have many a time felt that without the expectation of it life would be in its brightest station a burden too heavy to be borne. But these are topics too serious for this light handling. We are in the hands of an All-merciful Father. Let us live with hope in Him, and try to fill rightly the parts he has assigned us. Here is an anchor of the soul both sure and steadfast. By this let us abide, and vex ourselves with no needless fear.

Jack, poor Jack! I feel convinced is going to make a figure yet; he inherits a good head and an honest heart from his parents, and no bad habit of any kind has perverted these invaluable gifts. His only faults at present are his inexperience and the very excess of his good qualities. Our only subject of disagreement is the relative importance of worldly comforts and mental wealth. Jack decides, as a worthy fellow of twenty always will decide, that mere external rank and convenience are nothing; the dignity of the mind is all in all. I argue as every reasonable man of *twenty-eight*, that this is poetry in part, which a few years will mix pretty largely with prose. And there we differ and chop logic, an art for which Jack has been famous from his very cradle. Sometimes I make free to settle him with your finisher, 'Thou natural thou!' But on the whole he is getting more rational. His jolly presence has been of no small benefit to myself on many sad occasions. I have often absolutely wondered at the patience with which he has borne my black humours, when bad health and disturbance vexed me too much. He is certainly a prime honest 'Lord Moon,' [1] with all his faults.

Carlyle did not stay long in Edinburgh. He remained only till he had settled his business arrangements with Boyd, his publisher, and then went home to Mainhill to finish his translation of 'Meister' there. He was to receive 180*l.* on publication for the first edition. If a second edition was called for, Boyd was to pay him 250*l.* for a thousand copies, and after that the book was to be Carlyle's own. 'Any way, I am paid sufficiently for my labours,' he said. 'Am I a genius? I was intended for a horsedealer, rather.' The sheets of 'Meister' were sent to Haddington as they were printed. Miss Welsh refused to be interested in it, and thought more of the money which Carlyle was making than of the great Goethe and his novel. Carlyle admitted that she had much to say for her opinion.

[1] Name by which John Carlyle went in the family from the breadth of his face.

There is not (he said), properly speaking, the smallest particle of historical interest in it except what is connected with Mignon, and this you cannot fully see till near the very end. Meister himself is perhaps one of the greatest *ganaches* that ever was created by quill and ink. I am going to write a fierce preface disclaiming all concern with the literary or the moral merit of the work, grounding my claims to recompense or toleration on the fact that I have accurately copied a striking portrait of Goethe's mind—the strangest, and in many points the greatest, now extant. What a work! Bushels of dust and straw and feathers, with here and there a diamond of the purest water.

Carlyle was very happy at this time at Mainhill. He had found work that he could do, and had opened, as it seemed, successfully his literary career. The lady whom he had so long worshipped had given him hopes that his devotion might be rewarded. She had declined to find much beauty even in Mignon; but she might say what she pleased now without disturbing him.

To Miss Welsh.

Mainhill: April 15.

So you laugh at my venerated Goethe and my *Herzen's Kind* poor little Mignon. Oh, the hardness of man's, and still more of woman's heart! If you were not lost to all true feeling your eyes would be a fountain of tears in the perusing of 'Meister.' Have you really no pity for the hero, or the Count, or the Frau Melina, or Philina, or the Manager? Well, it cannot be helped. I must not quarrel with you. Do what you like. Seriously, you are right about the book. It is worth next to nothing as a novel. Except Mignon, who will touch you yet perhaps, there is no person in it one has any care about. But for its wisdom, its eloquence, its wit, and even for its folly and its dullness, it interests me much, far more the second time of reading than it did the first. I have not got as many ideas from any book for six years. You will like Goethe better ten years hence than you do at present. It is pity the man were not known among us. The English have begun to speak about him of late years, but no light has yet been thrown upon him; 'no light, but only darkness visible.' The syllables of Goethe excite an idea as vague and monstrous as the words Gorgon or Chimera.

It would do you good to see with what regularity I progress in translating. Clockwork is scarcely steadier. Nothing do I allow to interfere with me. My movements might be almost calculated like the moon's. It is not unpleasant work, nor is it pleasant. Original composition is ten times as laborious. It is an agitating, fiery, consuming business, when your heart is in it. I can easily conceive a man writing the soul out of him—writing till it evaporate like the snuff of a farthing candle when the matter interests him properly. I always recoil from again engaging with it. But this present business is cool and quiet. One feels over it as a shoemaker does when he sees the leather gathering into a shoe—as any mortal does when he sees the activity of his mind expressing itself in some external material shape. You are facetious about my mine of gold. It has often struck me as the most accursed item in men's lot that they had to toil for filthy lucre ; but I am not sure now that it is not the *ill-best* way it could have been arranged. Me it would make happy at least for half a year, if I saw the certain prospect before me of making 500*l.* per annum. A pampered Lord—*e.g.* Byron—would turn with loathing from a pyramid of ingots. I *may* be blessed in this way: he never. Let us be content.

It would edify you much to see my way of life here—how I write and ride and delve in the garden and muse on things new and old. On the whole I am moderately happy. There is rough substantial plenty here. For me there is heartfelt kindness in the breast of every living thing, from the cur that vaults like a kangaroo whenever he perceives me, and the pony that prances when he gets me on his back, up to the sovereign heads of the establishment. Better is a dinner of herbs with peace, than a stalled ox with contention. Better is affection in the smoke of a turf cottage than indifference amidst the tapestries of palaces.

I am often very calm and quiet. I delight to see these old mountains lying in the clear sleep of twilight, stirless as death, pure as disembodied spirits, or floating like cærulean islands, while the white vapours of the morning have hidden all the lower earth.

They are my own mountains. Skiddaw and Helvellyn, with their snowy cowls among their thousand azure brethren, are more to me than St. Gothard and Mont Blanc. Hartfell and Whitecombe raise their bald and everlasting heads into my native sky, and far beyond them, as I often picture, are Jane and her mother, sometimes thinking of me, cheering this dull earth for me with a distant spot of life and kindliness. . . . But, bless me! the sweet youth is growing quite poetical. *C'est assez.*

In this mood Carlyle heard of the end of Lord Byron. He had spoken slightingly of Byron in his last letter; he often spoke in the same tone in his own later years; but he allowed no one else to take the same liberties. Perhaps in his heart he felt at fourscore much what he wrote when the news came from Missolonghi. Both he and Miss Welsh were equally affected. She wrote, 'I was told it all alone in a room full of people. If they had said the sun or the moon was gone out of the heavens, it could not have struck me with the idea of a more awful and dreary blank in the creation than the words, ' Byron is dead.'

Carlyle answered—

Poor Byron! alas, poor Byron! the news of his death came upon my heart like a mass of lead; and yet, the thought of it sends a painful twinge through all my being, as if I had lost a brother. O God! that so many souls of mud and clay should fill up their base existence to its utmost bound; and this the noblest spirit in Europe should sink before half his course was run. Late so full of fire and generous passion and proud purposes; and now for ever dumb and cold. Poor Byron! and but a young man, still struggling amidst the perplexities and sorrows and aberrations of a mind not arrived at maturity, or settled in its proper place in life. Had he been spared to the age of three-score and ten, what might he not have done! what might he not have been! But we shall hear his voice no more. I dreamed of seeing him and knowing him; but the curtain of everlasting night has hid him from our eyes. We shall go to him; he shall not return to us. Adieu. There is a blank in your heart and a blank in mine since this man passed away.

CHAPTER XIII.

THE time for Carlyle's departure for London had now arrived. A letter came from Mrs. Buller begging his immediate presence. 'Meister' was finished and paid for.
A presentation copy was secured for Mainhill, and there
was no more reason for delay. The expedition was an
epoch in Carlyle's life. There was, perhaps, no one of
his age in Scotland or England who knew so much and
had seen so little. He had read enormously—history, poetry, philosophy ; the whole range of modern literature—
French, German, and English—was more familiar to him,
perhaps, than to any man living of his own age ; while
the digestive power by which all this spiritual food had
been digested and converted into intellectual tissue was
equally astonishing. And yet all this time he had never
seen any town larger than Glasgow, or any cultivated society beyond what he had fallen in with at occasional dinners with Brewster, or with the Bullers at Kinnaird.
London had hovered before him rather as a place of doubtful possibilities than of definite hope. The sanguine Irving would have persuaded him that it would open its arms
to a new man of genius. Carlyle knew better. He had
measured his own capabilities. He was painfully aware
that they were not of the sort which would win easy recognition, and that if he made his way at all it would be
slowly, and after desperate and prolonged exertion. He
would never go to bed unknown and wake to find himself
famous. His own disposition was rather towards some

quiet place in Scotland, where with fresh air and plain food he could possess his soul in peace and work undisturbed and unconfused. Still London was to be seen and measured. He was to go by sea from Leith, and for the first week or two after his arrival he was to be Irving's guest at Pentonville. A few happy days were spent at Haddington, and on Sunday morning, June 5, he sailed—sailed literally. Steamers had begun to run, but were not yet popular; and the old yacht, safe if tedious, was still the usual mode of transit for ordinary travellers. His fellow-passengers were—a Sir David Innes, a Captain Smith from Linlithgow; a M. Dubois, land-steward to Lord Bute; and two ladies who never left their cabins. This is Carlyle's account of his voyage.

To Miss Welsh.

I had the most melancholy sail to London. Cross winds, storms, and, what was ten times worse, dead calms, and the stupidest society in nature. Sir David Innes, if, indeed, he be a knight of flesh and blood, and not a mere shadowy personification of dullness, snored assiduously beside me all night, and talked the most polite ineptitudes all day. He had a large long head like a sepulchral urn. His face, pock-pitted, hirsute and bristly, was at once vast and hatchet-shaped. He stood for many hours together with his left hand laid upon the boat on the middle of the deck, and the thumb of his right hand stuck firmly with its point on the hip joint; his large blue and rheumy eyes gazing on vacancy, the very image of thicklipped misery. Captain Smith was of quite an opposite species, brisk, lean, whisking, smart of speech, and quick in bowing; but if possible still more inane than Dullness. . . . These two, Dullness and Inanity, contrived to tell me in the course of the voyage nearly all the truisms which natural and moral science have yet enriched the world withal. They demonstrated to me that sea-sickness was painful, that sea-captains ought to be expert, that London was a great city, that the Turks eat opium, that the Irish were discontented, that brandy would intoxicate. Oh, I thought I should have given up the ghost! M. Dubois, a Strasburger, Lord Bute's factotum, with his flageolet, his 'Vaillant Troubadour,' and his 'Es hatt' ein Bauer ein schönes Weib,' alone contributed to save me. I laughed at him every day about an hour. On Sunday do you suppose I was very gay ? The Bass was standing in sight all day, and I recollected where the Sunday before I had been sitting beside you in peace and quietness at home! But time and hours wear out the roughest day. Next Friday at noon we were winding slowly through the forest of masts in the Thames up to our station at Tower Wharf. The giant bustle, the coalheavers, the bargemen, the black buildings, the ten thousand times ten thousand sounds and movements of that monstrous harbour formed the grandest object I had ever witnessed. One man seems a drop in the ocean : you feel annihilated in the immensity of that heart of all the earth.

Carlyle has described in his ' Reminiscences ' his arrival in London, his reception in Irving's house, and his various adventures during his English visit. When written evidence rises before us of what we said and did in early life, we find generally that memory has played false to us, and has so shaped and altered past scenes that our actions have become legendary even to ourselves. Goethe called his autobiography ' Wahrheit und Dichtung,' being aware that facts stand in our recollection as trees, houses, mountains, rivers stand in the landscape ; that lights and shadows change their places between sunrise and sunset, and that the objects are grouped into new combinations as the point of vision alters. But none of these involuntary freaks of memory can be traced in Carlyle's ' Reminiscences.' After two and forty years the scenes and persons which he describes remain as if photographed precisely as they are to be found in his contemporary letters. Nothing is changed. The images stand as they were first printed, the judgments are unmodified, and are often repeated in the same words. His matured and epitomised narrative may thus be trusted as an entirely authentic record of the scenes which are recorded at fuller length in the accounts which he sent at the time to his family and friends. With Irving he was better pleased than he expected. Uneasiness Carlyle had felt about him—never, indeed, that the simplicity and truth of Irving's disposition could be impaired or tarnished, but that he might be misled and confused by the surroundings in which he was to find him. 'The orator,' he wrote, 'is mended since I saw him at Dunkeld. He begins to see that his honours are not supernatural, and his honest, practical warmth of heart is again becoming the leading feature of his character.' He was thrown at once into Irving's circle, and made acquaintance with various persons whom he had previously heard celebrated. Mrs. Strachey, Mrs. Buller's sister, he admired the most. Her husband, too, he met and liked, and her niece, Miss Kirkpatrick. To Miss Welsh he wrote a few days after his arrival :—

I have seen some notable characters. Mrs. Montagu [1] (do not tremble) is a stately matron, with a quick intellect and a taste for exciting sentiments, which two qualities, by dint of much management in a longish life, she has elaborated into the materials of a showy, tasteful, clearsighted, rigid, and, I fancy, cold manner of existence, intended rather for itself and being looked at than for being used to any useful purpose in the service of others. She loves and admires the Orator beyond all others : me she seems to like better than I like her. I have also seen and scraped acquaintance with Procter—Barry Cornwall. He is a slender, rough-faced, palish, gentle, languid-looking man, of three or four and thirty. There is a dreamy mildness in his eye ; he is kind and good in his manners, and I understand in his conduct. He is a poet by the ear and the fancy, but his heart and intellect are not strong. He is a small poet. I am also a nascent friend of Allan Cunningham's —my most dear, modest, kind, good-humoured Allan. He has his Annandale accent as faithfully as if he had never crossed the border. He seems not to know that he is anything beyond a reading mason. Yet I will send you his books and tell you of him, and you will find him a genius of no common make. I have also seen

[1] Mrs. Basil Montagu, of whom there is a full account in the *Reminiscences*, called by Irving 'the noble lady,' and already known through Irving's letters to Miss Welsh.

Thomas Campbell. Him I like worst of all. He is heartless as a little Edinburgh advocate. There is a smirk on his face which would befit a shopman or an auctioneer. His very eye has the cold vivacity of a conceited worldling. His talk is small, contemptuous, and shallow. The blue frock and trousers, the eyeglass, the wig, the very fashion of his bow, proclaim the literary dandy. His wife has black eyes, a fair skin, a symmetrical but vulgar face; and she speaks with that accursed Celtic accent—a twang which I never yet heard associated with any manly or profitable thought or sentiment, which to me is but the symbol of Highland vanity and filth and famine. 'Good heavens!' cried I, on coming out, 'does literature lead to this? Shall I, too, by my utmost efforts realise nothing but a stupid Gaelic wife, with the pitiful gift of making verses, and affections cold as those of a tinker's cuddie, with nothing to love but my own paltry self and what belongs to it? My proudest feelings rivalled, surpassed by Lord Petersham and the whole population of Bond Street? God forbid! Let me be poor and wretched if it must be so, but never, never let the holy feeling of affection leave me. Break my heart a hundred times, but never let it be its own grave!' The aspect of that man jarred the music of my mind for a whole day. He promised to invite me to his first 'literary *déjeuner*.' Curiosity attracts, disgust repels. I know not which will be stronger when the day arrives. Perhaps I am hasty about Campbell. Perhaps I am too severe. He was my earliest favourite. I hoped to have found him different. Of Coleridge and all the other originals I will not say a word at present. You are sated and more.

Coleridge naturally was an object of more than curiosity. He was then at the height of his fame—poet, metaphysician, theologian, accomplished, or supposed to be accomplished, in the arts in which Carlyle was most anxious to excel. Carlyle himself had formed a high if not the highest opinion of the merits of Coleridge, who was now sitting up at Highgate receiving the homage of the intellectual world, and pouring out floods of eloquence on all who came to worship in a befitting state of mind. The befitting state was not universal even in those who sincerely loved the great man. Leigh Hunt and Lamb had sate one night in the Highgate drawing room for long hours listening to the oracle discoursing upon the Logos. Hunt, as they stood leaning over a style in the moonlight, on their way home, said, 'How strange that a man of such indisputable genius should talk such nonsense!' 'Why, you see,' said Lamb, stammering, 'C-c-coleridge has so much f-f-fun in him.' The finished portrait of Coleridge is found in Carlyle's 'Life of Sterling.' The original sketch is a letter of the 24th of June to his brother John.

I have seen many curiosities; not the least of them I reckon Coleridge, the Kantian metaphysician and quondam Lake poet. I will tell you all about our interview when we meet. Figure a fat, flabby, incurvated personage, at once short, rotund, and relaxed, with a watery mouth, a snuffy nose, a pair of strange brown, timid, yet earnest-looking eyes, a high tapering brow, and a great bush of grey hair; and you have some faint idea of Coleridge. He is a kind good soul, full of religion and affection and poetry and animal magnetism. His cardinal sin is that he wants *will*. He has no resolution. He shrinks from pain or labour in any of its shapes. His very attitude bespeaks this. He never straightens his knee-joints. He stoops with his fat, ill-shapen shoulders, and in walking he does not tread, but shovel and slide. My father would call it 'skluiffing.' He is also always busied to keep, by strong and frequent inhalations, the water of his mouth from overflowing, and his eyes have a look of anxious impotence. He *would* do with all his heart, but he knows he dares not. The conversation of the man is much as I anticipated—a forest of thoughts, some true, many false, more *part* dubious, all of them ingenious in some degree, often in a high degree. But there is no method in his talk: he wanders like a man sailing among many currents, whithersoever his lazy mind directs him; and, what is more unpleasant, he preaches, or rather soliloquises. He cannot speak, he can only *tal-k* (so he names it). Hence I found him unprofitable, even tedious; but we parted very good friends, I promising to go back and see him some evening—a promise which I fully intend to keep. I sent him a copy of 'Meister,' about which we had some friendly talk. I reckon him a man of great and useless genius: a strange, not at all a great man.

While Carlyle was studying the leaders of literature in London with such indifferent satisfaction, the family at Mainhill were busy over his own first book. Never had Goethe's novel found its way into a stranger circle than this rugged, unlettered Calvinist household. But they had all strong natural understandings. Young and old alike read it, and in their way appreciated it, the mother most of all.

John Carlyle to Thomas Carlyle.

Mainhill : June 24.

You did well to send our father the neckerchief and tobacco with the spluichan, for he was highly pleased at the sight of them. The shawl, our mother says, suits very well, though she has no particular need of one at present. She bids me tell you she can never repay you for the kindness you have all along shown her, and then she has advices about religion to give you, the best of gifts in her estimation that she has to offer. She is sitting here as if under some charm, reading 'Meister,' and has nearly got through the second volume. Though we are often repeating honest Hall Foster's denouncement against readers of 'novels,' she still continues to persevere. She does not relish the character of the women, and especially of Philina : 'They are so wanton.' She cannot well tell what it is that interests her. I defer till the next time I write to give a full account of the impression it has made upon us all, for we have not got it fairly studied yet. We are unanimous in thinking it should succeed.

The Bullers were still uncertain about their future movements. One day they were to take a house at Boulogne, the next to settle in Cornwall, the next to remain in London, and send Carlyle with the boys into the country. As a temporary measure, ten days after his arrival he and Charles found themselves located in lodgings at Kew Green, which Carlyle soon grew weary of and Charles Buller hated; while Carlyle, though he appreciated, and at times even admired, Mrs. Buller's fine qualities, was not of a temper to submit to a woman's caprices.

To John Carlyle.

Kew Green : June 24, 1824.

The Bullers are essentially a cold race of people. They live in the midst of fashion and external show. They love no living creature. Our connection, therefore, has to sit a little loosely. I attach no portion of my hopes or thoughts of affection towards them ; they none to me. Nevertheless, I have engaged to go with them whithersoever they list for the next three months. After that, with regard to the French project, I shall pause before deciding. Indeed, so fitful and weather-cock-like in their proceedings are they, that it is very possible the whole scheme of Boulogne-sur-Mer may be abandoned long before the time for trying it comes round. Meanwhile, Mrs. B. has settled us here *for a fortnight only* in lodgings, and we have begun our studies. It is a pleasant village. We are within a bowshot of a Royal Palace, close by the south bank of the Thames, about six miles to the westward of London. A village here is not what it is with you. Here it is a quantity of houses scattered over a whole parish, each cluster connected with the rest by lanes of trees, with meadows and beautiful greens interspersed, sometimes ponds and lakes and hedges of roses, and commons with sheep and cuddies grazing on them. Many of the houses belong to rich people, and the whole has a very smart and pleasing air. Such is the village of Kew, especially the Green, the part of it which lies on the south side of the river, connected by the bridge with Kew proper. We form part of the periphery of an irregular square, measuring, perhaps, two furlongs in diagonal, intersected with one large and many foot roads, and into portions by thick, low, painted wooden palings, with breaks in it to admit the freest ingress and egress. The parish church, with its cluster of gravestones, stands a little to the right of our windows. Beyond it the northwest corner of the square is occupied by the Palace and the barracks of soldiers. This, with the many barges and lighters of the river, and the shady woods and green places all around, makes the place very pretty. What is better, our lodging seems to be very respectable. I have a good, clean, quiet bed, and the landlady, Mrs. Page, and her pretty granddaughter (sweet Anne Page), almost become as dead women every time we speak to them, so reverential are they and so prompt to help.

Mrs. Page was unlike the dames who had driven Car-

lyle so distracted in Edinburgh, and the contrast between
the respectful manners of English people and the hard
familiarity of his countrywomen struck him agreeably.
Time and progress have done their work whether for
good or evil, and it would at present be difficult to find
reverential landladies either at Kew Green or anywhere
in the British dominions; Kew Green has become vulgar-
ised, and the grace has gone from it; the main points of
the locality can be recognised from Carlyle's picture, but
cockneys and cockney taste are now in possession. The
suburban sojourn came to an early end, and with it Carlyle's relations with Mr. Buller and his family. He describes the close of the connection in words which did not
express his deliberate feeling. He knew that he owed
much to Mrs. Buller's kindness; and her own and Mr.
Buller's regard for him survived in the form of strong
friendship to the end of their lives. But he was irritated
at the abruptness with which he conceived that he had
been treated. He was proud and thin-skinned. His next
letter is dated from Irving's house at Pentonville, which
was again immediately opened to him, and contains the
history of the Buller break-up, and of a new acquaintance
which was about to take him to Birmingham.

4 Myddelton Terrace, Pentonville: July 6, 1824.

My dear Mother,—I suppose you are not expecting to hear from
me so soon again, and still less to hear the news I have got to tell
you. The last letter was dated from Kew Green; there will be
no more of mine dated thence. Last time I was complaining of
the irresolute and foolish fluctuations of the Bullers: I shall never
more have reason to complain of them and their proceedings. I
am now free of them for ever and a day. I mentioned the correspondence which had taken place between 'the fair Titania' (as
the Calcutta newspapers called her) and myself on the subject of
her hopeful son, and how it was arranged that we should live together till October, and then *see* about proceeding to Boulogne,
in France, or else abandoning our present engagement altogether.

The shifting and trotting about which she managed with so total a disregard to my feelings, joined to the cold and selfish style of the lady's general proceedings, had a good deal disaffected me; and when, in addition to all this, I reflected that nothing permanent could result from my engagement with them, and considered the horrid weariness of being in seclusion from all sense and seriousness, in the midst of sickness on my own part, mingled with frivolous and heartless dissipation on theirs, I had well nigh silently determined *not* to go to Boulogne, or even to stay with the people though they remained in England. My determination was called for sooner than I had anticipated. After a week spent at Kew in the most entire tedium, by which my health had begun to deteriorate rapidly, but which I determined to undergo without repining till October, Mrs. Buller writes me a letter signifying that they must know directly whether I would go with them to France or not; that if I could not, the boy might be sent to prepare for Cambridge; and that if I could, we must instantly decamp for Royston, a place in Hertfordshire about fifty miles off. I replied that the expected time for deciding was not yet arrived, but that if they required an immediate decision, of course there was nothing for it but to count on my declining the offer. Next day we met in town by appointment; there seemed to be the best understanding in the world betwixt us; it was agreed that I should quit them—an arrangement not a little grievous to old Buller and his son, but no wise grievous to his wife, one of whose whims was Cambridge University, in which whim, so long as she persists, she will be ready to stake her whole soul on the fulfilment of it. Buller offered me twenty pounds for my trouble. With an excess of generosity which I am not quite reconciled to since I thought of it maturely, I pronounced it to be too much, and accepted of *ten*. The old gentleman and I shook hands with dry eyes. Mrs. Buller gave me one of those 'Good mornings' with which fashionable people think it right to part with friends and foes alike. Charlie was in a passion of sadness and anger, to be forgotten utterly in three hours, and I went my way and they saw me no more. Such is my conclusion with the Bullers. I feel glad that I have done with them; their family was ruining my mind and body. I was selling the very quintessence of my spirit for 200*l.* a year. Twelve months spent at Boulogne in the midst of drivelling and discomfort would have added little to my stock of cash, and fearfully diminished my remnant of spirits, health, and affection.

The world must be fronted some time, soon as good as *syne!* Adieu, therefore, to ancient dames of quality, that flaunting, painting, patching, nervous, vapourish, jigging, skimming, scolding race of mortals.[1] Their clothes are silk, their manners courtly, their hearts are *kipper*. I have left the Bullers twelve months sooner than they would have parted with me had I liked. I am glad that we have parted in friendship; very glad that we are parted at all. She invited me to a rout (a grand, fashionable affair) next night. I did not go a foot length. I want to have no further trade with her or hers, at least except in the way of cold civility; for as to what affection means I do not believe there is one of them that even guesses what it means. Her sister, indeed (Mrs. Strachey),[2] likes me; but she is as opposite as day from night.

Thus you see, my dear mother, I am as it were once more upon the waters. I got my trunks hither last night, after having kept them just one week at Kew, and paid fourteen shillings for the trip to and fro. So much for having a spirited commander like Titania. I am settled with Irving, who presses me to stay with him all winter. That I certainly will not do, though I honour the kindness that prompts even an *invitation* of this sort. Irving and I are grown very intimate again, and have had great talking matches about many things. He speaks in glorious language of the wonderful things I am to accomplish here, but my own views are much more moderate.

Meanwhile let me assure you that I have not been so happy for a long while. I am at no loss for plans of proceeding, nor is the future overcast before me with any heavy clouds that I should feel or fear. I am once more free; and I must be a weak genius indeed if I cannot find an honest living in the exercise of my faculties, independently of favour from anyone. My movements for a while must be rather desultory. My first is to be northward. Among the worthy persons whom I have met with here is a Mr. Badams, a friend of Irving's, a graduate in medicine, though his

---

[1] Poor Mrs. Buller! a year back 'one of the most fascinating women he had ever met.' She was about forty, and probably had never flaunted, painted, or patched in her life.

[2] Of this lady he says in another letter : 'My chief favourite is Mrs. Strachey, a sister of Mrs. Buller; but she is serious and earnest and religious and affectionate, while the other is light, giddy, vain, and heartless. She and I will be sworn friends by and by.'

business is in chemical manufactures in Birmingham, where I understand he is rapidly realising a fortune. This man, one of the most sensible, clear-headed persons I have ever met with, seems also one of the kindest. After going about for a day or two talking about pictures and stomach disorders, in the cure of which he is famous, and from which he once suffered four years of torment in person, what does the man do but propose that I should go up to Birmingham and live for a month with him, that he might find out the make of me and prescribe for my unfortunate inner man. I have consented to go with him. I understand he keeps horses, &c., and is really the frank hospitable fellow he seems. Of his skill in medicine I augur favourably from his general talent, and from the utter contempt in which he holds all sorts of drugs as applied to persons in my situation. Regimen and exercise are his specifics, assisted by as little gentlest medicine as possible; on the whole I think I never had such a chance for the recovery of health. I intend to set off in about a week. There is a fine coach that starts from our very door, and carries one up between seven in the morning and seven at night for one guinea. I am going to take books and read and ride and stroll about Birmingham, and employ or amuse myself as seemeth best. Sometimes I think of beginning another translation, sometimes of setting about some original work. 'Meister,' I understand, is doing very well. Jack tells me you are reading 'Meister.' This surprises me. If I did not recollect your love for me, I should not be able to account for it.

CHAPTER XIV.

CARLYLE was now once more his own master, adrift from all engagements which made his time the property of others, and without means or prospect of support save what his pen could earn for him. Miss Welsh had expected with too sanguine ignorance that when his first writings had introduced him to the world, the world would rush forward to his assistance; that he would be seized upon for some public employment, or at worst would be encouraged by a sinecure. The world is in no such haste to recognise a man of original genius. Unless he runs with the stream, or with some one of the popular currents, every man's hand is at first against him. Rivals challenge his pretensions; his talents are denied; his aims are ridiculed; he is tried in the furnace of criticism, and it is well that it should be so. A man does not know himself what is in him till he has been tested; far less can others know; and the metal which glitters most on the outside most often turns out to be but pinchbeck. A longer and more bitter apprenticeship lay upon Carlyle than even he, little sanguine as he was, might at this time have anticipated. His papers on Schiller had been well received and were to be collected into a volume; a contemptuous review of 'Meister' by De Quincey appeared in the 'London Magazine,' but the early sale was rapid. He had been well paid for the first specimens of jewels which he had brought out of the German mines. An endless vein remained unwrought, and the field was for the present his own. Thus he went down to Birmingham to his friend with a light heart, anxious chiefly about his health, and convinced that if he could mend his digestion, all else would be easy for him. Birmingham with its fiery furnaces and fiery politics was a new scene to him, and was like the opening of some fresh volume of human life. He has given so full a history of his experiences when he was Mr. Badams' guest that there is no occasion to dwell upon it. The visit lasted two months instead of one. His first impression of the place, as he described it in a letter to his brother, is worth preserving as a specimen of his powers of minute word-painting, and as a description of what Birmingham was sixty years ago.

To John Carlyle.

Birmingham : August 10, 1824.

Birmingham I have now tried for a reasonable time, and I cannot complain of being tired of it. As a town it is pitiful enough —a mean congeries of bricks, including one or two large capitalists, some hundreds of minor ones, and, perhaps, a hundred and twenty thousand sooty artisans in metals and chemical produce. The streets are ill-built, ill-paved, always flimsy in their aspect— often poor, sometimes miserable. Not above one or two of them are paved with flagstones at the sides ; and to walk upon the little egg-shaped, slippery flints that supply their places is something like a penance. Yet withal it is interesting from some of the commons or lanes that spot or intersect the green, woody, undulating environs to view this city of Tubal Cain. Torrents of thick smoke, with ever and anon a burst of dingy flame, are issuing from a thousand funnels. 'A thousand hammers fall by turns.' You hear the clank of innumerable steam-engines, the rumbling of cars and vans, and the hum of men interrupted by the sharper rattle of some canal-boat loading or disloading ; or, perhaps, some fierce explosion when the cannon founders are proving their new-made ware. I have seen their rolling-mills, their polishing of teapots, and buttons, and gun-barrels, and fire-shovels, and swords, and all manner of toys and tackle. I have looked into their iron works where 150,000 men are smelting the metal in a district a few miles to the north ; their coal-mines, fit image of Avernus ;

their tubs and vats, as large as country churches, full of copperas and aqua fortis and oil of vitriol; and the whole is not without its attractions, as well as repulsions, of which, when we meet, I will preach to you at large.

But all the while Carlyle's heart was in Scotland, at Haddington—and less at Haddington than at Mainhill. The strongest personal passion which he experienced through all his life was his affection for his mother. She was proud and wilful, as he. He had sent her, or offered her, more presents, and she had been angry with him. She had not been well, and she was impatient of doctors' regulations.

To Mrs. Carlyle, Mainhill.

Birmingham: August 29, 1824.

I must suggest some improvements in your diet and mode of life which might be of service to *you*, who I know too well have much to suffer on your own part, though your affection renders you so exclusively anxious about me. You will say you cannot be *fashed.* Oh, my dear mother, if you did but think of what value your health and comfort are to us all, you would never talk so. Are we not all bound to you, by sacred and indissoluble ties? Am I not so bound more than any other? Who was it that nursed me and watched me in frowardness and sickness from the earliest dawn of my existence to this hour?—My mother. Who is it that has struggled for me in pain and sorrow with undespairing diligence, that has for me been up early and down late, caring for me, labouring for me, unweariedly assisting me?—My mother. Who is the *one* that never shrunk from me in my desolation, that never tired of my despondencies, or shut up by a look or tone of impatience the expression of my real or imaginary griefs? Who is it that loves me and will love me for ever with an affection which no chance, no misery, no crime of mine can do away?—It is you, my mother. As the greatest favour that I can beg of you, let me, now that I have in some degree the power, be of some assistance in promoting your comfort. It were one of the achievements which I could look back upon with most satisfaction from all the stages of my earthly pilgrimage, if I could make you happier. Are we not all of us animated by a similar love to you? Why then will you spare any trouble, any cost, in what is valuable beyond aught earthly to every one of us?

Eight weeks were passed with Badams, without, however, the advantage to Carlyle's health which he had looked for. There had been daily rides into the country, visits to all manner of interesting places—Hadley, Warwick, and Kenilworth. The society had been interesting, and Badams himself all that was kind and considerate. But the contempt of ' drugs ' which he had professed in London had been rather theoretic than practical; and the doses which had been administered perhaps of themselves accounted for the failure of other remedies. At the beginning of September an invitation came to Carlyle to join the Stracheys at Dover. The Irvings were to be of the party. Irving needed rest from his preaching. Mrs. Irving had been confined and had been recommended sea air for herself and her baby. The Stracheys and Miss Kirkpatrick had taken a house at Dover; the Irvings had lodgings of their own, but were to live with their friends, and Carlyle was to be included in the party. Mrs. Strachey was a very interesting person to him, still beautiful, younger than Mrs. Buller, and a remarkable contrast to her. Mrs. Buller was a sort of heathen ; Mrs. Strachey was earnestly religious. ' She is as unlike Mrs. Buller,' Carlyle told his mother, ' as pure gold is to gilt copper ; she is an earnest, determined, warm-hearted, religious matron, while the other is but a fluttering patroness of routs and operas.' An invitation to stay with her had many attractions for him. He wished to go, but was undecided. The last letter from Birmingham was on September 18.

To John Carlyle.

Badams and I go on very lovingly together. He calls me 'philosopher' by way of eminence; and I discuss and overhaul, and dissect all manners of subjects with him. A closer acquaintance diminishes the sublimity, but scarcely the pleasing quality of his character. A certain tendency to paint *en beau*, a sort of gasconading turn in describing his own achievements and purposes, is all the fault I can discover in him; his kindheartedness, his constant activity, and good humour are more and more apparent. In spite of all his *long-bow* propensities (his running away with the harrows, as our father would call it) he is a man of no ordinary powers, nor has he any particle of dishonesty in his nature, however he may talk. In fact, if I admire the man less than I once expected, I like him more. Strange that so many men should say *the thing that is not* without perceptible temptation! Hundreds do it out of momentary vanity—Frank Dickson and many others. It is the poorest of all possible resources in this world of makeshifts; thou and I will never try it.

With regard to health, it often seems to me that I am better than I have been for several years, though scarcely a week passes without a relapse for a while into directly the opposite opinion. The truth is, it stands thus : I have been bephysicked and bedrugged. I have swallowed, say about two stoupfuls of castor oil since I came hither : unless I dose myself with that oil of sorrow every fourth day, I cannot get along at all. . . . My resources are more numerous than they have been, and I am free to use them. Am I a man and can do nothing to ameliorate my destiny? Hang it, I will set up house in the country and take to gardening and translating, before I let it beat me. In general I am not unhappy —of late I have begun to grudge being so long idle. 'Schiller' is almost at a stand. I have been thinking of it and preparing improvements, but the Taylor creature is slow as a snail. . . . I wrote to Irving stating in distant terms a proposal to board with him through winter. He has not answered me, but I expect daily that he will. If he consent, I shall go with him and Mrs. Strachey to Dover. If not, I think hardly. My better plan will be to go to London and take lodgings till this pitiful book is off my hands, then return to the North or stay in London as I reckon best.

The journey back on the coach through the midland counties, which in late September are usually so beautiful, was spoilt by bad weather. On his way, however, Carlyle saw Stratford, and was long enough in the town to form a clear picture of it. His letters are the journal of his experiences.

To John Carlyle.

London : September 27, 1824.

Taking leave of Badams, who strictly charged me to come back for another month till he had completed his doctorial and castor oil system with me, I left the city of Tubal Cain on Thursday morning. My passage was of a mixed character. Some of Badams's drugs had not prospered with me, and I fell below par in point of health. The morning also was damp and the day proved rainy. To complete the matter it cleared up just when I had shifted my place to the interior of the vehicle, and exchanged the sight of High Wycombe and the lawns of Buckinghamshire for the inane prattle of a little black-eyed pretty blue-stocking Genevese, my sole travelling companion; so that when they set me down in Oxford Street, falsely said by the rascal guard to be the nearest point to Pentonville, from which it was three miles distant—Lad Lane being only one—I fell somewhat out of humour, a dissonance of spirit which increased to loud jarring as I followed my stout and fleet porter, who strode lustily along under cloud of night, through labyrinthine streets and alleys, with my portmanteau dangling at his back, and a travelling bag to balance it in front. Tramp, tramp, amidst the rattling of wains and coaches, and the unearthly cries of fruiterers and oystermen and piemen and all the mighty din of London, till I verily thought he would never reach a point of the city which my eyes had seen before.

Nevertheless, I had not been without my enjoyments on the road. I had got another glance of the heart of 'merry England,' with its waving knolls and green woody fields and snug hamlets and antique boroughs and jolly ale-drinking, beef-eating people. . . . It was not without some pleasurable imaginations that I saw Stratford-upon-Avon, the very hills and woods which the boy Shakespeare had looked upon, the very church where his dust reposes, nay, the very house where he was born ; the threshold over which his staggering footsteps carried him in infancy ; the very stones where the urchin played marbles and flogged tops. . . . It is a small grim-looking house of bricks, bound, as was of old the fashion, with beams of oak intersecting the bricks which are built into it and fill up its interstices as the glass does in a window. The old tile roof is cast by age, and twisted into all varieties of curvature. Half the house has been modernised and made a butcher's shop. The street where it stands is a simple-looking, short, everyday village street, with houses mostly new, and consisting, like the Shakespeare house, of two low stories, or rather a story and a half. Stratford itself is a humble, pleasant-looking place, the residence as formerly of woolcombers and other quiet artisans, except where they have brought an ugly black canal into it, and polluted this classical borough by the presence of lighters or trackboats with famished horses, sooty drivers, and heaps of coke and coal. It seems considerably larger and less showy than Annan. Shakespeare, Breakspeare, and for aught I know sundry other spears, are still common names in Warwickshire. I was struck on my arrival at Birmingham by a sign not far from Badams's, indicating the abode of William Shakespeare, boot and shoe maker, which boots and shoes the modern Shakespeare also professed his ability to mend 'cheap and neatly.' Homer, I afterwards discovered, had settled in Birmingham as a button maker.

But I must not wander thus, or I shall never have done. Of Oxford, with its domes and spires and minarets, its rows of shady trees, and still monastic edifices in their antique richness and intricate seclusion, I shall say nothing till I see you. I must rather hasten to observe that I found the orator at Pentonville sitting sparrowlike, companionless, in—not on—the housetop alone. His wife had left him, and had taken all the crockery and bedding and other household gear along with her. He extended to me the right hand of fellowship notwithstanding, and even succeeded in procuring me some genial tea with an egg, only half rotten, which, for a London egg, is saying much. . . . By-and-by, one Hamilton, a worthy and accomplished merchant from Sanquhar, came in and took me with him to his lodgings and treated me comfortably; and there, in a splendid bed, I contrived, in spite of agitation from within, and noise and bugs from without, to get six hours of deep slumber. Next morning I was fitter to do business.

On leaving Birmingham I had felt uncertain whether I should go to Dover with the Orator or not; and I had partly determined to be regulated in my yea or no by his acceptance or rejection of my proposal to board with him while in London. On coming to discuss the subject I soon discovered that his reverence was embarrassed by a conflicting proposal (to board at a very high rate some medical youth from Glasgow) which was not yet decided on, and was consequently in the way of any definite arrangement with me. The good priest—for with all his vanities and affectations he is really a good man, an excellent man, as men go—puckered up his face and eyebrows in much distress, and was just commencing with various articulate and inarticulate preparations, when I, discovering rapidly how the matter stood, begged him to consider my proposal unmade, and never to say, or even think, one other word upon the subject. The puckers disappeared at this announcement, but were succeeded by a continuous cloud of gloom and regret as he set about advising me to go with him to Dover, and to put off the consideration of lodging and all such matters till my return. After much canvassing I assented, upon the proviso of my being allowed to bear my own share of the expense, and to be his fellow-lodger and not his guest. With this salve to my pride, which I already almost begin to despise as a piece of cold selfishness, we struck the bargain that he should set out on Monday, and I should follow whenever my business was concluded.

The 'business' I could have in London may well surprise you; it was (alas! it is) the most pitiful that ever man had: nothing but the collecting of a few books for the completing of my poor 'Schiller.' You cannot think what trotting to and fro I have had to get a book or two of the most simple character. Messrs. Taylor and Henry pay me somewhere on the verge of 90*l.* down upon the nail for this book, the day when it is published. In about ten weeks from this date I expect to be free of London, to have ascertained how it will suit me, what hopes, what advantages it offers, and to decide for continuance or departure as shall seem to me best. If my health improve I shall be for remaining, especially if I can fasten upon any profitable employment; if not, scarcely. About the ultimatum I am by no means low-spirited, not often even dumpish. I feel pretty confident that I *can* recover my health in some considerable degree, perhaps wholly. If not here —*elsewhere.* While this is in progress I can at the worst translate for the London or Edinburgh market; and if I were well, I feel that some considerable desire to write might arise within me. I might, like Archy Halliday, 'fin' a kind of inclination to bark, and certainly there is no want of game. A miserable scrub of an author, sharking and writing 'articles' about town like Hazlitt, De Quincey, and that class of living creatures, is a thing which, as our mother says, 'I canna be.' Nor shall I need it. I have fifty better schemes.

As to not boarding with Irving, I hardly regret it now that it is past. His house would scarcely have been a favourable place for studying any science but the state of religion in general, and that of the Caledonian chapel in particular, as managed by various elders, delegates, and other nondescript personages. A very affected and not very beautiful sister of ——'s is also to stay with them through the winter. Her I might have found it a task to love. 'Pray, Mr. Carlyle,' said she, in a mincing, namby-pamby tone, the night she arrived, when I was sitting with my powers of patience screwed to the sticking place, being in truth very miserable and very much indisposed to make complaints; 'Pray, Mr. Carlyle, are you *really* sick now, or is it only fanciful?' 'Fancy, ma'am, fancy, nothing more,' said I, half-turning round, and immediately proceeding with some other topic, addressed to some other member of the company. Besides, Irving has a squeaking brat of a son, 'who indeed brings us many blessings,' but rather interrupts our rest at night. Bad luck to his blessings compared with natural rest! In short, I shall be more completely master in my own lodgings.

Carlyle himself was not an inmate whom any mistress not directly connected with him would readily welcome into her household ; so it was well perhaps for all parties that the proposed arrangement was abandoned. The Dover visit, however, was accomplished, and the unexpected trip to Paris which grew out of it. For this, too, the reader is mainly referred to the 'Reminiscences,' which need no correction from contemporary letters; and to which those letters, though written when the scenes were fresh, can still add little, save a further evidence of the extreme accuracy of his memory. But there is a humourous description of the gigantic Irving and his new-born baby, a pleasant sketch of others of the party, and an interesting account of the state of English farming and the English labourer, as Carlyle saw both before the days of economic progress. These, and some vivid pictures of the drive through France, justify a few extracts.

To James Carlyle, Mainhill.

Dover : October 4.

My dear Father,—I arrived in this corner of the seagirt land in the dusk of a bright and sharp autumnal day. There has been no fixed arrangement in our plans as yet. Mrs. Irving with her infant had come down with a Miss Kirkpatrick, a cousin of Mrs. Strachey, in whose kind house we are all living till the rest arrive, when the Irvings and I shall evacuate the place and seek lodgings of our own. I expect to be very snug and comfortable while here. The sea-bathing seems to agree with me as well as ever, and the people are all anxious to treat me as a kind of established invalid, whose concerns are to be attended to as a prime object.

The young Miss Kirkpatrick, with whom I was already acquainted, is a very pleasant and meritorious person—one of the kindest and most modest I have ever seen. Though handsome and young and sole mistress of 50,000*l*., she is meek and unassuming as a little child. She laughs in secret at the awkward extravagances of the Orator; yet she loves him as a good man, and busies herself with nothing so much as discharging the duties of hospitality to us all. . . . Of Irving, I have much kindness towards me to record. I like the man, as I did of old, without respecting him much less or more. He has a considerable turn for displays, which in reality are sheer vanity, though he sincerely thinks them the perfection of Christian elevation. But in these things he indulges very sparingly before me, and any little glimpses of them that do occur I find it easy without the slightest ill-nature arising between us to repress. We talk of religion and literature and men and things, and stroll about and smoke cigars, a choice stock of which he has been presented with by some friend. I reckon him much improved since winter. The fashionable people have totally left him, yielding like feathers and flying chaff to some new 'centre of attraction.' The newspapers also are silent, and he begins to see that there was really nothing supernatural in the former hurly-burly, but that he must content himself with patient welldoing, and liberal, though not immoderate, success; not taking the world by one fierce onslaught, but by patient and continual sapping and mining, as others do.

I for one am sincerely glad that matters have taken this change. I consider him a man of splendid gifts and good intentions, and likely in his present manner of proceeding to be of much benefit to the people among whom he labours. His Isabella also is a good, honest-hearted person and an excellent wife. She is very kind to me, and though without any notable gifts of mind or manners or appearance, contrives to be in general extremely agreeable.   Irving and she are sometimes ridiculous enough at present in the matter of their son, a quiet *wersh gorb* of a thing, as all children of six weeks are, but looked upon by them as if it were a cherub from on high.   The concerns of 'him' (as they emphatically call it) occupy a large share of public attention.   Kitty Kirkpatrick smiles covertly, and I laugh aloud at the earnest devotedness of the good Orator to this weighty affair.   'Isabella,' said he the other night, ' I would wash him, I think, with *warm* water tonight,' a counsel received with approving assent by the mother, but somewhat objected to by others.   I declared the washing and dressing of *him* to be the wife's concern alone ; and that, were I in her place, I would wash him with oil of vitriol if I pleased, and take no one's counsel in it.

When Mrs. Strachey comes I expect some accession of enjoyment.   She has taken a great liking to me, and is any way a singularly worthy woman.   I had a very kind note from her this day.

Kent is a delightful region, fertile and well cultivated, watered with clear streams, sufficiently and not excessively besprinkled with trees, and beautifully broken with inequalities of surface. The whole country rests on chalk.   They burn this mineral in kilns and use it as lime.   In its native state it lies in immense masses, divided into strata or courses by lumps of flint distributed in parallel seams.   The husbandry in Kent is beyond that in many counties in England, but a Scottish farmer would smile at many parts of it.   They plough with five horses and two men (one ca-ing), and the plough has wheels.   Many a time have I thought of Alick with his Lothian tackle and two horses setting these inefficient loiterers to the right about.   Yet here they are much better than in Warwickshire, where farming may be said to be an unknown art, where the fields are sometimes of half an acre, and of all possible shapes but square, and a threshing mill is a thing nearly unheard of.   Here a fifth part of the surface is not covered with gigantic and ill-kept fences ; but they grow their wheat and their beans and their hops on more rational principles.   In all cases, however, the people seem to realize a goodly share of solid comfort.   The English hind has his pork (often raw) or his beef, with ale and wheaten bread three times a day, and wears a ruddy and substantial look, see him where you will.   I have looked into the clean, brick-built, tile-flagged little cottages, and seen the people dining, with their jug of ale, their bacon, and other ware, and a huge loaf, like a stithy clog, towering over it all.   It is pleasant to see everyone so well provided for. There is nothing like the appearance of want to be met with anywhere.

To Miss Welsh, little dreaming of the relations between herself and Irving, Carlyle was still more dramatic in his sketches of the Orator. Miss Welsh, as she told him afterwards, had purposely misled him on this subject.

October 5.—The Orator is busy writing and bathing, persuading himself that he is scaling the very pinnacles of Christian sentiment, which in truth, with him, are little more than the very pinnacles of human vanity rising through an atmosphere of great native warmth and generosity. I find him much as he was before, and I suppose always will be, overspread with secret affectations, secret to himself, but kind and friendly and speculative and discursive as ever. It would do your heart good to look at him in the character of dry nurse to his first-born, Edward. Oh that you saw the Giant with his broad-brimmed hat, his sallow visage, and his sable, matted fleece of hair, carrying the little pepper-box of a creature folded in his monstrous palms along the beach, tick ticking to it, and dandling it, and every time it stirs an eyelid grinning horribly a ghastly smile, heedless of the crowds of petrified spectators that turn round in long trains, gazing in silent terror at the fatherly leviathan ; you would laugh for twelve months after, every time you thought of it. And yet it is very wrong to laugh if one could help it. Nature is very lovely: pity she should ever be absurd. On the whole I am pleased with Irving, and hope to love him and admire him and laugh at him as long as I live. There is a fund of sincerity in his life and character which in these heartless, aimless days is doubly precious. The cant of religion, conscious or unconscious, is a pitiable thing, but not the most pitiable. It often rests upon a groundwork of genuine, earnest feeling, and is, I think, in all except its very worst phases, preferable to that poor and mean spirit of contemptuous *persiflage* which forms the staple of fashionable accomplishment so far as I can discern it, and spreads like a narcotic drench over all the better faculties of the soul.

Mrs. Strachey came down after a few days. The little party was always together—walking on the beach or reading Fletcher's 'Purple Island.' Mrs. Strachey herself was in full sympathy with Irving, if no one else was. Then her husband came, who was especially wanting in sympathy. The difference of sentiment became perceptible. The French coast lay invitingly opposite. The weather was beautiful. A trip to Paris was proposed and instantly decided on. Mr. Strachey, Miss Kirkpatrick, and Carlyle were to go. Mrs. Strachey and the Irvings were to stay behind. A travelling carriage was sent across the Channel, post-horses were always ready on the Paris road, and Carlyle, who had but left Scotland for the first time four months before, and had been launched an entire novice into the world, was now to be among the scenes so long familiar to him as names. They went by Montreuil, Abbeville, Nampont, with Sterne's 'Sentimental Journey' as a guide book, when Murray was unknown. They saw the Cathedral at Beauvais, for which Carlyle did not care at all; they saw French soldiers, for which he cared a great deal. He himself could speak a little French; Strachey, like most Englishmen, almost none. Montmorency reminded him of Rousseau. From Montmartre they looked down on Paris: 'not a breath of smoke or dimness anywhere, every roof and dome and spire and chimney-top clearly visible, and the skylights sparkling like diamonds.' 'I have never,' he says, 'since or before, seen so fine a view of a town.' Carlyle, who could see and remember so much of Stratford, where he stayed only while the coach changed horses, coming on Paris fresh, with a mind like wax to receive impressions, yet tenacious as steel in preserving them, carried off recollections from his twelve days' sojourn in the French capital which never left him, and served him well in after years when he came to write about the Revolution. He saw the places of which he had read. He saw Louis Dix-huit lying in state, Charles Dix, Legendre (whose Geometry he had translated for Brewster), the great Laplace, M. de Chezy the Persian professor. He heard Cuvier lecture. He went to the Théâtre Français, and saw and heard Talma in ' Œdipe.' He listened to a sermon at Ste. Geneviève. A more impressive sermon was a stern old gray-haired corpse which he saw lying in the Morgue. He saw the French people, and the ways and works of them, which interested him most of all. These images, with glimpses of English travellers, were all crowded into the few brief days of their stay ; the richest in new ideas, new emotions, new pictures of human life, which Carlyle had yet experienced.

From the many letters which he wrote about it, I select one to his brother John.

To John Carlyle.

Dover : November 7.

My expedition to Paris was nearly as unexpected to myself as the news of it will be to you. Strachey, a little bustling, logic-chopping, good-hearted, frank fellow, came down to Dover three weeks ago, and finding himself, I suppose, rather dull in the region of the Cinque Ports, and tempted, moreover, by the persuasions of his cousin Kitty, as well as by the daily sight of the French coast, he determined at last on a journey thither, and after infinite pleadings and solicitations I was prevailed upon to be of the party. They were to travel in their own carriage, Kitty and her maid inside, Strachey on the coach-box to see the country. The additional expense for me would be nothing ; it would be *so* pleasant, and would do me *so* much good. In fine, after a world of perplexities and miscalculations and misadventures, I having first half consented, then wholly refused, then again consented, we at length all assembled by different routes on the sands of Boulogne in the afternoon of Thursday gone a fortnight, and set off with the utmost speed of three lean horses of the poste royale for Paris. After adventures and mistakes which will keep us laughing many a winter night when thou and I meet, we reached the capital on Saturday about four o'clock, and forthwith established ourselves in the Hôtel de Wagram, and proceeded to the great purpose of our journey—the seeing of the many sights with which the metropolis of France abounds beyond any other spot on the surface of the earth. By degrees we got into proper train, and everything went on wonderfully well. Strachey and I went out singly or in company to purvey for dinners and breakfasts in the cafés and *restaurateur* establishments, &c.

Sated at length with wonders, we left Paris last Wednesday, and after a not unprosperous journey arrived here yesterday afternoon. Irving and his household had left Dover a few hours before.[1] On the whole I cannot say I regret this jaunt. I have seen many strange things which may people my imagination with interesting forms, and, perhaps, yield some materials for reflection and improvement. France, as it presented itself to me on a most cursory survey, seemed a place rather to be looked at than tarried in. Oh that I had space to paint to you the strange pilgarlic figures that I saw breakfasting over a few expiring embers on roasted apples, ploughing with three ponies, with ploughs like peat barrows, or folded together in long trough-shaped wicker carts, wearing night caps, and dresses of blue calico, with a black stump of a pipe stuck between their jaws, and a drop hanging at their long thin noses, and faces puckered together into the most *weepy mouse* aspect; or the women riding on cuddies with wooden saddles; or the postilions with their leather shovel hats and their boots like moderate churns; often blind of one eye or broken-legged, and always the coolest liars in existence. But better than all was our own mode of treating them; and Strachey's French when he scolded the waiters and hosts of the inns. 'C'est bien imposant' (said he at Beauvais), 'c'est une rascalité, vous dis-je; vous avez chargé deux fois trop; vous êtes,' &c. To all which they answered with the gravity of judges passing the sentence of death: 'Monsieur, c'est impossible; on ne vous surfait nullement; on ne,' &c. 'Où est les chevaux,' shrieked he at the end of every post. 'Vont venir, monsieur,' said they. Kitty and I were like to split with laughing. At length Strachey himself gave up the cause entirely and took to speaking French English without disguise. When a man asked him for 'quelque chose à boire; je vous ai conduit très-bien,' Strachey answered, without looking at him, 'Nong! vous avez drivé devilish slow,' which suited just as well.

Of Paris I shall say nothing till we meet. It is the Vanity Fair of the Universe, and cannot be described in many letters. With few exceptions the streets are narrow and crowded and unclean, the kennel in the middle, and a lamp hanging over it here and

---

[1] In the *Reminiscences* he says that he found Irving still at Dover. This is the single error of fact which I have detected.

there on a rope from side to side. There are no footpaths, but an everlasting press of carriages and carts and dirty people hastening to and fro among them, amidst a thousand *gare-gares* and *sacrés* and other oaths and admonitions; while by the side are men roasting chestnuts in their booths, fruitshops, wineshops, barbers; silk merchants selling *à prix juste* (without cheating), *restaurateurs*, *cafés*, *traiteurs*, *magasins de bonbons*, billiard-tables, *estaminets* (gin-shops), *débits de tabac* (where you buy a cigar for a halfpenny and go out smoking it), and every species of *dépôt* and *entrepôt* and *magasin* for the comfort and refreshment of the physical part of the natural man, plying its vocation in the midst of noise and stink, both of which it augments by its produce and by its efforts to dispose of it. The Palais Royal is a spot unrivalled in the world, the chosen abode of vanity and vice, the true palace of the *tigre-singes* (tiger-apes), as Voltaire called his countrymen, a place which I rejoice to think is separated from me by the girdle of the ocean, and never likely to be copied in the British Isles. I dined in it often, and bought four little bone *étuis* (needle-cases) at a franc each for our four sisters at Mainhill. It is a sort of emblem of the French character, the perfection of the physical and fantastical part of our nature, with an absence of all that is solid and substantial in the moral, and often in the intellectual part of it. Looking-glasses and trinkets and fricassees and gaming tables seem to be the life of a Frenchman; his home is a place where he sleeps and dresses; he lives in the *salon du restaurateur* on the *boulevard*, or the garden of the Palais Royal. Every room you enter, destitute of carpet or fire, is expanded into boundlessness by mirrors; and I should think about fifty thousand dice-boxes are set a rattling every night, especially on Sundays, within the walls of Paris. There the people sit and chatter and fiddle away existence as if it were a raree show, careless how it go on so they have excitement, *des sensations agréables*. Their palaces and picture-galleries and triumphal arches are the wonder of the earth, but the stink of their streets is considerable, and you cannot walk on them without risking the fracture of your legs or neck.

But peace to the French! for here I have no room to express even my ideas about them, far less to do them any justice. Suffice it to observe that I contrived to see nearly all that could be seen within twelve days, and to carry off as much enjoyment as it was possible for sights to afford me at the expense of about five pounds sterling. I saw the Louvre gallery of pictures, the Tuileries palace, the Jardin des Plantes, the churches and cemeteries, and all that *could* be seen. I saw Talma the actor, and almost touched His Most Christian Majesty Charles X. What was most interesting, I heard Baron Cuvier deliver his introductory lecture on comparative anatomy. Cuvier himself pleased me much : he seems about fifty, with a fair head of hair growing grey, a large broad, not very high head, a nose irregularly aquiline, receding mouth, peaked chin, blue eyes, which he casts upwards, puckering the eyebrows with a look of great sweetness and wisdom ; altogether the appearance of an accomplished, kind, and gentlemanly person. His lecture lasted an hour and a half. I made out nine-tenths of it, and thought it very good and wonderfully fluent and correct for an extempore one. Nay, what do you think ? I made bold to introduce myself to Legendre, and was by him taken to a sitting of the Institute, and presented to Dupin, the celebrated traveller in England. Here also I saw Laplace and Lacroix, and Poisson the mathematician, and Vauquelin and Chaptal and Thénard the chemists, and heard Majendie read a paper. Dupin would have introduced me to Laplace and others, an honour which I declined, desiring only to impress myself with a picture of their several appearances.

Such was Carlyle's sudden visit to Paris—an incident of more importance to him than he knew at the moment. He complained before and he complained after of the hardness of fortune to him ; but fortune in the shape of friends was throwing in his way what very few young men better connected in life have the happiness of so early falling in with. The expedition created no small excitement at Mainhill. The old people had grown up under the traditions of the war. For a son of theirs to go abroad at all was almost miraculous. When they heard that he was gone to Paris, ' all the stoutness of their hearts' was required to bear it.

It matters little to the sufferers (wrote his brother Alexander) whether their evils are real or imaginary. Our anxiety was groundless, but this did little help till your letter to Jack arrived

We had inquired at the post-office every day for more than a fortnight before it came, and every new disappointment was, especially to our anxious mother, reason sufficient for darkening still
deeper the catalogue of her fears about your welfare. I really
believe that two or three days more of silence would have driven
her distracted well nigh. She had laid aside singing for more
than a fortnight; and even the rest of the women, if they attempted to sing or indulge in laughing, were reproached with un-
becoming lightness of heart. But, thanks to heaven, we are all
of us to rights again; and you have crossed and re-crossed the
blue ocean—yea, visited the once-powerful kingdom of the great
Napoleon, at whose frown Europe crouched in terror.

CHAPTER XV.

A.D. 1824. ÆT. 29.

THE holiday was over. Carlyle returned to London with the Stracheys, and settled himself in lodgings in South-hampton Street, near Irving. Here at any rate he intended to stay till Schiller was off his hands complete in the form of the book. That accomplished, the problem of his future life remained to be encountered. What was he to do? He was adrift, with no settled occupation. To what should he turn his hand? Where should he resolve to live? He had now seen London. He had seen Birmingham with its busy industries. He had seen Paris. He had been brought into contact with English intellectual life. He had conversed and measured strength with some of the leading men of letters of the day. He knew that he had talents which entitled him to a place among the best of them. But he was sick in body, and mentally he was a strange combination of pride and self-deprecation. He was free as air, but free only, as it seemed to him, because of his insignificance,—because no one wanted his help. Most of us find our course determined by circumstances. We are saved by necessity from the infirmity of our own wills. No necessity interfered with Carlyle. He had the world before him with no limitations but his poverty, and he was entirely at sea. So far only he was determined, that he would never sell his soul to the Devil, never speak what he did not wholly believe, never do what in his inmost heart he did not feel to be right, and that he would keep his independence, come what might.

As old Quixote said (he wrote at this time), and as I have often said after him, if it were but a crust of bread and a cup of water that Heaven has given thee, rejoice that thou hast none but them to thank for it. A man that is not standing on his own feet in regard to economical affairs soon ceases to be a man at all. Poor Coleridge is like the hulk of a huge ship—his masts and sails and rudder have rotted quite away.

Literature lay open. Nothing could hinder a man there save the unwillingness of publishers to take his wares; but of this there seemed to be no danger. 'Meister' seemed to be coming to a second edition; the 'Schiller,' such parts of it as had as yet appeared, had been favourably noticed; and Schiller's own example was specially encouraging. Schiller, like himself, had been intended for the ministry, had recoiled from it, had drifted, as he had done, into the initial stages of law, but had been unable to move in professional harness. Schiller, like himself again, had been afflicted with painful chronic disease, and, though it killed him early, his spirit had triumphed over his body. At the age at which Carlyle had now arrived, Schiller's name was known in every reading household in Germany, and his early plays had been translated into half the languages in Europe. Schiller, however, more fortunate than he, possessed the rare and glorious gift of poetry. Carlyle had tried poetry and had consciously failed. He had intellect enough. He had imagination—no lack of that, and the keenest and widest sensibilities; yet with a true instinct he had discovered that the special faculty which distinguishes the poet from other men, nature had not bestowed upon him. He had no correct metrical ear; the defect can be traced in the very best of his attempts, whether at translation or at original composition. He could shape his materials into verse, but without spontaneity, and instead of gaining beauty they lost their force and clearness. His prose at this time was, on the other hand, su premely excellent, little as he knew it. The sentences in his letters are perfectly shaped, and are pregnant with meaning. The more impassioned passages flow in rhythmical cadence like the sweetest tones of an organ. The style of the 'Life of Schiller' is the style of his letters. He was not satisfied with it; he thought it 'wretched,' 'bombastic,' 'not in the right vein.' It was in fact simple. Few literary biographies in the English language equal it for grace, for brevity, for clearness of portraiture, and artist-like neglect of the unessentials. Goethe so clearly recognised its merits, that in a year or two it was to be translated under his direction into German, and edited with a preface by himself. While England and Scotland were giving Carlyle at best a few patronising nods, soon to change to anger and contempt, Goethe saw in this young unknown Scotchman the characteristics of a true man of genius, and spoke of him 'as a new moral force, the extent and effects of which it was impossible to predict.'

The rewriting and arranging of the 'Life of Schiller' was more tedious than Carlyle expected. It was done at last, however, published and paid for. A copy was sent to Mainhill, with a letter to his mother.

I have at last finished that miserable book, on account of which I have been scolding printers and running to and fro like an evil spirit for the last three weeks. The 'Life of Schiller' is now fairly off my hands. I have not put my name to it, not feeling anxious to have the syllables of my poor name pass through the mouths of cockneys on so slender an occasion, though, if anyone lay it to my charge, I shall see no reason to blush for the hand I had in it. Sometimes of late I have bethought me of some of your old maxims about pride and vanity. I do see this same vanity to be the root of half the evil men are subject to in life. Examples of it stare me in the face every day.

The pitiful passion under any of the thousand forms which it assumes never fails to wither out the good and worthy parts of a man's character, and leave him poor and spiteful, an enemy to his own peace and that of all about him. There never was a wiser doctrine than that of Christian humility, considered as a corrective for the coarse unruly selfishness of man's nature. I know you will read the 'Schiller' with attention and pleasure. It contains nothing that I know of but truth of fact and sentiment, and I have always found that the honest truth of one mind had a certain attraction in it for every other mind that loved truth honestly. Various quacks, for instance, have exclaimed against the immorality of 'Meister;' and the person whom it delighted above all others of my acquaintance was Mrs. Strachey, exactly the most religious, pure, and true-minded person among the whole number. A still more convincing proof of my doctrine was the satisfaction you took in it.

The 'Schiller' was as welcome at Mainhill as 'Meister' had been, but I have anticipated the completion of it. It was not finished till the middle of the winter, all which time Carlyle was alone in his London lodgings. His personal history from the time of his return from Dover is told in his letters.

To Mrs. Carlyle, Mainhill.

23 Southampton Street, Pentonville :
November 12, 1824.

The Stracheys took me with them in their carriage to Shooter's Hill, and I made my way to the hospitable mansion of the Orator at Pentonville by various coaches as I best could. Next morning no entreaties for delay could detain me. I set out in quest of lodgings, determined to take no rest till I had found some place which I could call my own, where I might at last collect my scattered thoughts and see what yet remained to me to be accomplished or avoided. I found the task of seeking lodgings less abominable than I used to reckon it in Edinburgh. Irving and his wife went with me to one or two till I got into the way, after which I dismissed them, and proceeded on the search myself. Ere long I landed in Southampton Street, a fine, clean, quiet spot, and found a landlady and a couple of rooms almost exactly such as I was wanting.

Here I have fixed my abode for a space, and design to set seriously about remodelling my affairs. On the whole I am happy that I have got into a house of my own where I am lord and master, and can manage as I like without giving an account to anyone. Irving could not take me to board in his house, having engaged to admit one Parker from Glasgow (at a *very* high rate), who is coming here to study law. Indeed, after inspecting the state of his internal economy, I more than ceased to desire it. He himself is of rough and ready habits, and his wife is not by any means the pink of housekeepers. For one like me their house and table would have suited but indifferently in point of health, and their visitors and other interruptions would have sadly interfered with my standing business. Irving's kind and interesting conversation was the only thing that tempted me, and even this for the present could not have been got. The Orator's whole heart and soul seem for a while to have been set on two solitary objects—the Caledonian Chapel and the squealing brat of a child which his dear Isabella brought him three months ago. This smallest and *wershest* of his Majesty's subjects the worthy preacher dandles and fondles and dry-nurses and talks about in a way that is piteous to behold. He speculates on the progressive development of *his* senses, on the state of *his* bowels, on *his* hours of rest, his pap-spoons and his hippings. He asks you twenty times a day (me he dares not ask any longer) if *he* is not a pretty boy. He even at times attempts a hideous chaunt to the creature by way of lullaby. Unhappy *gorb!* I have wished it farther than I need repeat at present. Its mewing used to awaken me at night. Its history keeps me silent by day. Now that I am gone from its sphere I can wish it well as the offspring of my friend, whom after all I do not like much the worse that he is over-fond and foolish as a father. In my present situation, too, I can enjoy all that is enjoyable in his company and friendship. This house is within three minutes' walk of his, where I design to be a frequent visitor. They have been kind friends to me. I were a worthless creature to forget them.

I expect to pass my time neither unpleasantly nor unprofitably in this city. I have people enough here whom I wish to see and may see. Some of them are attractive by their talent and knowledge, several by their kindness. The Stracheys I have found to be friendly in a high degree. Mrs. Montagu (Irving's 'noble lady,' whom I do not like as well as Mrs. S.), had a note lying for me in Dover inviting me in very warm and high flown terms to come and live with them. The Bullers are here at present; they sent inviting me by Arthur their son to come and dine with them to-day. I would not *dine* with the King. But I engaged to go and take tea. Badams predicts that I will come back to him; but this I do not expect.

London pleased Carlyle less as he knew it better.

To John Carlyle.

23 Southampton Street: November 20, 1824.

Allen of York is here at present, setting up a sort of 'Asylum.' He wishes me to go out and live with him at his house in Epping Forest. He will board me and a horse for 40*l.* a year! That scheme will not answer. There is folly enough within my reach already without going to seek it among the professedly insane. Perhaps I may go and stay with him a week or so when I have finished the writing of this book. I have yet made but little progress in my survey of London. The weather has been very unpropitious, and I have had many things to do. I have several persons (Mrs. Montagu, Mrs. Strachey, Procter, &c.) whom I call on now and then, and might far oftener if I found it useful. They are kind persons, particularly the first two; but for rational employment of my mind in their company there is but very little. People of elevated minds and clear judgment seem to be as rare here as in the North. Anything approaching to a *great character* is a treasure I have yet to meet with. Yet such is life. The little that is good in it we ought to welcome, and forget how much better it might have been when we think how much worse it generally is. These two women and their families treat me as if I were a near relation, not a wandering stranger. I feel their kindness, and hope yet to profit more by it. Basil Montagu, the husband, was described to me as a philosopher. I find him to be an honest-hearted —— goose. Happy Irving, who sees in all his friends the pink of human excellence; and when he has found the nakedness of the land, can turn him round and seek a fresh supply. He is still fighting away as valiantly as ever—nursing and preaching. His popularity is growing steadier, and I think will ultimately settle into something comfortable and accordant with the nature of things.

The fashionable people have long ago forgot that he exists; and our worthy preacher has discovered, fortunately not too late, that many things since the Reformation have been more surprising than to grow a London lion for the space of three little months. I am glad with all my heart that this insane work is over. Irving is becoming known to men at large *as he is.* The sceptical and literary people find that he is *not* a quack ; and they honour him, or at least let him live at peace. There are many persons of warm hearts and half-cultivated heads who love him and admire him, and I think will stand by him firmly. All that have ever known him in private must and do like him. Delivered from the gross incense of preaching popularity, Irving will cultivate his mind in peace ; and may ray out a profitable mixture of light and darkness upon a much wider public than he has yet addressed by writing. After all he is a brave fellow—among the best, if not the very best, whom I have met in life. Success to him ! for though I laugh at him, I were a dog if I did not love him. Speak not of his popularity. Your words will be interpreted to mean, not that it is growing rational, but that it is over. At present I reckon the appearance of it better than it has ever been.

The correspondence with Miss Welsh had continued regularly since Carlyle left Scotland. Letters written under such circumstances are in their nature private, and so must for the most part remain. Miss Welsh, however, was necessarily a principal element in any scheme which Carlyle might form for his future life, and to her his views were exposed without the smallest reserve. The pensions or sinecures of which her too sanguine expectation had dreamt, he had known from the first to be illusions. He must live, if he lived at all, by his own hand. He had begun to think that both for body and mind London was not the place for him. He had saved between two and three hundred pounds, beyond what he had spent upon his brothers. His tastes were of the simplest. The plainest house, the plainest food, the plainest dress, was all that he wanted. The literary men whom he had met with in the metropolis did not please him. Some, like Hazlitt, were selling their souls to the periodical press. Even in Campbell and Coleridge the finer powers were dormant or paralysed, under the spell it seemed of London and its influences. Southey and Wordsworth, who could give a better account of their abilities, had turned their backs upon the world with its vain distinctions and noisy flatteries, and were living far away among the lakes and mountains. Carlyle was considering that he, too, would be better in Annandale. He would take a farm and stock it. His brother Alexander would manage it for him, while he could study and write. From these two sources, means sufficient could easily be provided for a simple and honourable existence. Before taking any decided step, however, it was necessary to consult the person who had promised to be his wife when he should find himself in a condition to maintain her in tolerable comfort. It is possible—though speculations of an interested kind influenced Carlyle as little as they ever influenced any man—that among their resources he had calculated her fortune would pass for something. There had been no occasion for her to tell him precisely the disposition which she had made of it. He had written to her effusively, and she had laughed at him. She had been afterwards slightly unwell, and had expressed penitence for her levity.

To Miss Welsh.

23 Southampton Street, Pentonville : November —.

Your sickness I have striven to make light of. I will not let myself believe that it is more than temporary ; and the serious mood you partly owe to it is that in which to me you are far most interesting.

Do not mock and laugh, however gracefully, when you can help it. For your own sake I had almost rather see you sad. It is the earnest, affectionate, warm-hearted, enthusiastic Jane that I love. The acute, sarcastic, clear-sighted, derisive Jane I can at best but admire. Is it not a pity that you had such a turn that way? 'Pity rather that the follies of the world, and yours among the number, Mr. Quack, should so often call for castigation.' Well, well! Be it so, then. A wilful man, and still more a wilful woman, will have their way. . . . Now let us turn over a new leaf —a new leaf in the paper, and still more in the subject. I am meditating with as rigid an intensity as ever on the great focus of all purposes at present—the arranging of my future life. Here is no light business, and no want of eagerness in me to see it done. As yet I have made no way, or very little; but already I am far happier than I was, from the mere consideration that my destiny, with all its manifold entanglements, perplexing and tormenting as they are, is now submitted to my own management. Of my projects I can give no description. They fluctuate from day to day, and many of them are not of a kind to be explained in writing. One item lies at the bottom of almost any scheme I form. It is determination to have some household of my own; some abode which I may be lord of, though it were no better than the Cynic's tub; some abiding home which I may keep myself in peace by the hope of improving—not of changing for another. I have lived too long in tents a wandering Bedouin, the fruit of my toils wasted or spent in the day that witnessed them. I am sick and must recover; and if so, sickness itself provides the helps for getting out of it. Till then my mind lies spell-bound, the best of my talents (bless the mark) shut up even from my own poor view, and the thought of writing anything beyond mere drudgery is vain. I see all this, but I also see the plan of conquering it if it can be conquered. I must settle myself down within reach of Edinburgh or London. I must divide my time between mental and bodily exercises. If the latter could be turned to profit, could be regularly fixed and ordered by necessity of any kind, I should regard the point as gained. Had I land of my own, I should instantly be tempted to become a—farmer! Laugh outright! But it is very true. I think how I should mount a horseback in the grey of the morning and go forth like a destroying angel among my lazy hinds,[1] quickening every sluggish hand, cultivating and cleaning, tilling and planting, till the place became a very garden round me. In the intermediate hours I could work at literature; thus compelled to live according to the wants of nature, in one twelvemonth I should be the healthiest man in three parishes, and then, if I said and did nothing notable, it were my own blame or nature's only.

This you say is Utopian dreaming, not the sober scheme of a man in his senses. I am sorry for it—sorry that nothing half so

[1] This is like his 'sluttish harlots' at Kinnaird. How did he know that his hinds would be lazy? But vehement language, which implied nothing but the impatience and irritability of his own mind, was as characteristic of Carlyle as it was of Johnson.

likely to save me comes within the circuit of my capabilities. A sinecure! God bless thee, my darling! I could not touch a sinecure though twenty of my friends should volunteer to offer it. *Keineswegs.* It is no part of my plan to eat the bread of idleness so long as I have the force of a sparrow left in me to procure the honest bread of industry. Irving, too! good Irving! His thoughts are friendly, but he expresses them like a goose. 'Help me to the uttermost'? If he can help himself to get along the path through life, it is all that I shall ask of him. If his own shins are safe at the journey's end (a point on which there are many doubts), let him hang a votive tablet up and go to bed in peace. I shall manage mine. There is no use in 'helps.' The grown-up man that cannot be his own help ought to solicit his discharge from the Church militant, and turn him to some middle region by the earliest conveyance. For affection, or the faintest imitation of it, a man should feel obliged to his very dog. But for the gross assistances of patronage or purse, let him pause before accepting them from anyone. Let him utterly refuse them except from beings that are enshrined in his heart of hearts, and from whom no chance can divide him. It is the law in Yarmouth that every herring hang by its own head. Except in cases singularly wretched or singularly happy, that judicious principle I think should also govern life.

A few days later he writes again :

Irving advises me to stay in London ; partly with a friendly feeling, partly with a half-selfish one, for he would fain keep me near him. Among all his followers there is none whose intercourse can satisfy him. Any other than him it would go far to disgust. Great part of them are blockheads, a few are fools. There is no rightly intellectual man among them. He speculates and speculates, and would rather have one contradict him rationally, than gape at him with the vacant stare of children viewing the Grand Turk's palace with his guards—all alive! He advises me, not knowing what he says. He himself has the nerves of a buffalo, and forgets that I have not. His philosophy with me is like a gill of ditch-water thrown into the crater of Mount Ætna. A million gallons of it would avail me nothing.

On the whole, however, he is among the best fellows in London, by far the best that I have met with. Thomas Campbell has a far clearer judgment, infinitely more taste and refinement, but there is no living well of thought or feeling in him. His head is a shop, not a manufactory; and for his heart, it is as dry as a Greenock kipper. I saw him for the second time the other night. I viewed him more clearly and in a kindlier light, but scarcely altered my opinion of him. He is not so much a man as the editor of a magazine. His life is that of an exotic. He exists in London, as most Scotchmen do, like a shrub disrooted and stuck into a bottle of water. Poor Campbell! There were good things in him too, but fate has pressed too heavy on him, or he has resisted it too weakly. His poetic vein is failing, or has run out. He has a Glasgow wife, and their only son is in a state of idiotcy. I sympathised with him, I could have loved him, but he has forgot the way to love. Procter here has set up house on the strength of his writing faculties, with his wife, a daughter of the Noble Lady. He is a good-natured man, lively and ingenious, but essentially a small. Coleridge is sunk inextricably in the depths of putrescent indolence. Southey and Wordsworth have retired far from the din of this monstrous city; so has Thomas Moore. Whom have we left? The dwarf Opium-eater, my critic in the 'London Magazine,' lives here in lodgings, with a wife and children living, or starving, on the scanty produce of his scribble far off in Westmoreland. He carries a laudanum bottle in his pocket, and the venom of a wasp in his heart. A rascal (——), who writes much of the blackguardism in 'Blackwood,' has been frying him to cinders on the gridiron of 'John Bull.' Poor De Quincey! He had twenty thousand pounds, and a liberal share of gifts from nature. Vanity and opium have brought him to the state of 'dog distract or monkey sick.' If I could find him, it would give me pleasure to procure him one substantial beefsteak before he dies. Hazlitt is writing his way through France and Italy. The ginshops and pawnbrokers bewail his absence. Leigh Hunt writes 'wishing caps' for the 'Examiner,' and lives on the lightest of diets at Pisa. But what shall I say of you, ye ——, and ——, and ——, and all the spotted fry that 'report' and 'get up' for the 'public press,' that earn money by writing calumnies, and spend it in punch and other viler objects of debauchery? Filthiest and basest of the children of men! My soul come not into your secrets; mine honour be not united unto you! 'Good heavens!' I often inwardly exclaim, 'and is this the literary world?' This rascal rout, this dirty rabble, destitute not only of high feeling and knowledge or intellect, but even of common honesty! The very best of them are ill-natured weaklings. They are not red-blooded men at all. They are only things for writing articles. But I have done with them for once. In railing at them let me not forget that if they are bad and worthless, I, as yet, am nothing; and that he who putteth on his harness should not boast himself as he who putteth it off. Unhappy souls! perhaps they are more to be pitied than blamed. I do not hate them. I would only that stone walls and iron bars were constantly between us.

Such is the literary world of London; indisputably the poorest part of its population at present.

While in this humour with English men of letters, Carlyle was surprised and cheered by a letter from one of the same calling in another country, the man whom above all others he most honoured and admired, Goethe himself. He had sent a copy of his translation of ' Meister' to Weimar, but no notice had been taken of it, and he had ceased to expect any. ' It was like a message from fairyland,' he said. He could at first scarcely believe ' that this was the real hand and signature of that mysterious personage whose name had floated through his fancy like a sort of spell since his boyhood, whose thoughts had come to him in maturer years almost with the impressiveness of revelations.' An account of this angel visitation, with a copy of the letter itself, was forwarded to Mainhill.

To John Carlyle.

Southampton Street : December 18.

The other afternoon, as I was lying dozing in a brown study after dinner, a lord's lackey knocked at the door and presented me with a little blue parcel, requiring for it a note of delivery. I opened it, and found two pretty stitched little books, and a letter from Goethe! I copy it and send it for your edification. The patriarchal style of it pleases me much :—[1]

' My dearest Sir,—If I did not acknowledge on the spot the arrival of your welcome present, it was because I was unwilling to

[1] The translation is mine; Carlyle copied the letter as it was written.

send you an empty acknowledgment merely, but I purposed to add some careful remarks on a work so honourable to me.

'My advanced years, however, burdened as they are with many indispensable duties, have prevented me from comparing your translation at my leisure with the original text—a more difficult undertaking, perhaps, for me than for some third person thoroughly familiar with German and English literature. Since, however, I have at the present moment an opportunity, through the Lords Bentinck, of forwarding this note safely to London, and at the same time of bringing about an acquaintance between yourself and the Lord B. which may be agreeable to both of you, I delay no longer to thank you for the interest which you have taken in my literary works as well as in the incidents of my life, and to entreat you earnestly to continue the same interest for the future also. It may be that I shall yet hear much of you. I send herewith a set of poems which you will scarcely have seen, but with which I venture to hope that you will feel a certain sympathy.

'With the most sincere good wishes,

'Your most obedient,

'J. W. GOETHE.' [1]

[1] In Goethe's German : —

'Wenn ich, mein werthester Herr, die glückliche Ankunft Ihrer willkommenen Sendung nicht ungesäumt anzeige, so war die Ursache dass ich nicht einen leeren Empfangschein ausstellen, sondern über Ihre mir so ehrenvolle Arbeit auch irgend ein geprüftes Wort beyzufügen die Absicht hatte.

'Meine hohen Jahre jedoch mit so vielen unabwendbaren Obliegenheiten immerfort beladen, hinderten mich an einer ruhigen Vergleichung Ihrer Bearbeitung mit dem Originaltext, welches vielleicht für mich eine schwerere Aufgabe seyn möchte, als für irgend einen dritten der deutschen und englischen Literatur gründlich Befreundeten. Gegenwärtig aber, da ich eine Gelegenheit sehe durch die Herren Grafen Bentinck gegenwärtiges Schreiben sicher nach London zu bringen, und zugleich beiden Theilen eine angenehme Bekanntschaft zu verschaffen, so versäume nicht meinen Dank für Ihre so innige Theilnahme an meinen literarischen Arbeiten, sowohl als an den Schicksalen meines Lebens, hierdurch treulich auszusprechen; und Sie um Fortsetzung derselben auch für die Zukunft angelegentlich zu ersuchen. Vielleicht erfahre ich in der Folge noch manches von Ihnen, und übersende zugleich mit diesem eine Reihe von Gedichten welche schwerlich zu Ihnen gekommen sind, von denen ich aber hoffen darf, dass sie Ihnen einiges Interesse abgewinnen werden.

'Mit den aufrichtigsten Wünschen,

'Ergebenst,

'J. W. GOETHE.'

This is the first of several letters which Carlyle received from Goethe; the earliest token of the attention which he had commanded from the leader of modern literature, an attention which deepened into regard and admiration when the 'Life of Schiller' reached Goethe's hands. The acquaintance which was to prove mutually interesting came of course to nothing. Carlyle heard no more of the 'Lord Bentinck.' The momentary consequence which attached to him as the correspondent of the poet-minister of the Duke of Weimar disappeared in England, where he seemed no more than an insignificant struggling individual, below the notice of the privileged circles.

The annals of this year, so eventful in Carlyle's history, may close with a letter to him from the poor farm-house in Annandale.

To Thomas Carlyle.

Mainhill: December 18, 1824.

Dear Son,—I take this opportunity to thank you for your unvarying kindness, though I fear it will hardly read. But never mind; I know to whom I am writing. It is a long time since we had a sight of each other; nevertheless I am often with you in thought, and I hope we shall meet at a throne of grace where there is free access to all who come in faith. Tell me if thou readest a chapter often. If not, begin; oh, do begin! How do you spend the Sabbath in that tumultuous city? Oh! remember to keep it holy; this you will never repent. I think you will be saying, 'Hold, mother!' but time is short and uncertain. Now, Tom, the best of boys thou art to me! Do not think I am melancholy, though I so speak. Be not uneasy on my account. I have great reason to be thankful. I am quite well, and happy too when I hear from London and Edinburgh. And pray do not let me want food: as your father says, I look as if I would eat your letters. Write everything and soon—I look for one every fortnight till we meet. I grudge taking up the sheet, so I bid thee goodnight, and remain

Your affectionate mother,.

MARGARET CARLYLE.

P.S. by Alexander Carlyle :—

You are very wise, we seriously think, in determining to live in the country, but how or where I do not pretend to say ; perhaps in some cottage with a grass park or cow attached to it for the nonce, and our mother or Mag for housekeeper. Or what say you of farming (marrying, I dare not speak to you about at all)? There are plenty of farms to let on all sides of the country. But tell me : are the warm hearts of Mainhill changed ? or are they less anxious to please ? I guess not. Yet after all, I do often think that you would be as comfortable here as anywhere.

CHAPTER XVI.

GOETHE's letter was more than a compliment. Goethe, who did not throw away his words in unmeaning polite-nesses, had noticed Carlyle ; and notice was more welcome from such a source than if it had come from ministers or kings. The master had spoken approvingly. The disci-ple was encouraged and invigorated. He had received an earnest that his intellectual career would not be a wholly unfruitful one. Pleasant as it was, however, it did not help the solution of the pressing problem, what was he immediately to do ? The prospect of a farm in Scotland became more attractive the more he thought of it. Free-dom, fresh air, plain food, and the society of healthy, pious people, unspoilt by the world and its contagion— with these life might be worth having and might be turned to noble uses. He had reflected much on his engagement with Miss Welsh. He had felt that perhaps he had done wrong in allowing her to entangle herself with a person whose future was so uncertain, and whose present schemes, even if realised successfully, would throw her, if she mar-ried him, into a situation so unlike what she had antici-pated, so unlike the surroundings to which she had been accustomed. In his vehement way he had offered to re-lease her if she wished it ; and she had unhesitatingly refused. As little, however, was her ambition gratified with the prospect of being mistress of a Scotch farm. She had mocked at his proposal. She had pointed out with serious truth his own utter unfitness for a farmer's occu-

pation.   She had jestingly told him that she had land of
her own at Craigenputtock.   The tenant was leaving.   If
he was bent on trying, let him try Craigenputtock.   He
took her jest in earnest.   Why should he not farm Craigenputtock?   Why should not she, as she was still willing
to be his life companion, live with him there?   Her father
had been born in the old manor-house, and had intended
to end his days there.   To himself the moorland life
would be only a continuance of the same happy mode of
existence which he had known at Mainhill.   In such a
household, and in the discharge of the commonest duties,
he had seen his mother become a very paragon of women.
He did not understand, or he did not wish to understand,
that a position which may be admirably suited to a person
who has known no other, might be ill-adapted to one who
had been bred in luxury and had never known a want un-
cared for.   The longer he reflected on it, the more desirable the plan of taking Craigenputtock appeared to him to
be.

To Miss Welsh.

Pentonville: Jan. 9, 1825.

I trust that the same cheerful spirit of affection which breathes
in every line of your last charming letter still animates you, and
disposes you kindly towards me.   I have somewhat to propose to
you which it may require all your love of me to make you look
upon with favour.   If you are not the best woman in the world, it
may prove a sorry business for both of us.

You bid me tell you how I have decided—what I mean to do.
It is you that must decide.   I will endeavour to explain to you
what I wish ; it must rest with you to say whether it can ever be
attained.   You tell me you have land which needs improvement.
Why not work on that?   In one word, then, will you go with me?
Will you be my own forever?   Say yes, and I embrace the project with my whole heart.   I send my brother Alick over to rent
that Nithsdale farm for me without delay ; I proceed to it the moment I am freed from my engagements here ; I labour in arranging it, and fitting everything for your reception ; and the instant

it is ready I take you home to my hearth, never more to part from me, whatever fate betide us.

I fear you think this scheme a baseless vision; and yet it is the sober best among the many I have meditated—the best for me, and I think also, so far as I can judge of it, for yourself. If it take effect and be well conducted, I look upon the recovery of my health and equanimity, and with these, of regular profitable and natural habits of activity, as things which are no longer doubtful. I have lost them by departing from nature; I must find them by returning to her. A stern experience has taught me this, and I am a fool if I do not profit by the lesson. Depend upon it, Jane, this literature which both of us are so bent on pursuing will not constitute the sole nourishment of any true human spirit. No truth has been forced upon me, after more resistance, or with more invincible impressiveness than this. I feel it in myself. I see it daily in others. Literature is the *wine* of life. It will not, cannot, be its food. What is it that makes blue-stockings of women, magazine hacks of men? They neglect household and social duties. They have no household and social enjoyments. Life is no longer with them a verdant field, but a *hortus siccus*. They exist pent up in noisome streets, amid feverish excitements. They despise or overlook the common blessedness which Providence has laid out for *all* his creatures, and try to substitute for it a distilled quintessence prepared in the alembic of painters and rhymers and sweet singers. What is the result? This *ardent spirit* parches up their nature. They become discontented and despicable, or wretched and dangerous. Byron and all strong souls go the latter way. Campbell and all the weak souls the former. 'Hinaus!' as the Devil says to Faust. 'Hinaus ins freie Feld!' There is no soul in these vapid 'articles' of yours. Away! be men before attempting to be writers.

You, too, are unhappy, and I see the reason. You have a deep, earnest, and vehement spirit, and no earnest task has ever been assigned it. You despise and ridicule the meanness of the things about you. To the things you honour you can only pay a fervent adoration which issues in no practical effect. Oh that I saw you the mistress of a house diffusing over human souls that loved you those clear faculties of order, judgment, elegance, which you are now reduced to spend on pictures and portfolios; blessing living hearts with that enthusiastic love which you must now direct to the distant and dimly seen. All this is in you. You have a heart and an intellect and a resolute decision which might make you the model of wives, however widely your thoughts and your experience have hitherto wandered from that highest distinction of the noblest women. I too have wandered wide and far. Let us return; let us return together. Let us learn through one another what it is to live. Let us set our minds and habitudes in order, and grow under the peaceful sunshine of nature, that whatever fruit or flowers have been implanted in our spirits may ripen wholesomely and be distributed in due season. What is genius but the last perfection of true manhood? the pure reflection of a spirit in union with itself, discharging all common duties with more than common excellence; extracting from the many-coloured scenes of life in which it mingles the beautifying principle which more or less pervades them all? The rose in its full-blown fragrance is the glory of the fields; but there must be a soil and stem and leaves, or there will be no rose. Your mind and my own have in them many capabilities; but the first of all their duties is to provide for their own regulation and contentment. If there be an overplus to consecrate to higher ends it will not fail to show itself. If there be none, it were better it should never attempt to show itself.

But I must leave these generalities and avoid romance, for it is an earnest practical affair we are engaged in, and requires sense and regulation, not poetries and enthusiasm. 'Where then,' you ask me, 'are the means of realising these results, of mastering the difficulties and deficiencies that beset us both?' This too I have considered; the black catalogue of impediments have passed again and again in review before me, but on the whole I do not think them insurmountable. If you will undertake to be my faithful helper, as I will all my life be yours, I fear not to engage with them.

The first, the lowest, but a most essential point, is that of funds. On this matter I have still little to tell you that you do not know. I feel in general that I have ordinary faculties in me, and an ordinary degree of diligence in using them, and that thousands manage life in comfort with even slenderer resources. In my present state my income, though small, might to reasonable wishes be sufficient; were my health and faculties restored, it *might* become abundant. Shall I confess to you this is a difficulty which we are apt to overrate. The essentials of even elegant comfort are not difficult to procure. It is only vanity that is insatiable in consuming. To my taste cleanliness and order are far beyond gilding and grandeur, which without them is an abomination; and for displays, for festivals, and parties I believe you are as indisposed as myself. What is the use of this same vanity? Where is the good of being its slaves? If thou and I love one another, if we discharge our duties faithfully and steadfastly, one labouring with honest, manful zeal to provide, the other with noble wife-like prudence in dispensing, have we not done all we can? Are we not acquitted at the bar of our own conscience? And what is it to us whether this or that Squire or Bailie be richer or poorer than we?

Two laws I have laid down to myself—that I must and will recover health, without which to think or even to live is burdensome or unprofitable; and that I will *not* degenerate into the wretched thing which calls itself an author in our capitals, and scribbles for the sake of lucre in the periodicals of the day. Thank Heaven, there are other means of living. If there were not, I for one should beg to be excused. . . . On the whole I begin to entertain a certain degree of contempt for the destiny which has so long persecuted me. I will be a man in spite of it. Yet it lies with you whether I shall be a *right* man, or only a hard and bitter Stoic. What say you? Decide for yourself and me. Consent if you dare trust me, and let us live and die together. Yet fear not to deny me if your judgment so determine. It will be a sharp pang that tears away from me for ever the hope which now for years has been the solace of my existence; but better to endure it and all its consequences than to witness and to cause the forfeit of your happiness. At times, I confess, when I hear you speak of your gay cousins, and contrast with their brilliant equipments my own simple exterior and scanty prospects, and humble, but to me most dear and honourable-minded kinsmen, whom I were the veriest dog if I ceased to love and venerate and cherish for their true affection and the rugged sterling worth of their character—when I think of all this I could almost counsel you to cast me utterly away, and to connect yourself with one whose friends and station are more analogous to your own. But anon in some moment of self-love, I say proudly there is a spirit in *me* which is worthy of this maiden, which shall be worthy of her. I will teach her, I will guide her, I will make her happy. Together we will share the joys and sorrows of existence.

Speak, then. . . . Think well of me, of yourself, of our circum-

stances, and determine—Dare you trust me, dare you trust your
fate with me, as I trust mine with you? Judge if I wait your answer with impatience. I know you will not keep me waiting. Of
course it will be necessary to explain all things to your mother,
and take her serious advice respecting them. For your other
friends, it is not worth while consulting one of them. I know
not that there is one among them that would give you as disinterested advice as even I, judging in my own cause. May God
bless you and direct you. Decide as you will.

Miss Welsh, after having lost Irving, had consented to
be Carlyle's wife as soon as he was in a fair position to
marry, in the conviction that she was connecting herself
with a man who was destined to become brilliantly distinguished, whom she honoured for his character and admired for his gifts, in whose society and in whose triumphs
she would find a compensation for the disappointment of
her earlier hopes. She was asked in this letter to be the
mistress of a moorland farming establishment. Had she
felt towards Carlyle as she had felt towards his friend,
she would perhaps have encountered cheerfully any lot
which was to be shared with the object of a passionate
affection. But the indispensable feeling was absent.
She was invited to relinquish her station in society, and
resign comforts which habit had made necessary to her,
and she was apparently to sacrifice at the same time the
very expectations which had brought her to regard a marriage with Carlyle as a possibility. She knew better than
he what was really implied in the situation which he offered her. She knew that if farming on a Scotch moor
was to be a successful enterprise, it would not be by morning rides, metaphorical vituperation of ' lazy hinds,' and
forenoons and evenings given up to poetry and philosophy. Both he and she would have to work with all their
might, and with their own hands, with all their time and
all their energy, to the extinction of every higher ambition.
Carlyle himself also she knew to be entirely unfit for any

such occupation. The privations of it might be nothing to him, for he was used to them at home, but he would have to cease to be himself before he could submit patiently to a life of mechanical drudgery. She told him the truth with the merciless precision which on certain occasions distinguished her.

To Thomas Carlyle.

Haddington : January 13, 1825.

I little thought that my joke about your farming Craigenputtock was to be made the basis of such a serious and extraordinary project. If you had seen the state of perplexity which your letter has thrown me into, you would have practised any self-denial rather than have written it. But there is no use in talking of what is done. *Cosa fatta ha capo.* The thing to be considered now is what to do.

You have sometimes asked me did I ever think ? For once in my life at least I have thought myself into a vertigo, and without coming to any positive conclusion. However, my mind, such as it is, on the matter you have thus precipitately forced on my consideration I will explain to you frankly and explicitly, as the happiness of us both requires. I love you, and I should be the most ungrateful and injudicious of mortals if I did not. But I am not *in love* with you ; that is to say, my love for you is not a passion which overclouds my judgment and absorbs all my regards for myself and others. It is a simple, honest, serene affection, made up of admiration and sympathy, and better perhaps to found domestic enjoyment on than any other. In short, it is a love which *influences*, does not *make* the destiny of a life.

Such temperate sentiments lend no false colouring, no 'rosy light' to your project. I see it such as it is, with all the arguments for and against it. I see that my consent under existing circumstances would indeed secure to *me* the only fellowship and support I have found in the world, and perhaps, too, shed some sunshine of joy on your existence, which has hitherto been sullen and cheerless ; but, on the other hand, that it would involve you and myself in numberless cares and difficulties, and expose me to petty tribulations which I want fortitude to despise, and which, not despised, would embitter the peace of us both. I do not wish for fortune more than is sufficient for my wants—my natural wants, and the artificial ones which habit has rendered nearly as importunate as the others. But I will not marry to live on less; because, in that case, every inconvenience I was subjected to would remind me of what I had quitted, and the idea of a sacrifice should have no place in a voluntary union. Neither have I any wish for grandeur; the glittering baits of titles and honours are only for children and fools. But I conceive it a duty which everyone owes to society, not to throw up that station in it which Providence has assigned him, and, having this conviction, I could not marry into a station inferior to my own with the approval of my judgment, *which* alone could enable me to brave the censures of my acquaintance.

And now let me ask you, have you any *certain* livelihood to maintain me in the manner I have been used to live in? any *fixed* place in the rank of society I have been born and bred in? No. You have projects for attaining both, capabilities for attaining both, and much more. But as yet you have not attained them. Use the noble gifts which God has given you. You have prudence —though, by the way, this last proceeding is no great proof of it. Devise then how you may gain yourself a moderate but *settled* income. Think of some more promising plan than farming the most barren spot in the county of Dumfriesshire. What a thing that would be to be sure! You and I keeping house at Craigenput- tock! I would as soon think of building myself a nest on the Bass rock. Nothing but your ignorance of the spot saves you from the imputation of insanity for admitting such a thought. Depend upon it you could not exist there a twelvemonth. For my part I could not spend a month at it with an angel. Think of something else then. Apply your industry to carry it into effect; your talents, to gild over the inequality of our births—and then we will talk of marrying. If all this were realised, I *think* I should have good sense enough to abate something of my romantic ideal, and to content myself with stopping short on this side idolatry. At all events I will marry no one else. This is all the promise I can or will make. A positive engagement to marry a certain per- son at a certain time, at all haps and hazards, I have always con- sidered the most ridiculous thing on earth. It is either altogether useless or altogether miserable. If the parties continue faithfully attached to each other, it is a mere ceremony. If otherwise, it becomes a fetter, rivetting them to wretchedness, and only to be broken with disgrace.

Such is the result of my deliberations on this very serious subject. You may approve of it or not, but you cannot either persuade me or convince me out of it. My decisions, when I do decide, are unalterable as the laws of the Medes and Persians. Write instantly, and tell me that you are content to leave the event to time and destiny, and in the meanwhile to continue my friend and guardian, which you have so long faithfully been, and *nothing more.*

It would be more agreeable to etiquette, and perhaps also to prudence, that I should adopt no middle course in an affair such as this; that I should not for another instant encourage an affection which I may never reward, and a hope I may never fulfil, but cast your heart away from me at once, since I cannot embrace the resolution which would give me a right to it for ever. This I would assuredly do if you were like the generality of lovers, or if it were still in my power to be happy independent of your affection. But, as it is, neither etiquette nor prudence can obtain this of me. If there is any change to be made in the terms on which we have so long lived with one another, it must be made by you, not by me.

An ordinary person who had ventured to make such a proposal as Miss Welsh had declined, would have been supremely foolish if he had supposed that it could be acceded to ; or supremely selfish if he had possessed sufficient influence with the lady whom he was addressing to induce her to listen to it. But Carlyle was in every way peculiar. Selfish he was, if it be selfishness to be ready to sacrifice every person dependent on him, as completely as he sacrificed himself to the aims to which he had resolved to devote his life and talents. But these objects were of so rare a nature, that the person capable of pursuing and attaining them must be judged by a standard of his own. His rejoinder to this letter throws a light into the inmost constitution of his character. He thanked Miss Welsh for her candour ; he was not offended at her resoluteness ; but also, he said, he must himself be resolute. She showed that she did not understand him. He was simply conscious that he possessed powers for the use of which he was responsible, and he could not afford to allow those powers to run to waste any longer.

To Miss Welsh.

Pentonville : Jan. 20, 1825.

It were easy for me to plant myself upon the pinnacle of my own poor selfishness, and utter a number of things proceeding from a very vulgar sort of pride. It were easy also to pour out over the affair a copious effusion of sentimental cant. But to express in simplicity the convictions of a man wishing at least with his whole heart to act as becomes him, is not easy. Grant me a patient hearing, for I have things to say that require earnest consideration from us both.

In the first place, however, I must thank you heartily for your candour. Your letter bears undoubted evidence within itself of being a faithful copy of your feelings at the moment it was written ; and this to me is an essential point. Your resoluteness does not offend me ; on the contrary I applaud it. Woe to us both if we cannot be resolute. The miserable man is he who halts between two opinions, who would and would not ; who longs for the merchandise and will not part with the price. He who has dared to look his destiny, however frightful, steadfastly in the face, to measure his strength with its difficulties, and once for all to give up what he cannot reach, has already ceased to be miserable.

Your letter is dictated by good sense and sincerity ; but it shows me that you have only an imperfect view of my present purposes and situation ; there are several mistakes in it, expressed or implied. It is a mistake to suppose that want of self-denial had any material share in causing this proposal. I hope that I should at all times rather suffer pain myself than transfer it to you ; but here was a very different case. For these many months the voice of every persuasion in my conscience has been thundering to me as with the Trump of the Archangel : Man ! thou art going to destruction. Thy nights and days are spent in torment ; thy heart is wasting into entire bitterness. Thou art making less of life than the dog that sleeps upon thy hearth. Up, hapless mortal ! Up and re-build thy destiny if thou canst ! Up in the name of God, that God who sent thee hither for other purposes than to wander to and fro, bearing the fire of hell in an unguilty bosom, to suffer in vain silence, and to die without ever having lived ! Now, in exploring the chaotic structure of my fortunes, I find my affection for you intertwined with every part of it ; connected with whatever is holiest in my feelings or most imperative in my duties.

It is necessary for me to understand completely how this matter stands; to investigate my own wishes and powers in regard to it; to know of you both what you will do and what you will not do. These things once clearly settled, our line of conduct will be clear also. It was in such a spirit that I made this proposal; not, as you suppose, grounded on a casual jest of yours, or taken up in a moment of insane selfishness; but deliberated with such knowledge as I had of it for months, and calmly decided on, as with all its strangeness absolutely the best for both of us. There was nothing in it of the love and cottage theory, which none but very young novel writers now employ their thoughts about. Had you accepted it, I should not by any means have thought the battle won. I should have hailed your assent, and the disposition of mind it bespoke, with a deep but serious joy; with a solemn hope as indicating the distinct possibility that two true hearts might be united and made happy through each other; might by their joint unwearied efforts be transplanted from the barren wilderness, where both seemed out of place, into scenes of pure and wholesome activity, such as nature fitted both of them to enjoy and adorn. You have rejected it, I think wisely; with your actual purposes and views we should both have been doubly wretched had you acted otherwise. Your love of me is completely under the control of judgment and subordinated to other principles of duty or expediency. Your happiness is not by any means irretrievably connected with mine. Believe me, I am not hurt or angry. I merely wished to know. It was only in brief moments of enthusiasm that I ever looked for a different result. My plan was no wise one if it did not include the chance of your denial as well as that of your assent.

The maxims you proceed by are those of common and acknowledged prudence; and I do not say that it is not wise in you to walk exclusively by them. But for me, my case is peculiar; and unless I adopt other than common maxims, I look upon my ruin as already sure. In fact I cannot but perceive that the stations from which we have looked at life, and formed our schemes of it, are in your case and mine essentially different. You have a right to anticipate excitement and enjoyment. The highest blessing I anticipate is peace. You are bound to pay deference to the criticisms of others, and expect their approbation; I, to pay comparatively little deference to their criticisms, and to overlook their contempt. This is not strange; but it accounts for the wide discrepancy in our principles and intentions and demands the serious study of us both.

In your opinion about sacrifices, *felt to be such*, I entirely agree; but at the same time need I remind your warm and generous heart that the love which will not make sacrifices to its object is no proper love? Grounded in admiration and the feeling of enjoyment, it is a fit love for a picture or a statue or a poem; but for a living soul it is not fit. Alas! without deep sacrifices on both sides, the possibility of our union is an empty dream. It remains for us both to determine what extent of sacrifice it is worth. To me, I confess the union with such a spirit as yours might be, is worth all price but the sacrifice of those very principles which would enable me to deserve and enjoy it.

Then why not make an effort, attain rank and wealth, and confidently ask what is or might be so precious to me? Now, my best friend, are you sure that you have ever formed to yourself a true picture of me and my circumstances; of a man who has spent seven long years in *incessant* torture, till his heart and head are alike darkened and blasted, and who sees no outlet from this state but in a total alteration of the purposes and exertions which brought it on. I must not and cannot continue this sort of life; my patience with it is utterly gone. It were better for me on the soberest calculation to be dead than to continue it much longer. Even of my existing capabilities I can make no regular or proper use till it is altered. These capabilities, I have long seen with regret, are painted in your kind fancy under far too favourable colours. I am not without a certain consciousness of the gifts that are in me; but I should mistake their nature *widely*, if I calculated they would ever guide me to wealth and preferment or even certainly to literary fame. As yet the best of them is very immature; and even if they should come forth in full strength, it must be to other and higher ends that they are directed. How then? Would I invite a generous spirit out of affluence and respectability to share with me obscurity and poverty? Not so. In a few months I might be realising from literature and other kindred exertions the means of keeping *poverty* at a safe distance. The elements of real comfort, which in your vocabulary and mine, I think, has much the same meaning, might be at my disposal; and farther than this I should think it injudicious to expect that external circumstances could materially assist me in the conduct of life. The rest must depend upon myself and the regulation of my own affections and habits.

Now this is what I would do were it in my power. I would ask a generous spirit, one whose happiness depended on seeing me happy, and whose temper and purposes were of kindred to my own —I would ask such a noble being to let us unite our resources—not her wealth and rank merely, for these were a small and unessential fraction of the prayer, but her judgment, her patience, prudence, her true affection, to mine ; and let us try if by neglecting what was not important, and striving with faithful and inseparable hearts after what was, we could not rise above the miserable obstructions that beset us both into regions of serene dignity, living as became us in the sight of God, and all reasonable men, happier than millions of our brethren, and each acknowledging with fervent gratitude that to the other he and she owed all. You are such a generous spirit. But your purposes and feelings are not such. Perhaps it is happier for you that they are not.

This, then, is an outline intended to be true of my unhappy fortunes and strange principles of action. Both, I fear, are equally repulsive to you, yet the former was meant for a faithful picture of what destiny has done to me, and the latter are positively the best arms which my resources offer me to war with her. I have thought of these things till my brain was like to crack. I do not pretend that my conclusions are indubitable, I am still open to better light. But this at present is the best I have. Do you also think of all this ? not in any spirit of anger, but in the spirit of love and noblemindedness which you have always shown me. If we must part, let us part in tenderness and go forth upon our several paths lost to the future, but in possession of the past.

T. CARLYLE.

The functions of a biographer are, like the functions of a Greek chorus, occasionally at the important moments to throw in some moral remarks which seem to fit the situation. The chorus after such a letter would remark, perhaps, on the subtle forms of self-deception to which the human heart is liable, of the momentous nature of marriage, and how men and women plunge heedlessly into the net, thinking only of the satisfaction of their own immediate wishes. . . . Self-sacrifice it might say was a noble thing. But a sacrifice which one person might properly make, the other might have no reasonable right to ask or to allow. It would conclude, however, that the issues of human acts are in the hands of the gods, and would hope for the best in fear and trembling. Carlyle spoke of self-denial. The self-denial which he was prepared to make was the devotion of his whole life to the pursuit and setting forth of spiritual truth ; throwing aside every meaner ambition. But apostles in St. Paul's opinion were better unwedded. The cause to which they give themselves leaves them little leisure to care for the things of their wives. To his mother Carlyle was so loving,

> That he might not beteem the winds of heaven
> Visit her face too roughly.

This was love indeed—love that is lost in its object, and thinks first and only how to guard and foster it. His wife he would expect to rise to his own level of disinterested self-surrender, and be content and happy in assisting him in the development of his own destiny ; and this was selfishness—selfishness of a rare and elevated kind, but selfishness still ; and it followed him throughout his married life. He awoke only to the consciousness of what he had been, when the knowledge would bring no more than unavailing remorse. He admired Miss Welsh ; he loved her in a certain sense ; but, like her, he was not *in love*. In a note-book written long after I find the following curious entry in her hand.

What the greatest philosopher of our day execrates loudest in Thackeray's new novel—finds indeed 'altogether false and damnable in it'—is that love is represented as spreading itself over our whole existence, and constituting the one grand interest of it; whereas love—*the thing people call love*—is confined to a very few years of man's life ; to, in fact, a quite insignificant fraction of it, and even then is but one thing to be attended to among many infinitely more important things. Indeed, so far as he (Mr. C.) has seen into it, the whole concern of love is such a beggarly futility, that in an heroic age of the world nobody would be at the pains to think of it, much less to open his mouth upon it.

A person who had known by experience *the thing called love*, would scarcely have addressed such a vehemently unfavourable opinion of its nature to the woman who had been the object of his affection. He admired Miss Welsh. Her mind and temper suited him. He had allowed her image to intertwine itself with all his thoughts and emotions; but with love his feeling for her had nothing in common but the name. There is not a hint anywhere that he had contemplated as a remote possibility the usual consequence of a marriage—a family of children. He thought of a wife as a companion to himself who would make life easier and brighter to him. But this was all, and the images in which he dressed out the workings of his mind served only to hide their real character from himself.

Miss Welsh's explanation of the limits of her regard had made so little impression that she found it necessary to be still more candid.

You assure me (she replied in answer to this long letter) that you are not hurt or angry. Does this imply that there is some room for your being hurt or angry—that I have done or said what might have angered another less generous than you? I think so. Now room for disappointment there *may* be, but surely there is none for mortification or offence. I have refused my immediate assent to your wishes because our mutual happiness seemed to require that I should refuse it. But for the rest I have not slighted your wishes; on the contrary, I have expressed my willingness to fulfil them at the expense of everything but what I deem essential to our happiness; and, so far from undervaluing you, I have shown you, in declaring that I would marry no one else, not only that I esteem you above all the men I have ever seen, but also that I am persuaded I should esteem you above all the men I may ever see. What, then, have you to be hurt or angry at?

The maxims I proceed by (you tell me) are those of common and acknowledged prudence; and you *do not say* it is unwise in me to walk by them exclusively. The maxims I proceed by are the convictions of my own judgment; and being so it would be unwise in me not to proceed by them whether they are right or wrong. Yet I am prudent, I fear, only because I am not strongly tempted to be otherwise. My heart is capable (I feel it is) of a love to which *no* deprivation would be a sacrifice—a love which would overleap that reverence for opinion with which education and weakness have begirt my sex, would bear down all the restraints which *duty* and *expediency* might throw in the way, and carry every thought of my being impetuously along with it. But the all-perfect mortal who could inspire me with a love so extravagant is nowhere to be found; exists nowhere but in the romance of my own imagination. Perhaps it is better for me as it is. A passion like the torrent in the violence of its course might perhaps too, like the torrent, leave ruin and desolation behind. In the meantime I should be mad to act as if from the influence of such a passion while my affections are in a state of perfect tranquillity. I have already explained to you the nature of my love for *you;* that it is deep and calm, more like the quiet river which refreshes and beautifies where it flows, than the torrent which bears down and destroys: yet it is materially different from what one feels for a statue or a picture.

'Then why not attain wealth and rank?' you say; and it is you who have said it, not I. Wealth and rank, to be sure, have different meanings, according to the views of different people; and what is bare sufficiency and respectability in the vocabulary of a young lady may be called wealth and rank in that of a philosopher. But it certainly was not wealth or rank according to *my* views which I required you to attain. I merely wish to see you earning a certain livelihood, and exercising the profession of a gentleman. For the rest, it is a matter of great indifference to me whether you have hundreds or thousands a year; whether you are a 'Mr.' or a 'Duke.' To me it seems that my wishes in this respect are far from unreasonable, even when your peculiar maxims and situation are taken into account.

Nor was it wholly with a view to improvement in your external circumstances that I have made their fulfilment a condition to our union, but also with a view to some improvement in my sentiments towards you which might be brought about in the meantime. In withholding this matter in my former letter I was guilty of a false and ill-timed reserve. My tenderness for your feelings betrayed me into an insincerity which is not natural to me. I thought that the most decided objection to your circumstances would pain you less than the least objection to yourself. While, in truth, it is in some measure grounded on *both*. I must be sincere, I find: at whatever cost.

As I have said, then, in requiring you to better your fortune, I had some view to an improvement in my sentiments. I am not sure that they are proper sentiments for a husband. They are proper for a brother, a father, a guardian spirit; but a husband, it seems to me, should be dearer still. At the same time, from the change which my sentiments towards you have already undergone during the period of our acquaintance, I have little doubt but that in time I shall be perfectly satisfied with them. One loves you, as Madame de Staël said, in proportion to the ideas and sentiments which are in oneself. According as my mind enlarges, and my heart improves, I become capable of comprehending the goodness and greatness which are in you, and my affection for you increases. Not many months ago I would have said it was *impossible* that I should ever be your wife. At present I consider this the most probable destiny for me, and in a year or two perhaps I shall consider it the only one. *Die Zeit ist noch nicht da!*

From what I have said it is plain (to me at least) what ought to be the line of our future conduct. Do *you* what you can to better your external circumstances; always, however, subordinately to your own principles, which I do not ask you to give up; which I should despise you for giving up whether I approved them or no —while I, on the other hand, do what I can, subordinately to nothing, to better *myself;* which I am persuaded is the surest way of bringing my wishes to accord with yours; and let us leave the rest to fate.

Miss Welsh had been perfectly candid; and had she ended there, Carlyle—if persons in such situations were ever as wise as they ought to be—would have seen from this frank expression of her feelings that a marriage with himself was not likely to be a happy one for her. He had already dimly perceived that the essential condition was absent. She did not love him as she felt that she could love. As little, however, could she make up her mind to give him up or consent that, as he had said, 'they should go forth their several ways.' She refused to believe that he could mean it. 'How could I,' she said, 'part from the only living soul that understands me ? I would marry you to-morrow rather ; our parting would need to be brought about by death or some dispensation of Providence. Were you to will it, to part would no longer be bitter. The bitterness would be in thinking you unworthy.'

The serious tone changed ; the mockery at the Craigenputtock farm project came back, with the strong sense playing merrily beneath it.

Will you be done with this wild scheme of yours? I tell you it will not answer, and you must play Cincinnatus somewhere else. With all your tolerance of places you would not find at Craigenputtock the requisites you require. The light of heaven to be sure is not denied it ; but for green grass ? Beside a few cattle fields there is nothing except a waste prospect of heather and black peat moss. Prune and delve will you ? In the first place there is nothing to prune : and for delving, I set too high a value on your life to let you engage in so perilous an enterprise. Were you to attempt such a thing there are twenty chances to one that you would be swallowed up in the moss, spade and all. In short, I presume, whatever may be your *farming* talents, you are not an accomplished cattle-drover, and nobody but a person of this sort could make the rent of the place out of it. Were *you* to engage in the concern, we should all be ruined together.

Part with Carlyle, however, she would not, unless he himself wished it.

I know not (she says in a following letter) how your spirit has gained such a mastery over mine, in spite of my pride and stubbornness. But so it is. Though self-willed as a mule with others, I am tractable and submissive towards you. I hearken to your voice as to the dictates of a second conscience hardly less awful to me than that which nature has implanted in my breast. How comes it then that you have this power over me ? for it is not the effect of your genius and virtue merely. Sometimes in my serious moods I believe it is a charm with which my good angel has fortified my heart against evil.

Thus matters drifted on to their consummation. The stern and powerful sense of duty in these two remarkable persons held them true through a long and trying life together to the course of elevated action which they had both set before themselves. He never swerved from the high aims to which he had resolved to devote himself. She, by never failing toil and watchfulness, alone made it possible for him to accomplish the work which he achieved. But we reap as we have sown. Those who seek for something more than happiness in this world must not complain if happiness is not their portion. She had the companionship of an extraordinary man. Her character was braced by the contact with him, and through the incessant self-denial which the determination that he should do his very best inevitably exacted of her. But she was not happy. Long years after, in the late evening of her laborious life, she said, 'I married for ambition. Carlyle has exceeded all that my wildest hopes ever imagined of him—and I am miserable.'

CHAPTER XVII.

A.D. 1825. ÆT. 29.

By the beginning of January the 'Life of Schiller' was finished. Carlyle lingered in London for a few weeks longer. The London publishers had their eye on him, and made him various offers for fresh translations from the German; for a life of Voltaire; for other literary biographies. For each or all of these they were ready to give him, as they said, fair terms. He postponed his decision till these terms could be agreed on. Meanwhile he was as usual moody and discontented; in a hurry to be gone from London, and its 'men of letters,' whom he liked less and less.

To John Carlyle.

London: January 22, 1825.

With regard to my own movements after the conclusion of this most small of literary labours, there is yet nothing fixed determinately. That I shall return to Scotland pretty soon is, I think, the only point entirely decided. Here is nothing adequate to induce my continuance. The people are stupid and noisy, and I live at the easy rate of five and forty shillings per week! I say the people are stupid not altogether unadvisedly. In point either of intellectual and moral culture they are some degrees below even the inhabitants of the 'modern Athens.' I have met no man of true head and heart among them. Coleridge is a mass of richest spices putrefied into a dunghill. I never hear him *tawlk* without feeling ready to worship him, and toss him in a blanket. Thomas Campbell is an Edinburgh '*small*,' made still smaller by growth in a foreign soil. Irving is enveloped with delusions and difficulties, wending somewhat down hill, to what depths I know not; and scarcely ever to be seen without a host of the most stolid of all his Majesty's Christian people sitting round him. I wonder often that he does not buy himself a tar-barrel, and fairly light it under the Hatton Garden pulpit, and thus once for all *ex fumo* giving *lucem*, bid adieu the gross train-oil concern altogether. The poor little ——. I often feel that were I as one of these people, sitting in a whole body by the cheek of my own wife, my feet upon my own hearth, I should feel distressed at seeing myself so *very* poor in spirit. Literary men! The Devil in his own good time take all such literary men. One sterling fellow like Schiller, or even old Johnson, would take half a dozen such creatures by the nape of the neck, between his finger and thumb, and carry them forth to the nearest common sink. Save Allan Cunningham, our honest Nithsdale peasant, there is not one *man* among them. In short, it does not seem worth while to spend five and forty shillings weekly for the privilege of being near such pen-men.

To live in London and become enrolled in the unillustrious fellowship, Carlyle felt to be once for all impossible. But what was to be the alternative? Miss Welsh had condemned the farming project; but the opinion at Mainhill was not so unfavourable. If a good farm could be found, his brother Alexander was ready to undertake to set it going. His mother or a sister would manage the house and dairy. To his father, who was experienced in such matters, that Tom should take to them as he had done appeared neither wild nor unfeasible. He might, indeed, go back to Edinburgh and take pupils again. Mr. Buller was prepared to send his son Arthur to him, and go on with the 200*l.* a-year. One of the Stracheys might come, and there were hopes of others; but Carlyle hated the drudgery of teaching, and was longing for fresh air and freedom.

He had sent 'Schiller' to his mother.

The point next to be considered (he wrote to her) is what shall be done with the author of this mighty work? He is a deserving youth, with a clear conscience, but a bad bad stomach. What shall be done with him? After much consideration, I had resolved in the first instance to *come home.* Irving wants a week of talk with me before I go. By the time that is done I shall have settled my affairs here, taken leave of the good people, and be about ready to take flight. I am not coming by sea, so take no thought of it. My last voyage satisfied me with sailing; with regard to my subsequent proceedings there must be some consideration, but not an hour of loitering. I have set out before my mind distinctly what I *want :* and this, as Goethe says, is half the game. I *will recover my health*, though all the books in the universe should go to smoke in the process. I will be a whole man ; no longer a piping, pining wretch, though I should knap stones by the wayside for a living. I had some thoughts of setting up house at Edinburgh, and taking two or three pupils whose education I might superintend at college. But I already perceive this project will not suit my chief purpose ; I recur to the old plan of farming and living in the country. This I really think might be made to do. What might hinder Alick and me to take a farm and move to it with you and some other of the younkers, furnishing up an apartment in the house for my writing operations, and going on in our several vocations with all imaginable energy ? You must take counsel with the whole senate on this matter. I *must* have a house of my own (a bit haddin o' my ain ——), where I can enjoy quiet and free air, and have liberty to do as I list ; and I see no scheme so likely in the actual state of matters as this. Tell Alick to look about him on all sides for such a thing ; a farm with a comfortable house to live in, and at a rent which we can front. I shall have 200*l.* in my pocket when I return, notwithstanding the horrible expensiveness of this place ; and that, with what we have already, ought to put us on some sort of footing. Were we once begun I could write at a moderate rate without injuring myself, and make a handsome enough thing of it within the year. And for my health, with riding, gardening, and so forth, it would to a certainty improve. Could I live without taking drugs for three months, I should even now be perfectly well. But drenching oneself with castor oil and other abominations, how can one be otherwise than weak and feckless ? I must and will come out of this despicable state ; nor on the whole have I any great doubts about succeeding. Often of late I have even begun to look upon my long dismal seven years of pain as a sort of blessing in disguise. It has kept me clear of many temptations to degrade myself; and really when I look back on my former state of mind, I scarcely see how, except by sickness or some most grinding calamity, I could have been delivered out of it into the state proper for a man in this world. Truly, as you say, the ways of that Being who guides our destiny are wonderful, and past finding out. Let us trust that for all of us this will prove the best.

The start of Schiller in the trade was less favourable than had been looked for, and the offers from the book-sellers for future work, when they came to be specified, were not satisfactory. Carlyle in consequence formed an ill opinion of these poor gentlemen.

The booksellers of the universe (he said) are bipeds of an erect form and speak articulately; therefore they deserve the name of men, and from me at least shall always get it. But for the rest, their thoughts are redolent of 'solid pudding.' They are as the pack-horses of literature; which the author should direct with a halter and a goad, and remunerate with clover and split beans. Woe to him if the process is reversed; if he, with a noose about his neck, is tied to their unsightly tail, and made to plash and sprawl along with them through every *stank* to which their love of provant leads them. Better it were to be a downright hairy cuddy, and crop thistles and gorse on any of the commons of this isle.

He was more successful in making an arrangement with the publishers of ' Wilhelm Meister ' for further transla-tions. It was arranged that he should furnish them with selections from Goethe, Tieck, Hoffmann, Jean Paul, and several others, enough to form the considerable book, which appeared in the following year, in four volumes, as speci-mens of German romance. With this work definitely in prospect, which he felt that he could execute with ease as a mechanical task, Carlyle left London at the beginning of March, and left it with dry eyes. He regretted nothing in it but Irving; and Irving having taken now to inter-pretation of prophecy, and falling daily into yet wilder speculations, was almost lost to him. Their roads had long been divergent—Irving straying into the land of dreams, Carlyle into the hard region of unattractive truth, which as yet presented itself to him in its sternest form.

The distance was becoming too wide for intimacy, although their affection for each other, fed on recollections of what had been, never failed either of them. Carlyle went down to Scotland, staying a day or two at Birmingham, and another at Manchester to see an old school-fellow. When the coach brought him to Ecclefechan he found waiting for him his little sister Jane, the poetess, who had been daily watching for his arrival. 'Her bonny little blush,' he wrote long after, ' and radiancy of look when I let down the window and suddenly disclosed myself, are still present to me.'

His relation with his family was always beautiful. They had been busy for him in his absence, and had already secured what he was longing after. Two miles from Mainhill, on the brow of a hill, on the right as you look towards the Solway, stands an old ruined building with uncertain traditions attached to it, called the Tower of Repentance. Some singular story lies hidden in the name, but authentic record there is none. The Tower only remains visible far away from the high slopes which rise above Ecclefechan. Below the Tower is the farm-house of Hoddam Hill, with a few acres of tolerable land attached to it. The proprietor, General Sharpe, was the landlord of whom the Carlyles held Mainhill. It had been occupied by General Sharpe's factor; but the factor wishing to leave, they had taken it at the moderate rent of 100*l.* a year for 'Tom,' and Alick was already busy putting in the crops, and the mother and sisters preparing the house to receive him. They would have made a home for him among themselves, and all from eldest to youngest would have done everything that affection could prompt to make him happy. But the narrow space, the early hours, the noises inseparable from the active work of a busy household, above all, the necessity of accommodating himself to the habits of a large family, were among the evils which he reckoned that he must avoid. He required a home of his own where he could be master of everything about him, and sit or move, sleep or rise, eat or fast, as he pleased, with no established order of things to interfere with him. Thus Hoddam Hill was taken for him, and there he prepared to settle himself.

This morning (he wrote to Miss Welsh from Mainhill on March 23) they woke me with the tumult of loading carts with apparatus for Hoddam, a farm of which I, or brother Alick for me, am actually tenant. Think of this and reverence my *savoir faire*. I have been to see the place, and I like it well so far as I am interested in it. There is a good house where I may establish myself in comfortable quarters. The views from it are superb. There are hard smooth roads to gallop on towards any point of the compass, and ample space to dig and prune under the pure canopy of a wholesome sky. The ancient Tower of Repentance stands on a corner of the farm, a fit memorial for reflecting sinners. My mother and two little sisters go with us at Whitsunday—we expect them to manage well. Here, then, will I establish my home till I have conquered the fiend that harasses me, and afterwards my place of retreat till some more suitable one shall come within my reach.

Miss Welsh had promised that as soon as he was settled she would pay him and his mother a visit at Hoddam, that she might become acquainted with her future relations, and see with her eyes the kind of home which he was inviting her to share with him. His own imagination had made it into fairyland.

I will show you (he wrote) Kirkconnell churchyard and Fair Helen's grave. I will take you to the top of Burnswark and wander with you up and down the woods and lanes and moors. Earth, sea, and air are open to us here as well as anywhere. The water of Milk [1] was flowing through its simple valley as early as the brook Siloa, and poor Repentance Hill is as old as Caucasus itself. There is a majesty and mystery in nature, take her as you will. The essence of all poetry comes breathing to a mind that

---

[1] One of the small tributaries of the Annan.

feels from every province of her empire. Is she not immovable, eternal and immense in Annandale as she is in Chamouni? The chambers of the East are opened in every land, and the sun comes forth to sow the earth with orient pearl. Night, the ancient mother, follows him with her diadem of stars; and Arcturus and Orion call *me* into the Infinitudes of space as they called the Druid priest or the shepherd of Chaldea. Bright creatures! how they gleam like spirits through the shadows of innumerable ages from their thrones in the boundless depths of heaven.

> Who ever gazed upon them shining,
> And turned to earth without repining,
> Nor wished for wings to fly away
> To mix with their ethereal ray.

The calm grace and even loveliness of this passage goes further than all his arguments to justify Carlyle's longing for a country home among his own people. It was already telling on the inmost fibres of his nature, and soothing into sleep the unquiet spirits that tormented him.

I avoid as far as possible quoting passages from the 'Reminiscences,' preferring the contemporary record of his letters which were written at the time; and because what is already there related does not need repeating. But in this year, when he was living among his own people, the letters are wanting, and one brief extract summing up the effects and experiences of the life at Hoddam may here be permitted.

Hoddam Hill was a neat compact little farm, rent 100*l*., which my father had leased for me, on which was a prettyish little cottage for dwelling house; and from the window such a view (fifty miles in radius from beyond Tyndale to beyond St. Bees, Solway Firth and all the fells to Ingleborough inclusive) as Britain or the world could hardly have matched. Here the ploughing, &c., was already in progress which I often rode across to see. Here I established myself,[1] set up my books and bits of implements, and took to doing German romance as my daily work—ten pages daily my stint, which I faithfully accomplished, barring some rare acci-

---

[1] May 26, 1825.

dents. Brother Alick was my practical farmer; my ever kind and beloved mother with one of the little girls was generally there. Brother John too, oftenest, who had just taken his degree—these with a little man and ditto maid were our establishment. . . . This year has a rustic dignity and beauty to me, and lies now like a not ignoble russet-coated idyll in my memory; one of the quietest on the whole, and, perhaps, the most triumphantly important of my life. I lived very silent, diligent, had long solitary rides on my wild Irish horse Larry, good for the dietetic part. My meditatings, musings, and reflections were continual; my thoughts went wandering or travelling through eternity, though time and space so far as poor I had scanned or known, and were now to my infinite solacement coming back with tidings to me. This year I found that I had conquered all my scepticisms, agonising doubtings, fearful wrestlings with the foul, vile, and soul-murdering mud-gods of my epoch; had escaped as from a worse than Tartarus, with all its Phlegethons and Stygian quagmires, and was emerging free in spirit into the eternal blue of ether, where, blessed be Heaven, I have, for the spiritual part, ever since lived, looking down upon the welterings of my poor fellow-creatures in such multitudes and millions still stuck in that fatal element, and have had no concern whatever in their Puseyisms, ritualisms, metaphysical controversies and cobwebberies, and no feeling of my own except honest silent pity for the serious or religious part of them, and occasional indignation for the poor world's sake at the frivolous, secular, and impious part with their universal suffrages, their nigger emancipations, sluggard and scoundrel protection societies, and unexampled prosperities for the time being. What my pious joy and gratitude then was, let the pious soul figure. In a fine and veritable sense, I, poor, obscure, without outlook, almost without worldly hope, had become independent of the world. What was death itself from the world to what I had come through? I understood well what the old Christian people meant by conversion—by God's infinite mercy to them. I had in effect gained an immense victory, and for a number of years, in spite of nerves and chagrins, had a constant inward happiness that was quite royal and supreme, in which all temporal evil was transient and insignificant, and which essentially remains with me still, though far oftener eclipsed, and lying deeper down than then. Once more, thank Heaven for its highest gift. I then felt, and still feel, endlessly indebted to Goethe in the business. He in his fashion, I perceived, had travelled the steep rocky road before me—the first of the moderns. Bodily health itself seemed improving. Bodily health was all I had really lost in the grand spiritual battle now gained; and that too I may have hoped would gradually return altogether—which it never did, and was far enough from doing. Meanwhile my thoughts were very peaceable, full of pity and humanity as they had never been before. Nowhere can I recollect of myself such pious musings, communings silent and spontaneous with fact and nature, as in those poor Annandale localities. The sound of the kirk-bell once or twice on Sunday mornings (from Hoddam kirk, about a mile on the plains below me) was strangely touching, like the departing voice of eighteen hundred years.[1]

The industry which Carlyle describes did not show itself immediately on his settlement at Hoddam. The excitement of the winter months had left him exhausted; and for the first few weeks at least he was recovering himself in an idleness which showed itself in the improvement of his humour. In *June* he wrote to Miss Welsh:—

I am gradually and steadily gathering health, and for my occupations they amount to zero. It is many a weary year since I have been so idle or so happy. I read Richter and Jacobi; I ride and hoe cabbages, and, like Basil Montagu, am 'a lover of all quiet things.' Sometimes something in the shape of conscience says to me, 'You will please to observe, Mr. Tummas, that time is flying fast away, and you are poor and ignorant and unknown, and verging towards nine and twenty.[2] What is to become of you in the long run, Mr. Tummas? Are you not partly of opinion that you are an ass? The world is running past you. You are out of the battle altogether, my pretty sir: no promotion, knowledge, money, glory!' To which I answer, 'And what the devil is the matter? What have knowledge, money, glory, done for me hitherto? Time, you say, is flying. Let it fly; twice as fast if it likes.' I hope this humour will not be my final one. It is rather a holy time—a *pax Dei*, which exhausted nature has conquered for herself from all the fiends that assaulted and beset her. As strength returns, the battle will again commence; yet never I trust with such fateful

[1] *Reminiscences*, p. 226 *et seq.*
[2] Thirty—he was born December 4, 1795.

eagerness as of old. I see the arena of my life lying round me desolate and quiet as the ashes of Mount Ætna. Flowers and verdure will again spring over its surface. But I know that fire is still beneath it, and that it, or I, have no foundation or endurance. Oh human life! Oh soul of man! But my paper is concluded.

Carlyle could not long be idle. The weariness passed off. He took up his translating work, and went on with it as he has related. An accident meanwhile precipitated the relations between himself and Miss Welsh, which had seemed likely to be long protracted, and, after threatening to separate them for ever, threw them more completely one upon the other.

When Irving first settled in London he had opened the secrets of his heart to a certain lady with whom he was very intimately acquainted. He had told her of his love for his old pupil, and she had drawn from him that the love had been returned. She had seen Irving sacrifice himself to duty, and she had heard that his resolution had been sustained by the person to whom the surrender of their mutual hopes had been as bitter as to himself. The lady was romantic, and had become profoundly interested. Flowing over with sympathy, she had herself commenced a correspondence with Haddington. To Carlyle she wrote occasionally, because she really admired him. To Miss Welsh she introduced herself as one who was eager for her confidence, who was prepared to love her for the many excellences which she knew her to possess, and to administer balm to the wounds of her heart.

Miss Welsh did not respond very cordially to this effusive invitation. It was not her habit to seek for sympathy from strangers; but she replied in a letter which her new friend found extremely beautiful, and which stirred her interest still deeper. The lady imagined that her young correspondent was still pining in secret for her lost lover, and she was tempted to approach closer to the subject which had aroused her sympathies. She thought it would be well slightly to disparage Irving. She painted him as a person whose inconstancy did not deserve a prolonged and hopeless affection. She too had sought to find in him the dearest of friends; but he had other interests and other ambitions, and any woman who concentrated her heart upon him would be disappointed in the return which she might meet with.

The lady's motive was admirable. She thought that she could assist in reconciling Miss Welsh to her disappointment. In perfect innocence she wrote confidentially to Carlyle on the same subject. She regarded him simply as the intimate friend both of Miss Welsh and Irving. She assumed that he was acquainted with their secret history. She spoke of the affection which had existed between them as still unextinguished on either side. For the sake of both of them she wished that something might be done to put an end to idle regrets and vain imaginings. Nothing she thought could contribute more to disenchant Miss Welsh than a visit to herself in London, where she could see Irving as he was in his present surroundings.[1]

Miss Welsh had for two years never mentioned Irving to Carlyle except bitterly and contemptuously; so bitterly indeed that he had often been obliged to remonstrate. Had he been less singleminded, a tone so marked and acid might have roused his suspicions. But that Irving and she had been more than friends, if he had ever heard a hint of it, had passed out of his mind. Even the lady's letter failed to startle him. He mentioned merely, when he next wrote to her, that the writer laboured under some strange

[1] No part of this language is the lady's own. The substance of her letters was repeated in the correspondence which followed between Carlyle and Miss Welsh. I have alluded to the subject only because Mrs. Carlyle said afterwards that but for the unconscious action of a comparative stranger her engagement with Carlyle would probably never have been carried out.

delusion about her secret history, and had told him in a letter full of eloquence that her heart was with Irving in London.

Miss Welsh felt that she must at least satisfy her ec- static acquaintance that she was not pining for another woman's husband. She was even more explicit. She had made up her mind to marry Carlyle. She told her intru- sive correspondent so in plain words, desiring her only to keep her secret. The lady was thunderstruck. In ordi- nary life she was high-flown, and by those who did not know her might have been thought affected and unreal ; but on occasions really serious she could feel and write like a wise woman. She knew that Miss Welsh could not love Carlyle. The motive could only be a generous hope of making life dearer, and want of health more endurable, to an honest and excellent man, while she might be seek- ing blindly to fill a void which was aching in her own heart. She required Miss Welsh, she most solemnly ad- jured her, to examine herself, and not allow one who had known much disappointment and many sorrows to dis- cover by a comparison of his own feelings with hers that she had come to him with half a heart, and had mistaken compassion and the self-satisfaction of a generous act for a sentiment which could alone sustain her in a struggle through life. Supposing accident should set Irving free, supposing his love to have been indestructible and to have been surrendered only in obedience to duty, and suppos- ing him, not knowing of this new engagement, to come back and claim the heart from which an adverse fate had separated him, what in such a case would her feeling be ? If she could honestly say that she would still prefer Car- lyle, then let her marry him, and the sooner the better. If, on the other hand, she was obliged to confess to her- self that she could still find happiness where she had hoped to find it, Irving might still be lost to her ; but in such a condition of mind she had no right to marry any-one else.

With characteristic integrity Miss Welsh, on receiving this letter, instantly enclosed it to Carlyle. She had been under no obligation, at least until their marriage had been definitely determined on, to inform him of the extent of her attachment to Irving. But sincere as she was to a fault in the ordinary occasions of life, she had in this matter not only kept back the truth, but had purposely misled Carlyle as to the nature of her feelings. She felt that she must make a full confession. She had deceived him — wilfully deceived him. She had even told him that she had never cared for Irving. 'It was false,' she said. She had loved him—once passionately loved him. For this she might be forgiven. 'If she had shown weakness in loving a man whom she knew to be engaged to another, she had made amends in persuading him to marry the other, and save his honour from reproach.' But she had disguised her real feelings, and for this she had no excuse. She who had felt herself Carlyle's superior in their late controversy, and had been able to rebuke him for selfishness, felt herself degraded and humbled in his eyes. If he chose to cast her off, she said that she could not say he was unjust; but her pride was broken; and very naturally, very touchingly, she added that he had never been so dear to her as at that moment when she was in danger of losing his affection and, what was still more precious to her, his respect.

If Carlyle had been made of common stuff, so unex-pected a revelation might have tried his vanity. The actual effect was to awaken in him a sense of his own un-worthiness. He perceived that Miss Welsh was probably accepting him only out of the motives which Mrs. Mon-tagu suggested. His infirmities, mental and bodily, might make him an unfit companion for her or indeed for any

woman. It would be better for her once for all to give
him up. He knew, he said, that he could never make her
happy. They might suffer at parting, but they would
have obeyed their reason, and time would deaden the
pain. No affection was unalterable or eternal. Men
themselves, with all their passions, sank to dust and were
consumed. He must imitate her sincerity. He said (and
he spoke with perfect truth) that there was a strange,
dark humour in him over which he had no control. If
she thought they were 'blue devils, weak querulous wail-
ings of a mind distempered,' she would only show that she
did not understand him. In a country town she had seen
nothing of life, and had grasped at the shadows that passed
by her. First, the rude, smoky fire of Edward Irving
seemed to her a star from heaven ; next, the quivering
ignis fatuus of the soul that dwelt in himself. The
world had a thousand noble hearts that she did not dream
of. What was he, and what was his father's house, that
she should sacrifice herself for him ?

It was not in nature—it was not at least in Miss Welsh's
nature—that at such a time and under such circumstances
she should reconsider her resolution. She was staying
with her grandfather at Templand when these letters were
interchanged. She determined to use the opportunity to
pay the Carlyles her promised visit, see him in his own
home and his own circle, and there face to face explain all
the past and form some scheme for the immediate future.
Like the lady in London, she felt that if the marriage was
to be, or rather since the marriage was to be, the sooner it
was over now the better for everyone. Carlyle was to
have met her on the road, and was waiting with horses ;
but there had been a mistake. She was dropped by the
coach the next morning at Kelhead Kilns, from which
she sent him a little characteristic note.

Kelhead Kilns : Friday, September 3, 1825.

Good morning, Sir. I am not at all to blame for your disappointment last night. The fault was partly your own, and still more the landlady's of the Commercial Inn, as I shall presently demonstrate to you *vivâ voce*. In the meantime I have billeted myself in a snug little house by the wayside, where I purpose remaining with all imaginable patience till you can make it convenient to come and fetch me, being afraid to proceed directly to Hoddam Hill in case so sudden an apparition should throw the whole family into hysterics. If the pony has any prior engagement, never mind. I can make a shift to walk two miles in pleasant company. Any way, pray make all possible despatch, in case the owner of these premises should think I intend to make a regular settlement in them.   Yours,
                                                                        JANE.

The great secret, which had been known from the first to Mrs. Carlyle and suspected by the rest, was now the open property of the family ; and all, old and young, with mixed feelings of delight and anxiety, were looking forward to the appearance of the lady who was soon to belong to them.

She stayed with us above a week (Carlyle writes), happy, as was very evident, and making happy. Her demeanour among us I could define as unsurpassable, spontaneously perfect. From the first moment all embarrassment, even my mother's, as tremulous and anxious as she naturally was, fled away without return. Everybody felt the all-pervading simple grace, the perfect truth and perfect trustfulness of that beautiful, cheerful, intelligent, and sprightly creature, and everybody was put at his ease. The questionable visit was a clear success. She and I went riding about, the weather dry and grey, nothing ever going wrong with us ; my guidance taken as beyond criticism ; she ready for any pace, rapid or slow, melodious talk never wanting. Of course she went to Mainhill, and made complete acquaintance with my father (whom she much esteemed and even admired, now and henceforth—a *reciprocal* feeling, strange enough), and with my two elder sisters, Margaret and Mary, who now officially kept house with my father there. On the whole, she came to know us all, saw face to face us and the rugged peasant element and way of life we had; and was *not* afraid of it, but recognised, like her noble self, what of intrinsic worth it might have, what of real human dignity. She charmed all hearts, and was herself visibly glad and happy, right loath to end these halcyon days, eight or perhaps nine the utmost appointed sum of them.

Two little anecdotes she used to tell of this visit, showing that under peasant's dresses there was in the Carlyles the essential sense of delicate high breeding. She was to use the girls' room at Mainhill while there; and it was rude enough in its equipments as they lived in it. Margaret Carlyle, doing her little best, had spread on the deal table for a cover a precious new shawl which some friend had given her. More remarkable was her reception by the father. When she appeared he was in his rough dress, called in from his farm work on the occasion. The rest of the family kissed her. The old man to her surprise drew back, and soon left the room. In a few minutes he came back again, fresh shaved and washed, and in his Sunday clothes. Now, he said, if Miss Welsh allows it, I am in a condition to kiss her too. When she left Hoddam, Carlyle attended her back to Dumfries.

As I rode with her (he says) she did not attempt to conceal her sorrow, and indeed our prospect ahead was cloudy enough. I could only say 'Espérons, espérons.' To her the Haddington element had grown dreary and unfruitful; no geniality of life possible there, and I doubt not many paltry frets and contradictions. We left our horses at the Commercial Inn; I walked with her, not in gay mood either, to her grandmother's threshold, and there had to say farewell. In my whole life I can recollect no week so like a Sabbath as that had been to me—clear, peaceful, mournfully beautiful, and as if sacred.

A few days after she was gone Carlyle wrote the following entry in his most intermittent journal:—

Hoddam Hill, September 21, 1825.—*A hiatus valde deflendus.* Since the last line was written, what a wandering to and fro! how many sad vicissitudes of despicable suffering and inaction have I undergone! This little book and the desk that carries it have passed a summer and winter in London since I last opened it; and I, their foolish owner, have roamed about the brick-built Babylon, the sooty Brummagem, and Paris, the Vanity Fair of our modern world. My mood of mind is changed. Is it improved? *Weiss nicht.* This stagnation is not peace; or is it the peace of Galgacus's Romans: 'Ubi solitudinem faciunt, pacem appellant.' How difficult it is to free one's mind from cant! How very seldom are the principles we act on clear to our own reason! Of the great nostrums, 'forgetfulness of self' and 'humbling of vanity,' it were better therefore to say nothing. In my speech concerning them I overcharge the impression they have made on me, for my conscience, like my sense of pain and pleasure, has grown dull, and *I secretly desire to compensate for laxity of feeling by intenseness of describing.* How much of these great nostrums is the product of necessity? Am I like a sorry hack, content to feed on heather while rich clover seems to lie around it at a little distance, because in struggling to break the tether it has almost hanged itself? Oh that I could go out of the body to philosophise! that I could ever feel as of old the glory and magnificence of things, till my own little *Me* (*mein kleines Ich*) was swallowed up and lost in them. (Partly cant!) But I cannot, I cannot. Shall I ever more? *Gott Weiss.* At present I am but an *abgerissenes Glied,* a limb torn off from the family of man, excluded from acting, with pain for my companion, and hope, that comes to all, rarely visiting me, and, what is stranger, rarely desired with vehemence. Unhappy man, in whom the body has gained the mastery over the soul! Inverse sensualist, not drawn into the rank of beasts by pleasure, but driven into it by pain! Hush! hush! Perhaps this *is* the truce which weary nature has conquered for herself to re-collect her scattered strength. Perhaps, like an eagle (or a goose) she will 'renew her mighty youth' and fly against the sun; or at least fish haddocks with equanimity, like other birds of similar feather, and no more lie among the pots, winged, maimed, and plucked, doing nothing but chirp like a chicken in the croup for the livelong day. 'Jook and let the jaw gae by,' my pretty sir. When this solitude becomes intolerable to you it will be time enough to quit it for the dreary blank which society and the bitterest activity have hitherto afforded you. You deserve considerable pity, **Mr. C.,** and likewise considerable contempt. Heaven be your comforter, my worthy sir! You are in a promising condition at this present: sinking to the bottom, yet laid down to sleep; destruction brandishing his sword above you, and you quietly desiring him to take your life but spare your rest. *Gott hilf Ihnen!* Now for Tieck and his Runenberg. But first one whiff of generous narcotic. 'How gladly we love to wander on the plain with the summit in our eye!' *Ach Du meine Einzige die Du mich liebst und Dich an mich anschmiegst, warum bin ich Dir wie ein gebrochenes Rohr! Sollst Du niemals glücklich werden? Wo bist Du heute Nacht? Mögen Friede und Liebe und Hoffnung deine Gefährten seyn! Leb' wohl.*

CHAPTER XVIII.

A.D. 1825. ÆT. 30.

Miss Welsh had now seen with her own eyes the realities of life in a small Scotch farm, and was no longer afraid of it. She doubtless distrusted as much as ever Carlyle's fitness in his own person for agricultural enterprises. But if his brother would take the work off his hands he could himself follow his own more proper occupations. She had recognised the sterling worth of his peasant family, and for her own part she was willing to share their method of existence, sharply contrasted as it was with the elegance and relative luxury of her home at Haddington. It was far otherwise with her mother. Mrs. Welsh's romantic days were not over. They were never over to the end of her life; but she had no romance about Carlyle. She knew better than her daughter how great the sacrifice would be, and the experience of fifty years had taught her that resolutions adopted in enthusiasm are often repented of when excitement has been succeeded by the wearing duties of hard every-day routine. She was a cultivated, proud, beautiful woman, who had ruled as queen in the society of a Scotch provincial town. Many suitors had presented themselves for her daughter's hand, unexceptionable in person, in fortune, in social standing. Miss Welsh's personal attractions, her talents, the fair if moderate fortune which, though for the present she had surrendered it, must be eventually her own, would have entitled her to choose among the most eligible matches in East Lothian. It was natural, it was inevitable, independ-

ent of selfish considerations, that she could not look without a shudder on this purposed marriage with the son of a
poor Dumfriesshire farmer, who had no visible prospects
and no profession, and whose abilities, however great they
might be, seemed only to unfit him for any usual or profitable pursuit. Added to this, Carlyle himself had not attracted her. She was accustomed to rule, and Carlyle
would not be ruled. She had obstinate humours, and
Carlyle, who never checked his own irritabilities, was impatient and sarcastic when others ventured to be unreasonable. She had observed and justly dreaded the violence
of his temper, which when he was provoked or thwarted
would boil like a geyser. He might repent afterwards of
these ebullitions; he usually did repent. But repentance
could not take away the sting of the passionate expressions, which fastened in the memory by the metaphors
with which they were barbed, especially as there was no
amendment, and the offence was repeated on the next
temptation. It will easily be conceived, therefore, that
the meeting between mother and daughter after the Hoddam visit, and Miss Welsh's announcement of her final
resolution, was extremely painful. Miss Welsh wrote to
Carlyle an account of what had passed. His letter in
reply bears the same emblem of the burning candle, with
the motto, '*Terar dum prosim,*' which he had before
sketched in his journal. He was fond of a design which
represented human life to him under its sternest aspect.'

To Miss Welsh.

Hoddam Hill: November 4, 1825.

. . . Let us be patient and resolute, and trust in ourselves and
each other. I maintain that the weal of every human being, not
perhaps his enjoyment or his suffering, but his true and highest
welfare, lies within himself. Oh that we had wisdom to put this
weighty truth in practice: to know our duty—for a duty every liv-

[1] See p. 159.

ing creature has—and to do it with our whole heart and our whole soul. This is the everlasting rock of man's security against which no tempest or flood shall prevail. ' Sufficiently provided for within,' the outward gifts or amercements of fortune are but the soft or the hard materials out of which he is to build his fairest work of art, a life worthy of himself and the vocation wherewith he is called. But I am verging towards cant, so I shall hasten to the right about.

Your mother is not wise or just in spoiling the stinted enjoyments of your present way of life by the reflections and remonstrances with which she pursues you. Her views of me and my connection with you I cannot justly blame : they coincide too nearly with my own. But what, one might ask her, does she mean you to *do ?* Anything ? If so, it were better that she simply proposed it, and backed it out by all attainable reasons in simplicity and quiet, that if just and fit you might go through with it at all haps and hazards instantly and completely. If nothing, then silence is the least that can be asked of her. Speech that leads not to action, still more that hinders it, is a nuisance on the earth. Let *us* remember this, as well as call on others to remember it. But, after all, where is the mighty grief ? *Is* it ruin for you to think of giving yourself to me, here as I am, in the naked undissembled meanness of my actual state ? Consider this with a cold clear eye, not in the purple light of love, but in the sharp still light of prudence. If your mind still have any wavering, follow the truth fearlessly, not heeding me, for I am ready with alacrity to forward your anticipated happiness in any way. Or was this your love of me no girlish whim, but the calm, deliberate self-offering of a woman to the man whom her reason and her heart had made choice of ? Then is it a crime in you to love me, whose you are in the sight of God and man ?

The story of my temper is not worth much. I actually do not think myself an ill-natured man, nor even, all things considered, very ill-tempered ! Really it is wearisome to think of these things. What counsel to give you I know not. Submission has its limits. When not based on conviction it degenerates into hypocrisy, and encourages demands which perhaps ought to be resisted. But in asserting your rights be meek and reasonable. What is this caprice and sullenness in your mother but unhappiness in herself—an effort to increase her own scanty stock of satisfaction at your expense ; or rather to shift a portion of her own suffering upon you ? She *cannot* cease to love you, and this is saying much. For me I beg you to take no thought. Her anger at me, her aversion to me, shall never be remembered against her. She thinks of me in the main, to the full as highly as she ought ; and these gusts of unreasonable caprice should be met by increased equability, and steady forgiving self-possession, as angry gusts of wind are rendered harmless not by other conflicting gusts, but by a solid wall of stone and mortar.

While on the Haddington side the contemplated alliance was so distasteful, two letters from Miss Welsh, one to Carlyle's mother, the other to his little sister Jane, show how playfully and prettily she had thrown herself into the ways of the Mainhill household, and adopted their expressions. With Jane she had assumed the privilege of an elder sister, and charged herself with the direction of her education. Carlyle has written a short preface to each.

To Mrs. Carlyle, Hoddam Hill.

[There are snatches of *coterie* speech in this letter, two quite of new date, brought from Hoddam Hill, which I must explain.

'Broad Atlantic of his countenance' was a phrase I had noticed in some stupidly adoring 'Life of Fox,' and been in use to apply to my brother John, whose face also was broad enough (and full of honesty and good humour, poor fellow!). From him also comes the other phrase, ' mixture of good and evil.' He was wont in his babbly way, while at breakfast with mother and me, to remark when the least thing was complained of or went wrong, 'Nothing but evil in the world, mother!' till one day mother took him sharply up on theological grounds. Ever onward from which he used to make it 'Nothing but a mixture of good and evil.' He had many mock utterances of this kind. 'Comes all to the same ultimately,' 'What d'ye think of life this morning ?' &c., over which we had our laughing and counter-laughing, borne with perfect gravity always, and perfect patience, but producing no abatement of the practice. One morning, however, he did get a retort, which rather stuck to him. Addressing his mother with 'What d'ye think of life, mother ?' 'What does t'ou (thou) think o' death tho'?' answered she with a veritably serious and crypto-contemptuous tone, which was not forgotten again.

'Christian *comfoart*' comes from a certain Mrs. Carruthers of Haregills, a cousin of my mother; Bell by maiden name, solid, rather stupid, farmer's wife by station. Meeting once with Frank Dickson (a speculative Tartar he, unluckily for her), she had been heard to wind up some lofty lilt with, 'Sir, it is the great *soorce* of Christian *comfoart*,' accent on the last syllable and sound *oa*, Annandale only.—T. C.]

George Square, Edinburgh: November 14.

My dear Mrs. Carlyle,—In the busy idleness of my present situation I have little leisure to write or to do any rational thing; but it is best I should fulfil my promise to you *now* rather than wait for a more quiet season, that you may know that even the turmoil of a great city cannot seduce me into forgetfulness of the Hill. Indeed, the more I am in the way of what is commonly called pleasure, the more I think of the calm days which I spent under your roof. I have never been so happy since; though I have been at several fine entertainments, where much thought and pains and money were expended to assemble the ingredients of enjoyment; and this is no wise strange, since affection is the native element of my soul, and *that* I found in your cottage warm and pure, while in more splendid habitations it is chilled with vanity, affectation, and selfishness. For 'there is nothing but a mixture of good and evil in the world, mother;' and thus some have 'the dinner of herbs where love is,' others 'the stalled ox and hatred therewith.'

I left Templand on Thursday last after many delays, but in no such downcast mood as at my departure from the Hill. Indeed, I was never in my life more pleased to turn my face homewards, where, if I have not suitable society any more than in Nithsdale, I can at least enjoy what is next best, solitude. But all my impatience to see Haddington failed to make the journey hither agreeable, which was as devoid of 'Christian comfoart' as anything you can suppose. Never was poor damsel reduced to such 'extremities of fate.' I was sick, woefully sick, and notwithstanding that I had on four petticoats, benumbed with cold. To make my wretchedness as complete as possible, we did not reach Edinburgh till many hours after dark. Sixteen miles more, and my wanderings for this season are at an end. Would that my trials were ended also! But no! Tell Mr. Carlyle my handsome cousin is coming to Haddington with his sister Phoebe, and his valet Henley, and his great dog Toby, over and above Dash,

Craigen, Fanny, and Frisk. My heart misgives me at the prospect of this inundation of company, for their ways are not my ways, and what is amusement to them is death to me. But I must just be patient as usual. Verily I should need to be Job, instead of Jane Welsh, to bear these everlasting annoyances with any degree of composure.

Mr. Carlyle must write next week without fail to Haddington, lest in vexation of spirit I curse God and die. Moreover, he must positively part with Larry, and get a horse of less *genius* in his stead, if he would not have me live in continual terror of his life.[1] If the fates are kind, and the good doctor[2] a man of his word, he will be in this city to-morrow, so that I have some hope to feast my eyes on 'the broad Atlantic of his countenance,' and hear all about my dear friends at the Hill before I go. How does Jane's Latin prosper? Tell her to write a postscript in her brother's next letter. You must excuse this hurried epistle. I am writing under many eyes and in the noise of many tongues. God bless you.

I am always affectionately yours,

JANE B. WELSH.

The next letter is to Jean Carlyle, which is prefaced by Carlyle thus.

This Jean Carlyle is my second youngest sister, then a little child of twelve. The youngest sister, youngest of us all, was Jenny (Janet), now Mrs. Robert Hanning, in Hamilton, Canada West. These little beings in their bits of grey speckled (black and white) straw bonnets, I recollect as a pair of neat brisk items, tripping about among us that summer at the Hill, especially Jean (only by euphemism Jane), the bigger of the two, who was a constant quantity there. The small Jenny (I think in some pet) had unexpectedly flung herself off and preferred native independence at Mainhill. Jean, from her black eyes and hair, had got the name of 'Craw Jean' among us, or often of 'Craw' simply. That was

---

[1] Larry had run away with Carlyle, thrown him, and dragged him some yards along the road. He rode up to a late period in his life; but he always had a loose seat, and his mind was busy with anything but attending to his horse. Fritz, his last, a present from Lady Ashburton, carried him safely for many years through the London streets, to the astonishment of most of his friends. I asked him once how he had escaped misadventure. 'It was Fritz,' he said. 'He was a very sensible fellow. I suppose he had not been brought up to think that the first duty of a horse was to say something witty.'

[2] John Carlyle.

my mother's complexion too ; but the other seven of us, like our father, were all of common blond. Jean was an uncommonly open-minded, gifted, ingenuous, and ingenious little thing, *true* as steel (never told a fib from her birth upwards), had, once or so, shown suddenly a *will* like steel too (when indisputably in the right, as I have heard her mother own to me), otherwise a most loving, cheerful, amenable creature, hungering and thirsting for all kinds of knowledge ; had a lively sense of the ridiculous withal, and already something of what you might call 'humour.' She was by this time in visible favour with me, which doubtless she valued sufficiently. One of the first things I had noted of her was five or six years ago in one of my rustications at Mainhill, when in the summer evenings brothers Alick and John and I used to go out wandering extensively and talking ditto till gloaming settled into dark, always I observed little Craw turned up, either at our starting or somewhere afterwards, trotting at my side, head hardly higher than my knee, but eagerly thrown back and listening with zeal and joy : no kind of 'sport' equal to this, for her, pursuit of knowledge under difficulties. Poor little Craw !

My darling took warmly to her for my sake and the child's own. This was the first time they had met. 'Such a child ought to be educated,' said she, with generous emphasis, and felt steadily, and, indeed, took herself, for some years onwards, a great deal of trouble and practical pains about it, as this letter may still indicate. Little Jean was had to Comely Bank,[1] for a good few months, got her lessons, &c., attended us to Craigenputtock, hoping to try farther there too ; but in the chaos of *incipience* there (a rather dark and even dismal chaos, had not *my* Jane been a daughter of the Sun) this was found impracticable ; and Scotsbrig, father's place,[2] coveting and almost grudging the little Jean's bits of labour within doors and without, she had to give the project up and return to her own way of life, which she loyally did ; grew up a peasant girl, got no further special education, though she has since given herself consciously and otherwise not a little, both of the practical and speculative sort ; and is at this day to be named fairly a superior woman, superior in extent of reading, culture, &c., and still better in veracity of character, sound discernment, and practical wisdom ; wife for above thirty-five years now[3] of

---

[1] Where Carlyle first lived, as will be seen, after his marriage.

[2] To which old Mr. Carlyle removed from Mainhill in the year following.

[3] Written in 1868.

James Aitken, a prosperous, altogether honest, valiant, intelligent and substantial man, house-painter in Dumfries by trade; parents they, too, of my bright little niece, Mary C. Aitken, who copies for me, and helps me all she can in this my final operation in the world.

To Miss Jane Carlyle, Hoddam Hill.

Haddington : November, 1825.

My affectionate Child,—It grieved me to learn from your good little postscript,[1] that the poor Latin was already come to a stand; for I would fain see the talents with which nature has entrusted you not buried in ignorance, but made the most of. Nevertheless, I do not *blame* you, because you have despaired of accomplishing an impossibility; for it *is* impossible for you, sure enough, to make any great attainment of scholarship in the circumstances in which you are already placed. You must on no account, however, abandon the idea of becoming a scholar, for good, because it is beyond your ability to carry it into effect just as soon as you wish; for your circumstances, by the blessing of Heaven, may be in process of time rendered more towardly; but should the noble desire of knowledge die away within you, you would indeed cruelly disappoint my hopes. Moreover, though the acquirement of a foreign language has proved too difficult a matter for you in the time being, I see nothing that there is to hinder you from reading many instructive books in your own. For your mother cannot be so hard a task-mistress, that she would refuse you two hours or so in the day to yourself, provided she saw that they were turned to a profitable account. Here is a copy of Cowper's Poems for you, with which I expect you will presently commence a regular course of reading. Your brother is able, and I am sure will be most willing, to direct you in the choice of books; and on this account you ought to be exceedingly thankful, as many for want of such direction have to seek knowledge by a weary circuit.

Had Providence been less kind to you in the relation you hold in life, you should get many an epistle from me full of the best advices I have to give; for I love you, my good little girl, from the bottom of my heart, and desire earnestly that it should be well with you in this world as well as in the world to come. But when I consider the piety and goodness of the mother who has

---

[1] 'Doubtless of some letter from me.—T. C.'

you in her bosom, and that he whose wisdom I bow myself before is your brother, I feel it idle and presumptuous in me to offer you any counsel, when in the precepts and example of those about you, you have already such a light to your path. Do but continue, my dear Jean, a dutiful daughter and a loving sister, and you are sure to grow up an estimable woman. If we can make you also an accomplished woman, so much the better.

One thing more when I am about it. Look sharp that you fulfil the written promise which you gave me at parting; for know that I am not disposed to remit you the smallest tittle of it. And now God bless and keep you.

I am always your attached friend,
JANE BAILLIE WELSH.

After the bright interlude of Miss Welsh's visit to Hoddam, life soon became as industrious as Carlyle has described. The mornings were spent in work over the German Tales, the afternoons in rides, Larry remaining still in favour notwithstanding his misdemeanours. In the evenings he and his mother perhaps smoked their pipes together, as they used to do at Mainhill, she in admiring anxiety laboring to rescue his soul from the temptations of the intellect; he satisfying her, for she was too willing to be satisfied, that they meant the same thing, though they expressed it in different languages. He was meditating a book, a real book of his own, not a translation, though he was still unable to fasten upon a subject; while the sense that he was in his own house, lord of it and lord of himself, and able if he pleased to shut his door against all comers, was delightful to him.

It is inexpressible (he wrote) what an increase of happiness and of consciousness, wholesome consciousness of inward dignity, I have gained since I came within the walls of this poor cottage— my own four walls—for in this state the primeval law of nature acts on me with double and triple force; and how cheaply it is purchased, and how smoothly managed. They simply admit that I am *Herr im Hause,* and act on this conviction. There is no grumbling about my habitudes and whims. If I choose to dine on fire and brimstone, they will cook it for me to their best skill, thinking only that I am an unintelligible mortal, perhaps in their secret souls a kind of humourist, *facheux* to deal with, but no bad soul after all, and *not* to be dealt with in *any* other way. My own four walls!

This expression, repeated twice, suggests the possible date of a poem—the only poem, perhaps, that Carlyle ever wrote which is really characteristic of him. It was written either at Hoddam or at Craigenputtock. In some respects—in the mention of a wife, especially—it suits Craigenputtock best. But perhaps his imagination was looking forward.

MY OWN FOUR WALLS.

The storm and night is on the waste,
    Wild through the wind the herdsman calls,
As fast on willing nag I haste
    Home to my own four walls.

Black tossing clouds with scarce a glimmer
    Envelope earth like sevenfold palls ;
But wifekin watches, coffee-pot doth simmer,
    Home in my own four walls.

A home and wife I too have got,
    A hearth to blaze whate'er befals ;
What needs a man that I have not
    Within my own four walls ?

King George has palaces of pride,
    And armed grooms must ward those halls ;
With one stout bolt I safe abide
    Within my own four walls.

Not all his men may sever this,
    It yields to friends', not monarchs', calls ;
My whinstone house my castle is—
    I have my own four walls.

When fools or knaves do make a rout
   With gigmen, dinners, balls, cabals,
I turn my back and shut them out;
   These are my own four walls.

The moorland house, though rude it be,
   May stand the brunt when prouder falls;
'Twill screen my wife, my books, and me,
   All in my own four walls.

In the autumn of this year Carlyle had a glimpse of
Irving at Annan.

I had next to no correspondence with Irving (he says); a little
note or so on business, nothing more. Nor was Mrs. Montagu
much more instructive on that head, who wrote me high-sounding
amiable things which I could not but respond to more or less,
though dimly aware of their quality. Nor did the sincere and ardent Mrs. Strachey, who wrote seldomer, almost ever touch upon
Irving. But by some occasional unmelodious clang in all the
newspapers (twice over I think in this year) we could sufficiently
and with little satisfaction construe his way of life. Twice over
he had leapt the barriers and given rise to criticisms of the customary idle sort, loudish universally and nowhere accurately just.
Case first was of preaching to the London Missionary Society
(Missionary I will call it, though it might be 'Bible,' or another).
On their grand anniversary these people had assigned him the
honour of addressing them, and were numerously assembled, expecting some flourishes of eloquence and flatteries to their illus-
trious, divinely blessed society, ingeniously done and especially
with fit brevity; dinner itself waiting, I suppose, close in the rear.
Irving emerged into his speaking place at the due moment; but
instead of treating men and office-bearers to a short, comfortable dose of honey and butter, opened into strict, sharp inquiries,
rhadamanthine expositions of duty and ideal, issuing, perhaps, in
actual criticism and admonition; gall and vinegar instead of
honey; at any rate, keeping the poor people locked up there 'for
above two hours,' instead of an hour or less, with dinners hot at
the end of it. This was much criticised: 'Plainly wrong, and
produced by love of singularity and too much pride in oneself,'
voted everybody. For, in fact, a man suddenly holding up the
naked inexorable ideal in the face of the clothed (and in England

generally plump, comfortable, and pot-bellied) reality is doing an unexpected and questionable thing.

The next escapade was still worse. At some public meeting, probably of the same 'Missionary Society,' Irving again held up his Ideal, I think not without murmurs from former sufferers by it, and ended by solemnly putting down, not his name to the subscription list, but an actual gold watch, which he said had just arrived to him from his beloved brother lately dead in India.[1] That of the gold watch tabled had in reality a touch of rash ostentation, and was bitterly crowed over by all the able editors for a time. On the whole one could gather too clearly that Irving's course was beset with pitfalls, barking dogs, and dangers and difficulties unwarned of; and that for one who took so little counsel with prudence, he perhaps carried his head too high. I had a certain harsh kind of sorrow about poor Irving, and my loss of him (and his loss of me on such poor terms as these seemed to me), but I carelessly trusted in his strength against whatever mistakes and impediments, and felt that for the present it was better to be absolved from corresponding with him.

That same year, late in autumn, he was at Annan only for a night and a day, returning from some farther journey, perhaps to Glasgow or Edinburgh, and had to go on again for London next day. I rode down from Hoddam Hill before nightfall, found him sitting in the snug little parlour beside his father and mother, beautifully domestic. I think it was the last time I ever saw those good old people. We sat only a few minutes, my thoughts sadly contrasting the beautiful affectionate safety here and the wild tempestuous hostilities and perils yonder. He left his blessing to each by name in a low soft voice. There was something almost tragical to me as he turned round, hitting his hat on the little door lintel, and next moment was on the dark street followed only by me. His plan of journey was to catch the Glasgow London mail at Gretna, and to walk thither, the night being dry. We stept over to Robert Dickson's, his brother-in-law's, and sate there still talking for perhaps an hour. He looked sad and serious, not in the least downhearted; told us, probably in answer to some question of mine, that the projected London University seemed to

[1] This brother was John, the eldest of the three, an Indian army surgeon, whom I remember once meeting on a common stair in Edinburgh, on return, I suppose, from a call on some comrade higher up: a taller man than even Edward, and with a blooming, placid, not very intelligent face.

be progressing towards fulfilment, and how, at some meeting, Poet Campbell, arguing loudly for a purely *secular* system, had on sight of Irving entering at once stopped short, and in the politest manner he could, sat down without another word on the subject. 'It will be *un*religious, secretly *anti*-religious all the same,' said Irving to us.

When the time had come for setting out, and we were all on foot, he called for his three little nieces, having their mother by him, made them each successively stand on a chair, laid his hand on the head first of one, with a 'Mary Dickson, the Lord bless you,' then of the next by name, and of the next; 'the Lord bless you,' in a sad, solemn tone, with something of elaborate noticeable in it too; which was painful and dreary to me; a dreary visit altogether, though an unabatedly affectionate on both sides—in what a contrast, thought I, to the old sunshiny visits when Glasgow was head-quarters, and everybody was obscure, frank to his feelings, and safe. Mrs. Dickson, I think, had tears in her eyes. Her too he doubtless blessed, but without hand on head. Dickson and the rest of us escorted him a little way. We parted in the howling of the north wind, and I turned back across the moors to Hoddam Hill to meditate in silence on the chances and changes of this strange whirlpool of a world.[1]

[1] The last paragraph is taken from a contemporary description of the scene. The rest, as most complete, is from the *Reminiscences*, p. 231, and is a curious illustration of the minute exactness of Carlyle's memory.

CHAPTER XIX.

A.D. 1826.   ÆT. 31.

The life at Hoddam Hill, singularly happy while it lasted, and promising to last, was not after all of long continuance. Differences with the landlord, General Sharpe, rose to a quarrel, in which old Mr. Carlyle took his son's part. Hoddam Hill was given up; the lease of Mainhill, expiring at the same time, was not renewed, and the whole family, Carlyle himself with the rest, removed to Scotsbrig, a substantial farm in the neighbourhood of Ecclefechan, where the elder Carlyles remained to the end of their lives, and where their youngest son succeeded them.

The break-up at Hoddam precipitated the conclusion of Carlyle's protracted relations with Miss Welsh.   He sums up briefly his recollections of the story of this year, which was in every way so momentous to him.

My translation (German Romance) went steadily on, the pleasantest labour I ever had ; could be done by task in whatever humour or condition one was in, and was day by day (ten pages a day, I think) punctually and comfortably so performed.   Internally, too, there were far higher things going on ; a grand and ever joyful victory getting itself achieved at last !   The final chaining down, trampling home ' for good,' home into their caves for ever of all my spiritual dragons, which had wrought me such woe, and for a decade past had made my life black and bitter.[1]   This year 1826 saw the end of all that, with such a feeling on my part as may be fancied.   I found it to be essentially what Methodist people call their ' conversion,' the deliverance of their souls from

[1] First battle won in the Rue de l'Enfer—Leith Walk—four years before. Campaign not ended till now.

the Devil and the pit; precisely enough *that*, in new form. And there burnt accordingly a sacred flame of joy in me, silent in my inmost being, as of one henceforth superior to fate, able to look down on its stupid injuries, with contempt, pardon, and almost with a kind of thanks and pity. This 'holy joy,' of which I kept silence, lasted sensibly in me for several years in blessed counterpoise to sufferings and discouragements enough; nor has it proved what I can call fallacious at any time since. My 'spiritual dragons,' thank heaven, do still remain strictly in their caves, forgotten and dead, which is indeed a conquest, and the beginning of conquests. I rode about a great deal in all kinds of weather that winter and summer, generally quite alone, and did not want for meditations, no longer of defiantly hopeless or quite impious nature.

Meanwhile, if on the spiritual side all went well, one poor item on the temporal side went ill: a paltry but essential item—our lease arrangements of Hoddam Hill. The lease had been hurriedly settled, on word of mouth merely, by my father, who stood well with his landlord otherwise, and had perfect trust in him. But when it came to practical settlement, to 'demands of outgoing tenant,' who was completely right as against his landlord, and completely wrong as against us, there arose difficulties which, the farther they were gone into, spread the wider. Arbitration was tried; much was tried; nothing would do. Arbitrators, little farmers on the neighbouring estates, would not give a verdict, but only talk, talk. Honourable landlord owes outgoing tenant (his and his father's old factor) say 150*l.*, and other just decision there was none. Factor was foolish, superannuated, impoverished, pressingly in want of his money. Landlord was not wise or liberal. Arbitrary and imperious he tried to be; wrote letters, &c., but got stiff answers; over the belly of justice would not be permitted to ride. The end was, after much babbling, in which I meddled little, and only from the background,[1] complete break ensued; Hoddam Hill to be given up, laid at his honour's feet May 26, 1826; ditto Mainhill when the lease also expired there. My father got, on another estate

[1] Not altogether. In a letter from Hoddam Hill Carlyle says: 'My kindred can now regard the ill-nature of our rural Ali Pacha with a degree of equanimity much easier to attain than formerly. Ali—I mean his honour General Sharpe—and I had such a *schane* the other day at this door. I made Graham of Burnswark laugh at it yesterday all the way from Annan to Hoddam Bridge. In short, Ali sank, in the space of little more than a minute, from 212° of Fahrenheit's thermometer to 32°, and retired even below the freezing-point.'

near by, the farm of Scotsbrig, a far better farm (where our people still are), farm well capable both of his stock and ours, with roomy house, &c., where, if anywhere in the country, I, from and after May, 1826, must make up my mind to live. To stay there till German Romance was done—clear as to that—went accordingly, and after a week of joinering resumed my stint of ten daily pages, steady as the town clock, no interruption dreaded or occurring. Had a pleasant, diligent, and interesting summer; all my loved kindred about me for the last time ; hottest and droughtiest summer I have ever seen, drier even than the last (of 1868), though seldom quite so intolerably hot. No rain from the end of March till the middle of August. Delightful morning rides (in the first months) are still present to me, ditto breakfasts in the kitchen, an antique baronial one, roomy, airy, curious to me. Cookery, company, and the cow with her produce always friendly to me. Nothing to complain of but want of the old silence ; noise and bustle of business now round me, and like to increase, not diminish; and this thought always too, here cannot be thy continuing city ! and then withal, my darling in noble silence getting so weary of dull Haddington. In brief, after much survey and consideration of the real interests and real feelings of both parties, I proposed, and it was gently acceded to, that German Romance once done (end of September or so) we should wed, settle at Edinburgh in some small suburban house (details and preparations there all left to her kind mother and her), and thenceforth front our chances in the world, not as two lots, but as one, for better for worse, till death us part !

In August Haddington became aware of what was toward a great enough event there, the loss of its loved and admired 'Jeannie Welsh, the Flower o' Haddington' (as poor old Lizzie Baldy, a notable veteran sewing woman, humble heroine, then sadly said), 'gaun to be here na mair !' In Annandale, such my entire seclusion, nothing was yet heard of it for a couple of months. House in Comely Bank[1] suitable as possible had been chosen; was being furnished from Haddington, beautifully, perfectly, and even richly, by Mrs. Welsh's great skill in such matters, aided by her daughter's, which was also great, and by the frank *wordless* generosity of both, which surely was very great! Mrs. Welsh had decided to give up house, quit Haddington, and privately even never see

---

[1] A row of houses to the north of Edinburgh, then among open fields between the city and the sea.

it more; to live at Templand thenceforth with her father and sister (Aunt Grizzie), where it was well judged her help might be useful. My brave little woman had by deed of law two years before settled her little estate (Craigenputtock) upon her mother for life, being clearly indispensable *there.* Fee simple of the place she had at the same time by will bequeathed to me if I survived her.

So Carlyle, at a distance of forty-two years, describes the prelude to his marriage—accurately so far as substance went, and with a frank acknowledgment of Mrs. Welsh's liberality, as the impression was left upon his memory. But, exactly and circumstantially as he remembered things which had struck and interested him, his memory was less tenacious of some particulars which he passed over at the time with less attention than perhaps they deserved, and thus allowed to drop out of his recollection. Details have to be told which will show him *not* on the most considerate side. They require to be mentioned for the distinct light which they throw on aspects of his character which affected materially his wife's happiness. There were some things which Carlyle was *constitutionally* incapable of apprehending, while again there are others which he apprehended perhaps with essential correctness, but on which men in general do not think as he thought. A man born to great place and great visible responsibilities in the world is allowed to consider first his position and his duties, and to regard other claims upon him as subordinate to these. A man born with extraordinary talents, which he has resolved to use for some great and generous purpose, may expect and demand the same privileges, but they are not so easily accorded to him. In the one instance it is assumed as a matter of course that secondary interests must be set aside; even in marriage the heir of a large estate consults the advantage of his family; his wife's pleasure, even his wife's comforts must be postponed to the supposed demands of her husband's situation. The claims of a man of genius are less tolerantly dealt with; partly perhaps because it is held an impertinence in any man to pretend to genius till he has given proof of possessing it; partly because, if extraordinary gifts are rare, the power of appreciating them is equally rare, and a fixed purpose to make a noble use of them is rarer still. Men of literary faculty, it is idly supposed, can do their work anywhere in any circumstances; if the work is left undone the world does not know what it has lost; and thus, partly by their own fault, and partly by the world's mode of dealing with them, the biographies of men of letters are, as Carlyle says, for the most part the saddest chapter in the history of the human race except the Newgate Calendar.

Carlyle, restless and feverish, was convinced that no real work could be got out of him till he was again in a home of his own, and till his affairs were settled on some permanent footing. His engagement, while it remained uncompleted, kept him anxious and irritated. Therefore he conceived that he must find some cottage suited to his circumstances, and that Miss Welsh ought to become immediately the mistress of it. He had money enough to begin housekeeping; he saw his way, he thought, to earning money enough to continue it on the scale on which he had himself been bred up—but it was on condition that the wife that he took to himself should do the work of a domestic servant as his own mother and sisters did; and he was never able to understand that a lady differently educated might herself, or her friends for her, find a difficulty in accepting such a situation. He was in love, so far as he understood what love meant. Like Hamlet he would have challenged Miss Welsh's other lovers 'to weep, to fight, to fast, to tear themselves, to drink up Esil, eat a crocodile,' or 'be buried with her quick in the earth;' but when it came to the question how he was himself to do the work which he intended to do, he chose to go his own way, and expected others to accommodate themselves to it.

Plans had been suggested and efforts made to secure some permanent situation for him. A newspaper had been projected in Edinburgh, which Lockhart and Brewster were to have conducted with Carlyle under them. This would have been something; but Lockhart became editor of the 'Quarterly Review,' and the project dropped. A Bavarian Minister had applied to Professor Leslie for someone who could teach English literature and science at Munich. Leslie offered this to Carlyle, but he declined it. He had set his mind upon a cottage outside Edinburgh, with a garden and high walls about it to shut out noise. This was all which he himself wanted. He did not care how poor it was so it was *his own*, entirely his own, safe from intruding fools.

Here he thought that he and his wife might set themselves up together and wish for nothing more. It did, indeed, at moments occur to him that, although he could be happy and rich in the midst of poverty, 'for a woman to descend from superfluity to live in poverty with a sick, ill-natured man, and not be wretched, would be a miracle.' But though the thought came more than once, it would not abide. The miracle would perhaps be wrought; or indeed without a miracle his mother and sisters were happy, and why should anyone wish for more luxuries than they had?

Mrs. Welsh being left a widow, and with no other child, the pain of separation from her daughter was unusually great. Notwithstanding a certain number of caprices, there was a genuine and even passionate attachment between mother and daughter. It might have seemed that a separation was unnecessary, and that if Mrs. Welsh could endure to have Carlyle under her own roof, no difficulty on his side ought to have arisen. Mrs. Welsh indeed, romantically generous, desired to restore the property, and to go back and live with her father at Templand; but her daughter decided peremptorily that she would rather live with Carlyle in poverty all the days of her life sooner than encroach in the smallest degree on her mother's independence. She could expect no happiness, she said, if she failed in the first duty of her life. Her mother should keep the fortune, or else Miss Welsh refused to leave her.

All difficulties might be got over, the entire economic problem might be solved, if the family could be kept together. As soon as the marriage was known to be in contemplation this arrangement occurred to everyone who was interested in the Welshes' welfare as the most obviously desirable. Mrs. Welsh was as unhappy as ever at an alliance that she regarded as not imprudent only, but in the highest degree objectionable. Carlyle had neither family nor fortune nor prospect of preferment. He had no religion that she could comprehend, and she had seen him violent and unreasonable. He was the very last companion that she would have selected for herself. Yet for her daughter's sake she was willing to make an effort to like him, and, since the marriage was to be, either to live with him or to accept him as her son-in-law in her own house and in her own circle.

Her consent to take Carlyle into her family removed Miss Welsh's remaining scruples, and made her perfectly happy. It never occurred to her that Carlyle himself would refuse, and the reasons which he alleged might have made a less resolute woman pause before she committed herself further. It would never answer, he said; 'two households could not live as if they were one, and he would never have any right enjoyment of his wife's company till she was all his own.' Mrs. Welsh had a large acquaintance. He liked none of them, and 'her visitors would neither be diminished in numbers nor bettered in quality.' No! he must have the small house in Edinburgh; and 'the moment he was master of a house, the first use he would turn it to would be to slam the door against nauseous intruders.' It never occurred to him, as proved too fatally to be the case, that he would care little for 'the right companionship' when he had got it; that he would be absorbed in his work; that, after all, his wife would see but little of him, and that little too often under trying conditions of temper; that her mother's companionship, and the 'intrusion' of her mother's old friends, might add more to her comfort than it could possibly detract from his own.

However deeply she honoured her chosen husband, she could not hide from herself that he was selfish—extremely selfish. He had changed his mind indeed about the Edinburgh house almost as soon as he had made it up—he was only determined that he would not live with Mrs. Welsh.

Surely (Miss Welsh wrote) you are the most tantalising man in the world, and I the most tractable woman. This time twelve-month nothing would content you but to live in the country, and though a country life never before attracted my desires, it nevertheless became my choice the instant it seemed to be yours. In truth I discovered a hundred beauties and properties in it which had hitherto escaped my notice; and it came at last to this, that every imagination of the thoughts of my heart was love in a cottage continually. *Eh bien!* and what then? A change comes over the spirit of your dream. While the birds are yet humming, the roses blooming, the small birds rejoicing, and everything is in summer glory about our ideal cottage, I am called away to live *in prospectu* in the smoke and bustle and icy coldness of Edinburgh. Now this I call a trial of patience and obedience—and say, could I have complied more readily though I had been your wedded wife ten times over? Without a moment's hesitation, without once looking behind, without even bidding adieu to my flowers, I took my way with you out of our Paradise, to raise another in the howling wilderness. A very miracle of love! Oh mind of man! And this too must pass away. Houses and walled gardens pass away like the baseless fabric of a vision; and lo! we are once more a solitary pair, 'the world all before us where to choose our place of rest.' Be Providence our guide. Suppose we take different roads and try how that answers. There is ——, with 50,000*l.* and a princely lineage, and 'never was out of humour in her life'—with such a 'singularly pleasing creature' you could hardly fail to find yourself admirably well off—while I, on the other hand, might better my fortune in many quarters. A certain handsome stammering Englishman I know of would give his ears to carry me away south with him. My second cousin, too, the doctor at Leeds, has set up a fine establishment, and writes to me that 'I am the very first of my sex.' Or, nearer home, I have an interesting young widower in view, who has no scruple in making me mother to his three small children, blue stocking though I be. But what am I talking about? as if we were not already married, married past redemption. God knows in that case what is to become of us. At times I am so disheartened that I sit down and weep.

Carlyle could just perceive that he had not been gracious, that Mrs. Welsh's offer had deserved ' more serious consideration,' and at least a more courteous refusal. He could recognize also, proud as he was, that he had little to offer in his companionship which would be a compensation for the trials which it might bring with it. He again offered to set the lady free.

To Miss Welsh.

Oh Jane, Jane, your half-jesting enumeration of your wooers does anything but make me laugh. A thousand and a thousand times I have thought the same thing in deepest earnest. That you have the power of making many good matches is no secret to me ; nay, it would be a piece of news for me to learn that I am not the very worst you ever thought of. And you add, with the same tearful smile, 'Alas! we are married already.' Let me cut off the interjection, and say simply what is true, that we are not married already ; and do you hereby receive further my distinct and deliberate declaration that it depends on yourself, and shall always depend on yourself, whether ever we be married or not.

God knows I do not say this in a vulgar spirit of defiance, which in our present relation were coarse and cruel ; but I say it in the spirit of disinterested affection for you, and of fear from the reproaches of my own conscience, should your fair destiny be marred by me, and you wounded in the house of your friend. Can you believe it with the good nature which I declare it deserves ? It would absolutely give me satisfaction to know that you thought yourself entirely free of all ties to me but those, such as they might be, of your own still renewed election. It is reasonable and right that you should be concerned for your future establishment. Look round with calm eyes on the persons you mention, and if there is any one among them whose wife you had rather be—I do not mean whom you love better than me, but whose wife, all things considered, you had rather be than mine— then I call upon you, I, your brother and friend through every fortune, to accept that man and leave me to my destiny. But if, on the contrary, my heart and my hand, with the barren and perplexed destiny which promises to attend them, shall after all appear the best that this poor world can offer you, then take me and be content with me, and do not vex yourself with struggling to alter what is unalterable—to make a man who is poor and sick suddenly become rich and healthy. You tell me you often weep when you think what is to become of us. It is unwise in you to weep. If you are reconciled to be *my* wife (not the wife of an ideal *me*, but the simple actual prosaic *me*), there is nothing frightful in the future. *I* look into it with more and more confidence and composure. Alas ! Jane, you do not know me. It is not the poor unknown rejected Thomas Carlyle that you know, but the prospective rich, known, and admired. I am reconciled to my fate as it stands, or promises to stand ere long. I have pronounced the word *unpraised* in all its cases and numbers, and find nothing terrific in it, even when it means unmoneyed, and even by the mass of his Majesty's subjects neglected or even partially contemned. I thank Heaven I have other objects in my eye than either their pudding or their breath. This comes of the circumstance that my apprenticeship is ending, and yours still going on. Oh Jane, I could weep too, for I love you in my deepest heart.

These are hard sayings, my beloved child, but I cannot spare them, and I hope, though bitter at first, they may not remain without wholesome influence. Do not be angry with me. Do not. I swear I deserve it not. Consider this as a true glimpse into my heart which it is good that you contemplate with the gentleness and tolerance you have often shown me. If you judge it fit, I will take you to my heart as my wedded wife this very week. If you judge it fit, I will this very week forswear you for ever. More I cannot do ; but all this, when I compare myself with you, it is my duty to do. Adieu. God bless you and have you in his keeping !

      I am yours at your own disposal for ever and ever,

                              T. CARLYLE.

That Carlyle could contemplate with equanimity being unpraised, unmoneyed, and neglected all his life, that he required neither the world's pudding nor its breath, and could be happy without them, was pardonable and perhaps commendable. That he should expect another person to share this unmoneyed, puddingless, and rather forlorn condition, was scarcely consistent with such lofty principles. Men may sacrifice themselves, if they please, to imagined high duties and ambitions, but they have no right to marry wives and sacrifice them. Nor were these ' hard sayings which could not be spared ' exactly to the point, when he had been roughly and discourteously rejecting proposals which would have made his *unmoneyed* situation of less importance.

He had said that Miss Welsh did not know him, which was probably true ; but it is likely also that he did not know himself. She had answered this last letter of his with telling him that she had chosen him for her husband, and should not alter her mind. Since this was so he immediately said, ' she had better wed her wild man of the woods at once, and come and live with him in his cavern in the hope of better days.' The cavern was Scotsbrig. When it had been proposed that he should live with Mrs. Welsh at Haddington, he would by consenting have spared the separation of a mother from an only child, and would not perhaps have hurt his own intellect by an effort of self-denial. It appeared impossible to him, when Mrs. Welsh was in question, that two households could go on together. He was positive that he must be master in his own house, free from noise and interruption, and have fire and brimstone cooked for him if he pleased to order it. But the two households were not, it seemed, incompatible when one of them was his own family. If Miss Welsh would come to him at Scotsbrig, 'he would be a new man;' 'the bitterness of life would pass away like a forgotten tempest,' and he and she 'would walk in bright weather thenceforward' to the end of their existence. This, too, was a mere delusion. The cause of his unrest was in himself; he would carry with him, wherever he might go or be, the wild passionate spirit, fevered with burning thoughts, which would make peace impossible, and cloud the fairest weather with intermittent tempests. Scotsbrig would not have frightened Miss Welsh. She must have perceived his inconsistency, though she did not allude to it. But if Carlyle had himself and his work to consider, she had her mother. Her answer was very beautiful.

To Thomas Carlyle.

Were happiness the thing chiefly to be cared for in this world, I would put my hand in yours now, as you say, and so cut the knot of our destiny. But oh! have you not told me a thousand times, and my conscience tells me also, that happiness is a secondary consideration? It must not, must not, be sought out of the path of duty. Should I do well to go into Paradise myself, and leave the mother who bore me to break her heart? She is looking forward to my marriage with a more tranquil mind in the hope that our separation is to be but nominal—that, by living where my husband lives, she may at least have every moment of my society which he can spare. And how would it be possible not to disappoint her of this hope if I went to reside with your people in Annandale? Her presence there would be a perpetual cloud. For the sake of all concerned, it would be necessary to keep her quite apart from us, yet so near.[1] She would be the most

[1] Templand, where Mrs. Welsh was to live if she returned to her father, was about fifteen miles from Ecclefechan.

wretched of mothers, the most desolate woman in the world.   Oh !
is it for me to make her so ? me who am so unspeakably dear to
her in spite of all her caprice, who am her only, only child, and
she a widow ? I love you, Mr. Carlyle, tenderly, devotedly. But I
may not put my mother away from me, even for your sake. I cannot do it. I have lain awake whole nights trying to reconcile
this act with my conscience. But my conscience will have nothing to say to it—rejects it with indignation.

What is to be done, then ? Indeed, I see only one way to escape out of all these perplexities. Be patient with me while I tell
you what it is. My mother, like myself, has ceased to feel any
contentment in this hateful Haddington, and is bent on disposing
of our house here as soon as may be, and hiring one elsewhere.
Why should it not be the vicinity of Edinburgh after all ? and
why should not you live with your wife in your mother's house ?
Because, you say, my mother would never have the grace to like
you, or let you live with her in peace ; because you could never
have any right enjoyment of my society, so long as you had me
not all to yourself ; and finally because you must and will ' have
a door of your own to slam in the face of all nauseous intruders.'
These are objections which sound fatal to my scheme; but I am
greatly mistaken if they are not more sound than substance. My
mother would like you, assuredly she would, if you came to live
with her as her son. Her terror is lest, through your means, she
should be made childless, and a weak imagination that you regard
her with disrespect—both which rocks of offence would be removed by this one concession. Besides, as my wedded husband,
you would appear to her in a new light. Her maternal affection,
of which there is abundance at the bottom of her heart, would of
necessity extend itself to him with whom I was become inseparably connected ; and mere common sense would prescribe a kind
motherly behaviour as the only expedient to make the best of
what could no longer be helped.

The arrangement was at least as reasonable as that
which he had himself proposed, and Carlyle, who was so
passionately attached to his own mother, might have been
expected to esteem and sympathise with Miss Welsh's affection for hers.   At Scotsbrig he would have had no
door of his own ' to slam against nauseous intruders ; ' his

father, as long as he lived, would be master in his own house; while the self-control which would have been required of him, had he resided with Mrs. Welsh as a son-in-law, would have been a discipline which his own character especially needed. But he knew that he was 'gey ill to live wi'.' His own family were used to him, and he in turn respected them, and could, within limits, conform to their ways. From others he would submit to no interference. He knew that he would not, and that it would be useless for him to try. He felt that he had not considered Mrs. Welsh as he ought to have done; but his consideration, even after he had recognized his fault remained a most restricted quantity.

To Miss Welsh.

April 2, 1826.

As we think mostly of our own wants and wishes alone in this royal project, I had taken no distinct account of your mother. I merely remembered the text of Scripture, 'Thou shalt leave thy father and mother and cleave unto thy husband, and thy desire shall be towards him all the days of thy life.' I imagined perhaps she might go to Dumfriesshire and gratify her heart by increasing the accommodations of her father, which she would then have ample means to do; perhaps that she might even——[1] in short, that she might arrange her destiny in many ways in which my presence must be a hindrance rather than a furtherance. Here I was selfish and thoughtless. I might have known that the love of a mother to her only child is indestructible and irreplaceable; that forcibly to cut asunder such was cruel and unjust.

Perhaps, as I have told you, I may not yet have got to the bottom of this new plan so completely as I wished; but there is one thing that strikes me more and more the longer I think of it—this, the grand objection of all objections, the head and front of offence, the soul of all my counterpleading— an objection which is too likely to overset the whole project. It may be stated in a word: '*The man should bear rule in the house, and not the woman.*' This is an eternal axiom, the law of nature, which no mortal departs from unpunished. I have meditated on this many years,

---

[1] He probably was going to say 'marry again,' but checked himself.

and every day it grows plainer to me. I must not, and I cannot, live in a house of which I am not head. I should be miserable myself, and make all about me miserable. Think not this comes of an imperious temper, that I shall be a harsh and tyrannical husband to thee. God forbid! But it is the nature of a man, if he is controlled by anything but his own reason, that he feels himself degraded and incited, be it justly or not, to rebellion and discord. It is the nature of a woman again (for she is entirely passive, not active) to cling to the man for support and direction, to comply with his humours and feel pleasure in doing so, simply because they are his, to reverence while she loves him, to conquer him not by her force, but by her weakness, and perhaps, the cunning gipsy, to command him by obeying him. . . . Your mother is of all women the best calculated for being a *wife*, and the worst for being a *husband*. I know her, perhaps better than she thinks; and it is not without affection and sincere esteem that I have seen the fundamental structure of her character, and the many light capricious half graces, half follies, that sport on the surface of it. I could even fancy that she might love me also and feel happy beside me, if her own true and kindly character were to come into fair and free communion with mine, which she might then find was neither false nor cruel any more than her own. But this could only be (I will speak it out at once and boldly, for it is the quiet and kind conviction of my judgment, not the conceited and selfish conviction of my vanity)—this could only be in a situation where she looked up to me, not I to her.

Now think, Liebchen, whether your mother will consent to forget her own riches and my poverty, and uncertain, more probably my scanty, income, and consent, in the spirit of Christian meekness, to make *me* her guardian and director, and be a second wife to her daughter's husband. If she can, then I say she is a noble woman, and in the name of truth and affection *let* us all live together and be one household and one heart, till death or her own choice part us. If she cannot, which will do anything but surprise me, then also the other thing cannot be, must not be; and for her sake no less than for yours and mine we must think of something else.

The Greek chorus would have shaken its head ominously, and uttered its musical cautions, over the temper displayed in this letter. Yet it is perfectly true that Carlyle would have been an unbearable inmate of any house, except his father's, where his will was not absolute. 'Gey ill to live wi',' as his mother said. The condition which he made was perhaps not so much as communicated to Mrs. Welsh, for whom it would have furnished another text for a warning sermon. The 'judicious desperation' which Carlyle recommended to her daughter brought her to submit to going to live at Scotsbrig. Under these circumstances Mrs. Welsh, in desperation too, decided that the marriage should be celebrated immediately and an end made. She comforted herself with the thought that being at Templand with her father, she would at least be within reach, and could visit Scotsbrig as often as she pleased. Here, however, new difficulties arose. Carlyle, it seems, had made the proposition without so much as consulting his father and mother. They at least, if not he, were sensible, when they heard of it, of the unfitness of their household to receive a lady brought up as Miss Welsh had been. 'Even in summer,' they said, 'it would be difficult for her to live at Scotsbrig, and in winter impossible;' while the notion that Mrs. Welsh should ever be a visitor there seemed as impossible to Carlyle himself. He had deliberately intended to bring his wife into a circle where the suggestion of her mother's appearance was too extravagant to be entertained.

You have misconceived (he said) the condition of Scotsbrig and our only possible means of existence there. You talk of your mother visiting us. By day and night it would astonish her to see this household. Oh, no. Your mother must not visit mine. What good were it? By an utmost exertion on the part of both they might learn, perhaps, to tolerate each other, more probably to pity and partially dislike each other. Better than mutual tolerance I could anticipate nothing from them. The mere idea of such a visit argued too plainly that you *knew nothing* of the family circle in which, for my sake, you were ready to take a place.

It is sad to read such words. Carlyle pretended that he knew Mrs. Welsh. Human creatures are not all equally unreasonable; and he knew as little of her as he said that her daughter knew of Scotsbrig. The two mothers, when the family connection brought them together, respected each other, could meet without difficulty, and part with a mutual regard which increased with acquaintance. Had the incompatibility been as real as he supposed, Carlyle's strange oblivion both of his intended wife's and his wife's mother's natural feelings would still be without excuse.

His mind was fixed, as men's minds are apt to be in such circumstances. He chose to have his own way, and since it was impossible for Miss Welsh to live at Scotsbrig, and as he had on his side determined that he would not live with Mrs. Welsh, some alternative had to be looked for. Once more he had an opportunity of showing his defective perception of common things. Mrs. Welsh had resolved to leave Haddington and to give up her house there immediately. The associations of the place after her daughter was gone would necessarily be most painful. All her friends, the social circle of which she had been the centre, regarded the marriage with Carlyle as an extraordinary *mésalliance*. To them he was known only as an eccentric farmer's son without profession or prospects, and their pity or their sympathy would be alike distressing. She had herself found him moody, violent, and imperious, and she at least could only regard his conduct as extremely selfish. Men in the situation of lovers often are selfish. It is only in novels that they are heroic or even considerate. It occurred to Carlyle that since Mrs. Welsh was going away the house at Haddington would do well for himself. There it stood, ready provided with all that was necessary. He recollected that Edinburgh was noisy and disagreeable, Haddington quiet, and connected with his own most pleasant recollections. It might have occurred to him that under such altered circumstances, where she would be surrounded by a number of acquaintances, to every one of whom her choice appeared like madness, Miss Welsh might object to living there as much as her mother. She made her objections as delicately as she could; but he pushed them aside as if they were mere disordered fancies; and the fear of 'nauseous intruders,' which had before appeared so dreadful to him, he disposed of with the most summary serenity. 'To me,' he calmly wrote, 'among the weightier evils and blessings of existence, the evil of impertinent visitors, and so forth, seems but a small drop of the bucket, and an exceedingly little thing. I have nerve in me to despatch that sort of deer for ever by dozens in the day.'

'That sort of deer' were the companions who had grown up beside Miss Welsh for twenty years. She was obliged to tell him peremptorily that she would not hear of this plan. It would have been happier and perhaps better both for her and for him had she taken warning from the unconscious exhibition which he had made of his inner nature. After forty years of life with him—forty years of splendid labour, in which his essential conduct had been pure as snow, and unblemished by a serious fault, when she saw him at length rewarded by the honour and admiration of Europe and America—she had to preach nevertheless to her younger friends as the sad lesson of her own experience, 'My dear, whatever you do, never marry a man of genius.' The mountain-peaks of intellect are no homes for quiet people. Those who are cursed or blessed with lofty gifts and lofty purposes may be gods in their glory and their greatness, but are rarely tolerable as human companions. Carlyle consented to drop the Haddington proposal, not, however, without showing that he thought Miss Welsh less wise than he had hoped.

The vacant house at Haddington (he said) occurred to my recollection like a sort of godsend expressly suited to our purpose. It seemed so easy, and on other accounts so indispensable, to let it stand undisposed of for another year, that I doubted not a moment but the whole matter was arranged. If it turned out, which I reckoned to be impossible if you were not distracted in mind, that you really liked better to front the plashes and puddles and the thousand inclemencies of Scotsbrig through winter than live another six months in the house where you had lived all your days, it was the simplest process imaginable to stay where we were. The loss was but of a few months' rent for your mother's house, and the certainty it gave us made its great gain. Even yet I cannot, with the whole force of my vast intellect, understand how my project has failed. I wish not to undervalue your objections to the place, or your opinion on any subject whatever, but I confess my inability with my present knowledge to reconcile this very peremptory distaste with your usual good sense.

Again the plans were all astray. An Annandale cottage was once more thought of, and once more, again, the difference in point of view became prominent.

I should have 200*l.* to begin with (Carlyle said), and many an honest couple has begun with less. I know that wives are supported, some in peace and dignity, others in contention and disgrace, according to their wisdom or their folly, on all incomes from 14*l.* a year to 200,000*l.*, and I trusted in Jane Welsh, and still trust in her, for good sense enough to accommodate her wants to the means of the man she has chosen before all others, and to live with him contented on whatever it should please Providence to allot him, keeping within their revenue, not struggling to get without it, and therefore *rich*, by whatever arithmetical symbol, whether tens, hundreds, or thousands, by which that same revenue might be expressed. This is not impossible, or even very difficult, provided the will be truly there. Say what we like, it is in general our stupidity that makes us straightened or contemptible. The sum of money is a very secondary matter. One of the happiest, most praiseworthy, and really most enviable families on the earth at present lives within two bowshots of me—that of Wightman, the hedger—on the produce of fifteenpence per diem, which the man earns peacefully with his mattock and bill, not counting himself any philosopher for so doing. Their cottage on our hill is as tidy as a cabinet. They have a black-eyed boy whom few squires can parallel. Their *girnel* is always full of meal. The man is a true, honest, most wisely-conditioned man, an elder of the congregation, and meekly but firmly persuaded that he shall go to heaven when his hedging here below is done. What wan these knaves that a king should have?

If Carlyle had looked into the economics of the Wight-man household, he would have seen that the wife made her own and her husband's and the child's clothes, that she cooked the meals, swept and cleaned the house that was 'tidy as a cabinet,' washed the flannels and the linen, and weeded the garden when she required fresh air—that she worked in fact at severe bodily labour from sunrise to sunset. Had he inquired into this, it is possible (though it would have depended on his mood) that he might have asked himself whether Miss Welsh, setting aside her education and habits, was physically capable of these exertions, and whether he had a right to expect her to undertake them. Happily neither she nor her mother had completely parted with their senses. They settled the matter at last in their own fashion. The Haddington establishment was broken up. They moved to Edinburgh, and took the house in Comely Bank which Carlyle mentioned. Mrs. Welsh undertook to pay the rent, and the Haddington furniture was carried thither. She proposed to remain there with her daughter till October, and was then to remove finally to her father's house at Templand, where the ceremony was to come off. Carlyle when once married and settled in Edinburgh would be in the way of any employment which might offer for him. At Comely Bank, at any rate, Mrs. Welsh could be received occasionally as a visitor. For immediate expenses of living there was Carlyle's 200*l*., and such additions to it as he could earn. Miss Welsh recovered hope and spirit, and wrote in June from the new home, describing it and its position.

It is by no means everything one might wish (she said) ; but it is by much the most suitable that could be got, particularly in situation, being within a few minutes' walk of the town, and at the same time well out of its smoke and bustle. Indeed it would be quite country-looking, only that it is one of a range ; for there is a real flower garden in front, overshadowed by a fair spreading tree, while the windows look out on the greenest fields with never a street to be seen. As for interior accommodation, there are a dining room and a drawing room, three sleeping rooms, a kitchen, and more closets than I can see the least occasion for unless you design to be another Blue Beard. So you see we shall have apartments enough, on a small scale indeed, almost laughably small ; but if this is no objection in your eyes, neither is it any in mine.

Carlyle was supremely satisfied. The knotty problem which had seemed so hopeless was now perfectly solved.

To Miss Welsh.

Scotsbrig: July 19, 1826.

It is thus the mind of man can learn to command the most complex destiny, and like an experienced steersman (to speak in a most original figure) to steer its barque through all imaginable currents, undercurrents, quicksands, reefs, and stormy weather. Here are two swallows in the corner of my window that have taken a house (not at Comely Bank) this summer ; and in spite of drought and bad crops, are bringing up a family together with the highest contentment and unity of soul. Surely, surely, Jane Welsh and Thomas Carlyle here as they stand have in them conjunctly the wisdom of many swallows. Let them exercise it then, in God's name, and live happy as these birds of passage are doing. It is not nature that made men unhappy, but their own despicable perversities. The Deuce is in the people ! Have they not food and raiment fit for all the wants of the body ; and wives, and children, and brothers, and parents, and holiest duties for the wants of the soul ? What ails them then, the ninnies ? Their vanity, their despicable, very despicable *self-conceit*, conjoined with, or rather grounded on, their lowness of mind. They want to be happy, and by happiness they mean *pleasure*, a series of *passive* enjoyments. If they had a quarter of an eye they would see that there not only was not, but could not be such a thing in God's creation. I often seriously thank this otherwise my infernal distemper for having helped to teach me these things. They are not to be learned without sore affliction. Happy he to whom even affliction will teach them! And here ends my present lecture.

The great business having been once arranged, the rest of the summer flew swiftly by. 'German Romance' was finished, and paid for the marriage expenses. The world was taken into confidence by a formal announcement of what was impending: Miss Welsh, writing for the first time to her relations, sent a description of her intended husband to the wife of her youngest uncle, Mrs. George Welsh. She was not blinded by affection—no one ever less so in her circumstances. I have not kept back what I believe to have been faults in Carlyle, and the lady to whom he was to be married knew what they were better than anyone else can know; yet here was her deliberate opinion of him.—He stood there such as he had made himself: a peasant's son who had run about barefoot in Ecclefechan street, with no outward advantages, worn with many troubles bodily and mental. His life had been pure and without spot. He was an admirable son, a faithful and affectionate brother, in all private relations blamelessly innocent. He had splendid talents, which he rather felt than understood; only he was determined, in the same high spirit and duty which had governed his personal conduct, to use them well, whatever they might be, as a trust committed to him, and never, never to sell his soul by travelling the primrose path to wealth and distinction. If honour came to him, honour was to come unsought. I as if feel in dwelling on his wilfulness

> I did him wrong, being so majestical,
> To offer him the show of violence.

But I learnt my duty from himself: to paint him as he was, to keep back nothing and extenuate nothing. I never knew a man whose reputation, take him for all in all, would emerge less scathed from so hard a scrutiny.

Miss Welsh's letter was sent to Carlyle after her death in 1866. It came to him, as he said, ' as a flash of radiance from above.' One or two slight notes which he attached are marked with his initials, T. C.

To Mrs. George Welsh, Boreland, Dumfries.

Templand : September, 1826.

My dear Mrs. Welsh,—You must think me just about the most faithless character in the nation ; but I know, myself, that I am far from being so bad as I seem. The truth is, the many strange things I have had to do and think of in late months left me no leisure of mind for writing mere complimentary letters ; but still you, as well as others of my friends, have not been remembered by me with the less kindness that you have seen no expression of my remembrance on paper. So pray do not go to entertain any hard thoughts of me, my good little aunt, seeing that at bottom I deserve nothing but loving-kindness at your hands. Better add a spice of long-suffering to your loving-kindness, which will make us the very best friends in the world.

It were no news to you what a momentous matter I have been busied with. ' Not to know that would argue yourself unknown.' For a marriage is a topic suited to the capacities of all living ; and in this, as in every other known instance, has been made the most of. But, forasmuch as much breath has been wasted on ' my situation,' I have my own doubts whether they have given you any right idea of it. They would tell you, I should suppose, first and foremost, that my intended is *poor* (for that it requires no great depth of sagacity to discover) ; and in the next place, most likely, indulge in some criticisms scarce flattering on his birth,[1] the more likely if their own birth happened to be mean or doubtful ; and if they happened to be vulgar fine people with disputed pretensions to good looks, they would to a certainty set him down as unpolished and ill-looking. But a hundred chances to one they would

---

[1] ' Gracie, of Dumfries, kind of "genealogist by trade," had marked long since (of his own accord, not knowing me) my grandfather to be lineally descended from the "first Lord Carlyle," and brings us down from the brother of the murdered Duncan. What laughing my darling and I had when that document arrived.—T. C.'

not tell you he is among the cleverest men of his day—and not the cleverest only, but the most enlightened; that he possesses all the qualities I deem essential in my husband—a warm, true heart to love me, a towering intellect to command me, and a spirit of fire to be the guiding star of my life.[1] Excellence of this sort always requires some degree of superiority in those who duly appreciate it. In the eyes of the *canaille*, poor soulless wretches, it is mere *foolishness;* and it is only the *canaille* who babble about other people's affairs.

Such, then, is this future husband of mine—not a great man according to the most common sense of the word, but truly great in its natural proper sense: a scholar, a poet, a philosopher, a wise and noble man, one 'who holds his patent of nobility from Almighty God, and whose high stature of manhood is not to be measured by the inch rule of Lilliputs. Will you like him? No matter whether you do or not, since I like him in the deepest part of my soul.[2]

I would invite you to my wedding if I meant to invite anyone; but to my taste such ceremonies cannot be *too* private. Besides, by making distinctions amongst my relations on the occasion, I should be sure to give offence; and by God's blessing I will have no one there who does not feel kindly both towards *him* and *me*.

My affectionate regards to my uncle; a kiss to wee John; and believe me always,

Your sincere friend and dutiful niece,

JANE WELSH.[3]

The wedding day drew on; not without (as was natural) more than the usual nervousness on both sides at the irrevocable step which was about to be ventured. Carlyle knew too well 'that he was a perverse mortal to deal with,' 'that the best resolutions made shipwreck in practice,' and that 'it was a chance if any woman could be happy with him.' 'The brightest moment of his existence,' as in anticipation he had regarded his marriage, was within three

[1] 'Alas! alas!—T. C.'

[2] 'God bless thee, dear one!—T. C.'

[3] 'Letter read now—January 24, 1868—after a sleepless night withal such as has too often befallen latterly, cuts me through the soul with inexpressible feelings—*remorse* no small portion of them. Oh! my ever dear one! How was all this fulfilled for thee —— fulfilled!!—T. C.'

weeks of him, yet he found himself 'splenetic, sick, sleepless, void of faith, hope, and charity—in short, altogether
bad and worthless.' 'I trust Heaven I shall be better
soon,' he said; 'a certain incident otherwise will wear a
quite original aspect.' Clothes had to be provided, gloves
thought of. Scotch custom not recognising licenses in
such cases, required that the names of the intending pair
should be proclaimed· in their respective churches; and
this to both of them was intolerable. They were to be
married in the morning at Templand church, and to go
the same day to Comely Bank.

Carlyle, thrifty always, considered it might be expedient 'to take seats in the coach from Dumfries.' The
coach would be safer than a carriage, more certain of arriving, &c. So nervous was he, too, that he wished his
brother John to accompany them on their journey—at
least part of the way. In her mind the aspect of the affair
varied between tragic and comic, Carlyle's troubles over
the details being ludicrous enough.

I am resolved in spirit (she said), and even joyful—joyful in the
face of the dreaded ceremony, of starvation, and of every horrible
fate. Oh, my dearest friend, be always so good to me, and I shall
make the best and happiest wife. When I read in your looks and
words that you love me, then I care not one straw for the whole
universe besides. But when you fly from me to smoke tobacco,
or speak of me as a mere circumstance of your lot, then indeed
my heart is troubled about many things.

Miss Welsh, too, as well as Carlyle, had a fiery temper.
When provoked she was as hard as flint, with possibilities
of dangerous sparks of fire. She knew her tendencies and
made the best resolutions :—

I am going really to be a very meek-tempered wife (she wrote
to him). Indeed, I am begun to be meek-tempered already. My
aunt tells me she could live for ever with me without quarrelling,
I am so reasonable and equable in my humour. There is some-

thing to gladden your heart withal. And more than this, my grandfather observed, while I was supping my porridge last night, that 'she was really a douce peaceable body that Pen.' Do you perceive, my good sir, the fault will be wholly your own if we do not get on most harmoniously together.

The grandfather, as Carlyle was coming into his family, was studying what he had already written.

My grandfather (she added) has been particularly picturesque these two days. On coming down stairs on Sunday evening I found him poring over 'Wilhelm Meister.' 'A strange choice,' I observed, by way of taking the first word with him, 'for Sunday reading.' He answered me quite sharply, 'Not at all, miss ; the book is a very good book ; it is all about David and Goliah.'

Jest as she would, however, Miss Welsh was frightened and Carlyle was frightened. The coach suggestion had sent a shiver through her. They comforted one another as if they were going to be executed.

To Thomas Carlyle.

Templand : October 10.

You desired me to answer your letter on Thursday, but I have waited another post that I might do it better, if indeed any good thing is to be said under such horrid circumstances. Oh do, for Heaven's sake, get into a more benignant humour, or the incident will not only wear a very original aspect, but likewise a very heart-breaking one. I see not how I am to go through with it. I turn quite sick at the thought. But it were Job's comfort to vex you with my anxieties and 'severe affection.' I will rather set before you, by way of encouragement, that the purgatory will soon be past, and would speak peace where there is no peace, only that you would easily see through such affected philosophy. There is nothing for us then but, like the Annan congregation, to pray to the Lord.

I have said that I delayed writing that I might do it more satisfactorily for this reason. I expected to know last night when my mother is to come from Edinburgh, in which case I should have been able to name some day, though not so early a one as that proposed ; but alas! alas! my mother is dilatory and uncertain as ever, and the only satisfaction I can give you at this time is to promise I will soon write again. What has taken her to Edinburgh so inopportunely! to set some fractions of women cutting out white gowns, a thing which might have been done with all convenience when we were there last month. But some people are wise, and some are otherwise, and I shall be glad to get the gowns any way, for I should like ill to put you to charge in that article for a very great while. Besides, you know it would be a bad omen to marry in mourning. When I first put it on, six years ago,[1] I thought to wear it for ever; but I have found a second father, and it were ungrateful not to show, even externally, how much I rejoice in him.

I fear you must be proclaimed to your own parish. Pity, since you are so ashamed of me! but I will enlighten you on that head also in my next.

With respect to the journey part of the business, I loudly declare for running the risk of being stuck up part of the way (which at this season of the year is next to none) rather than undergo the unheard-of horror of being thrown into the company of strangers in such severe circumstances, or possibly, which would be still worse, of some acquaintance in the stage coach. For the same reason I prohibit John from going with us an inch of the road; and he must not think there is any unkindness in this. I hope your mother is praying for me. Give her my affectionate regards.

JANE WELSH.

Carlyle, on his side, tried to allay his fears of what Miss Welsh called 'the odious ceremony' by reading Kant, and had reached the hundred and fiftieth page of the 'Kritik der reinen Vernunft,' when he found that it was too abstruse for his condition, and that Scott's novels would answer better. With this assistance he tried to look more cheerfully on the adventure.

After all (he said) I believe we take this impending ceremony far too much to heart. Bless me! Have not many people been married before now? and were they not all carried through with some measure of Christian *comfoart*, and taught to see that marriage was simply nothing—but marriage? Take courage, then, and let no 'cold shudder' come over you; and call not this an odious ceremony, but rather a blessed ordinance sanctioning by

[1] For her father. She had worn mourning ever since.

earthly laws what is already sanctioned in heaven; uniting two souls for worldly joy and woe which in God's sight have chosen one another from amongst all men. Can any road be dark which is leading thither? You will see it will be all 'smooth as oil,' notwithstanding our forebodings. Consider Goethe's saying, 'We look on our scholars as so many swimmers, each of whom in the element that threatened to devour him, unexpectedly feels himself borne up and able to make progress; and so it is with all that man undertakes'—with marriage as with other things. By all reason, therefore, German and English, I call on you to be composed in spirit, and to fear no evil in this really blessed matter.

To your arrangements about the journey and the other items of the how and when, I can only answer as becomes me. Be it as thou hast said. Let me know your will and it shall be my pleasure. And so by the blessing of Heaven we shall roll along side by side with the speed of post-horses till we arrive at Comely Bank. I shall only stipulate that you will let me, by the road, as occasion serves, *smoke three cigars* without criticism or reluctance, as things essential to my perfect contentment. Yet if you object to this article, think not that I will break off the match on that account, but rather, like a dutiful husband, submit to the everlasting ordinance of Providence, and let my wife have her way.

You are very kind, and more just than I have reason to expect, in imputing my ill-natured speeches (for which Heaven forgive me) to their true cause—a disordered nervous system. Believe me, Jane, it is not I, but the Devil speaking out of me, which could utter one harsh word to a heart that so little deserves it. Oh, I were blind and wretched if I could make thee unhappy. But it will not and shall not be, for I am not naturally a villain; and at bottom I do love you well. And so when we have learnt to know each other as we are, and got all our arrangements accomplished and our household set in order, I dare promise you that it will all be well, and we shall live far happier than we have ever hoped. Sickness is the origin, but no good cause, of indiscriminating spleen; if we are wise we must learn, if not to resist, at least to evade its influences—a science in which even I in the midst of my own establishment fancy I have made some progress, and despair not of making more.

As to the proclamation, on which I expect your advice, I protest I had rather be proclaimed in all the parish churches of the empire than miss the little bird I have in my eye, whom I see not how I am to do without. So get the gowns made ready and loiter not, and tell me, and in a twinkling *me voilà !* Thank your aunt for her kind invitation, which I do not refuse or accept till the next letter, waiting to see how matters turn. I was surely born to be a Bedouin. Without freedom 'I should soon die and do nocht ava.' My chosen abode is in my own house in preference to the palace of Windsor; and next to this shall I not, with the man in the play, take my ease at mine inn?

My mother's prayers (to speak with all seriousness) are, I do believe, not wanting either to you or to me, and if the sincere wishes of a true soul can have any virtue, we shall not want a blessing. She bids me send you the kindest message I can contrive, which I send by itself without contrivance. She says she will have one good *greet* when we set off, and then be at peace. Now then what remains but that you appoint the date, that you look forward to it with trust in me and trust in yourself, and come with trust to your husband's arms and heart, there to abide through all chances for ever? Oh, we are two ungrateful wretches, or we should be happy. Write soon, and love me for ever; and so good night, *mein Herzenskind.* Thine *auf ewig,*

T. CARLYLE.

So the long drama came to its conclusion. The banns were published, the clothes made, the gloves duly provided. The day was the 17th of October, 1826. Miss Welsh's final letter, informing Carlyle of the details to be observed, is humourously headed, ' *The last Speech and marrying Words of that unfortunate young woman, Jane Baillie Welsh.*'

Truly (answered Carlyle), a most delightful and swanlike melody is in them—a tenderness and warm devoted trust worthy of such a maiden bidding farewell to the unmarried earth of which she was the fairest ornament. Let us pray to God that our holy purpose is not frustrated. Let us trust in Him and in each other, and fear no evil that can befall us.

They were married in the parish church of Templand in the quietest fashion, the minister officiating, John Carlyle the only other person present except Miss Welsh's family. Breakfast over, they drove off, *not* in the coach, but in a post-chaise, and without the brother. No delays or difficulties befell them on the road. Whether Carlyle did or did not smoke his three cigars remains unrecorded. In the evening they arrived safely at Comely Bank.

Regrets and speculations on 'the might have beens' of life are proverbially vain. Nor is it certain that there is anything to regret. The married life of Carlyle and Jane Welsh was not happy in the roseate sense of happiness. In the fret and chafe of daily life the sharp edges of the facets of two diamonds remain keen, and they never wear into surfaces which harmoniously correspond. A man and a woman of exceptional originality and genius are proper mates for one another only if they have some other object before them besides happiness, and are content to do without it. For the forty years which these two extraordinary persons lived together, their essential conduct to the world and to each other was sternly upright. They had to encounter poverty in its most threatening aspect— poverty which they might at any moment have escaped if Carlyle would have sacrificed his intellectual integrity, would have carried his talents to the market, and written down to the level of the multitude. If he ever flagged, it was his wife who spurred him on; nor would she ever allow him to do less than his very best. She never flattered anyone, least of all her husband; and when she saw cause for it the sarcasms flashed out from her as the sparks fly from lacerated steel. Carlyle, on his side, did not find in his marriage the miraculous transformation of nature which he had promised himself. He remained lonely and dyspeptic, possessed by thoughts and convictions which struggled in him for utterance, and which could be fused and cast into form only (as I have heard him say) when his whole mind was like a furnace at white heat. The work which he has done is before the world, and the world has long acknowledged what it owes to him. It would not have been done as well, perhaps it would never have been done at all, if he had not had a woman at his side who would bear, without resenting it, the outbreaks of his dyspeptic humour, and would shield him from the petty troubles of a poor man's life—from vexations which would have irritated him to madness—by her own incessant toil.

The victory was won, but, as of old in Aulis, not without a victim. Miss Welsh had looked forward to being Carlyle's intellectual companion, to sharing his thoughts and helping him with his writings. She was not over-rating her natural powers when she felt being equal to such a position and deserving it. The reality was not like the dream. Poor as they were, she had to work as a menial servant. She, who had never known a wish ungratified for any object which money could buy; she, who had seen the rich of the land at her feet, and might have chosen among them at pleasure, with a weak frame withal which had never recovered the shock of her father's death—she after all was obliged to slave like the wife of her husband's friend Wightman, the hedger, and cook and wash and scour and mend shoes and clothes for many a weary year. Bravely she went through it all; and she would have gone through it cheerfully if she had been rewarded with ordinary gratitude. But if things were done rightly, Carlyle did not inquire who did them. Partly he was occupied, partly he was naturally undemonstrative, and partly she in generosity concealed from him the worst which she had to bear. The hardest part of all was that he did not see that there was occasion for any special acknowledgment. Poor men's wives had to work. She was a poor man's wife, and it was fit and natural that she should work. He had seen his mother and his sisters doing the drudgery of his father's household without expecting to be admired for doing it. Mrs. Carlyle's life was entirely lonely, save so far as she had other friends. He consulted her judgment about his writings, for he knew the value of it, but in his conceptions and elaborations he chose to be always by himself. He said truly that he was a Bedouin. When he was at work he could bear no one in the room ; and, at least through middle life, he rode and walked alone, not choosing to have his thoughts interrupted. The slightest noise or movement at night shattered his nervous system; therefore he required a bedroom to himself; thus from the first she saw little of him, and as time went on less and less ; and she, too, was human and irritable. Carlyle proved, as his mother had known him, 'ill to live with.' Generous and kind as he was at heart, and as he always showed himself when he had leisure to reflect, 'the Devil,' as he had said, 'continued to speak out of him in distempered sentences,' and the bitter arrow was occasionally shot back.

Miss Welsh, it is probable, would have passed through life more pleasantly had she married someone in her own rank of life ; Carlyle might have gone through it successfully with his mother or a sister to look after him. But, after all is said, trials and sufferings are only to be regretted when they have proved too severe to be borne. Though the lives of the Carlyles were not happy, yet if we look at them from the beginning to the end they were grandly beautiful. Neither of them probably under other conditions would have risen to as high an excellence as in fact they each achieved ; and the main question is not how happy men and women have been in this world, but what they have made of themselves. I well remember the bright assenting laugh with which she once responded to some words of mine when the propriety was being discussed of relaxing the marriage laws. I had said that the true way to look at marriage was as a discipline of character.

CHAPTER XX.

MARRIED LIFE had begun; and the first eighteen months of his new existence Carlyle afterwards looked back upon as the happiest that he had ever known. Yet the rest which he had expected did not come immediately. He could not rest without work, and work was yet to be found. Men think to mend their condition by a change of circumstances. They might as well hope to escape from their shadows. His wife was tender, careful, thoughtful, patient, but the spirit which possessed her husband, whether devil or angel he could hardly tell, still left him without peace.

I am still dreadfully confused (he wrote to his mother a few days after his arrival at Comely Bank), I am still far from being at home in my new situation, but I have reason to say that I have been mercifully dealt with; and if an outward man worn with continual harassments and spirits wasted with so many agitations would let me see it, that I may fairly calculate on being far happier than I have ever been. The house is a perfect model, furnished with every accommodation that heart could desire, and for my wife, I may say in my heart that she is far better than any wife, and loves me with a devotedness which it is a mystery to me how I have ever deserved. She is gay and happy as a lark, and looks with such soft cheerfulness into my glooomy countenance, that new hope passed into me every time I met her eye. In truth I was very sullen yesterday, sick with sleeplessness, nervous, bilious, splenetic, and all the rest of it.

His days were spent in solitary wanderings by the sad autumnal sea. He begged his brother John to come to him.

I am all in a maze (he said), scarce knowing the right hand from the left in the path I have to walk. I am still insufficiently supplied with sleep; no wonder therefore that my sky should be tinged with gloom. Tell my mother, however, that I do believe I shall get hefted to my new situation, and then be one of the happiest men alive. Tell her also that by Jane's express request I am to read a sermon and a chapter with commentary, at least every Sabbath day, to my household, also that we are taking seats in church, and design to live soberly and devoutly as beseems us. On the whole this wife of mine surpasses my hopes. She is so tolerant, so kind, so cheerful, so devoted to me: oh that I were worthy of her! Why am I not happy then? Alas! Jack, I am bilious. I have to swallow salts and oil; the physic leaves me pensive yet quiet in heart, and on the whole happy enough; but the next day comes a burning stomach and a heart full of bitterness and gloom.

The entries in his diary are still more desponding.

December 7, 1826.—My whole life has been a continual nightmare, and my awakening will be in hell.—TIECK.

There is just one man unhappy: he who is possessed by some idea which he cannot convert into action, or still more which restrains or withdraws him from action.—GOETHE.

The end of man is an action, not a thought.—ARISTOTLE.

Adam is fabled by the Talmudists to have had a wife before Eve: she was called Lilith, and their progeny was all manner of aquatic and aerial—devils.—BURTON.

As he grew more composed, Carlyle thought of writing some kind of didactic novel. He could not write a novel, any more than he could write poetry. He had no *invention*. His genius was for fact: to lay hold on truth, with all his intellect and all his imagination. He could no more invent than he could lie. Still he laboured at it in his thoughts, and in the intervals he threw himself into a course of wide and miscellaneous reading. Sir Thomas Browne, Raleigh, Shaftesbury, Herder, Tieck, Hans Sachs, Werner, Sir William Temple, Scaliger, Burton, Alison, Mendelssohn, Fichte, Schelling, Kant, Heine, Italian books,

Spanish books, French books, occupied or at least distracted him, and short extracts or observations mark his steps as he went along.

December 3, 1826.—The conclusion of the essay on Urn-burial (Sir Thomas Browne) is absolutely beautiful: a still elegiac mood, so soft, so deep, so solemn and tender, like the song of some departed saint flitting faint under the everlasting canopy of night; an echo of deepest meaning 'from the great and famous nations of the dead.' Browne must have been a good man. What was his history? What the real form of his character? *Abiit ad plures.* 'He hath gone to the greater number.' Two infants reasoning in the womb about the nature of this life might be no unhandsome type of two men reasoning here about the life that is to come. I should like to know more of Browne; but I ought to understand his time better also. What are we to make of this old English literature? Touches of true beauty are thickly scattered over these works; great learning, solidity of thought; but much, much that now cannot avail any longer. Certainly the *spirit* of that age was far better than that of ours. Is the form of our literature an improvement intrinsically, or only a form better adapted to our actual condition? I often think the latter. Difficulty of speaking on these points without affectation. We know not what to think, and would gladly think something very striking and pretty.

Sir Walter Raleigh's 'Advice to his Son,' worldly wise, sharp, far-seeing. The motto, 'Nothing like getting on.' Of Burghley's 'Advice' the motto is the same; the execution, if I rightly remember, is in a gentler and more loving spirit. Walsingham's 'Manual' I did not read. These men of Elizabeth's are like so many Romans or Greeks. Were we to seek for the Cæsars, the Ciceros, Pericles, Alcibiades of England, we should find them nowhere if not in that era. Wherefore are these things hid, or worse than hid, presented in false tinsel colours, originating in affected ignorance and producing affected ignorance? Would I knew rightly about it and could present it rightly to others. For 'hear, alas! this mournful truth, nor hear it with a frown.' There in that old age lies the *only* true *poetical* literature of England. The poets of the last age took to pedagogy (Pope and his school), and shrewd men they were; those of the present age to ground and lofty tumbling, and it will do your heart good to see how they vault.

It is a damnable heresy in criticism to maintain either expressly or implicitly that the ultimate object of poetry is sensation. That of cookery is such, but not that of poetry. Sir Walter Scott is the great intellectual *restaurateur* of Europe. He might have been numbered among the Conscript Fathers. He has chosen the worser part, and is only a huge Publicanus. What are his novels—any one of them? A bout of champagne, claret, port, or even ale drinking. Are we wiser, better, holier, stronger? No. We have been amused. Oh, Sir Walter, thou knowest so well that *Virtus laudatur et alget!* Byron—good generous hapless Byron! And yet when he died he was only a *Kraftmann* (*Powerman* as the Germans call them). Had he lived he would have been a poet.

What shall I say of Herder's 'Ideen zur Philosophie der Geschichte der Menschheit'? An extraordinary book, yet one which by no means wholly pleaseth me. If Herder were not known as a devout man and clerk, his book would be reckoned atheistical. Everything is the effect of circumstances or organisation. *Er war was er seyn konnte.* The breath of life is but a higher intensation of light and electricity. This is surely very dubious, to say no worse of it. Theories of this and kindred sorts deform his whole work—immortality not shown us, but left us to be hoped for and to be believed by faith. This world sufficiently explainable without reference to another. Strange ideas about the Bible and religion; passing strange we think them for a clergyman. Must see more of Herder. He is a new species in some degree.

December 7.—Chateaubriand, Friedrich Schlegel, Werner, and that class of man among ourselves, are one of the distinctive features of the time. When Babylon the Great is about to be destroyed, her doom is already appointed by infidelity; and religion, too much interwoven with that same Babylon, has not yet risen on her mind, but seems rather, only seems, as if about to perish with her. A curious essay might be written on the customary grounds of human belief. Yes, it is true. The decisions of reason (*Vernunft*) are superior to those of understanding (*Verstand*). The latter vary in every age (by what law?), while the former last for ever, and are the same in all forms of manhood.

Oh Parson Alison, what an essay 'On Taste' is that of thine! Oh most intellectual Athenian, what accounts are those you give us of Morality and Faith, and all that really makes a man a man? Can you believe that the 'Beautiful' and 'Good' have no deeper root in us than 'association,' 'sympathy,' 'calculation'? Then, if so, whence, in Heaven's name, comes this sympathy, the pleasure of this association, the *obligancy* of this utility? You strive, like the witch in Hoffmann, to work from the outside inwards, and two inches below the surface you will never get.

The philosophy of Voltaire and his tribe exhilarates and fills us with glorying for a season—the comfort of the Indian who warmed himself at the flames of his bed.

A clown that killed his ass for drinking up the moon, *ut lunam mundo redderet. In Lud. vives.* True of many critics of sceptics. The sceptics have not drunk up the moon, but the reflection of it in their own dirty puddles ; therefore need not be slain.

January, 1827.—Read Mendelssohn's 'Phædon,' a half translation, half imitation of Plato's ' Phædon,' or last thoughts of Socrates on the immortality of the soul. On the whole a good book— and convincing? *Ay de mi !* These things, I fear, are not to be proved but believed ; not seized by the understanding, but by faith. However, it is something to remove errors if not introduce truths ; and to show us that our analogies drawn from corporeal things are entirely inapplicable to the case. For the present, I will confess it, I scarce see how we can reason with absolute certainty on the nature or fate of anything, for it seems to me we only see our own perceptions and their relations ; that is to say, our soul sees only its own partial reflex and manner of existing and conceiving.

Sapientia prima est stultitiâ caruisse. Fully as well thus, *Stultitia prima est sapientiâ caruisse :* the case of all materialist metaphysicians, most utilitarians, moralists, and generally all negative philosophers, by whatever name they call themselves. It was God that said Yes. It is the Devil that forever says No.

Leibnitz and Descartes found all truth to rest on our seeing and believing in God. We English have found our seeing and believing in God to rest on all truth, and pretty work we have made of it.

Is not political economy useful? and ought not Joseph Hume and Macculloch to be honoured of all men? My cow is useful, and I keep her in the stable, and feed her with oilcake and ' chaff and dregs,' and esteem her truly. But shall she live in my parlour? No ; by the Fates, she shall live in the stall.

Virtue *is* its own reward, but in a very different sense than you suppose, Dr. Gowkthrapple. The *pleasure* it brings! Had you ever a diseased liver? I will maintain, and appeal to all competent judges, that no evil conscience with a good nervous system ever caused a tenth part of the misery that a bad nervous system, conjoined with the best conscience in nature, will always produce. What follows, then? Pay off your moralist, and hire two apothecaries and two cooks. Socrates is inferior to Captain Barclay; and the 'Enchiridion' of Epictetus must hide its head before Kitchener's 'Peptic Receipts.' Heed not the immortality of the soul so long as you have beefsteaks, porter, and—blue pills. *Das hole der Teufel!* Virtue is its own reward, because it needs no reward.

To prove the existence of God, as Paley has attempted to do, is like lighting a lantern to seek for the sun. If you look hard by your lantern, you may miss your search.

An historian must write, so to speak, in *lines;* but every event is a *superficies.* Nay, if we search out its causes, a *solid.* Hence a primary and almost incurable defect in the art of narration, which only the very best can so much as approximately remedy. N.B. I understand this myself. I have known it for years, and have written it now, with the purpose, perhaps, of writing it at large elsewhere.

The courtesies of political life too often amount to little more than this, ' Sir, you and I care not two brass farthings the one for the other. We have and can have no friendship for each other. Nevertheless, let us enact it if we cannot practise it. Do you tell so many lies, and I shall tell so many; and depend on it, the result will be of great service to both. For is not this December weather very cold? And though our grates are full of ice, yet if you keep a picture of fire before yours, and I another before mine, will not this be next to a real coal and wood affair?'

Goethe ('Dichtung und Wahrheit,' ii. 14) asserts that the sublime is natural to all young persons and peoples; but that daylight (of reason) destroys it unless it can unite itself with the Beautiful; in which case it remains indestructible—a fine observation.

The economies, all this time, had to be attended to, and the prospect refused to brighten; and this did not mend Carlyle's spirits.

No talent for the market, thought I—none; the reverse rather (so he says of himself, looking back in later years). Indeed, I was conscious of no considerable talent whatever, only of infinite shyness and abstruse humour, veiled pride, &c., and looked out oftenest on a scene that was abundantly menacing to me. What folly was in all this, what pusillanimity and beggarly want of hope. Nothing in it now seems respectable except that of 'unfitness for the market,' &c., namely, the faith I had in me, and never would let go, that it was better to perish than do dishonest work, or do one's honest work otherwise than well. All the rest I may now blush for, and perhaps pity; blush for especially.

One piece of good fortune the Carlyles had. He had some friends in Edinburgh and she many; and he was thus forced out of himself. He was not allowed after all to treat visitors as 'nauseous intruders.' His wife had a genius for small evening entertainments; little tea parties such as in after days the survivors of us remember in Cheyne Row, over which she presided with a grace all her own, and where wit and humour were to be heard flashing as in no other house we ever found or hoped to find. These began in Edinburgh; and no one who had been once at Comely Bank refused a second invitation. Brewster came and De Quincey, penitent for his article on 'Meister,' and Sir William Hamilton and Wilson, (though Wilson for some reason was shy of Carlyle), and many more.

Carlyle, finding no employment offered him, was trying to make it. He sketched a prospectus for a literary Annual Register, 'a work which should perform for the intelligent part of the reading world such services as " Forget-me-Nots," " Souvenirs," &c. seemed to perform for the idle part of it.' ' It was to exhibit a compressed view of the actual progress of *mind* in its various manifestations during the past year.' The subjects were to be ' biographical portraits of distinguished persons lately deceased,' 'essays, sketches, miscellanies of various sorts, illustrating the existing state of literature, morals, and manners—on which points,' Carlyle thought, 'several things might be adduced not a little surprising to the optimists and the mob of gen-

tlemen that wrote with ease.' 'Thirdly, critiques with extracts from the few really good books produced in England,
Germany, and France, an essence of reviewing, a spirit of
the literary produce of the year.' 'Fourthly, a similar account might be given of works of art and discoveries of
science.' 'Fifthly, though politics were to be excluded, any
incidents, misfortunes, delusions, crimes, or heroic actions
illustrative of the existing spiritual condition of man,
might be collected and preserved.' Poetry was to be admitted if it could be had good of its kind, only ' with rigid
exclusion of Odes written at ——, Verses to ——, and the
whole genus of Songs by a Person of Quality.'

Pity that no Edinburgh or London publisher could see his
way to assisting Carlyle in this enterprise; for he would
have written most of it himself, and such a record would
now be of priceless value. But he was unknown and un-
prepossessing. Neither the Meister nor the Schiller were
selling as well as had been expected. The booksellers
hung back, and they judged rightly, perhaps, for their own
interests. Carlyle, like all really original writers, had to
create the taste which could appreciate him. The scheme
came to nothing, and his small capital was slowly melting
away.

The picture of the Comely Bank life given in the 'Reminiscences' may be supplemented from the family letters.

Jane Welsh Carlyle to Mrs. Carlyle, Scotsbrig.[1]

Comely Bank : December 9, 1826.

My dear Mother,—I must not let the letter go without adding
my 'Be of good cheer.' You would rejoice to see how much better my husband is since we came hither. And we are really very
happy. When he falls on some work we shall be still happier.
Indeed I should be very stupid or very thankless if I did not
congratulate myself every hour of the day on the lot which it has
pleased Providence to assign me. My husband is so kind, so in

[1] Being a postscript to a letter of Carlyle's own.

all respects after my own heart. I was sick one day, and he nursed me as well as my own mother could have done, and he never says a hard word to me unless I richly deserve it. We see great numbers of people, but are always most content alone. My husband reads then, and I read or work, or just sit and look at him, which I really find as profitable an employment as any other. God bless you and my little Jean, whom I hope to see at no very distant date.

Thomas Carlyle to Mrs. Carlyle, Scotsbrig.

Comely Bank : January 2, 1827.

My dear Mother,—At length Tait (the publisher) has given me an opportunity of sending off the weary book,[1] and along with it a word or two to assure you of my welfare. The German Romance I have inscribed to my father, though I know he will not read a line of it. From you, however, I hope better things ; and at any rate I have sent you a book which I am sure you *will* read, because it relates to a really good man, and one engaged in a cause which all men must reckon good. You must accept this 'Life of Henry Martyn' as a new year's gift from me; and while reading it believe that *your* son is a kind of missionary in his way—not to the heathen of India, but to the British heathen, an innumerable class whom he would gladly do something to convert if his perplexities and manifold infirmities would give him leave. . . . We must wait patiently and study to do what service we can, not despising the day of small things, but meekly trusting that hereafter it may be the day of greater.

I am beginning to be very instant for some sort of occupation, which, indeed, is my chief want at present. I must stir the waters and see what is to be done. Many many plans I have, but few of them, I doubt, are likely to prove acceptable at present ; the times are so bad, and bookselling trade so dull. Something, however, I will fix upon, for work is as essential to me as meat and drink. Of money we are not in want. The other morning Mrs. Welsh sent us a letter with sixty pounds enclosed, fearing lest cleanness of teeth might be ready to overtake us. I thought it extremely kind and handsome ; but we returned the cash with many thanks, wishing to fight our own battle at least till the season of need arrive.

I have not said a word yet about your kind Scotsbrig package.

[1] German Romance.

It was all right and in order, only that a few of the eggs (the box not being completely stuffed firm) had suffered by the carriage. Most part of them Jane has already converted into custards, pancakes, or the other like ware ; the others I am eating and find excellent. A woman comes here weekly with a fresh stock to us, and I eat just one daily, the price being 15*d.* per dozen. Now, my dear mother, you must make Alick write to me, and tell me all that is going on with himself or you. Wish all hands a happy new year in my name, and assure them all, one by one, that I will love them truly all my days.

Thomas Carlyle to Alexander Carlyle.

Comely Bank : February 3.

Our situation at Comely Bank continues to be unexceptionable —nay, in many points truly enviable. Ill health is not harder on us than usual, and all other things are about as one could wish them. It is strange, too, how one gets habituated to sickness. I bear my pain as Christian did his pack in the 'Pilgrim's Progress,' strapped on too tightly for throwing off ; but the straps do not gall as they once did ; in fact, I believe I am rather better, and certainly I have not been happier for many a year. Last week, too, I fairly began—a book.[1] Heaven only knows what it will turn to, but I have sworn to finish it. You shall hear about it as it proceeds, but as yet we are only got through the first chapter. You would wonder how much happier steady occupation makes us, and how smoothly we all get along. Directly after breakfast the good wife and the Doctor [2] retire upstairs to the drawing-room, a little place all fitted up like a lady's workbox, where a spunk of fire is lit for the forenoon ; and I meanwhile sit scribbling and meditating and wrestling with the powers of dullness, till one or two o'clock, when I sally forth into the city or towards the sea-shore, taking care only to be home for the important purpose of consuming my mutton chop at four. After dinner we all read learned languages till coffee (which we now often take at night instead of tea), and so on till bedtime ; only that Jane often sews ; and the Doctor goes up to the celestial globe, studying the fixed stars through an upshoved window, and generally comes down to his porridge about ten with a nose dropping at the extremity. Thus pass our days in our trim little cottage, far from all the up-

[1] The novel.

[2] John Carlyle, now staying with them.

roars and putrescences (material and spiritual) of the reeky town, the sound of which we hear not, and only see over the knowe the reflection of its gaslights against the dusky sky, and bless ourselves that we have neither part nor lot in the matter. Many a time on a soft mild night I smoke my pipe in our little flower-garden, and look upon all this, and think of all absent and present friends, and feel that I have good reason 'to be thankful I am not in Purgatory.'

Of society we might have abundance. People come on foot, on horseback, and even in wheeled carriages to see us, most of whom Jane receives upstairs, and despatches with assurances that the weather is good, bad, or indifferent, and hints that their friend-ship passes the love of women. We receive invitations to dinner also; but Jane has a circular—or rather two circulars—one for those she values, and one for those she does not value ; and one or the other of these she sends in excuse. Thus we give no dinners and take none, and by the blessing of heaven design to persist in this course so long as we shall see it to be best. Only to some three or four chosen people we give notice that on Wednesday nights we shall *always* be at home, and glad if they will call and talk for two hours with no other entertainment but a cordial wel-come and a cup of innocent tea. Few Wednesday evenings pass accordingly when some decent soul or other does not step in and take his place among us ; and we converse and really, I think, enjoy ourselves more than I have witnessed at any beef-eating and wine-bibbing convention which I have been trysted with attending.

I had almost forgot to tell you that I have in my pocket a letter of introduction to Jeffrey of the 'Edinburgh Review.' It was sent to me from Procter of London. One of these days I design presenting it, and you shall hear the result.

Jane Welsh Carlyle to Mrs. Carlyle, Scotsbrig.

21 Comely Bank : February 17.

My husband is busy below stairs, and I, it seems, am this time to be the writer—with greater willingness than ability, indeed, for I have been very stupid these some days with cold. But you must not be left in the idea that we are so neglectful as we have seemed. A little packet was actually written to go by the carrier on Wednesday ; when the rain fell and the wind blew, so that no living creature dared venture to his quarters. The Doctor pro-ceeded thither as early as was good for his health, in case fortune in the shape of bad weather, or whisky, had interposed delay. By that time, however, carrier, boxes, and Bobby were all far on the road ; so you see there was nothing for it but to write by post, which I lose no time in doing.

And now let me thank you for the nice eggs and butter, which arrived in best preservation and so opportunely—just as I was lamenting over the emptied cans as one who had no hope. Really it is most kind in you to be so mindful and helpful of our town wants, and most gratifying to us to see ourselves so cared for.

The new book is going on at a regular rate, and I would fain persuade myself that his health and spirits are at the same regular rate improving. More contented he certainly is since he applied himself to this task, for he was not born to be anything but miserable in idleness. Oh that he were indeed well, well beside *me*, and occupied as he ought. How plain and clear life would then lie before us ! I verily believe there would not be such a happy pair of people on the face of the whole earth. Yet we must not wish this too earnestly. How many precious things do we not already possess which others have not, have hardly an idea of ! Let us enjoy thêm then, and bless God that we are permitted to enjoy them rather than importune his goodness with vain longing for more. Indeed we had a most quiet and even happy life here. Within doors all is warm, is swept and garnished, and without the country is no longer winter like, but beginning to be gay and green. Many pleasant people come to see us ; and such of our visitors as are *not* pleasant people have at least the good effect of enhancing the pleasures to us of being alone. *Alone* we are never weary. If I have not Jean's enviable gift of talking, I am at least among the best listeners in the kingdom, and my husband has always something interesting and instructive to say. Then we have books to read—all sorts of them, from Scott's Bible down to novels—and I have sewing-needles, and purse-needles, and all conceivable implements for ladies' work. There is a piano, too, for ' soothing the savage breast ' when one cares for its charms ; but I am sorry to say neither my playing nor my singing seems to give Mr. C. much delight. I console myself, however, with imputing the blame to his want of taste rather than to my want of skill.

So Jean is not coming yet. Well, I am sorry for it ; but I hope the time is coming. In the mean time she must be a good girl, and read as much as she has time for, and above all things cultivate this talent of speech. It is my husband's worst fault to me that I will not or cannot speak. Often when he has talked for an hour without answer, he will beg for some signs of life on my part, and the only sign I can give is a little kiss. Well, that is better than nothing; don't you think so?

She might well say, 'He has talked for an hour without answer.' It was not easy to answer Carlyle. Already it seems his power of speech, unequalled so far as my experience goes by that of any other man, had begun to open itself. ' Carlyle first, and all the rest nowhere,' was the description of him by one of the best judges in London, when speaking of the great talkers of the day. His vast reading, his minute observation, his miraculously retentive memory, gave him something valuable to say on every subject which could be raised. What he took into his mind was dissolved and recrystallised into original combinations of his own. His writing, too, was as fluent as his speech. His early letters—even the most exquisitely finished sentences of them—are in an even and beautiful hand without erasure or alteration of a phrase. Words flowed from him with a completeness of form which no effort could improve. When he was excited it was like the eruption of a volcano, thunder and lightning, hot stones and smoke and ashes. He had a natural tendency to exaggeration, and although at such times his extraordinary metaphors and flashes of Titanesque humour made him always worth listening to, he was at his best when talking of history or poetry or biography, or of some contemporary person or incident which had either touched his sympathy or amused his delicate sense of absurdity. His laugh was from his whole nature, voice, eyes, and even his whole body. And there was never any malice in it. His own definition of humour, 'a genial sympathy with the under side,' was the definition also of his own feeling about all things and all persons, when it was himself that was speaking, and not what he called the devil that **was** occasionally in possession. In the long years that I was intimate with him I never heard him tell a malicious story or say a malicious word of any human being. His language was sometimes like the rolling of a great cathedral organ, sometimes like the softest flute-notes, sad or playful as the mood or the subject might be; and you listened— threw in, perhaps, an occasional word to show that you went along with him, but you were simply charmed, and listened on without caring to interrupt. Interruption, indeed, would answer little purpose, for Carlyle did not bear contradiction any better than Johnson. Contradiction would make him angry and unreasonable. He gave you a full picture of what was in his own mind, and you took it away with you and reflected on it.

This singular faculty—which, from Mrs. Carlyle's language, appears to have been shared in some degree by his sister Jean—had been the spell which had won his wife, as Othello's tales of his adventures won the heart of Desdemona; and it was ready brightening the evenings at Comely Bank. She on her side gives an imperfect idea of her own occupations when she describes herself as busy with needlework and books and the piano. They kept but one servant, and neither she nor her husband could endure either dirt or disorder, while Carlyle's sensitive stomach required a more delicate hand in the kitchen than belonged to a maid of all work. The days of the loaf—her first baking adventure, which she watched as Benvenuto Cellini watched his Perseus—were not yet. Edinburgh bread was eatable, and it was not till they were at Craigenputtock that she took charge of the oven. But Carlyle himself has already described her as making the damaged Scotsbrig eggs into custards and puddings. 'When they married,' Miss Jewsbury says, 'she had determined that he should never write for money, but only when he had something to say, and that she would make whatever money he gave

her answer for all needful purposes. She managed so well
that comfort was never absent from her house, and no one
looking on could have guessed whether they were rich or
poor. Whatever she had to do she did with a peculiar
personal grace that gave a charm to the most prosaic details. But she had to put her hand to tasks of the rudest
kind. No one who in later years saw her lying on the
sofa in broken health and languor would guess the amount
of energetic hard work she had done in her life. Her insight was like witchcraft. When she was to make her
first pudding she went into the kitchen and locked the
door on herself, having got the servant out of the road.
It was to be *such* a pudding—not just a common pudding
but something special, and it was good, being made with
care by weight and measure.'

Thus prettily Carlyle's married life began, the kind
friends at Scotsbrig sending weekly supplies by the carrier.
But even with Mrs. Carlyle to husband them the visible
financial resources were ebbing and must soon come to low
water; and on this side the prospect resolutely refused to
mend. The novel was a failure and eventually had to be
burnt. The hope which had vaguely lingered of some
regular and salaried appointment faded away. Overtures
of various kinds to London publishers had met with no
acceptance. German Romance was financially a failure
also, and the Edinburgh publishers would make no future
ventures. Under these conditions it is not wonderful that
(resolved as he was never to get into money difficulties)
Carlyle's mind reverted before long to his old scheme of settling at Craigenputtock. He no longer thought of turning
farmer himself. His wife's ridicule would have saved him
from any rash enterprise of that kind. But his brother
Alick was still willing to undertake the farm and to make
a rent out of it. For himself he looked to it only as a
cheap and quiet residence. His Hoddam experience had

taught him the superior economy of a country life. At Craigenputtock he could have his horse, pure air, milk diet, all really or theoretically essential to his health. Edinburgh society he considered was of no use to him; practical Edinburgh, he was equally sure, would do nothing for him; and away on the moors 'he could go on with his literature and with his life-task generally in the absolute solitude and pure silence of nature, with nothing but loving and helpful faces round him under clearly improved omens.' To his wife he did recognize that the experiment would be unwelcome. She had told him before her marriage that she could not live a month at Craigenputtock with an angel, while at Comely Bank she had little to suffer and something to enjoy.

Her modest days (he says), which never demanded much to make them happy, were beginning to have many little joys and amusements of their own in that bright scene, and she would have to change it for one of the loneliest, mooriest, and dullest in nature. To her it was a great sacrifice, if to me it was the reverse; but at no moment, even by a look, did she ever say so. Indeed I think she never felt so at all. She would have gone to Nova Zembla with me, and found *it* the right place had benefit to me or set purpose of mine lain there.

Only one recommendation Craigenputtock could have had to Mrs. Carlyle—that it was her own ancestral property, and that her father had been born there. Happily her mother, when the scheme was mentioned to her, approved heartily. Templand was but fifteen miles from Craigenputtock gate, not more than a morning's ride, and frequent meetings could be looked forward to. The present tenant of Craigenputtock was in arrears with his rent, and was allowing house and fences to go to ruin. Some change or other had become indispensable, and Mrs. Welsh was so anxious to have the Carlyles there that she undertook to put the rooms in repair and to pay the expenses of the move.

After a week or two of consideration Carlyle joined his brother Alick in the middle of April at Dumfries, Mrs. Welsh paying her daughter a visit during his absence. They drove out together and examined the place, and the result was that the tenant was to go, while Carlyle was to enter into possession at Whitsuntide; the house was to be made habitable, and, unless some unforeseen good luck should befall Carlyle meanwhile, he and his wife were to follow when it was ready to receive them. One pretty letter from her has been preserved, which was written to her husband when he was absent on this expedition.

To Thomas Carlyle.

Comely Bank: April, 1827.

Dear, Dear—Cheap, Cheap,[1]—I met the postman yesterday morning, and something bade me ask if there were any letters. Imagine my agitation when he gave me yours four and twenty hours before the appointed time. I was so glad and so frightened, so eager to know the *whole* contents that I could hardly make out any part. In the little tobacconist's, where I was fain to seek a quiet place, I did at length, with much heart-beating, get through the precious paper, and found that you still loved me pretty well, and that the 'Craig o' Putta' was still a hope; as also that if you come not back to poor Goody on Saturday it will not be for want of will.[2] Ah! nor yet will it be for want of the most fervent prayers to Heaven that a longing Goody can put up; for I am sick —sick to the heart—of this absence, which indeed I can only bear in the faith of its being brief. . . .

Alas, the poor Craig o' Putta! What a way it is in with these good-for-nothing sluggards! I need not recommend to you to do all that is possible—nay, 'to do the impossible'—to get them out. Even suppose we did not wish the place for ourselves, it would be miserable to consign it to such hands. You will use all fair means, therefore, to recover it from them—that is, all honest means; for,

---

[1] 'Cheap! Cheap!' was an answer with which Carlyle had replied once to some endearment of hers.

[2] Goody was Carlyle's name for his wife at this time.

as to the tenderness and delicacy which would have been becoming towards a worthy tenant, it were here out of place. I shall be very anxious until I hear from you again. Would to heaven the business was settled, and in the way we wish! These perplexities and suspenses are not good for bilious people : indeed, they are making *me* positively ill. How often since you went have I been reminded of your figure about the *hot ashes* (?), and my head has ached more continuously than at any time these six months. But health and spirits will come back when my husband comes back with good news—or rather, when he comes back at all, whether his news be good or bad. . . . To be separated from you one week is frightful as a foretaste of what it *might* be, but I will not think of this if I can help it; and after all why should I think of life without you? Is not my being interwoven with yours so close that it can have no separate existence? Yes, surely, we will live together and die together and be together through all eternity. But you will be calling this 'French sentimentality,' I fear; and even 'the style of mockery is better than that.'

I have not been altogether idle since we parted, though I threatened I would take to bed. I have finished my review, the representation of female character in the Greek poets, and the comparison between Cæsar and Alexander, with all that I could understand of the 'Friend;' over and above which I have transacted a good deal of shaping and sewing, the result of which will be complete, I hope, by the day of your return, and fill you with 'weender and amazement.' [1] Gilbert Burns is gone. Mr. Brodie told us of his death last week. Besides him, Mrs. Binnie, the Bruce people, and Mrs. Aitken, we have had no visitors, and I have paid no visits. Last night I was engaged to Mrs. Bruce, but I wrapped a piece of flannel about my throat and made my mother carry an apology of *cold*. But I may cut short these insipidities. My kindest love to all, from the wee'est up to Lord Moon. [2]

Here is Carlyle's answer, coming from his best, his re. l self—the true Carlyle, which always lay below, however irritable or moody the surface.

[1] 'Report of little Jean's of some preacher who had profusely employed that locution, pronounced as here.—T. C.' This is one of the letters specially annotated by Carlyle for publication.

[2] 'The Lord Moon is brother John=the Lord Mohun of Hamilton's tragic ballad, which is still sung in those parts. Epithet from brother Alick indicating breadth of face.—T. C.'

To the *Wife.*

Scotsbrig: April 17, 1827.

Not unlike what the drop of water from Lazarus's finger might have been to Dives in the flame was my dearest Goody's letter to her husband yesterday afternoon.   Blacklock[1] had retired to the bank for fifteen minutes ; the whirlwind was sleeping for that brief season, and I smoking my pipe in grim repose, when Alick came back with your messenger.   No ; I do not love you in the least— only a little *sympathy* and *admiration,* and a certain *esteem.*   Nothing more ! oh my dear best wee woman—but not a word of all this.

Such a day I never had in my life, but it is all over and well, and now ' Home, brothers, home ! '

Oh, Jeannie, how happy shall we be in this Craig o' Putta ! Not that I look for an Arcadia or a Lubberland there ; but we shall sit under our bramble and our saugh tree, and none to make us afraid ; and my little wife will be there for ever beside me, and I shall be well and blest, and ' the latter end of that man will be better than the beginning.'

Surely I shall learn at length to prize the pearl of great price which God has given to me unworthy.   Surely I already know that to me the richest treasure of this sublunary life has been awarded—the heart of my own noble Jane.   Shame on me for complaining, sick and wretched though I be.   Bourbon and Braganza, when I think of it, are but poor men to me.   Oh Jeannie ! oh my wife ! we will never part, never through eternity itself ; but I will love thee and keep thee in my heart of hearts ! that is, unless I grow a very great fool—which, indeed, this talk doth somewhat betoken.

God bless thee !   Ever thine,

T. CARLYLE.

[1] The outgoing tenant of Craigenputtock.

CHAPTER XXI.

A.D. 1827.   ÆT. 32.

ALEXANDER CARLYLE, with his sister Mary, went into occupation of Craigenputtock at Whitsuntide 1827. His
brother had intended to join him before the end of the
summer, but at this moment affairs in Edinburgh began
to brighten and took a turn which seemed at one time
likely to lead into an entirely new set of conditions. Carlyle had mentioned that he had a letter of introduction
to Jeffrey. He had delayed presenting it, partly, perhaps,
on account of the absolute silence with which some years
before Jeffrey had received a volunteered contribution
from him for the 'Edinburgh Review.' Irving had urged
the experiment, and it had been made. The MS. was not
only not accepted, but was neither acknowledged nor returned. Carlyle naturally hesitated before making another advance where he had been repulsed so absolutely.
He determined, however, shortly after his return from his
Craigenputtock visit, to try the experiment. He called on
the great man and was kindly received. Jeffrey was struck
with him; did not take particularly to his opinions; but
perceived at once, as he frankly said to him, that 'he was
a man of original character and right heart,' and that he
would 'be proud and happy to know more of him.' A
day or two after he called with Mrs. Jeffrey at Comely
Bank, and was as much—perhaps even more—attracted
by the lady whom he found there, and whom he discovered to be some remote Scotch kinswoman. It was the
beginning of a close and interesting intimacy, entered up-

on, on Jeffrey's part, with a genuine recognition of Carlyle's qualities and a desire to be useful to him, which, no doubt, would have assumed a practical form had he found his new friend amenable to influence or inclined to work in harness with the party to which Jeffrey belonged. But Jeffrey was a Benthamite on the surface, and underneath an Epicurean, with a good-humoured contempt for enthusiasm and high aspirations. Between him and a man so 'dreadfully in earnest' as Carlyle, there could be little effective communion, and Carlyle soon ceased to hope, what at first he had allowed himself to expect, that Jeffrey might be the means of assisting him into some independent situation.

The immediate effect of the acquaintance, however, was Carlyle's admission, freely offered by the editor, into the 'Edinburgh Review,' a matter just then of infinite benefit to him, drawing him off from didactic novels into writing the series of Essays, now so well known as the Miscellanies, in which he tried his wings for his higher flights, and which in themselves contain some of his finest thoughts and most brilliant pictures. His first contribution was to be for the number immediately to appear, and Jeffrey was eager to receive it.

Carlyle was not particularly elated, and mentions the subject slightly in a letter to his brother Alick about the establishment at Craigenputtock.

To Alexander Carlyle.

Comely Bank : June 3.

It gave us much pleasure to find that you had in very deed made a settlement in your new abode, and were actually boiling your pot at the Craig o' Putta under circumstances however unpropitious. Your tears for parting (from Scotsbrig) will scarcely be dried yet, but in a little while you will look upon this movement in its real light, not as a parting, but as a truly blessed reunion for us all, where, I hope and believe, many good days are in store for every one of us. It will not be long till you have scrubbed up the old Craig, put in the broken slates, and burnt or buried the rotten rags of the late housewife, who, I am told, is indeed a slattern, and not only so, but a drunkard, which is far worse. Mary's nimble fingers and an orderly head will have introduced new arrangements into the mansion; things will begin to go their usual course, and the mavis and tomtit will no longer sing to sad hearts. Poor Mary! Be good to her in this her first removal from home, and remember that you are not only a brother to her, but, as it were, a husband and father.

As to the house, I think with you it were better if we all saw it before the plans were settled. Jane and I are both for coming down shortly. We shall not be long in seeing you. The only thing that absolutely detains me is a little article which I have to write before the end of this month for the 'Edinburgh Review'— a very brief one—which I begin to-morrow.

To his brother John he was more explicit.

To John Carlyle.

Comely Bank: June 4.

Of my own history since I wrote last I need mention only one or two particulars. Everything goes its course. I fight with dullness and bile in the forenoons as of old; I still walk diligently, talk *de omni scibili* when I can find fit or unfit audience, and so live on in the old light and shadow fashion much as you knew me before, only with rather more comfort and hope than with less. Our evening parties continue their modest existence. Last Wednesday we had Malcolm[1] and one Paterson, said to be 'the hope of the Scottish Church,' a very feckless young man so far as externals go, for his voice is the shrillest treble, he wears spectacles, and would scarcely weigh six stone avoirdupois; but evidently shrewd, vehement, modest, and, on the whole, well gifted and conditioned. . . .

One day I resolutely buckled myself up and set forth to the Parliament House for the purpose of seeing our Reviewer (Jeffrey). The little Jewel of Advocates was at his post. I accosted him, and, with a little explanation, was cheerfully recognised. 'The Article—where is the Article?' seemed to be the gist of his talk to me: for he was to all appearance anxious that I would undertake the task of Germanising the public, and ready even to let me do it *con amore*, so I did not treat the whole earth not yet Ger-

[1] See *Reminiscences*, p. 210.

manised as 'a parcel of blockheads,' which surely seemed a fair enough request. We walked to his lodgings discussing these matters. Two days after, having revolved the thing, I met him again with notice that I would 'undertake.' The next number of the 'Review,' it appeared, was actually in the press, and to be printed off before the end of June, so that no large article could find place there till the succeeding quarter. However, I engaged, as it were for paving the way, to give him in this present publication some little short paper, I think on the subject of Jean Paul, though that is not quite settled with myself yet. And thus, oh Jack, thou see'st me occupied with a new trade! On the whole I am rather glad of this adventure, for I think it promises to be the means of a pleasant connection. Certainly Jeffrey is by much the most lovable of all the literary men I have seen, and he seemed ready, nay desirous, if time would but permit, to cultivate a further intimacy.

Jean Paul was decided on, to be followed in the autumn by a more elaborate article on the general state of German literature. It was written at once, and forms the first of the Miscellaneous Essays in the collected edition of Carlyle's works. Carlyle's 'style,' which has been a rock of offence to so many people, has been attributed to his study of Jean Paul. No criticism could be worse founded. His style shaped itself as he gathered confidence in his own powers, and had its origin in his father's house in Annandale. His mode of expressing himself remained undistinguished by its special characteristics till he had ceased to occupy himself with the German poets. Of his present undertaking Carlyle says :—

Perhaps it was little De Quincey's reported admiration of Jean Paul—Goethe a mere corrupted pigmy to him—that first put me upon trying to be orthodox and admire. I dimly felt poor De Quincey, who passed for a mighty seer in such things, to have exaggerated, and to know, perhaps, but little of either Jean Paul or Goethe. However, I held on reading and considerably admiring Jean Paul on my own score, though always with something of secret disappointment. I could now wish, perhaps, that I hadn't. My first favourite books had been Hudibras and Tristram Shandy.

Everybody was proclaiming it such a feat for a man to have wit, to have humour above all. There was always a small secret something of affectation, which is not now secret to me, in that part of my affairs. As to my poor style, Edward Irving and his admiration of the old Puritans and Elizabethans—whom at heart I never could entirely adore, though trying hard—his and everybody's doctrine on that head played a much more important part than Jean Paul upon it. And the most important by far was that of nature, you would perhaps say, if you had ever heard my father speak, or my mother, and her inward melodies of heart and voice.

Carlyle's acquaintance with Wilson—Christopher North —had been slight, Wilson, perhaps, dreading his radicalism. In the course of the summer, however, accident threw them more closely together, and one of their meetings is thus described.

To John Carlyle.

21 Comely Bank.

Last night I supped with John Wilson, Professor of Moral Philosophy here, author of the 'Isle of Palms,' &c., a man of the most fervid temperament, fond of all stimulating things, from tragic poetry down to whisky punch. He snuffed and smoked cigars and drank liquors, and talked in the most indescribable style. It was at the lodging of one John Gordon, a young very good man from Kirkcudbright, who sometimes comes here. Daylight came on us before we parted; indeed, it was towards three o'clock as the Professor and I walked home, smoking as we went. I had scarcely either eaten or drunk, being a privileged person, but merely enjoyed the strange volcanic eruptions of our poet's convivial genius. He is a broad sincere man of six feet, with long dishevelled flax-coloured hair, and two blue eyes keen as an eagle's. Now and then he sank into a brown study, and seemed dead in the eye of law. About two o'clock he was sitting in this state smoking languidly, his nose begrimed with snuff, his face hazy and inert; when all at once flashing into existence, he inquired of John Gordon, with an irresistible air, 'I hope, Mr. Gordon, you don't believe in universal damnation?' It was wicked, but all hands burst into inextinguishable laughter. But I expect to see Wilson in a more philosophic key ere long; he has promised to call on me, and is, on the whole, a man I should like to know better. Geniuses of any sort, especially of so kindly a sort, are so very rare in this world.

Another and yet brighter episode of this summer was a second and far more remarkable letter from Goethe. Carlyle had sent the 'Life of Schiller' to Weimar, and afterwards the volumes of German Romance. They were acknowledged with a gracious interest which went infinitely beyond his warmest hopes. There was not a letter only, but little remembrances for himself and his wife; and better even than the presents, a few lines of verse addressed to each of them.

Carlyle sends the account to his mother.

Comely Bank: August 18.

News came directly after breakfast that a packet from Goethe had arrived in Leith. Without delay I proceeded thither, and found a little box carefully overlapped in wax cloth, and directed to me. After infinite wranglings and perplexed misdirected higglings I succeeded in rescuing the precious packet from the fangs of the Custom House sharks, and in the afternoon it was safely deposited in our little parlour—the daintiest boxie you ever saw—so carefully packed, so neatly and tastefully contrived was everything. There was a copy of Goethe's poems in five beautiful little volumes for 'the valued marriage pair Carlyle;' two other little books for myself, then two medals, one of Goethe himself and another of his father and mother; and, lastly, the prettiest wrought-iron necklace with a little figure of the poet's face set in gold for 'my dear spouse,' and a most dashing pocket-book for me. In the box containing the necklace, and in each pocket of the pocket-book were cards, each with a verse of poetry on it in the old master's own hand. All these I will translate to you by-and-by, as well as the long letter which lay at the bottom of all, one of the kindest and gravest epistles I ever read. He praises me for the 'Life of Schiller' and the others ; asks me to send him some account of my own previous history, &c. In short, it was all extremely graceful, affectionate and patriarchal. You may conceive how much it pleased us. I believe a ribbon with the order of the Garter would scarcely have flattered either of us more.

The letter from Goethe was this :[1]—

To Thomas Carlyle.

Weimar : July 20, 1827.

In a letter of the 15th of March which I sent by the post, and which I trust has reached you safely, I mentioned the great pleasure which your present had given me. It found me in the country where I could study and enjoy it with greater leisure. I now am enabled to send a packet to you likewise, which I hope that you will be kind enough to accept from me.

Let me, in the first place, tell you, my dear sir, how very highly I esteem your ' *Biography* of Schiller.' It is remarkable for the

---

[1] In einem Schreiben vom 15. März, welches ich mit der Post absendete und Sie hoffentlich zu rechter Zeit werden erhalten haben, vermeldete ich wie viel Vergnügen mir Ihre Sendung gebracht. Sie fand mich auf dem Lande, wo ich sie mit mehrerer Ruhe betrachten und geniessen konnte. Gegenwärtig sehe ich mich in dem Stande, auch ein Packet an Sie abzuschicken mit dem Wunsche freundlicher Aufnahme.

Lassen Sie mich vorerst, mein Theuerster, von Ihrer Biographie Schillers das Beste sagen. Sie ist merkwürdig, indem sie ein genaues Studium der Vorfälle seines Lebens beweist, so wie denn auch das Studium seiner Werke und eine innige Theilnahme an denselben daraus hervorgeht. Bewundernswürdig ist es wie Sie sich auf diese Weise eine genügende Einsicht in den Character und das hohe Verdienstliche dieses Mannes verschafft, so klar und so gehörig als es kaum aus der Ferne zu erwarten gewesen.

Hier bewahrheitet sich jedoch ein altes Wort: ' Der gute Wille hilft zu vollkommener Kenntniss.' Denn gerade dass der Schottländer den deutschen Mann mit Wohlwollen anerkennt, ihn verehrt und liebt, dadurch wird er dessen treffliche Eigenschaften am sichersten gewahr, dadurch erhebt er sich zu einer Klarheit zu der sogar Landsleute des Trefflichen in früheren Tagen nicht gelangen konnten ; denn die Mitlebenden werden an vorzüglichen Menschen gar leicht irre : das Besondere der Person stört sie, das laufende bewegliche Leben verrückt ihre Standpunkte und hindert das Kennen und Anerkennen eines solchen Mannes.

Dieser aber war von so ausserordentlicher Art, dass der Biograph die Idee eines vorzüglichen Mannes vor Augen halten und sie durch individuelle Schicksale und Leistungen durchführen konnte, und sein Tagewerk dergestalt vollbracht sah.

Die vor den *German Romances* mitgetheilten Notizen über das Leben Musäus, Hoffmanns, Richters &c. kann man in ihrer Art gleichfalls mit Beyfall aufnehmen ; sie sind mit Sorgfalt gesammelt, kürzlich dargestellt und geben von eines jeden Autors individuellem Character und der Einwirkung desselben auf seine Schriften genugsame Vorkenntniss.

Durchaus beweist Herr Carlyle eine ruhige, klare Theilnahme an den deutschen poetisch-literarischen Beginnen ; er giebt sich hin an das eigenthümliche Bestreben der Nation, er lässt den Einzelnen gelten, jeden an seiner Stelle.

careful study which it displays of the incidents of Schiller's life, and one clearly perceives in it a study of his works and a hearty sympathy with them. The complete insight which you have thus obtained into the character and high merits of this man is really admirable, so clear it is, and so appropriate, so far beyond what might have been looked for in a writer in a distant country.

Here the old saying is verified, ' a good will helps to a full understanding.' It is just because the Scot can look with affection on a German and can honour and love him, that he acquires a sure eye for that German's finest qualities. He raises himself into a clearness of vision which Schiller's own countrymen could not arrive at in earlier days. For those who live with superior men are

Sey mir nun erlaubt allgemeine Betrachtungen hinzuzufügen, welche ich längst bey mir im Stillen hege und die mir bey den vorliegenden Arbeiten abermals frisch aufgeregt worden.

Offenbar ist das Bestreben der besten Dichter und ästhetischen Schriftsteller aller Nationen schon seit geraumer Zeit auf das allgemein Menschliche gerichtet. In jedem Besondern, es sey nun historisch, mythologisch, fabelhaft, mehr oder weniger willkührlich ersonnen, wird man durch Nationalität und Persönlichkeit hindurch jenes Allgemeine immer mehr durchleuchten und durchschimmern sehn.

Da nun auch im practischen Lebensgange ein gleiches obwaltet und durch alles Irdisch-Rohe, Wilde, Grausame, Falsche, Eigennützige, Lügenhafte sich durchschlingt, und überall einige Milde zu verbreiten trachtet, so ist zwar nicht zu hoffen dass ein allgemeiner Friede dadurch sich einleite, aber doch dass der unvermeidliche Streit nach und nach lässlicher werde, der Krieg weniger grausam, der Sieg weniger übermüthig.

Was nun in den Dichtungen aller Nationen hierauf hindeutet und hinwirkt, diess ist es was die übrigen sich anzueignen haben. Die Besonderheiten einer jeden muss man kennen lernen, und sie ihr zu lassen, um gerade dadurch mit ihr zu verkehren ; denn die Eigenheiten einer Nation sind wie ihre Sprache und ihre Münzsorten, sie erleichtern den Verkehr, ja, sie machen ihn erst vollkommen möglich.

Verzeihen Sie mir, mein Werthester, diese vielleicht nicht ganz zusammenhängenden noch alsbald zu überschauenden Aeusserungen ; sie sind geschöpft aus dem Ocean der Betrachtungen, der um einen jeden Denkenden mit den Jahren immer mehr anschwillt. Lassen Sie mich noch Einiges hinzufügen, welches ich bey einer andern Gelegenheit niederschrieb, das sich jedoch hauptsächlich auf Ihr Geschäfft unmittelbar beziehen lässt.

Eine wahrhaft allgemeine Duldung wird am sichersten erreicht, wenn man das Besondere der einzelnen Menschen und Völkerschaften auf sich beruhen lässt, bey der Ueberzeugung jedoch festhält, dass das wahrhaft Verdienstliche sich dadurch auszeichnet dass es der ganzen Menschheit angehört. Zu einer solchen Vermittlung und wechselseitigen Anerkennung tragen die Deutschen seit langer Zeit schon bey.

Wer die deutsche Sprache versteht und studirt befindet sich auf dem **Markte**

easily mistaken in their judgment. Personal peculiarities irritate them. The swift changing current of life displaces their points of view, and hinders them from perceiving and recognising the true worth of such men.

Schiller's character, however, was so extraordinary that his biographer could start with the idea of an excellent man before him. He could carry that idea through all individual destinies and achievements, and thus see his task accomplished.

The notices, prefixed to 'German Romance,' of the lives of

wo alle Nationen ihre Waaren anbieten. Er spielt den Dolmetscher indem er sich selbst bereichert.

Und so ist jeder Uebersetzer anzusehen, dass er sich als Vermittler dieses allgemein geistigen Handels bemüht, und den Wechseltausch zu befördern sich zum Geschäfft macht. Denn was man auch von der Unzulänglichkeit des Uebersetzens sagen mag, so ist und bleibt es doch eines der wichtigsten und würdigsten Geschäffte in dem allgemeinen Weltwesen.

Der Koran sagt: 'Gott hat jedem Volke einen Propheten gegeben in seiner eignen Sprache.' So ist jeder Uebersetzer ein Prophet seinem Volke. Luther's Bibelübersetzung hat die grössten Wirkungen hervorgebracht, wenn schon die Kritik daran bis auf den heutigen Tag immerfort bedingt und mäkelt. Und was ist denn das ganze ungeheure Geschäfft der Bibelgesellschaft als das Evangelium einem jeden Volke in seiner eignen Sprache zu verkündigen?

Hier lassen Sie mich schliessen, wo man ins Unendliche fortfahren könnte, und erfreuen Sie mich bald mit einiger Erwiederung, wodurch ich Nachricht erhalte, dass gegenwärtige Sendung zu Ihnen gekommen ist.

Zum Schlusse lassen Sie mich denn auch Ihre liebe Gattin begrüssen, für die ich einige Kleinigkeiten, als Erwiederung ihrer anmuthigen Gabe, beyzulegen mir die Freude mache. Möge Ihnen ein glückliches Zusammenleben viele Jahre bescheert seyn.

Nach allem diesem finde ich mich angeregt Einiges hinzuzufügen: Möge Herr Carlyle alles obige freundlich aufnehmen und durch anhaltende Betrachtung in ein Gespräch verwandeln, damit es ihm zu Muthe werde als wenn wir persönlich einander gegenüber ständen.

Habich ihm ja sogar noch für die Bemühung zu danken, die er an meine Arbeiten gewendet hat, für den guten und wohlwollenden Sinn mit dem er von meiner Persönlichkeit und meinen Lebenereignissen zu sprechen geneigt war. In dieser Ueberzeugung darf ich mich denn auch zum voraus freuen, dass künftighin, wenn noch mehrere von meinen Arbeiten ihm bekannt werden, besonders auch wenn meine Correspondenz mit Schiller erscheinen wird, er weder von diesem Freunde noch von mir seine Meinung ändern, sondern sie vielmehr durch manches Besondere noch mehr bestätigt finden wird.

Das Beste herzlich wünschend

Treu theilnehmend,

J. W. GOETHE.

Weimar, a. 20. Jul. 1827.

Musæus, Hoffmann, Richter, &c., can be approved of equally in their several kinds. They are compiled with care, are briefly set out, and provide an adequate notion of each author's personal character, and of the effect of it upon his writings.

Mr. Carlyle displays throughout a calm, clear sympathy with poetical literary activity in Germany. He throws himself into the special national tendency, and gives individuals their credit each in his place.

Let me add a few general observations which I have long harboured in silence, and which have been stirred up by these present works.

It is obvious that for a considerable time the efforts of the best poets and æsthetic writers throughout the world have been directed towards the general characteristics of humanity. In each particular sphere, be it history, mythology, fiction, more or less arbitrarily conceived, the universal is made to show and shine through what is merely individual or national.

In practical life we perceive the same tendency, which pervades all that is of the earth earthy, crude, wild, cruel, false, selfish, and treacherous, and tries everywhere to spread a certain sereneness. We may not, indeed, hope from this the approach of an era of universal peace ; but yet that strifes which are unavoidable may grow less extreme, wars less savage, and victory less overbearing.

Whatever in the poetry of all nations aims and tends towards this, is what the others should appropriate. And one must study and make allowances for the peculiarities of each nation, in order to have real intercourse with it. The special characteristics of a people are like its language and its currency. They facilitate exchange ; indeed, they first make exchange possible.

Pardon me, my dear sir, for these remarks, which perhaps are not quite coherent, nor to be scanned all at once ; they are drawn from the great ocean of observations, which, as life passes on, swells up more and more round every thinking person. Let me add some more observations which I wrote down on another occasion, but which apply specially to the business on which you are now engaged.

We arrive best at a true general toleration when we can let pass individual peculiarities, whether of persons or peoples, without quarrelling with them ; holding fast nevertheless to the conviction that genuine excellence is distinguished by this mark, that it belongs to all mankind. To such intercourse and mutual recognition the Germans have long contributed.

He who knows and studies German finds himself in the market where the wares of all countries are offered for sale; while he enriches himself, he is officiating as interpreter.

A translator therefore should be regarded as a trader in this great spiritual commerce, and as one who makes it his business to advance the exchange of commodities. For say what we will of the inadequacy of translation, it always will be among the weightiest and worthiest factors in the world's affairs.

The Koran says that God has given each people a prophet in its own tongue. Each translator is also a prophet to his people. The effects of Luther's translation of the Bible have been immeasurable, though criticism has been at work picking holes in it to the present day. What is the enormous business of the Bible Society but to make known the Gospel to every nation in its own tongue?

But from this point we might be led into endless speculations. Let me conclude.

Oblige me with an early reply, that I may know that my packet has reached your hands.

Commend me to your excellent wife, for whom I send a few trifles. Give me pleasure by accepting them in return for her charming present. May your life together be happy, and may many years be your portion.

I have yet something to add. May Mr. Carlyle take in friendly part what I have said above. May he consider it well, and throw it into dialogue, as if he and I had been conversing in person together.

I have now to thank him for the pains which he has taken with my own writings, and for the good and affectionate tone in which he has been pleased to speak of myself and of my history. I may thus gratify myself with a belief that hereafter, on more complete acquaintance with my works, and after the publication especially of my correspondence with Schiller, he will not alter his opinion either of my friend or of me, but will find it confirmed by fresh particulars. Wishing him from my heart all good things, and with genuine sympathy with him,

J. W. Goethe.

Such was Goethe's letter, which so much and so justly delighted Carlyle. On a card in the pocket-book was writ-

ten, 'Mr. Carlyle will give me especial pleasure by some
account of his past life.'

On another card were the lines—

> Augenblicklich aufzuwarten
> Schicken Freunde solche Karten ;
> Diesmal aber heissts nicht gern,
> Euer Freund ist weit und fern.—GOETHE.

Weimar, 20. Juli, 1827.

A third card was in the box with the wrought-iron necklace which was intended for Mrs. Carlyle. On this was
written—

> Wirst du in den Spiegel blicken
> Und vor deinen heitern Blicken
> Dich die ernste Zierde schmücken :
> Denke dass nichts besser schmückt
> Als wenn man den Freund beglückt.—G.

The 'books' were 'Faust,' the first five volumes of the
latest edition of Goethe's works, and the last published
number of 'Kunst und Alterthum.' There were two
medallions, as Carlyle had told his mother—one of them
of Goethe with an eagle on the reverse ; the other of himself also, with his father and mother on the reverse. The
whole present, Carlyle said, was most tasteful, and to him
as precious as *any* such present could possibly be.

A still more charming, because unintended, compliment
was to follow from the same quarter. When the purposed
removal to Craigenputtock came to be talked of among
Carlyle's Edinburgh friends, it seemed to them 'considerably fantastic and unreasonable.'

Prospects in Edinburgh (he says) had begun to brighten economically and otherwise ; the main origin of this was our acquaintance with the brilliant Jeffrey, a happy accident rather than a
matter of forethought on either side. My poor article on Jean
Paul, willingly enough admitted into his 'Review,' excited a considerable, though questionable, sensation in Edinburgh, as did the
next still weightier discharge of 'German Literature' in that un-

expected vehicle, and at all events denoted me as a fit head for that kind of adventure. In London, shortly after, had arisen a 'Foreign Quarterly Review,' and then in a month or two, on some booksellers' quarrel, a 'Foreign Review,' on both of which I was employed, courted, &c., till their brabble healed itself. This and the like of this formed our principal finance fund during all the Craigenputtock time. For nothing had shaken our determination to the new home. Very well, very well, I said to all this. It will go much further there instead of straitened as here.

The article on German literature reached Weimar. It was of course anonymous. Goethe read it, and, curious to know the authorship of such an unexpected appearance, wrote to Carlyle for information. 'Can you tell me,' he said, 'who has written the paper on the state of German literature in the "Edinburgh Review"? It is believed here to be by Mr. Lockhart, Sir Walter Scott's stepson. They are both serious, well-disposed men, and equally deserving of honour.'[1] Goethe could not be suspected of insincere politeness, and every sentence of the previous letter was a genuine expression of true feeling; but this indirect praise was so clearly undesigned that it was doubly encouraging.

Carlyle was still determined on Craigenputtock, but various causes continued to detain him in Edinburgh. The acquaintance with Jeffrey ripened into a warm intimacy. Jeffrey was a frequent visitor in Comely Bank; the Carlyles were as often his guests at Craigcrook. They met interesting persons there, whose society was pleasant and valuable. Jeffrey was himself influential in the great world of politics, and hopes revived—never, perhaps, very ardently in Carlyle himself, but distinctly in his wife and among his friends—that he would be rescued by some fitting appointment from banishment to the Dumfriesshire

[1] I am sorry that of this letter from Goethe only this single passage is preserved. Indeed, as I have already said, the originals of all Goethe's letters to Carlyle have disappeared, and there remain only the copies of some of them which he sent to his brother.

moors.   Carlyle was now famous in a limited circle, and
might reasonably be selected for a professorship or other
similar situation ; while other possibilities opened on various sides to which it was at least his duty to attend.
Meanwhile demands came in thick for fresh articles: Jeffrey wanted one on Tasso; the ' Foreign Quarterly' wanted
anything that he pleased to send, with liberal offers of
pay.   He could not afford at such a moment to be out of
the reach of libraries, and therefore for the present he left
his brother alone in the moorland home.

In the summer he and his wife ran down for a short
holiday at Scotsbrig, giving a few brief days to Templand,
and a glance at Craigenputtock.   By August they were
again settled in Comely Bank.   The Carlyles, as he said
long before, were a clannish set, and clung tenaciously together.   The partings after ever so brief a visit were always sorrowful.

To Mrs. Carlyle, Scotsbrig.

21 Comely Bank : August.

My dear Mother,—It was pity that we were all so *wae* that day
we went off; but we cannot well help it.   This life is but a series
of meetings and partings, and many a tear one might shed, while
these ' few and evil days ' pass over us.   But we hope there is another scene to which this is but the passage, where good and holy
affections shall live as in their home, and for true friends there
shall be no more partings appointed.   God grant we may all have
our lot made sure in that earnest and enduring country ; for surely
this world, the more one thinks of it, seems the more fluctuating,
hollow, and unstable.   What are its proudest hopes but bubbles
on the stream of time, which the next rushing wave will scatter
into air ?   You have heard of Canning's death—the Prime Minister of Britain, the skilful statesman on whom all eyes in England
and Europe were expectingly fixed.

> What is life ? a thawing ice board
> On a sea with sunny shore ;
> Gay we sail, it melts beneath us ;
> We are sunk and seen no more.

But I must leave these moralities, in which, perhaps, I am too apt to indulge. Before this time Mary will be with you and have reported progress up to Monday last, the day when I left Craigenputtock. She will have told you how Jane and I were overtaken by rain at Dumfries, and how we spent the night with the hospital man in Academy Street, and how his daft maid came bouncing into the room after we were in bed, to the astonishment of Goody, altogether unaccustomed to such familiarity. For the rest, however, we did as well as might be, and the order of 'Mary Stuart's' apartment was considerably admired. On Monday evening, after parting with the Doctor, I cantered along without adventure to Templand ; was met two bow-shots from the house by a young wife well known to me and glad to get me back, and next morning by ten o'clock both she and I were safely mounted *on the roof* of the Edinburgh coach, where, the day being fine, we continued comfortably enough seated, till about half-past eight the natural progress of the vehicle landed us safe and sound in our own neighbourhood. The house was standing quiet and almost overgrown with flowers. Next day everything returned to its old routine, and we were sitting in our bright still little cottage as if we had never stirred out of it. I set to work to trim the garden till my mind should settle after its wanderings, but as yet I am not half through with it.

You *must come hither in winter*, that is a settled point. My father and you may journey together by Hawick in many ways. Alick was even calculating the relative costs and profits of coming to Edinburgh himself with a cartload of potatoes and other necessaries. In case of his visiting us, you might all then come together. But *any way you* MUST come. It would be a grievous disappointment if I could not have the pleasure of showing you this city and its wonders, and if we missed this opportunity there is no saying when another might occur. So settle it with yourself that you *are* to come, and in the meantime consider when you can do it best, and we will study to conform.

I went on Saturday to see Jeffrey, but found him from home for a week. So soon as I have got Goethe a letter written, and various other little odd things transacted, I design sitting down to my *large* article for his 'Review ;' after which I shall be ready for the *poor book*,[1] which, alas ! has been dreadfully overlooked of late. It is a pity one had not twenty minds and hands ; double

---

[1] Not yet consciously abandoned, but never again taken up.

pity one did not faithfully employ the mind and hands one has; but I will turn a new leaf shortly, for idle I cannot and must not be. *The sweat of the brow* is not a curse but the wholesomest blessing in life. Remember me in warmest affection to everyone at Scotsbrig. I would give a shilling for a long letter. Surely you may club one up amongst you.

I am ever, my dear mother's son,

T. CARLYLE.

With reputation growing, and economics looking less gloomy, Carlyle's spirits were evidently rising. We hear no more of pain and sickness and bilious lamentations, and he looked about him in hope and comfort. The London University was getting itself established, offering opportunities for Nonconformist genius such as England had never before provided. Professors were wanted there in various departments of knowledge. He was advised to offer himself to be one of them, and he wrote to Irving to inquire, with no particular result:—

To John Carlyle.

Comely Bank : September 5.

I had a letter from Edward Irving the other day about the Æsthetical Professorship in the London University.[1] In a strange, austere, puritanical, yet on the whole honest and friendly looking style, he advises me to proceed and make the attempt. 'The Lord,' he says, blesses him; his Church rejoices in 'the Lord;' in fact, the Lord and he seem to be quite hand and glove. He looks unhappy, for his tone sounds hollow, like some voice from a sepulchral aisle ; yet I do honestly believe there is much worth among his failings, much precious truth among all this *cant*. I must even regret that he goes into those matters with so very disunited a heart; but there where he stands, I wish I and every one of us were half as good men. As to this 'projection,' as he calls it, I have not yet taken any steps, being indeed too busy for doing anything. I was to write to him again, but have not. I wait for counsel from Jeffrey, whom I have not since seen.

---

[1] It was not yet decided what the chair was to be—Rhetoric, Taste, Moral Philosophy, English Literature, or what.

In appointments to the London University, the great Brougham, not yet Chancellor or peer, but member for Yorkshire, and greatest orator in the House of Commons, was likely to be omnipotent. Jeffrey, it was equally probable, would carry weight with Brougham; and Jeffrey, when Carlyle consulted him, expressed the utmost personal willingness to be of use to Carlyle. But his reply illustrates what Goethe had just observed about Schiller, that genius rarely finds recognition from contemporaries as long as it can possibly be withheld. At all times, Jeffrey said, he would be willing to recommend Carlyle as a man of genius and learning; he did not conceal, however, that difficulties would lie in the way of his success in this especial enterprise. Carlyle, he said, was a sectary in taste and literature, and was inspired with the zeal by which sectaries were distinguished. He was inclined to magnify the special doctrines of his sect, and rather to aggravate than reconcile the differences which divided them from others. He confessed, therefore, that he doubted whether the patrons either would or ought to appoint such a person to such a charge. The sincerity and frankness of Carlyle's character increased the objection, for such a person would insist the more peremptorily on the articles of his philosophic creed—a creed which no one of the patrons adopted, and most of them regarded as damnable heresy. It was therefore but too likely that this would prove an insuperable obstacle. In all other respects Jeffrey considered Carlyle fully qualified, and likely, if appointed, to do great credit to the establishment. But he was afraid that Carlyle would not wish to disguise those singularities of opinion from which he foresaw the obstructions to his success; and as a further difficulty he added that the chair at which Carlyle was aiming had long been designed for Thomas Campbell, and would probably be given to him.

Jeffrey invited Carlyle and his wife to dinner, however,

to talk the chances over. Carlyle assured Jeffrey 'that there was no sectarianism or heresy in the matter. He was more open to light,' he said, ' than others of his craft ; and he was satisfied for himself that the patrons of the University would do excellently well to make him professor.' ' Jeffrey,' Mrs. Carlyle thought, ' was in his heart of the same opinion.' She was herself uncertain whether she wished her husband to succeed or not ; but London would at all events be an escape from Craigenputtock. Reflection had not tended to make the moor more palatable to her. Her little sister-in-law Jean had just been sent out thither to keep her brother company.

'Poor Jean !' Mrs. Carlyle wrote about this. ' She is seeing the world all on a sudden. What will the creature make of herself at Craigenputtock ? I hope they took her garters from her, and everything in the shape of hemp or steel.'

Jeffrey did what he could, perhaps not with very great ardour, but with vigour enough to save him from the charge of neglecting his friend. He went on a visit to Brougham in the autumn. He mentioned Carlyle, and in high terms of praise. He 'found Brougham, however, singularly shy on the subject, and though the subject was introduced half a dozen times during Jeffrey's stay, Brougham was careful to evade it, in a way that showed that he did not wish to be pressed for an answer even by an intimate friend.'

'I may add in confidence,' Jeffrey said, ' that he made very light of Irving's recommendation, and it was not likely to be of much weight with any of the other directors either.'

Notwithstanding these discouragements, Carlyle silently nourished some hope of success.

I believe (he wrote to his brother in October) that no appointment to the London chair will take place for a considerable time, and in the meanwhile Brougham will keep his eye on me, and if he

finds that I prosper may apply to me ; if not, will leave me standing. At all events the thing is right. I am before these people
in some shape, perhaps as near my real one as I could expect ;
and if they want nothing with me, 'the Deil be in me,' as daft
Wull said, if I want anything with them either. I am still as undetermined as ever whether their acceptance of me would be for
my good or not.

He came to know Brougham better in after years.
There was probably no person in England less likely to
recognise Carlyle's qualities ; and the more distinguished
Carlyle became, the more Brougham was sure to have con-
gratulated himself on having kept his new University
clear of such an influence. It must be admitted that the
'*disesteem*' was equally marked on both sides.

Carlyle meanwhile did not rest on the vain imagination
of help from others. He worked with all his might on
the new line which had been opened to him, and here I
have to mention one of those peculiarly honourable characteristics which meet us suddenly at all turns of his
career. He had paid his brother's expenses at the University out of his salary as the Bullers' tutor. He was
now poor himself with increased demands upon him, but
the first use which he made of his slightly improved
finances was to send John Carlyle to complete his education in the medical schools in Germany. He estimated
John's talents with a brother's affection, and he was resolved to give him the best chances of distinguishing himself. The cost was greater than he had calculated on, but
he was not discouraged.

To John Carlyle.

Comely Bank : November 29, 1827.

Do not, good brother, let thy heart be cast down for the Mammon of this world. A few more hard sovereigns we are yet, thank
Heaven, in a condition to furnish. Write for what is necessary
and it will be sent. Above all do not neglect dissection and sur-

gery for the sake of any poor thrift there might be in the omission of it. Go on and prosper. Learn all and everything that is to be learned; and if you come home to us a good well-appointed man and physician, we will not think the money ill-bestowed.

The remainder of the same letter carries on the picture of daily life at Comely Bank.

The 'Edinburgh Review' is out some time ago, and the 'State of German Literature' has been received with considerable surprise and approbation by the Universe. Thus, for instance, De Quincey praises it in his ' Saturday Post.' Sir William Hamilton tells me it is ' cap-tal,' and Wilson informs John Gordon that it ' has done me a deil o' good.' De Quincey was here last Wednesday and sate till midnight. He is one of the smallest men you ever in your life beheld ; but with a most gentle and sensible face, only that the teeth are destroyed by opium, and the little bit of an under lip projects like a shelf. He speaks with a slow, sad, and soft voice in the politest manner I have almost ever witnessed, and with great gracefulness and sense, were it not that he seems decidedly given to prosing. Poor little fellow! It might soften a very hard heart to see him so courteous, yet so weak and poor; retiring *home* with his two children to a miserable lodging-house, and writing all day for the king of donkeys, the proprietor of the ' Saturday Post.' I lent him Jean Paul's autobiography, which I got lately from Hamburgh, and advised him to translate it for Blackwood, that so he might raise a few pounds, and fence off the Genius of Hunger yet a little while. Poor little De Quincey! He is an innocent man, and, as you said, extremely *washable* away.

CHAPTER XXII.

WHILE Carlyle was taking care of his brother, an active interest was rising in Edinburgh about himself. Scotch people were beginning to see that a remarkable man had appeared among them, and that they ought not to let him slip through their hands. A new opening presented itself which he thus describes to his father.

To Mr. James Carlyle, Scotsbrig.

Comely Bank: December 22.

There has been a fresh enterprise started for me, no less than to attempt to be successor to Dr. Chalmers in the St. Andrew's University. He, Chalmers, is at present Professor of Moral Philosophy there, but is just removing to Edinburgh to be Professor of Divinity, and I have been consulting with my friends whether it would be prudent in me to offer myself as a candidate for the vacant office. They all seem to think sincerely that if the election proceeded on fair principles I might have a chance of rather a good sort; but this proviso is only a doubtful one, the custom having long been to decide such things by very *un*fair principles. As yet nothing is determined; but my patrons are making inquiries to see how the land lies; and some time next week we shall know what to do. Most part are inclined to think I ought to try.

Among those who encouraged Carlyle in this ambition, and lent active help, Jeffrey was now the first, and, besides general recommendations, wrote most strongly in his favour to Dr. Nicol, the Principal of the University. Equal testimonials, viewed by the intrinsic quality of the givers, to those which were collected or spontaneously offered on this occasion, were perhaps never presented by any candidate for a Scotch professorship. Goethe himself wrote one, which in these times might have carried the day; but Goethe was then only known in Scotland as a German dreamer. Carlyle, though again personally pretending indifference, exerted himself to the utmost, and was, perhaps, more anxious than he was aware of being

To Mrs. Carlyle, Scotsbrig.

Comely Bank: January, 1821.

I am as diligent as possible storming the battlements of St. Andrew's University for *the* professorship for which I have actually eight days ago declared myself formally a candidate! This was after all due investigation conducted by Jeffrey and others, from which, if I could gather no fixed hope of my succeeding, it seemed at least that there was no fixed determination against me; that I might try without censure—nay, in my circumstances, ought to try. I accordingly wrote off to St. Andrews, and next day to all the four winds, in quest of recommendations—to Goethe, to Irving, to Buller, to Brewster, &c. These same recommendations are now beginning to come in upon me. I had one from Brewster two days ago (with the offer of further help), and this morning came a decent testificatory letter from Buller, and a most majestic certificate in three pages from Edward Irving. The good orator speaks as from the heart, and truly says, as he has ever done, that he thinks me a most worthy man—not forgetting to mention among my other advantages the 'prayers of religious parents,' a blessing which, if I speak less of it, I hope I do not feel less than he. On the whole it is a splendid affair this of his; and being tempered by the recommendation of John Leslie,[1] may do me much good. Before the end of next week I expect to have all my testimonials sent off; and there the matter may for a long time rest, the period of election being still unfixed. Of my hopes and calculations as to success I can say nothing, being myself able to form no judgment. I am taught to believe that if merit gain it, I shall gain; which is a proud belief and ought to render failure a matter of comparative indifference to me; more especially as, like the weather in Cowthwaites' calculations, I can do

---

[1] Sir John Leslie, Professor of Mathematics in Edinburgh, who had been Carlyle's teacher.

' owther way.' I often care not sixpence whether I get it or no ; but we shall see. If it is laid out for me it *will* come ; if not, not.

Jeffrey had been alert making inquiries. The nomination he had found to rest in substance with the Principal, Dr. Nicol, an active, jobbing, popular man, who had placed most of the present professors and conferred obligations on all, and who, through his influence in earlier days with Lord Melville, had acquired an absolute ascendency in the St. Andrew's Senate. Nicol secured, the rest of the votes might be counted on ; without Nicol they could not. The Principal was described by Jeffrey as good-natured, sensible, and worldly, not without some sense of the propriety of attracting men of talent and reputation into the University staff ; but cautious and prudent, possessing neither genius nor learning, and without reverence for them. In Church matters Nicol was moderate, with distrust and contempt for every kind of enthusiasm. It was not unlikely, therefore, that he had already cast his eyes on some decent, manageable, and judicious priest for the office. With such a man testimonials from Irving would be rather injurious than useful. Men of rank would weigh most, and next to them men of repute for learning.

There is a certain humour in the claims of Thomas Carlyle, supported by the most famous man of letters in Europe, being submitted to be tried in the scales by such a person as this. But so it was, and is, and perhaps must be, in constitutional countries, where high office may fall on the worthy, but rarely or never on the most worthy. It is difficult everywhere for the highest order of merit to find recognition. Under a system of popular election it is almost impossible.

My testimonials (Carlyle wrote to his brother John)[1] are in such terms that if I cannot carry the place I think it may seem vain to attempt to carry *any* such place by means of testimonials to *merit*

[1] Feb. 1, 1828.

alone. The dear little Duke[1]—Jane says she could kiss him—has written me a paper which might of itself bring me any professorship in the island. Irving also spends five heroical pages on my merits, and Wilson says there is no man known to him fitter for the office; so what more can I do but let the matter take its course and await the issue 'with indescribable composure.' The truth is, I hardly care which way it go. A man, if you give him meat and clothes, is, or ought to be, sufficient for himself in this world; and his culture is but beginning if he think that any outward influence of person or thing can either make him or mar him. If I do not go thither (which, after all, is very likely; for ——, an old stager, talks of applying), why then *I* shall not go, and *they* will not get me; and the sun will rise and set, and the grass will grow, and I shall have eyes to see and ears to hear notwithstanding. Do all that you can in honesty, and reckon the result indubitable; for the *inward* result will not fail if rightly endeavoured: and for the *outward*, 'non flocci facias,' do not value it a rush.

After a few weeks the suspense was over. Carlyle was not appointed; someone else was; and someone else's church was made over to another someone else whom it was desirable to oblige; 'and so the whole matter was rounded off in the neatest manner possible.' Such at least was Carlyle's account of what he understood to be the arrangement. Perhaps the 'someone else' was a fitter person after all. Education in countries so jealous of novelty as Great Britain is, or at least was sixty years ago, follows naturally upon lines traced out by custom, and the conduct of it falls as a matter of course to persons who have never deviated from those lines. New truths are the nutriment of the world's progress. Men of genius discover them, insist upon them, prove them in the face of opposition, and if the genius is not merely a phosphorescent glitter, but an abiding light, their teaching enters in time into the University curriculum. But out of new ideas time alone can distinguish the sound and real from the illusive and imaginary; and it was enough that Carlyle was described

[1] Duke of Craigcrook, the name by which Jeffrey went.

as a man of original and extraordinary gifts to make college patrons shrink from contact with him.

Carlyle himself dimly felt that St. Andrew's might not be the best place for him. It seemed hard to refuse promotion to a man because he was too good for it, and no doubt he would have been pleased to be appointed. But for the work which Carlyle had to do a position of intellectual independence was indispensable, and his apprenticeship to poverty and hardship had to be prolonged still further to harden his nerves and perhaps to test his sincerity. The loss of this professorship may be regretted for Mrs. Carlyle's sake, who did not need the trials which lay before her. Carlyle himself in a University chair would have been famous in his day, and have risen to wealth and consequence, but he might not have been the Carlyle who has conquered a place for himself among the Immortals.

So ended the only fair prospect which ever was opened to him of entering any of the beaten roads of life; and fate having thus decided in spite of the loud remonstrance of all friends, of Jeffrey especially, Carlyle became once more bent on removing to Craigenputtock.

The certificate of the angel Gabriel (he said) would not have availed me a pin's worth. The Devil may care; I can still live independent of all persons whatever. At the Craig, if we stick together as we have done, we may fairly bid defiance to the constable. Praised be heaven! for of all curses that of being baited for debt, or even frightened of falling into it, is surely the bitterest.

The repairs in the old house were hastened forward, that it might be ready for them in the spring.

The domestic scene in Comely Bank had been meantime brightened by the long-talked-of event of the visit of old Mrs. Carlyle to Edinburgh. In all her long life she had never yet been beyond Annandale, had never seen the interior of any better residence than a Scottish farmhouse. To the infinite heaven spread above the narrow circle of her horizon she had perhaps risen as near on wings of prayer and piety as any human being who was upon the earth beside her; but of the earth itself, of her own Scotland, she knew no more than could be descried from Burnswark Hill. She was to spend Christmas week at Comely Bank. She arrived at the beginning of December.

To James Carlyle, Scotsbrig.

Comely Bank: December 22, 1827.

My dear Father,—My mother will not let me rest any longer till I write to you; she says it was promised that a letter should go off the very night Jean and she arrived; and nevertheless it is a melancholy fact that above two weeks have elapsed since that event, and no better tidings been sent you than a word or two in the blank line of the ' Courier.' I would have written sooner had I been in right case, or indeed had there been anything more to communicate than what so brief an announcement might convey as well as a much larger one.

The two wayfarers did *not* find me waiting for them at the coach that Wednesday evening. Unhappily it was quite out of my power to keep that or any other appointment. I had been seized about a week before with a most virulent sore-throat, which detained me close prisoner in the house. All that I could do under these circumstances was to send out a trusty substitute, a Mr. Gordon, who kindly undertook the office. But he, mistaking one coach for another, went and waited at the *wrong* inn ; so that our beloved pilgrims were left to their own resources, and had to pilot their way hither under the guidance of the porter who carried their box. This, however, they accomplished without difficulty or accident, and rejoiced us all by their safe and, in part at least, unexpected arrival.

Since then all things have gone on prosperously. Jane has been busy, and still is so, getting ready suitable apparel of bonnets and frocks. My mother has heard Andrew Thomson in his ' braw kirk,' not much to her satisfaction, since ' he had to light *four* candles before even he could strike.' She has also seen old Mrs. Hope, the Castle of Edinburgh, the Martyrs' Graves, John Knox's house, and who knows how many other wonders, of which I doubt not she will give you a true and full description when she returns. As yet, however, the half has not been seen. The weather has been so stormy that travelling out was difficult, and I have been in no high condition for officiating as guide. In stormy days she *smokes* along with me, or sews wearing raiment, or reads the wonderful articles of my writing in the 'Edinburgh Review.' She has also had a glimpse of Francis Jeffrey, the great critic and advocate, and a shake of the hand from a true German doctor.

Nevertheless she is extremely anxious about getting home, and indeed fails no day to tell us several times that she ought to be off. 'She is doing nothing,' she says; 'and they'll a' be in a hubble o' work' at home. I tell her she was never idle for two weeks in her life before, and ought therefore to give it a fair trial; that 'the hubble at home' will all go on rightly enough in her absence; that, in short, she should not go this year but the next. So I am in hopes we shall get her persuaded to stay where she is till after New Year's Day, which is now only nine or ten days distant, and then we will let her go in peace. The two Janes and she are all out in the town at present buying muslin for sundry necessary articles of dress which we have persuaded the mother to undertake the wearing of. These may keep her, I hope, in some sort of occupation; for idle, I see, she cannot and will not be. We will warn you duly when to expect her.

I trust *you* will soon be well enough for a journey hither; for you too, my dear father, *must* see Edinburgh before we leave it. I have thought of *compelling* you to come back with me when I come down.

I am ever, your affectionate son,

T. CARLYLE.

James Carlyle did not come. He was with his son once afterwards at Craigenputtock, but he never saw Edinburgh.

My mother (Carlyle wrote to his brother on the 1st of February) stayed about four weeks, then went home by Hawick, pausing a few days there. She was in her usual health, wondered much at Edinburgh, but did not seem to relish it excessively. I had her at the pier of Leith and showed her where your ship vanished, and she looked over the blue waters eastward with wettish eyes, and asked the dumb waters 'when he would be back again.' Good mother! but the time of her departure came on, and she left us stupefied by the magnitude of such an enterprise as riding over eighty miles in the 'Sir Walter Scott' without jumping out of the window, which I told her was the problem. Dear mother! let us thank God that she is still here in the earth spared for us, and, I hope, to see good. I would not exchange her for any ten mothers I have ever seen. Jane (Jean) the less she left behind her, ' to improve her mind.' The creature seems to be doing very fairly, and is well and contented. *My* Jane, I grieve to say, is yet far enough from well, but I hope much from summer weather and a smart pony in the south. She is not by any means an estab- lished *valetudinarian*, yet she seldom has a day of true health, and has not gained strength entirely since you left her.

I give a few more extracts from letters written to his brother during the remainder of the Comely Bank time.

To John Carlyle.

Comely Bank : March 7.

Explain to me how I may send you a matter of twenty pounds, or such other sum as you may require, to bring you home to us again. I have no want of money for all needful purposes at pres- ent ; and (I thank God for it) I am able to earn more ; neither is there any investment for it half so good as these in the bank of affection, where perishable silver and gold is converted into im- perishable remembrances of kind feelings. Speak, therefore, plainly and speedily and it shall be done. . . .

I am glad to find that you admire Schelling, and know that you do not understand him. That is right, my dear Greatheart. Look into the deeply significant regions of Transcendental phi- losophy (as all philosophy *must* be) and feel that there are wonders and mighty truths hidden in them ; but look with your clear grey Scottish eyes and shrewd Scottish understanding, and refuse to be mystified even by your admiration. Meanwhile, Diligence, Truth ; Truth, Diligence. These are our watchwords, whether we have ten talents or only a decimal fraction of one.

I have not a syllable to tell you about the London University except that according to all human probability the people neither now nor at any other time will have the least to do with me. I heard the other day from Charles Buller the younger. He says that, hearing of my purpose, he went to Mill (the British India Philister), who is one of the directors, and spoke with him ; but found that my German metaphysics were an unspeakable stone of stumbling to that great thinker, whereby Buller began to perceive that my chances had diminished to the neighbourhood of zero.

It appears, however, that I am become a sort of newspaper *Literatus* in London on the strength of these articles (bless them), and that certain persons wonder what manner of man I am. A critic in the 'Courier' (apparently the worst in nature from the one sentence that I read of him) says I am 'the supremest German scholar in the British Empire.' *Das hole der Teufel!* However, I am rather amused at the *naïveté* with which Crabb Robinson talks to me on this subject. He characterises the papers as a splendid instance of literary *ratting* on the part of the editor, and, imputing the whole composition to a Sir — Hamilton, advocate, says it has some eloquence, and though it cuts its own throat (to speak as a figure), will do GOOD.

The 'Foreign Review' gave me 47*l*. for my trash on Werner.[1] I have sent them a far better paper on Goethe's 'Helena,'[2] for which I shall not get so much. I have engaged to send in a long paper on Goethe's character generally, this of 'Helena' being a sort of introduction.

How matters stand at Craigenputtock I can only guess, but am going down to see. I am in no small uncertainty. This Edinburgh is getting more agreeable to me, more and more a sort of home; and I *can* live in it, if I like to live perpetually unhealthy, and strive for ever against becoming a *hack;* for that I cannot be. On the other hand, I should have liberty and solitude for aught I like best among the moors—only Jane, though like a good wife she says nothing, seems evidently getting more and more afraid of the whole enterprise. She is not at all stout in health. But I must go and look at things with my own eyes, and now as ever there is need of mature resolve, and steadfast when mature.

March 12.

Jeffrey and I continue to love one another like a new Pylades and Orestes. At least, such is often my feeling towards him. Good little Duke! There are few men like thee in this world, Epicurean in creed though thou be, and living all thy days among Turks in grain.

Wilson I can get little good of, though we are as great as ever. Poor Wilson! It seems as if he shrunk from too close a union with anyone. His whole being seems hollowed out, as it were, and false and counterfeit in his own eyes. So he encircles himself with wild cloudy sportfulness, which to me often seems reck-

[1] *Miscellanies*, vol. i. p. 101.   [2] *Ibid.* p. 171.

less and at bottom full of sharp sorrow. Oh that a man would not halt between two opinions. How can anyone love poetry and rizzered haddocks with whisky toddy, outwatch the Bear with Peter Robinson, and at the same time with William Wordsworth? For the last four weeks he has been very unwell, and his friends are not without apprehension for him. He purposes to visit Switzerland in summer and take De Quincey with him. I called yesterday on De Quincey about two o'clock and found him invisible in bed. His landlady, a dirty, very wicked looking woman, said, if he arose at all, it was usually about five o'clock. Unhappy little opium eater, and a quicker little fellow, or of meeker soul (if he had but lived in Paradise or Lubberland) is not to be found in these parts.

The intellectual city is at present entertaining itself not a little with the Apocrypha controversy, in which Grey the minister and Thomson the minister are exhibiting the various manner of offence and defence, to the edification of all parties interested. Translated into the language of the shambles, where their spirit clearly enough originates, these pamphlets of theirs mean simply, ' Sir, you are a d—d rascal,' and 'No, sir, *you* are a d—d rascal.' Happily I have read next to nothing of the whole, and heard as little of it as I possibly could. But now some private wag has taken up the task of caricaturing in pictorial wise these reverend persons; and a crowd shoving and shouldering for a clear and clearer view may be seen at all printshop windows contemplating the distorted figures of their *pawstors* depicted as bulldogs and greyhounds, as preachers and prizefighters climbing the steeple like orthodox men, or throttling one another like exasperated fishwomen; for there are said to be twelve caricatures in the course of publication, and a fresh one comes out every now and then. What Thomson and Grey say to it I know not. For myself I should only say in the words of the old poem—

> May the Lord put an end unto all cruel wars,
> And send peace and contentment unto all British tars.

Eager as Carlyle was to be gone from Edinburgh, he confessed that in his wife's manner he had detected an unwillingness to bury herself in the moors. The evident weakness of her health alarmed him, and he could scarcely have forgotten the aversion with which she had received his first suggestion of making Craigenputtock their home. For himself his mind was made up; and usually when Carlyle wished anything he was not easily impressed with objections to it. In this instance, however, he was evidently hesitating. Craigenputtock, sixteen miles from the nearest town and the nearest doctor, cut off from the outer world through the winter months by snow and flood, in itself gaunt, grim, comfortless, and utterly solitary, was not a spot exactly suited to a delicate and daintily nurtured woman. In the counter scale was her mother, living a few miles below in Nithsdale. But for this attraction Mrs. Carlyle would have declined the adventure altogether; as it was she trembled at the thought of it.

The house in Comely Bank was held only by the year. They were called on to determine whether they would take it for another twelve months or not. Before deciding they resolved to see Craigenputtock together once more. Little Jean was left in charge at Edinburgh, and Carlyle and Mrs. Carlyle went down to Dumfriesshire. 'I still remember,' he said in the 'Reminiscences,' 'two grey blusterous March days at Craigenputtock with the proof-sheets of Goethe's "Helena" in my hand, and Dumfries architects chaotically joined therewith.'

On a blusterous March day Craigenputtock could not look to advantage. They left it still irresolute, and perhaps inclining to remain among their friends. But the question had been settled for them in their absence; on returning to Comely Bank they found that their landlord, not caring to wait longer till they had made up their minds, had let the house to another tenant, and that at all events they would have to leave it at Whitsuntide. This ended the uncertainty.

We found all well at Comely Bank (Carlyle wrote to his mother, when he came back), only the fire a little low, and the maid gone out seeking places, so that it was some space before tea could be raised. The wise young stewardess[1] had sunk considerably into pecuniary embarrassments, but in all other points was well and happy, and had managed herself throughout with a degree of prudence and *gumption* far beyond her years. Indeed both Jane and I were surprised at the acuteness the little crow had displayed in all emergencies, and perhaps still more at the strange growth she had made in manner and bearing during our absence, for she seemed to have enlarged into a sort of woman during that period of self-direction. The best of our news is that we *are* coming down to the Craig this Whitsunday to take up our abode there. This house was found to have been *let* during our absence. Since we had to flit any way, whither should we flit but to our own house on the moor? We are coming down then against the term, to *neighbour* you. Will you be good neighbours or bad? I cannot say, Mrs. Carlyle, but I jealouse you, I jealouse you. However, we are to try; for Jane and I were out this very day, buying paper for the two rooms, which is already on its way to Dumfries; and the painters we trust are busy, and Alick and Uncle John doing great things, that the mansion house may be swept and smooth by the 26th of May, when we will visit it with bag and baggage, we hope as a permanent home.

I anticipate with confidence (he wrote at the same time to his brother) a friendly and rather comfortable arrangement at the Craig, in which, not in idleness, yet in peace and more self-selected occupations, I may find more health, and, what I reckon weightier, more scope to improve and worthily employ myself, which either here or there I reckon to be the great end of existence and the only happiness.

So ended the life at 21 Comely Bank—the first married home of the Carlyles; which began ominously, as a vessel rolls when first launched, threatening an overturn, and closed with improved health and spirits on Carlyle's part, and prospects which, if not brilliant, were encouraging and improving. He had been fairly introduced into the higher walks of his profession, and was noticed and talked about. Besides the two articles on Jean Paul and on German literature, he had written the paper on Werner, the essay on

[1] Jean, his sister.

Goethe's 'Helena,' and the more elaborate and remarkable essay on Goethe himself, which now stand among the 'Miscellanies.'[1] Goethe personally remained kind and attentive. He had studied Carlyle's intellectual temperament, and had used an expression about him in the St. Andrews testimonial which showed how clear an insight he had gained into the character of it. Carlyle was resting, he said, on an *original foundation*, and was so happily constituted that he could develop out of himself the requirements of what was good and beautiful[2]—*out of himself*, not out of contact with others. The work could be done, therefore, as well, or perhaps better, in solitude. Along with the testimonial had come a fresh set of presents, with more cards and verses and books, and with a remembrance of himself which Carlyle was to deliver to Sir Walter Scott. It was a proud tribute, and proud he was to report of it to Scotsbrig.

I must tell you (he wrote) of the arrival of Goethe's box, with such a catalogue of rarities as would astonish you. There was a bracelet and gold breast-pin (with the poet's bust on a ground of steel), besides two gilt books for Jane, and for the husband I know not how many verses and cards and beautiful volumes, the whole wrapped in about half a quire of German newspapers. Sir Walter Scott's medals are not yet delivered, the baronet being at present in London; but I have written to him announcing what lies here for his acceptance, and in some week or two I cannot but expect that I shall speak with the great man and, having delivered my commission, wish him good morning. To Goethe I have already written to thank him for such kindness.

This was the last of Comely Bank. A few days later the Carlyles were gone to the Dumfriesshire moorland where for seven years was now to be their dwelling-place.

[1] Vol. i. p. 233.

[2] 'Wodurch an den Tag gelegt wird, dass er auf einem originalen Grund beruhe, und die Erfordernisse des Guten und Schönen aus sich selbst zu entwickeln das Vergnügen habe.' This, so far as I know, is the only sentence of this testimonial which survives.

Carlyle never spoke to Scott, as he hoped to do ; nor did Sir Walter even acknowledge his letter. It seems that the medals and the letter to Scott from Goethe were entrusted to Wilson, by whom, or by Jeffrey, they were delivered to Scott on the arrival of the latter soon after in Edinburgh. Carlyle's letter, of which Wilson had also taken charge, was perhaps forgotten by him.

VOL. I.—23

THE END OF THE FIRST VOLUME.

THOMAS CARLYLE

VOL. II.

JANE WELSH CARLYLE.

From a miniature in possession of J.A.Froude Esq.

THOMAS CARLYLE

A HISTORY OF THE FIRST FORTY YEARS OF HIS LIFE

1795–1835

BY

JAMES ANTHONY FROUDE, M.A.

FORMERLY FELLOW OF EXETER COLLEGE, OXFORD

TWO VOLUMES IN ONE

VOL. II.

NEW YORK

CHARLES SCRIBNER'S SONS

1882

[*All rights reserved*]

LIFE OF

THOMAS CARLYLE.

CHAPTER I.

A.D. 1828. ÆT. 33.

GOETHE had said of Carlyle that he was fortunate in having in himself an originating principle of conviction, out of which he could develop the force that lay in him unassisted by other men. Goethe had discerned what had not yet become articulately clear to Carlyle himself. But it is no less true that this principle of conviction was already active in his mind, underlying his thoughts on every subject which he touched. It is implied everywhere, though nowhere definitely stated in his published writings. We have arrived at a period when he had become master of his powers, when he began distinctly to utter the 'poor message,' as he sometimes called it, which he had to deliver to his contemporaries. From this time his opinions on details might vary, but the main structure of his philosophy remained unchanged. It is desirable, therefore, before pursuing further the story of his life, to describe briefly what the originating principle was. The secret of a man's nature lies in his religion, in what he really believes about this world, and his own place in it. What was Carlyle's religion? I am able to explain it, partly from his conversations with myself, but happily not from this source only, into which alien opinions might too probably intrude. There remain among his unpublished papers the fragments of two unfinished essays which he was never able to complete satisfactorily to himself, but which he told me were, and had been, an imperfect expression of his actual thoughts.

We have seen him confessing to Irving that he did not believe, as his friend did, in the Christian religion, and that it was vain to hope that he ever would so believe. He tells his mother, and he so continued to tell her as long as she lived, that their belief was essentially the same, although their language was different. Both these statements were true. He was a Calvinist without the theology. The materialistic theory of things—that intellect is a phenomenon of matter, that conscience is the growth of social convenience, and other kindred speculations, he utterly repudiated. Scepticism on the nature of right and wrong, as on man's responsibility to his Maker, never touched or tempted him. On the broad facts of the Divine government of the universe he was as well assured as Calvin himself; but he based his faith, not on a supposed revelation, or on fallible human authority. He had sought the evidence for it, where the foundations lie of all other forms of knowledge, in the experienced facts of things interpreted by the intelligence of man. Experienced fact was to him revelation, and the only true revelation. Historical religions, Christianity included, he believed to have been successive efforts of humanity, loyally and nobly made in the light of existing knowledge, to explain human duty, and to insist on the fulfilment of it; and the reading of the moral constitution and position of man, in the creed, for instance, of his own family, he believed to be truer far, incommensurably truer, than was to be found in the elaborate metaphysics of utilitarian ethics. In revelation, technically so called, revelation confirmed by his-

torical miracles, he was unable to believe—he felt himself
forbidden to believe—by the light that was in him. In
other ages men had seen miracles where there were none,
and had related them in perfect good faith in their eagerness to realise the divine presence in the world. They
did not know enough of nature to be on their guard
against alleged suspensions of its unvarying order. To
Carlyle the universe was itself a miracle, and all its phenomena were equally in themselves incomprehensible.
But the special miraculous occurrences of sacred history
were not credible to him. 'It is as certain as mathematics,' he said to me late in his own life, 'that no such
thing ever has been or can be.' He had learnt that effects
succeeded causes uniformly and inexorably without intermission or interruption, and that tales of wonder were as
little the true accounts of real occurrences as the theory of
epicycles was a correct explanation of the movements of
the planets.

So far his thoughts on this subject did not differ widely
from those of his sceptical contemporaries, but his further
conclusions not only were not their conclusions, but were
opposed to them by whole diameters; for while he rejected the literal narrative of the sacred writers, he believed as strongly as any Jewish prophet or Catholic saint
in the spiritual truths of religion. The effort of his life
was to rescue and reassert those truths which were being
dragged down by the weight with which they were encumbered. He explained his meaning by a remarkable illustration. He had not come (so far as he knew his own purpose) to destroy the law and the prophets, but to fulfil them,
to expand the conception of religion with something wider,
grander, and more glorious than the wildest enthusiasm
had imagined.

The old world had believed that the earth was station-
ary, and that the sun and stars moved round it as its guar-

dian attendants. Science had discovered that sun and stars, if they had proper motion of their own, yet in respect of the earth were motionless, and that the varying aspect of the sky was due to the movements of the earth itself. The change was humbling to superficial vanity. 'The stars in their courses' could no longer be supposed to fight against earthly warriors, or comets to foretell the havoc on fields of slaughter, or the fate and character of a prince to be affected by the constellation under which he was born. But if the conceit of the relative importance of man was diminished, his conception of the system of which he was a part had become immeasurably more magnificent; while every phenomenon which had been actually and faithfully observed remained unaffected. Sun and moon were still the earthly time-keepers ; and the mariner still could guide his course across the ocean by the rising and setting of the same stars which Ulysses had watched upon his raft.

Carlyle conceived that a revolution precisely analogous to that which Galileo had wrought in our apprehension of the material heaven was silently in progress in our attitude towards spiritual phenomena.

The spiritual universe, like the visible, was the same yesterday, to-day, and for ever, and legends and theologies were, like the astronomical theories of the Babylonians, Egyptians, or Greeks, true so far as they were based on facts, which entered largely into the composition of the worst of them—true so far as they were the honest efforts of man's intellect and conscience and imagination to interpret the laws under which he was living, and regulate his life by them. But underneath or beyond all these speculations lay the facts of spiritual life, the moral and intellectual constitution of things as it actually was in eternal consistence. The theories which dispensed with God and the soul Carlyle utterly abhorred. It was not credible to him, he said, that intellect and conscience could have been placed in him by a Being which had none of its own. He rarely spoke of this. The word God was too awful for common use, and he veiled his meaning in metaphors to avoid it. But God to him was the fact of facts. He looked on this whole system of visible or spiritual phenomena as a manifestation of the will of God in constant forces, forces not mechanical but dynamic, interpenetrating and controlling all existing things, from the utmost bounds of space to the smallest granule on the earth's surface, from the making of the world to the lightest action of a man. God's law was everywhere: man's welfare depended on the faithful reading of it. Society was but a higher organism, no accidental agreement of individual persons or families to live together on conditions which they could arrange for themselves, but a natural growth, the conditions of which were already inflexibly laid down. Human life was like a garden, 'to which the will was gardener,' and the moral fruits and flowers, or the immoral poisonous weeds, grew inevitably according as the rules already appointed were discovered and obeyed, or slighted, overlooked, or defied. Nothing was indifferent. Every step which a man could take was in the right direction or the wrong. If in the right, the result was as it should be; if in the wrong, the excuse of ignorance would not avail to prevent the inevitable consequence.

These in themselves are but commonplace propositions which no one denies in words; but Carlyle saw in the entire tone of modern thought, that practically men no longer really believed them. They believed in expediency, in the rights of man, in government by majorities; as if they could make their laws for themselves. The law, did they but know it, was already made; and their wisdom, if they wished to prosper, was not to look for what was convenient to themselves, but for what had been decided already in Nature's chancery.

Many corollaries followed from such a creed when sincerely and passionately held. In arts and sciences the authority is the expert who understands his business. No one dreamt of discovering a longitude by the vote of a majority; and those who trusted to any such methods would learn that they had been fools by running upon the rocks. The science of life was no easier—was harder far than the science of navigation: the phenomena were infinitely more complex; and the consequences of error were infinitely more terrible. The rights of man, properly understood, meant the right of the wise to rule, and the right of the ignorant to be ruled. 'The gospel of force,' of the divine right of the strong, with which Carlyle has been so often taunted with teaching, merely meant that when a man has visibly exercised any great power in this world, it has been because he has truly and faithfully seen into the facts around him; seen them more accurately and interpreted them more correctly than his contemporaries. He has become in himself, as it were, one of nature's forces, imperatively insisting that certain things must be done. Success may blind him, and then he mis-sees the facts and comes to ruin. But while his strength remains he is strong through the working of a power greater than himself. The old Bible language that God raised up such and such a man for a special purpose represents a genuine truth.

But let us hear Carlyle himself. The following passages were written in 1852, more than twenty years after the time at which we have now arrived. Figure and argument were borrowed from new appliances which had sprung into being in the interval. But the thought expressed in them was as old as Hoddam Hill when they furnished the armour in which he encountered Apollyon.

They are but broken thoughts, flung out as they presented themselves, and wanting the careful touch with which Carlyle finished work which he himself passed through the press; but I give them as they remain in his own handwriting.

SPIRITUAL OPTICS.

Why do men shriek so over one another's creeds? A certain greatness of heart for all manner of conceptions and misconceptions of the Inconceivable is now if ever in season. Reassure thyself, my poor assaulted brother. Starting from the east, a man's road seems horribly discordant with thine, which is so resolutely forcing itself forward by tunnel and incline, victorious over impediments from the western quarter. Yet see, you are both struggling, more or less honestly, towards the centre—all mortals are unless they be diabolic and not human. Recollect with pity, with smiles and tears, however high thou be, the efforts of the meanest man. Intolerance coiled like a dragon round treasures which were the palladium of mankind was not so bad; nay, rather was indispensable and good. But intolerance, coiled and hissing in that horrid manner, now when the treasures are all fled, and there are nothing but empty pots new and old—pots proposing that they shall be filled, and pots asserting that they were once full—what am I to make of that? Intolerance with nothing to protest but empty pots and eggs that are fairly addle, is doubly and trebly intolerable. I do not praise the tolerance talked of in these times; but I do see the wisdom of a Truce of God being appointed, which you may christen tolerance, and everywhere proclaim by drum and trumpet, by public cannon from the high places, and by private fiddle, till once there be achieved for us something to be intolerant about again. There are a few men who have even at present a certain right, call it rather a certain terrible duty, to be intolerant, and I hope that these will be even more, and that their intolerance will grow ever nobler, diviner, more victorious. But how few are there in all the earth! Be not so much alarmed at the opulences, spiritual or material, of this world. Whether they be of the hand or the mind, whether consisting of St. Katherine's docks, blooming cornfields, and filled treasuries, or of sacred philosophies, theologies, bodies of science, recorded heroisms, and accumulated conquests of wisdom and harmonious human utterances—they have all been amassed by little and little. Poor insignificant transitory bipeds little better than thyself have ant-wise accumulated them all. How inconsiderable was the contribution of each; yet working with hand or with head in the strenuous ardour of their heart, they did what was in them; and here, so magnificent, overwhelming, almost divine and immeasurable, is the summed-up result. Be modest towards it; loyally reverent towards it: that is well thy part. But begin at last to understand withal what thy own real relation to it is; and that if it, in its greatness, is divine, so then in thy littleness art thou [not so?] *Lass Dich nicht verblüffen*, 'Don't let thyself be put upon' [no]. 'Stand up for thyself withal.' That, say the Germans, is the eleventh commandment; and truly in these times for an ingenuous soul there is not perhaps in the whole Decalogue a more important one.

And in all kinds of times, if the ingenuous soul could but understand that only in proportion to its own divineness can any part or lot in those divine possessions be vouchsafed it, how inexpressibly important would it be! Such is for ever the fact; though not one in the hundred now knows it or surmises it. Of all these divine possessions it is only what thou art become equal to that thou canst take away with thee. Except thy own eye have got to see it, except thy own soul have victoriously struggled to clear vision and belief of it, what is the thing seen and the thing believed by another or by never so many others? Alas, it is not thine, though thou look on it, brag about it, and bully and fight about it till thou die, striving to persuade thyself and all men how much it is thine. Not *it* is thine, but only a windy echo and tradition of it bedded in hypocrisy, ending sure enough in tragical futility, is thine. What a result for a human soul! In all ages, but in this age, named of the printing press, with its multiform pulpits and platforms, beyond all others, the accumulated sum of such results over the general posterity of Adam in countries called civilised is tragic to contemplate; is in fact the raw material of every insincerity, of every scandal, platitude, and ignavia to be seen under the sun. If men were only ignorant and knew that they were so, only void of belief *and sorry for it*, instead of filled with sham belief and proud of it—ah me!!

The primary conception by rude nations in regard to all great attainments and achievements by men is that each was a miracle and the gift of the gods. Language was taught man by a heavenly power. Minerva gave him the olive, Neptune the horse, Triptolemus taught him agriculture, &c. The effects of *optics* in this strange camera obscura of our existence, are most of all singular! The grand centre of the modern revolution of ideas is even this— we begin to have a notion that all this *is* the effect of optics, and that the intrinsic fact is very different from our old conception of it. Not less 'miraculous,' not less divine, but with an altogether totally new (or hitherto unconceived) *species* of divineness; a divineness lying much nearer home than formerly; a divineness that does not come from Judæa, from Olympus, Asgard, Mount Meru, but is in man himself; in the heart of everyone born of man—a grand revolution, indeed, which is altering our ideas of heaven and earth to an amazing extent in every particular whatsoever. From top to bottom our spiritual world, and all that depends on the same, which means nearly everything in the furniture of our life, outward as well as inward, is, as this idea advances, undergoing change of the most essential sort, is slowly getting 'overturned,' as they angrily say, which in the sense of being gradually turned over and having its vertex set where its base used to be, is indisputably true, and means a 'revolution' such as never was before, or at least since letters and recorded history existed among us never was. The great Galileo, or numerous small Galileos, have appeared in our spiritual world too, and are making known to us that the sun stands still; that as for the sun and stars and eternal immensities, they do not move at all, and indeed have something else to do than dance round the like of us and our paltry little dog-hutch of a dwelling place; that it is we and our dog-hutch that are moving all this while, giving rise to such phenomena; and that if we would ever be wise about our situation we must now attend to that fact. I would fain sometimes write a book about all that, and try to make it plain to everybody. But alas! I find again there is next to nothing to be said about it in words at present—and indeed till lately I had vaguely supposed that everybody understood it, or at least understood me to mean it, which it would appear that they don't at all.

A *word* to express that extensive or universal operation of referring the motion from yourself to the object you look at, or *vice versâ*? Is there none?

A notable tendency of the human being in case of mutual motions on the part of himself and another object, is to misinterpret the said motion and impute it to the wrong party. Riding in this whirled vehicle, how the hedges seem to be in full gallop on each side of him ; how the woods and houses, and all objects but the fixed blue of heaven, seem to be madly careering at the top of their speed, stormfully waltzing round transient centres, the whole earth gone into menadic enthusiasm, he himself all the while locked into dead quiescence ! And again, if he is really sitting still in his railway carriage at some station when an opposite train is getting under way, his eye informs him at once that *he* is at length setting out and leaving his poor friends in a stagnant state. How often does he commit this error? It is only in exceptional cases, when helps are expressly provided, that he avoids it and judges right of the matter.

It is very notable of the outward eye, and would be insupportable, did not the experience of each man incessantly correct it for him, in the common businesses and locomotions of this world. In the uncommon locomotion it is not so capable of correction. During how many ages and æons, for example, did not the sun and the moon and the stars go all swashing in their tremendously rapid revolution every twenty-four hours round this little indolent earth of ours, and were evidently *seen* to do it by all creatures, till at length the Galileo appeared, and the Newtons in the rear of him. The experience necessary to correct that erroneous impression of the eyesight was not so easy of attainment. No. It lay far apart from the common businesses, and was of a kind that quite escaped the duller eye. It was attained nevertheless ; gradually got together in the requisite quantity ; promulgated, too, in spite of impediments, holy offices, and such like ; and is now the general property of the world, and only the horses and oxen cannot profit by it. These are notable facts of the outward eyesight and the history of its progress in surveying this material world.

But now, will the favourable reader permit me to suggest to him a fact which, though it has long been present to the consciousness of here and there a meditative individual, has not, perhaps, struck the favourable reader hitherto—that with the inward eyesight and the spiritual universe there is always, and has always, been the same game going on. Precisely a similar game, to infer motion of your own when it is the object seen that moves ; and rest of your own with menadic storming of all the gods and demons ; while it is yourself with the devilish and divine impulses that you have, that are going at express train speed ! I say the Galileo of this, many small Galileos of this, have appeared some time ago—having at length likewise collected (with what infinitely greater labour, sorrow, and endurance than your material Galileo needed) the experience necessary for correcting such illusions of the *inner* eyesight in its turn—a crowning discovery, as I sometimes call it, the essence and summary of all the sad struggles and wrestlings of these last three centuries. No man that reflects need be admonished what a pregnant discovery this is; how it is the discovery of discoveries, and as men become more and more sensible of it will remodel the whole world for us in a most blessed and surprising manner. Such continents of sordid delirium (for it is really growing now very sordid) will vanish like a foul Walpurgis night at the first streaks of dawn. Do but consider it. The delirious dancing of the universe is stilled, but the universe itself (what scepticism did not suspect) is still all there. God, heaven, hell, are none of them annihilated for us, any more than the material woods and houses. Nothing that was divine, sublime, demonic, beautiful, or terrible is in the least abolished for us as the poor pre-Galileo fancied it might be; only their mad dancing has ceased, and they are all reduced to dignified composure; any madness that was in it being recognised as our own henceforth.

What continents of error, world-devouring armies of illusions and of foul realities that have their too true habitation and too sad function among such, will disappear at last wholly from our field of vision, and leave a serener veritable world for us. Scavengerism, which under Chadwick makes such progress in the material streets and beneath them, will alarmingly but beneficently reign in the spiritual fields and thoroughfares; and deluges of spiritual water, which is light, which is clear, pious vision and conviction, will have washed our inner world clean too with truly celestial results for us. Oh, my friend, I advise thee awake to that fact, now discovered of the inner eyesight, as it was long since of the outer, that not the sun and the stars are so rapidly dashing round; nor the woods and distant steeples and country mansions are deliriously dancing and waltzing round accidental centres: that it is thyself, and thy little dog-hole of a planet or dwelling-place, that are doing it merely.

It was God, I suppose, that made the Jewish people and gave them their hook-noses, obstinate characters, and all the other gifts, faculties, tendencies, and equipments they were launched upon the world with. No doubt about that in any quarter. These were the general outfit of the Jews, given them by God and none else whatever. And now, if in the sedulous use of said equipments, faculties, and general outfit, with such opportunities as then were, the Jew people did in the course of ages work out for themselves a set of convictions about this universe which were undeniable to them, and of practices grounded thereon which were felt to be salutary and imperative upon them, were not the Jew people bound at their peril temporal and eternal to cherish such convictions and observe said practices with whatever strictest punctuality was possible, and to be supremely thankful that they had achieved such a possession ? I fancy they would do all this with a punctuality and devoutness and sacred rigour in exact proportion to the quantity of obstinate human method, piety, persistence, or of that Jewhood and manhood, and general worth and wisdom, that were in them ; for which be they honoured as Jews and men. And if now they please to call all this by the highest names in their vocabulary, and think silently, and reverently speak of it, as promulgated by their great Jehovah and Creator for them, where was the harm for the time being? Was it not intrinsically true that their and our unnameable Creator *had* revealed it to them ? having given them the outfit of faculties, character, and situation for discerning and believing the same? Poor souls ! they fancied their railway carriage (going really at a great rate, I think, and with a terrible noise through the country) was perfectly motionless, and that they at least saw the landscape, discerned what landscape there was dancing and waltzing round them. Their error was the common one incidental to all passengers and movers through this world—except those overloaded busy eating individuals that make their transit sleeping. Yes: fall well asleep ; you will not think the landscape waltzes ; you will see no landscape, but in their dim vastness the turbid whirlpools of your own indigestions and nightmare dreams. You will be troubled with no *mis*conceptions of a Godhood, Providence, Judgment Day, eternal soul of night, or other sublimity in this world. Looking into your own digestive apparatus when sleep has melted it into the immense, you snore quietly and are free from all that.

So far Carlyle had written, and then threw it aside as unsatisfactory, as not adequately expressing his meaning, and therefore not to be proceeded with. But a very intelligible meaning shines through it ; and when I told him that I had found and read it, he said that it contained his real conviction, a conviction that lay at the bottom of all his thoughts about man and man's doings in this world. A sense lay upon him that this particular truth was one which he was specially called on to insist upon, yet he could never get it completely accomplished. On another loose sheet of rejected MS. I find the same idea stated somewhat differently :—

Singular what difficulty I have in getting my poor message de-livered to the world in this epoch : things I imperatively need still to say.

1. That all history is a Bible—a thing stated in words by me more than once, and adopted in a sentimental way ; but nobody can I bring fairly into it, nobody persuade to take it up practically as a *fact*.

2. Part of the 'grand Unintelligible,' that we are now learning spiritually too—that the earth *turns*, not the sun and heavenly spheres. One day the spiritual astronomers will find that *this* is the infinitely greater miracle. The universe is not an orrery, theo-logical or other, but a universe ; and instead of paltry theologic brass spindles for axis, &c., has laws of gravitation, laws of attrac-tion and repulsion ; is not a Ptolemaic but a Newtonian universe. As Humboldt's 'Cosmos' to a fable of children, so will the new world be in comparison with what the old one was, &c.

3. And flowing out of this, that the work of genius is not *fiction* but fact. How dead are all people to that truth, recognising it in word merely, not in deed at all ! Histories of Europe ! Our own history ! Eheu ! If we had any vivacity of soul and could get the old Hebrew spectacles off our nose, should we run to Judæa or Houndsditch to look at the doings of the Supreme ? Who con-quered anarchy and chained it everywhere under their feet ? Not the Jews with their morbid imaginations and foolish sheepskin Targums. The Norse with their steel swords guided by fresh val-iant hearts and clear veracious understanding, it was *they* and not the Jews. The supreme splendour will be seen *there*, I should imagine, not in Palestine or Houndsditch any more. Man of genius to interpret history ! After interpreting the Greeks and Romans for a thousand years, let us now try our own a little. (How clear this has been to myself for a long while !) Not one soul, I believe, has yet taken it into him. Universities founded

by monk ages are not fit at all for this age. 'Learn to read Greek, to read Latin'! You cannot be *saved* (religiously speaking too) with those languages. What of reason there *was* in that! Beautiful loyalty to the ancients Dante and Virgil, *il duca mio.* Beautiful truly so far as it goes! But the superfœtation is now grown perilous, deadly, horrible, if you could see it!

Old piety was wont to say that God's judgments tracked the footsteps of the criminal; that all violation of the eternal laws, done in the deepest recesses or on the conspicuous high places of the world, was absolutely certain of its punishment. You could do no evil, you could do no good, but a god would repay it to you. It was as certain as that when you shot an arrow from the earth, gravitation would bring it back to the earth. The all-embracing law of right and wrong was as inflexible, as sure and exact, as that of gravitation. Furies with their serpent hair and infernal maddening torches followed Orestes who had murdered his mother. In the still deeper soul of modern Christendom there hung the tremendous image of a Doomsday—*Dies iræ, dies illa*—when the All-just, without mercy now, with only terrific accuracy now, would judge the quick and the dead, and to each soul measure out the reward of his deeds done in the body—eternal Heaven to the good, to the bad eternal Hell. The Moslem too, and generally the Oriental peoples, who are of a more religious nature, have conceived it so, and taken it, not as a conceit, but as a terrible fact, and have studiously founded, or studiously tried to found, their practical existence upon the same.

My friend, it well behoves us to reflect how true essentially all this still is: that it continues, and will continue, fundamentally a fact in all essential particulars—its certainty, I say its infallible certainty, its absolute justness, and all the other particulars, the eternity itself included. He that has with his eyes and soul looked into nature from any point—and not merely into distracted theological, metaphysical, modern philosophical, or other cobweb representations of nature at second hand—will find this true, that only the vesture of it is changed for us; that the essence of it cannot change at all. Banish all miracles from it. Do not name the name of God; it is still true.

Once more it is in religion with us, as in astronomy—we know now that the earth moves. But it has not annihilated the stars for us; it has infinitely exalted and expanded the stars and universe. Once it seemed evident the sun did daily rise in the east;

the big sun—a sun-god—did travel for us, driving his chariot over the crystal floor all days: at any rate the sun *went*. Now we find it is only the earth that goes. So too all mythologies, religious conceptions, &c., we begin to discover, are the necessary products of man's godmade mind.

I need add little to these two fragments, save to repeat that they are the key to Carlyle's mind; that the thought which they contain, although nowhere more articulately written out, governed all his judgments of men and things. In this faith he had 'trampled down his own spiritual dragons.' In this faith he interpreted human history, which history witnessed in turn to the truth of his convictions. He saw that now as much as ever the fate of nations depended not on their material development, but, as had been said in the Bible, and among all serious peoples, on the moral virtues, courage, veracity, purity, justice, and good sense. Nations where these were honoured prospered and became strong; nations which professed well with their lips, while their hearts were set on wealth and pleasure, were overtaken, as truly in modern Europe as in ancient Palestine, by the judgment of God.

'I should not have known what to make of this world at all,' Carlyle once said to me, 'if it had not been for the French Revolution.'

This might be enough to say on Carlyle's religion; but there is one aspect of religion on which everyone who thinks at all will wish to know his opinion. What room could there be for prayer in such a scheme of belief as his? In one form or other it has been a universal difficulty. How should ignorant man presume to attempt to influence the will of his Creator, who by the necessity of his nature cannot change, and must and will on all occasions and to all persons do what is just and right?

Reason cannot meet the objection. Yet nevertheless men of the highest powers have prayed and continue to pray. I am permitted to publish the following letters, which show what Carlyle thought about it in 1870. And as he thought in 1870, he thought in 1828. His mind when it was once made up never wavered, never even varied.

From George A. Duncan to Thomas Carlyle.

4 Eyre Place, Edinburgh : June 4, 1870.

Honoured Sir,—I am a stranger to you, but my grandfather, Dr. Henry Duncan, of Ruthwell, was not, and it is a good deal on that ground that I rest my plea for addressing you. Of all the things I possess there is none I value more than a copy of your translation of 'Meister's Apprenticeship,' presented to my grandfather by you, and bearing on its fly-leaf these to me thrice precious words :—' To the Rev. Dr. Duncan, from his grateful and affectionate friend T. Carlyle.' I show it to all my friends with the utmost pride. But I have another plea. I was one of those Edinburgh students to whom, as a father to his sons, you addressed words which I have read over at least six times, and mean, while I live, to remember and obey. I have still one plea more. You know that in this country, when people are perplexed or in doubt, they go to their minister for counsel : you are my minister, my only minister, my honoured and trusted teacher, and to you I, having for more than a year back ceased to believe as my fathers believed in matters of religion, and being now an inquirer in that field, come for light on the subject of prayer. There are repeated expressions in your works which convince me that in some form or other you believe in prayer, and the fact that the wisest men, Luther, Knox, Cromwell, and that greater Man whose servants they were, were pre-eminently men of prayer, is at variance with the thought which still forces itself upon me, that to attempt to change the Will of Him who is Best and Wisest (and what is prayer, if it is not that?) is in the last degree absurd. The only right prayer, it seems to me, is 'Thy will be done ; ' and that is a needless one, for God's will shall assuredly be done at any rate. Is it too much to hope that you will kindly write me a few lines throwing light on this subject ? I have read Goethe's ' Confessions of a Fair Saint,' and also what you say with regard to Cromwell's prayers, but still I have not been able to arrive at a conviction. Lest these remarks should seem to you intolerably shallow, I must inform you that I am only twenty.

Would it interest you in any measure to read some letters written by you to Mr. Robert Mitchell when this old century was in its teens, and thus recall from your own beloved past a thousand persons, thoughts, and scenes and schemes bygone ? Mr. M. left my grand-uncle, Mr. Craig, one of his trustees, and among the papers which thus fell into Mr. Craig's hands were several letters from you to Mr. Mitchell. Mr. C.'s daughters lately gave them to one of my sisters, and I believe that if you expressed the slightest wish to see them, I should be able to persuade her to let me send them to you, though she guards them very jealously.

Believe me, yours ever gratefully,

GEO. A. DUNCAN.

Thomas Carlyle to George A. Duncan.

Chelsea : June 9, 1870.

Dear Sir,—You need no apology for addressing me ; your letter itself is of amiable ingenuous character ; pleasant and interesting to me in no common degree. I am sorry only that I cannot set at rest, or settle into clearness, your doubts on that important subject. What I myself practically, in a half-articulate way, believe on it I will try to express for you.

First, then, as to your objection of setting up *our* poor wish or will in opposition to the will of the Eternal, I have not the least word to say in contradiction of it. And this seems to close, and does, in a sense though not perhaps in all senses, close the question of our prayers being *granted*, or what is called 'heard ;' but that is not the whole question.

For, on the other hand, prayer is and remains always a native and deepest impulse of the soul of man ; and correctly gone about, is of the very highest benefit (nay, one might say, indispensability) to every man aiming morally high in this world. No prayer no *religion*, or at least only a *dumb* and lamed one ! Prayer is a turning of one's soul, in heroic reverence, in infinite desire and *endeavour*, towards the Highest, the All-Excellent, Omnipotent, Supreme. The modern Hero, therefore, ought *not* to give up praying, as he has latterly all but done.

Words of prayer, in this epoch, I know hardly any. But the act of prayer, in great moments, I believe to be still possible ; and that one should gratefully accept such moments, and count them blest, when they come, if come they do—which latter is a most rigorous preliminary question with us in all cases. '*Can I pray* in this moment' (much as I may *wish* to do so)? 'If not, then NO!' I can at least stand silent, inquiring, and *not* blasphemously *lie* in this Presence!

On the whole, Silence is the one safe form of prayer known to me, in this poor sordid era—though there are ejaculatory words too which occasionally rise on one, with a felt propriety and veracity; words very welcome in such case! Prayer is the aspiration of our poor struggling heavy-laden soul towards its Eternal Father; and, with or without words, ought *not* to become impossible, nor, I persuade myself, need it ever. Loyal sons and subjects *can* approach the King's throne who have no 'request' to make there, except that they may continue loyal. Cannot they?

This is all I can say to you, my good young friend; and even this, on my part and on yours, is perhaps too much. Silence, silence! 'The Highest cannot be spoken of in words,' says Goethe. Nothing so desecrates mankind as their continual babbling, both about the speakable and the unspeakable, in this bad time!

Your grandfather was the amiablest and kindliest of men; to me pretty much a *unique* in those young years, the one cultivated man whom I could feel myself permitted to call *friend* as well. Never can I forget that Ruthwell Manse, and the beautiful souls (your grandmother, your grand-aunts, and others) who then made it bright to me. All vanished now, all vanished!

Please tell me *whose* son you are—not George John's, I think, but Wallace's, whom I can remember only as a grave boy? Also whether bonny little 'Barbara Duncan' is still living; or indeed if she ever lived to be your aunt? I have some sad notion No. I will not trouble you about the Mitchell letters: I wrote many letters to the good Mitchell; but I fear now they were all of a foolish type, fitter to burn than to read at present. Tell me also, if you like, a little more about yourself, your pursuits and endeavours, your intended course in the world. You perceive I expect from you one more letter at least, though it is doubtful whether I can *answer* any more, for *reasons* you may *see* sufficiently!

Believe me, dear Sir,

Yours with sincere good wishes,

T. CARLYLE.

CHAPTER II.

I HAVE already described Craigenputtock as the dreariest spot in all the British dominions. The nearest cottage is more than a mile from it; the elevation, 700 feet above the sea, stunts the trees and limits the garden produce to the hardiest vegetables. The house is gaunt and hungry-looking. It stands with the scanty fields attached as an island in a sea of morass. The landscape is unredeemed either by grace or grandeur, mere undulating hills of grass and heather, with peat bogs in the hollows between them. The belts of firs which now relieve the eye and furnish some kind of shelter were scarcely planted when the Carlyles were in possession. No wonder Mrs. Carlyle shuddered at the thought of making her home in so stern a solitude, delicate as she was, with a weak chest, and with the fatal nervous disorder of which she eventually died already beginning to show itself. Yet so it was to be. She had seen the place in March for the first time in her life, and then, probably, it had looked its very worst. But in May, when they came to settle, the aspect would have scarcely been mended. The spring is late in Scotland; on the high moors the trees are still bare. The fields are scarcely coloured with the first shoots of green, and winter lingers in the lengthening days as if unwilling to relax its grasp. To Mrs. Carlyle herself the adventure might well seem desperate. She concealed the extent of her anxiety from her husband, though not entirely from others. Jeffrey especially felt serious alarm. He feared not without reason that Carlyle was too much occupied with his own thoughts to be trusted in such a situation with the charge of a delicate and high-spirited woman, who would not spare herself in the hard duties of her situation.

The decision had been made, however, and was not to be reconsidered. Jeffrey could only hope that the exile to Siberia would be of short duration. When the furniture at Comely Bank was packed and despatched, he invited Mr. and Mrs. Carlyle to stay with him in Moray Place, while the carts were on the road. After two days they followed, and in the last week of May they were set down at the door of the house which was now to be their home. The one bright feature in the situation to Carlyle was the continual presence of his brother at the farm. The cottage in which Alexander Carlyle lived was attached to the premises; and the outdoor establishment of field, stall, and dairy servants was common to both households.

I resume the letters.

To John Carlyle.

Craigenputtock : June 10, 1828.

My dear Jack,—We received your much-longed-for letter two days ago before leaving Edinburgh in such a scene of chaotic uproar as I had never witnessed, and do earnestly hope I shall never witness again, for the house was full of mats and deal boxes and straw and packthread, and there was a wrapping and a stitching and a hammering and tumbling; and Alick and Jamie came with six carts to take away our goods; and all things were wrenched from their old fixtures, and dispersed and scattered asunder, or united only by a common element of dust and noise. What would the sack of a city be, when the dismantling of a house is such! From all packers and carpenters, and flittings by night or day, Good Lord deliver us.

I have waited here above two weeks in the vain hope that some calmness would supervene. But painters and joiners still dese-

crate every corner of our dwelling, and I write in the midst of
confusion worse confounded as better than not writing at all.

We have arrived at Craigenputtock and found much done, but
still much to do; we must still rush and run with carts and sad-
dlehorses to Dumfries every second day, and rejoice when we
return if the course of events have left us a bed to sleep on.
However, by the strength of men's heads and arms a mighty improvement is and will be accomplished, and one day we calculate
a quiet house must stand dry and clean for us amid this wilderness; and the philosopher will hoe his potatoes in peace on his
own soil, and none to make him afraid. Had we come hither out
of whim one might have sickened and grown melancholy over
such an outlook; but we came only in search of food and raiment,
and will not start at straws. Away then with *Unmuth und Ver-
druss!* Man is born to trouble and toil as the sparks fly upwards.
Let him toil, therefore, as his best is, and make no noise about the
matter. Is the day wearisome, dusty, and full of *midges* that the
galled limbs are like to fail?

> Ein guter Abend kommt heran,
> Wenn ich den ganzen Tag gethan. . . .

Next evening, after the arrival of your letter, I wrote to Messrs.
Black and Young, booksellers, London (of the 'Foreign Review'),
directing them to pay twenty out of forty pounds which they had
ordered me to draw on them for, into the hands of Messrs. Ran-
some & Co. to be paid to the Baron von Eichthal at Munich.[1] I
hope the money may have reached you by this time. I sent these
booksellers a long paper on Goethe for their next still unprinted
number; the forty pounds was for an essay on his 'Helena.' I
meant to send them another piece (on the life of Heyne) for this
number; but where is the cunning that could write a paper here
in the midst of uncreated night? But I am getting very sick, and
must leave you till after dinner, and go *stick* some rows of peas
which are already flourishing in our new garden.

. . . Alas! Jack, there is no sticking of peas for me at this
hour, the cutting-tools being all in active operation elsewhere; so
I sit down to talk with you again, still *impransus*, though in better health than I was an hour ago. Indeed, I have been in considerably better health ever since I came hither, and found my red
chestnut Irish doctor (though ill) saddled, waiting for me in his
stall. By degrees I do think I shall grow as sound as another

---

[1] With whom John Carlyle was then living.

man; and then, when the German doctor is settled within sight of me at Dumfries,[1] and we see him twice a week, and all is fixed on its own footing, will not times be brighter than they have been with us? One blessing we have always to be thankful for—unity and brotherly love, which makes us, though a struggling, still a united family—and are we not all spared together in this wonderful existence still to hope as we struggle? Let us ever be grateful to the Giver of all good, and struggle onward in the path He directs. Some traces of our presence may also be left behind us in this pilgrimage of life, some grains added to the great pyramid of human endeavour. What more has man to wish for?

Of the Craig o' Putta I cannot yet rightly speak till we have seen what adjustment matters will assume. Hitherto, to say truth, all prospers as well as we could have hoped. The house stands heightened and white with rough cast, a light hewn porch in front and canns on the chimney-heads; and within it all seems firm and sound. During summer, as we calculate, it will dry, and the smoke we have reason to believe is now pretty well subdued, so that on this side some satisfaction is to be looked for. We appear also to have been rather lucky in our servants. An active maid came with us from Edinburgh. A dairywoman, also of good omen, comes to us to-morrow from Thornhill; and a good-humoured slut of a byre-woman was retained after half a year's previous trial. Then we have two sufficient farming men and a bonneted stripling skilful in sheep, from this glen. Alick himself is an active little fellow as ever bent ——, and though careworn is diligent, hearty, and compliant. He lives in his little room, which is still but half-furnished like the rest of the house.[2] Mary has been visiting at Scotsbrig, and is now learning to sew at Dumfries. Jane the lesser (Jean) has taken her place here and furnishes butter and *afterings* (*jibbings*)[3] for tea, though we are still in terrible want of a cheeseboard, and by the blessing of Heaven shall get one to-morrow afternoon. Jane (the greater) is surveying all things, proving all things, that she may hold fast to what is good. She watches over her joiners and painters with an eye like any hawk's, from which nothing crooked, unplumb or otherwise irregular can hide itself a moment. And then, to crown our felicity,

[1] John Carlyle's present intention.

[2] Not yet in occupation of his own cottage.

[3] Annandale expressions, meaning—what? The explanatory word itself requires explaining.

we have two fowls hatching in the wood, a duck with twelve eggs, and a hen with (if I mistake not) eleven, from which, for they are properly fed and cared for, great things are expected. Nay, it was but these three nights ago that we slew a Highland stot and salted him in a barrel, and his puddings even now adorn the kitchen ceiling.

From Edinburgh or other peopled quarters of the world I have yet heard nothing. We left Edward Irving there preaching like a Boanerges, with (as Henry Inglis very naively remarked) the town divided about him, ' one party thinking that he was quite mad, another that he was an entire humbug.' For my own share I would not be intolerant of any so worthy a man; but I cannot help thinking that if Irving is on the road to truth, it is no straight one. We had a visit from him, and positively there does seem a touch of extreme exaltation in him. I do not think he will go altogether mad, yet what else he will do I cannot so well conjecture. Cant and enthusiasm are strangely commingled in him. He preaches in steamboats and all open places, wears clothes of an antique cut (his waistcoat has flaps or tails midway down the thigh) and in place of ordinary salutation bids ' the Lord bless you.' I hear some faint rumour of his out-heroding Herod since we left the North, but we have not yet got our newspaper, and so know nothing positive. So ' the *Laurt* bless HIM !' for the present, and if you pass through London on your return, you are engaged to go and see him, and, I think he said, ' abide with him' or ' tarry with him' on your way.

The last two nights we spent in Edinburgh were spent—where think you? In the house of Francis Jeffrey, surely one of the kindest little men I have ever in my life met with. He and his household (wife and daughter) have positively engaged to come and pay us a visit here this very summer! I am to write him an article on Burns as well as on Tasso. But alas, alas! all writing is as yet far from my hand. Walter Scott I did not see because he was in London ; nor hear of, perhaps because he was a busy or uncourteous man, so I left his Goethe medals to be given him by Jeffrey.[1] Lockhart had written a kind of ' Life of Burns,' and men in general were making another uproar about Burns. It is this book, a trivial one enough, which I am to *pretend* reviewing. Further, except continued abuse of Leigh Hunt for his ' Lord

---

[1] They had been originally entrusted to Wilson. How they had been passed to Jeffrey I do not know.

Byron, and some of his Contemporaries,' there seemed no news in
the literary world, or rather universe; for was there ever such a
world as it has grown?

Be steady and active and of good cheer, my dear Doctor, and
come home and live beside us, and let us all be as happy as we
can.

I am ever, your true brother,

T. CARLYLE.

The carpenters and plasterers were at last dismissed.
Craigenputtock became tolerable, if not yet 'cosmic,' and
as soon as all was quiet again, Carlyle settled himself to
work.[1] Tasso was abandoned, or at least postponed, but

[1] It was now that the 'bread' problem had to be encountered, of which
Miss Jewsbury speaks in her 'Recollections of Mrs. Carlyle.' Carlyle could
not eat such bread as the Craigenputtock servants could bake for him, or as
could be bought at Dumfries, and Mrs. Carlyle had to make it herself. Miss
Smith, an accomplished lady living at Carlisle, has kindly sent me a letter in
which the story is characteristically told by Mrs. Carlyle herself. It is
dated January 11, 1857—after an interval of nearly thirty years. Mrs. Carlyle
writes:—

'So many talents are wasted, so many enthusiasms turned to smoke, so
many lives split for want of a little patience and endurance, for want of
understanding and laying to heart what you have so well expressed in your
verses—the meaning of *the Present*—for want of recognising that it is not the
greatness or littleness of "the duty nearest hand," but the spirit in which
one does it, that makes one's doing noble or mean. I can't think how people
who have any natural ambition and any sense of power in them escape going
mad in a world like this without the recognition of that. I know I was
very near mad when I found it out for myself (as one has to find out for
oneself everything that is to be of any real practical use to one).

'Shall I tell you how it came into my head? Perhaps it may be of comfort
to you in similar moments of fatigue and disgust. I had gone with my husband to live on a little estate of *peat bog* that had descended to me all the way
down from John Welsh the Covenanter, who married a daughter of John
Knox. *That* didn't, I am ashamed to say, make me feel Craigenputtock a
whit less of a peat bog, and a most dreary, untoward place to live at. In fact,
it was sixteen miles distant on every side from all the conveniences of life,
shops, and even post office. Further, we were very *poor*, and further and
worst, being an only child, and brought up to "great prospects," I was sublimely ignorant of every branch of useful knowledge, though a capital Latin
scholar, and very fair mathematician!! It behoved me in these astonishing
circumstances to learn to sew! Husbands, I was shocked to find, wore their
stockings into holes, and were always losing buttons, and *I* was expected to
"look to all that;" also it behoved me to learn to *cook!* no capable servant

the article on Burns was written—not so ungraciously, so far as regarded Lockhart, as the epithet 'trivial' which had been applied to his book might have foreboded. But it is rather on Burns himself than on his biographer's account of him that Carlyle's attention was concentrated. It is one of the very best of his essays, and was composed with an evidently peculiar interest, because the outward circumstances of Burns's life, his origin, his early surroundings, his situation as a man of genius born in a farmhouse not many miles distant, among the same people and the same associations as were so familiar to himself, could not fail to make him think often of himself while he was writing about his countryman. How this article was judged by the contemporary critics will be presently seen. For

choosing to live at such an out-of-the-way place, and my husband having bad digestion, which complicated my difficulties dreadfully. The *bread*, above all, brought from Dumfries, "soured on his stomach" (oh Heaven!), and it was plainly my duty as a Christian wife to bake at home. So I sent for Cobbett's *Cottage Economy*, and fell to work at a loaf of bread. But knowing nothing about the process of fermentation or the heat of ovens, it came to pass that my loaf got put into the oven at the time that myself ought to have been put into bed; and I remained the only person not asleep in a house in the middle of a desert. One o'clock struck, and then two, and then three; and still I was sitting there in an immense solitude, my whole body aching with weariness, my heart aching with a sense of forlornness and *degradation*. That I, who had been so petted at home, whose comfort had been studied by everybody in the house, who had never been required to *do* anything but *cultivate my mind*, should have to pass all those hours of the night in watching *a loaf of bread*—which mightn't turn out bread after all! Such thoughts maddened me, till I laid down my head on the table and sobbed aloud. It was then that somehow the idea of Benvenuto Cellini sitting up all night watching his Perseus in the furnace came into my head, and suddenly I asked myself: "After all, in the sight of the Upper Powers, what is the mighty difference between a statue of Perseus and a loaf of bread, so that each be the thing one's hand has found to do? The man's determined will, his energy, his patience, his resource, were the really admirable things of which his statue of Perseus was the mere chance expression. If he had been a woman living at Craigenputtock, with a dyspeptic husband, sixteen miles from a baker, and he a bad one, all these same qualities would have come out more fitly in a *good* loaf of bread.

'I cannot express what consolation this germ of an idea spread over my uncongenial life during the years we lived at that savage place, where my two immediate predecessors had gone *mad*, and the third had taken to *drink*.'

himself, it is too plain that before he came to the end of it the pastoral simplicities of the moorland had not cured Carlyle of his humours and hypochondrias. He had expected that change of scene would enable him to fling off his shadow. His shadow remained sticking to him; and the poor place where he had cast his lot had as usual to bear the blame of his disappointment. In his diary there stands a note: 'Finished a paper on Burns, September 16, 1828, at this Devil's Den, Craigenputtock.'

Meanwhile, though he complained of hearing little from the world outside, his friends had not forgotten him. Letters came by the carrier from Dumfries, and the Saturday's post was the event of the week. Jeffrey especially was affectionate and assiduous. He reproached Carlyle for not writing to him, complained of being so soon forgotten, and evidently wished to keep his friend as close to him as possible. The papers on German literature had brought a pamphlet upon Jeffrey about Kant, from 'some horrid German blockhead;' but he was patient under the affliction and forgave the cause. King's College had been set on foot in London on orthodox principles, under the patronage of the Duke of Wellington and the bishops. He offered to recommend Carlyle to them as Professor of Mysticism; although mysticism itself he said he should like less than ever if it turned such a man as Carlyle into a morbid misanthrope, which seemed to be its present effect. Sir Walter had received his medals and had acknowledged them; had spoken of Goethe as his master, and had said civil things of Carlyle, which was more than he had deserved. Jeffrey cautioned Carlyle to be careful of the delicate companion who had been trusted to him; offered his services in any direction in which he could be of use, and throughout, and almost weekly, sent to one or other of the 'hermits' some note or letter, short or long, but always sparkling, airy, and honestly affectionate. I am sorry that I am not at liberty to print these letters *in extenso;* for they would show that Jeffrey had a genuine regard and admiration for Carlyle, which was never completely appreciated. It was impossible from their relative positions that there should not be at least an appearance of patronage on Jeffrey's part. The reader has probably discovered that Carlyle was proud, and proud men never wholly forgive those to whom they feel themselves obliged.

Late in the summer there came a letter from the young Charles Buller, now grown to intellectual manhood, and thinking about entering public life. He and his old tutor had not forgotten each other. Carlyle had watched him through Cambridge, and had written to caution him against certain forms of Liberal opinion towards which Mrs. Strachey had seen with alarm that her brilliant nephew was tending. Buller replies :—

To Thomas Carlyle.

August 31, 1828.

I can hardly say I feel sorry for your disappointment respecting St. Andrews and the London University, since you seem to have been utterly careless of success. The former I suppose went almost solely by ministerial influence ; and as my father has not quite arrived at the degree of Toryism and baseness which would make a man support the Duke of Wellington's Government, he could hardly have done any good in that way. You have, I see, left Edinburgh. Which and where is the awfully cacophonious place where you have taken up your residence? I would venture to hint that you have kept a perplexing silence respecting the posture of your present life.

I see the London University allows people to give lectures in some manner of connection with them without being appointed by them. Suppose you were to propose to give lectures on German literature and philosophy, I should think you would get an innumerable quantity of pupils. I do not know whether the new ' King's College' is closed to all teachers by M.A.'s and Reverends. If not, I should think you might possibly stand a good chance of getting some appointment there, and it would certainly be a great thing to have one person in that establishment who knows anything beyond that slender and antique lore which the two venerable Universities of Oxford and Cambridge impart to their *élèves*. But I only mention this, for I am utterly ignorant whether this new King's College is to teach anything beyond loyalty and Church of Englandarianism, or to have any teachers except a Greek and Latin lecturer, and perhaps one in Divinity to explain the Catechism. But if you think it worth while I would obtain information from the Bishop of Llandaff, who is the best of the people who have anything to do with it.

We forwarded your letter to Mrs. Strachey, who I dare say will not have acknowledged it, because she has just had the misfortune of—a tenth child. We have some expectation of seeing Miss Kirkpatrick soon, but she is in great trouble. Her brother William, perhaps you already know, died in May after a lingering and painful illness. His poor young wife has gone mad, and Kitty, after all this, has been involved in a very wearisome and distressing dispute with Mrs. Kirkpatrick's sister respecting the care of her brother's children.

And now I refer once more to what you said in your letter to me about myself. You seem to hope that my Utilitarianism and blankness in religion will not last long. If they are wrong, that is, not a true conclusion of my reason, I hope that I may abandon them, and that soon. But I have adopted Utilitarianism because I think it affords the best explanation of men's opinions on morals, and because on it may be built, I think, the best framework on which we may form and instruct the natural feelings of men to do that which produces peace and good will among them.

I think, moreover, that the doctrines of the Utilitarians, whether promulgated under that name or under others, have already done no little good in shaming the world out of some of its worst theories of right and wrong respecting most important matters of practice. That many of the Utilitarians are grossly intolerant I am very ready to admit. But is not this the invariable concomitant (except in the very first geniuses) of zeal for the truth? and especially so when men have, like the Utilitarians, to keep their new principles by main force of logic against the intolerance of the stupid champions of orthodoxy, and the general disfavour even of the better and wiser part of the community?

With regard to my blankness in religion—you call by a mild name a set of opinions to which men usually attach a name that burns worse than Inquisitor's fire and faggot—I have fixed myself in that, because I have not yet found that faith which I could believe, and none among the creeds of this world that I could *wish* to be true. I could picture to myself a bright creed truly; but to think that it could be real because it was pretty would be childish indeed.

But my steed awaits me.

> Believe me, ever yours sincerely,
> CHARLES BULLER.

July this year had been intensely hot. Jeffrey had complained of being stifled in the courts, and for the moment had actually envied his friends their cool mountain breezes. The heat had been followed in August by rain. It had been 'the wettest, warmest summer ever known.' Alexander Carlyle had been living hitherto with his brother, the cottage which he was to occupy with one of his sisters not being yet ready. The storms had delayed the masons; while the article on Burns was being written the premises were still littered with dirt, and Carlyle's impatience with small misfortunes perhaps had inspired the unpleasant epithet of Devil's Den with which he had already christened his home. He appears to have remained, however, in a—for him—tolerable humour.

To John Carlyle.

August 25, 1828.

In this mansion we have had a battle like that of St. George and the Dragon. Neither are we yet conquerors. Smoke and wet and chaos. The first we have subdued; the last two we are subduing. May the Lord keep all Christian men from flitting.

As to literature, which also is bread-making, I have done nothing since Whitsunday but a shortish paper on Heyne [1] for the 'Foreign Review,' which will appear in No. 4. A long article on Goethe is just publishing in No. 3,[2] which has been, for want of cash, I believe, exceedingly delayed; and at this very date I am very busy, and third part done, with a 'fair, full, and free' essay on Burns for the 'Edinburgh Review.' None can say how bilious I am, and

---

[1] *Miscellanies*, vol. ii. p. 75. [2] *Ibid.*, vol. i. p. 233.

am like to be; but I have begun to ride daily on Larry,[1] and so Jeffrey shall have his article at the appointed time. That wonderful little man is expected here very soon with *Weib und Kind*. He takes no little interest in us, writes often, and half hates, half loves me with the utmost sincerity. Nay, he even offers me in the coolest, lightest manner the use of his purse, and evidently rather wishes I would use it. *Proh Deûm atque hominum fidem!* This from a Scotchman and a lawyer! Jane is in considerable trepidation getting the house fully equipped for these august visitors. Surely I think she will succeed. Nay, already we are very smart. Here is a drawing-room with Goethe's picture in it, and a piano, and the finest papering on the walls; and I write even now behind it, in my own little library, *out* of which truly I can see nothing but a barn-roof, tree tops, and empty hay-carts, and under it perhaps a stagnant midden, cock with hens, overfed or else dazed with wet and starvation; but *within* which I may see a clear fire (of peats and Sanquhar coals), with my desk and books and every accoutrement I need in fairest order. Shame befall me if I ought to complain, except it be of my own stupidity and pusillanimity. Unhappily we still want a front door road, and the lawn is mostly a quagmire.

Several weeks ago I had a long letter from Goethe[2] enclosing another from Dr. Eckermann, his secretary, full of commendations and congratulations about my criticism of his 'Helena.' I ought to have written to him long ago, but cannot and must not, till I have done with Burns. If you pass within any manageable distance of Weimar you will surely wait on this sage man. Seriously, I venerate such a person considerably more not only than any king or emperor, but than any man that handles never so expertly the tools of kings and emperors. *Sein Excellenz* already knows you by name, and will welcome you in his choicest mood.

Did you hear of the horrible accident at Kirkcaldy? Irving was going to preach there, and the kirk fell and killed eight and twenty persons. 'What think'st a he means,' said my father, 'gawn up and down the country tevelling and screeching like a wild bear?' Heaven only knows completely. Walter Welsh wonders they do not 'lay him up.' I add no more.

Your brother,   T. CARLYLE.

[1] The Irish horse of 'genius,' who had thrown him at Hoddam Hill.

[2] I find no copy of this letter. The original appears to be lost among the rest.

The Jeffreys were to have come in September, while the weather was still fine, but they had gone first to the western Highlands, and their visit was put off till the next month. Meanwhile the article on Burns had been sent off, and before the appearance of the visitors at Craigenputtock a sharp altercation had commenced between the editor and his contributor on certain portions of it, which was not easily ended. On the article itself the world has pronounced a more than favourable verdict. Goethe considered it so excellent that he translated long passages from it, and published them in his collected works; [1] but, as Goethe had observed about Schiller, contemporaries always stumble at first over the writings of an original man. The novelty seems like presumption. The editor of the 'Edinburgh Review' found the article long and diffuse, though he did not deny that 'it contained much beauty and felicity of diction.' He insisted that it must be cut down—cut down perhaps to half its dimensions. He was vexed with Carlyle for standing, as he supposed, in his own light, misusing his talents and throwing away his prospects. He took the opportunity of reading him a general lecture.

'I suppose,' he said, 'that you will treat me as something worse than an ass when I say that I am firmly persuaded the great source of your extravagance, and of all that makes your writings intolerable to many and ridiculous to not a few, is not so much any real peculiarity of opinions, as an unlucky ambition to appear more original than you are, or the humbler and still more delusive hope of converting our English intellects to the creed of Germany and being the apostle of another Reformation. I wish to God I could persuade you to fling away these affectations, and be contented to write like your famous countrymen of all ages: as long at least as you write to

[1] Goethe's *Works*, vol. xxxiii. pp. 181 *et seq.*

your countrymen and for them.   The nationality for which you commend Burns so highly might teach you, I think, that there are nobler tasks for a man like you than to vamp up the vulgar dreams of these Dousterswivels you are so anxious to cram down our throats ; but which I venture to predict no good judge among us will swallow, and the nation at large speedily reject with loathing.'

So spoke the great literary authority of the day.   The adventurous Prince who would win the golden water on the mountain's crest is always assailed by cries that he is a fool and must turn back, from the enchanted stones which litter the track on which he is ascending.   They too have once gone on the same quest.   They have wanted faith, and are become blocks of rock echoing commonplaces ; and if the Prince turns his head to listen to them, he too becomes as they.   Jeffrey tried to sweeten his admonitions by compliments on the article upon Goethe ; but here too he soon fell to scolding.   'Though I admire,' he said, ' the talent of your paper, I am more and more convinced of the utter fallacy of your opinions and the grossness of your idolatry.   I predict too, with full and calm assurance, that your cause is hopeless, and that England never will admire, nor indeed endure, your German divinities.   It thinks better and more of them indeed than it ever will again.   Your eloquence and ingenuity a little mask their dull extravagance and tiresome presumption.   As soon as they appear in their own persons everybody will laugh.   I am anxious to save you from this *fœda superstitio*.   The only harm it has yet done you is to make you a little verbose and prone to exaggeration.   There are strong symptoms of both in your Burns.   I have tried to staunch the first, but the latter is in the grain, and we must just risk the wonder and the ridicule it may bring on us.'

This was not merely the protest of an editor, but the

reproach of a sincere friend. Jeffrey ardently desired to recommend Carlyle and to help him forward in the world. For Carlyle's own sake, and still more for the sake of his young and delicate relative, he was vexed and irritated that he should have buried himself at Craigenputtock. He imagined, and in a certain sense with justice, that Carlyle looked on himself as the apostle of a new faith (to a clever man of the world the most absurd and provoking of illusions), which the solitude of the moors only tended to encourage.

With October the promised visit was accomplished. How he came with Mrs. Jeffrey and his daughter, how the big carriage stood wondering how it had got there in the rough farm-yard, how Carlyle and he rode about the country, with what astonishment he learnt that his dinner had been cooked for him by his hostess's own hands, how he delighted them all in the evenings with his brilliant anecdotes and mimicries—all this has been told elsewhere and need not be repeated. Those two days were a sunny island in the general dreariness, an Indian summer before winter cut the Carlyles off from the outside world and wrapped them round with snow and desolation. During the greater part of the Jeffreys' stay controverted subjects were successfully avoided. But Carlyle's talk had none the less provoked Jeffrey. He himself, with a spiritual creed which sat easy on him, believed nevertheless that it was the business of a sensible man to make his way in the world, use his faculties to practical purposes, and provide for those who were dependent upon him. He saw his friend given over as he supposed to a self-delusion which approached near to foolish vanity, to have fallen in love with clouds like Ixion, and to be begetting chimæras which he imagined to be divine truths. All this to a clear practical intelligence like that of Jeffrey was mere nonsense, and on the last night of his stay he ended a long argument in a tone of severe reproach for which he felt himself afterwards obliged to apologise. His excuse, if excuse was needed, was a genuine anxiety for Carlyle's welfare, and an equal alarm for his wife, whose delicacy, like enough, her husband was too much occupied with his own thoughts to consider sufficiently. 'I cannot bring myself to think,' he said in a letter which he wrote after he had left them, 'that either you or Mrs. Carlyle are naturally placed at Craigenputtock; and though I know and reverence the feelings which have led you to fix there for the present, I must hope it will not be long necessary to obey them in that retreat. I dare not advise, and do not even know very well what to suggest to a mind so constituted as yours; but I shall be proud to give you my views upon anything that occurs to yourself, and pray understand that few things in this world can give me more gratification than being able to be of any serious use to you. Take care of the fair creature who has trusted herself so entirely to you. Do not let her ride about in the wet, nor expose herself to the wintry winds that will by-and-by visit your lofty retreat; and think seriously of taking shelter in Moray Place [1] for a month or two, and in the meantime be gay and playful and foolish with her, at least as often as you require her to be wise and heroic with you. You have no *mission* upon earth, whatever you may fancy, half so important as to be innocently happy—and all that is good for you of poetic feeling and sympathy with majestic nature will come of its own accord without your straining after it. That is my creed, and right or wrong I am sure it is both a simpler and a humbler one than yours.'

The trouble with the article on Burns was not over. Jeffrey, as editor, had to consider the taste of the great

[1] Jeffrey's house in Edinburgh.

Liberal party in literature and politics, and to disciples of
Bentham, as indeed to the average reader of any political
persuasion, Carlyle's views were neither welcome nor intelligible. When the proof sheets came, he found 'the first
part cut all into shreds—the body of a quadruped with the
head of a bird, a man shortened by cutting out his thighs
and fixing the knee-caps on the hips.' Carlyle refused to
let it appear 'in such a horrid shape.' He replaced the
most important passages, and returned the sheets with an
intimation that the paper might be cancelled, but should
not be mutilated. Few editors would have been so forbearing as Jeffrey when so audaciously defied. He complained, but he acquiesced. He admitted that the article
would do the Review credit, though it would be called
tedious and sprawling by people of weight whose mouths
he could have stopped. He had wished to be of use to
Carlyle by keeping out of sight in the Review his mannerism and affectation; but if Carlyle persisted he might have
his way.

Carlyle was touched; such kindness was more than he
had looked for. The proud self-assertion was followed by
humility and almost penitence, and the gentle tone in
which he wrote conquered Jeffrey in turn. Jeffrey said
that he admired and approved of Carlyle's letter to him in
all aspects. 'The candour and sweet blood' which was
shown in it deserved the highest praise; and, as the dying
pagan said in the play, 'If these are Christian virtues I am
a Christian,' so Jeffrey, hating as he did what he called
Carlyle's mysticism, was ready to exclaim, if these were
mystic virtues he was mystic. 'But your virtues are your
own,' he said, 'and you possess them not in consequence of
your mysticism, but in spite of it. You shall have anything you like. I cannot chaffer with such a man, or do
anything to vex him; and you shall write mysticism for

me if it will not be otherwise, and I will print it too at all hazards with very few and temperate corrections. I think you have a great deal of eloquence and talent, and might do considerable things if —— But no matter; I will not tire of you; after all, I believe there are many more things as to which we agree than about which we differ, and the difference is not radical, but formal chiefly.'

CHAPTER III.

A.D. 1829. ÆT. 34.

So the winter settled down over Craigenputtock. The
weekly cart struggled up when possible from Dumfries
with letters and parcels, but storms and rain made the
communications more and more difficult. Old James Carlyle came over from Scotsbrig for a week after the Jeffreys
went, an Edinburgh friend followed for three days more,
and after that few faces save those of their own household
were seen at the Carlyles' door. Happily for him he was
fully employed. The 'Foreign Review' and the 'Edinburgh' gave him as much work as he could do. He had
little need of money; Scotsbrig supplied him with wheat
flour and oatmeal, and the farm with milk and eggs and
hams and poultry. There was little that needed buying
save tea and sugar and tobacco; and his finances (for his
articles were long and handsomely paid for) promised for
a time to be on an easy footing in spite of the constant expenses of his brother John at Munich. There were two
horses in the stable—Larry, the Irish horse of 'genius,'
and Harry, Mrs. Carlyle's pony.[1] In fine weather they

[1] Carlyle told me a story of these two horses, illustrative of the sense of
humour in animals. I cannot date it either by day or year, and therefore I
give it in a note. They had a vicious old sow, who was the tyrant and the
terror of the farm-yard. One day Carlyle was smoking his pipe outside his
front door, when he heard shrieks of rage and agony combined from the back
of the house. He went round to see what was the matter. A deep drain had
been opened across the yard, the bottom of which was stiff clay. Into this
by some unlucky curiosity the sow had been tempted to descend, and being
there found a difficulty in getting out. The horses were loose. The pony

occasionally rode or walked together. But the occasions
grew rarer and rarer. Carlyle was essentially solitary.
He went out in all weathers, indifferent to wet and, in
spite of his imagined ill-health, impervious to cold. But
he preferred to be alone with his thoughts, and Mrs. Carlyle was left at home to keep the house in proper order.
She by education, and he by temperament, liked everything to be well kept and trim. He was extremely dainty
about his food. He did not care for delicacies, but cleanliness and perfect cookery of common things he always insisted on, and if the porridge was smoked, or the bread
heavy, or the butter less than perfect, or a plate or a dish
ill-washed, he was entirely intolerable. Thus the necessary imperfections of Scotch farm-servant girls had to be
supplemented by Mrs. Carlyle herself. She baked the
bread, she dressed the dinner or saw it dressed, she cleaned
the rooms. Among her other accomplishments she had
to learn to milk the cows, in case the byre-woman should
be out of the way, for fresh milk was the most essential
article of Carlyle's diet. Nay, it might happen that she
had to black the grates to the proper polish, or even scour
the floors while Carlyle looked on encouragingly with his
pipe. In addition to this she had charge of dairy and
poultry ; not herself necessarily making butter or killing
fowls, but directing what was to be done and seeing that
it was done properly. Her department, in short, was the
whole establishment. This winter she was tolerably well,
and as long as her health lasted she complained of nothing. Her one object was to keep Carlyle contented, to
prevent him from being fretted by any petty annoyance,

saw the opportunity—the sow was struggling to extricate herself. The pony
stood over her, and at each effort cuffed her back again with a stroke of the
fore hoof. The sow was screaming more from fury than pain. Larry stood
by watching the performance and smiling approval, nodding his head every
time that the beast was knocked back into the clay, with (as Carlyle declared)
the most obvious and exquisite perception of the nature of the situation.

and prevent him also from knowing with how much labour to herself his own comfort was secured.

Thus the months passed on pleasantly. The 'tempests,' about which Jeffrey had been so anxious, howled over the moors, but did not much affect them. Carlyle's letters were written in fair spirits. The Devil's Den had become a tolerable home. Mrs. Carlyle, it seems, when she could spare time, galloped down alone to Templand (15 miles) to see her mother.

To John Carlyle.

Craigenputtock : November 26, 1828.

This house, bating some outskirt things, which must be left till spring, is really substantial, comfortable, and even half elegant. I sit here in my little library and laugh at the howling tempests, for there are green curtains and a clear fire and papered walls. The 'old kitchen' also is as tight a dining room as you would wish for me, and has a black clean barred grate, at which, when filled with Sanquhar coals, you might roast Boreas himself. The good wife too is happy and contented with me and her solitude, which I believe is not to be equalled out of Sahara itself. You cannot figure the stillness of these moors in a November drizzle. Nevertheless I walk often under cloud of night, in good Ecclefechan clogs, down as far as Carstammon Burn, sometimes to Sandy Wells, conversing with the void heaven in the most pleasant fashion. Besides Jane also has a pony now which can canter to perfection even by the side of Larry. To-morrow she is going over to Templand with it, and it is by her that I send this letter. Grace, our servant, a tight tidy careful sharp-tempered woman, is the only other inmate of the house.

I write hard all day, and then Jane and I, both learning Spanish for the last month, read a chapter of 'Don Quixote' between dinner and tea, and are already half through the first volume and eager to persevere. After tea I sometimes write again, being dreadfully slow at the business, and then generally go over to Alick and Mary and smoke my last pipe with them ; and so I end the day, having done little good, perhaps, but almost no ill that I could help to any creature of God's.

So pass our days, except that sometimes I stroll with my axe or bill in the plantations, and when I am not writing I am reading.

We had Henry Inglis here for three days, and our father for a week lately, both of whom seemed highly contented with this wonderful Craig. Alick and Mary, you already understand, live in their own cottage, or rather double farmhouse, for were it once dried it will be the bieldest, tightest mansion of its sort within some miles of it. They have two man-servants and two maid-servants, are fattening, or merely boarding, quantities of black cattle, have almost a dozen pigs, and plenty of weak corn, and about eighty cartloads of potatoes, to say nothing of turnip acres, to feed them with. Alick is about thatching a cattle shed, long since built (of dry stones), down near the moor, and we have had roadsmen for many weeks gravelling the front of this door (a most marked improvement), making us a proper road to it, and thoroughly repairing the old road. Thus you see chaos is rolling himself back from us by degrees, and all winter we are to have stone-diking, and planting, and draining (if I can write for the cash), till by-and-by I think this hermitage will positively become a very tolerable place. For the rest we drink tea together every Sunday night and live in good brotherhood, having no neighbours that do not wish us well.

As to my writing, it is only at present a most despicable 'article' entitled 'German Playwrights,' with which I expect to be done in a week.

Next I mean to write one on Novalis, and probably a larger one on Voltaire. Some day these roads will be made and sky-lights mended, and all tight and pargetted, and I shall have leisure to cease reviewing, and try to give work for reviewing.

Our news, beyond our own household, are mostly of a sombre cast. James Anderson, the young Laird of Straquhar, our kind neighbour and acquaintance, died after two days' illness a few weeks ago. John Grier, of the Grove, is gone to his long home. He also died suddenly, but like a just man, and with entire composure. Is not this world a mystery, and grand with terror as well as beauty?[1] My letter, you will see, ends in sable, like the life of man. My own thoughts grow graver every day I live.

When Carlyle was in good spirits, his wife had a pleas-ant time with him. 'Ill to live wi',' impatient, irritable

[1] In a previous letter Carlyle, speaking of another death, says : 'Oh God, it is a fearful world, this we live in, a film spread over bottomless abysses, into which no eye has pierced.' The same expression occurs in the *French Revolution*. The image had already impressed itself into his mind.

over little things, that he always was; but he was charming, too; no conversation in my experience ever equalled his; and unless the evil spirit had possession of him, even his invectives when they burst out piled themselves into metaphors so extravagant that they ended in convulsions of laughter with his whole body and mind, and then all was well again. Their Spanish studies together were delightful to both. His writing was growing better and better. She—the most watchful and severest of critics,—who never praised where praise was not deserved, was happy in the fulfilment of her prophecies, and her hardest work was a delight to her when she could spare her husband's mind an anxiety or his stomach an indigestion. At Christmas she had a holiday, going down to her mother and grandfather at Templand. But while away among her own people her heart was on the Craig. This is one of the letters which Carlyle himself annotated, in the sad days when she was lost to him for ever.

To Thomas Carlyle.

Templand : December 30, 1828.

Goody, Goody, dear Goody,—You said you would weary, and I do hope in my heart you are wearying. It will be so sweet to make it all up to you in kisses when I return. You will *take me* and hear all my bits of experiences, and your heart will beat when you find how I have longed to return to you. Darling, dearest, loveliest, 'The Lord bless you.'[1] I think of you every hour, every moment. I love you and admire you, like—like anything. My own Good-Good. But to get away on Sunday was not in my power: my mother argued, entreated, and finally *grat* (wept). I held out on the ground of having appointed Alick to meet me at church; but that was untenable. John Kerr[2] could be sent off at break of day to tell that I could not come. I urged that the household would find themselves destitute of every Christian *comfoart*, unless I were home before Wednesday. That could be

[1] 'Poor Edward Irving's practice and locution, suspect of being somewhat too solemn ! T. C.'

[2] The Templand man-servant.

taken care of by sending anything that was wanted from here. Tea, sugar, butchers' meat, everything was at my service. Well, but I wanted, I said, to be your *first-foot* on New Year's Day. I might be gratified in this also. She would hire a post-chaise and take me over for that day on condition I returned at night!

In short, she had a remedy ready for everything but death, and I could not without seeming very unkind and ungracious, refuse to stay longer than I proposed. So I write this letter 'with my own hand' [Ed. Irving] that you may not be disappointed from day to day; but prepare to welcome me 'in your choicest mood' on Sunday. If the day is at all tolerable, perhaps Alick or you will meet me at church. Mrs. Crichton, of Dabton, was very pressing that you and I should spend some days with them just now, 'when their house was full of company.' But I assured her it would be losing labour to ask you. However, by way of consolation, I have agreed to 'refresh' a party for her with my presence on Friday, and held out some hope that you would visit them at your leisure. 'I am sure the kindness of those people ——' 'The Lord bless them!'[1]

Dearest, I wonder if you are getting any victual. There must be cocks at least, and the chickens will surely have laid their eggs. I have many an anxious thought about you; and I wonder if you sleep at nights, or if you are wandering about—on, on—smoking and killing mice. Oh, if I was there I could put my arms so close about your neck, and hush you into the softest sleep you have had since I went away. Good night. Dream of me.

> I am ever,
> Your own GOODY.

The first year of Craigenputtock thus drew to an end. The storms of December were succeeded by frost, and the moors were bound fast in ice. Carlyle continued as busy as ever at what he called 'the despicable craft of reviewing,' but doing his very best with it. No slop-work ever dropped from his pen. He never wrote down a word which he had not weighed, or a sentence which he had not assured himself contained a truth. Every one of the articles composed on this bare hill-top has come to be reprinted unaltered, and most of them have a calmness too

[1] Irving.

often absent from his later writings. Handsome pay, as I said, came in, but not more than was needed. Brother John was a constant expense; and even in the 'Dunscore wilderness' life was impossible without money. 'Alas!' Carlyle said, 'for the days when Diogenes could fit up his tub, and let the "literary world" and all the other worlds except the only true one within his own soul wag hither and thither at discretion.'

Voltaire was now his subject. His mind was already turning with an unconscious fascination towards the French Revolution. He had perceived it to be the most note-worthy phenomenon of modern times. It was interesting to him, as an illustration of his conviction that untruthful-ness and injustice were as surely followed by divine retribu-tion as the idolatries and tyrannies of Biblical Egypt and Assyria; that the Power which men professed on Sundays to believe in was a living Power, the most real, the most tremendous of all facts. France had rejected the Reforma-tion. Truth had been offered her in the shape of light, and she would not have it, and it was now to come to her as lightning. She had murdered her prophets. She had received instead of them the scoffing Encyclopædists. Yet with these transcendental or 'mystic' notions in his head, Carlyle could write about the most worldly of all men of genius, as himself a man of the world. He meets Voltaire on his own ground, follows him into his private history with sympathising amusement; falls into no fits of horror over his opinions or his immoralities; but regards them as the natural outcome of the circumstances of the time. In Voltaire he sees the representative Frenchman of the age, whose function was to burn up unrealities, out of the ashes of which some more healthy verdure might eventually spring. He could not reverence Voltaire, but he could not hate him. How could he hate a man who had fought man-fully against injustice in high places, and had himself many a time in private done kind and generous actions? To Carlyle, Voltaire was no apostle charged with any divine message of positive truth. Even in his crusade against what he believed to be false, Voltaire was not animated with a high and noble indignation. He was simply an instrument of destruction, enjoying his work with the pleasure of some mocking imp, yet preparing the way for the tremendous conflagration which was impending. There is, of course, audible in this article a deep undertone of feeling. Yet the language of it is free from everything like excited rhetoric. In the earlier part of his career Carlyle sympathised with and expected more from the distinctive functions of revolution than he was able to do after longer experience. 'I thought,' he once said to me, 'that it was the abolition of rubbish. I find it has been only the kindling of a dunghill. The dry straw on the outside burns off; but the huge damp rotting mass remains where it was.'

Thinking on these momentous subjects, Carlyle took his nightly walks on the frozen moor, the ground crisp under his feet, the stars shining over his head, and the hills of Dunscore (for advantage had been taken of the dryness of the air) 'gleaming like Strombolis or Etnas with the burning of heath.' 'Craigenputtock otherwise silent, solitary as Tadmore in the wilderness; yet the infinite vault still over it, and the earth a little ship of space in which he was sailing, and man everywhere in his Maker's eye and hand.'

The new year perhaps did not bring many letters; for Carlyle's friends were still few, and his intimate friends who would write on such occasions were very few. One letter, however, could not fail to come from the faithful Jeffrey, who sent, as a New Year greeting, 'kind thoughts and good wishes,' with a laughing lecture against 'dogmatism,' and 'the desperate darkness of audacious mysticism.' From this Jeffrey passed to moralising on human life and things in general. Edinburgh and the whole of Britain had been shaken by the Burke and Hare business. With the light touch, half jesting and half serious, which is the charm of Jeffrey's style, he spoke of himself as living in fear of fever and dissection, yet not less gaily, less carelessly than usual. Men, he said, were naturally predestinarians, and ran their risks patiently because they could not avoid them. The pestilent and murdering angels had passed him so far, and he was grateful for his escape. Carlyle had been reading 'Don Quixote,' and in writing to Jeffrey had alluded to it, contrasting old times with new. Jeffrey protested against Carlyle's damnable heresy, insisting that there were plenty of shabby fellows whining over petty aches and finding life irksome in the age and country of Cervantes, and that in the Britain of George IV. there were stout-hearted, bright-spirited men who bore up against captivity and worse ills as cheerily as he did. He invited Carlyle to come and stay with him in Edinburgh, and shake off his sickly fancies. They might furnish swelling themes for eloquence, but were out of date and never convinced anybody ; and as for Carlyle's notion that a man ought to have *a right creed as to his relations with the universe,* he would never persuade anyone that the regulation of life was such a laborious business as he would make it, or that it was not better to go lightly through it *with the first creed that came to hand,* than spend the better half of it in an anxious verification of its articles. It would matter less if Carlyle was but amusing himself with paradoxes, but he was ' so dreadfully in earnest.' He was neutralising half the fame and all the use of his talents, and keeping aloof from him most of the men who were fittest for his society.

Never had Jeffrey written to Carlyle with more warmth. The provocation to which he confessed was but the overflowing of good will to which his friend's views prevented him from giving the effect which he desired. The good will, though perfectly genuine, was not entirely disinterested. Carlyle's essays had drawn the notice of the distinguished band of men who were then the chief contributors to the 'Edinburgh Review.' They had recognised that he had extraordinary talents; that if he could be brought to his senses and would subscribe the articles of the Whig faith, he might be an invaluable recruit to the great party of Reform. Jeffrey himself was about to retire from the editorship of the 'Edinburgh Review,' and to become Dean of the Faculty. His advice, though not decisive, would be of weight in the choice of his successor, and he had seriously thought of recommending Carlyle. Brougham, Macaulay, Sydney Smith would all have more or less to be consulted; and perhaps the political chiefs as well; yet if his friend would only be amenable, burn his Goethe, renounce his mysticism, and let his talents and virtues have fair play, Jeffrey must have thought that the objections in those quarters would not be insurmountable.

So was Carlyle tempted in his hermitage, like another St. Anthony, by the spirit of this world, and in a more seductive dress than that in which it assailed the Christian saint. There was no situation in the empire more attractive to literary ambition than the editorship of the 'Edinburgh Review' in those its palmy days of glory and power. To have been even thought of for such an office implied that the attention of the Reform leaders had been drawn to him; and that if not in this way, yet in some others, he might, if he pleased, be advanced to some lucrative and honourable office. The difficulty was not on their side, it was on his. The way which they called heresy he called truth, and the kind, honest, but seducing angel assailed him in vain.

Carlyle, though in the 'Reminiscences of Lord Jeffrey' he has acknowledged a general wish on Jeffrey's part to serve him, which was thwarted by his own persistency, has passed over without mention this particular instance of it. He never mentioned it even in conversation to myself. But the fact was so. Jeffrey is himself the witness. The publishers of the 'Review' came down to Edinburgh to consult with him. Carlyle was not actually proposed. The prudent and cautious views of the Longmans, and Jeffrey's wish to spare Carlyle the mortification of being rejected, prevented his pretensions from being brought directly under discussion. But the inflexibility and independence of Carlyle's character were the chief, perhaps the only obstacles. Jeffrey was bitterly disappointed. The person selected was Macvey Napier, the editor of the 'Encyclopædia,' 'a safe man at all events.' Jeffrey, writing to Carlyle, could not hide his mortification. 'It was with mixed sorrow and anger,' he said, that he saw his friend renouncing his natural titles to distinction for such fantastical idolatry. The folly of his own fair cousin's ancestors, who threw away their money in improving and adorning Craigenputtock, was but a faint type of Carlyle's. But he could not help him; he would pray for him if it would do any good.

A further effect of the change of editorship was that it threatened at first the close of Carlyle's connection with the 'Review,' even as a contributor. Jeffrey continued to edit till the middle of 1829, and so long as he was in the chair Carlyle's help was still solicited. The Voltaire had been written for the 'Edinburgh,' if the 'Edinburgh' would have it, and a corresponding article was in contemplation upon Johnson, Voltaire's direct antithesis. Neither of these subjects pleased Jeffrey. Carlyle, he thought, perhaps in this case with some want of judgment, could have nothing new to say on either of them. But as the time of his withdrawal drew near he begged hard for a parting contribution for his last number. The Voltaire would have answered well for him, but he did not even ask to look at it. On any other subject Carlyle might write what he pleased ; mysticism of the worst kind should not be rejected. He was really ambitious, he said, of having a morsel of mysticism. He was going to take advantage of his approaching abdication by plaguing Brougham with an attack on Utilitarianism ; and it was but reasonable that he should use the same retreat from responsibility in encouraging Carlyle to commit a fresh outrage on the rational part of his readers. Any topic would serve as a text. Jeffrey suggested ' Vivian Grey ' or ' Pelham.' ' Vivian Grey ' he considered better than the best novel which any German had ever written. Carlyle proposed Southey, but Macaulay had forestalled him. In the end Carlyle wrote the ' Signs of the Times,' the first of the essays in which he brought out his views of the condition of modern English society—a most signal outrage indeed, if that was what Jeffrey wanted, on ' the Philosophy of Progress ' which was preached so continuously from the Edinburgh pulpit. He gave Jeffrey full warning of what was coming. Jeffrey only encouraged him with visibly malicious amusement. But the cautious character which he ascribed to Napier made it probable that this article might be his last in that periodical.

Of outward incidents meanwhile the Craigenputtock history was almost entirely destitute. The year 1829 rolled by without interruption to the tranquil routine of daily life. John Carlyle came home from Germany and became sometimes his brother's guest till a situation as doctor could be found for him. Carlyle himself wrote and rode and planted potatoes. His wife's faculty for spreading grace about her had extended to the outside premises, and behind the shelter of the trees she had raised a rose garden. An old but strong and convenient gig was added to the establishment. When an article was finished Car-

lyle allowed himself a fortnight's holiday: he and Mrs.
Carlyle driving off with Larry either to Templand or to
Scotsbrig; the pipe and tobacco duly arranged under cover
on the inner side of the splashboard. The Jeffreys passed
through Dumfries in the summer. Their friends from the
Craig drove down to see them, and were even meditating
afterwards an expedition in the same style throughout
England as far as Cornwall.

Carlyle was full of thoughts on the great social questions
of the day. He wished to see with his own eyes the actual condition of the people of England, as they lived in
their own homes. The plan had to be abandoned for
want of means, but he had set his own heart upon it, and
Mrs. Carlyle would have been glad too of a change from a
solitude which was growing intolerably oppressive. Carlyle's ill humours had not come back, but he was occupied
and indifferent. There is a letter from his wife to old
Mrs. Carlyle at Scotsbrig, undated, but belonging evidently to March of this year, in which she complains of
the loneliness. 'Carlyle,' she says, 'never asks me to go
with *him*, never even looks as if he desired my company.'

One visitor, however, came to Craigenputtock in the
summer whose visit was more than welcome. Margaret,
the eldest of Carlyle's sisters, had the superiority of mind
and talent which belonged to her brother, and she had
along with it an instinctive delicacy and nobleness of
nature which had overcome the disadvantages of her education. She had become a most striking and interesting
woman, but unhappily along with it she had shown symptoms of consumption. In the preceding autumn the family
had been seriously alarmed about her. She had been ill
all through the winter, but she had rallied with the return
of warm weather. The cough ceased, the colour came
back to her cheeks, she was thought to have recovered
entirely, and in June or July she rode over with her

brother John from Scotsbrig to Craigenputtock, picking
up on the way a precious letter which was waiting at
Dumfries post-office.

I remember (Carlyle writes) one beautiful summer evening,
1829, as I lounged out of doors smoking my evening pipe, silent
in the great silence, the woods and hill tops all gilt with the flaming splendour of a summer sun just about to set, there came a
rustle and a sound of hoofs into the little bending avenue on my
left (sun was behind the house and me), and the minute after
brother John and Margaret direct from Scotsbrig, fresh and handsome, as their little horses ambled up, one of the gladdest sights
and surprises to me. 'Mag, dear Mag, once more.' [1] John had
found a letter from Goethe for me at the post-office, Dumfries.
This, having sent them in doors, I read in my old posture and
place, pure white the fine big sheet itself, still purer the noble
meaning all in it, as if mutely pointing to eternity—letter fit to be
read in such a place and time.[2] Our dear Mag stayed some
couple of weeks or more (made me a nice buff-coloured cotton
waistcoat, I remember). She was quietly cheerful, and complained of nothing; but my darling, with her quick eye, had noticed too well (as she then whispered to me) that the recovery was
only superficial, and that worse might be ahead. It was the last
visit Margaret ever made.

Nothing more of special moment happened this year.
Life went on as usual; but the autumn brought anxieties
of more than one description. The letters that remain are
few, for his wife and his brother Alexander, to whom he
wrote most confidentially, were both at Craigenputtock, and
his brother John also was for several months with him.
He was trying to produce something better than review
articles, and was engaged busily with an intended history
of German literature, for which he had collected a large
quantity of books. But John Carlyle, who was naturally
listless, had to be stimulated to exertion, and was sent to
London to look for employment. Employment would not

[1] The account is taken from the *Reminiscences.* The concluding words are
inserted from a letter.
[2] I discover no trace of this letter. Perhaps it may yet be found.

come; perhaps was less assiduously looked for than it might have been. The expense of his maintenance fell on Carlyle, and the reviews were the only source to which he could look. More articles therefore had to be produced if a market could be found for them. Jeffrey, constant in his friendship, consulted the new editor of the 'Edinburgh,' and various subjects were suggested and thought over. Carlyle proposed Napoleon, but another contributor was in the way. Jeffrey was in favor of Wycliffe, Luther, or 'the Philosophy of the Reformation.' Napier thought a striking article might be written on some poetical subject; but when Jeffrey hinted to him some of Carlyle's views on those topics, and how contemptuously he regarded all the modern English singers, the new editor 'shuddered at the massacre of the innocents to which he had dreamt of exciting him.' Still, for himself, Jeffrey thought that if Carlyle was in a relenting mood, and wished to exalt or mystify the world by a fine rhapsody on the divine art, he might be encouraged to try it.

Liking Jeffrey as Carlyle did, he was puzzled at so much interest being shown in him. He called it a mystery. Jeffrey humourously caught up the word, and accepted it as the highest compliment which Carlyle could pay. In a humbler sense, however, he was content to think it natural that one man of a kind heart should feel attracted towards another, and that signal purity and loftiness of character, joined to great talents and something of a romantic history, should excite interest and respect.

Jeffrey's anxiety to be of use did not end in recommendations to Napier. He knew how the Carlyles were situated in money matters. He knew that they were poor, and that their poverty had risen from a voluntary surrender of means which were properly their own, but which they would not touch while Mrs. Welsh was alive. He knew also that Carlyle had educated and was still supporting his brother out of his own slender earnings. He saw, as he supposed, a man of real brilliancy and genius weighed down and prevented from doing justice to himself by a drudgery which deprived him of the use of his more commanding talents; and with a generosity the merit of which was only exceeded by the delicacy with which the offer was made, he proposed that Carlyle should accept a small annuity from him. Here again I regret that I am forbidden to print the admirable letter in which Jeffrey conveyed his desire, to which Carlyle in his own mention of this transaction has done but scanty justice. The whole matter he said should be an entire secret between them. He would tell no one—not even his wife. He bade Carlyle remember that he too would have been richer if he had not been himself a giver where there was less demand upon his liberality. He ought not to wish for a monopoly of generosity, and if he was really a religious man he must do as he would be done to; nor, he added, would he have made the offer did he not feel that in similar circumstances he would have freely accepted it himself. To show his confidence he enclosed 50*l.*, which he expected Carlyle to keep, and desired only to hear in reply that they had both done right.

Carlyle was grateful, but he was proud. He did not at the time, or perhaps ever, entirely misconstrue the spirit in which Jeffrey had volunteered to assist him; but it is hard, perhaps it is impossible, for a man to receive pecuniary help, or even the offer of pecuniary help, from a person who is not his relation without some sense that he is in a position of inferiority; and there is force in the objection to accepting favours which Carlyle thus describes, looking back over forty years:—

Jeffrey generously offered to confer on me an annuity of 100*l.*, which annual sum had it fallen on me from the clouds would have been of very high convenience at the time, but which I could not for a moment have dreamt of accepting as gift or sub-ventionary help from any fellow-mortal. It was at once in my handsomest, gratefullest, but brief and conclusive way declined from Jeffrey. 'Republican equality,' the silently fixed law of human society at present : each man to live on his own resources, and have an equality of economics with every other man ; danger-ous, and not possible except through cowardice or folly to depart from said clear rule till perhaps a better era rise on us again.

From a letter written at the time there appears through his genuine gratitude a faint but perceptible tinge of wounded feeling.

Do but think of Jeffery (he wrote to his brother, who was really the cause that he was in difficulties). A letter was lying here from him offering in the daintiest style to settle a hundred a year on unworthy me. I have just sent the meekest, friendliest, but most emphatic refusal for this and all coming times. Do not mention this, for you see it has never gone beyond the length of a flourish of rhetoric, and is scarcely fit to mention. Only when-ever we think of our Dean of the Faculty let us conceive him as a *multum in parvo* that does credit to Scotland and humanity.

If anyone thinks that Carlyle was deficient in gratitude, let him remember that gratitude is but one of many feel-ings which are equally legitimate and reputable. The gentleman commoner at Pembroke College meant only kindness when he left the boots at Johnson's door ; but Johnson, so far from being grateful, flung the boots out of the window, and has been praised by all mankind for it.

From his brother himself Carlyle was careful to con-ceal the scanty state to which his resources were reduced. From his notebook I find that at one time in 1830 he had but five pounds left with which to face the world. Yet he still wrote cheerfully, and remittances were still sent, with no word except of kind exhortation to exertion.

To John Carlyle, London.

Craigenputtock : February 11, 1830.

Your last letter, dear brother, though but of a sable texture, gave me more real satisfaction than any you had written. It exhibits you in a figure of decided action, which after so many weeks of storm-bound inactivity we all heartily longed and prayed to see you in. Spite of all difficulties, and these are too many and too heavy, I now doubt not a moment that you will find yourself a settlement and ultimately prosper there. But you are now at the pinch of the game, Jack, and must *not* falter. Now or never! Oh, my dear brother, do not loiter, do not linger, trusting to the chapter of chances and help from other men. Know and feel that you are still there yourself; *one* heart and head that will never desert your interests. I know the many difficulties and hesitations, how wretched you are while others only fancy you sluggish. But, thank Heaven, you are now afoot, fairly diligent and intent. What way it is in you to make you will make; and already I can well believe you are far happier; for evil, as Jean Paul truly says, is like a nightmare—the instant you begin to *stir* yourself it is already gone.

Meanwhile do not fret yourself over much; a period of probation and adventure is appointed for most men, is good for all men. For your friends especially—and testifying by deeds your affection to them—give yourself *no* sorrow. There is not a friend you have, Jack, who doubts for an instant of your affection; neither is their wish with regard to you to see you rich and famous, but to see you self-collected, diligent, and wise, steering your way manfully through this existence, resolutely and with clear heart as beseems a man, as beseems *such* a man. Whether you ride in carriages and drink Tokay, and have crowds to follow after you, or only walk in Scotch clogs like the rest of us, is a matter—so you *do* walk—of far smaller moment. 'Stout heart to a stay brae' then, my brave boy! There is nothing in the world to frighten a clear heart. They can refuse you guinea fees, but the godlike privilege of alleviating wretchedness, of feeling that you are a true man, let the whole host of gigmen say to it what they will, no power on earth, or what is under it, can take from you. Oh then, my brother, up and be doing! Be my real stout brother as of old, and I will take you to my heart and name you proudly, though in the world's eye you were the lowest of the low. What charm is in a name? Physician, surgeon, apothecary—all but quack—is honourable. There are plenty of poor to practise on. If you gain but twenty shillings during the first half year do not despair. As for the poor ten pounds you get from me, you are heartily welcome to it thrice over. My only grief is that in the present posture of affairs I can furnish nothing more. The Blacks have not so much as paid me yet. However, times will not always be so bad, and while I have help to give depend on it as your own.

Your affectionate brother,

T. C.

The Fates this winter were doing their very worst to Carlyle. His wife had escaped harm from the first season at Craigenputtock, but was not to be let off so easily a second time. All went well till the close of December; a fat goose had been killed for the new year's feast; when the snow fell and the frost came, and she caught a violent sore-throat, which threatened to end in diphtheria. There was no doctor nearer than Dumfries, and the road from the valley was hardly passable. Mrs. Welsh struggled up from Templand through the snow-drifts; care and nursing kept the enemy off, and the immediate danger in a few days was over; but the shock had left behind it a sense of insecurity, and the unsuitableness of such a home for so frail a frame became more than ever apparent. The old father at Scotsbrig fell ill, too, this January and showed signs of breaking, and beside the illness of those dear to him, the repose of the country was startled by more than one frightful tragedy. The death of a Craigenputtock neighbour affected Carlyle much.

Rob Clerk of Craigmony (he wrote to his brother John) had been drinking at Minny hire, perhaps the day you were departing. He tumbled off his chair with a groan, gave a snort or two on the floor, and was by his companions reckoned to be dead drunk. At their convenient leisure they hoisted him and his boy, also drunk, into the cart, which Johnny McCawe's 'lassie' (happily sober) drove home under cloud of night to his aunt. Rob spoke none, moved none, and his aunt carried him in on her back and laid him on the bed, and after hours of sedulous ministering discovered him to be—dead! Rob was once a man that could have tuned markets with his own purse, and he would not 'taste' in those days. But he failed in trade twice; since then has led a strange wet and dry existence, drunk in all corners of Britain from Sussex to Sutherland, and *so* found his end at length. Is it not a wild world this? Who made it? who governs it? who gets good of it? Without faith I think a man were forced to be an atheist.

The next letter, one of the very few which Carlyle ever addressed to a public journal, explains itself.

To the Editor of the 'Dumfries and Galloway Courier.'

April 12, 1830.

Mr. Editor,—Some time last autumn a 'fatal accident' stood recorded in the newspapers, of a young man having come by his death at a place called Knockhill, near Ecclefechan, in this county, under somewhat singular circumstances. The young man, it appeared, had been engaged in some courtship with one of the maid-servants of the house; had come that night to see her in the fashion common, or indeed universal, with men of his station in that quarter, was overheard by the butler, was challenged, pursued, and, refusing to answer any interrogatory, but hastening only to escape, was shot dead by him on the spot. No man who has lived three weeks in the south of Scotland can be ignorant that such visits occur nightly everywhere, and have occurred from time immemorial. It is a custom by many blamed, by some applauded. In the romantic spirit sometimes displayed in it; in the long journeyings and wistful waitings for an interview; in the faithfulness with which the rustic wooer at all hazards keeps his secret which is also another's, Dr. Currie traces among our peasants some resemblance to the gallantry of a Spanish Cavalier. In company with the butler so fatally watchful on this occasion were two men to have assisted him in any defence, in any seizure. Whether he knew the individual fugitive, then within some feet of his gun, is uncertain; that he guessed his errand there is scarcely so. Enough the poor young man who had refused to speak fell to the ground exclaiming only, Oh, lasses, lasses!" and in a few instants was no more.

> Ready or not ready, no delay!
> On to his Judge's bar he must away.

Last week I looked over your circuit intelligence with some anxiety to see how this case had been disposed of, but unfortunately without effect. There was no notice of it there. Interesting trials enough we have had, trials for attempting to shoot rabbits, for writing marriage lines, for stealing a pair of breeches; but for the 'shedder of blood' there was no trial. To none of his Majesty's justiciars, it would seem, has any hint of that transaction been communicated. Whether it was ever so much as glanced at, much less thoroughly sifted by any official personage, high or low, appears not from the record—nowhere the smallest whisper of it.

May I ask in the name of all that is wonderful how this has been? Is it lawful, then, to put to death any individual whom you may find flirting with your maid after ten at night? Nay, is it *so* lawful that no inquiry can be needed on the subject; but the whole matter may be hushed up into insignificance, with a few bows or shrugs? If we have an Act of Parliament to that purport it is well; only let us understand clearly how it runs. May any British subject, the poorest cotter, keep his loaded gun for our rural Celadons, and shoot them with less ceremony than he dare do snipes? Or is it only men possessing certain 'ploughgates of land' that enjoy such a privilege? If so, might not it be well that they were bound to take out some licence or game certificate first?

Of your Public Prosecutor I know not even the name. The master of that Knockhill mansion, the unhappy creature his servant, are, if possible, still more unknown to me. Hatred of them, love of them, fear or hope of them, have I none. Neither say I, nor know I, whether in that act the wretched homicide did right or did wrong. But in the name of God, let all official courtesies and hole and corner work be far from us when 'man's blood' is on our floor! Let the light in on it, the clear eye of public inquiry, or the spot will blacken there for ever. Let the law with its fifteen good men and true speak forth an open verdict, that the muttered curses of a whole district may cease.

Vox.

CHAPTER IV.

THE outward life of a man of letters is in his works.   But in his works he shows only so much of himself as he considers that the world will be benefited or interested by seeing; or rather, if he is true artist he does not show his own self at all.   The more excellent the thing produced, the more it resembles a work of nature in which the creation is alone perceived, while the creating hand is hidden in mystery.   Homer and Shakespeare are the greatest of poets, but of the men Homer and Shakespeare we know next to nothing.   'The blind old bard of Chio's rocky isle' has been even criticised out of existence, and ingenious inquirers have been found to maintain that the Stratford player furnished but a convenient name, and that the true authors of 'Henry IV.' or 'Hamlet,' were Queen Elizabeth's courtiers and statesmen.

Men of genius do not care to hang their hearts upon their sleeve for daws to peck at; yet if they have left anywhere their written conversations with themselves, if they have opened a door into the laboratory where the creative force can be seen in its operation, and the man himself can be made known to us as he appeared in undress and in his own eyes, the public who are interested in his writings may count it as a piece of rare good fortune.   No man who has any vital force in him ever lies to himself.   He may assume a disguise to others ; but the first condition of success is that he be true to his own soul and has looked his own capacities and his own faults fairly in the face.   I have already given some extracts from Carlyle's Journal. The entries are irregular, sometimes with a blank of several years. For 1829 and 1830 it is unusually ample, and that the story may not be interrupted I place before the reader collectively the picture which it gives of Carlyle's mind. Some incidents are alluded to which have still to be related. The reader will learn what he may find wanting in the chapter which will follow.

Extracts from a Diary Kept at Craigenputtock.
1829—1830.

February, 1829.—Has the mind its cycles and seasons like nature, varying from the fermentation of *werden* to the clearness of *seyn,* and this again and again, so that the history of a man is like the history of the world he lives in? In my own case I have traced two or three such vicissitudes. At present, if I mistake not, there is some such thing at hand for me.

Above all things I should like *to know England;* the essence of social life in this same little island of ours. But how? No one that I speak to can throw light on it; not he that has worked and lived in the midst of it for half a century. The blind following the blind! Yet each cries out, 'What glorious sunshine we have!' The 'old literature' only half contents me. It is ore and not metal. I have not even a *history* of the country half precise enough. With Scotland it is little better. To me there is nothing poetical in Scotland but its religion. Perhaps because I know nothing else so well. England, with its old chivalry, art, and 'creature comfort,' looks beautiful, but only as a cloud country, the distinctive features of which are all melted into one gay sunny mass of hues. After all we are a world 'within ourselves,' a 'self-contained house.'

The English have never had an artist except in poetry: no musician; no painter. Purcell (was he a native?) and Hogarth are not exceptions, or only such as confirm the rule.

He who would understand England must understand her Church—for that is half of the whole matter. Am I not conscious of a prejudice on that side? Does not the very sight of a shovel hat in some degree indispose me to the wearer thereof? Shut up my heart against him? This must be looked into. Without love there is no knowledge.

Do I not also partly despise, partly hate, the aristocracy of Scotland? I fear I do, though under cover. This too should be remedied. On the whole I know little of the Scottish gentleman, and more than enough of the Scottish *gigman.* All are not mere rent-gatherers and game-preservers.

Have the Scottish gentry lost their national character of late years, and become mere danglers in the train of the wealthier English? Scott has seen certain characters among them of which I hitherto have not heard of any existing specimen.

Is the true Scotchman the peasant and yeoman; chiefly the former?

Shall we actually go and drive through England, to see it? Mail coaches are a mere mockery.

A national character, that is, the description of one, tends to realise itself, as some prophecies have produced their own fulfilment. Tell a man that he is brave, and you help him to become so. The national character hangs like a pattern in every head; each sensibly or insensibly shapes himself thereby, and feels pleased when he can in any manner realise it.

Is the characteristic strength of England its love of justice, its deep-seated universally active sense of fair play? On many points it seems to be a very stupid people; but seldom a hide-bound, bigoted, altogether unmanageable and unaddressable people.

The Scotch have more enthusiasm and more consideration; that is, at once more sail and ballast. They seem to have a *deeper* and *richer* character as a nation. The old Scottish music, our songs, are a highly distinctive feature.

Read Novalis' 'Schriften' for the second time some weeks ago, and wrote a review of them. A strange mystic unfathomable book, but full of matter for most earnest meditation. What is to become (next) of the world and the sciences thereof? Rather, what is to become of *thee* and thy sciences? Thou longest to *act* among thy fellow men, and canst yet scarcely *breathe* among them.

Friedrich Schlegel dead at Dresden on the 9th of January. Poor Schlegel, what a toilsome seeking was thine! Thou knowest now whether thou hast found—or thou carest not for knowing!

What am I to say of Voltaire? His name has stood at the top of a sheet for three days and no other word! Writing is a dreadful labour, yet not so dreadful as *idleness*.

Every living man is a visible mystery; he walks between two eternities and two infinitudes. Were we not blind as moles we should value our humanity at ∞, and our rank, influence, &c. (the trappings of our humanity) at 0. Say I am a man, and you say all. Whether king or tinker is a mere appendix.—'Very true, Mr. Carlyle, but then——' we must believe truth and practice error?

Pray that your eyes be opened, that you may *see* what *is* before them! The whole world is built, as it were, on light and glory— only our *spiritual* eye must discern it; to the bodily eye Self is as a perpetual *blinder*, and we see nothing but darkness and contradiction.

Luther, says Melanchthon, would often, though in robust health, go about for *four days* eating and drinking—nothing! 'Vidi continuis quatuor diebus, cum quidem recte valeret, prorsus nihil edentem aut bibentem. Vidi sæpe alias multis diebus quotidie exiguo pane et halece contentum esse.' Content for many days with a little piece of bread and herring. *O tempora! O mores!*

Luther's character appears to me the most worth discussing of all modern men's. He is, to say it in a word, a great man in every sense; has the soul at once of a conqueror and a poet. His attachment to music is to me a very interesting circumstance; it was the channel for many of his finest emotions, for which words, even words of prayer, were but an ineffectual exponent. Is it true that he did leave Wittenberg for Worms with nothing but his Bible and his flute? There is no scene in European history so splendid and significant. I have long had a sort of notion to

write some life or characteristic of Luther. A picture of the public thought in those days, and of this strong lofty mind overturn-
ing and new moulding it, would be a fine affair in many senses.
It would require immense research. Alas! alas! when are we to
have another Luther? Such men are needed from century to
century; there seldom has been more need of one than now.

Wrote a paper on Voltaire for the 'Foreign Review.' It appears to have given some, very slight, satisfaction; pieces of it
breathe afar off the right spirit of composition. When shall I
attain to write wholly *in that spirit?*

Paper on Novalis for F. R. just published. Written last January amid the frosts. Generally poor. Novalis is an anti-mechan-
ist—a deep man—the most perfect of modern spirit-seers. I
thank him for somewhat.

August 5, 1829.—Also just finished an article on the 'Signs of
the Times' for the 'Edinburgh Review,' as Jeffrey's last speech.
Bad in general, but the best I could make it under such incubus
influences.

Every age appears surprising and full of vicissitudes to those
that live therein—as indeed it is and must be—vicissitudes from
nothingness to existence; and from the tumultuous wonders of
existence forward to the still wonders of death.

Politics are not our life—which is the practice and contemplation of goodness—but only the *house* wherein that life is led. Sad
duty that lies on us to *parget* and continually repair our houses,
saddest of all when it becomes our sole duty.

An institution, a law of any kind, may became a *deserted* edifice;
the walls standing, no life going on within but that of bats, owls,
and unclean creatures. It will then be pulled down if it stand
interrupting any thoroughfare. If it do not so stand, people may
leave it alone till a grove of natural wood grow round it; and no
eye but that of the adventurous antiquarian may know of its existence, such a tangle of *brush* is to be struggled through before it
can be come at and viewed.

All language but that concerning *sensual* objects is or has been
figurative. Prodigious influence of metaphors! Never saw into

it till lately; a truly useful and philosophical work would be a good 'Essay on Metaphors.'

Begin to think more seriously of discussing Martin Luther. The only inspiration I know of is that of genius. It was, is, and will always be of a divine character.

Wonderful universe! Were our eyes but opened, what a 'secret' were it that we daily see and handle without heed!

Understanding is to reason as the talent of a beaver (which can build houses, and uses its tail for a trowel) to the genius of a prophet and poet. Reason is all but extinct in this age; it can never be altogether extinguished.

'Das Seligseyn ist um eine Ewigkeit älter als das Verdammt-seyn.'—Jean Paul.

'The mixture of those things by speech which by nature are divided is the mother of all error.'—Hooker.

Error of political economists about improving waste lands as compared with manufacturing. The manufacture is worn and *done*. The machine itself dies. The improved land remains an addition to the estate *for ever*. What is the amount of this error? I see not, but reckon it something considerable.

Is it true that of all quacks that ever quacked (boasting themselves to be somebody) in any age of the world, the political economists of this age are, for their intrinsic size, the loudest? Mercy on us, what a quack-quacking; and their egg, even if *not* a wind one, is of value simply one halfpenny.

Their whole philosophy (!) is an arithmetical computation performed in words; requires, therefore, the intellect, not of Socrates or Shakespeare, but of Cocker or Dilworth. Even if this were right—which it scarcely ever is, for they miss this or the other item, do as they will, and must return to practice and take the low *posteriori* road after all—the question of money-making, even of national money-making, is not a high but a low one; as they treat it, among the highest. Could they tell us how wealth is and should be *distributed*, it were something; but they do not attempt it.

Political philosophy? Political philosophy should be a scientific revelation of the whole secret mechanism whereby men cohere together in society; should tell us what is meant by 'country' (*patria*), by what causes men are happy, moral, religious, or the contrary. Instead of all which it tells us how 'flannel jackets' are exchanged for 'pork hams,' and speaks much about 'the land last taken into cultivation.' They are the hodmen of the intellectual edifice, who have got upon the wall and will insist on building as if they were masons.

The Utilitarians are the 'crowning mercy' of this age, the summit (now first appearing to view) of a mass of tendencies which stretch downwards and spread sidewards over the whole intellect and morals of the time. By-and-by the clouds will disperse, and we shall see it all in dead nakedness and brutishness; our Utilitarians will pass away with a great noise. You think not? Can the reason of man be trodden under foot for ever by his sense? Can the brute in us prevail for ever over the angel?

The Devil has his elect.

'Pero digan lo que quisieren los historiadores; que desnudo naci, desnudo mi hallo, ni pierdo ni gano, aunque por verme puesto in libros y andar por ese mundo de mano en mano, no se me da un trigo, que digan de mi todo lo que quisieren,' says Sancho.—'Quixote,' iv. 117.

January 14, 1830.—Does it seem hard to thee that thou shouldst toil in dulness, sickness, isolation? Whose lot is not even thus? Toil then, and *tais-toi*.

Either I am degenerating into a *caput mortuum*, and shall never think another reasonable thought; or some new and deeper view of the world is about to arise in me. Pray heaven the latter! It is dreadful to live without vision. When there is no light the people perish.

With considerable sincerity I can pray at this moment, 'Grant me, O Father, enough of wisdom to live well; prosperity to live easily grant me or not, as Thou seest best.' A poor, faint *prayer* as such, yet surely a kind of wish, as indeed it has generally been with me; and now a kind of comfort to feel it still in my otherwise too withered heart.

I am a 'dismembered limb,' and feel it again too deeply. Was I ever other? Stand to it tightly, man, and do thy utmost. Thou hast little or no hold on the world; promotion will never reach thee, nor true fellowship with any active body of men; but hast thou not still a hold on thyself? *Ja, beym Himmel!*

Religion, as Novalis thinks, is a social thing. Without a church there can be little or no religion. The action of mind on mind is mystical, infinite; religion, worship can hardly (perhaps not at all) support itself without this aid. The derivation of *Schwärmerey* indicates some notion of this in the Germans. To *schwärmen* (to be enthusiastic) means, says Coleridge, to *swarm*, to crowd together and excite one another.

What is the English of all quarrels that have been, are, or can be, between man and man? Simply this. Sir, you are taking more than your share of pleasure in this world, something from *my* share; and by the gods you shall not—nay, I will fight you rather. Alas! and the whole lot to be divided is such a beggarly account of empty boxes, truly a 'feast of shells,' not eggs, for the yolks have all been blown out of them. Not enough to fill half a stomach, and the whole human species famishing to be at them. Better we should say to our brother, 'Take it, poor fellow, take that larger share which I reckon mine, and which thou so wantest; take it with a blessing. Would to Heaven I had but enough for thee!' This is the moral of the Christian religion; how easy to write, how *hard* to practise.

I have now almost done with the Germans. Having seized their opinions, I must turn me to inquire *how* true are they? That truth is in them no lover of truth will doubt; but how much? And after all one needs an intellectual scheme (or ground plan of the universe) drawn with one's own instruments. I think I have got rid of materialism. Matter no longer seems to me so ancient, so unsubduable, so *certain* and palpable as mind. *I* am mind; whether matter or not I know not, and can not. Glimpses into the spiritual universe I have sometimes had (about the true nature of religion), the possibility after all of supernatural (really natural) influences. Would they could but stay with me, and ripen into a perfect view.

Miracle? What is a miracle? Can there be a thing more miraculous than any other thing? I myself am a standing wonder. It is the inspiration of the Almighty that giveth us understanding.

What is poetry? Do I really love poetry? I sometimes fancy almost not. The jingle of maudlin persons with their mere (even genuine) sensibility is unspeakably fatiguing to me. My greatly most delightful reading is where some Goethe musically *teaches* me. Nay, any fact relating especially to man is still valuable and pleasing. My memory, which was one of the best, has failed sadly of late years (principally the last two); yet not so much by defect in the faculty, I should say, as by want of earnestness in using it. I attend to few things as I was wont; few things have any interest for me. I live in a sort of waking dream. Doubtful it is in the highest degree whether ever I shall make men hear my voice to any purpose or not. Certain only that I shall be a *failure* if I do not, and unhappy; nay, unhappy enough (that is, with suffering enough) even if I do. My own talent I cannot in the remotest degree attempt at estimating. Something superior often does seem to lie in me, and hitherto the world has been very kind; but *many* things inferior also; so that I can strike no balance. Hang it, try and leave this *Grübeln*. *What we have done* is the only mirror that can show us what we *are*. One great desideratum in every society is a man to hold his peace.

> Oh Time, how thou fliest;
> False heart, how thou liest;
> Leave chattering and fretting,
> Betake thee to doing and getting.

April 17.—Got dreadfully ill on with a most tremendous speculation on history, intended first as an introduction to my German work, then found at last that it would not do there, and so cut it out after finishing it, and gave it to my wife. I carry less weight now, and skim more smoothly along. Why cannot I write books (of that kind) as I write letters? They are and will be of only temporary use.

Francis Jeffrey the other week offered me a hundred a year, having learned that this sum met my yearly wants. He did it neatly enough, and I had no doubt of his sincerity. What a state of society is this in which a man would rather be shot through the heart twenty times than do both himself and his neighbour a *real ease*. How separate pride from the natural necessary feeling of self? It is ill to do, yet may be done. On the whole I have been somewhat in the wrong about 'independence;' man is not independent of his brother. Twenty men united in love can accomplish much that to two thousand isolated men were impossible. Know this, and know also that thou hast a power of thy own, and standest with a Heaven above even *Thee*. And so *im Teufel's Namen*, get to thy work then.

June 8.—Am about beginning the second volume of that German Lit. History; dreadfully lazy to start. I know and feel that it will be a trivial insignificant book, do what I can; yet the writing of it sickens me and inflames my nerves as if it were a poem! Were I done with this, I will endeavour to *compile* no more.

Is not the Christian religion, is not every truly vital interest of mankind (?), a thing that *grows?* Like some Nile whose springs are indeed hidden, but whose full flood, bringing gladness and fertility from its mysterious mountains, is seen and welcomed by all.

Received about four weeks ago a strange letter from some Saint Simonians at Paris, grounded on my little 'Signs of the Times.' [1] These people have strange notions, not without a large spicing of truth, and are themselves among the *Signs*. I shall feel curious to know what becomes of them. *La classe la plus pauvre* is evidently in the way of rising from its present deepest abasement. In time it is likely the world will be better divided, and he that has the toil of ploughing will have the first cut at the reaping.

A man with 200,000*l.* a year eats the whole fruit of 6666 men's labour through a year; for you can get a stout spadesman to work and maintain himself for the sum of 30*l.* Thus we have private individuals whose wages are equal to the wages of seven or eight thousand other individuals. What do those highly beneficed individuals *do* to society for their wages?—*Kill partridges.* CAN this last? No, by the soul that is in man it cannot, and will not, and shall not!

Our political economists should collect statistical *facts;* such as, 'What is the lowest sum a man can live on in various countries? What is the highest he gets to live on? How many people work with their hands? How many with their heads? How many not at all? and innumerable such. What all want to know

[1] Just appeared in the *Edinburgh Review*, and reprinted in the *Miscellanies.*

is the condition of our fellow men; and strange to say it is the thing least of all understood, or to be understood as matters go. The present 'science' of political economy requires far less intellect than successful bellows mending; and perhaps does less good, if we deduct all the evil it brings us. Though young it already carries marks of decrepitude—a speedy and soft death to it.

You see two men fronting each other. One sits dressed in red cloth, the other stands dressed in threadbare blue; the first says to the other, 'Be hanged and anatomised!' and it is forthwith put in execution, till Number Two is a skeleton. Whence comes it? These men have no *physical hold* of each other; they are not in contact. Each of the bailiffs, &c., is included in his own *skin*, and not hooked to any other. The reason is, *Man is a spirit.* Invisible influences run through *Society*, and make it a mysterious whole full of life and inscrutable activities and capabilities. Our individual existence is mystery; our social, still more.

Nothing can act but where it is? True—if you will—only *where is it?* Is not the distant, the dead, whom I love and sorrow for HERE, in the genuine spiritual sense, as really as the table I now write on? Space is a mode of our sense, so is time (this I only half understand); *we* are—we know not what—light sparkles floating in the æther of the Divinity! So that this solid world after all is but an air-image; our *me* is the only reality, and all is godlike or God.

Thou wilt have no mystery and mysticism; wilt live in the daylight (rushlight?) of truth, and see thy world and understand it? Nay, thou wilt laugh at all that believe in a mystery; to whom the universe is an oracle and temple, as well as a kitchen and cattle-stall? *Armer Teufel!* Doth not thy cow calve, doth not thy bull gender? Nay, peradventure, dost not thou thyself gender? Explain me that, or do one of two things: retire into private places with thy foolish cackle; or, what were better, give it up and weep, not that the world is mean and disenchanted and prosaic, but that thou art vain and blind.

Is anything more wonderful than another, if you consider it maturely? *I* have *seen* no men rise from the dead; I have seen some thousands rise from *nothing*. I have not force to fly into the sun, but I *have* force to lift my hand, which is equally strange.

Wonder is the basis of worship; the reign of wonder is perennial, indestructible ; only at certain stages (as the present) it is (for some short season) *in partibus infidelium.*

August, 1830.—What is a man if you look at him with the mere logical sense, with the understanding? A pitiful hungry biped that wears breeches. Often when I read of pompous ceremonials, drawing-room levées, and coronations, on a sudden the *clothes* fly off the whole party in my fancy, and they stand there straddling in a half ludicrous, half horrid condition!

September 7.—Yesterday I received tidings that my project of cutting up that thrice wretched 'History of German Literature' into review articles, and so realising *something* for my year's work, will *not* take effect. The 'course of Providence' (nay, sometimes I almost feel that there *is* such a thing even for *me*) seems guiding my steps into new regions ; the question is coming more and more towards a decision. Canst thou, there as thou art, accomplish aught good and true ; or art thou to die miserably as a vain pretender? It is above a year since I wrote one sentence that came from the right place ; since I did one action that seemed to be really worthy. The want of money is a comparatively insignificant affair ; were I doing well otherwise, I could most readily consent to go destitute and suffer all sorts of things. On the whole I am a——. But tush!

The moral nature of a man is not a composite factitious concern, but lies in the very heart of his being, as his very self of selves. The first alleviation to irremediable pain is some conviction that it has been merited, that it comes from the All-just— from God.

What am I but a sort of ghost? Men rise as apparitions from the bosom of night, and after grinning, squeaking, gibbering some space, return thither. The earth they stand on is bottomless ; the vault of their sky is infinitude ; the life-*time* is encompassed with eternity. O wonder! And they buy cattle or seats in Parliament, and drink coarser or finer fermented liquors, as if all this were a city that had foundations.

I have strange glimpses of the power of spiritual union, of association among men of like object. Therein lies the true element of religion. It is a truly supernatural climate. All wondrous things, from a Pennenden Heath or Penny-a-week Purgatory Society, to the foundation of a Christianity, or the (now obsolete) exercise of magic, take their rise here. Men work godlike miracles thereby, and the horridest abominations. Society is a wonder of wonders, and politics (in the right sense far, very far, from the common one) is the noblest science. *Cor ne edito!* Up and be doing! Hast thou not the strangest, grandest of all talents committed to thee, namely, LIFE itself? O heaven! And it is momentarily rusting and wasting, if thou use it not. Up and be doing! and pray (if thou but can) to the unseen Author of all thy strength to guide thee and aid thee; to give thee, if not victory and possession, unwearied activity and *Entsagen.*

Is not every thought properly an inspiration? Or how is one thing more inspired than another? Much in this.

Why should politeness be peculiar to the rich and well born? Is not every man *alive*, and is not every man infinitely venerable to every other? 'There is but one temple in the universe,' says Novalis, 'and that is the body of man.'

Franz von Sickingen was one of the noblest men of the Reformation period. He defended Ulrich von Hutten, warred against perfidious Würtemberg, was the terror of evildoers, the praise of whoso did well. Hutten and he read Luther together: light rising in darkness! He also stood by Götz von Berlichingen, and now walks in poetry. But why I mention him here is his transcendent good breeding. He was at feud with his superior the Bishop of Triers, and besieged by him, and violently defending himself against injustice at the moment when he received his death wound. His castle was surrendered; Triers and others approached the brave man, over whose countenance the last paleness was already spreading: he took off his cap to Triers, there as he lay in that stern agony. What a picture!

Nulla dies sine lineâ. Eheu, eheu! Yesterday accordingly I wrote a thing in dactyls, entitled the 'Wandering Spirits,' which now fills and then filled me with 'detestation and abhorrence.' No matter—to-day I must do the like. *Nulla dies sine lineâ.* To the persevering, they say, all things are possible. Possible or impossible, I have no other implement for trying.

Last night I sat up very late reading Scott's 'History of Scotland.' An amusing narrative, clear, precise, and I suppose accurate : but no more a history of Scotland than I am Pope of Rome. A series of palace intrigues and butcheries and battles, little more important than those of Donnybrook Fair; all the while that *Scotland*, quite unnoticed, is holding on her course in industry, in arts, in culture, as if 'Langside' and 'Clean-the-Causeway' had remained unfought. Strange that a man should think that he was writing the history of a nation while he is chronicling the amours of a wanton young woman called queen, and a sulky booby recommended to kingship for his fine limbs, and then blown up with gunpowder for his ill behaviour! Good heaven! let them fondle and pout and bicker *ad libitum :* what has God's fair creation and man's immortal destiny to do with them and their trade?

One inference I have drawn from Scott : that the people in those old days had a singular talent for nicknames : King *Toom-Tabard, Bell-the-Cat* (less meritorious), the *Foul Raid*, the *Round-about Raid, Clean-the-Causeway*, the *Tulchan* Prelates, &c. &c. Apparently there was more humour in the national mind than now.

For the rest the 'Scottish History' looks like that of a gipsy encampment—industry of the rudest, largely broken by sheer indolence ; smoke, sluttishness, hunger, scab and—blood. Happily, as hinted, Scotland herself *was not there.*

Lastly, it is noteworthy that the nobles of the country have maintained a quite despicable behaviour from the times of Wallace downwards. A selfish, ferocious, famishing, unprincipled set of hyænas, from whom at no time and in no way has the country derived any benefit. The day is coming when these our modern hyænas (though *toothless*, still mischievous and greedy beyond limit) will (quietly I hope) *be paid off : Canaille fainéante, que faites-vous là ?* Down with your double-barrels; take spades, if ye can do no better, and work or die.

The quantity of pain thou feelest is indicative of the quantity of life, of talent thou hast : a stone feels no pain. (Is that a fact?)

September 9.—Wrote a fractionlet of verse entitled 'The Beetle'[1] (a real incident on Glaisters Moor), which, alas! must stand for the *linea*, both of Tuesday and Wednesday. To-day I am to try I know not what. Greater clearness will arrive. I make far

---

[1] *Miscellanies*, vol. i., Appendix II., No. 6.

most progress when I *walk*, on solitary roads—of which there are enough here.

Last night came a whole bundle of 'Fraser's Magazines,' &c. : two little papers by my brother in them, some fables by me ; and on the whole such a hurly-burly of rhodomontade, punch, loyalty, and Saturnalian Toryism as eye hath not seen. This out-Black-woods Blackwood. Nevertheless, the thing has its meaning—a kind of wild popular lower comedy, of which John Wilson is the inventor. It may perhaps (for it seems well adapted to the age) carry down his name to other times, as his most remarkable achievement. All the magazines (except the 'New Monthly') seem to aim at it ; a certain quickness, fluency of banter, not excluding sharp insight, and Merry Andrew drollery, and even humour, are available here ; however, the grand requisite seems to be im-pudence, and a fearless committing of yourself to talk in your drink. *Literature* has *nothing* to do with this ; but printing has ; and printing is now no more the peculiar symbol and livery of lit-erature than writing was in Gutenberg's day.

Great actions are sometimes historically barren ; smallest ac-tions have taken root in the moral soil and grown like banana for-ests to cover whole quarters of the world. Aristotle's philoso-phy and the Sermon on the Mount (and both too had *fair trial*), the 'Mécanique Céleste' and the 'Sorrows of Werter,' Alexander's expedition, and that of Paul the Apostle of the Gentiles ! Of these, however, Werter is half a *gourd*, and only by its huge *de-cidua* (to be used as manure) will fertilise the future. So, too, with the rest ; all are *deciduous*, and must at last make manure, only at longer dates. Yet of some the root also (?) seems to be undying.

What are Schiller and Goethe if you try them in that way ? As yet it is too soon to try them. No true effort *can* be lost.

One thing we see : the moral nature of man is deeper than his intellectual ; things planted down into the former may grow as if for ever ; the latter as a kind of drift mould produces only an-nuals. What is Jesus Christ's significance ? *Altogether moral.* What is Jeremy Bentham's significance ? Altogether intellectual, logical. I name him as the representative of a class important only for their numbers, intrinsically wearisome, almost pitiable and pitiful. Logic is their sole foundation, no other even recognised as possible ; wherefore their system is a *machine* and cannot *grow* or endure ; but after thrashing for a little (and doing good service that way) must thrash itself to pieces and be made fuel. Alas, poor England ! stupid, purblind, pudding-eating England ! Bentham with his *Mills* grinding thee out morality ; and some Macaulay, also be-aproned and a grinder, testing it, and decrying it,[1] because—it is not his own Whig established Quern-morality—I mean that the Utilitarians *have* logical machinery, and do grind fiercely and potently, *on their own foundation ;* whereas the Whigs have no foundation, but must stick up their handmills, or even pepper mills, on what fixture they can come at, and then grind as it pleases Heaven. The Whigs are amateurs, the Radicals are guild-brethren.

The sin of this age is dilettantism ; the Whigs and all ' moderate Tories ' are the grand dilettanti. I begin to feel less and less patience for them. This is no world where a man should stand trimming his whiskers, looking on at work or touching it with the point of a gloved finger. *Man sollte greifen zu !* There is more hope of an atheist utilitarian, of a superstitious ultra (Tory), than of such a lukewarm withered mongrel. He would not believe though one rose from the dead. He is wedded to idols—let him alone.

September, about the 28*th.*[2]—Rain ! rain ! rain ! The crops all lying tattered, scattered, and unripe ; the winter's bread still under the soaking clouds ! God pity the poor !

It was a wise regulation which ordained that certain days and times should be set apart for seclusion and meditation—whether as fasts or not may reasonably admit of doubt ; the business being to get *out* of the body to philosophise. But on the whole there is a deep significance in SILENCE. Were a man forced for a length of time but to *hold his peace,* it were in most cases an incalculable benefit to his insight. Thought works in silence, so does virtue. One might erect statues to Silence. I sometimes think it were good for me, who after all cannot err much in loquacity here, did I impose on myself at set times the duty of not speaking for a day. What folly would one avoid did the tongue lie quiet till the mind had finished and was calling for utterance. Not only our good

[1] Macaulay's Essay on James Mill.
[2] Even a regular count of days was lost at Craigenputtock.

thoughts, but our good purposes also, are frittered asunder, and dissipated by unseasonable speaking of them. Words, the strangest product of our nature, are also the most potent. Beware of speaking. Speech is human, silence is divine, yet also brutish and dead : therefore we must learn both arts ; they are both difficult. Flower roots *hidden* under soil. Bees working in darkness, &c. The soul, too, in silence. Let not thy left hand know what thy right hand doeth. Indeed, secresy is the element of all goodness ; every virtue, every beauty is mysterious. I hardly understand even the surface of this. . . .

October 28.—Written a strange piece 'On Clothes.'[1] Know not what will come of it.

> Gutes Pferd
> Ist's Hafer's werth (myself ? November 24).

Received the 'ornamented Schiller' from Goethe, and wondered not a little to see poor old Craigenputtock engraved at Frankfort-on-the-Main. If I become anything, it will look well; if I become nothing, a piece of kind dotage (on his part). Sent away the 'Clothes,' of which I could make a kind of book, but cannot afford it. Have still the book *in petto* (?), but in the most chaotic shape.

The Whigs in office, and Baron Brougham Lord Chancellor! Haystacks and cornstacks burning over all the south and middle of England! Where will it end? Revolution on the back of revolution for a century yet? Religion, the cement of *society*, is not here : we can have no permanent beneficent arrangement of affairs.

Not that we want *no* aristocracy, but that we want a *true* one. While the many work with their hands, let the few work with their heads and hearts, *honestly*, and not with a shameless villany pretend to work, or even openly steal. Were the landlords all hanged and their estates given to the poor, we should be (economically) much happier perhaps for the space of thirty years. But the population would be doubled then ; and again the hunger of the unthrifty would burn the granary of the industrious. Alas ! that there is no Church, and as yet no apparent possibility of one.

The divine right of squires is equal to the divine right of kings,

---

[1] First sketch of *Sartor Resartus*, intended for a review article.

and not superior? A word has made them, and a word can un-make them.

I have no *property* in anything whatsoever; except, perhaps (if I am a virtuous man) in my own free will. Of my body I have only a life rent; of all that is without my skin only an accidental possession, so long as I can keep it. Vain man! Are the stars *thine* because thou lookest on them? Is that piece of earth thine because thou hast eaten of its fruits? Thy proudest palace what is it but a tent: pitched not indeed for days but for years? The earth is *the Lord's.* Remember this, and seek other duties than game preserving, wouldst thou not be an interloper, sturdy beggar, and even thief.

> Faules Pferd
> Keines Hafers werth.

The labourer is worthy of his hire, and the idler of his also, namely, of starvation.

Byron we call 'a dandy of sorrows and acquainted with grief.' That is a brief definition of him.

What *is* art and poetry? Is the beautiful really higher than the good? A higher *form* thereof? Thus were a poet not only a priest, but a high priest.

When Goethe and Schiller say or insinuate that art is higher than religion, do they mean perhaps this? That whereas religion represents (what is the essence of truth for man) the good as *in-finitely* (the word is emphatic) different from the evil, but sets them in a state of hostility (as in heaven and hell), art likewise admits and inculcates this quite infinite difference, but *without* hostility, with peacefulness, like the difference of two poles which *cannot* coalesce yet do not quarrel—nay, should not quarrel, for both are essential to the whole. In this way is Goethe's morality to be considered as a *higher* (apart from its comprehensiveness, nay, universality) than has hitherto been promulgated? *Sehr einseitig!* Yet perhaps there is a glimpse of the truth here.

Examine by logic the import of thy life and of all lives. What is it? A making of meal into manure, and of manure into meal. To the *cui bono* there is no answer from logic.

December 29, 1830.—The old year just expiring; one of the most worthless years I have spent for a long time. *Durch eigne und anderer Schuld!* But words are worse than nothing. To thy *review* (Taylor's 'Hist. Survey'). Is it the most despicable of work? Yet is it not too good for *thee?* Oh, I care not for poverty, little even for disgrace, nothing at all for want of renown. But the horrible feeling is when I cease my own struggle, lose the consciousness of my own strength, and become positively quite worldly and wicked.

In the paths of fortune (fortune!) I have made no advancement since last year; but, on the contrary (owing chiefly to that German Literary History one way and another), considerably retrograded. No matter: had I but progressed in the other better path! But alas, alas! howsoever, *pocas palabras! I* am still here.

Bist *Du* glücklich, Du Gute, dass Du unter der Erde bist? Wo stehst Du? Liebst Du mich noch? God is the God of the dead as well as of the living. The dead as the living are—where *He wills.*

This Taylor is a wretched atheist and Philistine. It is *my* duty (perhaps) to put the flock whom he professes to lead on their guard. Let me do it *well!*

February 7, 1831.—Finished the review of *Taylor* some three weeks ago, and sent it off. It is worth little, and only partially in a right spirit.

Sent to Jack to liberate my 'Teufelsdröckh' from editorial durance in London, and am seriously thinking to make a book of it. The thing is not right—not *art;* yet perhaps a nearer approach to art than I have yet made. We ought to try. I want to get it done, and then translate 'Faust,' as I have partially promised to Goethe. Through 'Teufelsdröckh' I am yet far from seeing my way; nevertheless materials are partly forthcoming.

No sense from the 'Foreign Quarterly Review;' have nearly determined on opening a correspondence on the matter of that everlasting MS.[1] with Bowring of the 'Westminster.' Could write also a paper on the Saint Simonians. One too on Dr. Johnson, for Napier. Such are the financial aspects. *N.B. I have some five pounds to front the world with*—and expect no more for months. Jack, too, is in the neap tide. Hand to the oar.

---

[1] German Literature.

All Europe is in a state of disturbance, of revolution. About this very time they may be debating the question of British 'Reform' in London. The Parliament opened last week. Our news of it expected on Wednesday. The times are big with change. Will *one* century of constant fluctuation serve us, or shall we need two? Their Parliamentary reforms and all that are of small moment; a beginning (of good and evil), nothing more. The whole frame of society is rotten, and must go for fuel wood—and where is the new frame to come from? I know not, and no man knows.

The only sovereigns of the world in these days are the literary men (were there any such in Britain)—the prophets. It is always a theocracy: the king has to be anointed by the priest; and now the priest, the Goethe for example, will not, cannot consecrate the existing king who therefore is a usurper, and reigns only by sufferance. What were the bet that King William were the last of that profession in Britain, and Queen Victoria never troubled with the sceptre at all? Mighty odds: yet nevertheless not infinite; for what thing is certain now? No mortal cares twopence for any king, or obeys any king except through *compulsion;* and society is not a ship of war. Its government cannot always be a press-gang.

What are the episcopal dignitaries saying to it? Who knows but Edward Irving may not yet be a bishop! They will clutch round them for help, and unmuzzle all manner of bull-dogs when the thief is at the gate. Bull-dogs with teeth. The generality have no teeth in that kennel.

Kings *do* reign by divine right, or not at all. The king that were God-appointed would be an emblem of God and could *demand* all obedience from us. But where is that king? The *best man,* could we find him, were he. Tell us, tell us, O ye codifiers and statists and economists, how we shall find him and raise him to the throne: or else admit that the science of polity is worse than unknown to you.

Earl *(Jarl—Yärl),* count, duke, knight, &c., are all titles derived from *fighting.* The honour-titles in a future time will derive themselves from *knowing* and well-*doing.* They will also be conferred with more deliberation and by better judges. This is a prophecy of mine.

God is above us, else the future of the world were well-nigh desperate. Go where we may, the deep *heaven* will be round us.

Jeffrey is Lord-Advocate and M.P. Sobbed and shrieked at taking office, like a bride going to be married. I wish him altogether well, but reckon he is on the wrong course ; Whiggism, I believe, is all but for ever done. Away with Dilettantism and Machiavellism, though we should get atheism and Sansculottism in their room ! The latter are at least substantial things, and do not build on a continued wilful falsehood. But oh ! but oh ! where is Teufelsdröckh all this while ? The south-west is busy thawing off that horrible snowstorm. Time rests not—thou only art idle. To pen ! to pen !

'Benvenuto Cellini' a very worthy book ; gives more insight into Italy than fifty Leo Tenths would do. A remarkable man Benvenuto, and in a remarkable scene. Religion and art with ferocity and sensuality ; polished respect with stormful independence ; faithfully obedient subjects to popes who are not hierarchs but plain scoundrels ! Life was far sunnier and richer then ; but a time of change, loudly called for, was advancing, and but lately has reached its crisis. Goethe's essay on Benvenuto quite excellent.

Pope's 'Homer's Odyssey,' surely a very false, and though ingenious and talented, yet bad translation. The old epics are great because they (musically) show us the *whole world* of those old days. A modern epic that did the like would be equally admired, and for us far more admirable. But where is the genius that can write it ? Patience ! patience ! he will be here one of these centuries.

Is Homer or Shakespeare the greater genius ? It were hard to say. Shakespeare's world is the more complex, the more spiritual, and perhaps his mastery over it was equally complete. ' *We are such stuff* as dreams are made of.' There is the basis of a whole poetic universe. To that mind all forms and figures of men and things would become ideal.

What is a *whole* ? or how specially *does* a poem differ from prose ? Ask not a definition of it in words, which can hardly express common logic correctly. Study to create in thyself a *feeling* of it ; like so much else it cannot be made clear, hardly even to thy thought (?).

I see some vague outline of what a *whole* is: also how an individual delineation may be 'informed with the Infinite;' may appear hanging in the universe of time and space (partly): in which case is it a poem and a whole? Therefore are the true heroic poems of these times to be written with the *ink of science?* Were a correct philosophic biography of a man (meaning by philosophic *all* that the name can include) the only method of celebrating him? The true history (had we any such, or even generally any dream of such) the true epic poem? I partly begin to surmise so. What after all is the true proportion of St. Matthew to Homer—of the Crucifixion to the fall of Troy?

On the whole I wish I could define to myself the true relation of moral genius to poetic genius; of religion to poetry. Are they one and the same—different forms of the same; and if so, which is to stand higher, the Beautiful or the Good? Schiller and Goethe seem to say the former, as if it included the latter, and might supersede it: how truly I can never well see. Meanwhile that the *faculties* always go together seems clear. It is a gross calumny on human nature to say that there ever was a mind of surpassing talent that did not also surpass in *capability* of virtue; and *vice versâ.* Nevertheless, in both cases there are female geniuses too, minds that admire and receive, but can hardly create. I have observed that in these also the taste for religion and for poetry go together. The most wonderful words I ever heard of being uttered by man are those in the four Evangelists by Jesus of Nazareth. Their intellectual talent is hardly inferior to their moral. On this subject, if I live, I hope to have much to say.

And so ends my first note-book after nigh eight years, here at Craigenputtock, at my *own* hearth, and though amid trouble and dispiritment enough, yet with better outlooks than I had then. My outward world is not much better (yes it is, though I have far less money), but my inward *is*, and I can promise myself never to be *so* miserable again. Farewell, ye that have fallen asleep since then; farewell, though distant, perhaps near me! Welcome the good and evil that is to come, through which God assist me to struggle wisely. What have I to look back on? Little or nothing. What forward to? My own small sickly force amid wild enough whirlpools! The more diligently apply it then. Νὺξ ἔρχεται.

CHAPTER V.

IT appears from the journal that early in 1830 Carlyle
had advanced so far with his History of German Literature that he was hoping soon to see it published and off
his hands.   A first sketch of 'Teufelsdröckh'—the egg out
of which 'Sartor Resartus' was to grow—had been offered
without result to London magazine editors.   Proposals
were made to him for a Life of Goethe.   But on Goethe
he had said all that for the present he wished to say.
Luther was hanging before him as the subject which he
wanted next to grapple, could he but find the means of
doing it.   But the preliminary reading necessary for such
a work was wide and varied.   The books required were
not to be had at Craigenputtock; and if the literary history could once be finished, and any moderate sum of
money realised upon it, he meditated spending six months
in Germany, taking Mrs. Carlyle with him, to collect materials.   He had great hopes of what he could do with
Luther.   An editor had offered to bring it out in parts in
a magazine, but Carlyle would not hear of this.

I rather believe (he said) that when I write that book of the
great German lion, it shall be the best book I have ever written,
and go forth, I think, on its own legs.   Do you know we are actually talking of spending the next winter in Weimar, and preparing all the raw material of a *right Luther* there at the fountain-
head—that is, of course, if I can get the history done and have
the cash.

Jeffrey started at the idea of the winter at Weimar—at

least for Mrs. Carlyle—and suggested that if it was carried out she should be left in his charge at Edinburgh. He was inclined; he said, to be jealous of the possible influence of Goethe, who had half bewitched her at a distance—unless indeed the spell was broken by the personal presence of him. But Jeffrey's fears were unnecessary. There was no Weimar possible for Carlyle, and no Life of Luther. The unfortunate 'German Literature' could not find a publisher who would so much as look at it. Boyd, who had brought out the volumes of 'German Romance,' wrote that he would be proud to publish for Carlyle upon almost any other subject except German Literature. He knew that in this department Carlyle was superior to any other author of the day, but the work proposed was not calculated to interest the British public. Everyone of the books about German literature had been failures, most of them ruinous failures. The feeling in the public mind was that everything German was especially to be avoided, and with the highest esteem for Carlyle's talent he dared not make him an offer. Even cut up into articles he still found no one anxious to take it. There was still another hope. Carlyle's various essays had been greatly noticed and admired. An adventurous bookseller might perhaps be found who would bid for a collected edition of them. The suggestion took no effect however. The 'Teufelsdröckh' had to be sent back from London, having created nothing but astonished dislike. Nothing was to be done therefore but to remain at Craigenputtock and work on, hoping for better times. Fresh articles were written, a second on Jean Paul, a slight one on Madame de Staël, with the first of the two essays on history which are published in the 'Miscellanies.' He was thus able to live, but not so far as money was concerned to overtake the time which he had spent over his unsaleable book; his finances remained sadly straitened, and he needed all his energy to fight on against discouragement. One bright gleam of comfort came to him from Weimar in the summer of this year. Communication had been kept up constantly with Goethe since the Comely Bank time. In the winter 1829–30, Mrs. Carlyle, writing to her mother-in-law at Scotsbrig, says:

Carlyle is over head and ears in business to-night writing letters to all the four winds. There is a box to be despatched for Goethe containing all manner of curiosities, the most precious of which is a lock of my hair. There is also a smart Highland bonnet for his daughter-in-law, accompanied by a nice little piece of poetry professing to be written by me, but in truth I did not write a word of it.

> Scotland prides her in the bonnet blue
> That brooks no stain in love or war;
> Be it on Ottilie's head a token true
> Of Scottish love to kind Weimar.

Goethe's answer reached Craigenputtock about June.[1]

[1] Das werthe Schatzkästlein, nachdem es durch den strengsten Winter vom Continent lange abgehalten worden, ist endlich um die Hälfte März glücklich angelangt.

Um von seinem Gehalt zu sprechen, erwähne zuerst die unschätzbare Locke, die man wohl mit dem theuren Haupte verbunden möchte gesehen haben, die aber hier einzeln erblickt mich fast erschreckt hätte. Der Gegensatz war zu auffallend; denn ich brauchte meinen Schädel nicht zu berühren um zu wissen dass daselbst nur Stoppeln sich hervorthun; es war mir nicht nöthig vor dem Spiegel zu treten, um zu erfahren dass eine lange Zeitreise ihnen ein missfarbiges Ansehen gegeben. Die Unmöglichkeit der verlangten Erwiederung fiel mir aufs Herz, und nöthigte mich zu Gedanken deren man sich zu entschlagen pflegt. Am Ende aber blieb mir doch nichts übrig als mich an der Vorstellung zu begnügen: eine solche Gabe sey dankbarlichst ohne Hoffnung irgend einer genügenden Gegengabe anzunehmen. Sie soll auch heilig in der ihrer würdigen Brieftasche aufbewahrt bleiben, und nur das Liebenswürdigste ihr zugesellt werden.

Der schottische elegante Turban hat, wie ich versichern darf, zu manchem Vergnüglichen Gelegenheit gegeben. Seit vielen Jahren werden wir von den Einwohnern der drey Königreiche besucht, welche gern eine Zeit lang bey uns verweilen und gute Gesellschaft geniessen mögen. Hierunter befinden sich zwar weniger Schotten, doch kann es nicht fehlen dass nicht noch das Andenken an einen solchen Landsmann sich in einem schönen Herzen so lebendig finde, um die National-Prachtmütze, die Distel mit eingeschlossen, als einen wünschenswerthesten Schmuck anzusehen; und die gütige Senderinn hätte

To Thomas Carlyle.

The precious casket, after having been long detained from the Continent through the most severe winter, has at last safely arrived towards the middle of March. With regard to its contents, I mention first the inestimable lock of hair, which one would have wished to have seen together with the dear head, but which as here seen by itself had almost frightened me. The contrast was too

sich gewiss gefreut das lieblichste Gesicht von der Welt darunter hervorgucken zu sehen. Ottilie aber dankt zum allerverbindlichsten, und wird, sobald unsere Trauertage vorüber sind, damit glorreich aufzutreten nicht ermangeln.

Lassen Sie mich nun eine nächste Gegensendung ankündigen, welche zum Juni als der günstigsten Jahreszeit sich wohl wird zusammengefunden haben. Sie erhalten :—

1. Das Exemplar Ihres übersetzten Schiller, geschmückt mit den Bildern Ihrer ländlichen Wohnung (by day and night!), begleitet von einigen *Bogen* in meiner Art, wodurch ich zugleich dem Büchlein offnen Eingang zu verschaffen, besonders aber die Communication beyder Länder und Literaturen lebhafter zu erregen trachte. Ich wünsche dass diese nach Kenntniss des Publicums angewandten Mittel Ihnen nicht misfallen, auch der Gebrauch, den ich von Stellen unserer Correspondenz gemacht, nicht als Indiscretion möge gedeutet werden. Wenn ich mich in jüngern Jahren von dergleichen Mittheilungen durchaus gehütet, so ziemt es dem höhern Alter auch solche Wege nicht zu verschmähen. Die günstige Aufnahme des Schillerischen Briefwechsels gab mir eigentlich hiezu Anlass und Muth.

Ferner finden Sie beygelegt :—

2. Die vier noch fehlende Bände gedachter Briefe. Mögen Sie Ihnen als Zauberwagen zu Dienste stehen, um sich in der damaligen Zeit in unsere Mitte zu versetzen, wo es eine unbedingte Strebsamkeit galt, wo niemand zu fordern dachte und nur zu verdienen bemüht war. Ich habe mir die vielen Jahre her den Sinn, das Gefühl jener Tage zu erhalten gesucht und hoffe es soll mir fernerhin gelingen.

3. Eine fünfte Sendung meiner Werke liegt sodann bey, worin sich wohl manches unterhaltende, unterrichtende, belehrende, brauchbar anzuwendende finden wird. Man gestehe zu dass es auch Ideal-Utilitarier gebe, und es sollte mir sehr zur Freude gereichen, wenn ich mich darunter zählen dürfte. Noch eine Lieferung, dann ist vorerst das beabsichtigte Ganze vollbracht, dessen Abschluss zu erleben ich mir kaum zu hoffen erlaubte. Nachträge giebt es noch hinreichend. Meine Papiere sind in guter Ordnung.

4. Ein Exemplar meiner Farbenlehre und der dazu gehörigen Tafeln soll auch beygfügt werden ; ich wünsche, dass Sie den zweyten, als den *historischen* Theil, zuerst lesen. Sie sehen da die Sache herankommen, stocken, sich aufklären und wieder verdüstern. Sodann aber ein Bestreben nach neuem Lichte ohne allgemeinen Erfolg. Alsdann würde die erste Hälfte des ersten Theils, als die *didactische* Abtheilung, eine allgemeine Vorstellung geben wie ich die Sache angegriffen wünsche. Freylich ist ohne Anschauung der Experimente hier nicht durchzukommen ; wie Sie es mit der *polemischen* Ab-

striking, for there was no need for my touching my skull in order to know that stubbles only would show themselves there. It was not necessary for me to stand before the looking-glass in order to know that the long passage of time had imparted to my hair a discoloured appearance. The impossibility of the asked-for return troubled my heart, and drove me to thoughts which one is wont to put aside. In the end, however, nothing remained to me but to be satisfied with the thought that such a gift must be gratefully accepted, without the hope of any sufficient return. It shall remain sacredly kept, in a pocket-book worthy of it, and only the most loved shall ever bear it company.

The elegant Scotch turban has, as I may assure you, been the occasion of much enjoyment. For many years we have had visits from the inhabitants of the three kingdoms, who like to stay with us for a time and enjoy good society. Though there are fewer Scots among them, it cannot be but that the memory of one such countryman should be so vivid in some one beautiful heart *here* as to make it look on that splendid national head-dress, including the thistle, as a most desirable ornament. The kind sender would, no doubt, have been delighted to see the most charming face in the world looking out from under it. Ottilie sends her most grateful thanks, and will not fail, as soon as our mourning is over, to make a glorious appearance in it.

Let me now in return announce to you an approaching despatch, which I hope to have put together by June, as the most favourable time of the year. You receive :—

1st. The copy of your translated Schiller, adorned with the

theilung halten wollen und können, wird sich alsdann ergeben. Ist es mir möglich, so lege besonders für Sie ein einleitendes Wort bey.

5. Sagen Sie mir etwas zunächst wie Sie die Deutsche Literatur bey den Ihrigen einleiten wollen ; ich eröffne Ihnen gern meine Gedanken über die Folge der Epochen. Man braucht nicht überall ausführlich zu seyn : gut aber ist's auf manches vorübergehende Interessante wenigstens hinzudeuten, um zu zeigen dass man es kennt.

Dr. Eckermann macht mit meinen Sohn eine Reise gegen Süden und bedauert, nicht wie er gewünscht hatte, diesmal beyhülflich syn zu können. Ich werde gern, wie obgesagt, seine Stelle vertreten. Diesen Sommer bleib ich zu Hause und sehe bis Michael Geschäfte genug vor mir.

Gedenken Sie mit Ihrer lieben Gattinn unserer zum besten und empfangen wiederholten herzlichen Dank für die schöne Sendung.

Treu angehörig,

J. W. GOETHE.

Weimar, den 13. April, 1830.

prctures of your country home (by day and night), accompanied by some sheets in my own style, whereby I try to gain a ready entrance for the little book, and more especially to infuse greater life into the intercourse of the two countries and literatures. I hope that the means which I have employed according to my knowledge of the public may not displease you, and that the use which I have made of some passages of our correspondence may not be taken as an indiscretion. Though in my earlier years I have carefully abstained from such communications, it behoves a more advanced age not to despise even such ways. It was really the favourable reception of my correspondence with Schiller which gave me the impulse and courage for it. Further, you will find added—

2nd. The four volumes, still wanting, of those letters. May they serve as a magic chariot to transport you into our midst at that period, when we thought of nothing but striving, where no one thought of asking for rewards, but was only anxious to deserve them. I have tried for these many years to keep alive the sense and the feeling of those days. I hope I shall succeed in this for the future also.

3rd. A fifth copy of my works is also there, in which I hope may be found many things amusing, instructive, improving, and fit for use. Let it be admitted that there exist ideal utilitarians also, and it would give me much pleasure if I might count myself among them. Still one number, and I shall have finished the whole of what I intended for the present, and the completion of which I hardly allowed myself to hope I should see. Supplements there are plenty, and my papers are in good order.

4th. A copy of my ' Treatise on Colour,' with the tables belonging to it, shall also be added ; and I wish you to read the second, as the *historical* part, first. You see how the subject arose, how it came to a standstill, how it grew clear, and how it became dark again ; then a striving after new light, without a general success. Afterwards, the first half of the first part, being the *didactic* section, would give a general idea how I wish to see the subject taken up. Only without seeing the experiments, it is impossible to get on here. You will then see what you wish and are able to do with the *polemical* portion. If it is possible I shall add an introductory word especially for you.

5th. Please to tell me first how you wish to introduce German literature among your people. I shall then open my thoughts to you on the succession of the epochs. It is not necessary to be very exhaustive everywhere, but it is well to point at least to many things which had a passing interest, in order to show that one knows them. Dr. Eckermann is making a journey with my son, southwards, and regrets that this time he is not able to be useful as he had wished. I should gladly, as I said just now, take his place. I shall stay at home this summer, and until Michaelmas have plenty of work before me.

May you and your dear wife keep us in best remembrance, and receive once more my hearty thanks for the beautiful presents.

Sincerely yours,
J. W. GOETHE.

Weimar : April 13, 1830.

Attached to the letter to Carlyle were a few additional lines on the request of Mrs. Carlyle for a lock of his hair, to which he had been unable to accede. The original remains preserved among her treasures, the only autograph of Goethe which I have succeeded in finding.[1]

An incomparable black ringlet demands a few more words from me. I have to say with real regret that the desired exchange is, alas ! impossible. Short and miscoloured, and robbed of all its grace, old age must be content if the inner man can still throw out a flower or two when the outward bloom has departed. I would gladly find a substitute, but as yet I have not succeeded. My fairest greetings to the admirable wife. I trust the box has arrived safe. G.

Goethe had already spoken of his inability to comply in his first letter. This little note was perhaps intended for the *surrogat* which he had been vainly looking for ; as an autograph which Mrs. Carlyle might keep for herself.

---

[1] Eine unvergleichliche schwarze Haarlocke veranlasst mich noch ein Blättchen beyzulegen, und mit wahrhaftem Bedauern zu bemerken dass die verlangte Erwiederungleider unmöglich ist. Kurz und missfarbig, alles Schmuckes entbehrend, muss das Alter sich begnügen wenn sich dem Innern noch irgend eine Blüthe aufthut, indem die Aeussere verschwunden ist. Ich sinne schon auf irgend ein Surrogat ; ein solches zu finden hat mir aber noch nicht glücken wollen. Meine schönsten Grüsse der würdigen Gattinn.

Möge das Kästchen glücklich angekommen seyn.

G.

If the box came at the time which he intended, the pleasure which it must have given was soon clouded. The journal alludes to the death of the most dearly loved of all Carlyle's sisters. The Carlyles as a family were passionately attached to each other. Margaret Carlyle's apparent recovery was as delusive as her sister-in-law had feared. In the winter she fell ill again ; in the spring she was carried to Dumfries in the desperate hope that medical care might save her. Carlyle has written nothing more affecting than the account of her end in the ' Reminiscences of Irving.' A letter written at the time to his brother, if wanting the mellow beauty which the scene had assumed in his memory, is even more impressive from the greater fulness of detail.

To John Carlyle.

Craigenputtock : June 29, 1830.

It was on Monday night when Alick took leave of our sister. On Tuesday, if I remember rightly, she felt ' better,' but was evidently fast growing weaker. In the afternoon it was pretty evident to everyone that she was far gone. The doctor, who was unwearied in his assiduities, formed a worse opinion at every new examination. All hope of a complete cure had vanished some days before. Our mother asked her in the afternoon if she thought herself dying. She answered, ' I dinna ken, mother, but I never was so sick in my life.' To a subsequent question about her hopes of a future world, she replied briefly, but in terms that were comfortable to her parents. It was about eight at night when John Currie was despatched to go and seek a horse and proceed hither ; where, as you already know, he arrived about midnight. By this time the sick-room was filled with sympathising relatives. The minister, Mr. Clyde, also came and feelingly addressed her. She recognised everyone, was calm, clear as she had ever been ; sometimes spoke in whispers, directing little services to be done to her ; once asked where Mary was, who had gone out for a moment. Twice she asked for the ' drops,' I believe that ' mixture' I spoke of. The first time, our mother, who now cared chiefly for her soul's weal, and that sense and recollection might be given her in that stern hour, answered dissuasively, but said if she asked for them a second time they should be given her. Some hours before, our mother had begged her forgiveness if she had ever done her anything wrong; to which the dying one answered, 'Oh no, no, mother, never, never,' earnestly, yet quietly, and without tears. About a quarter-past ten she asked again for the drink (or drops, which were taken in water), and took the glass which Mary also held in her own hand. She whispered to Mary, 'Pour up,' swallowed about half the liquid, threw her head on the pillow, looking out with her usual look ; but her eyes quickly grew bright and intense, the breath broke into long sighs, and in about two minutes a slight quiver in the under lip gave token that the fight was fought and the wearied spirit at its goal. I saw her in the winding-sheet about six o'clock, beautiful in death, and kissed her pale brow, not without warm tears which I could not check. About mid-day, when she was laid in the coffin, I saw her face once more for the last time.

Our mother behaved in what I must call an heroic manner. Seeing that the hour was now come, she cast herself and her child on God's hand, and endeavoured heartily to say, 'His will be done.' Since then she has been calmer than any of us could have hoped—almost the calmest of us. No doubt the arrow still sticks in her heart, and natural sorrow must have its course ; but I trust she seeks and finds the only true balm, howsoever named, by which man's woe can be healed and made blessed to him.

Thus, dear brother, has our eldest and best sister been taken from us, mercifully, as you said, though sorrowfully, having been spared much suffering, and carried in clear possession of her sense and steadfastness through that last solemn trial. We all wept sore for her as you have done and now do, but will endeavour to weep no more. I have often thought she had attained all in life that life could give her—a just, true, meekly invincible completed character, which I and so many others, by far more ambitious paths, seek for in vain. She was in some points, I may say deliberately, superior to any woman I have ever seen. Her simple clearness of head and heart, her perfect fairness, and quiet, unpretending, brief decisiveness in thought, word, and act (for in all these she was remarkable) made up so true and brave a spirit as, in that unaffected guise, we shall hardly look upon again. She might have been wife to a Scottish martyr, and spoken stern truths to the ear of tyrants, had she been called to that work. As it is, she sleeps in a pure grave, and our peasant maiden to us who knew her is more than a king's daughter. Let us for ever remember her and love her, but cease from henceforth to mourn for her. She was mercifully dealt with—called away when her heart if not unwounded was yet unseared and fresh, amidst pain and heaviness it is true, but not in any agony or without some peaceful train of hope enlightening her to the end. The little current of her existence flowed onward like a Scottish brook through green simple fields. Neither was it caught into the great ocean over chasms and grim cataracts, but gently and as among thick clouds whereon hovered a rainbow.

I might tell you something of the funeral arrangements, and how the loss has left the rest of us. Early on Tuesday our mother and Mary set off for Scotsbrig in one of Alick's carts which happened to be there. A coffin was speedily got ready, with burial litter, &c.; and it was agreed that Alick and I should attend the body down to Scotsbrig next day, where it was to lie till Saturday, the day of the funeral. All Wednesday these things kept him and me incessantly busy; the poor Alick was sick to the heart, and cried more that day than I had ever seen him do in his life. At night I had to return hither and seek Jenny. I was the messenger of heavy and unexpected tidings. Jane too insisted on going with us; so next morning (Thursday) we set out hence, Jenny and I in a gig, Jane riding behind us. At Dumfries, where Alick had remained to watch all night, we found Jacob with a hearse. About two o'clock we moved off, the gig close following the hearse, Jane and Alick riding behind us. We reached Scotsbrig about six. Poor Robert Crow was dreadfully affected. He waked every night, spoke earnestly and largely on the subject of the deceased, and by his honesty and sensibility and pure sincere religious bearing endeared himself to everyone. On Saturday about half-past one the procession moved away. Our mother stood like a priestess in the door, tearless when all were weeping. Our father and Alick went in the gig. The former, ill in health, looked resolute, austere, and to trivial condolers and advisers almost indignant. The coffin was lowered into a very deep grave on the east side of our headstone in the Ecclefechan churchyard, and the mourners, a numerous company, separated; W. Graham and a few others accompanying us home to that stupid horrid ceremony, a funeral tea, which in our case was speedily transacted.

Yesterday morning we set out on our return. It had been settled that Mary was to stay yonder for a fortnight or ten days, our mother and Jenny to come hither. I drove the former in the gig; Jenny came in a cart with Bretton. We settled various accounts, &c., at Dumfries, and arrived here about eleven, all well. Mother had a good sleep, and is pretty well in health. She talked of returning to the Sacrament. Our father was complaining much, and evidently suffering somewhat severely. His appetite is bad. He has a cold, coughs a little, and is in bad spirits when left to himself. I bought him some paregoric, but he was breathless, dispirited, and could not eat. We hope the good weather would mend him would it come. The rest of us are well. God bless you, dear brother. T. CARLYLE.

We are all sad and dull (he wrote a fortnight later) about her that is laid in the earth. I dream of her almost nightly, and feel not indeed sorrow, for what is life but a continual dying? Yet a strange obstruction and haunting remembrance. Let us banish all this, for it is profitless and foolish.

> Thy quiet goodness, spirit pure and brave,
>   What boots it now with tears to tell ;
> The path to rest lies through the grave :
>   Loved sister, take our long farewell.

We shall meet again, too, if God will. If He will *not*, then better we should not meet.

From the ' Journal ' I add a few more words.

On the 22nd of June my sister Margaret died at Dumfries, whither she had been removed exactly a week before for medical help. It was a Thursday night, about ten minutes past ten. Alick and I were roused by express about midnight, and we arrived there about four. That solstice night, with its singing birds and sad thoughts, I shall never forget. She was interred next Saturday at Ecclefechan. I reckoned her the best of all my sisters—in some respects the best woman I had ever seen.

> Whom bring ye to the still dwelling ?
> 'Tis a tired playmate whom we bring you ;
> Let her rest in your still dwelling
> Till the songs of her heavenly sisters awaken her.

And so let me betake myself again with what energy I can to the commencement of my task. Work is for the living, rest is for the dead.

Margaret Carlyle sleeps in Ecclefechan churchyard. Her father followed soon, and was laid beside her. Then after him, but not for many years, the pious, tender, original, beautiful-minded mother. John Carlyle was the next of their children who rejoined them, and next he of whom I am now writing. The world and the world's business scatter families to the four winds, but they collect again in death. Alick lies far off in a Canadian resting-place; but in his last illness, when the memory wanders, he too had travelled in spirit back to Annandale and the old days when his brother was at college, and with the films of the last struggle closing over his eyes he asked anxiously if 'Tom was come back from Edinburgh.'

The loss of this sister weighed heavily on Carlyle's spirits, and the disappointment about his book fretted him on the side to which he might naturally have turned to seek relief in work. Goethe's steady encouragement was of course inspiriting, but it brought no grist to the mill, and the problem of how he was to live was becoming extremely serious. Conscious though he was of exceptional powers, which the most grudging of his critics could not refuse to acknowledge, he was discovering to his cost that they were not marketable. He could not throw his thoughts into a shape for which the Sosii of the day would give him money. He had tried poetry, but his verse was cramped and unmelodious. He had tried to write stories, but his convictions were too intense for fiction. The 'dreadful earnestness' of which Jeffrey complained was again in his way, and he could have as little written an entertaining novel as St. Paul or St. John. His entire faculty—intellect and imagination alike—was directed upon the sternest problems of human life. It was not possible for him, like his friend at Craigcrook, to take up with the first creed that came to hand and make the best of it. He required something which he could really believe. Thus his thoughts refused to move in any common groove. He had himself to form the taste by which he could be appreciated, and when he spoke his words provoked the same antagonism which every original thinker is inevitably condemned to encounter—antagonism first in the form of wonder, and when the wonder ceased of irritation and angry enmity. He taught like one that had authority—a tone which men naturally resent, and must resent, till the teacher has made his pretensions good. Every element was absent from his writing which would command popularity, the quality to which book-sellers and review editors are obliged to look if they would live themselves. Carlyle's articles were magnetic enough, but with the magnetism which repelled, not which attracted. His faith in himself and in his own purposes never wavered; but it was becoming a subject of serious doubt to him whether he could make a living, even the humblest, by literature. The fair promises of the last year at Comely Bank had clouded over; instead of invitations to write, he was receiving cold answers to his own proposals. Editors, who had perhaps resented his haughty style, were making him 'feel the difference,' neglecting to pay him even for the articles which had been accepted and put in type. His brother John, finding also patients who would pay slow in sending for him, and not willing to give his services gratuitously, was thinking that he too would become a man of letters, and earn his bread by writing for magazines. Carlyle warned him off so dangerous an enterprise with the most impressive earnestness.

To John Carlyle.

Craigenputtock: August 6, 1830.

I sympathise in your reluctance to enter on the practice of medicine, or indeed of any professional duty; well understanding the difficulties that lie at the porch of all and threaten the solitary adventurer. Neither can I be surprised at your hankering after a literary life, so congenial as I have often heard you hint it would be to your tastes. Nevertheless it *would* greatly astonish me if beyond mere preliminary reveries these feelings produced any influence on your conduct. The voice of all experience seems to be in favour of a profession. You sail there as under convoy in the middle of a fleet, and have a thousandfold chance of reaching port. Neither is it Happy Islands and halcyon seas alone that you miss, for literature is thickly strewed with cold Russian Nova Zemblas, where you shiver and despair in loneliness; nay often, as in the case of this 'Literary History of Germany,' you anchor on some slumbering whale and it ducks under and leaves you spinning in the eddies. To my mind nothing justifies me for having adopted the trade of literature, except the remembrance that I had no other but these two—that of a schoolmaster or that of a priest: in the one case with the fair prospect of speedy maceration and starvation; in the other of *perjury*, which is infinitely worse. As it is, I look confidently forward to a life of poverty, toil, and dispiritment, so long as I remain on this earth, and hope only that God will grant me patience and strength to struggle onwards through the midst of it, working out his will as I best can in this lonely clay-pit where I am set to dig. The pitifullest of all resources is complaining, which accordingly I strive not to practice: only let these things be known for my brother's warning, that he may order his life better than I could do mine.

For the rest I pretend not to thwart your own judgment, which ought to be mature enough for much deeper considerations; neither would I check these overflowings of discouragement, poured as they naturally should be into a brother's ear; but after all that is come and gone I expect to learn that your medical talent, sought over all Europe, and indisputably the most honourable a man can have, is no longer to be hidden in a napkin, still less to be thrown away into the lumber-room; but to come forth into the light of day for your own profit and that of your fellow men.

Tell me, therefore, dear Jack, that you are in your own lodging resolute, compacted, girt for the fight, at least endeavouring to do your true duty. Now, as ever I have predicted that success was certain for you, my sole fear is that such wavering and waiting at the pool may in the end settle into a habit of fluctuation and irresolution far enough from your natural character; a fear which of course every new week spent in drifting to and fro tends to strengthen.

Fear nothing, Jack. Men are but poor spindle-shanked whiffling *wonners*, when you clutch them through the mass of drapery they wear. To throw plenty of them over the house-ridge were no such feat for a right fellow. Neither is their favour, their envy, their admiration, or anything else the poor devils can give or withhold, our life or our death. Nay, the worst we and they fear is but a bugbear, a hollow shadow, which if you grasp it and smite it dissolves into air. March boldly up to it and to them; strong and still like the stars, 'Ohne Hast doch ohne Rast.'[1] There is a soul in some men yet, even yet, and God's sky is above us, and God's commandment is in us—

> Und wenn die Welt voll Teufel wär',
> Und wollt' uns gar verschlingen,
> So fürchten wir uns nicht so sehr :
> Es muss uns doch gelingen.[2]

Up and be doing. Be my brother and life companion, not in word and feeling only, but in deepest deed!

With regard to that manuscript of the Literary History of Germany, get it out of ——'s claws if you have not as I trust already done so. To which now add an article on Schiller that Fraser has, that he talked of giving to some magazine or other, but that I desire to have the privilege of giving or retaining myself, being minded, as I said already, to have no more business transactions with that gentleman. Get the two MSS. therefore, dear Jack, and wrap them up tightly till I send for them. The Schiller by-and-by I intend for the 'Foreign Quarterly Review.'[3] About the history I wrote to Gleig,[4] Colburn's editor of some 'Library of General Knowledge,' three weeks ago, and again to-day, having received no answer. Fraser offered to negotiate for me there in a letter he sent me last week, but he need not mingle further in the matter, I think. If I do not hear in a week I shall decide for myself, and cut Gleig as I have done other editors, and try some different method of realising a pound or two. Get you the MSS. in the first place. Tait, to whom I wrote, declines. I am now got

[1] Without haste, yet without rest.
[2] From Luther's Hymn.
[3] It was, however, published after all in *Fraser's Magazine*, and stands now in the third volume of the *Miscellanies*.
[4] Afterwards the well-known Chaplain-General.

as far as Luther, and if I can get no bookseller I will stop short there, and for the present slit it up into review articles, and publish it that way.[1] Magazine Fraser has never offered me a doit for Richter's critique, and not even printed it at all. If you can get any cash from the fellow it will come in fine stead just now, when I have above 200*l.* worth of writing returned on my hands, and no Fortunatus' hat close by. Adieu, Jack. We are poor men, but nothing worse.

Your brother,

T. CARLYLE.

To a proud gifted man it was no pleasant thing to chaffer with publishers and dun for payments, which were withheld perhaps to bend the spirit of their too independent contributor. Carlyle bore his humiliation better than might have been expected. Indeed, as a rule, all serious trials he endured as nobly as man could do. When his temper·failed it was when some metaphorical gnat was buzzing in his ear. John Carlyle succeeded in extorting the few pounds that were owing from Fraser.

To John Carlyle.

Craigenputtock : August 21, 1830.

In returning from Scotsbrig this day week, whither I had gone on the Thursday before, I found your letter lying safe for me at Dumfries, and in spite of its valuable enclosure only bearing single postage. That last circumstance was an error on the part of his Majesty which it did not strike me in the least to rectify. We hear that Providence is a rich provider, and truly in my case I may thankfully say so. Many are the times when some seasonable supply in time of need has arrived when it was not in the least looked for. I was not by any means quite out of money when your bank paper came to hand ; but I saw clearly the likelihood, or rather the necessity, of such an event, which now by this ' sea-

---

[1] Partially accomplished in the following years, after many difficulties. The Nibelungen Lied appeared in the *Westminster Review*, and Early German Literature in the *Foreign Quarterly*. These essays, which are still the best upon their special subjects which exist in the English language, are specimens of the book which could find no publisher. They too are in the third volume of the *Miscellanies*.

sonable interposition' is put off to a safer distance. Pity that poor fellows should hang so much on cash! But it is the general lot, and whether it be ten pounds or ten thousand that would relieve us, the case is all the same, and the tie that binds us equally mean. If I had money to carry me up and down the world in search of good men and fellow-labourers with whom to hold communion, and heat myself into clearer activity, I should think myself happier; but in the mean time I have *myself* here for better or worse; and who knows but my imprisonment in these moors, sulkily as I may sometimes take it, is really for my good? If I have any right strength it will. If not, then what is the matter whether I sink or swim? Oh that I had but a little real wisdom ; then would all things work beautifully together for the best ends. Meanwhile the Dunscore Patmos is simply the place where of all others in the known world I can live *cheapest*, which in the case of a man living by literature, with little saleable talent, and who would very fain not prove a liar and a scoundrel, this is a momentous point. So let us abide here and work, or at least rest and be thankful.

I am happy to tell you that if this Literary History is not finished, it is now at least concluded. On Tuesday last I had a very short note from Captain, or rather Curate ———, which had been twice requested from him, stating that he found 'the publishers averse,' chiefly on the score of terms (which terms I had never hinted at), and indicating that he himself was averse chiefly on the score of size, as *one* volume would have suited the Library better. Further, it appeared from this note that the Reverend Editor was in all human probability a cold-hearted, shabbyish, dandy parson and lieutenant, who, being disappointed that I would not work for him at low wages, and any kind of work, wished to have nothing more to do with me, in which implied wish I could not but heartily, though sorrowfully, coincide, so that nothing remains for you but to send me back that ill-starred MS. as soon as you can, that I may consign it to its ultimate distinction.

Assure Fraser that I feel no shadow of spleen against him, but a true sentiment of friendship and regret at all the trouble he has had. For your satisfaction understand I am positively glad this intolerable business is done, nay, glad that it is done in this way rather than another. What part of the MS. I can split into review articles I will serve in that way ; for the present leaving the whole narrative complete down to Luther, to serve as an Introduction to my various essays on German Literature, in the compass of which essays (had I one or two more, for example Luther, Lessing, Herder) there already lies the best History of German Literature that I can easily write; and so were there a flourishing prophetic and circumspective essay appended by way of conclusion, we had a very fair *Geschichte,* or at least a *zur Geschichte,* all lying cut and dry, which can be published at any time if it is wanted; if not in my lifetime, then in some other, till which consummation it will lie here eating no bread. And so for all things, my brother, let us be thankful. I will work no more in 'Libraries,' or, if I can help it, in compilation. If my writing cannot be sold, it shall at least have been written out of my own heart. Also henceforth I will endeavour to be my own editor, having now arrived at the years for it. Nay, in the Devil's name, have I not a kail garden here that will grow potatoes and onions? The highest of men have often not had so much.

Too much of your sheet is already filled with my own concerns. At Scotsbrig, as I must tell you, matters wore a more tolerable aspect than I anticipated. Our mother was as well as usual, rather better, having been out at hay-making. Our father was still weak and somewhat dispirited, but as far as I could see he had no disease working on him, save loss of appetite and the general feebleness belonging to those years he has now arrived at. He sits most of the day, reading miscellaneously enough, wanders sometimes among the labourers, or even does little jobs himself. He seemed much quieter and better tempered.

Alick has written that he cannot keep this farm longer than Whitsunday, finding it a ruinous concern. Let Mrs. Welsh arrange the rest herself. Alick knows not well what he is to turn him to. Other farms might be had, but it is a ticklish business taking farms at present. Poor outlook there, nothing but loss and embarrassment. I often calculate that the land is all let some thirty per cent. too high; and that before it can be reduced the whole existing race of farmers must be ruined: that is, the whole agricultural tools (which are capital) broken in pieces and burnt in the landlords' fire, to warm his pointers with.

Ach Gott! The time is sick and out of joint. The perversities and mismanagements, moral and physical, of this best-of-all stage of society are rising to a head; and one day, see it who may, the whole concern will be blown up to Heaven, and fall thence to Tartarus, and a new and fairer era will rise in its room. Since the time of Nero and Jesus Christ there is no record of such embarrassments and crying, or, what is still worse, silent abominations. But the day, as we said, *will* come; for God is still in Heaven, whether Henry Brougham and Jeremiah Bentham know it or not; and the gig, and gigmania [1] must rot or start into thousand shivers, and bury itself in the ditch, that *Man* may have clean roadway towards the goal whither through all ages he is tending. *Fiat, fiat!*

Make my kindest compliments to my old friend your landlord, [2] whose like, take him for all in all, I have not yet looked upon. Tell him that none more honestly desires his welfare. Oh were I but joined to such a man! Would the Scotch Kirk but expel him, and his own better genius lead him far away from all Apocalypses, and prophetic and theologic chimæras, utterly unworthy of such a head, to see the world as it here lies visible, and is, that we might fight together for God's *true* cause even to the death! With one such man I feel as if I could defy the earth. But patience! patience! I shall find one, perhaps. At all events, courage! courage! What have we to look for but toil and trouble? What drivellers are we to whimper when it comes, and not front it, and triumph over it.

God for ever bless you, dear brother.

Heartily yours,

T. CARLYLE.

[1] Allusion to Thurtell's trial: 'I always thought him a respectable man.' 'What do you mean by respectable?' 'He kept a gig.'

[2] Irving, who had taken John Carlyle to live with him.

CHAPTER VI.

TRIALS had fallen sharply on Carlyle, entirely, as Jeffrey
had said, through his own generosity.   He had advanced
240*l.* in the education and support of his brother John.
He had found the capital to stock the farm at Craigenputtock, and his brother Alick thus had received from him
half as much more—small sums, as rich men estimate such
matters, but wrung out by Carlyle as from the rock by
desperate labour, and spared out of his own and his wife's
necessities.   John (perhaps ultimately Alexander, but of
this I am not sure) honourably repaid his share of this
debt in the better days which were coming to him, many
years before fortune looked more kindly on Carlyle himself.   But as yet John Carlyle was struggling almost penniless in London.   Alick's farming at Craigenputtock, which
Carlyle had once rashly thought of undertaking for himself, had proved a disastrous failure, and was now to be
abandoned.[1]   The pleasant family party there had to be
broken up, and his brother was to lose the companionship
which softened the dreariness of his solitude.   Alick

---

[1] Carlyle, however, had brought his genius to bear on the cultivation in a
single instance, though he could not save the farm.   A field at Craigenputtock
was made useless by a crop of nettles which covered the whole of it.   They
had been mowed down many times, but only grew the thicker ; and to root
them out would have been a serious expense.   It struck Carlyle that all plants
were exhausted by the effort of flowering and seeding, and if an injury would
ever prove mortal to the nettle it would be at that particular crisis.   He
watched the field till the seed was almost ripe, then mowed it once more, and
with complete success.   So at least he described the experiment to me.   Gar-
deners will know if the success was accidental or was due to some other cause.

Carlyle had the family gift of humour. His letters show that had he been educated he too might have grown into something remarkable. Alick could laugh with all his heart and make others laugh. His departure changed the character of the whole scene. Carlyle himself grew discontented. An impatient Radicalism rings through his remarks on the things which were going on round him. The political world was shaken by the three glorious days in Paris. England, following the example, was agitating for Reform, and a universal and increasing distress flung its ominous shadow over the whole working community. Reports of it all, leaking in through chance visitors, local newspapers, or letters of friends, combined with his own and his brother's indifferent and almost hopeless prospects, tended too naturally to encourage his gloomy tendencies. Ever on the watch to be of use to him, the warm-hearted Jeffrey was again at hand to seduce him into conformity with the dominant Liberal ways of thinking; that in the approaching storm he might at least open a road for himself to his own personal advancement. In August Jeffrey pressed his two friends in his most winning language to visit him at Craigcrook. Carlyle, he said, was doing nothing, and could employ himself no better than to come down with his blooming Eve out of his 'blasted Paradise,' and seek shelter in the lower world. To Mrs. Carlyle he promised roses and a blue sea, and broad shadows stretching over the fields. He said that he felt as if destined to do them real service, and could now succeed at last. Carlyle would not be persuaded; so in September the Jeffreys came again unlooked for to Craigenputtock. Carlyle was with his family at Scotsbrig.

Returning (he said, Sept. 18, 1830) late in the evening from a long ride, I found an express from Dumfries that the Jeffreys would be all at Craigenputtock that night. Of the riding and running, the scouring and scraping and Caleb Balderstone arranging my unfortunate but shifty and invincible Goody must have had, I say nothing. Enough, she is the cleverest of housewives, and might put innumerable *blues* to shame. I set out next morning, and on arriving here actually found the Dean of the Faculty with his adherents, sitting comfortably in a house swept and garnished awaiting my arrival. Of the *shine* itself I have room for no description. It all went prosperously on, and yesterday morning they set out homewards, reducing us instantly to our own more *commodious farthing rushlight*, which is our usual illumination. The worthy Dean is not very well, and I fear not very happy. We all like him better than we did. He is the most sparkling, pleasant little fellow I ever saw in my life.

How brilliant Jeffrey was, how he delighted them all with his anecdotes, his mockeries, and his mimicries, Carlyle has amply confessed; and he has acknowledged the serious excellence which lay behind the light exterior. It was on this occasion that he sent the 50*l.* to Hazlitt which came too late and found poor Hazlitt dying. It was on this occasion that he renewed his generous offer to lift Carlyle for a time over his difficulties out of his own purse, and when he could not prevail, promised to help John Carlyle in London, give him introductions, and if possible launch him in his profession. He charged himself with the Literary History, carried it off with him, and undertook to recommend it to Longman. From all this Jeffrey had nothing to gain: it was but the expression of hearty good will to Carlyle himself for his own sake and for the sake of his wife, in whom he had at least an equal interest. He wrote to her as cousin: what the exact relationship was I know not; but it was near enough, as he thought, to give him a right to watch over her welfare; and the thought of Carlyle persisting, in the face of imminent ruin, in what to him appeared a vain hallucination, and the thought still more of this delicate woman degraded to the duties of the mistress of a farmhouse, and obliged to face another winter in so frightful a climate, was simply horrible to him. She had not concealed from him that she was not happy at Craigenputtock; and the longer he reflected upon it the more out of humour he became with the obstinate philosopher who had doomed her to live there under such conditions.

It is evident from his letters that he held Carlyle to be gravely responsible. He respected many sides of his character, but he looked on him as under the influence of a curious but most reprehensible vanity, which would not and could not land him anywhere but in poverty and disappointment, while all the time the world was ready and eager to open its arms and lavish its liberality upon him if he would but consent to walk in its ways and be like other men. In this humour nothing that Carlyle did would please him. He quarrelled with the 'Literary History.' He disliked the views in it; he found fault with the style. After reading it, he had to say that he did not see how he could be of use in the obstetrical department to which he had aspired in its behalf.

Hang them! (said Carlyle bitterly, as one disappointment trod on the heels of another), hang them! I have a book in me that will cause ears to tingle, and one day out it must and will issue. In this valley of the shadow of magazine editors we shall not always linger. Courage! Not hope—for she was always a liar— but courage! courage!

An account of Jeffrey's visit is inserted in the Journal. Carlyle was evidently trying to think as well as he could about his *great* friend, and was not altogether succeeding.

The Jeffreys were here for about a week. Very good and interesting beyond wont was our worthy Dean. He is growing old, and seems dispirited and partly unhappy. The fairest cloak has its wrong side where the seams and straggling stitches afflict the eye! Envy no man. *Nescis quo urit.* Thou knowest not where the shoe pinches.

Jeffrey's essential talent sometimes seems to me to have been that of a Goldoni, some comic dramatist, not without a touch of fine lyrical pathos. He is the best mimic in the lowest and highest senses I ever saw. All matters that have come before him he has taken up in little dainty comprehensible forms ; chiefly logical— for he is a Scotchman and a lawyer—and encircled with sparkles of conversational wit or *persiflage;* yet with deeper study he would have found poetical forms for them, and his *persiflage* might have incorporated itself with the love and pure human feeling that dwells deeply in him. This last is his highest strength, though he himself hardly knows the significance of it ; he is one of the most loving men alive ; has a true kindness not of blood and habit only, but of soul and spirit. He cannot *do* without being loved. He is in the highest degree social ; and in defect of this *gregarious;* which last condition he in these bad times has for the most part had to content himself withal. Every way indeed he has fallen on evil days : the prose spirit of the world—to which world his kindliness draws him so strongly and so closely—has choked up and all but withered the better poetic spirit he derived from nature. Whatever is highest he entertains, like other Whigs, only as an ornament, as an appendage. The great business of man he, intellectually, considers, as a wordling does, *to be happy.* I have heard him say, ' If folly were the happiest I would be a fool.' Yet his daily life belies this doctrine, and says—' Though goodness were the most wretched, I would be good.'

In conversation he is brilliant, or rather sparkling, lively, kind, willing either to speak or listen, and above all men I have ever seen ready and copious, on the whole exceedingly pleasant in light talk—yet alas ! light, light, too light. He will talk of nothing *earnestly,* though his look sometimes betrays an earnest feeling. He starts contradictions in such cases, and argues, argues. Neither is his arguing like that of a thinker, but of the advocate—victory, not truth. A right *terræ filius* would feel irresistibly disposed to wash him away. He is not a strong man in any shape, but nimble and tough.

He stands midway between God and Mammon, and his preaching through life has been an attempt to reconcile them. Hence his popularity—a thing easily accountable when one looks at the world and at him, but little honourable to either. Literature ! poetry ! Except by a dim indestructible instinct which he has never dared to avow, yet being a true poet in his way could never eradicate, he knows not what they mean. A true newspaper critic on the great scale ; no priest, but a concionator.

Yet on the whole he is about the *best man* I ever saw. Sometimes I think he will abjure the devil if he live, and become a pure light. Already he is a most tricksy, dainty, beautiful little spirit. I have seen gleams on the face and eyes of the man that let you look into a higher country. God bless him! These jottings are as sincere as I could write them; yet too dim and inaccurately compacted. I see the nail, but have not here hit it on the head.

Meanwhile, and in the midst of Jeffrey's animadversions, Carlyle himself was about to take a higher flight. He 'had a book in him which would cause ears to tingle.' Out of his discontent, out of his impatience with the hard circumstances which crossed, thwarted, and pressed him, there was growing in his mind 'Sartor Resartus.' He had thoughts fermenting in him which were struggling to be uttered. He had something real to say about the world and man's position in it to which, could it but find fit expression, he knew that attention must be paid. The 'clothes philosophy,' which had perhaps been all which his first sketch contained, gave him the necessary form. His own history, inward and outward, furnished substance; some slight invention being all that was needed to disguise his literal individuality; and in the autumn of the year he set himself down passionately to work. Fast as he could throw his ideas upon paper the material grew upon him. The origin of the book is still traceable in the half fused, tumultuous condition in which the metal was poured into the mould. With all his efforts in calmer times to give it artistic harmony he could never fully succeed. 'There are but a few pages in it,' he said to me, 'which are rightly done.' It is well perhaps that he did not succeed. The incompleteness of the smelting shows all the more the actual condition of his mind. If defective as a work of art, 'Sartor' is for that very reason a revelation of Carlyle's individuality.

The idea had first struck him when on a visit with Mrs.

Carlyle at Templand. Customs, institutions, religious creeds, what were they but *clothes* in which human creatures covered their native nakedness, and enabled men themselves to live harmoniously and decently together? Clothes, dress, changed with the times; they grew old, they were elaborate, they were simple; they varied with fashion or habit of life; they were the outward indicators of the inward and spiritual nature. The analogy gave the freest scope and play for the wilfullest and wildest humour. The Teufelsdröckh, which we have seen seeking in vain for admission into London magazines, was but a first rude draft. Parts of this perhaps survive as they were originally written in the opening chapters. The single article, when it was returned to him, first expanded into two; *then* he determined to make a book of it, into which he could project his entire self. The 'Foreign Quarterly' continued good to him. He could count on an occasional place in 'Fraser.' The part already written of his 'Literary History,' slit into separate articles, would keep him alive till the book was finished. He had been well paid for his 'Life of Schiller.' If the execution corresponded to the conception, that 'Sartor' would be ten times better.

On the 19th of October he described what he was about to his brother. 'I am leading the stillest life, musing amidst the pale sunshine, or rude winds of October Tirl the Trees, when I go walking in this almost ghastly solitude, and for the rest writing with impetuosity. I think it not impossible that I may see you this winter in London. I mean to come whenever I can spare the money, that I may look about me among men for a little. What I am writing at is the strangest of all things. A very singular piece, I assure you. It glances from heaven to earth and back again, in a strange satirical frenzy, whether fine or not remains to be seen.'

Near the same date he writes to his mother:—

The wife and I are very quiet here, and accustoming ourselves as fast as we can to the stillness of winter which is fast coming on. These are the greyest and most silent days I ever saw. My besom, as I sweep up the withered leaves, might be heard at a furlong's distance. The woods are getting very parti-coloured; the old trees quite bare. All witnesses that another year has travelled away. What good and evil has it brought us? May God sanctify them both to every one of us! I study not to get too *wae;* but often I think of many solemn and sad things, which indeed I do not wish to forget. We are all in God's hand; otherwise this world, which is not wholly a valley of the shadow of death, were too frightful. Why should we fear? Let us hope. We are in the place of hope. Our life is a hope. But far better than all rea- sonings for cheerfulness is the diligence I use in following my daily business. For the last three weeks I have been writing my task-work again, and get along wonderfully well. What it is to be I cannot yet tell—whether a book or a string of magazine articles. We hope the former; but in either case it may be worth some- thing.

'Sartor' was indeed a free-flowing torrent, the outburst- ing of emotions which as yet had found no escape. The discontent which in a lower shape was rushing into French Revolutions, Reform Bills, Emancipation Acts, Socialism, and Bristol riots and rick burnings, had driven Carlyle into far deeper inquiries—inquiries into the how and why of these convulsions of the surface. The Hebrew spiritual robes he conceived were no longer suitable, and that this had something to do with it. The Hebrew clothes had become 'old clothes'—not the fresh wrought garments adapted to man's real wants, but sold at second-hand, and gaping at all their seams. Radical also politically Carlyle was at this time. The constitution of society, as he looked at it, was unjust from end to end. The workers were starving; the idle were revelling in luxury. Radicalism, as he understood it, meant the return of Astræa—an ap- proach to equity in the apportionment of good and evil in

this world; and on the intellectual side, if not encouragement of truth, at least the withdrawal of exclusive public
support of what was not true, or only partially true. He
did then actually suppose that the Reform Bill meant
something of that kind; that it was a genuine effort of
honourable men to clear the air of imposture. He had not
realised, what life afterwards taught him, that the work
of centuries was not to be accomplished by a single political change, and that the Reform Bill was but a singeing
of the dungheap. Even then he was no believer in the
miraculous effects to be expected from an extended suf-
frage. He knew well enough that the welfare of the State,
like the welfare of everything else, required that the wise
and good should govern, and the unwise and selfish should
be governed; that of all methods of discovering and pro
moting your wise man the voice of a mob was the least
promising, and that if Reform meant only liberty, and the
abolition of all authority, just or unjust, we might be
worse off perhaps than we were already. But he was impatient and restless; stung no doubt by resentment at the
alternative offered to himself either to become a humbug
or to be beaten from the field by starvation; and the
memorable epitaph on Count Zaehdarm and his achievements in this world showed in what direction his intellectual passions were running.

It seems that when Jeffrey was at Craigenputtock Carlyle must have opened his mind to him on these matters,
and still more fully in some letter afterwards. Jeffrey,
who was a Whig of the Whigs, who believed in liberty,
but by liberty meant the right of every man to do as he
pleased with his own as long as he did not interfere with
his neighbour, had been made seriously angry. Mysticism
was a pardonable illusion, provoking enough while it lasted,
but likely to clear off, as the morning mist when the sun
rises higher above the horizon; but these political views,

taken up especially by a man so determined and so passionately in earnest as Carlyle, were another thing, and an
infinitely more dangerous thing. Reform within moderate limits was well enough, but these new opinions if they
led to anything must lead to revolution. Jeffrey believed
that they were wild and impracticable ; that if ever misguided missionaries of sedition could by eloquence and
resolute persistence persuade the multitude to adopt notions
subversive of the rights of property, the result could only
be universal ruin. His regard and even esteem for Carlyle seem to have sensibly diminished from this time. He
half feared him for the mischief which he might do, half
gave him up as beyond help—at least as beyond help from
himself. He continued friendly. He was still willing to
help Carlyle within the limits which his conscience allowed,
but from this moment the desire to push him forward in
the politico-literary world cooled down or altogether ceased.

He tried the effect, however, of one more lecture, the
traces of which are visible in ' Sartor.' He had a horror
of Radicalism, he said. It was nothing but the old feud
against property, made formidable by the intelligence and
conceit of those who had none. . . . Carlyle's views
either meant the destruction of the right of property altogether, and the establishment of a universal co-operative
system—and this no one in his senses could contemplate—
or they were nonsense. Anything short of the abolition
of property, sumptuary laws, limitation of the accumula-
tion of fortunes, compulsory charity, or redivision of land,
would not make the poor better off, but would make all
poor ; would lead to the destruction of all luxury, elegance,
art, and intellectual culture, and reduce men to a set of
savages scrambling for animal subsistence. The institution of property brought some evils with it, and a revolting spectacle of inequality. But to touch it would entail
evils still greater ; for though the poor suffered, their lot

was only what the lot of the great mass of mankind must necessarily be under every conceivable condition. They would escape the pain of seeing others better off than they were, but they would be no better off themselves, while they would lose the mental improvement which to a certain extent spread downwards through society as long as culture existed anywhere, and at the same time the hope and chance of rising to a higher level, which was itself enjoyment even if it were never realised. Rich men after all spent most of their income on the poor. Except a small waste of food on their servants and horses, they were mere distributors among frugal and industrious workmen.

If Carlyle meant to be a politician, Jeffrey begged him to set about it modestly and patiently, and submit to study the questions a little under those who had studied them longer. If he was a Radical, why did he keep two horses himself, producing nothing and consuming the food of six human creatures, that his own diaphragm might be healthily agitated ? Riding-horses interfered with the subsistence of men five hundred times more than the unfortunate partridges.[1] So again Carlyle had adopted the Radical objections to machinery. Jeffrey inquired if he meant to burn carts and ploughs—nay, even spades too, for spades were but machines ? Perhaps he would end by only allowing men to work with *one* hand,[2] that the available work might employ a larger number of persons. Yet for such aims as these Carlyle thought a Radical insurrection justifiable and its success to be desired. The very first enactments of a successful revolution would be in this spirit : the overseers of the poor would be ordered to give twelve or twenty shillings to every man who could

[1] See the Zaehdarm Epitaph.
[2] A curiously accurate prophecy on Jeffrey's part, not as regarded Carlyle, but as to the necessary tendency of the unionist theory.

not, or said he could not, earn as much by the labour to which he had been accustomed.

Speculations on these and kindred subjects are found scattered up and down in 'Sartor.' Jeffrey was crediting Carlyle with extravagances which it is impossible that even in his then bitter humour he could have seriously entertained. He was far enough from desiring insurrection, although a conviction did lay at the very bottom of his mind that incurably unjust societies would find in insurrection and conflagration their natural consummation and end. But it is likely that he talked with fierce exaggeration on such subjects. He always did talk so. It is likely, too, that he had come to some hasty conclusions on the intractable problems of social life, and believed changes to be possible and useful which fuller knowledge of mankind showed him to be dreams. Before a just allotment of wages in this world could be arrived at—just payment according to real desert—he perceived at last that mankind must be themselves made just, and that such a transformation is no work of a political revolution. Carlyle too had been attracted to the St. Simonians. He had even in a letter to Goethe expressed some interest and hope in them ; and the wise old man had warned him off from the dangerous illusion. 'Von der Société St. Simonien bitte Dich fern zu halten,' Goethe had said. 'From the Society of the St. Simonians I entreat you to hold yourself clear.'[1] Jeffrey's practical sense had probably suggested difficulties to Carlyle which he had overlooked ; and Goethe carried more weight with him than Jeffrey. 'Sartor' may have been improved by their remonstrances ; yet there lie in it the germs of all Carlyle's future teaching—a clear statement of problems of the gravest import, which cry for a solution, which insist on a solution, yet on

[1] This sentence alone survives of Goethe's letter on the occasion, extracted in one of Carlyle's own.

which political economy and Whig political philosophy fail utterly to throw the slightest light. I will mention one to which Carlyle to his latest hour was continually returning. Jeffrey was a Malthusian. He had a horror and dread of over-population. 'Sartor' answers him with a scorn which recalls Swift's famous suggestion of a remedy for the distresses of Ireland.

The old Spartans had a wiser method, and went out and hunted down their Helots, and speared and spitted them, when they grew too numerous. With our improved fashions of hunting, now, after the invention of firearms and standing armies, how much easier were such a hunt. Perhaps in the most thickly peopled countries some three days annually might suffice to shoot all the able-bodied paupers that had accumulated within the year. Let Government think of this. The expense were trifling; the very carcases would pay it. Have them salted and barrelled. Could you not victual therewith, if not army and navy, yet richly such infirm paupers, in workhouses and elsewhere, as enlightened charity, dreading no evil of them, might see good to keep alive?

And yet there must be something wrong. A full-formed horse will in any market bring from twenty to two hundred friedrichs d'or. Such is his worth to the world. A full-formed man is not only worth nothing to the world, but the world could afford him a good round sum would he simply engage to go and hang himself. Nevertheless, which of the two was the more cunningly devised article, even as an engine? Good heavens! a white European man, standing on his two legs, with his two five-fingered hands at his shacklebones, and miraculous head on his shoulders, is worth, I should say, from fifty to a hundred horses!

What portion of this inconsiderable terraqueous globe have ye actually tilled and delved till it will grow no more? How thick stands your population in the pampas and savannas of America, round ancient Carthage and in the interior of Africa, on both slopes of the Atlantic chain, in the central platform of Asia, in Spain, Greece, Turkey, Crim Tartary, and the Curragh of Kildare? One man in one year, as I have understood it, if you lend him earth, will feed himself and nine others. Alas! where are now the Hengsts and Alarics of our still growing, still expanding Europe, who when their home is grown too narrow will enlist, and

like fire-pillars guide onwards those superfluous masses of indomitable living valour, equipped not now with the battle-axe
and war-chariot, but with the steam-engine and ploughshare?
Where are they?   Preserving their game!

When Carlyle published his views on 'the Nigger question,' his friends on both sides of the Atlantic were astonished and outraged.   Yet the thought in that pamphlet
and the thought in 'Sartor' is precisely the same.   When
a man can be taught to work and made to work, he has a
distinct value in the world appreciable by money like the
value of a horse.   In the state of liberty where he belongs
to nobody, and his industry cannot be calculated upon, he
makes his father poorer when he is born.   Slavery might
be a bad system, but under it a child was worth at least as
much as a foal, and the master was interested in rearing it.
Abolish slavery and substitute anarchy in the place of it,
and the parents, themselves hardly able to keep body and
soul together, will bless God when a timely fever relieves
them of a troublesome charge.

This fact, for fact it is, still waits for elucidation, and I
often heard Carlyle refer to it; yet he was always able to
see 'the other side.'   No Hengst or Alaric had risen in the
fifty years which had passed since he had written 'Sartor;'
yet not long before his death he was talking to me of
America and of the success with which the surplus population of Europe had been carried across the sea and distributed over that enormous continent.   Frederick himself,
he said, could not have done it better, even with absolute
power and unlimited resources, than it had 'done itself'
by the mere action of unfettered liberty.

CHAPTER VII.

A CHANGE meanwhile came over the face of English politics. Lord Grey became Prime Minister, and Brougham Chancellor, and all Britain was wild over Reform and the coming millennium. Jeffrey went into Parliament and was rewarded for his long services by being taken into the new Government as Lord Advocate. Of course he had to remove to London, and his letters, which henceforward were addressed chiefly to Mrs. Carlyle, were filled with accounts of Cabinet meetings, dinners, Parliamentary speeches—all for the present going merry as a marriage bell. Carlyle at Craigenputtock continued steady to his work. His money difficulties seemed likely to mend a little. Napier was overcoming his terror, and might perhaps take articles again from him for the 'Edinburgh.' The new 'Westminster' was open to him. The 'Foreign Quarterly' had not deserted him, and between them and 'Fraser' he might still find room enough at his disposal. The Literary History was cut up as had been proposed; the best parts of it were published in the coming year in the form of Essays, and now constitute the greater part of the third volume of the 'Miscellanies.' A second paper on Schiller, and another on Jean Paul, both of which had been for some time seeking in vain for an editor who would take them, were admitted into the 'Foreign Review' and 'Fraser.' Sufficient money was thus ultimately obtained to secure the household from starvation. But some months passed before these arrangements could be completed, and

'Sartor' had to go on with the prospect still gloomy in the extreme. Irving had seen and glanced over the first sketch of it when it was in London, and had sent a favourable opinion. Carlyle himself, notwithstanding his work, found time for letters to his brother, who was still hankering after literature.

To John Carlyle.

Craigenputtock: February 26, 1831.

Till Wednesday I am preparing 'Reineke' and various little etceteras, after which I purpose seriously inclining heart and hand to the finishing of 'Teufelsdröckh'—if indeed it be finishable. How could you remember Irving's criticism so well? Tell him it was quite like himself; he said all that was friendly, flattering, and encouraging, yet with the *right* faults kindly indicated—a true picture painted *couleur de rose*. I will make the attempt. And now, dear Jack, as to the last fraction of the letter; a word about you. Sorry am I to see your supplies running so low, and so little outlook for bettering them : yet what advice to give you? I have said a thousand times when you could not believe me, that the trade of literature was worse as a trade than that of honest street sweeping; that I know not how a man without some degree of prostitution could live by it, unless indeed he were situated like me, and could live upon potatoes and point if need were—as indeed need has been, is, and will be, with better men than me. If the angels have any humour I am sure they laughed heartily to-day, as I myself have repeatedly done, to see Alick setting off with twelve pence of copper, a long roll like a pencase, the whole disposable capital of both our households. I realised six, he six, so he was enabled to go. I was for keeping three, but he looked wistfully, and I gave him them with loud laughter. He had borrowed all our money and did *not* get payments last Wednesday, but surely will on Monday. . . . I could also prove that a life of scribbling is the worst conceivable for cultivating thought, which is the noblest, and the only noble thing in us. Your ideas never get root, cannot be sown, but are ground down from day to day. Oh that I heard of any medicine for your practising, were it only on the lower animals. However, patience—courage. The time is coming—dear Jack, keep a stout heart; I think I notice in you a considerable improvement since you left us; a far more manly bearing. Never despond. If you see no feasible method of ever fairly attempting to get professional employment in London, why then I think I would leave London. Do not fall into straits. Do not involve yourself in debt. Come out of it. Come *hither*. Share our provisions, such as the good God gives us—our roof and our welcome, and we will consider which way you are next to try it. Above all hide nothing from me, and I will hide it from the Scotsbrig people whenever you bid me.

And so God bless you, dear brother. Fear nothing but behaving unwisely.

T. CARLYLE.

Alick Carlyle was to leave Craigenputtock at Whitsuntide, a neighbouring grazier having offered the full rent for the farm, which Alick was unable to afford. Where he was to go and what was to become of him was the great family anxiety.

Little things (said Carlyle) are great to little men, to little man; for what was the Moscow expedition to Napoleon but the offering also for a new and larger farm whereon to till? and this too was but a mere clout of a farm compared with the great farm whose name is *Time,* or the quite boundless freehold which is called Eternity. Let us feel our bits of anxieties therefore, and make our bits of efforts, and think no shame of them.

Both brothers were virtually thrown upon his hands, while he seemingly was scarce able to take care of himself and his wife. When Alick was gone he and she would be left 'literally *unter vier Augen,* alone among the whinstone deserts; within fifteen miles not one creature they could so much as speak to,' and 'Sartor' was to be written under such conditions. Another winter at Craigenputtock in absolute solitude was a prospect too formidable to be faced. They calculated that with the utmost economy they might have 50*l.* in hand by the end of the summer, 'Teufelsdröckh' could by that time be finished. Mrs. Carlyle could stay and take care of Craigenputtock, while Carlyle himself would visit ' the great beehive and wasp's nest of London,' find a publisher for his book, and then see whether there was any other outlook for him. If none offered, there was still a resource behind, suggested perhaps by the first success of Irving and advised by Charles Buller.

I have half a mind (he wrote to John, warning him at the same time to be secret about it) to start when I come there, if the ground promise well, and deliver a dozen lectures in my own Annandale accent with my own God-created brain and heart, to such audience as will gather round me, on some section or aspect of this strange life in this strange era, of which my soul, like Eliphaz the Temanite's, is getting fuller and fuller. Does there seem to thee any propriety in a man that has organs of speech and even some semblance of understanding and sincerity sitting for ever, mute as a milestone, while quacks of every colour are quacking as with lungs of brass? True, I have no pulpit; but as I once said, cannot any man make him a pulpit simply by inverting the nearest tub? And what are your Whigs, and Lord Advocates, and Lord Chancellors, and the whole host of unspeakably gabbling parliamenteers and pulpiteers and pamphleteers, if a man suspect that there is fire enough in his belly to burn up the entire creation of such? These all build on mechanism; one spark of dynamism, of inspiration, were it in the poorest soul, is stronger than they all.

As for the Whig Ministry with whom Jeffrey might appear to connect me, I partly see two things: first, that they will have nothing in any shape to do with me, did I show them the virtue of a Paul; nay, the more virtue the less chance, for virtue is the will to choose the good, not tool-usefulness, to forge at the expedient: secondly, that they, the Whigs, except perhaps Brougham and his implements, will not endure. The latter, indeed, I should wonder little to see one day a second Cromwell. He is the cunningest and the strongest man in England now, as I construe him, and with no better principle than a Napoleon has—a worship and self-devotion to power. God be thanked that I had nothing to do with his University and its committees. So that Providence seems saying to me, 'Thou wilt never find pulpit, were it but a rhetoric chair, provided for thee. Invert thy tub, and speak if thou hast aught to say.'

Keep this inviolably secret, and know meanwhile that if I can raise 50*l.* at the right season, to London I will certainly come.

John Carlyle on his own account needed fresh admonition. Patients he could hear of none. The magazine editors were inclining for his name's sake to listen to him. Carlyle's feeling about it was like that of the rich man in torment.

To John Carlyle.

Craigenputtock : March 27, 1831.

I am clear for your straining every sinew simply to get *medical employment,* whether as assistant surgeon or in *any* other honest capacity. Without any doubt as the world now stands your safety lies there. Neither are you so destitute of friends and influence that on any given reasonable plan a considerable force of help could not be brought to bear. There are several, of weight, that would on more than one ground rejoice to do their best for you. Your world of London lies too dim before me for specification in this matter. Towards this, however, all your endeavours ought doubtless to be directed. Think and scheme and inquire, or rather continue to do so : once foiled is nothing like final defeat. So long as life is in a man there is strength in him. *Ein anderes Mal wollen wir unsere Sache besser machen*—' the next time we will manage our affairs better'—this was Fritz's *Wahlspruch;* and in this place of hope, where indeed there is nothing for us but hope, every brave man in reverses says the like.

For your success with the ' New Monthly,' or even with Napier, I care little, except so far as it might enable you to continue longer in London on the outlook. In other respects I am nearly sure failure would even be for your good. Periodical writing is, as I have often said, simply the worst of all existing employments. No mortal that had another noble art, the noblest with but one single exception, but would turn from it with abhorrence and cleave with his whole heart to the other. I am of opinion that you have a talent in you, perhaps far deeper than you yourself have often suspected; but also that it will never come to growth in that way. Incessant scribbling is inevitable death to thought. What can grow in the soil of that mind which must all be riddled monthly to see if there are any grains in it that will sell ? A hack that contents himself with gathering any offal of novelty or the like, and simply spreads this out on a stand and begs the passengers to buy it, may flourish in such craft ; an honest man, much more a man of any original talent, cannot. Thoughts fall on us, as I said, like seed. This you will find to be true. It is time only and silence that can ripen them. So convinced am I of the dangerous, precarious, and on the whole despicable and ungainly nature of a life by scribbling in any shape, that I am resolved to investigate again whether even I am for ever doomed to it.

I will not leave literature; neither should you leave it. Nay, had I but two potatoes in the world, and one true idea, I should hold it my duty to part with one potato for paper and ink, and live upon the other till I got it written. To such extremities may a *mere* man of letters be brought in Britain at present; but no wise *you*, who have another footing, and can live in a steady genial climate till experience have evoked into purity what is in you—*then* to be spoken with authority in the ears of all.

Such lesson, my dear brother, had you to learn in London before even the right effort could begin. It is a real satisfaction that, however bitterly you are learning or have learnt it, henceforth your face and force are turned in the true direction. If not to-day, then to-morrow you must and will advance prosperously and triumph. Forward, then, *festen Muth's und frohen Sinn's*, and God be with you. Fear nothing ; *die Zeit bringt Rosen.*

Of public matters I could write much ; but, greatly as the spectacle of these times—a whole world quitting its old anchorage and venturing into new untried seas with little science of sailing aboard—solicits one's attention, they do not interest either of us chiefly. I have signed no petition ; nay, I know not whether, had I the power by speaking a word to delay that consummation or hasten it, I would speak the word. It is a thing I have either longed for passionately or with confidence carelessly predicted any time these fifteen years. If I with any zeal approve of it now, it is simply on the ground of this incontrovertible aphorism which the state of all the industrious in these quarters too lamentably confirms—

> Hungry guts and empty purse
> May be better, can't be worse.

There is no logic yet discovered that can get behind this. Yes, in God's name, *let* us try it the other way. Jane 'salutes you with greetings and sisterly blessings.'[1] Adieu, dear Jack, *für jetzt.*

Ever your brother,

T. CARLYLE.

[1] Phrase of Edward Irving's.

In this period of 'potatoes and point' and 'farthing rushlights' for illumination after dark, the reader may be anxious to know how Mrs. Carlyle was getting on. Little can be said about this, for Carlyle tells next to nothing of her save in sad letters to Jeffrey, the nature of which, for they have not been preserved, can only be conjectured from Jeffrey's replies to them. We are left pretty much to guess her condition; and of guesses, the fewer that are ventured the better. Here, however, is one letter of her own inquiring after a servant for her mother—one of the collection which Carlyle has himself made, and has attached notes and preface to it.

To Miss Jean Carlyle, Scotsbrig.

[Betty Smail, mother of the two servant girls treated of here, was a dependant and cottager at Scotsbrig, come of very honest farmer people, though now reduced. She was herself a hardy, striving, noteworthy, lithe body, stood a great deal of sorrow and world-contradiction well, and died, still at Scotsbrig, very deaf, and latterly gone quite blind, age about ninety, only last year (1868), or the year before. Her girl Jean did not go, I think. Both these poor girls died in their mother's lifetime: one, probably Jean, soon after this of sudden fever; the other still more tragically of some *neuralgic* accident—suicide, thought not to be voluntary, hardly two weeks before my own great loss. Ah me!—T. C.]

Craigenputtock : Spring, 1831.

My dearest Jean,—I was meaning to write you a long letter by Alick, but I have been in bed all day with a headache, and am risen so confused and dull that for your sake as well as my own I shall keep my speculations—news I have none—till another opportunity, merely despatching in a few words a small piece of business I have to trouble you with, which will not wait.

My mother is wanting a woman at next term to take charge of her few cattle, work out, and assist at the washings. Not wishing to hire one out of Thornhill, she has requested me to look about for her, and would have liked Betty Smail, whom I formerly recommended, provided she had been leaving the Andersons. But I was happy to find (having been the means of placing there) that she is not leaving them, and continues to give great satisfaction by her honest, careful, obliging character. Miss Anderson happened to mention to Betty that I had been inquiring about her for my mother, when she suggested that her sister Jean, who is out of a place, might possibly answer. You know this Jean. Is she still disengaged? would she be willing to come? and do you think she would be fit for the place?

That you may be better able to form a judgment in the matter, I must tell you my mother has already *one* Jean, who is a *favourite* of some standing; and you know there is not houseroom at Templand for *two* favourites at once.

The present Jean maintains her ground partly by good service, partly by *wheedling*. To get the good-will of her mistress, and so have a comfortable life, the new comer, besides the usual requisites in a byre-woman, should possess the art of wheedling in a still higher degree,[1] or she should be an obtuse, imperturbable character that would take 'the good the gods provided,' and for the rest 'jouk until the jaw gaed by,' would go on honestly milking her cows and ' clatting' her byre 'in maiden meditation fancy free,' till under a change of ministry, which always comes at last, she might find herself suddenly promoted in her turn.

Now all this is very ill-natured, and you will mind it only so far as you see sense in it. It means simply that if Jean Smail be a very sensitive or quarrelsome character, and at the same time without *tact*, she would not be likely to prosper. Send me word by Alick what you think. I need hardly add that a servant who *pleases* could not possibly find a better place.

Tell your mother, with my love, that the hen she has sent to be *eaten* has laid the first egg of our whole stock.

God bless you. More next time, as the Doctor says.

Ever affectionately yours,

JANE W. CARLYLE.

Meanwhile the affairs of the poor Doctor were coming to extremity. Excellent advice might be given from Craigenputtock; but advice now was all that could be af-

---

[1] 'Truish—emphatic for business' sake.—T. C.'

forded. Even his magazine articles, for which he had been rebuked for writing, could not be sold after all. It was time clearly for a *deus ex machinâ* to appear and help him. Happily there was a *deus* in London able and willing to do it in the shape of Jeffrey. Though he had failed in inducing Carlyle to accept pecuniary help from him, he could not be prevented from assisting his brother, and giving him or lending him some subvention till something better could be arranged. Here, too, Carlyle's pride took alarm. It was pain and humiliation to him that any member of his family should subsist on the bounty of a stranger. He had a just horror of debt. The unlucky John himself fell in for bitter observations upon his indolence. John, he said, should come down to Scotland and live with him. There was shelter for him and food enough, such as it was. He did not choose that a brother of his should be degraded by accepting obligations. But this time Jeffrey refused to listen. It might be very wrong, he admitted, for a man to sit waiting by the pool till an angel stirred the water, but it was not necessarily right therefore that because he could not immediately find employment in his profession, he should renounce his chances and sit down to eat potatoes and read German at Craigenputtock. He had no disposition to throw away money without a prospect of doing good with it, but he knew no better use to which it could be put than in floating an industrious man over the shoals into a fair way of doing good for himself. Even towards Carlyle, angry as he had been, his genuine kindness obliged him to relent. If only he would not be so impracticable and so arrogant! If only he could be persuaded that he was not an inspired being, and destined to be the founder of a new religion! But a solitary life and a bad stomach had so spoilt him, all but the heart, that he despaired of being able to mend him.

Jeffrey was so evidently sincere that even Carlyle could

object no longer on his brother's account. 'My pride,' he said, 'were true pride—savage, satanic, and utterly damnable—if it offered any opposition to such a project when my own brother and his future happiness was concerned.' Jeffrey did not mean to confine himself to immediate assistance with his purse. He was determined to find, if possible, some active work for John. Nothing could be done immediately, for he was obliged to leave London on election business. Help in money at least was to be given as soon as he returned; Carlyle using the interval for another admonition.

Consider your situation (he wrote to his brother on the 8th of May) with unprejudiced, fearless mind, listening no moment to the syren melodies of hope, which are only melodies of sloth, but taking cold prudence and calculation with you at every step. *Nimm Dich zusammen.* Gather yourself up. Feel your feet upon the rock before you rest, not upon the quicksand, where resting will but engulph you deeper. In your calculations, too, I would have you throw out literature altogether. Indeed, I rather believe it were for your good if you quite burnt your magazine pen and devoted yourself exclusively and wholly to medicine, and nothing but medicine. Magazine work is below street-sweeping as a trade. Even I, who have no other, am determined to try by all methods whether it is not possible to abandon it.

At Craigenputtock the most desperate pinch was not yet over. One slip of the Literary History came out in the April number of the 'Edinburgh' in the form of a review of Taylor's 'Historic Survey of German Poetry,'[1] but payment for it was delayed or forgotten. Meanwhile the farm-horses had been sold. Old Larry, doing double duty on the road and in the cart, had laid himself down and died—died from overwork. So clever was Larry, so humorous, that it was as if the last human friend had been taken away. The pony had been parted with also, though it was recovered afterwards; and before payment

[1] *Miscellanies,* vol. iii.

came from Napier for the article they were in real extremity. Alick by his four years of occupation was out
of pocket 300*l.* These were the saddest days which Carlyle had ever known.

The summer came, and the Dunscore moors grew beautiful in the dry warm season. 'So pure was the air, the
foliage, the herbage, and everything round him,' that he
said, if Arcadianly given, he 'might fancy the yellow
buttercups were asphodel, and the whole scene a portion
of Hades—some outskirt of the Elysian Fields, the very
perfection of solitude.' Between the softness of the scene
and the apparent hopelessness of his prospects, Carlyle's
own heart seems for a moment to have failed. He wrote
to Jeffrey in extreme depression, as if he felt he had lost
the game, and that there was nothing for it but to turn
cynic and live and die in silence. The letter I have not
seen, and I do not know whether it has been preserved,
but Jeffrey's answer shows what the tone of it must have
been. 'The cynic tub,' 'the primitive lot of man,' Jeffrey
frankly called an unseemly and unworthy romance. If
Carlyle did not care for himself, he ought to think of his
young and delicate wife, whose great heart and willing
martyrdom would make the sacrifice more agonising in
the end. It was not necessary. He should have aid—
effective aid; and if he pleased he might repay it some
day ten times over. Something should be found for him
to do neither unglorious nor unprofitable. He was fit for
many things, and there were more tasks in the world fit
for him than he was willing to believe. He complimented
him on his last article in the 'Edinburgh.' Empson had
praised it warmly. Macaulay and several others, who had
laughed at his 'Signs of the Times,' had been struck with
its force and originality. If he would but give himself
fair play, if he could but believe that men might differ
from him without being in damnable error, he would

make his way to the front without difficulty. If Jeffrey had been the most tender of brothers he could not have written more kindly. Carlyle if one of the proudest was also one of the humblest of mortals. He replied, 'that he was ready to work at any honest thing whatsoever;' 'that he did not see that literature could support an honest man otherwise than *à la* Diogenes.' 'In this fashion he meant to experiment if nothing else could be found, which however through all channels of investigation he was minded to try for.'

It is not easy to see precisely what kind of employment Jeffrey had really in view for Carlyle. At one time no doubt he had thought of recommending him strongly to the Government. At another he had confessedly thought of him as his own successor on the 'Edinburgh Review.' But he had been frightened at Carlyle's Radicalism. He had been offended at his arrogance. Perhaps he thought that it indicated fundamental unsoundness of mind. He little conjectured that the person for whom he was concerning himself was really one of the most remarkable men in Europe, destined to make a deeper impression upon his contemporaries than any thinker then alive. This was not to be expected; but it must be supposed that he was wishing rather to try the sincerity of Carlyle's professions than that he was really serious in what he now suggested. He gave a list of possible situations : a clerkship at the Excise or the Board of Longitude or the Record Office, or a librarianship at the British Museum, or some secretaryship in a merchant's house of business. He asked him which of these he would detest the least, that he might know before he applied for it.

Poor Carlyle ! It was a bitter draught which was being commended to his lips. But he was very meek; he answered that he would gratefully accept any one of them : but even such posts as these he thought in his despondency to be beyond his reach. He was like the pilgrim in the valley of humiliation. 'I do not expect,' he told his mother, 'that he will be able to accomplish anything for me. I must even get through life *without a trade*, always in poverty, as far better men have done. Our want is the want of faith. Jesus of Nazareth was not poor, though he had not where to lay his head. Socrates was rich enough. I have a deep, irrevocable, all-comprehending Ernulphus curse to read upon Gigmanity : that is the Baal worship of our time.'

Though brought down so low, he could not entirely love the hand which had made him feel where he stood in the world's estimation. His unwillingness that John should accept money from Jeffrey was not removed.

To John Carlyle.

Craigenputtock : July 7, 1831.
Help towards work I would solicit from any reasonable man. Mere pecuniary help for its own sake is a thing one should always be cautious of accepting. Few are worthy to give it, still fewer capable of worthily receiving it. Such is the way of the time we live in. Meanwhile, relax not your own efforts for a moment. Think, project, investigate. You are like a soul struggling towards birth ; the skilfullest accoucheur (pardon the horrible figure) can but help the process. Here, too, the Cæsarean operation, as I have seen, is oftenest fatal to the fœtus. In short, Jack, there lie the rudiments of a most sufficient man and doctor in thee : but wise *will* must first body them forth. Oh, I know the thrice-cursed state you are in—hopeless grim death-defying thoughts ; a world shut against you by inexpugnable walls. Rough it out ; toil it out ; other way of making a *man* have I never seen. One day you will see it all to have been needed, and your highest, properly your only blessing.

I must not take all your encomiums about my scriptorial genius. Nevertheless, I am coming up to look about me, and if possible even to establish myself in London. This place is as good as done ; not even the last advantage, that of living in any pecuniary sufficiency, for I never was as poor. Naso,[1] the blockhead, has

[1] Napier, of the *Edinburgh Review.*

neither paid me nor written to me. But we are in no strait. I shall even raise the wind for a London voyage without much difficulty. I can write to Naso, if he will not to me. I have some thoughts of cutting him and his calcined *caput mortuum*—dead men's ashes of Whiggism—at any rate. But fair and soft. I now see through Teufel, write at him literally night and day, yet cannot be done within—say fifteen days. Then I should like to have a week's rest, for I am somewhat in the inflammatory vein. As to the Teufel itself, whereof 122 solid pages lie written off, and some 40 above half ready are to follow, I cannot pretend to prophecy. My humour is of the stoical sort as concerns it. Sometimes I think it goodish, at other times bad; at most times the best I can make it here. A strange book all men will admit it to be. Partially intended to be a true book I know it to be. It shall be printed if there is a possibility. You anticipate me in the suggestion of lodgings. There must I live, and nowhere as a guest. *Dreitägiger Gast wird eine Last.* A guest after three days is a burden. Have you no little bedroom even where you are; and one little parlour would serve us both. I care about nothing but a bed where I can sleep. That is to say, where are no bugs and no noises about midnight; for I am pretty invincible when once fairly sealed. The horrors of nerves are somewhat laid in me, I think; yet the memory of them is frightfully vivid. For the rest, my visit to London is antigigmanic from heart to skin. The venerable old man (Goethe) sends me ten days ago the noblest letter I ever read.[1] Scarcely could I read it without tears. Let me die the death of the righteous; let my last end be like his. Goethe is well and serene. Another box on the way hither. We all salute you.

T. C.

The picture of Carlyle's condition—poor, almost without hope, the companions which had made the charm of his solitude—his brother Alick, his horse Larry—all gone or going, the place itself disenchanted—has now a peculiar interest, for it was under these conditions that 'Sartor Resartus' was composed. A wild sorrow sounds through its sentences like the wind over the strings of an æolian harp. Pride, too, at intervals fiercely defiant, yet yielding

---

[1] Not to be found.

to the inevitable, as if the stern lesson had done its work. Carlyle's pride needed breaking. His reluctance to allow his brother to accept help from Jeffrey had only plunged him into worse perplexities. John had borrowed money, hoping that his articles would enable him to repay it. The articles had not been accepted, and the hope had proved a quicksand. Other friends were willing to lend what was required, but he would take nothing more; and the only resource left was to draw again upon Carlyle's almost exhausted funds.

To John Carlyle.

Craigenputtock : July 12, 1831.

I wrote last Thursday under cover to the Lord Advocate, which letter you have before this received. However, not knowing the right address, I was obliged to address the M.P. at 'London,' so that some delay may have occurred. Alick and I[1] were down at the kirk on Sunday. I went for the first time these many months, on account of the Irish collection : and there your letter was lying which demands a quite instantaneous reply. I regretted greatly that no device of mine could take effect sooner than to-night; but as if it had been some relief, I made ready another letter for your behoof (of which anon) that very night, and have had it lying here sealed ever since. It was a letter to Bowring, requesting him to pay the Nibelungen article[2] forthwith into your hands. I did this as courteously as possible, and imagine he will not fail. However, a day or two may elapse ; and in the meantime you have nothing. Had I been at Dumfries I would have got a Bank of England note ; but there is none such here : we have not even a better than this of *one* pound, though I tried to borrow a *five* in vain. So you must receive it as our poor *non plus ultra*. Take it to William Hamilton in Cheapside. Say your brother was sending you money, and requested that he would give you a sovereign for this. If Bowring do not send before it is done, I think you may call on him. I suppose there will be three sheets, and their pay is only ten guineas. Take off it what you have need of till I come.

---

[1] Alick Carlyle, unable to find another farm or occupation, had come back for a time, and was living in a small room in the yard at Craigenputtock.

[2] I.e., the money due for it.

Write also a word on the papers to say how it is,[1] and how you are. I have had you little out of my head since Sunday last.

Shocking as your situation is, however, we all here agree that it is more hopeful than we have ever yet had clear argument to think it. Thank God you have done no wrong. Your conscience is free, and *you yourself* are there. We all reckon that your conduct in that matter of Jeffrey's 20*l.* was entitled to be called *heroic.* Sooner or later, my dear brother, it must have come to this, namely, that your own miscellaneous industry could not support you in London, and that you ceased to borrow, better, we say, now than never. Bear up; front it bravely. There are friendly eyes upon you, and hearts praying for you. Were we once together it will be peremptorily necessary to consider how the land lies and what is to be done. In all situations (out of Tophet) there is a *duty*, and our highest blessedness lies in doing it. I know not whether Jeffrey may be able to do anything for you. He speaks to me rather more hopefully than he seems to have done to you.

I shall study to be with you about the beginning of August. I have written as you suggested to Napier for a note to Longman, also for payment of what he owes me. I am struggling forward with Dreck, sick enough, but not in bad heart. I think the world will no wise be enraptured with this medicinal *Devil's-dung;* that the critical republic will cackle vituperatively, or perhaps maintain total silence—*à la bonne heure!* It was the best I had in me. What God has given me, that the Devil shall not take away. Be of good cheer, my brother. Behave wisely, and continue to trust in God. No doubt *He* sent you hither to work out His will. It is man's mission and blessedness could he but rightly walk in it. Write to me. Trust in me.

Ever your brother,

T. CARLYLE.

Once more on the 17th of the same month—

I am labouring at Teufel with considerable impetuosity, and calculate that, unless accidents intervene, I may be actually ready to get under way at the end of the month. But there will not be a minute to lose. I sometimes think the book *will* prove a kind of medicinal *assafœtida* for the pudding stomach of England, and produce new secretions there. *Jacta est alea!* I will speak out

[1] The Carlyles communicated with one another by cipher on newspapers, to save postage.

what is in me, though far harder chances threatened. I have no other trade, no other strength or portion in this earth. Be it so. Hourly you come into my head, sitting in your lone cabin in that human chaos with *mehr als ein Schilling* and bread and water for your dinner; and I cannot say but I respect you more and love you more than ever I did. Courage! Courage! *Tapferkeit*, 'deliberate valour' is God's highest gift, and comes not without trial to any. Times will mend; or, if times never mend, then in the Devil's name let them stay as they are, or grow worse, and *we* will mend. I know but one true wretchedness—the want of work (want of wages is comparatively trifling), which want, however, in such a world as this planet of ours *cannot* be permanent unless we continue blind therein. I must to my Dreck, for the hours go. *Gott mit Dir!*

It was a sad, stern time to these struggling brothers; and it is with a feeling like what the Scots mean by *wae* that one reads the letters that Jeffrey was writing during the worst of it to Mrs. Carlyle. He had done what he was allowed to do. Perhaps he thought they understood their own matters best; and it was not easy to thrust his services on so proud a person as Mrs. Carlyle's husband, when they were treated so cavalierly; but he did not choose to let the correspondence fall, and to her he continued to write lightly and brilliantly on London gaieties and his own exploits in the House of Commons. The tone of these letters must have been out of harmony with the heavy hearts at Craigenputtock, but he was still acting as a real friend and remained on the watch for opportunities to be of use, if not to Carlyle himself, yet at least to his brother.

So July ran out and 'Sartor' was finished, and Carlyle prepared to start, with the MS. and the yet unpublished sections of the Literary History in his portmanteau, to find a publisher for one or both of them; to find also, if possible, some humble employment to which his past work might have recommended him; to launch himself, at any

rate, into the great world, and light on something among
its floating possibilities to save him from drowning, which
of late had seemed likely to be his fate. With Craigenputtock as a home he believed that he had finally done.
The farm which was to have helped him to subsist had
proved a failure, and had passed to strangers. Living retired in those remote moorlands, he had experienced too
painfully that from articles in reviews he could count on
no regular revenue, while the labour lost in the writing
led to nothing. Work of such a kind, if it was to be profitable, must become an intellectual prostitution; and to escape from this was the chief object of his London journey.
He had so far swallowed his pride as to accept after all a
loan of 50*l.* from Jeffrey for his expenses. The sums due
to him would provide food and lodging during his stay.
Such hopes as he still may have entertained of the realisa-
tion of his old dream of making a mark in the world lay
in the MS. of 'Sartor.' 'It is a work of genius, dear,'
Mrs. Carlyle said to him as she finished the last page—
she whose judgment was unerring, who flattered no one,
and least of all her husband. A work of genius! Yes;
but of genius so original that a conventional world, measuring by established rules, could not fail to regard it as a
monster. Originality, from the necessity of its nature,
offends at its first appearance. Certain ways of acting,
thinking, and speaking are in possession of the field and
claim to be the only legitimate ways. A man of genius
strikes into a road of his own, and the first estimate of
such a man has been, is, and always will be, unfavourable.
Carlyle knew that he had done his best, and he knew the
worth of it. He had yet to learn how hard a battle still
lay ahead of him before that worth could be recognised by
others. Jeffrey compared him to Parson Adams going to
seek his fortune with his manuscript in his pocket. Charles
Buller, more hopeful, foretold gold and glory. Jeffrey, at

any rate, had made it possible for him to go; and, let it be added, John Carlyle, notwithstanding his struggles to avoid obligations, had been forced to accept pecuniary help from the same kind hand.

Night before going (he wrote in 1866), how I still remember it! I was lying on my back on the sofa in the drawing room. She sitting by the table late at night, packing all done, I suppose. Her words had a guise of sport, but were profoundly plaintive in meaning. 'About to part; and who knows for how long, and what may have come in the interim.' This was her thought, and she was evidently much out of spirits. 'Courage, dear—only for a month,' I would say to her in some form or other. I went next morning early, Alick driving; embarked at Glencaple Quay. Voyage as far as Liverpool still vivid to me. The rest, till arrival in London, gone—mostly extinct.

CHAPTER VIII.

A.D. 1831. ÆT. 36.

Extracts from Carlyle's Note Book, begun in London 1831.

August 4th.—Left Craigenputtock and my kind little wife, Alick driving me, at two o'clock in the morning. Shipped at Glencapel; hazy day; saw Esbie in the steerage; talked mysticism with him during six weary hours we had to stay at Whitehaven. Reimbarkment there amidst bellowing and tumult and fiddling unutterable, all like a spectral vision. 'She is not there.' St. Bees Head. Man with the nose. Sleep in the steamboat cabin : confusion worse confounded. Morning views of Cheshire—the Rock, Liverpool, and steamboats.

August 5th, 9.30 in the morning.—Land at Liverpool; all abed at Maryland Street.[1] Boy Alick[2] accompanies me over Liverpool. Exchange, dome : dim view there. Dust, toil, cotton bags, hampers, repairing ships, disloading stones. Carson a hash : melancholy body of the name of Sloan. Wifekin's assiduity in caring for me.

August 6th (Saturday).—Taken to one Johnstone, a frenchified Lockerby man, who leads me to Change. Place in 'Independent Tally Ho,' Sir! See George Johnstone, surgeon, whom I had unearthed the night before. Patient of his. He dines with us. Walk on the Terrace, near the Cemetery. Have seen the steam coaches in the morning. Liverpool a dismembered aggregate of streets and sand-pits. Market! hubbub!

August 8th.—Go out to find Esbie. He calls on me. Confused family dinner; ditto tea. G. Johnstone again; talk; to bed.

August 9th.—Off on Monday morning. Shipped through the Mersey; coached through Eastham, Chester, Overton (in Wales),

---

[1] Liverpool home of Mrs. Carlyle's uncle John,—the uncle who was made bankrupt through a fraudulent partner, and afterwards paid all his creditors in full.

[2] John's son.

Ellesmere, Shrewsbury, Wolverhampton, Birmingham; attempt at tea there. Discover, not without laughter, the villany of the Liverpool coach bookers. Henley-in-Arden. Stratford-on-Avon (horses lost there). Get to sleep. Oxford at three in the morning. Out again there; chill but pleasant. Henley, Maidenhead, &c. Arrive, full of sulphur, at White Horse Cellar, Piccadilly. Dismount at the Regent Circus, and am wheeled (not whirled) hither [1] about half-past ten. Poor Jack waiting all the while at the Angel, Islington. Talk together when he returns; dine at an eating-house among Frenchmen, one of whom ceases eating to hear me talk of the St. Simonians. Leave my card at the Lord Advocate's, with promise to call next morning. Sulphurous enough.

These extracts supply the lost places in Carlyle's memory, and serve as a frame into which to fit the following letter to his wife. The intense affection which he felt for her is visible in every line.

To Mrs. Carlyle, Craigenputtock.

6 Woburn Buildings, Tavistock Square : August 11, 1831.

Dearest and Wife,—I have got a frank for you and will write from the heart whatever is in the heart. A blessing it was that you made me give such a promise; for I feel that an hour's speech in speaking with my own will do me infinite good. It is very sweet in the midst of this soul-confusing phantasmagoria to know that I have a fixed possession elsewhere; that my own Jeannie is thinking of me, loving me; that her heart is no dream like all the rest of it. Oh love me, my dearest—always love me. I am richer with thee than the whole world could make me otherwise.

But to be practical. Expect no connected or even intelligible narrative of all the chaotic sights, sounds, movements, countermovements I have experienced since your lips parted from mine on our threshold—still less of all the higher chaotic feelings that have danced their wild torch dance within me. For the present I must content myself, like Sir William Hamilton, with 'stating a fact or two.' Understand then, Goodykin, that after infinite confusion, I arrived at Liverpool about eight o'clock on the morning

---

[1] To 6 Woburn Buildings, Tavistock Square—the house of George Irving, Edward Irving's brother, where John Carlyle lodged.

after I left you, quite sleepless, and but for your dinner (which I parted with a certain 'Esbie,' whom Alick knows well, whom I found in the boat and preached mysticism to for six hours), quite victual-less. The Maryland Street people[1] were not up, but soon rose and received me well. Delightful it was to get into a room and—have my face washed; and then on opening my trunk to find everywhere traces of my good 'coagitor's'[2] care and love. The very jujube box with its worsted and darning needle did not escape me; it was so beautiful I could almost have cried over it. Heaven reward thee, my clear-headed, warm-hearted, dearest little Screami-kin!

John Welsh was the same substantial, honest fellow whom we have always known him: he and I got along, as we always do, beautifully together.

The Auntie was loud, talkative, argumentative, infinitely bus-tling, but also very assiduous in showing me kindness. To make a long tale short, I left them on Sunday morning at half-past seven with many blessings and two cups of sufficient coffee, which the good housewife would not be prevented from making me at that early hour.

Which last hospitality I may well say was doubly blest; for it so turned out this was the only refection I received till my arri-val in London on the following day about ten o'clock! I must except a penny loaf snatched from the landlady of an inn in Shrop-shire; and a cup of hot sugar and water (as the whole time proved only fifteen minutes), for which I had the pleasure of paying half-a-crown in the village of Birmingham. How all this happened, and I was sent circulating over the whole West of England, set my watch by the Shrewsbury clock, and saw portions of Wales, and had the delightfulest drive, only no victual, or knowledge by what route I was bound—all this depended on the art of the Liver-pool coach agents, at which, villanous as it was, I could not help laughing, when, after leaving Birmingham, I came to see into the mystery. There are men in Liverpool who will *book* you to go by any coach you like, and to enter London at any place and hour *you* like, and then send you thither by any coach or combination of coaches *they* like. I was booked for a certain imaginary 'Tally Ho,' went by seven successive vehicles none of which had that name, and entered London three hours later and by quite the op-

---

[1] Mr. John Welsh and his family.
[2] His wife. Somebody's pronunciation of 'coadjutor.'

posite side than I had appointed John to wait at. Sulphurous enough. However, I have now had sleep and am well. The only mischief done *was the breaking of the eggs*, which, however, the warehouseman has now made good again. So do not grieve thyself, dearest. The broken eggs are dearer to me than the whole ones would have been. There is a pathos in them, and I love Jeannie more.

With little difficulty I conveyed myself and luggage to Jack's old lodgings, and there learnt his actual address at no great distance, and, to my astonishment, in the upper floor of George Irving's house, who also lets lodgings. It is a very beautiful sitting-room, an immense bedroom above (and John sleeps with George), for which we are to pay 25s. weekly. Quiet and airy, and among known people. All is right in this respect.

The first day I did little; yet walked over to the Duke's,[1] found him out, and left my card with a promise for next morning. It is between two and three miles from this. On arriving there I was asked my name and then instantly ushered in and welcomed in their choicest mood by the whole family. Mrs. Jeffrey was as kind as ever; Charlotte too came simpering in and looked as if she would let me live. The Advocate retired and re-entered with your picture, which was shown round; for little I could have *grat* over it. After a time by some movements I got the company dispersed, and the Advocate by himself, and began to take counsel with him about 'Teufelsdröckh.' He thought Murray, in spite of the Radicalism, would be the better publisher; to him accordingly he gave me a line, saying that I was a genius and would likely become eminent; further, that he (Jeffrey) would like well to confer with him about that book. I directly set off with this to Albemarle Street; found Murray out; returned afterwards and found him in, gave an outline of the book, at which the Arimaspian smiled, stated also that I had nothing else to do here but the getting of it published, and was above all anxious that his decision should be given soon. He answered that he would begin this very afternoon, and that on Wednesday next he would give me an answer. I then went off; despatched my 'Teufelsdröckh' with *your* tape round him. Of the probable issue I can form no conjecture: only Murray seemed to know me, and I dare say is very anxious to keep well with Ministers, so will risk what he dares.

[1] Jeffrey's house in Jermyn Street.

Napier's letter is also come, with a note to Rees, which I think I shall perhaps not deliver (perhaps, too, I may) till after next Wednesday.

Badams called here an hour after I came : he brought his wife next day. I was out, but saw them in the evening. She is a good woman, and good-looking, whom I think you will like. *He* is in no good way, I doubt; yet not without hope. I have also seen Mrs. Montagu; talked longer with her than I shall speedily do again, for she seems to me embittered and exasperated; and what have I to do with her quarrels? Jack she seems positively to have cut, because he would not turn with her in a day from a transcendental apotheosis of Badams to excommunication. All things go round and round. For me, as I told her, I would continue to love all parties and pity all, and hate or quarrel with none.

Jack stands *glowering o'er me,* as you know is his wont. Tell Alick all my news ; read him the letter (so much of it as you can read), and give to everyone my kindest brotherly love.

August 15.

Your kind precious letter came to me on Friday like a cup of water in the hot desert. It is all like yourself : so clear, precise, loving, and true to the death. I *see* poor Craigenputtock through it, and the best little Goodykin sitting there, hourly meditating on me and watching my return. Oh, I am very rich were I without a penny in the world! But the Herzen's Goody must not fret herself and torment her poor sick head. I will be back to her ; not an hour will I lose. Heaven knows the sun shines not on the spot that could be pleasant to me where she were not. So be of comfort, my Jeannie, and with thy own sweet orderly spirit make calmness out of confusion, and the dawn (as it does in some climates) to shine through the whole night till it be morning, and the sun once more embraces his fair kind earth. For the rest, thou canst not be too 'Theresa-like ;'[1] it is this very fidelity to practical nature that makes the charm of the picture. . . .

I am getting a little more composed in this whirlpool, and can tell you better how it whirls.

On Friday morning, the day after I wrote, Jack walked down with me to Longmans, and I delivered Napier's note to a staid, cautious, business-like man, who read it with an approving smile,

---

[1] Theresa, in *Wilhelm Meister.*

listened to my description of the 'German Literary History' with the same smile in a *fixed* state, and then (like a barbarian as he was) 'declined the article.' He was polite as possible, but seemed determined on risking *nothing*. If Murray fail me (as Wednesday will probably show), I have calculated that it will be hardly worth while to offer these people Dreck, but that I must try some other course with him. *I hope not at all*, therefore hardly think that Murray will accept (so lucky were it), and am already looking out what I can for other resources in the worst issue. Dreck shall be printed if a man in London will do it; if not with, then without, 'fee or reward.' I even conjecture still that this is the time for him : everybody I see participates in the feeling that society is nigh done; that she is a Phœnix perhaps not so many conjecture. I agree with my prophetess in thinking that some *young* adventurous bookseller were the hopefullest. We shall see soon.

Saturday morning I wrote to Goethe (with kindest love from you too); also to Charles Buller and to Fraser (notifying my presence), then off for Shooter's Hill some ten miles away, where we arrived in time for dinner. Strachey is as alert as ever. In his poor lady I had room to mark the doings of time. She wore a sad secluded look; I learnt she had been for three years violently dyspeptical. Our recognition was franker on my part than on hers; only her eyes spoke of gladness; nay, she seemed to have a kind of fear of me, and in a little *special* conversation I had it all to myself. She inquired kindly for you, whom I described as one that she would like, *a hater of lies*, to begin with. Poor Julia Strachey! She is like a flower frozen among ice, and now contented with such soil : a hitherto unnoticed girl had rushed up to a woman, and in the long black locks I noticed a streak of grey. Fleeting time! Here too might I partly discern that *my* place was changed, though still (not ?) *empty*. A 'female friend,' skilled, it is said, in the Greek tragedians (*credat Apella*), was there, brim full of intolerant Church of Englandism—a little grey-eyed, ill-bred, fat button of a creature (very like a certain white sempstress in Ecclefechan) : with her in the course of the evening I was provoked for one moment, so pert was she, to run tilt, and I fear transfix her. Strachey was beginning a hoarse laugh, but suddenly checked himself, as a landlord should : and little Button went off to bed without good-night, but was blithe again next morning. That *such* should be the only friend of such! Let not us, dear Jeannie, com-

plain of solitude. I have still *you*, with really a priceless talent
for silence, as Mrs. S. too has. I say priceless, for this Button
wants it wholly, and thereby I felt would have driven me in three
days to blank despair.

The orator was at Leamington when I arrived. He only returned
Saturday night, has already been up here to see me, and left a
message that he would be at home all day. From all I can see,
Irving seems to have taken his part: is forgotten by the intellectual
classes, but still flourishes as a green bay-tree (or rather green
cabbage-tree) among the fanatical classes, whose ornament and
beacon he is. Strangely enough it is all fashioned among these
people: a certain everlasting *truth*, ever new truth, reveals itself
in them, but with a *body* of mere froth and soap-suds and other
the like ephemeral impurities. Yet I love the man, and can
trustfully take counsel of him. His wife I saw some nights ago—
leaner, clearer-complexioned, I should say clearer-hearted also, and
clearer-headed, but, alas! *very* straitlaced, and living in the *suds*
element.

I forced myself out this morning to go and breakfast with the
Advocate, and was there before anyone was up. Charlotte the
younger and the elder received me in their choicest mood. In
the midst of breakfast a side door opened, and the poor Duke looked
in in his night-gown (for they have made the back drawing-room
into a bed-room) to ask for me, and with the old quizzicality in
his little face declared, 'Why, Charley, I've got the cholera, I believe.' He called me afterwards into his bed-room to ask how I
was progressing, thought it likely that Murray would publish at
some time or other, spoke of John, asked for your health, and what
I had prescribed for you. Letters arriving, I got your frank and
withdrew, straitly charged to return. I am to take tea this evening at Badams's, where Godwin is promised.

Wednesday, August 17.

I left off on the eve of seeing Irving and taking tea with Godwin. The first object I accomplished. Irving, with his huge
fleece of now grizzled hair, was eager to talk with me and see me
often. I was with him last night, and being quite in his neighbourhood (within three minutes), shall take frequent opportunities
of seeing him. He is bent on our coming to London, of which I
myself can yet say nothing. Some vague schemes of settling within some miles of it (as at Enfield, where Badams is to live) are

hovering about me, which I will overhaul and see through. It will all depend on this, can I get work here and money for it to keep any sort of house ? which question is yet far from answered or answerable. However, I hope, and fear not.

Next came Godwin. Did you not grudge me that pleasure, now ? At least, mourn that you were not there with me ? Grudge not, mourn not, dearest Jeannie ; it was the most unutterable stupidity ever enacted on this earth. We went, Jack and I, to the huge Frenchwoman Mrs. Kenny's (once Mrs. Hólcroft), Badams's mother-in-law, a sort of more masculine *Aurelia* ('Wilhelm Meister '), who lives, moves, and has her being among plays, operas, dilet-tantes, and playwrights. Badams and his wife had not returned from the country, but in a few minutes came. Mrs. Godwin al-ready sate gossiping in the dusk—an old woman of no signifi-cance ; by-and-by dropped in various playwrightesses and play-wrights, whom I did not even look at; shortly before candles Godwin himself (who had been drinking *good* green tea by his own hearth before stirring out). He is a bald, bushy-browed, thick, hoary, hale little figure, taciturn enough, and speaking when he does speak with a certain *epigrammatic* spirit, wherein, except a little shrewdness, there is nothing but the most commonplace character. (I should have added that he wears spectacles, has full grey eyes, a very large blunt characterless nose, and ditto chin.) By degrees I hitched myself near him, and was beginning to open him and to open on him, for he had stared twice at me, when sud-denly enough began a speaking of French among the Kennys and Badamsinas (for they are all French-English), and presently Godwin was summoned off to—take a hand at whist ! *I* had al-ready flatly declined. There did the philosopher sit, and a swarm of noisy children, chattering women, noisy dilettantes round him ; and two women literally crashing hoarse thunder out of a piano (for it was louder than an iron forge) under pretext of its being music by Rossini. I thought of my own piano, and the far differ-ent fingering it got; looked sometimes not without sorrow at the long-nosed whist-player, and in the space of an hour (seeing sup-per about to be laid in another room) took myself away.

Next morning (Tuesday) I went to Bowring's. Figure to your-self a thin man about my height and bent at the *middle* into an angle of 150°, the *back* quite straight, with large grey eyes, a huge turn-up nose with straight nostrils to the very point, and large projecting close-shut mouth : figure such a one walking restlessly about the room (for he had been thrown out of a gig, and was in pain), frank of speech, vivid, emphatic, and *verständig*. Such is the Radical Doctor. We talked copiously, he utterly utilitarian and Radical, I utterly mystical and Radical; and parted about noon with a standing invitation on his part to come again, and promise to introduce me to the 'Examiner' editor (Fonblanque); and a certain trust on my part and disposition to cultivate further acquaintance. He named several booksellers whom I might apply to in case Murray baulked me, as I calculate he is but too like to do.

Wednesday morning I put on clean raiment (nothing but the white trowsers are wearable here for the heat, and I have still only two pairs), and drawing myself a chart on a slip of paper, started off to Albemarle Street according to bargain. The dog of a bookseller gone to the country. I leave my card with remonstrances and inquiries when? The clerk talks of 'Mr. Murray writing to you sir?' I will call again to-morrow morning and make Mr. M. speak to me, I hope. . . .

Thursday.—I went to the House of Commons last night and found at the door a Speaker's order awaiting me from the Duke. It is a pretty apartment that of theirs; far smaller than I expected,[1] hardly larger than some drawing-rooms you have seen, with some four ranges of benches rising high behind each other like pews in a church gallery, an oval open space in the middle, at the farther extremity of which sits the Speaker in what seemed a kind of press (like our wardrobe, only oaken); opposite him is the door. A very narrow gallery runs all round atop for reporters, strangers, &c. I was seated on the ground floor below this. Althorp spoke, a thick, large, broad-whiskered, farmer-looking man; Hume also, a powdered, clean, burly fellow; and Wetherell, a beetle-browed, sagacious, quizzical old gentleman; then Davies, a Roman-nosed dandy, whom I left *jannering*, having left it all in some three-quarters of an hour. O'Connell came and spoke to an individual before me. You would call him a well-doing country shopkeeper, with a bottle-green frock or great coat, and brown scratch wig. I quitted them with the highest contempt; our poor Duke, or any known face, I could not see.

This morning I returned to Albemarle Street; the bookseller was first denied to me, then showed his broad one-eyed face, and with fair speeches signified that his family were all ill, and he had

[1] The old house, before the fire.

been called into the country ; and my manuscript—lay still un-opened ! I reminded him not without emphasis of the engage-ment made, and how I had nothing else to do here but see that matter brought to an end, to all which he pleaded hard in extenu-ation, and for two or three days' further allowance. I made him *name* a new day : ' Saturday *first ;* ' then I am to return and learn how the matter stands. He is said to be noted for procrastination, but also for honourableness, even munificence. My prospects apart from him are not brilliant ; however, loss of time is the worst of all losses ; he shall not keep me dancing round him very long, go how it may. Of the Duke I would gladly take counsel ; but find no opportunity to speak—a visit profits almost nothing. Happily, however, I can take counsel of *myself*.

I am to dine with Drummond the banker to-morrow, an admirer of mine whom I have never seen. On Saturday with Allan Cun-ningham. These are my outlooks for the present.

August 22.

My dearest little Comforter,—Your dear kind letter arrived that Thursday night, though not till late—with the very latest of the ' Twopennies,' I think ; which invaluable class of men keep trav-elling here all day from eight in the morning till ten at night. My blessings on thee, little Goody, for the kind news thou send-est ! It is all a living picture, and the dear Screamikin artist standing in the middle of it, both acting it and drawing it for my sake. I saw your half-insane beer-barrel of a Fyffe,[1] and the midges all buzzing round him in the sultry morning ; the racket of the Macturk chaise, your rushing forth to the post-office, your eager devouring of my letter, and all the rest of it, in which, alas ! the headache and the two hours of sleep did not escape me. Com-pose thyself, my darling ; we *shall* not be separated, come of it what may. And how should we do, think'st thou, with an eternal separation ? O God, it is fearful ! fearful ! But is not a little temporary separation like this needful to manifest what *daily* mercy is in our lot which otherwise we might forget, or esteem as a thing of course ? Understand, however, once more that I have yet taken up with no other woman. Nay, many as I see—light air-forms tripping it in satin along the streets, or plumed amazons curbing their palfreys in the park with pomp and circumstance

---

[1] A Haddington doctor, one of Miss Welsh's many suitors before her mar-riage.

enough—there has no one yet fronted me whom even to look at I would exchange with my own. *Ach Gott!* there is not such a one extant. Yes, as proud as I am grown (for the more the Devil pecks at me, the more vehemently do I wring his nose), and standing on a kind of basis which I feel to be of adamant, I perceive that of all women my own Jeannie is the wife for me ; that in her true bosom (once she were a mystic) a man's head is worthy to lie. Be a mystic, dearest ; that is, stand with me on this everlasting basis, and keep thy arms around me : through life I fear nothing.

But I must proceed with my journal of life in London. My narrative must have finished on Thursday night about five o'clock. Jack and I went out to walk and make calls after that ; found no one at home but Mrs. Badams, who was nigh weeping when she spoke to us of her husband. Poor thing, she has a ticklish game to play ; for Badams seems to me to be hovering on the verge of ruin—uncertain as yet whether he will turn back, or only plunge down, down. I tell all this in one word : he is in the habit of daily drinking brandy till his head gets confused. He began this accursed practice not many months ago for the sake of an intolerable headache he had, and which brandy (then nauseous enough to him) was wont to cure ; but now I suspect the nauseousness has ceased, and the brandy is chiefly coveted because it yields stupefaction. His volition seems gone, or quite dormant ; his *gig* has broken down with him all to shivers, at full speed.[1]

With the Montagus I have somewhat less sympathy. It seems still uncertain whether they will lose anything by him,[2] and their ferocity (except from Basil) is quite transcendental. On the whole my original impression of that 'noble lady' was the true one. * * * * * * * * * * * She goes upon words—words. I called once more and left my card, and shall continue at rare intervals to do the like ; but for trust or friendship it is now more clearly than ever a chimæra. I smiled (better than the Duke did) at her offer of 'giving you money' to come hither. *Jane Welsh Carlyle* a taker of money in this era of the gigmen ! *Nimmer und nimmermehr.* *

Tush ! it is all stuff and fudge and fiddle-faddle, of which I begin to grow aweary. Oh no, my dearest ; we will have no meet-

---

[1] Badams—once one of Carlyle's truest and most useful friends—died miserably soon after.

[2] Badams had led them into some speculation which had not been successful.

ings that we cannot purchase for ourselves. We shall meet; nay, perhaps, ere long thou shalt see London and thy husband in it, on earnings of our own. From all which the practical inference is, 'let us endeavour to clear our minds of cant.'

Friday I spent with Irving in the *animali parlanti* region of the *supernatural.* Understand, ladykin, that the 'gift of tongues' is here also (chiefly among the women), and a positive belief that God is still working miracles in the Church—by hysterics. Nay, guess my astonishment when I learned that poor Dow of Irongray[1] is a wonder-worker and speaker with tongues, and had actually 'cast out a devil' (which however returned again in a week) between you and Dumfries! I gave my widest stare; but it is quite indubitable. His autograph letter was read to me, detailing all that the '*Laart*' had done for him. Poor fellow! it was four days after his wife's death. I was very wae for him, and not a little shocked. Irving hauled me off to Lincoln's Inn Fields to hear my double (Mr. Scott), where I sate directly behind a speakeress with tongues, who unhappily, however, did not perform till after I was gone. My double is more like 'Maitland,' the cotton-eared, I hope, than me; a thin, black-complexioned, vehement man, earnest, clear, and narrow as a tailor's listing. For a stricken hour did he sit expounding in the most superannuated dialect (of *Chroist* and so forth), yet with great heartiness the meaning of that one word *Entsagen.* The good Irving looked at me wistfully, for he knows I cannot take miracles in; yet he looks so piteously, as if he implored me to believe. Oh dear! oh dear! was the Devil ever busier than now, when the supernatural must either depart from the world, or reappear there like a chapter of Hamilton's 'Diseases of Females'?

At night I fondly trusted that we had done with the miraculous; but no, Henry Drummond too is a believer in it. This Drummond, who inhabits a splendid mansion in the west, proved to be a very striking man. Taller and leaner than I, but erect as a plummet, with a high-carried, quick, penetrating head, some five-and-forty years of age, a singular mixture of all things—of the saint, the wit, the philosopher—swimming, if I mistake not, in an element of dandyism. His dinner was dandiacal in the extreme: a meagre series of pretentious kickshaws, on which no hungry jaw could satisfactorily bite, flunkies on all hands, yet I had to ask four times before I could get a morsel of bread. His wife has had

[1] A Craigenputtock neighbour.

'twenty miscarriages,' and looks pitiful enough. Besides her we were five : Spencer Percival, Member of the House (of Stupids, called of Commons) ; Tudor, a Welshman, editor of the 'Morning Watch ;' our host, Irving, and I. They were all prophetical, Toryish, ultra-religious. I emitted, notwithstanding, floods of Teufelsdröckhist Radicalism, which seemed to fill them with *ween-der* and amazement, but was not ill received, and indeed refused to be gainsayed. We parted with friendliest indifference, and shall all be happy to meet again, and to part again. This Drummond, who is a great pamphleteer, has 'quoted' me often, it seems, &c. He is also a most munificent and beneficent man—as his friends say.

On Saturday morning I set out for Albemarle Street. Murray, as usual, was not in ; but an answer lay for me—my poor 'Teufels-dröckh,' wrapped in new paper, with a letter stuck under the packthread. I took it with a silent fury and walked off. The letter said he regretted exceedingly, &c. ; all his literary friends were out of town ; he himself occupied with a sick family in the country ; that he had conceived the finest hopes, &c. In short, that 'Teufelsdröckh' had never been looked into ; but that if I would let him keep it for a month, he would *then* be able to say a word, and by God's blessing a favourable one.

I walked on through Regent Street and looked in upon James Fraser, the bookseller. We got to talk about 'Teufelsdröckh,' when, after much hithering and thithering about the black state of trade, &c., it turned out that honest James would publish the book for me on this principle : if I would give *him* a sum not exceeding 150*l.* sterling ! 'I think you had better wait a little,' said an Edinburgh advocate to me since, when he heard of this proposal. 'Yes,' I answered, 'it is my purpose to wait to the end of eternity for it.' 'But the public will not buy books.' 'The public has done the wisest thing it could, and ought never more to buy what they call books.'

Spurning at destiny, yet in the mildest terms taking leave of Fraser, I strode through the streets carrying Teufelsdröckh openly in my hand. I took a pipe and a glass of water, and counsel with myself. I was bilious and sad, and thought of my dear Jeannie, for whom also were these struggles. Having rested a little, I set out again to the Longmans, to hear what they had to say. The German Literary History having soon been despatched, I describe Teufelsdröckh, bargain that they are to look at it themselves, and send it back again in two days : that is to-morrow. They are honest, rugged, punctual-looking people, and will keep their word, but the chance of declining seems to me a hundred to one. *A la bonne heure!* I have a problem which *is* possible : either to get Dreck printed, or to ascertain that I *cannot,* and so tie him up and come home with him. So fear nothing, love. I care not a doit for the worst ; and thou too hast the heart of a heroine—art worthy of me were I the highest of heroes. Nay, my persuasion that Teu- felsdröckh is in his place and his time here, grows stronger the more I see of London and its philosophy. The doctrine of the Phœnix, of Natural Supernaturalism, and the whole Clothes Phi- losophy (be it but well stated) is exactly what all intelligent men are wanting.

Sunday morning had a snip of a note from Empson. Walked over to Jermyn Street ; saw the Duke ; had to tell him openly (or not at all) how it stood with my manuscript ; felt clear and sharp as a war weapon, for the world was not brotherly to me. The Charlottes were at church. I consulted the Duke about Napier ; found my own idea confirmed that he was anxious enough to have me write, but afraid lest I committed him ; so that 'agreeing about subjects' would be the difficulty. Jeffrey asked to see my MS. when the Longmans had done with it : he would look through it and see what he could *talk* to Murray concerning it. I gladly con- sented ; and thus for a while the matter rests. Murray is clearly the man if he will ; only I have lost ten days by him already, for he might have told me what he did finally tell in one day.

Carlyle, little sanguine as he was, had a right to be sur- prised at the difficulty of finding a publisher for his book. Seven years before he had received a hundred pounds for his 'Life of Schiller.' It had been successful in England. It had been translated into German under the eye of Goethe himself. 'Sartor' Carlyle reckoned to be at least three times as good, and no one seemed inclined to look at it.

Meanwhile, on another side of his affairs the prospect unexpectedly brightened. His brother had been the heav- iest of his anxieties. A great lady, 'the Countess of Clare,' was going abroad and required a travelling physician. Jeff- rey heard of it, and with more real practical kindness than Carlyle in his impatience had been inclined to credit him with, successfully recommended John Carlyle to her. The arrangements were swiftly concluded. The struggling, penniless John was lifted at once into a situation of responsibility and security, with a salary which placed him far beyond need of further help, and promised to enable him to repay at no distant time both his debt to Jeffrey, and all the money which Carlyle had laid out for him. Here was more than compensation for the other disappointments. Not only Carlyle had no longer to feel that he must divide his poor earnings to provide for his brother's wants in London, but he could look without anxiety on his own situation. He even thought himself permitted, instead of returning to Craigenputtock, to propose that Mrs. Carlyle should join him in London without the help of Mrs. Montagu. He was making friends; he was being talked about as a new phenomenon of a consequence as yet unknown. Review and magazine editors were recovering heart, and again seeking his assistance. He could write his articles as well in a London lodging as in the snowy solitudes of Dunscore, while he could look about him and weigh at more leisure the possibilities of finally removing thither. He wrote to propose it, and awaited his wife's decision. Meanwhile his letters continue his story.

To Mrs. Carlyle, Scotsbrig.

London: August 26, 1831.

My dear Mother,—As Jack proposes writing to my father, doubtless he will mention the good tidings he has to tell, namely, of an appointment to be travelling physician to a lady of great rank, the Countess of Clare, with a salary of 300 guineas a year, all travelling expenses included. This is the work of the Lord Advocate, Jeffrey, and is looked on by everyone as a piece of real good fortune. For yourself, my dear mother, I know how you dislike foreign voyaging, and that all your maternal fears will be awakened by this arrangement. However, you too will reflect that anything in honesty is better than forced *idleness*, which was poor

Doil's [1] condition here; also you may take my word for it that the dangers of such a course of travel are altogether trifling—not equal to those of walking the London streets, and running, every time you cross, lest coaches break a limb of you. The lady herself is an invalid, and must journey with every convenience. Italy, whither they are bound, is the finest of climates; and the sailing part of it is simply of three hours' continuance—in whole, *twenty-five miles.* I have seen some people who know the Countess, and all give her a good character. She is young (perhaps thirty-three), courteous, and has behaved in this transaction with great liberality. Jack also is much more prudent and manly in his ways than he was; so that I think there is a fair prospect of his even doing the poor lady some good, and getting into a friendly relation to her, which also may eventually do himself much good. Something mysterious there is in the condition of this high personage. She was married some years ago, and shortly after that event she parted from her husband (they say by her own determination), the nearest friends know not for what reason; and now she lives in a sort of widowhood (her husband is Governor of Bombay, and said to be 'a very good sort of man'), so that being farther in ill-health she is probably unhappy enough, and has need of good counsel every way.

The business of the book proceeds but crabbedly. The whole English world I find has ceased to read books, which, as I often say to the booksellers, is the wisest thing the English world could do, considering what wretched froth it has been dosed with for many years, under the false title of 'books.' Every mind is engrossed with political questions, and in a more earnest mood than to put up with such stuff as has been called literature. Meanwhile, though I cannot but rejoice in this state of public opinion, yet the consequences to myself are far from favourable. The present, too, I find, is the deadest part of the whole year for business, so that every way the matter moves heavily, and I require to have my own shoulder at it always or it would not move at all. Hitherto I have made no approximation to a bargain, except finding that man after man will not *act*, and only at best demands 'time for consideration,' which, except in very limited measure, I cannot afford to give him. The MS. is at present in Jeffrey's hands, whence I expect to receive it in some two days with a favourable, or at worst an unfavourable judgment—in either of which

---

[1] Family nickname of John Carlyle.

cases I shall find out what to do. Little money, I think, will be had for my work, but I will have it printed if there be a man in London that will do it, even without payment to myself. If there be no such man, why then what is to be done but tie a piece of good *skeenyie* about my papers, stick the whole in my pocket, and march home again with it, where at least potatoes and onions are to be had, and I can wait till better times. Nay, in any case I find that either in possession or pretty certain expectation, I am otherwise worth almost 100*l.* of cash; so that while the whinstone house stands on the moor, what care I for one of them, or for all of them with the arch-Enemy at their head?

Of any permanent settlement here there is as yet nothing definite to be said. I see many persons here, some of them kind and influential, almost all of them ignorant enough, and in need of a teacher; but no offer that can be laid hold of presents itself or fixedly promises itself. This also I will see through. If God who made me and keeps me alive have work for me here, then here must I pitch my tent; if not, then elsewhere, still under his kind sky, under his all-seeing eye, to me alike where. I am rather resolute sometimes, not without a touch of grimness, but never timid or discouraged; indeed, generally quite quiet and cheerful. If I see no way of getting home soon, I have some thoughts of bringing Jane up hither, for she must be very lonely where she is. We shall see.

Thus, my dear mother, does it stand with us. I write you all this to satisfy your anxieties. Be of good cheer; trust for us, as for all things, in the Giver of good, who will order *all* things *well.* Assure my father of my entire love; and say that I hope to tell him many things when I return.

My kindest love to all, not forgetting Jean or any of the girls. God keep you and all of them. That is ever my heart's prayer. Many times, too, does *she* that is not now with us [1] revisit my thoughts: inexpressibly sad, inexpressibly mild; but I mourn not. I rather rejoice that *she* is now safe in the land of eternity, not in the troublous, ever-shifting land of time and of dreams. Oh, often I think that she is *with* me in my heart whispering to me to bear and forbear even as she did, to endure to the end, and then we shall meet *again* and part no more. Even as God will be it!

I conclude mournfully but not unhappily. Shall not the Great Father wipe away the tears from all eyes? Again and again I

[1] His sister Margaret.

say, let us trust in Him and Him only. Let us ever live in hope, in faith! God bless you all!

I am, dear mother, your affectionate son,

T. CARLYLE.

To Mrs. Carlyle, Craigenputtock.

August 29.

Dearest Wife,—This is Monday, and I have already, taking no counsel with flesh and blood, discharged two little duties: first gone and seen Empson (whom I had heretofore missed) *before* breakfast; second, arranged my washerwoman's goods, and made an invoice thereof that she may call for them, which duty it were my dear Goody's part to do were I not for a time Goodyless; so that now at noontide I can sit down with a clear conscience, and talk heartily and heartsomely with my own child about all things and about nothing, as is my wont and my delight. Thus in this spectre crowded desert I have a living person whose heart I can clasp to mine, and so feel that I too am alive. Do you not love me better than ever now? I feel in my own soul that thou dost and must. Therefore let us never mourn over this little separation which is but to make the reunion more blessed and entire.

Your two letters are here in due season, like angels (angel means heavenly *messenger*) from a far country. The first, as I prophesied, lay waiting for me at my return; the second I found lying on the Duke's table on Saturday, and snatched it up and read it in the hubbub of Piccadilly so soon as I could tear myself out into the solitude of crowds. Bless thee, my darling! I could almost wish thee the pain of a ride to Dumfries weekly for the sake of such a letter. But *had* you actually to faint all the way up? Heaven forbid! And the 'disease' on that fair face—how is it? If no better, never mind; I swear that it shall and will get better, or if it do not, that I will love you more than ever while it lasts. Will that make amends? It is no vain parade of rhetoric; it is a serious *fact:* my love for you does not depend on looks, and defies old age and decay, and, I can prophesy, will grow stronger the longer we live and toil together. Yes, Jeannie, though I have brought you into rough, rugged conditions, I feel that I have saved you: as Gigmaness you could not have lived; as woman and wife you need but to see your duties in order to do them, and to say from the heart, It is good for me to be here. So keep thy arms round me, and be my own prophetess and second self, and fear nothing, let the Devil do his worst. Poor Elizabeth![1] I fear, as you fear, that it is not well with her. Nevertheless, who knows the issues of life and death? Let us hope the best. Above all, do not you be a coward. I love you for your *bravery*, and because you have the heart of a valiant woman. Oh, my darling, is it conceivable that we should live divided in this unfriendly scene? Crown me with all laurels that ever decorated man's brow: were it other than the bitterest of mockeries if *she* who had struggled with me were not there to share it?

But I must check this lyrical tendency. Of history there is little to be told. Slowly, slowly does the business of poor Dreck get along, let me push it as I may. Heaven bless my own prophetess, who has from the first prophesied only good of it. Yes, good will come of it; for it was honestly meant, and the best we could do. Meanwhile do but mark how sluggishly it loiters.

Yesterday I returned (to Jermyn Street), found the family coach at the door, and all in the act of drawing on gloves to go out, except the Duke, with whom, after some gabblement with the others, I had the unwonted satisfaction of a private conversation—for ten minutes. Inquiring for Teufelsdröckh, as I was privileged to do, the critic professed that he had 'honestly read' twenty-eight pages of it (surprising feat); that he objected to the dilatoriness of the introductory part (as *we* both did also), and very much admired the scene of the sleeping city; further, that he would write to Murray that very day,[2] as I gather from Empson he has since done, to appoint a meeting with him, and if possible attain some finish with that individual at least. He (Jeffrey) would look through the book further in the interim, &c. &c.

Patience, patience! Hard times I said, dearest, for literary men. Nevertheless, let us take them as they come. Nay, Allan Cunningham advises me that it were almost 'madness' to press forward a literary work at this so inauspicious season and not to wait for a while—which, nevertheless, I cannot listen to. Why wait? *Rusticus expectat;* besides, Dreck must be *printed* as the first condition. Whether we get any money for him, or how much, is a quite secondary question. I have nothing for it but to *try*— try to the uttermost—and in the villanous interval of expectation to explore this wild, immeasurable chaos, and ascertain whether I can build aught in it. Such remains my outlook hitherto. Jeff-

---

[1] I do not know to whom this refers.
[2] Longman, after looking through the MS., had civilly declined it.

rey and I also spoke about the 'place under Government.' *Davon wird Nichts,* 'All filled up;' 'Applicants;' 'Economical Ministry,' &c. &c.—all which the Devil is welcome to, if he like. *Aide-toi, le ciel t'aidera.* I think of these things with considerable composure, at times with a certain silent ferocity. 'That *my* wife should walk on foot!' Yet, is she not my wife, and shall I not love her the more that she shares evil with me as if it were good? Let us fear nothing. I have the strength of 20,000 Cockneys while thou art with me. Let hard come to hard as it will; we will study to be ready for it. . . .

Of all the deplorables and despicables of this city and time the saddest are the 'literary men.' *Infandum! Infandum!* It makes my heart sick and wae. Except Churchill, and perhaps chiefly because he liked *me*, I have hardly found a man of common sense or common honesty. They are the Devil's own vermin, whom the Devil in his good time will snare and successively eat. The creature —— called again; the most insignificant *haddock* in nature— a dirty, greasy cockney apprentice, altogether empty, and nonextant except for one or two metaphysical quibbles (about every law*r* of nature being an idea*r* of the mind, &c.), and the completest outfit of innocent blank self-conceit I ever in life chanced to witness. He is a blown bladder, wherein no substance is to be sought. And yet a curious figure, intrinsically *small*, small; yet with a *touch* of geniality which far apart from Coleridge and cockneyism might have made him a small *reality*. God be with him! He was almost as wearisome as ——, and *very much detached*, as it struck me; knew nothing of men or things more than a sucking dove, at the same time looked out with an occasional gleam of geniality in his eyes; seemed even to like me, though I had barbarously enough entreated him.

The more comfortable was it to meet Empson this morning, in whom I at least found *sanity*, and what I have all along had to dispense with, the bearing of at least a *gentleman*. I am glad I went to Empson—went through two miles of tumultuous streets; found Empson in the solitude of the Temple, reading a newspaper in a flannel nightgown (which reminded me of Goody's, for it had a *belt*, only it was twice as large); a tall, broad, thin man, with wrinkled face, baldish head, and large mild melancholy dreamy blue eyes under bushy brows. He has a defect in his *trachea*, and can only mumble in speech, which he does with great copiousness in a very kindly style, confused enough, at the same time listening with the profoundest attention and toleration to whatever you offer in reply. He is, as I thought, on the threshold of mysticism, but I think will go deeper. Probably enough one might grow to like such a man; at all events I will try, and so I think will you; with your mother (were she more cultivated, or he more ignorant) he were the man according to God's heart. Of young Mill (the Spirit of the Age man) he speaks very highly, as of a converted Utilitarian who is studying German; so we are all to meet, along with a certain Mrs. Austin, a young Germanist and mutual intercessor (between Mill and Empson), and breakfast some day in the Templar's lodgings. *Quod felix faustumque sit!* It does my soul good to meet a true soul. Poor inexperienced Glen is the only phenomenon of that sort I have yet seen here, but I will riddle creation till I find more. Thus before your arrival (if such be our decision) I may perhaps have a little pleasant circle to present you to, for of the *old* there is very *little* to be made; Irving alone stands true, and he (poor fellow!) is working miracles, while the Montagus, Stracheys, &c., have mostly, I fear, drifted quite to leeward.

About your journey to London I myself know not what to say. The persuasion grows more and more upon me that we should *spend the winter* here. Say, Goody, would it not be pleasant to THEE? Tell me distinctly; and yet I already know it would, but that (as beseems a good wife) you subordinate your wishes to the common good, and will not even speak of them. Well, but here in this lodging we live actually (Jack and I) for some two guineas a week; or suppose in the winter season, and with many little gracefulnesses which Goody would superadd, it cost *us* two—three guineas: what then? It is little more than we used to spend in Edinburgh including rent; and we can thoroughly investigate London. I cannot promise you the comforts of our own poor Craig; yet it is a handsome lodging, and with purely honest people. Our drawing-room (for such it is) will be of the coldest, I doubt; but coals are not so very dear, and the female mind can devise thicker clothes. How then? shall it be decided on? We have to go somewhither: why not come *hither*, where my part of the going is already finished? Thyself shalt say it. Use thy prophetic gift. If it answer yes, then will I strive to obey.

To the Same.

September 4.

Thursday was the wettest of wet days, even till after bedtime;

the first day wherein I did not once stir out (except after dark to Irving's, who was not at home). Highgate and Coleridge were not to be thought of. After reading Goody's letter, I sate diligently over my proof-sheets—the day unvisited by any adventure except a little message from Mrs. Austin.

On Friday Jack and I walked over to the House of Lords; saw the Chancellor sitting between two Lords (two are necessary : one of them Earl Ferrers, son of him that was hanged, and the ugliest man extant, very like David Laing), a considerable handful of listeners and loiterers, and the poor little darling (Jeffrey) with a grey wig on it, and queer coatie with bugles or buttons on the cuffs, snapping away and speaking there in a foreign country among entire strangers. The fat Rutherford sate also within the ring, with Dr. Lushington (the divorcer) and certain of the clerk species. I declare I was partly touched with something of human feeling. However, our little darling seemed as gleg as ever; the '*trachea*' in moderate order; and was telling his story like a little king of elves. The Chancellor is a very particularly ignoble-looking man; a face not unlike your uncle Robert's, but stonier, and with a deeper, more restless, more dangerous eye ; *nothing* but business in his face—no ray of genius, and even a considerable tincture of insincerity. He was yawning awfully, with an occasional twitching up of the corners of the upper lip and point of the nose. A politician truly and *nothing* more. Learning that the Duke's speech would not end for two hours, I willingly took myself away.

After dinner came your letter, which I read twice; then had tea (black tea of my own) ; then off to the Austins, where I knew there would be green tea, which I had privately determined not to have. The Frau Austin herself was as loving as ever—a true Germanised spiritual *screamikin*. We were five of a party : her husband, a lean grey-headed painful-looking man, with large earnest timid eyes and a clanging metallic voice, that at great length set forth Utilitarianism *steeped* in German metaphysics, not dissolved therein ; a very worthy sort of limited man and professor of law. Secondly, a Frenchman, of no importance whatever, for he uttered not a word except some compliments in his own tongue. Thirdly, John Mill, 'Spirit-of-the-Age.' The other two you know already. This young Mill, I fancy and hope, is 'a *baying* you can love.' A slender, rather tall and elegant youth, with small clear Roman-nosed face, two small earnestly-smiling eyes ; modest, remarkably gifted with precision of utterance, enthusiastic, yet lucid, calm ; not a great, yet distinctly a gifted and amiable youth. We had almost four hours of the best talk I have mingled in for long. The youth walked home with me almost to the door; seemed to profess, almost as plainly as modesty would allow, that he had been converted by the head of the Mystic School, to whom personally he testified very hearty-looking regard. Empson did not appear (having caught cold, or something of that sort), but by letter (while we were together) engaged Mill and me to breakfast with him on Tuesday. I met poor Empson to-day riding towards Holborn, the large melancholy eyes of the man turned downwards, so that he did not observe me. On the whole, Goodykin, these rudiments of a mystic school (better than I anticipated here) are by far the most cheering phenomenon I see in London. Good will come of it. Let us wait and see in what way.

At the Duke's this morning, where I found Rutherford and Jayme Relish, the Galloway stot, who stared at me as if minded to gore, or afraid of being gored, till I bowed. I was led by his lordship into a private room, and there indulged with ten minutes' private talk on the subject of ' Teufelsdröckh.' The short of it is this : Murray will print a short edition (750 copies) of Dreck on the half-profits system (that is, I getting *nothing*, but also giving nothing) ; after which the sole copyright of the book is to be mine ; which offer he makes, partly out of love to ' your lordship ; ' chiefly from ' my great opinion of the originality,' &c. A poorish offer, Goody, yet perhaps after all the best I shall get. Better considerably than *my* giving 150*l.* for the frolic of having written such a work ! I mean to set off to-morrow morning to Colburn and Bentley (whom Fraser has prepared for me), and ascertain whether they will pay me *anything* for a first edition. Unless they say about 100*l.* I will prefer Murray. Murray *wished* me to try everywhere. You shall hear to-morrow how I speed, and then prophesy upon it.

I have this day written off to Napier to say that I have an article on *Luther* ready to write, and ask whether he will have it. Fifty pounds will be highly useful (thank God, not yet quite indispensable), and I can gain it handsomely in this way. These, dearest, are all my news. It is all very wooden, and would be dull to anyone but her it is written for. She will not think it dull, but interesting as the Epistle of a Paul to the church which is at Craig o' Putto.

Monday, 4 *o'clock.*—I was at Colburn's about eleven. After waiting a weary hour in the Bentleian apartments saw a muddy character enter, to whom I explained myself and Dreck.[1] The muddy man uttered the common cant of compliments, hinted at the sole object of publishers being money, the difference between talent and popularity, &c. &c. The purport will be that we shall have nothing to do with one another. So much I could gather partly from the muddy man. I shall go over and see Murray to-morrow morning, and if he will put his hand to the plough and get on with the printing forthwith, I mean to close with him and have done. The offer is not so bad : 750 copies for the task of publishing poor Dreck, and the rest of him *our own*. If he do not succeed, how could I ask any man to do more? If he do, then we have opening for another bargain. Let us hope nothing, Goody ; then we fear nothing. By one or the other means our poor little pot *will* keep boiling, and shall, though the Devil himself said nay.

Anticipating slightly, I may finish here the adventures of 'Sartor' or Dreck, and for the present have done with it. Murray at Jeffrey's instance had agreed to take the book on the terms which Carlyle mentioned—not, however, particularly willingly. Jeffrey himself, who had good practical knowledge of such things, thought that it 'was too much of the nature of a rhapsody to command success or respectful attention.' Murray perhaps rather wished to attach to himself a young man of unquestionable genius, whose works might be profitable hereafter, than expected much from this immediate enterprise. He decided to run the risk, however. The MS. was sent to the printer, and a page was set in type for consideration, when poor Murray, already repenting of what he had done, heard that while he was hesitating 'Sartor' had been offered to Longman, and had been declined by him. He snatched at the escape, and tried to end his bargain. He professed to think, and perhaps he really thought, that he had been treated unfairly. The correspondence that ensued must have made Murray more and more wonder what strange

[1] Neither Colburn nor Bentley in person, as appeared after.

being he was in contact with, and may be preserved as a curiosity.

To Thomas Carlyle, Esq.

Ramsgate : September 17.

Dear Sir,—Your conversation with me respecting the publication of your MS. led me to infer that you had given me the preference, and certainly not that you had already submitted it to the greatest publishers in London, who had declined to engage in it. Under these circumstances it will be necessary for me also to get it read by some literary friend before I can in justice to myself engage in the printing of it.

I am, dear Sir,

Your faithful servant,

JOHN MURRAY.

The apparent reflection on a want of sincerity in Carlyle was not altogether generous on Murray's part, but perhaps only too natural.

Carlyle answers :—

To John Murray, Esq.

Sir,—I am this moment favoured with your note of the 17th from Ramsgate, and beg to say in reply—

First, that your idea derived from conversation with me of my giving you the preference to all other publishers was perfectly correct : I had heard you described as a man of honour, frankness, and even generosity, and knew you to have the best and widest connections; on which grounds I might well say and can still well say that a transaction with you would please me better than a similar one with any other member of the trade.

Secondly, that your information of my having submitted my manuscript to the greatest publishers in London, if you mean thereby that after it first came out of your hands it lay two days in those of Messrs. Longman and Rees, and was from them delivered over to the Lord Advocate, is also perfectly correct. If you mean anything else, incorrect.

Thirdly, that if you wish the bargain which I had understood myself to have made with you unmade, you have only to cause your printer who is now working on my manuscript to return the same without danger or delay, and consider the business as finished.

To Thomas Carlyle.

Albemarle Street : Wednesday.

My dear Sir,—Had I been informed that during the interval in which I had returned the MS. to you it had been offered to Messrs. Longman and sent back after remaining with them two days, I certainly should have requested permission to have had it left to me for perusal before I determined upon its publication, and I only wish to be placed in the same position as I should have been had I been previously informed of that fact.

I am, my dear Sir,

Your obliged servant,

JOHN MURRAY.

Rough Draft of Reply.

Sir,—Though I cannot well discover what damage or alteration my MS. has sustained by passing through the hands of Messrs. Longman and Rees, I with great readiness enter into your views, and shall cheerfully release you from all engagement or shadow of engagement with me in regard to it, the rather as it seems reasonable for me to expect some higher remuneration for a work that has caused me so much effort, were it once fairly examined. Such remuneration as was talked of between *us* can, I believe, at all times be procured.

Perhaps you could now fix some date at which I might look for your decision on a quite new negotiation, if you incline to engage in such. I shall then see whether the limited extent of my time will still allow me to wait yours.

If not, pray have the goodness to cause my papers to be returned with the least possible delay.

The result was the letter from the ' bookseller,' enclosing the critical communication from his literary adviser, which Carlyle with pardonable malice attached as an Appendix to ' Sartor ' when it was ultimately published, and which has been thus preserved as a singular evidence of critical fallibility. But neither is Murray to be blamed in the matter nor his critic. Their business was to ascertain whether the book, if published, would pay for the printing ; and it was quite certain, both that the taste which could appreciate Carlyle did not exist till he himself created it, and that to 'Sartor,' beautiful and brilliant as it now seems, the world would then have remained blind. Carlyle himself, proud, scornful, knowing if no one else knew the value of the estimate 'of the gentleman in the highest class of men of letters' who had been consulted in the matter, judged Murray after his fashion far too harshly. In a letter to his wife he says:—

The printing of 'Teufelsdröckh,' which I announced as commencing, and even sent you a specimen of, has altogether stopped, and Murray's bargain with me has burst into air. The man behaved like a pig, and was speared, not perhaps without art; Jack and I at least laughed that night *à gorge déployée* at the answer I wrote his base *glare* of a letter : he has written again in much politer style, and I shall answer him, as McLeod advised my grandfather's people, 'sharp but mannerly.' The truth of the matter is now clear enough ; Dreck cannot be disposed of in London at this time. Whether he lie in my trunk or in a bookseller's coffer seems partly indifferent. Neither, on the whole, do I know whether it is not better that we have stopped for the present. Money I was to have none; author's vanity embarked on that bottom I have almost none ; nay, some time or other that the book can be *so* disposed of it is certain enough.

Carlyle was not alone in his contempt for the existing literary taste. Macvey Napier, to whom he had expressed an opinion that the public had been for some time ' fed with froth,' and was getting tired of it, agreed that ' he saw no indication in that vast body of any appetite for solid aliments.' Nay, he added (and the words deserve to be remarked), ' I am thoroughly convinced that were another Gibbon to appear and produce another such work as the " Decline and Fall," the half of an impression of 750 copies would be left to load the shelves of its publisher.'

The article on Luther which Carlyle had offered for the ' Edinburgh ' could not get itself accepted. Napier recognised that Luther was a noble subject, but he could not spare space for the effective treatment of it. He recommended instead a review of Thomas Hope's book on Man; and Carlyle, accepting the change, made Hope the text for the paper which he called 'Characteristics.' This essay, more profound and far-reaching even than 'Sartor,' was written in these autumn weeks in London.

CHAPTER IX.

A.D. 1831. ÆT. 36.

Mrs. Carlyle had entered eagerly into the scheme for joining her husband in London. Six weeks' solitude at Craigenputtock, with strangers now in occupation of the farm, had tried even her fortitude beyond her strength, and Alick and Jean Carlyle had gone from Scotsbrig to take care of her.

To Mrs. Carlyle, Scotsbrig.

Craigenputtock : September, 1831.

A thousand thanks, my dear kind mother, for sending Jean and Alick to my rescue. If some such mercy had not been vouchsafed me I think I must soon have worked myself into a fever or other violent disorder ; for my talent for fancying things, which is quite as great as your own, had so entirely got the upper hand of me that I could neither sleep by night nor rest by day. I have slept more, since they came and have kept me from falling into dreams, than I had done for a fortnight before.

I have news, if you have not heard it already, more joyful to me, I suspect, than to you : I am going to my husband, and as soon as I can get ready for leaving. Now do not grieve that he is not to return so soon as we expected. I am sure it is for his good, and, therefore, for all our goods. Here he was getting more and more unhappy, more and more dissatisfied with the world and himself. I *durst* not have counselled him to such a step ; but whenever he proposed it himself, I cordially approved. But I will tell you all about this and other matters when I come and see you all again before I set out.

Carlyle wants me to bring some butter, oatmeal, &c., which are not to be got good in London for love or money, and without the smallest remorse I apply to you to help me. I *have* some butter of our own cows; but as it has been salted in small quantities, sometimes in warm weather and by my own hands, which are not the most expert, I am afraid it will not be good enough; at all rates, inferior to the Scotsbrig thing.

Jean is going with me to Templand to-day, as a sort of protection against my mother's agitations. Next week she will help me to pack.

Your affectionate
JANE W. CARLYLE.

Carlyle, meanwhile, continued his account of himself in his letters. Napier had not then written conclusively about his article, and he was restless.

To Mrs. Carlyle, Craigenputtock.

London: September 11.

My days flow rather uselessly along. If Naso do not write soon I will seek some other task, were it the meanest. No one can force you to be idle, but only yourself. Neither is the world *shut* against anyone; but it is HE that is shut. God grant us some little touch of wisdom; let Fate turn up what card she likes, so we can play it well. I feel as if I had yet much to suffer, but also something to do. Do thou help me, my little woman; thou art worthy of that destiny, and perhaps it is appointed thee. These are fearful times, yet is there greatness in them. Now is the hour when he that feels himself a man should stand forth and prove himself such. Oh, could I but live in the light of that holy purpose and keep it ever present before me, I were happy—too happy!

Meanwhile, unfortunately for these many months, and now as formerly, I am rather wicked. Alas! Why should I dwell in the element of contempt and indignation, not rather in that of patience and love? I was reading in Luther's 'Tischreden,' and absolutely felt ashamed. What have I suffered? What did he suffer? One should actually, as Irving advises, 'pray to the Lord,' did one but know how to do it. The *best* worship, however, is stout working. *Frisch zu!*

I have not seen the Duke for a week. I acknowledge in myself a certain despicable tendency to think crabbedly of the poor Duke: a quite vulgar feeling it is. Merely as if he were not kind enough to *me*. Is he not kinder than most other men are? Shame on me! Out of various motives, among which love is not wholly wanting, he really wishes to do me good. Are not all others of his order indifferent to me? Should not he be at all times *more* and not *less?* Yet his path is not my path, nor are his thoughts my thoughts. It is more and more clear to me that we shall never do any good together. Let him come and sit with you in that 'flowerpot tub,' if he like; let us do him what kindness we can, which is not much, and stand ever with kind looks in that direction, yet always, too, on our side of the Strand. Frivolous gigmanity *cannot* unite itself to our stern destiny; let it pass by on the other side. But oh, my dear Jeannie, do help me to be a little softer, to be a little merciful to *all* men, even gigmen. Why should a man, though bilious, never so 'nervous,' impoverished, bugbitten, and bedevilled, let Satan have dominion over him? Save me, save me, my Goody! It is on this side that I am threatened; nevertheless we *will* prevail, I tell thee : by God's grace we will and shall.

September 14.

On Monday night I walked round from putting in your letter and borrowed me the last 'Quarterly Review,' to read the article there on the Saint Simonians, by Southey; it is an altogether miserable article, written in the spirit not of a philosopher but of a parish precentor. He knows what they are *not,* so far at least as the Thirty-nine Articles go; but nothing whatsoever of what they *are.* 'My brother, I say unto thee, thou art a poor creature.' The rest of the 'Review' is also despicable enough—blind, shovel-hatted, hysterically lachrymose. Lockhart, it seems, edits it out of Roxburghshire, rusticating by some 'burn' in that country. Tuesday night John Mill came in and sate talking with me till near eleven—a fine clear enthusiast, who will one day come to something; yet to nothing poetical, I think : his fancy is not rich; furthermore, he cannot *laugh* with any compass. You will like Mill. Glen[1] is a man of greatly more natural material; but hitherto he is like a blind Cyclops, *ill* educated, yet capable of good education; he may perhaps reap great profit from us.

Edward Irving is graver than usual, yet has still the old faculty of laughter; on the whole, a true sufficient kind of man, very anxious to have me stay here, where 'in two years or so' I should not

[1] 'Glen, who was mentioned before, was a young graduate of Glasgow studying law in London, of very considerable though utterly confused talent. Ultimately went mad, and was boarded in a farmhouse near Craigenputtock, within reach of us, where in seven or eight years he died.—T. C.'

fail to find some appointment. What I lament is that such a mind should not be in the van, but wilfully standing in the rear, bringing up the tagrag and bobtail, however well he do it. 'Miracles' are the commonest things in the world here. Irving said to Glen, '*When* I work miracles.' He and I have never fastened upon that topic yet, but by-and-by he shall hear my whole mind on it, for he deserves such confidence.

I gave your compliments to Empson, who received them with wreathed smiles and mumbles of heartiest welcome. I think you will like him—a bushy-faced kind-looking creature with most melancholy short-sighted eyes. He is from Lincolnshire ; walks much, I take it, with women, men being too harsh and contradictory with him. He was sitting in yellow nightgown, without neckcloth, shaggy enough, and writing with his whole might for Naso (Napier).

Of Macaulay I hear nothing very good—a sophistical, rhetorical, ambitious young man of talent ; 'set in there,' as Mill said, ' to make flash speeches, and he makes them.' It seems to me of small consequence whether we meet at all.

To Mrs. Carlyle, Scotsbrig.

September 19, 1831.

My dear Mother,—. . . Jane will have told you how languidly everything proceeds with me—how the 'people are all out of town,' everything stagnating because of this Reform Bill, the book trade in particular nearly altogether at a standstill, and lastly, how I, as the best thing I could do, have been obliged to give my poor book away (that is, the first edition of it),[1] and am even glad to see it printed on these terms. This is not very flattering news of the encouragement for men of my craft ; nevertheless, I study to say with as much cheerfulness as I can, *Be it so!* The Giver of all Good has enabled me to write the thing, and also to do *without* any pay for it : the pay would have been wasted away and flitted out of the bit as other pay does ; but if there stand any truth recorded there, *it* will not 'flit.' Nay, if there be even no truth (as where is the man that can say with confidence the inspiration of the Almighty has given *me* understanding), yet it was the nearest approach to such that I could make ; and so in God's name let it take its fortune in the world, and sink or swim

[1] This was written a day or two before the final collapse with Murray.

as the All-disposer orders. There remains for ever the maxim, 'In all thy ways acknowledge Him.'

I am earnestly expecting Jane, that some sort of establishment may be formed here, where we can spend the winter with more regularity and composure than I have hitherto enjoyed. Then we can look about us over this whirlpool, and I, in the meantime, shall most probably write some considerable essay for the 'Edinburgh Review,' that so, when we return, *Mall* may not be altogether out of *shafts*. Of any permanent appointment here I as yet see, with my own eyes, not the slightest outlook ; neither, indeed, is my heart set on such, for I feel that the King's palace with all it holds would in good truth do little for me ; and the prayer I ever endeavour to make is, 'Show me my duty, and enable me to do it.' If my duty be to endure a life of poverty and what 'light afflictions' attend on it, this also will not terrify me.

Meanwhile, I am not without my comforts ; one of the greatest of which is to have found various well-disposed men, most of them young men, who can feel a sort of scholarship towards me. My poor performances in the writing way are better known here than I expected ; clearly enough, also, there *is* want of instruction and light in this mirk midnight of human affairs ; such want as probably for eighteen hundred years there has not been. If *I* have any light to give them, let me give it ; if none, then what is to be done but seek for it, and hold my peace till I find it.

To Mrs. Carlyle, Liverpool.[1]

London : September 23.

My poor Goody,—All yesterday my thoughts were with thee in thy lone voyage, which now I pray the great Giver of Good may have terminated prosperously. Never before did I so well understand my mother's anxious forecasting ways. I felt that my best possession was trusted to the false sea, and all my cares for it could avail nothing. Do not wait a moment in writing. I shall have no peace till I know that you are safe. Meanwhile, in truth there is no use in tormenting myself ; the weather, here at least, was good. I struggle while I can to believe that it has all passed without accident, and that you are now resting in comparative safety in your uncle's house among friends.

Of rest I can well understand you have need enough. I grieve

[1] His wife had gone by water from Annan to her uncle's house at Liverpool : from thence to proceed by coach to London.

to think how harassed you have been of late, all which, I fear, has acted badly on your health; these bustlings and tossings to and fro are far too rough work for you. I can see, by your two last letters especially, that it is not well with you; your heart is, as it were, choked up, if not depressed. You are agitated and pro-voked, which is almost the worse way of the two. Alas! and I have no soft Aladdin's Palace here to bid you hasten and take re-pose in. Nothing but a noisy, untoward lodging-house, and no better shelter than my own bosom. Yet is not this the best of all shelters for you? the only safe place in this wide world? Thank God, this still is yours, and I can receive you there without dis-trust, and wrap you close with the solacements of a true heart's love. Hasten thither, then, my own wife. Betide what may, we will not despair, were the world never so unfriendly. *We* are in-divisible, and will help each other to endure its evils, nay to con-quer them.

Mrs. Carlyle arrived in London on the first of October, a good deal shattered by the journey and the charge of the miscellaneous cargo of luggage which she had brought with her: oatmeal, hams, butter, &c., supplied by the generous Scotsbrig to lighten the expense of the London winter. George Irving's lodgings, being found to contain bugs, were exchanged for others. John Carlyle departed with Lady Clare for Italy. Carlyle and his wife quartered themselves at Ampton Street, turning out of Gray's Inn Road, where they had two comfortable rooms in the house of an excellent family named Miles, who belonged to Ir-ving's congregation. Here friends came to see them: Mill, Empson, later on Leigh Hunt, drawn by the article on Hope ('Characteristics') which Carlyle was now assidu-ously writing, Jeffrey, and afterwards many more, the Carlyles going out into society, and reconnoitring literary London. Mrs. Carlyle in her way was as brilliant as her husband was in his own; she attracting every one, he wondered at as a prodigy, which the world was yet uncer-tain whether it was to love or execrate.

Carlyle's 'Journal' tells us generally what was passing

within him and round him, how London affected him, &c.
His and Mrs. Carlyle's letters fill out the picture.

Extracts from Journal.

October 10.—Wife arrived ten days ago. We here quietly
enough in 4 Ampton Street, and the world jogging on at the old
rate. Jack must be by this time in Paris. 'Teufelsdröckh,' after
various perplexed destinies, returned to me, and now lying safe in
his box. The book contents me little ; yet perhaps there is material in it ; in any case, I did my best.

The Reform Bill lost (on Saturday morning at six o'clock) by a
majority of forty-one. The politicians will have it the people must
rise. The people will do nothing half so foolish—for the present.
London seems altogether quiet. Here they are afraid of Scotland,
in Scotland of us.

On Saturday saw Sir James Mackintosh (at Jeffrey's), and
looked at and listened to him, though without speech. A broadish, middle-sized, grey-headed man, well-dressed, and with a plain
courteous bearing ; grey intelligent (unhealthy yellow-whited)
eyes, in which plays a dash of cautious vivacity (uncertain whether
fear or latent ire), triangular unmeaning nose, business mouth and
chin ; on the whole, a sensible official air, not without a due spicing of hypocrisy and something of pedantry, both no doubt involuntary. The man is a Whig philosopher and politician, such
as the time yields, our best of that sort, which will soon be extinct. He was talking mysteriously with other 'Hon. Members'
about 'what was to be done'—something *à la* Dogberry the thing
looked to me, though I deny not that it is a serious conjuncture,
only believe that change has some chance to be for the better, and
so see it all with composure.

Meanwhile, *what* was the true duty of a man? Were it to stand
utterly aloof from politics (not ephemeral only, for that of course,
but generally from all speculation about social systems, &c.), or is
not perhaps the very want of this time an infinite want of Gov-
ernors, of knowledge how to govern itself? Canst thou in any
measure spread abroad reverence over the hearts of men? That
were a far higher task than *any* other. Is it to be done by art?
or are men's minds as yet shut to art, and open only at best to

oratory? not fit for a *Meister*, but *only for a better and better Teu-felsdröckh? Think and be silent.*

'Mary Wollstonecraft's Life,' by Godwin. An Ariel imprisoned in a brickbat! It is a real tragedy and of the deepest. Sublimely virtuous endowment; in practice, misfortune, suffering, death . . . by destiny, and also by desert. An English Mignon; Godwin an honest boor that loves her, but cannot guide or save her.

Strange tendency everywhere noticeable to speculate on *men*, not on *man*. Another branch of the mechanical temper. Vain hope to make mankind happy by politics! You *cannot* drill a regiment of knaves into a regiment of honest men, enregiment and organise them as cunningly as you will. Give us the honest men, and the well-ordered regiment comes of itself. Reform one man —reform thy own inner man; it is more than scheming out reforms for a nation.

John told me of having seen in Holborn a man walking steadily along with some six baskets all piled above each other, his name and address written in large characters on each, so that he exhibited a statue of some twelve feet, and so by the six separate announcements had his existence sufficiently proclaimed. The trade of this man was basket-making; but he had found it needful to study a quite new trade—that of walking with six baskets on his head in a crowded street.

In like manner Colburn and Bentley, the booksellers, are known to expend ten thousand pounds annually on what they call advertising, more commonly called *puffing*. Puffing (which is simply the *second* trade, like that of basket-carrying) flourishes in all countries; but London is the true scene of it, having this one quality beyond all other cities—a quite immeasurable size. It is rich also, stupid, and ignorant beyond example; thus in all respects the true Goshen of quacks.

Every man I meet with mourns over this state of matters; no one thinks it remediable. You must do as the others do, or they will get the start of you or tread you under foot. 'All true, Mr. Carlyle BUT': I say, 'All true, Mr. Carlyle AND.' The first beginning of a remedy is that some *one* believe a remedy possible; believe that if he cannot live by truth, then he can *die* by it. Dost *thou* believe it? Then is the new era begun!

How men are hurried here ; how they are hunted and terrifically chased into double-quick speed; so that in self-defence they *must not* stay to look at one another! Miserable is the scandal-mongery and evil speaking of the country population : more frightful still the total ignorance and mutual heedlessness of these poor souls in populous city pent. 'Each passes on quick, transient, regarding not the other or his woes.' Each must button himself together, and take no thought (not even for evil) of his neighbour. There in their little cells, divided by partitions of brick or board, they sit strangers, unknowing, unknown, like passengers in some huge ship; each within his own cabin. Alas! and the ship is life; and the voyage is from eternity to eternity.

Everywhere there is the most crying want of *government,* a true all-ruining anarchy. No one has any *knowledge* of London, in which he lives. It is a huge aggregate of little systems, each of which is again a small anarchy, the members of which do not *work* together, but *scramble* against each other. The soul (what can be properly called the soul) lies dead in the bosom of man ; starting out in mad, ghastly night-walkings—e.g. the gift of tongues. Ignorance eclipses all things with its owlet wings. Man walks he knows not whither ; walks and wanders till he walks into the jaws of death, and is then devoured. Nevertheless, *God is in it.* Here, even here, is the revelation of the Infinite in the Finite ; a majestic poem (tragic, comic, or epic), couldst thou but read it or recite it! Watch it then; study it ; catch the secret of it; and proclaim the same in such accent as is given thee. Alas! the spirit is willing, but the flesh is weak.

On Thursday night last (this is Monday), the 28th of October, dined with Fonblanque, editor of the 'Examiner.' An honourable Radical; might be something better. London bred. Limited by education more than by nature. Something metallic in the tone of his voice (like that of Professor Austin). For the rest, a tall, loose, lank-haired, wrinkly, wintry, vehement-looking flail of a man. I reckon him the best of the fourth estate now extant in Britain. Shall see him again.

Allan Cunningham with us last night. Jane calls him a genuine Dumfriesshire mason still ; and adds that it is delightful to see a genuine man of any sort. Allan was, as usual, full of Scottish anecdotic talk. Right by instinct ; has *no* principles or *creed* that I can see, but excellent old Scottish *habits* of character. An interesting man.

Walter Scott left town yesterday on his way to Naples. He is to proceed from Plymouth in a frigate, which the Government have given him a place in. Much run after here, it seems ; but he is old and sick, and cannot enjoy it ; has had two shocks of palsy, and seems altogether in a precarious way. To me he is and has been an object of very minor interest for many, many years. The novelwright of his time, its favourite child, and *therefore* an almost worthless one. Yet is there something in his deep recognition of the worth of the past, perhaps better than anything he has *expressed* about it, into which I do not yet fully see. Have never spoken with him (though I might sometimes without great effort) ; and now probably never shall.

What an advantage has the pulpit where you address men already arranged to hear you, and in a vehicle which long use has rendered easy ; how infinitely harder when you have all to create—not the ideas only and the sentiments, but the symbols and the mood of mind ! Nevertheless, in all cases where man addresses man, on his spiritual interests especially, there is a *sacredness*, could we but evolve it, and think and speak in it. Consider better what it is thou meanest by a *symbol ;* how far thou hast insight into the nature thereof.

Is *Art* in the old Greek sense possible for men at this late era ? or were not perhaps the founder of a religion our true Homer at present ? The *whole soul* must be illuminated, made harmonious. Shakespeare seems to have had no religion but his poetry.

Where is To-morrow resident even now ? Somewhere or somehow it *is*, doubt not of that. On the common theory thou mayest think thyself into madness on this question.

November 2.—How few people speak for Truth's sake, even in its humblest modes ! I return from Enfield, where I have seen Lamb, &c. &c. Not one of that class will tell you a straightforward story or even a credible one about any matter under the sun. All must be packed up into epigrammatic contrasts, startling exaggerations, claptraps that will get a plaudit from the galleries ! I have heard a hundred anecdotes about William Hazlitt for example ; yet cannot by never so much cross-questioning even form to myself the smallest notion of how it really stood with him.

Wearisome, inexpressibly wearisome to me is that sort of clatter; it is not walking (to the end of time you would never advance, for these persons indeed have no WHITHER); it is not bounding and frisking in graceful, natural joy; it is dancing—a St. Vitus's dance. Heigh ho! Charles Lamb I sincerely believe to be in some considerable degree insane. A more pitiful, ricketty, gasping, staggering, stammering Tomfool I do not know. He is witty by denying truisms and abjuring good manners. His speech wriggles hither and thither with an incessant painful fluctuation, not an opinion in it, or a fact, or a phrase that you can thank him for—more like a convulsion fit than a natural systole and diastole. Besides, he is now a confirmed, shameless drunkard; *asks* vehemently for gin and water in strangers' houses, tipples till he is utterly mad, and is only not thrown out of doors because he is too much despised for taking such trouble with him. Poor Lamb! Poor England, when such a despicable abortion is named genius! He said there are just two things I regret in England's history: first, that Guy Fawkes' plot did not take effect (there would have been so glorious an *explosion*); second, that the Royalists did not hang Milton (then we might have laughed at them), &c. &c. *Armer Teufel!*

Carlyle did not know at this time the tragedy lying behind the life of Charles Lamb, which explained or extenuated his faults. Yet this extravagantly harsh estimate is repeated—scarcely qualified—in a sketch written nearly forty years after.

Among the scrambling miscellany of notables that hovered about us, Leigh Hunt was probably the best, poor Charles Lamb the worst. He was sinking into drink, poor creature; his fraction of 'humour,' &c., I recognised, and recognised—but never could accept for a great thing, a genuine, but essentially small and cockney thing; and now with gin, &c., superadded, one had to say 'Genius! This is not genius, but diluted insanity. Please remove this!'

The gentle Elia deserved a kinder judgment. Carlyle considered 'humour' to be the characteristic of the highest order of mind. He had heard Lamb extravagantly praised, perhaps, for this particular quality, and he was provoked to find it combined with habits which his own stern Calvinism was unable to tolerate.

To return to the letters:—

To Mrs. Carlyle, Scotsbrig.

4 Ampton Street, Mecklenburgh Square, London :
October 20, 1831.

My dear Mother,—We have nestled down here in our tight little lodging, and are as quiet as we could wish to be. Jane is in better health than she has enjoyed for many months; I, too, am fully better. We live thriftily, have companions and conversation of the best that can be had; and except that I cannot honestly tell myself that I am *working* (though I daily make the attempt to work and keep scraffling and feltering), we ought to call ourselves very well off indeed. The people of the house are cleanly, orderly, and seem honest—no noises, no bugs disturb us through the night; on the whole it is among the best places for *sleep* I have been in, as you may judge by this fact, that more than once we have slept almost ten hours at a stretch—a noble spell of sleeping, of which, however, both of us, so long disturbed and tost about, had need enough. The worst thing about our establishment is its *hamperedness*, which is so much the more sensible to us coming from the desert vastness of the moor at Craigenputtock. I have a sort of feeling as if I were tied up in a *sack* and could not get my fins *stirred*. No doubt this will wear off, for one needs but little room to work profitably in; my craft especially requires nothing but a chair, a table, and a piece of paper. Were I once fairly heated at my work, I shall not mind what sort of harness I am in. Napier writes to me that he expects a 'striking essay' from my hand for his next 'Edinburgh Review,' so I must bestir me, for there is little more than a month to work in.

Some of my friends here are talking of possible situations for me, but as yet on no ground that I can fairly see with my own eyes. I let it be known to every one who takes interest in me that I am very desirous to work at *any* honest employment I am acquainted with; but for the rest, able to hold on my way whether I find other employment or not. If I can earn myself a more liberal livelihood, I hope I shall be thankful for it, and use it as it beseems me; nay, I would even live in London for the sake of such a blessing; but if nothing of the kind turn up, as is most likely, then I can also, with all contentment, return to the Whinstone Craig, and rejoice that this city of refuge is left me. Truly thankful ought I to be that the Giver of all Good has imparted to me this highest of all blessings ; light to discern His hand in the confused workings of this evil world ; and to follow fearlessly whithersoever He beckons ! Ever be praised God for it ! I was once the miserablest of all men, but shall not be so any more. On the whole, however, there is work in abundance for me here—men ignorant on all hands of me of what it most concerns them to know ; neither will I turn me from the task of teaching them as it is given me. Had I once investigated the ground fully, I may perhaps lift up my voice so that it shall be heard a little farther than heretofore. But I wish to do nothing rashly, to take no step which I might wish in vain to retrace.

Meanwhile, my book, withdrawn from all bookselling consultations, lies safe in the box, waiting till the book-trade revive before I make a farther attempt. The *Reform Bill*, I suppose, must be disposed of first ; and when that may be I know not, neither, indeed, care. If the world will not have my bit-book, then, of a truth, my bit-book can do without the world. One good thing in the middle of all this stagnation is that we are perfectly peaceable here, though the contrary was by some apprehended. The newspapers will tell you, as their way is, about wars and rumours of wars ; but you need not believe them, or heed them. I see no symptom of revolting among the people, neither do I believe that anything short of hunger will raise them—of which, happily, there is as yet no approach. So keep yourself perfectly easy, my dear mother, and know that we are as safe as we could anywhere be ; nay, at the first stir of 'revolution' cannot we hasten to the *Craig* and sit there and see them revolve it out for their own behoof.

I dare say you have not seen in the newspapers, but will soon see something extraordinary about poor Edward Irving. His friends here are all much grieved about him. For many months he has been puddling and muddling in the midst of certain insane jargonings of hysterical women, and crackbrained enthusiasts, who start up from time to time in public companies, and utter confused stuff, mostly 'Ohs' and 'Ahs,' and absurd interjections about 'the body of Jesus ;' they also pretend to 'work miracles,' and have raised more than one weak bedrid woman, and cured people of 'nerves,' or as they themselves say, 'cast devils out of them.' All which poor Irving is pleased to consider as the 'work of the Spirit,' and to janner about at great length, as making *his* church the peculiarly blessed of Heaven, and equal to or greater than the primitive one at Corinth. This, greatly to my sorrow and that of many, has gone on privately a good while, with increasing vigour; but last Sabbath it burst out publicly in the open church; for one of the 'Prophetesses,' a woman on the verge of derangement, started up in the time of worship, and began to speak with tongues, and, as the thing was encouraged by Irving, there were some three or four fresh hands who started up in the evening sermon and began their ragings; whereupon the whole congregation got into foul uproar, some groaning, some laughing, some shrieking, not a few falling into swoons: more like a Bedlam than a Christian church. Happily, neither Jane nor I were there, though we had been the previous day. We had not even heard of it. When going next evening to call on Irving, we found the house all decked out for a 'meeting,' (that is, about this same 'speaking with tongues'), and as we talked a moment with Irving, who had come down to us, there rose a shriek in the upper story of the house, and presently he exclaimed, 'There is one prophesying; come and hear her!' We hesitated to go, but he forced us up into a back room, and there we could hear the wretched creature raving like one possessed: *hoo*ing, and *ha*ing, and talking *as* sensibly as one would do with a pint of brandy in his stomach, till after some ten minutes she seemed to grow tired and become silent.

Nothing so shocking and altogether unspeakably deplorable was it ever my lot to hear. Poor Jane was on the verge of fainting, and did not recover the whole night. And now the newspapers have got wind of it and are groaning loudly over it, and the congregation itself is like to split on the matter; and for poor Irving in any case dark mad times are coming. You need not speak of all this, at least not be the first to speak of it; most likely it will be too public. What the final issue for our most worthy, but most misguided friend may be, I dare not so much as guess. Could I do anything to save him, it were well my part, but I despair of being able to accomplish anything. I began a letter to him yesterday, but gave it up as hopeless when I heard that the newspapers had interfered, for now Irving I reckon *will not* draw back, lest it should seem fear of men rather than of God. The unhappy man! Let us nevertheless hope that he is not utterly lost, but only gone astray for a time. Be thankful also that our wits are still in some measure left with us.

．　　．　　．　　．　　．　　．

　The newspapers call on Irving's people for the honour of Scotland to leave him or muzzle him. The most general hypothesis is that he is a quack, the milder that he is getting cracked. Poor George is the man I pity most; he spoke to us of it, almost with tears in eyes, and earnestly entreated me to deal with his brother, which, when he comes hither (by appointment on Tuesday), I partly mean to attempt, though now I fear it will be useless. It seems likely that all the Loselism of London will be about the church next Sunday, that his people will quarrel with him; in any case that troublous times are appointed him. My poor friend! And yet the punishment was not unjust, that he who believed without inquiry should now believe against all light, and portentously call upon the world to admire as inspiration what is but a dancing on the verge of bottomless abysses of madness. I see not the end of it—who does?

　Carlyle did attempt, as he has related in the 'Reminiscences,' and as he tells in his letters, to drag Irving back from the precipice; but it proved as vain as he had feared; and all that he could do was but to stand aside and watch the ruin of his true and noble-minded friend. The last touch was added to the tragedy by the presence of Mrs. Carlyle to witness the catastrophe.

　Meanwhile London was filling again after the holidays; and the autumn brought back old faces of other friends whom Carlyle was glad to see again. The Bullers were among the earliest arrivals. Charles Buller, then beginning his brief and brilliant career, was an advanced Radical in politics, and equally advanced in matters of speculation. He had not yet found a creed, as he had said, which he could even wish to believe true. He had a generous scorn of affectation, and did not choose, like many of his contemporaries, to wear a mask of veiled hypocrisy. The hen is terrified when the ducklings she has hatched take to water. Mrs. Buller, indeed, shared her son's feelings and felt no alarm; but her sister, Mrs. Strachey, who, a good religious woman, was shocked at a freedom less common then than it is now, because it could be less safely avowed, and in despair of help from the professional authorities, to whom she knew that her nephew would not listen, she turned to Carlyle, whose opinions she perhaps imperfectly understood, but of whose piety of heart she was assured.

Carlyle was extremely fond of Charles Buller. He was the only person of distinction or promise of distinction with whom he came in contact that he heartily admired; and he, too, had regretted to see his old pupil rushing off into the ways of agnosticism. Well he knew that no man ever came, or ever could come, to any greatness in this world in irreverent occupation with the mere phenomena of earth. The agnostic doctrines, he once said to me, were to appearance like the finest flour, from which you might expect the most excellent bread; but when you came to feed on it you found it was powdered glass and you had been eating the deadliest poison. What he valued in Buller was his hatred of cant, his frank contempt of insincere professions. But refusal even to appear to conform with opinions which the world holds it decent to profess, is but the clearing of the soil from weeds. Carlyle, without waiting to be urged by Mrs. Strachey, had long been labouring to sow the seeds in Buller of a nobler belief; but a faith which can stand the wear and tear of work cannot be taught like a mathematical problem, and if Carlyle had shown Mrs. Strachey the condition of his own mind, she would scarcely have applied to him for assistance. Buller died before it had been seen to what seed sown such a mind as his might eventually have grown.

Thomas Carlyle to Mrs. Carlyle, Scotsbrig.

November 10, 1831.

. . . .

I feel in some measure getting to my feet again after so long stumbling. Some time ago, I actually began a paper for the 'Edinburgh Review,' at which I am daily working. My hand was sadly out; but by resolute endeavour I feel that it will come in again, and I shall perhaps make a tolerable story of it. So long as I can work it is all well with me: I care for nothing. The only thing I have to struggle against is idleness and falsehood. These are the two Devil's emissaries that, did I give them heed, would work all my woe. A considerable paper of mine came out in the 'Foreign Quarterly Review' (Cochrane's), which, with several other things that you have not yet seen, I hope to show you and get you to read when I return. Cochrane's pay will serve to keep *Mall in shaft* till we turn northward. Meanwhile all goes on as well as we could hope; our lodgings continue very comfortable and very cheap; so that we can *both* live for little more than it used in my last London residence to cost me alone. The people are very cleanly, polite, decent-minded people; they have seen better days, and seem to have a heart above their lot. Both of us sleep well; our health is fully of the old quality: we eat and breathe, and have wherewith to eat and breathe; for honest thinking and honest acting the materials are *everywhere* laid down to one.

Except the printing of my book, or rather the trying for it so long as there seems any good chance, I have no special call at London. Nevertheless, there are many profitable chances for me here; especially many persons with whom I find much encouragement and perhaps improvement in associating. A considerable knot of *young* men in particular I discover here that have had their eyes on me, and wish for insight from me; with these it seems quite possible some good may be done. Among the number was my landlord this morning,[1] a secretary in one of the Government offices, whom I met with for the first time. He had a whole party to meet me: four of the best mannered, most pleasant persons I have for a long time seen: all ingenuous persons 'lying,' what so few do, 'open to light.' The disciple or associate I have most to do with is one John Mill (the son of a Scotchman of eminence), acquainted with the Bullers, &c., who is a great favourite here. It was he that brought about my meeting this morning with my secretary (Taylor) and his friends, whom I hope to see again. Charles Buller also has come to town; he made his appearance here the other day, was in about an hour followed

---

[1] Henry (now Sir Henry) Taylor, with whom he had been at breakfast.

by Mill, and the two made what Jane called 'a pleasant forenoon
call of seven hours and a half.' Charles is grown a great tower
of a fellow, six feet three in height, a yard in breadth, shows
great talent and great natural goodness, which I hope he will by-
and-by turn to notable account. I met him and Strachey amid
the raw, frosty fog of Piccadilly this morning, and expect to see
him some evening soon. Mrs. Strachey is just returned from Devonshire, whence she had written us a very kind and true-looking
letter, and we *expect* to see her soon. The Montagus go hovering much about us; but their intercourse is of inferior profit :
their whole way of life has a certain hollowness, so that you nowhere find firm bottom. One must try to take the good out of
each and keep aloof from the evil that lies everywhere mixed
with it.

Irving comes but little in our way; and one does not like to go
and seek him in his own house in a whole posse of enthusiasts,
ranters, and silly women. He was here once, taking tea, since
that work of the 'Tongues' began. I told him with great earnestness my deep-seated, unhesitating conviction that it was *no* special work of the Holy Spirit, or of any spirit, save of that black,
frightful, unclean one that dwells in Bedlam. He persists, mildly
obstinate, in his course, greatly strengthened therein by his wife,
who is reckoned the beginner of it all. What it will all lead to I
pretend not to prophesy. I do not think it can spread to any extent even among the vulgar here at this time of day ; only a small
knot of ravers now rave in that old worn-out direction. But for
Irving himself the consequences frighten me. That he will lose
his congregation seems calculated on by his friends ; but perhaps
a far darker fear is not out of the question, namely that he may
lose his own wits. God guard him from such a consummation !
None of you, I am sure, will join in any ill-natured clamours
against him. Defend him rather with brotherly charity, and hope
always that he will yet be delivered from this real delusion of
the Devil.

Jane wanted me to tell you of the 'Examiner' editor,[1] but I
have not space here. The poor fellow has been thrown out of a
gig, and is tediously lame; so I have not yet seen him here,
neither was he at home when I pilgrimed over the other day, but
gone to Brighton for sea air. My ideas, therefore, were only
formed by candle-light. He is a long, thin, *tawtie*-headed man,

[1] Fonblanque.

with wrinkly, even baggy face, keen, zealous-looking eyes, a sort of well toned, honestly argumentative voice; very much the air of a true-hearted Radical. He was all braced with straps, moving on crutches, and hung together loosely, you would have said, as by *flail-cappins*. However, we got along bravely together, and parted, after arguing and assenting and laughing and mourning at consider-able length, with mutual purposes to meet again. I rather like the man; there is far more in him than in most of Radicals; besides, he means *honestly*, and has a real feeling where the shoe pinches, namely, that the grand misery is the condition of the poor classes.

I had much to write about the state of matters here, and to quiet your fears especially about the cholera, which so many tor-ment themselves with. It is in truth a disease of no such terrific quality, only that its effect is sudden, and the people have heard so much about it. Scarcely a year but there is a *typhus fever* in Glasgow or Edinburgh that kills far *more* than the cholera does in like cases. For my part, I am even satisfied that it has reached our coasts (where I have long inevitably expected it), and that now the reality which is measurable will succeed the terror which is unmeasurable, and doing great mischief both to individual peace of mind and all kinds of commercial intercourse. The worst effect here will be that same interruption; thus already the coals which come from Northumberland are beginning to rise. On the whole, however, it is our purpose to run no unnecessary risks; therefore, should the danger really come near us, and the disease break out in London under a shape in any measure for-midable, we will *forthwith bundle our gear*, and return to Puttock till it is over. This we have resolved on, so disquiet not yourself, my dear mother; there is no peril for the moment; nay, it is a hundred miles nearer *you* than us. As to *rioting* and all that sort of matter, there is no symptom of it here; neither in case of its actual occurrence have persons like us anything to fear. We are safer here, I take it, than we should be in Dunscore itself. . . . I will write, if aught notable happen, *instantly*. Farewell, dear mother. God bless you all. T. CARLYLE.

To John Carlyle.

November 13, 1831.

. . . .

As to Irving, expect little tidings of him. I think I shall hence-forth see little of him. His 'gift of tongues' goes on apace. Glen says there was one performing yesterday; but, on the whole, the

Cockneys are too old for such lullabies—they simply think he is gone distracted, or means to 'do' them; and so, having seen it once, come no more back. Edward himself came here about a fortnight ago to tea, and I told him solemnly, with a tone of friendly warning such as he well merited from me, what I thought of that scandalous delusion. He was almost at crying, but remained—as I expected him to remain. It sometimes appears to me the *darkest* fears are actually not groundless in regard to him. God deliver him! If that is not the Devil's own work, then let the Devil lay down the gun.

I know not whether you get any *Galignani's Messenger* or the like, so whether it is worth while to send you any public news. There have been *frightful* riots at Bristol, some hundreds of lives lost, all the public buildings burnt, and many private houses—quite a George Gordon affair—on occasion of Wetherell's arrival there as Recorder, whom unhappily they took that method of convincing that there was *not* 'a reaction' (in regard to Reform). Oh, the unspeakable, blundering, braying, brass-throated, leather-headed fool and fools! If they do not pass that Bill of theirs soon, the country will be a chaos, and 200 Tory lords crying out, Who shall deliver us? The Duke of Northumberland is actually *fortifying* his house here. Other riots there have been at Coventry, at Worcester, &c. Swing also is *as* busy as last winter; all London, all Britain, is organising itself into political unions. Finally, the cholera has actually arrived at Sunderland; a precious outlook! Truly the political aspects of England give even me alarms. A second edition of the French Revolution is distinctly within the range of chances; for there is nowhere any tie remaining among men. Everywhere, in court and cathedral, brazen falsehood now at length stands convicted of a lie, and famishing Ignorance cries, Away with her, away with her! God deliver us. Nay, God will deliver us; for this is His world, not the Devil's. All is perfectly quiet in London hitherto; only great apprehension, swearing-in of constables. Neither is the cholera yet dangerous. It has not spread from Sunderland, where it has now been some ten days. Should the danger grow imminent, we two have determined to fly to Puttock. Meanwhile, I cannot say that twenty choleras and twenty Revolutions ought to terrify one. The crash of the whole solar and stellar systems could only kill you once. 'I have cast away base fear from me for ever,' says Dreck, and he is seldom wholly wrong.

To Mrs. Welsh,[1] *Maryland Street, Liverpool.*

4 Ampton Street : Tuesday, December, 1831.

My dear Aunt,—When I returned from Enfield, where I had been for a week, I found the box containing the memorials of my heedlessness [2] awaiting me on the top of a cistern outside our staircase window ; and our landlady assured me with the utmost self-complacency that she had done all she could for it in the way of keeping it cool ! She looked rather blank when, after duly commending her care, I informed her it was probably a cloak and shawl, which she might now bring in out of the rain with all despatch. Only to the intellect of a Cockney would a deal box have suggested the exclusive idea of game.

The cloak I got dyed a more sober colour and lined and furred, so as effectually to exclude the cold, no slight conquest of Art over Nature in these days. Some people here have the impudence or ignorance to congratulate me on the agreeable change of climate I have made ; but truly, if my contentment depended mainly on weather, I should wish myself back to our own hill-top without delay. Regarded as a place merely, this noble city is simply the most detestable I ever lived in—one day a ferocious frost, the next a fog so thick you might put it in your pocket ; a Dead Sea of green-coloured filth under foot, and above an atmosphere like one of my uncle's sugar boilers. But, as the French say, *il faut se ranger ;* and so day after day I rush forth with desperate resignation, and even find a sort of sublimity in the infinite horror through which I must make my way, or die of indigestion.

If I am inclined to reflect on the *place,* however (perhaps not without a touch of national prejudice), it is certainly my bounden duty to speak well of the people. Nowhere have I found more worth, more talent, or more kindness ; and I must doubly regret the ill-health I have been suffering under, since it has so curtailed my enjoyment of all this. Nevertheless, though I dare seldom accept an invitation out, I have the pleasantest evenings at home. Scarce a night passes that some acquaintance, new or old, does not drop in at tea ; and then follow such bouts at talking ! Not of our ' Book ' (as my uncle named Carlyle) but of several books.

I have seen most of the literary people here, and, as Edward Irving said after his first interview with Wordsworth, ' I think not of them so highly as I was wont.'

[1] Wife of Mrs. Carlyle's Liverpool uncle.
[2] Things which she had left at Liverpool in passing through.

These people, who have made themselves snug little reputations, and on the strength of such hold up their heads as 'one and somewhat,' are by no means the most distinguished that I meet with either for talent or cultivation; some of them, indeed (Charles Lamb for instance), would not be tolerated in any society out of England. . . .

. . . My kindest love to my uncle and all the weans. Happy New Year and many of them; always the last the best! God bless you all!

Your affectionate

JANE W. CARLYLE.

To Miss Jean Carlyle, Scotsbrig.

4 Ampton Street: December, 1831.

My dear Jean,—You do not write to *me;* but you write, and I am content. The proverb says 'It is not lost that a friend gets;' to which I readily accede, the more readily because a letter with us is always regarded as a common good.

I do not forget you in London, as you predicted. My recollections of all I love are more vivid than at any former period. Often when I have been lying ill here among strangers, it has been my pleasantest thought that there were kind hearts at home to whom my sickness would not be a weariness; to whom I could return out of all this hubbub with affection and trust. Not that I am not kindly used here; from 'the noble lady'[1] down to the mistress of the lodging, I have everywhere found unlooked-for civility, and at least the show of kindness. With the 'noble lady,' however, I may mention my intercourse seems to be dying an easy natural death. Now that we *know* each other, the 'fine enthu-si-asm' cannot be kept alive without more hypocrisy than one of us at least can bring to bear on it. Mrs. Montagu is an actress. I admire her to a certain extent, but friendship for such a person is out of the question.

Mrs. Austin I have now seen, and like infinitely better. She is coming to tea to-morrow night. If I 'swear everlasting friendship' with any woman here, it will be with her.

But the most interesting acquaintances we have made are the St. Simonians.[2] You may fancy how my heart beat when a card

[1] Mrs. Montagu.

[2] 'The St. Simonians, Detrosier, &c., were stirring and conspicuous objects in that epoch, but have now fallen all dark and silent again.—T. C., 1866.'

bearing the name of *Gustave d'Eichthal* was sent up the other day, when I happened to be alone. Our meeting was most cordial; and, as he talks good English, we contrived to carry on a pretty voluble conversation till Carlyle came home and relieved me. He (Gustave) is a creature to love at first sight—so gentle and trustful and earnest-looking, ready to do and suffer all for his faith. A friend accompanies him, whom we had here to-day along with Mill and Detrosier; a stronger, perhaps nobler MAN than Gustave, with whom Carlyle seems to be exceedingly taken. *He* (Duverrier I think they call him) is at first sight ugly: all pitted with the small-pox; but by-and-by you wonder at your first impression, his countenance is so prepossessing and commanding. We hope to see a great deal of these men before we leave London. Both seem to entertain a high respect for Carlyle—as indeed everybody I see does. Glen continues to come a great deal about us; and *blethers* more like a man growing mad than one growing wiser. Carlyle maintains in opposition to me that there is 'method in his madness,' but his idea of the quantity seems daily diminishing.

Of the Irvings we see nothing and hear little good. Carlyle dined at a literary party the other day, where he met Hogg, Lockhart, Galt, Allan Cunningham, &c.

And now God bless you, one and all of you! My love to everyone.

Your affectionate

JANE W. CARLYLE.

CHAPTER X.

A.D. 1831.   ÆT. 36.

Extracts from Note Book.

November 2.—All the world is in apprehension about the cholera pestilence, which, indeed, seems advancing towards us with a
frightful, slow, unswerving constancy. For myself I cannot say
that it costs me great suffering ; we are all appointed once to die.
Death is the grand sum total of it all. Generally, now it seems to
me as if this life were but the inconsiderable portico of man's existence, which afterwards, in new mysterious environment, were to
be continued without end. I say, 'seems to me,' for the proof of
it were hard to state by logic ; it is the fruit of faith ; begins to
show itself with more and more decisiveness the instant you have
dared to say, 'Be it *either* way !' But on the whole our conception of immortality depends on that of *time,* which latter is the
deepest belonging to philosophy, and the one perhaps wherein
modern philosophy has earned its best triumph. Believe that
properly there *is* no space and no time, how many contradictions
become reconciled.

Sports are all gone from among men ; there is now no holiday
either for rich or poor. Hard toiling, then hard drinking or hard
fox-hunting. This is not the era of sport, but of martyrdom and
persecution. Will the new morning never dawn ? It requires a
certain vigour of the imagination and of the social faculties before
amusement, popular sports, can exist, which vigour at this era is
all but total inanition. Do but think of the Christmas carols and
games, the Abbots of Unreason, the Maypoles, &c. &c. Then look
at your Manchesters on Saturdays and Sundays.

'Education' is beyond being so much as despised. We must
praise it, when it is not *D*education, or an utter annihilation
of what it professes to foster. The best *educated* man you will

often find to be the artisan, at all rates the man of business. For why? He has put forth his hand and operated on Nature; must actually attain some true insight, or he cannot live. The worst educated man is usually your man of fortune. He has not put forth his hand upon anything except upon his bell rope. Your scholar proper, too, your so-called man of letters, is a thing with clearer vision, through the hundredth part of an eye. A Burns is infinitely better educated than a Byron.

A common persuasion among serious ill-informed persons that the *end of the world* is at hand—Henry Drummond, Edward Irving, and all that class. So it was at the beginning of the Christian era, say rather at the *termination* of the Pagan one. Which is the most ignorant creature of his class even in Britain? Generally speaking the Cockney, the London-bred man. What does the Cockney boy know of the muffin he eats? Simply that a hawker brings it to the door and charges a penny for it. The country youth sees it grow in the fields, in the mill, in the bakehouse. Thus of *all* things pertaining to the life of man.

November 4.—To it thou *Taugenichts*. Gird thyself! stir! struggle! forward! forward! thou art bundled up here and tied as in a sack. On, then, as in a sack race, 'Running, not raging.' *Gott sey mir gnädig.*

November 12.—Have been two days as good as idle—hampered, disturbed, quite out of sorts, as it were quite stranded; no tackle left, no tools but my ten fingers, nothing but accidental drift-wood to build even a raft of. 'This is no my ain house.' Art thou aware that no man and no thing, but simply thy own self, can permanently keep this down? Act on that conviction.

How sad and stern is all life to me! Homeless! homeless! would my *task* were *done*. I think I should not care to die; in real earnestness should care very little; this earthly sun has shown me only roads full of mire and thorns. Why cannot I be a kind of artist? Politics are angry, agitating. What have I to do with it? will any Parliamentary Reform ever reform *me?*

This I begin to see, that evil and good are everywhere, like shadow and substance; inseparable (for men), yet not hostile, only opposed. There is considerable significance in this fact, perhaps the *new* moral principle of our era. (How?) It was familiar to Goethe's mind.

November 17.—The nobleness of silence. The highest melody dwells only in silence (the sphere melody, the melody of health); the eye cannot see shadow, cannot see light, but only the two combined. General law of being. Think farther of this.

As it is but a small portion of our thinking that we can articulate into thoughts, so again it is but a small portion, properly only the outer surface of our morality, that we can shape into action, or into express rules of action. Remark farther that it is but the correct coherent shaping of this outward surface, or the incorrect, incoherent, monstrous shaping of it, and no wise the moral force which shaped it, which lies under it, vague, indefinite, unseen, that constitutes what in common speech we call a moral conduct or an immoral. Hence, too, the necessity of tolerance, of insight, in judging of men. For the correctness of that same outer surface may be out of all proportion to the inward depth and quantity; nay, often enough they are in inverse proportion; only in some highly favoured individuals can the great endowment utter itself without irregularity. Thus in great men, with whom inward and as it were latent morality must ever be the root and beginning of greatness, how often do we find a conduct defaced by many a moral impropriety, and have to love them with sorrow? Thus, too, poor Burns must record that almost the only noble-minded men he had ever met with were among the class named Blackguards.

Extremes meet. Perfect morality were no more an object of consciousness than perfect immorality, as pure light cannot any more be seen than pure darkness. The healthy moral nature loves virtue, the unhealthy at best makes love to it.

December 23.—Finished the 'Characteristics' about a week ago; baddish, with a certain beginning of deeper insight in it.

January 13, 1832.—Plenty of magazine editors applying to me, indeed sometimes pestering me. Do not like to break with any, yet must not close with any. Strange state of literature, periodical and other! A man must just lay out his manufacture in one of those old clothes shops and see whether any one will buy it. The *Editor* has little to do with the matter except as commercial broker; he sells it and pays you for it.

Lytton Bulwer has not yet come into sight of me. Is there aught more in him than a dandiacal philosophist? Fear not. Of the infatuated Fraser, with his dog's meat tart of a magazine, what? His pay is certain, and he means honestly, but he is a goose. It was he that sent me Croker's Boswell; am I bound to offer him the (future) article? or were this the rule in such cases; write thy best and the truth. Then publish it where thou canst best. An indubitable rule, but is it rule enough?

Last Friday saw my name in large letters at the 'Athenæum' office in Catherine Street, Strand; hurried on with downcast eyes as if I had seen myself in the pillory. Dilke (to whom I had entrusted Dreck to read it, and see if he could help me with it) asked me for a scrap of writing with my *name*. I could not quite clearly see my way through the business, for he had twice or thrice been civil to me, and I did reckon his 'Athenæum' to be the bad best of literary syllabubs, and thought I might harmlessly say so much; gave him *Faust's curse*, which hung printed there. Inclined now to believe that I did wrong; at least imprudently. Why yield even half a hair's breadth to puffing? Abhor it, utterly divorce it, and kick it to the Devil.

Singular how little wisdom or light of any kind I have met with in London. Do not find a single creature that has communicated an idea to me; at best one or two that can understand an idea. Yet the sight of London works on me strongly. I have not perhaps lost my journey hither.

Hayward of the Temple, a small but active and vivacious 'man of the time,' by a strange impetus takes to me; the first time, they say, he ever did such a thing, being one that lives in a chiar'-oscuro element of which good-humoured contempt is the basis. Dined in his rooms (over Dunning's) with a set of Oxonian Templars, stupid (in part), limited (wholly), conceited. A dirty evening; I at last sunk utterly silent. None of the great personages of letters have come in my way here, and except as sights they are of little moment to me. Jeffrey says he 'praised me to Rogers,' who, &c. &c. It sometimes rather surprises me that his lordship does not think it would be kind to show me the faces of those people. Something discourages or hinders him; what it is I know not, and indeed care not. The Austins, at least the (Lady) Austin, I like; *eine verständige herzhafte Frau.* Empson, a diluted, good-natured, languid *Anempfinder*. The strongest

young man, one Macaulay (now in Parliament, as I from the first
predicted), an emphatic, hottish, really forcible person, but unhappily without divine idea. Rogers (an elegant, politely malig-
nant old lady, I think) is in town and probably I might see him.
Moore is I know not where, a lascivious triviality of great name.
Bentham is said to have become a driveller and garrulous old
man. Perhaps I will try for a look of him. I have much to see
and many things to wind up in London before we leave it.

I went one day searching for Johnson's place of *abode*. Found
with difficulty the house in Gough (Goff) Square, where the Dictionary was composed. The landlord, whom Glen and I incidentally inquired of, was just scraping his feet at the door, invited
us to walk in, showed us the garret rooms, &c. (of which he
seemed to have the obscurest traditions, taking Johnson for a
schoolmaster), interested us much; but at length (dog of a fellow)
began to hint that he had all these rooms to let as lodgings.

Biography is the only history. Political history as now written
and hitherto, with its kings and changes of *tax-gatherers*, is little
(very little) more than a mockery of our want. This I see more
and *more*.

The world grows to me even more as a magic picture—a true
supernatural revelation, infinitely stern, but also infinitely grand.
Shall I ever succeed in copying a little therefrom.

January 18.—Came upon Shepherd, the Unitarian parson of
Liverpool, yesterday for the first time at Mrs. Austin's. A very
large, purfly, flabby man; massive head with long thin grey
hair; eyes *both* squinting, both overlapped at the corners by a
little roof of a brow, giving him (with his ill-shut mouth) a kind
of lazy, good-humoured aspect. For the rest, a Unitarian Radical, clear, steadfast, but every way limited. One rather trivial-
looking young lady, and another excessively ill-looking, sat opposite to him, seeming to belong to him. He said Jeffrey did not
strike him as 'a very taking man.' Lancashire accent, or some
provincial one. Have long known the Unitarians *intus et in cute*,
and never got any *good of them*, or any ill.

January 21.—Yesterday sat scribbling some stuff close on the
borders of nonsense, about biography as a kind of introduction to
'Johnson.' How is it to be? I see not well; know only that it

should be light, and written (by way of experiment) *currente calamo.* I am sickly, not dispirited, yet sad, as is my wont. When did I laugh last? Alas! 'light laughter like heavy money has altogether fled from us.' The reason is, we have *no communion;* company enough, but no fellowship. Time brings roses. Meanwhile, the grand perennial *Communion of Saints* is ever open to us. Enter and worthily comport thyself there.

Nothing in this world is to me more mournful, distressing, and in the end intolerable, than mirth not based on earnestness (for it is false mirth), than wit pretending to be wit, and yet not based on wisdom. Two objects would reduce me to gravity had I the spirits of a Merry Andrew—a death's head and a modern London wit. The besom of destruction should be swept over these people, or else perpetual silence (except when they needed victuals or the like) imposed on them.

In the afternoon Jeffrey, as he is often wont, called in on us; very lively, quick, and light. Chatted about cholera, a subject far more interesting to him than it is to us. Walked with him to Regent Street in hurried assiduous talk. O'Connell I called a real specimen of the almost obsolete species *demagogue.* Why should it be obsolete, this being the very scene for it? Chiefly because we are all dilettantes, and have no heart of faith, even for the coarsest of beliefs. His 'cunning' the sign, as cunning ever is, of a *weak* intellect or a weak character.

Soon after my return home Arthur Buller called with a *mein bester Freund!* A goodish youth, affectionate, at least attached; not so handsome as I had expected, though more so than enough. He walked with me to Fraser's dinner in Regent Street, or rather to the door of Fraser's house, and then took leave, with stipulation of speedy re-meeting. Enter through Fraser's bookshop into a back-room, where sit Allan Cunningham, W. Fraser (the only two known to me personally), James Hogg (in the easy chair of honour), Galt, and one or two nameless persons, patiently waiting for dinner. Lockhart (whom I did not know) requests to be introduced to me—a precise, brief, active person of considerable faculty, which, however, had shaped itself *gigmanically* only. Fond of quizzing, yet not *very* maliciously. Has a broad black brow, indicating force and penetration, but a lower half of face diminishing into the character at best of distinctness, almost of triviality. Rather liked the man, and shall like to meet him again. Galt looks old, is deafish, has the air of a sedate Greenock burgher; mouth indicating sly humour and self-satisfaction; the eyes, old and without lashes, gave me a sort of *wae* interest for him. He wears spectacles, and is hard of hearing; a very large man, and eats and drinks with a certain west country gusto and research. Said little, but that little peaceable, clear, and *gutmüthig.* Wish to see him also again. Hogg is a little red-skinned stiff sack of a body, with quite the common air of an Ettrick shepherd, except that he has a highish though sloping brow (among his yellow grizzled hair), and two clear little beads of blue or grey eyes that sparkle, if not with thought, yet with animation. Behaves himself quite easily and well; speaks Scotch, and mostly narrative absurdity (or even obscenity) therewith. Appears in the mingled character of zany and raree show. All bent on bantering him, especially Lockhart; Hogg walking through it as if unconscious, or almost flattered. His vanity seems to be immense, but also his good-nature. I felt interest for the poor 'herd body,' wondered to see him blown hither from his sheepfolds, and how, quite friendless as he was, he went along cheerful, mirthful, and musical. I do not well understand the man; his significance is perhaps considerable. His poetic talent is authentic, yet his intellect seems of the weakest; his morality also limits itself to the precept 'be not angry.' Is the charm of this poor man chiefly to be found herein, that he *is* a real product of nature, and able to speak naturally, which not one in a thousand is? An 'unconscious talent,' though of the smallest, emphatically *naïve.* Once or twice in singing (for he sung of his own) there was an emphasis in poor Hogg's look—expression of feeling, almost of enthusiasm. The man is a very curious *specimen.* Alas! he is a *man;* yet how few will so much as treat him like a *specimen,* and not like a mere wooden *Punch* or *Judy!* For the rest, our talk was utterly despicable: stupidity, insipidity, even not a little obscenity (in which all save Galt, Fraser, and myself seemed to join) was the only outcome of the night. Literary *men!* They are not worthy to be valets of such. Was a thing said that did not even solicit in mercy to be forgotton? Not so much as the attempt or wish to speak profitably. *Trivialitas trivialitatum, omnia trivialitas!* I went to see, and I saw; and have now said, and mean to be silent, or try if I can speak elsewhere.

Charles Buller entertained as unfavourable an opinion of London magazine writers as Carlyle himself. Mrs.

Strachey's alarm about Buller's theories of life may be corrected by a letter from himself. The Bullers were at this time at Looe, in Cornwall. They came to town in October.

To Thomas Carlyle.

Looe: September 12, 1831.

My dear Friend,—I am very happy to hear from Mrs. Austin that you had called on her, because I was really anxious that you should know so admirable a specimen of the disciples of Bentham and be known to her. But I felt half afraid to introduce you because I did not know how you would get on with—not herself, because she being a Benthamite has taken on herself human form and nature, and is a most delightful specimen of the union of Benthamite opinions and human feelings—but with the more regular Radicals who render the approach to her house dangerous. Conceive how great was my pleasure at learning from her that you had called on her ; that you had come for the purpose of making acquaintance with John Mill ; and that you had met him to your mutual delight. I knew well that to make you esteem one another, nothing was wanting but that you should understand each other. But I did not do sufficient justice to the Catholicism of both of you to feel quite confident that this would be the certain effect of your meeting. In this world of sects people rarely talk to each other for any purpose but to find out the sectarian names which they may fasten on each other; and if the name but differs, they only spend their time in finding out the various ramifications of each other's dissensions. In names and professed doctrines you and John Mill differ as widely as the poles ; but you may well meet on that point where all clear spirits find each other, the love of truth, which all must attain in their road to truth. To you without any fear I point out John Mill as a true Utilitarian, and as one who does honour to his creed and to his fellow believers ; because it is a creed that in him is without sectarian narrowness or unkindness, because it has not impaired his philosophy or his relish for the beautiful, or repressed any one of those good honest feelings which God gave all men before Bentham made them Utilitarians.

I am delighted at the certain prospect which you hold out to me of seeing you, and of making the acquaintance of Mrs. Carlyle. I shall be delighted to talk once more of old times, and of those

which are coming, to tell of what we used to do and think together, and of all that we have done and learned and planned since
we have wandered many a weary foot from one another. Thus I
shall learn from you what are the outlines of the great work which
you are now committing to the judgment of a thoughtless age;
and what manner of life you have been leading in the North, and
what kind of one you propose now. I, in my turn, will tell you
of some little time well employed, and of much misspent; of various studies, and creeds, and theories, of many great designs, and
of a very small portion of successful fulfilment thereof. I will
tell you of my assiduous study of the law, of how the worthy
burghers of Liskeard have come to me and offered me a seat for
this borough whenever the Reform Bill shall be passed, and of all
that I propose to do when I become the most eminent of lawyers
and the most furious of demagogues. These matters I promise
myself to talk over with you in the city of smoke and season of
fog, where I trust I shall meet you in exactly a month.

I rejoice that you think so highly of John Mill. I have just
heard from him, and I am happy that he understands and esteems
you, as you do him. This is as it should be. I do not see how it
matters to one right-minded man in what course the opinions of
another fly as long as both spring from the same sacred well of
love of truth. I do not believe that you really differ very much
in opinion; sure I am that you will find none of any set of men
more deserving to think rightly than John Mill, who thinks deeply
and honestly always. He is very different from the herd of creatures whom you have been pestered with in that great mart of
conceited folly, where the hawkers of every kind of shallowness
and quackery vend their wares in such numbers and with such
clamour. This age is the millennium of fools. They have certainly by some means or another obtained a mastery over better
men. I do believe that in this land of ours there still exists the
good old spirit of industry, and thoughtfulness, and honesty which
used to animate our fathers. Yet in literature we are represented
by our magazine writers and reviewers (*verbo sit venia*), and annals,
and fashionable novels, and fashionable metaphysics and philosophy : and our concerns are managed by the creatures whom you
heard gabbling in the House of Commons with a gravity and an
ignorance which are not found combined even in the servants'
hall.

I do believe with you that the end of this world of Insipids is coming. We must kick away the distaff of Omphale and get up and bestir ourselves to rid the world of monsters. Whether we shall labour to good purpose, or only show our strength as Hercules did in tearing ourselves to pieces, it is not yet given us to know ; but whenever there is a day of awakening, I trust that all good men and true will unite against the fools, and take at least 30,000 of them into the valley of salt and slay them.

All other matters I reserve for our meeting, which will certainly take place before long unless the cholera or such like curse severs us, or unless the Reform Bill is thrown out, in which case I shall assuredly remain here with any two or three who may be found to fight against the ' Rotten-hearted Lords.' But there will be more than that ; almost as many as there are men.

Adieu ! with my father's and mother's and Arthur's best regards.

Yours sincerely,

CHARLES BULLER.

CHAPTER XI.

A GREAT catastrophe was now impending in Carlyle's life.
His father had been ailing for more than two years, sometimes recovering a little, then relapsing again; and after
each oscillation he had visibly sunk to a lower level. The
family anticipated no immediate danger, but he had himself been steadily contemplating the end as fast approaching him, as appears plainly from a small feeble note which
had been written on the 21st of September of this year,
and remains fastened into his son's note-book, where it is
endorsed as ' My father's last letter—perhaps the last thing
he ever wrote.'

My dear Son,—I cannot write you a letter, but just tell you that
I am a frail old sinner that is very likely never to see you any
more in this world. Be that as it may, I could not help telling
you that I feel myself gradually drawing towards the hour appointed for all living. And, O God! may that awful change be
much at heart with every one of us. May we be daily dying to
sin and living to righteousness. And may the God of Jacob be
with you and bless you, and keep you in his ways and fear. I add
no more, but leave you in his hands and care.

JAMES CARLYLE.

The old man at parting with his son in the summer
gave him some money out of a drawer with the peculiar
manner which the Scotch call *fey*—the sign of death when
a man does something which is unlike himself. Carlyle
paid no particular attention to it, however, till the meaning of the unusual action was afterwards made intelligible
to him. The reports from Scotsbrig in the autumn and

early winter had been more favourable than usual. On the 13th of December Carlyle sent him, evidently without any great misgiving, the last letter which he on his side ever wrote to his father.

4 Ampton Street, London : December 13, 1831.

My dear Father,—I have long proposed to myself the pleasure of writing you a letter, and must now do it much more hurriedly than I could have wished. I did not mean to undertake it till next week, for at present I am engaged every moment *against time*, finishing an article for the 'Edinburgh Review,' and can expect no respite till after Saturday night. However, our Lord Advocate having called to-day and furnished me with a frank, I embrace the opportunity lest none so good occur afterwards.

Alick informed me in general about ten days ago that you were 'all well.' In the last newspaper [1] stood a word from Jean that she 'would write soon.' I can only pray that she would do so, and hope in the meantime that she may have no worse news to tell me. This weather is very unhealthy—the worst of the whole year ; I often think how my mother and you are getting on under it. I hope at least you will take every care, and do not needlessly or needfully expose yourself ; it is bad policy to brave the weather, especially for you at this season. I pray you keep much within doors ; beware of cold, especially of damp feet. A cup of tea night and morning I should also think a good preventive. But perhaps Jean will be able to inform me that 'all is well ;' one of the blessings I ought to be most thankful for, as it is among the most precious for me.

We are struggling forward here as well as we can. My health is not worse than it was wont to be. I think I am even clearer and fresher than when you saw me last. Jane has been complaining somewhat, but is not regularly *sick*. Her cold has left her, and now she has a little occasional cough with weakliness, the like of which is very prevalent here at present. George Irving has been attempting to prescribe for her ; she even let him draw a little blood. I rather think, however, that her faith in physicians is somewhat on a level with my own ; that she will give them no more of her blood, but trust to exercise, diet, and the return of settled weather.

[1] The family still communicated with one another by hieroglyphics on the newspapers.

I cannot get on with the publishing of my book. Nobody will so much as look at a thing of the sort till this Reform business be done. Nay, I begin to doubt whether I shall at all during the present posture of affairs get my speculation put into print. There is only a limited time that I will consent to wait looking after it. If they *do not* want it, why then let them leave it alone. Either way will do for me; I only want to know which. Meanwhile I am making what little attempts about it seem prudent. If I altogether fail here, I may still have Edinburgh to try in. One way or another, I wish to be at the end of it, and will be so. Our Advocate, who is now quite recovered again and as brisk as a bee, would fain do something useful for me—find me some place or other that would keep me here. I know he has spoken of me to Chancellors and Secretaries of State, and would take all manner of pains; nevertheless I compute simply that the result of it all will be—Nothing; and I still look back to my whinstone fortress among the mountains as the stronghold wherefrom I am to defy the world. I have applications enough for writing, some of them new since I came hither. So long as I can wag the pen there is no fear of me. I also incline to think that something might and perhaps should be done by such as me in the way of lecturing; but not at this time—not under these circumstances. We will wait, and if it seems good try it again. On the whole I always return to this. As the great Guide orders, so be it! While I can say *His will be mine*, there is no power in earth or out of it that can put me to fear.

I could describe our way of life here, which is very simple, had I room. Plenty of people come about us; we go out little to anything like parties, never to dinners; or anywhere willingly except for *profit*. I transact sometimes immense quantities of *talk*—indeed, often talk more than I listen; which course I think of altering. It is and continues a wild wondrous chaotic den of discord, this London. I am often *wae* and awestruck at once to wander along its crowded streets, and see and hear the roaring torrent of men and animals and carriages and waggons, all rushing they know not whence, they know not whither! Nevertheless there *is* a deep divine meaning in it, and God is in the midst of it, had we but eyes to see. Towards two o'clock I am about laying down my pen, to walk till as near dinner (at four) as I like; then comes usually resting stretched on a sofa, with such small talk as may be going till tea; after which, unless some interloper drop in (as happens fully oftener than not), I again open my desk and work till bedtime—about eleven. I have had a tough struggle indeed with this paper; but my hand is now *in* again, and I am doing better. Charles Buller comes now and then about us; a fine honest fellow, among the best we see. There is also one Glen (a young *unhewed* philosopher, a friend of Jack's), and one Mill, a young *hewed* philosopher and partial disciple of mine: both great favourites here. W. Graham, of Barnswark, was in our neighbourhood for three weeks, and will be arriving in Glasgow again about this very night, unless he have struck in by Ecclefechan and home. He is busy with some American patents, and so forth; from which he is sure of a salary for one year, but I think scarcely of anything more. The American Consulship, of which he hoped much, has gone another road. He is fresh and healthy, and I hope will fall in with something. Irving does not come much here; only once since that gift of tongues work began, and we have not been even once with *him.* It was last week that he called. He looked hollow and haggard; thin, grey-whiskered, almost an old man; yet he was composed and affectionate and patient. I could almost have wept over him, and did tell him my mind with all plainness. It seems likely they will take his church from him, and then difficulties of all sorts may multiply on him; but I do not think he will altogether lose his wits—at least not so as to land in Bedlam; and perhaps he may yet see his way through all this, and leave it all behind him. God grant it be so. I have hardly another scrap of room here. I must scrawl my mother a line, and then bid you all good night.

> I remain always, my dear Father,
> > Your affectionate Son,
> > > T. CARLYLE.

John Carlyle was now with Lady Clare at Rome. To him, busy as he was, his brother continued to write with anxious fulness. John Carlyle, with considerable talent, had shown an instability of purpose, for which he received, if he did not require, a steadily sustained stream of admonition.

It was very gratifying to us (Carlyle wrote on the 20th of December) to learn that all went tolerably with you, both as person and as doctor; continue to wish honestly with your whole heart to act rightly, and you will not go far wrong: no other advice is needed, or can be given. I have never despaired, and now I feel more and more certain, of one day seeing you *a man;* this too in a time like ours when such a result is of all others the hardest to realize. One has to learn the hard lesson of *martyrdom,* and that he has arrived in this earth, not to *receive,* but to *give.* Let him be ready then 'to spend and be spent' for God's cause ; let him, as he needs must, 'set his face like a flint' against all dishonesty and indolence and puffery and quackery and malice and delusion, whereof earth is full, and once for all flatly refuse to do the Devil's work in this which is God's earth, let the issue be simply what it may. 'I must live, Sir,' say many ; to which I answer, 'No, Sir, you need not live ; if your body cannot be kept together without selling your soul, then let the body fall asunder, and the soul be unsold.' In brief, Jack, defy the Devil in all his figures, and spit upon him ; he cannot hurt you.

The good old mother at Scotsbrig was fluttered about her scattered children.

Our mother (wrote one of the sisters) has been healthier than usual this winter, but terribly hadden down wi' anxiety. She told me the other day the first gaet she gaed every morning was to London, then to Italy, then to Craigenputtock,[1] and then to Mary's, and finally began to think them at hame were, maybe, no safer than the rest. When I asked her what she wished me to say to you, she said she had a thousand things to say if she had you here ; 'and thou may tell them, I'm very little fra' them.' You are to pray for us all daily, while separated from one another, that our ways be in God's keeping. You are also to tell the Doctor, when you write, with her love, that he is to read his Bible carefully, and not to forget that God sees him in whatever land he may be.

This message Carlyle duly sent on, and with it the continued diary of his own doings.

To John Carlyle.

I have had such a bout as never man had in finishing a kind of paper for Macvey.[2] I called the thing 'Characteristics,' and despatched it, according to engagement, by the Saturday mail coach.

---

[1] Where Alexander Carlyle was still staying, without the farm ; having found no other in its place.

[2] Napier, for the *Edinburgh.*

Whether Napier will have it or not is uncertain to me ; but no matter, or only a secondary one, for the thing has some truth in it, and could find vent elsewhere. It is Teufelsdröckh, and preaches from this text : ' The healthy know not of their health, but only the sick.' As to Teufelsdröckh himself, hope has not yet risen for him ; nay, rather, certainly begins to show itself that he has no hope. Glen read the MS. ' with infinite satisfaction ; ' John Mill with fears that ' the world would take some time to see what meaning was in it.' ' Perhaps all eternity,' I answered. For the rest we have partially made up our minds here and see the course we have to follow. Preferment there is none to be looked for ; living here by literature is either serving the Devil, or fighting against him at fearful odds ; in lecturing it is also quite clear there could no profitable audience be had as yet, where every lecturer is by nature a quack and tinkling cymbal. So what will remain but to thank God that our whinstone castle is still standing among the mountains ; and return thither to work there, till we can make a new sally. God be thanked, neither my wife nor I am capable of being staggered by any future that the world can proffer. ' From the bosom of eternity shine for us radiant guiding stars.' Nay, our task is essentially high and glorious and happy ; God only give us strength to do it well ! Meanwhile, offers in the literary periodical way come thick enough. Three or four weeks ago Procter wrote to me that E. L. Bulwer had 'some disposition' to employ me in the 'New Monthly Magazine,' of which he is editor, and that it would be advisable for me to call on him ; to which proposal of course there could be no answer, except mild silence—*der Inbegriff aller Harmonieen.* Whereupon in ten days more the mystagogue of the dandiacal body wrote to me a most bland and euphuistically flattering note, soliciting an interview as my 'admirer.' I answered that for some days I was too busy to call, but would when I had leisure, as I yesterday did ; and found him from home. I have also looked into his magazine, and find it polished, sharp, and barren—yet not *al*together—the work as of gig-men, or rather gig-*boys* and whig-boys aiming blindly enough towards something higher : *Ahndungen einer bessern Zeit !* My business being to *see* all men, I will in time look towards the ' Inspired Penman ' once more and ascertain better what his relation to me really is. I have articles in my head, but if Naso (Napier) behave himself he shall have the pick of them.

Napier unexpectedly and even gratefully accepted 'Characteristics.' He confessed that he could not understand it; but everything which Carlyle wrote, he said, had the indisputable stamp of genius upon it, and was therefore most welcome to the 'Edinburgh Review.' Lytton Bulwer pressed for an article on Frederick the Great; Hayward was anxious that a final article should be written on Goethe, to punish Wilson for his outrages against the great German in the 'Noctes Ambrosianæ.' Hayward, too, had done Carlyle a still more seasonable service, for he had induced Dr. Lardner to promise to take Carlyle's 'History of German Literature' for the 'Cabinet Encyclopædia.' The articles on the subject which had already appeared were to form part of it; some new matter was to be added to round off the story; and the whole was to be bound up into a *Zur Geschichte*, for which Carlyle was to receive 300*l*. To Hayward then and always he was heartily grateful for this piece of service, though eventually, as will be seen, it came to nothing. These brightening prospects were saddened by the deaths of various eminent persons whom he held in honour. Dr. Becker died of cholera at Berlin, then Hegel from cholera also; and still worse, his old friend Mr. Strachey, whom he had met lately in full health, was seized with inflammation of the lungs, and was carried off in a few days.

Worst of all—the worst because entirely unlooked for —came fatal news from Scotsbrig, contained in a sternly tender characteristic note from his sister Jean.

To Thomas Carlyle.

Scotsbrig: January 22, 1832.

My dear Brother,—It is now my painful duty to inform you that our dear father took what we thought was a severe cold last Monday night; he had great difficulty in breathing, but was always able to sit up most of the day, and sometimes to walk about. Last night he was in the kitchen about six o'clock, but he was evidently turning very fast worse in breathing. He got only one right night's sleep since he turned ill, and had been sometimes insensible, but when one spoke to him he generally recollected himself. But last night he fell into a sort of stupor about ten o'clock, still breathing higher and with greater difficulty. He spoke little to any of us. Seemingly unconscious of what he did, he came over the bedside, and offered up a prayer to Heaven in such accents as it is impossible to forget. He departed almost without a struggle this morning at half-past six. The funeral is to be on Friday; but my mother says she cannot expect you to be here. However, you must write to her directly. She needs consolation, though she is not unreasonable; but it was very unexpected. The Doctor durst do nothing. Oh, my dear brother, how often have we written ' all well!' I cannot write more at present.

Your affectionate Sister,
Jean Carlyle.

Subjoined were these few words:—

It is God that has done it; be still my dear children.
Your affectionate Mother.

The common theme
Is death of fathers; reason still hath cried,
From the first corse till he that died to-day,
This must be so;

yet being so common, it was still 'particular' to Carlyle. The entire family were knit together with an extremely peculiar bond. Their affections, if not limited within their own circle, yet were reserved for one another in their tenderest form. Friendship the Carlyles might have for others; their love was for those of their own household; while again, independently of his feeling as a son, Carlyle saw, or believed he saw, in his father personal qualities of the rarest and loftiest kind. Though the old man had no sense of poetry, Carlyle deliberately says that if he had been asked whether his father or Robert Burns had the finest intellect, he could not have answered. Carlyle's style, which has been so much wondered at, was learnt in the Annandale farmhouse; and beyond the intellect there was an inflexible integrity, in word and deed, which Carlyle honoured above all human qualities. The aspect in which he regarded human life, the unalterable conviction that justice and truth are the only bases on which successful conduct, either private or public, can be safely rested, he had derived from his father, and it was the root of all that was great in himself.

Being unable to be present at the funeral, he spent the intervening days in composing the memoir which has been published as the first of his 'Reminiscences.' He was now himself the head of the family, and on him also fell the duty of addressing the remaining members of it on the loss which had befallen them.

As the subject is 'common,' so all that can be said upon it—the sorrows, the consolations, and the hopes—are common also. The greatest genius that ever was born could have nothing new to say about death. Carlyle could but travel along the well-worn road; yet what he wrote is still beautiful, still characteristic, though the subject of it is hackneyed.

London: January 26, 1832.

My dear Mother,—I was downstairs this morning when I heard the postman's knock, and thought it might be a letter from Scotsbrig. Hastening up, I found Jane with the letter open and in tears. The next moment gave me the stern tidings. I had written you yesterday a light hopeful letter, which I could now wish you might not read in these days of darkness. Probably you will receive it just along with this; the first red seal so soon to be again exchanged for a black one. I had a certain misgiving, not seeing Jane's customary 'all well;' and I thought, but did not write (for I strive usually to banish vague fears), 'the pitcher goes often to the well, but it is broken at last.' I did not know that this very evil had actually overtaken us.

As yet I am in no condition to write much. The stroke, all unexpected though not undreaded, as yet painfully crushes my heart together. I have yet hardly had a little relief from tears. And yet it will be a solace to me to speak out with you, to repeat along with you that great saying which, could we lay it rightly to heart, includes all that man can say, 'It is God that has done it.' God supports us all. Yes, my dear mother, it is God has done it ; and our part is reverent submission to His will, and trustful prayers to Him for strength to bear us through every trial.

I could have wished, or I had too confidently hoped, that God had ordered it otherwise ; but what are our wishes and wills ? I trusted that I might have had other glad meetings and pleasant communings with my honoured and honourworthy father in this world, but it was not so appointed. We shall meet no more till we meet in that *other* sphere where God's Presence more immediately is ; the nature of which we know not, only we know that it is God's appointing, and therefore altogether *good*. Nay, already, had we but faith, our father is not parted from *us*, but only withdrawn from our bodily eyes. The dead and the living, as I often repeat to myself, are alike with God. He, fearful and wonderful, yet good and infinitely gracious, encircles alike both them that we see and them that we cannot see. Whoso trusteth in Him has obtained the victory over death ; the King of Terrors is no longer terrible.

Yes, my dear mother, and brothers and sisters, let us see also how mercy has been mingled with our calamity. Death was for a long time ever present to our father's thought ; daily and hourly he seemed meditating on his latter end. The end, too, appears to have been mild as it was speedy ; he parted as gently as most do from this vale of tears ; and, oh ! in his final agony he was enabled to call with his strong voice and strong heart on the God that had made him to have mercy on him ! Which prayer, doubt not one of you, the All-merciful *heard*, and, in such wise as infinite mercy might, gave answer to. And what is the death of one near to us, as I have often thought, but the setting out on a journey an hour before us, which journey we have all to travel ? What is the longest earthly life to the eternity, the endless, the beginningless which encircles it ? The oldest man and the new-born babe are but divided from each other by a single hair's breadth. For myself, I have long continually meditated on death till by God's grace it has grown transparent for me, and holy and great rather than terrific ; till I see that death, what mortals call death, is properly the beginning of life. One other comfort we have to take the bitterness out of our tears—this greatest of all comforts, and properly the only one : that our father was not called away till he had done his work, and done it faithfully. Yes, we can with a holy pride look at our father there where he lies low, and say that his task was well and manfully performed ; the strength that God had given him he put forth in the ways of honesty and well-doing ; no eye will ever see a hollow, deceitful work that *he* did ; the world wants one true man since he was taken away. When we consider his life, through what hardships and obstructions he struggled, and what he became and what he did, there is room for gratitude that God so bore him on. Oh, what were it now to us that he had been a king ? now, when the question is not, What *wages* hadst thou for thy work ? but, How was thy work done ?

My dear brothers and sisters, sorrow not, I entreat you—sorrow is profitless and sinful ; but meditate deeply every one of you on this : none of us but started in life with *far* greater advantages than our dear father had ; we will not weep for him, but we will go and do as he has done. Could I write my books as he built his houses, and walk my way so manfully through this shadow world, and leave it with so little blame, it were more than all my hopes. Neither are you, my beloved mother, to let your heart be heavy. Faithfully you toiled by his side, bearing and forbearing as you both could. All that was sinful and of the earth has passed away ; all that was true and holy remains for ever, and the parted shall meet together again with God. *Amen ! so be it !* We, your children, whom you have faithfully cared for, soul and body, and brought up in the nurture and admonition of the Lord, we gather round you in this solemn hour, and say, Be of comfort ! well done, hitherto ; persevere and it shall be well ! We promise here, before God, and the awful yet merciful work of God's hand, that we will continue to love and honour you, as sinful children can. And now, do you pray for us all, and let us all pray in such language as we have for one another, so shall this sore division and parting be the means of a closer union. Let us and everyone know that though this world is full of briars, and we are wounded at every step as we go, and one by one must take farewell and weep bitterly, yet ' there remaineth a *rest* for the people of God.' Yes, for the people of God there remaineth a rest, that rest which in this world they could nowhere find.

And now again I say, do not grieve any one of you beyond what nature forces and you cannot help. Pray to God, if any of you have a voice and utterance; all of you pray always, in secret and silence—if faithful, ye shall be heard openly. I cannot be with you to speak, but read in the Scriptures as I would have done. Read, I especially ask, in Matthew's Gospel, that passion, and death, and farewell blessing and command of Jesus of Nazareth; and see if you can understand and feel what is the 'divine depth of sorrow,' and how even by suffering and sin man is lifted up to God, and in great darkness there shines a light. If you cannot read it aloud in common, then do each of you take his Bible in private and read it for himself. Our business is not to lament, but to improve the lamentable, and make it also peaceably work together for greater good.

I could have wished much to lay my honoured father's head in the grave; yet it could have done no one good save myself only, and I shall not ask for it. Indeed, when I remember, that right would have belonged to John of Cockermouth, to whom I offer in all heartiness my brotherly love. I will be with you in spirit if not in person. I have given orders that *no one* is to be admitted here till after the funeral on Friday. I mean to spend these hours in solemn meditation and self-examination, and thoughts of the Eternal; such seasons of grief are sent us even for that end. God knocks at our heart: the question (is), will we open or not? I shall think every night of the candle burning in that sheeted room, where our dear sister also lately lay. Oh God, be gracious to us, and bring us all one day together in himself! After Friday I return, as you too must, to my worldly work; for that, also, is work appointed us by the heavenly taskmaster. I will write to John to-night or to-morrow. Let me hear from you again as soon as you have composure. I shall hasten all the more homewards for this. For the present, I bid God ever bless you all! Pray for me, my dear mother, and let us all seek consolation *there*.

I am ever, your affectionate,

T. CARLYLE.

The promised letter to his brother was written, and lies before me; but a few sentences only need be extracted from what is essentially a repetition of the last.

Our father's end was happy; he had lived to do all his work, and he did it manfully. His departure, too, was soft and speedy; that last strong cry of his in the death-struggle to God for deliverance, that is one of the things we must remember for ever. Was it not the fit end of a life so true and brave? For a true and brave man, such as there are too few left, I must name my father. If we think what an element he began in, how he with modest un-wearied endeavour turned all things to the best, and what a little world of good he had created for himself, we may call his life an honourable, a noble one. In some respects there is perhaps no man like him left. Jane and I were just remarking two days ago that we did not know any man whose spiritual faculties had such a stamp of natural strength. Alas! we knew not that already he was hidden from our eyes. I call such a man, bred up in poor Annandale, with nothing but what the chances of poor Annandale gave him, the true preacher of a gospel of freedom—of what men can do and be. Let his memory be for ever holy to us: let us each in his several sphere go and do likewise.

For myself, death is the most familiar of all thoughts to me—my daily and hourly companion. Death no longer seems terrible; and though the saddest remembrances rise round you, and natural grief will have its course, we can say with our heroic mother: 'It is God that has done it.' Death properly is but a hiding from *us*, from our fleshly organs. The departed are still with us; are not both they and we in the hand of God? A little while and we shall all meet; nay, perhaps see one another again! As God will! He is great; He is also good. There we must leave it, weep and murmur as we will.

I feel, my dear brother, how this stroke must pain you. Speak of it as we may, death is a stern event; yet also a great and sacred one. How holy are the dead! They do rest from their labours, and their works follow them. A whole section of the past seems departed with my father—shut out from me by an impassable bar-rier. He could tell me about old things, and was wont most graphically to do so when I went to Scotsbrig. Now he will do so no more: it is past, past! The force that dwelt in him had expended itself; he is lost from our eyes in that ocean of time wherein our little islet of existence hangs suspended, ever crum-bling in, ever anew bodying itself forth. Fearful and wonderful! Yet let us know that under time lies eternity; if we appear and are (while here) in time and through time, which means change, mortality, we also stand rooted in eternity, where there is no change, no mortality. Be of comfort, then; be of courage! 'The fair flowers of our garland,' said Novalis, 'are dropping off here one by one, to be united again yonder fairer and forever.' Let it be so, please God. His will, not ours, be done!

To Mrs. Carlyle, Scotsbrig.

4 Ampton Street : January 30.

My dear Mother,—I have determined to write you a few lines to-day, my mind, and I trust yours also, being in a state of composure ; though there is specially nothing more to be said, the very sound of my voice will do you good.

Since I wrote last I have been in Scotsbrig more than in London : the tumult of this chaos has rolled past me as a sound, all empty, with which I had nothing to do. My thought was in the house of mourning, present with you and with the departed. We had excluded *all* external communication from us till the funeral should be passed. I dwelt with my deceased father. Our whole speech and action was of high solemn matters. I walked out alone or with my wife, meditating, peaceably conversing of that great event. I have reason to be very thankful that much composure has been vouchsafed me. I never so saw my honoured father and his earnest, toilsome, manful life as now when he was gone from me ; I never so loved him, and *felt* as if his spirit were still living in me—as if my life was but a continuation of his, and to be led in the same valiant spirit that in a quite other sphere so distinguished him. Be the great Father thanked for His goodness ; chiefly for this, if He have given us any light and faith, to discern and reverence His mysterious ways, and how from the depths of grief itself there rises mildly a holy eternal joy.

Edward Irving on sending up his name was admitted to me on Friday afternoon. His wife was with him. He prayed with us I think about the time they would be in the churchyard. I felt that he meant kindly ; yet cannot say that either his prayer or his conversation worked otherwise on me than disturbingly. I had partly purposed sending for him, but was then thankful I had not done it. His whole mind is getting miserably crippled and weakened ; his insane babble about his tongues and the like were for me like froth to the hungry and thirsty. My father was a *Man*, and should be mourned for like a man. We had to forget our well-meaning visitors, and again take counsel with ourselves, and I trust with the God that dwells in us—were this last done only in *silence*. My father's memory has become very holy to me ; not sorrowful, but great and instructive. I could repeat, though with tears yet with softly resolved heart, ' Blessed are the dead that die in the Lord ; they do rest from their labours, and their works follow them.' Yes, their *works* are not lost; no grain of truth that was in them but belongs to eternity and cannot die.

Jane faithfully bore and suffered with me. We spoke much. I trust that she, too, is one day to 'become perfect through suffering,' and even in this earth to struggle unweariedly towards perfection as towards the one thing needful. We talked of death and life, with the significance of each; of the friends we had lost; of the friends still mercifully left us, and the duties we owed to them. In our two fathers we found a great similarity with so much outward difference. Both were *true* men, such as the world has not many to show now; both faithfully laboured according to their calling in God's vineyard (which this world is); both are now in the land of truth and light, while we still toil in that of falsehood and shadows. A little while, and we too 'shall reap if we faint not.' Of the other world it seems to me we do know this, and this only: that it too is God's world; and that for us and for our buried ones He hath done, and will do, all things *well*. Let us rest here; it is the anchor of the soul both sure and steadfast; other safety there is none.

To you also, my dear mother, I trust the call has not been made in vain. I know that you have borne yourself with heroism, for you have the true strength in you. Sad, doubtless, will your mood long be—sadder, perhaps, than ours, than mine. Your loss is the keenest. The companion that had pilgrimed by your side for seven and thirty years is suddenly called away. Looking on that hand you now see yourself *alone*. Not alone, dear mother, if God be with you! Your children also are still round you to bear up your declining years, to protect and support you, to love you with the love we owed *both* our parents. Oh, Providence is very merciful to us!

Neither let any one of us looking back on the departed mourn uselessly over our faults towards him, as in all things we err and come short. How holy are the dead! How willingly we take *all* the blame on ourselves which in life we were so willing to divide! I say, let us not lament and afflict ourselves over these things. They were of the earth earthy. Now *he* has done with them; they do him (nay, except for his own earthly sinfulness, they *did* him) no evil. Let us remember only, one and all of us, this truth, and lay it well to heart in our whole conduct: that the living also will one day be dead!

On the whole, it is for the living only that we are called to live

—'to work while it is still to-day.' We will dismiss vain sorrows, and address ourselves with new heart and purer endeavour to the tasks appointed us in life. Forward! forward! Let us *do* more faithfully than ever what yet remains to be done. All else is unprofitable and a wasting of our strength.

We two are purposing to come homeward early in March, and shall most likely come to Scotsbrig first. I have (or found I had already) as good as concluded that bargain about the 'Literary History.' I have a paper on Johnson to write, and many little odds and ends to adjust; after which we seem to have no business to do here, and shall march and leave it for the time. For myself, I fear not the world, or regard it a jot, except as the great task-garden of the Highest; wherein I am called to do *whatever* work the Task-master of men (wise are they that can hear and obey Him) shall please to appoint me. What are its frowns or its favours? What are its difficulties and falsehoods and hollow threatenings to me? With the spirit of my father I will front them and conquer them. Let us fear nothing; only being the slaves of sin and madness: these are the only real slaves.

Jane is out, or she would have sent you her blessing, her affection. She is distinctly growing better, and I hope will have recovered her usual strength ere long. Perhaps she too needed affliction, as which of us does not? Remember us always, as we do you. God ever bless you all.

I remain, dear mother, your affectionate son,

T. CARLYLE.

To John Carlyle, Rome.

4 Ampton Street: February 16, 1832.

. . . I wrote copiously twice to our mother. A letter has since come full of composure and peace. The survivors, our mother in particular, are all well, and knit the closer for this breach among them. Jamie,[1] it seems, as I had partly advised him, makes worship regularly in the household; Alick has promised to do the like in his. John of Cockermouth[2] parted from them at Burnfoot, exhorting them with affectionate tears in his eyes to live all united, as they had heretofore done, and mindful and worthy of the true man whose name they bore. Thus has the scene in mild solemnity closed. When the news first reached me I sat silent some minutes, the word 'τέλος!' pealing mournfully

[1] The youngest brother.
[2] The half brother. Only son of Mr. James Carlyle's first marriage.

through my heart till tears and sobs gave me relief. Death has long been hourly present with me ; I have long learned to look upon it as properly the beginning of life ; its dark curtain grows more and more transparent ; the departed, I think, are only hidden—they are still here. Both they and we, as I often repeat, 'are with God.' I wrote down in my note-book all that I could remember as remarkable about my father ; his life grew wonderfully clear to me, almost like the first stage of my own. I had great peace and satisfaction in thinking of him. Let us in our wider sphere live worthy of a father so true and so brave ; hope too that in some inscrutable way an eternal re-union is appointed us, for with God nothing is impossible ; at all events, 'that He will do all things well.' Therein lies the anchorage that cannot prove deceitful.

Your last letter seemed to me the best I had ever got from you —perhaps among the best I have ever got from any one. There is so much heartiness and earnestness ; the image of a mind honestly, deeply labouring, in a healthy and genuine position towards nature and men. Continue in that right mood; strive unweariedly, and all that is yet wanting will be given you. Go on and prosper. *Klarheit, Reinheit, 'Im Ganzen, Guten, Wahren resolut zu leben.'* This is *all* that man wants on earth ; even as of old, 'the one thing needful.' Well do I understand, my dear brother, those thoughts of yours on the Pincian Hill.[1] They tore my inward man in pieces for long years, and literally well nigh put an end to my life, till by Heaven's great grace I got the victory over them—nay, changed them into precious everlasting possessions. I wish you could have read my book [2] at this time, for it turns precisely (in its way) on these very matters ; in the paper 'Characteristics' also, some of my latest experiences and insights are recorded ; these I still hope you will soon see. Meanwhile be not for a moment discouraged ; for the victory is *certain* if you desire it honestly ; neither imagine that it is by forgetting such high questions that you are to have them answered. Unless one is an animal they cannot be forgotten. This also however is true, that logic will never resolve such things ; the instinct of logic is *to say No.* Remember always that the deepest truth, the truest of all, is actually 'unspeakable,' cannot be argued of, dwells far below the region of articulate demonstration ; it must be felt by trial and indubitable direct experience ; then it is known once and for ever. I wish I could have speech of

[1] Relating to religious difficulties, of the usual kind.
[2] *Sartor Resartus.*

you from time to time; perhaps I might disentangle some things for you. Yet after all the victory must be gained by *oneself*. '*Dir auch gelingt es Dich durchzuarbeiten.*' I will here only mention a practical maxim or two which I have found of chief advantage. First, I would have you know this: that '*doubt* of any sort can only be removed by *action*.' But what to act on? you cry. I answer again in the words of Goethe, 'Do the duty which lies nearest;' do it (not merely pretend to have done it); the next duty will already have become clear to thee. There is great truth here; in fact it is my opinion, that he who (by whatever means) has ever seen into the *infinite* nature of duty has seen all that costs difficulty. The universe has then become a temple for him, and the divinity and all the divine things thereof will infallibly become revealed. To the same purport is this saying, *die hohe Bedeutung des Entsagens*, once understand *entsagen*, then life *eigentlich beginnt*. You may also meditate on these words, 'the divine depth of sorrow,' 'the sanctuary of sorrow.' To me they have been full of significance. But on the whole, dear brother, study to clear your heart from all selfish *desire*, that *free will* may arise and reign absolute in you. True vision lies in thy *heart;* it is by this that the *eye* sees, or for-ever only fancies that it sees. Do the duty that lies there clear at hand. I must not spend your whole sheet in preaching, and will add only this other precept, which I find more important every day I live. Avoid all idle, untrue talk, as you would the pestilence. It is the curse and all-deforming, all-choking leprosy of these days. For health of *mind* I have the clearest belief that there is no help except in this which I have been inculcating in you: action—religious action. If the mind is cultivated, and cannot take in religion by the old vehicle, a new one must be striven after. In this point of view German literature is quite priceless. I never cease to thank Heaven for such men as Richter, Schiller, Goethe. The latter especially was my evangelist. His works, if you study them with due earnestness, are as the day-spring visiting us in the dark night. Perhaps Lady Clare may profit much by them—only keep away *dilettantism;* sweep it out of being; this is no world for it; this is no revelation of a world for it. Among Goethe's admirers here I find *no* one possessed of almost the smallest feeling of what lies in him. They have eyes but see not, hearts but understand not; as indeed the whole world almost has. Let them go their way, do thou go thine.

CHAPTER XII.

A.D. 1832.   ÆT. 37.

A FEW weeks only now remained of Carlyle's stay in London. The great change at Scotsbrig recommended, and perhaps required, his presence in Scotland. His brother Alick had finally left Craigenputtock to settle on a farm elsewhere, and the house on the moor could not be left unprotected. In London itself he had nothing further to detain him. He had failed in the object which had chiefly brought him there. 'Sartor Resartus' had to lie unpublished in his desk. On the other hand, he had made new and valuable acquaintances—John Mill, Leigh Hunt, Hayward, Lytton Bulwer—for the first three of whom at least he entertained considerable respect. He had been courted more than ever by magazines. Owing to the effect of his personal presence, he had as much work before him as he was able to undertake, and by Hayward's help Dr. Lardner was likely to accept on favourable terms his 'Literary History.' He had learnt, once for all, that of promotion to any fixed employment there was no hope for him. Literature was and was to be the task of his life. But the doubt of being able to maintain himself honourably by it was apparently removed. His thrifty farmhouse habits made the smallest certain income sufficient for his wants. His wife had parted cheerfully with the luxuries in which she had been bred, and was the most perfect of economical stewardesses. His brother John was now in circumstances to repay the cost of his education, and thus for two years at least he saw his way clearly before him. Some editorship or share of editorship might have been attainable had he cared to seek such a thing; but the conditions of the London literary profession disinclined him to any close connection with it; and he had adjusted his relations with Napier, Fraser, Lytton Bulwer, and the rest, on terms more satisfactory to himself than complimentary to them. With Napier he was on a really pleasant footing. The 'Characteristics' had been published without a word being altered or omitted. He liked Napier, and excepted him from his general censures. He was now writing his review of Croker's 'Life of Johnson,' which he had promised Fraser as the last piece of work which he was to do in London. 'This is the way that I have adjusted myself,' he wrote. 'I say will *you* or your dog's carrion cart take this article of mine and sell it unchanged? With the carrion cart itself I have and can have no personal concern.' 'For Fraser I am partly bound as to this piece on Johnson. Bulwer, if he want anything on similar terms, and I feel unoccupied, shall have it; otherwise not he.' In such scornful humour he prepared to retreat once more for another two years to his whinstone castle, and turn his back on London and the literary world.

My attitude towards literary London, he said in a letter to John (February 18), is almost exactly what I could wish; great respect, even love, from some few; much matter of thought given me for instruction and high edification by the very baseness and ignorance of the many. I dined at Magazine Fraser's some five weeks ago; saw Lockhart, Galt, Cunningham, Hogg. Galt has since sent me a book (new, and worth little); he is a broad gawsie Greenock man, old-growing, lovable with pity; Lockhart a dandiacal, not without force, but barren and unfruitful; Hogg, utterly a singing goose, whom also I pitied and loved. The conversation was about the basest I ever assisted in. The Scotch here afterwards got up a brutish thing by way of a 'Burns dinner,' which has since been called the 'Hogg dinner,' to the number of 500; famished gluttony, quackery, and stupidity were the elements of the work, which has been laughed at much. Enough of literary life. The Montagus live *far* from us ; both Jane and the noble lady seem to have *seen* each other, and found that an interview once in the six weeks was enough. I have been there some thrice since you went. Procter regards me as a proud mystic ; I him (mostly) as a worn-out dud ; so we walk on separate roads. The other Montagus are mostly mere *simulacra*, and not edifying ones. Peace be to all such. Of male favourites Mill stands at the top. Jeffrey, from his levity, a good deal lower ; yet he is ever kind and pleasant. I saw Irving yesternight. He is still good-natured and patient, but enveloped in the vain sound of the 'Tongues.' I am glad to think he will not go utterly mad (not madder than a Don Quixote was), but his intellect seems quietly settling into a superstitious *caput mortuum*. He has no longer any opinion to deliver worth listening to on any secular matter. The Chancellor can eject him. It is provided by the original deed of his chapel that the worship there shall be that of the Established Church of Scotland. His managers I know have already consulted Sugden. Whether and how soon they may drive the matter to extremities is not to be guessed. I pity poor Irving, and cannot prophesy of him. His 'Morning Watch,' which he gave me yesternight, is simply the howling of a Bedlamite.

To Alexander Carlyle.

4 Ampton Street : February 19.

· · · · · ·

We are coming home as early as possible in the month of March. We are busy, very busy, and in our usual health ; Jane, though still complaining, rather better than she has long been. I do not think she is to be *strong* again till she has got into her home and native air, which of course will quicken our motions the more.

We have both of us determined to take better care of our health were we once home again ; I feel it to be a real point of duty, were it only for the greater quantity and better quality of work which good health enables us to do. We are also minded to try if we cannot be a little more domesticated among the moors of Puttock—to take a greater interest in the people there (who are all immortal creatures, however poor and defaced), and to feel as if the place were a *home* for us. Such as it is, I feel it a great blessing that we have it to go to. For the whole summer and on-wards to winter I already see plenty of *work* before me : how we turn ourselves afterwards need not yet be decided on. I was very glad to learn that you had promised to my mother to keep religion in your house : without religion constantly present in the heart, I see not how a man can live otherwise than unreasonably—than desperately. I think that you do really in heart wish to be a good man ' as the one thing needful ; ' also that you will more and more ' lay aside every weight,' and be found running the race faithfully for the true and only prize of manhood. This is my hope and trust of you, dear brother ; God turn it for both of us more and more into fulfilment. Believe me ever,

Your faithfully affectionate brother,

T. Carlyle

The Carlyles left London on the 25th of March. They returned to Scotland by Liverpool, staying a few days with Mr. Welsh in Maryland Street, and then going on as they had come by the Annan steamer. Mrs. Carlyle suffered frightfully from sea-sickness. She endured the voyage for economy's sake ; but she was in bad health and in worse spirits. The Craigenputtock exile, dreary and disheartening, was again to be taken up ; the prospect of release once more clouded over. Her life was the dreariest of slaveries to household cares and toil. She was without society, except on an occasional visit from a sister-in-law or a rare week or so with her mother at Templand. Carlyle, intensely occupied with his thoughts and his writing, was unable to bear the presence of a second person when busy at his desk. He sat alone, walked alone, generally rode alone. It was necessary for him some time or other in the day to discharge in talk the volume of thought which oppressed him. But it was in vehement soliloquy, to which his wife listened with admiration perhaps, but admiration dulled by the constant repetition of the dose, and without relief or comfort from it. The evenings in London, with the brilliant little circle which had gathered about them, served only to intensify the gloom of the desolate moor, which her nerves, already shattered with illness, were in no condition to encounter. Carlyle observed these symptoms less than he ought to have done. His own health, fiercely as at times he complained of it, was essentially robust. He was doing his own duty with his utmost energy. His wife considered it to be part of hers to conceal from him how hard her own share of the burden had become. Her high principles enabled her to go through with it; but the dreams of intellectual companionship with a man of genius in which she had entered on her marriage had long disappeared; and she settled down into her place again with a heavy heart. Her courage never gave way; but she had a bad time of it. They stayed a fortnight at Scotsbrig, where they heard the news of Goethe's death. At the middle of April they were on the moor once more, and Carlyle was again at his work. The 'Characteristics' and the article on Johnson had been received with the warmest admiration from the increasing circle of young intellectual men who were looking up to him as their teacher, and with wonder and applause from the reading London world. He sat down with fresh heart to new efforts. 'The Death of Goethe' was written immediately on his return for Lytton Bulwer. *Das Mährchen,* 'THE Tale,' so called in Germany, as if there were no other fit to be compared with it, was translated for 'Fraser,' with its singular explanatory notes.[1] His great concluding article on Goethe himself, on Goethe's position and meaning in European history, had to be written next for the 'Foreign Quarterly;' another for the 'Edinburgh' on Ebenezer Elliot, the Corn-law Rhymer; and lastly the essay on Diderot, for which he had been collecting materials in London. He had added to his correspondents the new friend John Mill, between whom and himself there had sprung up an ardent attachment.

[1] Carlyle told me that he had asked Goethe whether he was right in his interpretation of this story, but that he could never get an answer from him about it.

His letters to Mill are not preserved, but Mill's to him remain. Between Jeffrey and Mrs. Carlyle also the communication began again, Mrs. Carlyle apparently telling her cousin more of her inner state of feeling than she pleased to show to anyone else. Jeffrey had been an almost daily visitor in Ampton Street : he saw and felt for her situation, he regarded himself as, in a sense, her guardian, and he insisted that she should keep him regularly informed of her condition. In London he had observed that she was extremely delicate ; that the prospect of a return to Craigenputtock was intolerable to her. Carlyle's views and Carlyle's actions provoked him more and more. He thought him as visionary as the Astronomer in ' Rasselas,' and confessed that he was irritated at seeing him throwing away his talent and his prospects.

Carlyle, after his reception in London circles, was less than ever inclined to listen to Jeffrey's protests. If in the midst of his speculations he could have spared a moment to study his wife's condition, the state of things at Craigenputtock might have been less satisfactory to him. He was extremely fond of her : more fond, perhaps, of her than of any other living person except his mother. But it was his peculiarity, that if matters were well with himself, it never occurred to him that they could be going ill with anyone else ; and, on the other hand, if he was uncomfortable, he required everybody to be uncomfortable along with him. After a week of restlessness he was at his work in vigorous spirits—especially happy because he found that he could supply Larry's place, and again afford to keep a horse.

Carlyle now takes up his own story.

To Mrs. Carlyle, Scotsbrig.

Craigenputtock : May 2, 1832.

My dear Mother,—We are getting along quite handsomely here, though in the midst of chaos and confusion worse confounded :

Jemmy Aitkin and his man and innumerable oilpots being in full operation. They are painting the dining-room, lobby, and staircase ; and, to avoid such a *slaister* for the future, doing it in oil. We live in the drawing-room meanwhile, and I, for my part, study to 'jook and let the jaw go by,' minding my own business as much as possible, and what is not my own business as little as possible.

Betty Smeal[1] and Mary, of whose safe arrival we were somewhat relieved to hear, would tell you more minutely than my little note how all stood with us a fortnight ago. Jane had sent off to Templand for a maid, but began to regret she had not endeavoured to bargain with the other, who, awkward as she was, seemed faithful and punctual. However, on the Monday a new figure made her appearance ; one 'Nancy' from Thornhill, a most assiduous, blithe, fond little stump of a body, who will do excellently well. The cow, too, is mending. Jane is far heartier now that she has got to work : to bake ;[2] and, mark this, to *preserve eggs* in lime-water ; so that, as I said, the household stands on a quite tolerable footing.

For a week I felt exceedingly out of my element ; inclined to be wretched and sulky : no work would prosper with me : I had to burn as fast as I wrote. However, by degrees I got *hefted* again, and took obediently to the *gang* and the *gear*. I have got one piece of work done and sent off to London ; the other I have now fairly on the anvil, hot before me, and will soon hammer it out. One that is still in the middle ought not, as you know, to *crow day*. However, I think I can calculate on being pretty well through before this week end ; so that Jane may tell Alick that I shall be *ready for a horse* any time after Wednesday next he likes. I have seen or heard nothing, since his letter, of the Dumfries beast, and will wait now till I be there at any rate, if we are not provided otherwise in the mean time.

This I believe, dear mother, is the main purpose of my letter— that I am to see you again so soon. We will then go through everything by the more convenient method.

I have rooted out a thousand docks with my dock spade, which I find to be an invaluable tool.

Let me pray that I may find you as well as Jane described,

---

[1] A Scotsbrig maid, who had been in charge of Craigenputtock in the winter.

[2] A mistake on Carlyle's part. Mrs. Carlyle had not strength for household work. She did it ; but it permanently broke down her health.

mending the Rackburn road? I add no more but the message of my wife's true love to one and all of you. My own heart's wishes are with you always.

> I remain, my dear Mother,
>> Ever your affectionate,
>>> T. CARLYLE.

Jane wishes Jemmy to be on the outlook for a pig for her; she would not like to go *beyond* ten shillings, only *wishes* a good one could be had so, and come up with Alick's cart. I know not whether the scheme is feasible.—T. C.

To John Carlyle, Naples.

May 22.

We are contented with the appearance of your domestic position, and would fain see further into it. Your noble patient seems to suffer more than we anticipated. A certain real pity for her forlorn fortune, so gorgeous outwardly, within so desolate, comes over me; one could fancy it no despicable task to struggle towards rectifying a life wherein are such capabilities of good. But, alas! how little can be done! Therein, as in so many other cases, must the patient minister to herself. He whom experience has not taught innumerable *hard* lessons, will be wretched at the bottom of Nature's cornucopia; and some are so dull at taking up! On the whole, the higher classes of modern Europe, especially of actual England, are true objects of compassion. Be thou compassionate, patiently faithful, leave no means untried; work for thy wages, and it will be well with thee. Those *Herzensergiessungen eines Einsamen*, which the late letters abound in, are not singular to me. The spirit that dwells in them is such as I can heartily approve of. It is an earnest mind seeking some place of rest for itself, struggling to get its foot off the quicksand and fixed on the rock. The only thing I regret or fear is that there should be so much occupation of the mind upon itself. Turn *outward*. Attempt not the impossibility to 'know thyself,' but solely 'to know what thou canst work at.' This last is a possible knowledge for every creature, and the only profitable one; neither is there any way of attaining it except *trial*, the attempt *to work*. Attempt honestly; the result, even if unsuccessful, will be infinitely instructive. I can see, too, you have a great want in your present otherwise so prosperous condition: you have not anything like enough *to do*. I dare say many a poor riding apothecary, with five times your labour and the fifth part of your income, is happier. Nevertheless, stand to it tightly; every time brings its duty. Think of this, as you are wont, but think of it with a practical intent. All speculation is beginningless and endless. Do not let yourself into *Grübeln*, even in your present state of partial inaction. I well, infinitely too well, know what *Grübeln* is: a wretched sink of darkness, pain, a paralytic fascination. Cover it up; that is to say, neglect it for some outward piece of action; go resolutely forward, you will not heed the precipices that gape on the right hand of you and on the left. Finally, dear brother, 'be alive!' as my Shrewsbury coachman told a Methodist parson; *be alive!* all is included in that. And so, God keep you and me! and make us all happy and honourable to one another, and 'not ashamed to live' (as a voice we have often heard was wont to pray), 'nor afraid to die.' Amen.

I was at Scotsbrig last week, and found them all struggling along, much as of old. Our dear mother holds out well; is in fair health, not more dispirited than almost any one would be under her bereavement, and peaceful, with a high trust in the great Guide of all. We expect her here in about a week, with Alick, who is bringing up the cart with some sort of a horse he was to buy for me. We settled everything at Scotsbrig; the departed had left it all ready for settlement. Your name or mine (as I had myself requested)[1] is not mentioned in the will: it was all between my mother and the other five. Each had to claim some perhaps 120*l.*—each of the five. Our mother has the houses with some 28*l.* yearly during life.

Of ourselves here there is not much new to be said. Jane seemed to grow *very greatly* better when she set foot on her native heath; is now not so well again, but better than in London. I have written two things—a short *Funeral Oration* on Goethe: it is for Bulwer's magazine of June (the 'New Monthly'), and pleases the lady much better than me; then a paper on certain Corn-law Rhymes for Napier, of some twenty-five pages. I am now beginning a far more extensive essay on *Goethe*, for the 'Foreign Quarterly Review.' I am apt to be rather stupid, but do the best I can. Venerable, dear Goethe! but we will not speak a word here. Our pastoral establishment is much like what it was; duller a little

---

[1] Carlyle explains in his journal. He had represented to his father that he and his brother John had received their share of his fortune in their education, and that the rest ought to be divided among those who, by working on the farm, had assisted in earning it.

since Alick went, but also quieter. Our new neighbours have nothing to do with us except little kind offices of business. Articulate speech I hear little, my sole comfort and remedy is work. Work! rather an unnatural state, but not to be altered for the present. With many blessings, too: a kind, true-hearted wife, with whom a true man may share *any* fortune, fresh air, food, and raiment fit for one. The place is even a beautiful place in its kind, and may serve for a workshop as well as another. Let us work then, and be thankful.

The Whig Ministry is all out and gone to the devil, Reform Bill and all. Newspapers will tell you enough. For us here it is little more than a matter of amusement: 'Whoiver's King I'se be soobject.' The country is all in a shriek, but will soon compose itself when it finds that things are—just where they were. Incapable dilettantes and capable knaves—which is worse? Excuse my dulness, dear John. Love me always, and may God bless you.

T. CARLYLE.

P.S. by Mrs. Carlyle:—

My husband says: 'I have written the dullest letter; do take the pen and underline it with something lively!' But alas! dear brother, I have dined—on a peppery pie! and judge whether what he requires be possible: *console-toi.* I will write you a long letter some day, and all out of my own head, as the children say. In the meantime, believe that my affections and heartiest good wishes are with you now and always.

Your sister,
JANE W. C.

Pleasant letters came from London. John Mill, young, ingenuous, and susceptible, had been profoundly impressed by Carlyle. He had an instinct for recognising truth in any form in which it might be presented to him. Charles Buller had foretold that although Mill's and Carlyle's methods of thought were as wide asunder as the poles, they would understand and appreciate each other. They sympathised in a common indignation at the existing condition of society, in a common contempt for the insincere professions with which men were veiling from themselves and from one another their emptiness of spiritual belief;

and neither Mill nor Carlyle as yet realised how far apart their respective principles would eventually draw them. The review of Boswell's ' Life of Johnson' had delighted Mill. He had read it so often that he could almost repeat it from end to end. He recognised the immense superiority of intellectual honesty to intellectual power. He recognised the shallowness and feebleness of modern thought in the midst of its cant of progress. He professed himself a humble disciple of Carlyle, eager to be convinced (which as yet he admitted that he was not) of the greatness of Goethe ; eager to admit with innocent modesty Carlyle's own superiority to himself.

The letters from Mill were agreeable interludes in the life at Craigenputtock, pictures of which Carlyle continued regularly to send to his brother, while he recorded in his Diary the workings of his own mind.

To John Carlyle, Naples.

Craigenputtock: July 31, 1832.

My dear Brother,—Goodwife Macadam brought us your letter of the 4th from church with her on Sunday evening. It is the way the three last have happened to come, so we shall esteem it a happy omen when our neighbour thinks of getting a sermon. God be thanked, it is all right. You are well, and have now heard that we are well. Another letter, sent off through the Advocate by the Foreign Office, will be already in your hands. We shall henceforth eschew William Fraser as we would the genius of impotence itself, and trust mainly to the Post, which, though it has loitered, has never yet absolutely deceived us. I lament for poor Fraser— a worthy, friendly creature, but whose utter unpunctuality in a world *built* on time will frustrate every endeavour he may engage in, except the last—that of quitting life—which will probably be transacted in *right* season. I am angry, too, as well as sorry ; the idle losing of letters is a stretch of carelessness to which even the peasants of Glenessland are superior. Entrust any of them with a letter, he knows it *must* be attended to. Fraser to all appearance has also wasted my last letter to Goethe ; at least no message yet reaches me from Weimar, and I wrote to Eckermann last week on that hypothesis. Fie, fie, the foolish Fraser! And now, Doctor, taking to ourselves this practical lesson to be for our share in all things doubly and trebly punctual, we will leave the unfortunate man. All is right at last.

Both of us were heartily gratified with your letter. I have the cheering sight before me of a prophecy, often pronounced and asserted, realising itself. Jack is to be a man after all. Your outward relations seem all prosperous and well managed. Your character is unfolding itself into true self-subsistence. In the work appointed you to do you not only seem to work but actually work. For the rest, let us be patient under this delay and separation. Both were perhaps necessary; in any case, if we improve them, will turn to good fruits. I quarrel not with your solitude, nor with anything you do, so it bring yourself contentment and the feeling of profit. This is the best and only *rôle* you can have. Nevertheless, I have always found that companionship with *any* man that will speak out truly his experiences and persuasions (so he have such) was a most precious ingredient in the history of one's life; a thing one turns back to, and finds evermore new meaning in; for indeed this is real, and therefore inexhaustible. God made that man you speak with; all else is more or less theoretical and incomplete. Indeed, in every sense one is but an unhealthy fraction while alone; only in society with his equals a whole. For which reason it gratifies me that you make acquaintance with Gell and old Squares, the doctor. I could like well to know both of them. Sir W. (*ein Bornirter den man muss gelten lassen*) will make an excellent cicerone; can tell you all about Troy, too, and who knows what itineraries. Quadri will satirically show you Italian quackery, and how an ardent, hot temperament demeans itself therein. I must also esteem it no small felicity you naturally have: that of associating with a thoroughly courteous society-cultivated woman. No higher piece of art is there in the world. *Schone sie! Verehre sie!* Your whole law lies there. The weak, lovely one will be loved, honoured and protected. Is not in truth a noble woman (noblewoman or not) *Gottes lieblichster Gedanke*, and worth reverencing? Be diligent with your journal. Note everything, let it seem noteworthy or not. Have no eye towards publication, but only towards self enlightenment and pleasant recollection. Publication, if it seems needful, will follow of its own accord. Goethe's Italian travels are a fine model. *Alles rein angeschaut, wie es ist, und seyn muss.* I often figure you

in the Toledo street with lemonade-booths and macaroni cook-
eries, and loud singing, loud speaking multitudes on the loveliest
spot of earth's surface. I here on the Glaisters hillside, in the
warm dusk, the wilderness all vapoury and silent except a curlew
or two, the great heaven above me, around me only the spirits of
the distant, of the dead—all has a preternatural character unspeakably earnest, sad, but nowise wretched. You may tell me,
if you like, what German books your lady reads; and on the
whole be more and more minute in picturing out to me the current
of your natural day. I want to know what clothes you wear, what
sort of victual you subsist on.

To turn now the Scottish side of the leaf. I have finished
'Goethe's Works,' and corrected the proof of it since I wrote—a
long, desultory, rhapsodic concern of forty-four pages in the
'F. Q. Review.' These are no days for speaking of Goethe. I
next went over to Catlinns,[1] and Scotsbrig, leaving Jane at Templand (who rued much that she had volunteered to stay behind
me). The Catlinns agriculture was all green and prospering.
The farmer, with wife and child, had gone over to Brand's of
Craighorn, whither I followed them; and, strange enough, was
shortly after joined by Jamie and my mother, all engaged that
evening to have tea there! Everything was as one could have
hoped: crops all excellent, good health, good agreement, good
weather. I drove our mother to Annan next forenoon in the clatch,
as we call the old gig, which the new grey mare briskly draws
along: went and bathed there at the 'back of the hill,' in the very
spot where I was near drowned six and twenty years ago, whither
I will not return: found Ben Nelson (it was market day); dined
with him and talked immeasurably all afternoon, though I had
much rather have listened if he had liked.

I was at Annan another bathing day, but missed Ben. However,
we chanced to meet on Dodbeck Heights next Wednesday morning as I was returning home: appointed a rendezvous at our inn
and then over a thimbleful of brandy and water talked again for
the space of two stricken hours. Waugh I now asked for and
heard the strangest history. Lying among the pots, forgotten of
men, he sees his Aunt Margaret die (poor old Peg!) and himself
thereby put in possession of 50*l.* as inheritance. Whereupon,
shaving his beard and putting on change of raiment, he walks
down to Benson's, and there orders fodder and stall of the best;

---

[1] Alexander Carlyle's new farm.

reigns among the bagmen to heart's content ; shifts after a season to the King's Arms, Dumfries, and there or in some similar establishment is perhaps even now burning his fifty pound candle to the socket, and going out in stench ! Saw ever mortal the like ? The man, Doctor, is once for all deprived of understanding, the greatest misfortune, properly the only one, that can befall a man. He hath said to the father of No Work and Darkness, 'Behold I am thine.' Let me mention here more specially, before quitting Annandale, that at Scotsbrig all was busy and right ; hay harvest was at its height the day I came off, and prospering well. Our mother seemed in better than usual health, was delighted with her two bathes, and should have (had another) but the clatch failed and needed repairs. She said after, 'I kenna how many kind things I wanted to bid (thee say for) me to John ; and thou was ay gane first.' I said you understood them all, and I constantly (wrote with) pains about Scotsbrig and her. I am to write thither this night and send your letter. Alick also I write to : our boy is going to exchange horses with him for a week (when) we get the rest of our coals carted. Our newspapers go between these households and sometimes from one to the other ; there is all community we can kept up : frequent messages, constant good wishes.

Since I returned I have been employed translating a little piece named 'Novelle,' from the fifteenth volume of Goethe, and revising an old translation of 'THE Mährchen,' with intent to add some commentary ; and offer both papers to James Fraser. I have an essay to write on Diderot (for Cochrane), and all his twenty-one octavos lying here to read first : shall do it, any way, *invitâ Minervâ*, and may as well begin even now. I have upwards of a hundred pages to put out of me before winter. Stand to it ? *Nulla dies sine lineâ.* As to Dreck, he lies here quite calm bound up in twine. My partial purpose is to spend another 50*l.* on him, and have him printed by-and-by myself. I in some measure see through the matter, not yet wholly. One thing I imagine to be clear enough, that *bookselling*, slain by puffery, is dead, and will not come alive again, though worms may for some time live in the carcase. What method writers who have something to write shall next take is now the question. In a generation or two the answer (summed up from the procedure of wise, inventive men) will be forthcoming. To us any way *martyrdom* is the thing appointed ; in this and all other generations only the degree of it, the outward figure of it, vary. Thank God we have still food and vesture, and *can* still get a thing spoken out and printed ; more we need not covet, more is not necessary. I have a thing to send Napier on all this, but it is *in petto* yet. Meanwhile we get along tolerably enough ; all, as you fancied, is tight, tidy, and peaceable here—a flourishing garden, with blackbirds devouring the fruit, even apples a basket or two ; roses innumerable ; a park walled in (this was poor Alick's last act here) so that the ' rowantree gate' and all gates but the outer one are removed, and cow and horses graze at ease ; a monstrous peat-stack against grim winter ; money in one's purse, faith in one's heart. What is there wanting ? So we live here, a *wunderliches, abgesondertes Wesen.* Jane drives down to Dumfries to-morrow with the boy, and takes this letter. She is far enough from perfect health still, yet certainly improving. She greets you affectionately; was much pleased with your letter, especially that part where you speak so sensibly about *a good wife* and the blessedness she brings. I have some thought that we shall be in Edinburgh this winter, printing of Dreck and what not. I have Mill, and Mrs. Austin Jane has, as occasional correspondents in London. Mill and Glen are acquainted, though it is mostly on Mill's side ; Glen is so *fencible* a character, so near madness moreover. Mill's letters are too speculative ; but I reckon him an excellent person, and his love to *me* is great. He tells me Glen got your Naples letter, was much contented therewith, and well. His other news are the decease, or at least paralysis, of St. Simonianism ; and London politics, for which I care less every day. Buller is trying for Liskeard borough with hopes. The election will not be for several months ; no dissolution all winter. George Irving was at Annan at his father's funeral for two days. Edward, it seems, is summoned to answer for himself before the Annan Presbytery, and will come, and be deposed. The time is near; whether I shall see him uncertain. He is preaching in the fields about London ; at Hampstead Heath, his precentor in a tree (last account I saw). There was also a paragraph about building him a new church. His old congregation have offered *somebody* 1,000*l.* a year. Whether he takes it, not said. The Dows are *both* out, the last of them resigned. It is wholly a beastly piece of ignorance and stupidity, too stupid even for the gross heads of England. That the high, the holy, can find no other lodging than that swinish one is even the misery. God mend it, and us. Of Badams no news since we left him in Bartlett's Buildings ; gone from Enfield, with no good outlook moral or domestic. Poor Badams, *wie gern möcht' ich Dich retten!* Graham is still in Glasgow, no tidings could I get of him farther. Burnswark unsold. So goes the world here, dear brother. The weather is hot, the year is fertile beyond all example. The simple hope from the Reform Bill. Electioneering flourishes, in which I take no interest. Cholera is at Carlisle, and somewhat worse than ever in London. None of us are in the least *alarmed* at it. Be not you either. I paid Alick 45*l*. 8*s*. of your money. The 25*l*. 8*s*. was a tailor's account; and now you owe him nothing. I sent Jeffrey word that you had remitted the 43*l*. 10*s*. (specifying the items) to pay him, and that *I*, not you, was now (till I could get the Dumfries banker near) his debtor. He answers, gratified by your punctuality, and I will now clear him off the first time I am at Dumfries. He says you have justified what I thought unjustifiable. *Gott sey Dank!* I am in *no* need of money, otherwise I would freely take your help, and will continue as ready if you prove worthy. I can now pay the Advocate my own debt (had I once got my accounts in), and have a 50*l*. over. Another 100*l*., to be earned as fast as may be, will clear Edinburgh and even print Dreck. As Dreck can be unprinted till the means be lent me, so one hand will wash the other, and we shall do very well. Jeffrey is perhaps on his way to Edinburgh to-day. He is a candidate for the Membership there, and has a Radical opponent and a Tory. All men are disappointed in him a little, but remember his *past* services.

Jane says she will write you a complete letter next time. This is the thing she *says*. Let us see whether she will perform. I will not fail to remind her, if that will do. And now, dear brother, adieu.

Valeas mei memor,

T. CARLYLE.

Extracts from Journal.

May 18.—About beginning an essay on Goethe's life. All still dark, or rather all void; yet thin films, of bulk enough had they become substances, hover here and there. Have been well nigh idle again for a fortnight. Nothing spurs me but an *evil conscience*.

I have often remarked that the present generation has lost the faculty of *giving names*. The modern streets of towns (London for a chief example) and innumerable other things are proofs of this. They are reduced to name streets by the owner of the land,

by the builder, or in some other mechanical way, almost as if by
formula. Thus in Dumfries they have made their old Lochmaben
Gate into *English Street*, they have their *Irish Street*, and so forth.
In Manchester they have taken the ready-made London names,
have their Piccadilly and the like. In Liverpool they have named
streets by herbs (Vine Street, &c., &c.), by poets (Pope Street),
and by other desperate methods. What talent is specially requisite for giving a name? A certain geniality of insight, whereby
some real property of the thing reveals itself. A very little will
do, but some little is requisite; then, so useful are names, even
an indifferent one sticks. We cannot now give so much as a *nickname*. Giving a NAME, indeed, is a poetic art; all poetry, if we
go to that with it, is but a giving of *names*.

What a sad want I am in of libraries, of books to gather facts
from! Why is there not a Majesty's library in every county town?
There is a Majesty's jail and gallows in every one.

Wednesday, May 23.—Came news that Wellington has not been
able to get on, so violent was the spirit of the country and Parliament, so had given up the concern, and 'our friends' were once
more all in their places, with liberty to create peers or do what
they liked. *A la bonne heure!* Democracy gets along with accel-
erated pace—whither? Old borough-mongers seemingly quite
desperate; meetings, resolutions, black flags and white flags
(some even mount a petticoat in reference to the Queen), threatenings, solemn covenants (to oust Toryism), run their course over
all the Isles. I purely an on-looker, in any other capacity there
being *no need* of me.

Thus, then, after eighteen months of discussion and concussion
(enough to shake a far firmer than our worm-eaten constitution to
pieces) is this grand question to be decided in the affirmative?
Shall we give ourselves a chance to begin to try whether we can
help the maladies of England, or shall we not give ourselves a
chance?

Earl Grey and his squadron have moved along like honest, solid-
lying—luggage. Tumbled back they had always fallen on a resolute unanimous people, and been borne forward again. Could
they have passed a Catholic Bill, any 'Bill' requiring the smallest
address or management? Wellington is at the stake (in effigy) in
all market towns; undeservedly, as I imagine. The man seems a

Tory *soldier;* otherwise a person of great intrepidity, strategic-diplomatic faculty, soldierly (Dalgettyish) principle, and even directness and plainness of speech. Fond of employment doubtless, fond of power. Perhaps one of the most honest men in the House of Lords. Earl Grey can speak; act he apparently cannot. He should resign *directly* after passing his Bill, if he would avoid becoming the most unpopular man in England, which poor W. now is. *Basta!*

Wednesday, June 6.—Was at Templand yesterday; over the 'Bogra Craig' in the morning, and returned at night by the Lag road. Fine scent of hawthorns and green summer herbs; old-fashioned thatched cottages, clean, whitened, warm-looking in their *häusliche Eingezogenheit.* Woman with her children peeling potatoes by the water side, down in the chasm at Scarbridge. At night, hawthorn blossoms again, queen of the meadows, glowworms in Glenessland, a waning moon, and gusty north-easter. My own thoughts sad enough, yet not of that hateful *emptiness.* They are thoughts, not mere *sensations.* Mother and Jane waiting my (late) return.

Sir James Mackintosh is dead. A Whig of the highest order, the result of whose life is well-nigh exhausted with himself. Henceforth no man of such faculty is doomed to that unfortunate part of a 'supposer,' well paid for plainly *supposing,* and so *seeming* plausibly to act, but may become a *believer,* and actually set about doing. I saw Mackintosh only once, and never spoke to him, only heard him speaking.

Very kind letter from Mill, whose zealous and quite credible approbation and appropriation of *Johnson* gratifies me, I doubt, far more than it should. Unspeakable is the importance of man to man. A tailor at Thornhill, who had vehemently laid to heart the Characteristics, was also a glad phenomenon to me. Let a million voices cry out, 'How clever!' it is still nothing; let one voice cry out, 'How true!' it lends us quite a new force and encouragement.

I have no books, cannot by any convenient contrivance get any books; a little money in this, as in one or two other matters, might do something for me. Hast thou not the Book of Nature? A page of it; but here, in the Dunscore Moss, well-nigh a blank leaf. Not wholly so. Read it well.

The most stupendous of gigmen was Phaeton ; drove the bravest gig, and with the sorrowfullest results. An instance, too, of what the law of inheritance produces. He had built no sun chariot (could not build a wheelbarrow), but would and could insist on *driving* one, and so broke his own neck and set fire to the world.

July 21.—A strange feeling of *supernaturalism*, of 'the fearfulness and wonderfulness' of life, haunts me and grows upon me. Saw Ben Nelson at Annan; long talk with him. Unluckily my habit (and the people's habit with me) is rather to speak than to listen; I mean it no wise so, but so I often find it has proved.

'Society for the Diffusion of Common Honesty' were the usefullest of all societies could it take *effect*.

July 22.—A foolish puppet figure, which I saw in a huckster's shop-window at London in some lane, has awakened thoughts in me which I have not yet found any words for ! To imagine; *bilden!* That is an unfathomable thing.

As yet I have never risen into the region of creation. Am I approaching it ? *Ach Gott! sich nähern dem unaussprechlichen.*

Was there ever a more merry-andrew-looking thing (if we consider it) than for a wretched creature named man, or gigman, alighting for one instant on this 'everlasting earth,' to say, it is mine ! *It;* consider what *it* (the earth) properly is—*the reflex of the living spirit of man*, the joint production of man and God—

> Natur ist Schall und Rauch
> Umnebelnd Himmelsgluth.

The greatest of all past or present anti-gigmen was Jesus Christ. This age is quite especially wrecked and sunk in gigmanism.

Homer's 'Iliad' would have brought the author, had he offered it to Mr. Murray on the half-profit system, say five-and-twenty guineas. The Prophecies of Isaiah would have made a small article in a review, which, paying not under the rate of three guineas a sheet (excluding extracts, whereof there are none in Isaiah), could cheerfully enough have remunerated him with a five pound note. To speak of paying the writer of a true book is, on the whole, delirium. The thing is unpayable ; the whole world could not buy it. Could the whole world induce him by fee or reward to write it otherwise—opposite wise ? Then is he no writer, only a deplorable despicable scribbler, waiting till the besom of destitution sweep him away.

Authors are martyrs—witnesses for the truth—or else nothing. Money cannot make or unmake them. They are made or unmade, commanded and held back by God Almighty alone, whose inspiration it is that giveth them understanding; yet for the world whom they address, for the fitness of their language towards it, their clearness of insight into its interests, and the ear *it* shall give them—for all in short that respects their revelation *of* themselves (not their existence *in* themselves)—money, as the epitome and magic talisman of all mechanical endeavour whatsoever, is of incalculable importance. Money cannot hire the writing of a book, but it can the printing of it. The existence of a public library, or non-existence thereof, in the circle where a thinker is born will forward his thinking or obstruct and prevent it. When the thinker has discovered truth, it depends on money whether the world shall participate in such discovery or not participate. In how many other ways (as when your nascent wise man is poor, solitary, uneducated, &c.) can the ' talisman of power ' cut away impediments and open out the path ! Many a fallen spark too is quenched, or lives only as a spark, which could have been fanned into a cheerful light and fire. (No end to all this, which is to go into that paulo post future essay on *Authors*.)

Cholera at Carlisle ; a case talked of in Annandale. The cowardice or bravery of the world manifests itself best in such a season. Nothing lies in *cholera*, with all its collapses, spasms, blueness of skin, and what else you like, except *death*, which may lie equally in a common catarrh—in the wheel of the nearest hackney coach. Yet here death is original ; the dunce who, blinded by custom, has looked at it in the usual forms, heedless, unreasoning, now *sees* it for the first time, and shudders at it as a novelty.[1]

' The special, sole, and deepest theme of the world's and man's

---

[1] The cholera fell very heavily on Dumfries. For want of accommodation the sick were crowded together in a single large building, out of which few who had entered came out alive. The town was terror struck. Carlyle told me that the panic at last reached the clergy, who were afraid to go within the door of that horrible charnel house to help the dying in their passage into eternity, but preached to them from the outside through the open windows. He had no love for Catholic priests and what he called their poisoned gingerbread consolations ; but in this instance he bore an ungrudging testimony that the only minister of religion who ventured in among the sick beds was a poor priest ; and the poor priest, alas ! caught the infection and died.

history, whereto all other themes are subordinated, remains the conflict of unbelief and belief. All epochs wherein belief prevails, under what form it will, are splendid, heart-elevating, fruitful for contemporaries and posterity. All epochs, on the contrary, where unbelief, in what form soever, maintains its sorry victory, should they even for a moment glitter with a sham splendour, vanish from the eyes of posterity, because no one chooses to burden himself with a study of the unfruitful.'—'Goethe's Works,' vi. 159, on Moses and his Exodus.

These notes show how powerfully Carlyle's intellect was working, how he was cutting out an original road for himself, far away from the Radicalism of the day. But it is in the nature of such thoughts that they draw off a man's attention from what is round him, and prevent him from attending to the thousand little things and the many great things of which the commonplaces of life are composed. Vocal as he was—pouring out whatever was in him in a stream of talk for hours together—he was not the cheerfullest of companions. He spoke much of *hope*, but he was never hopeful. The world was not moving to his mind. His anticipations were habitually gloomy. The persons with whom he had come in contact fell short of the demands which the sternness of his temper was inclined to make on them, from the drudge who had ill-cleaned a vegetable dish, to the man of letters who had written a silly article, *or* the Phaeton who was driving the State chariot through the wrong constellations. Thus, although indigestion, which interfered with his working, recalled his impatience to himself, he could leave his wife to ill-health and toil, assuming that all was well as long as she did not complain; and it was plain to every one of her friends, before it was suspected by her husband, that the hard, solitary life on the moor was trying severely both her constitution and her nerves.

Carlyle saw, and yet was blind. If she suffered she concealed her trials from him, lest his work should suffer also. But she took refuge in a kind of stoicism, which was but a thin disguise for disappointment and at times for misery. It was a sad fate for a person so bright and gifted; and if she could endure it for herself, others, and especially Jeffrey, were not inclined to endure it for her. Jeffrey had been often in Ampton Street, claiming the privileged intimacy of a cousin. Eyes so keen as the Lord Advocate's could not fail to see how things were going with her. She herself perhaps did not hide from him that the thought of being again immured in Craigenputtock was horrible to her. Liking and even honouring Carlyle as he did, he did not like his faults, and the Lord Advocate was slightly irritated at the reception which Carlyle had met with in London, as tending to confirm him in the illusion that he was a prophet of a new religion. He continued to write to Mrs. Carlyle tenderly and even passionately, as he would have written to a daughter of his own. It was intolerable to him to think of her with her fine talents lost to all the enjoyments that belonged to her age and character, and provoking to feel that it was owing to moody fancies too long cherished, and fantastic opinions engendered and fed in solitude. She made the best of her position, as she always did. She had been greatly interested in the daughter of her landlady in Ampton Street, Miss Eliza Miles, who had so romantically returned Mrs. Carlyle's regard, that she had proposed to go back with her as a servant to Craigenputtock. Mrs. Carlyle knew too well what Craigenputtock was to allow her to accept Miss Miles's offer. She wrote to her occasionally, however, in the summer which followed their stay in London, and invited her to pay the place a visit.

To Miss Eliza Miles.

Craigenputtock: June 16, 1832.

My dear Eliza,—I could wager you now think the Scots a less amiable nation than you had supposed, least of all to be commended on the score of good faith. Is it not so? Has not my whole nation suffered in your opinion through my solitary fault. In February I made a voluntary engagement to write to you, which now in June remains to be fulfilled. Still I am fulfilling it, which proves that it is not altogether 'out of sight out of mind' with me; and could I give you an idea of the tumult I have been in since we parted, you would find me excusable if not blameless. I never forgot my gentle Ariel in Ampton Street; it were positive sin to forget her, so helpful she, so trustful, so kind and good. Besides, this is the place of all others for thinking of absent friends, where one has so seldom any present to think of. It is the stillest, solitariest place that it ever entered your imagination to conceive, where one has the strangest shadowy existence. Nothing is actual in it but the food we eat, the bed one sleeps on, and, praised be Heaven, the fine air one breathes. The rest is all a dream of the absent and distant, of things past and to come. I was fatigued enough by the journey home, still more by the bustling which awaited me there—a dismantled house, no effectual servants, weak health, and, worse than the seven plagues of Egypt, a necessity of painters. All these things were against me. But happily there is a continual tide in human affairs; and if a little while ago I was near being swept away in the hubbub, so now I find myself in a dead calm. All is again in order about us, and I fold my hands and ask what is to be done next?

'The duty nearest hand will show itself in course.' So my Goethe teaches. No one who lays the precept to heart can ever be at a stand. Impress it on your 'twenty' children (that I think was the number you had fixed upon). Impress it on the whole twenty from the cradle upwards, and you will spare your sons the vexation of many a wild-goose chase, and render your daughters for ever impracticable to *ennui*. Shame that such a malady should exist in a Christian land: should not only exist, but be almost general throughout the whole female population that is placed above the necessity of working for daily bread. If I have an antipathy for any class of people it is for *fine ladies*. I almost match my husband's detestation of partridge-shooting gentlemen. Woe to the fine lady who should find herself set down at Craigenputtock for the first time in her life left alone with her own thoughts—no '*fancy bazaar*' in the same kingdom with her; no place of amusement within a day's journey; the very church, her last imaginable resource, seven miles off. I can fancy with what horror she would look on the ridge of mountains that seemed to enclose her from all earthly bliss ; with what despair in her accents she would inquire if there was not even a ' charity sale ' within reach. Alas, no ! no outlet whatever for ' lady's work,' not even a book for a fine lady's understanding. It is plain she would have nothing for it but to die as speedily as possible, and so relieve the world of the expense of her maintenance. For my part I am very content. I have everything here my heart desires that I could have anywhere else, except society, and even that deprivation is not to be considered wholly an evil. If people we like and take pleasure in do not come about us here as in London, it is thankfully to be remembered that ' here the wicked cease from troubling, and the weary are at rest.' If the knocker make no sound for weeks together, it is so much the better for my nerves. My husband is as good company as reasonable mortal could desire. Every fair morning we ride on horseback for an hour before breakfast. My precious horse knew me again, and neighed loud and long when he found himself in his old place. And then we eat such a surprising breakfast of homebaked bread and eggs, &c. &c. as might incite anyone that had breakfasted so long in London to write a pastoral. Then Carlyle takes to his writing, while I, like Eve, ' studious of household good,' inspect my house, my garden, my live stock, gather flowers for my drawing-room, and lapfuls of eggs, and finally betake myself also to writing or reading or making or mending, or whatever work seems fittest. After dinner, and only then, I lie on the sofa (to my shame be it spoken), sometimes sleep, but oftenest dream waking. In the evening I walk on the moor—how different from Holborn and the Strand!—and read anything that does not exact much attention. Such is my life, agreeable as yet from its novelty if for nothing else. Now would you not like to share it? I am sure you would be happy beside us for a while, and healthy, for I would keep all drugs from your lips, and pour warm milk into you. Could you not find an escort and come and try? At all rates write and tell me how you are, what doing, what intending. I shall always be interested in all that concerns you. My health is slowly mending.

> Yours affectionately,
> JANE CARLYLE.

This is pretty, and it shows Craigenputtock on its fairest side. But there was a reverse of the picture. I have not seen any of Mrs. Carlyle's letters to Jeffrey, but in one of them she sent some verses. It was summer, for there were rose leaves along with them, for which Jeffrey seem? to have asked. That the verses below were written at Craigenputtock is certain, for they are dated from 'The Desert.' Time, circumstances, and Jeffrey's own acknowledgment that she had sent him verses of some kind, make it almost certain that they belong to this particular period. I find them among loose fragments in her own portfolio :—

To a Swallow building under our Eaves.

Thou too hast travelled, little fluttering thing—
Hast seen the world, and now thy weary wing
    Thou too must rest.
But much, my little bird, couldst thou but tell,
I'd give to know why here thou lik'st so well
    To build thy nest.

For thou hast passed fair places in thy flight ;
A world lay all beneath thee where to light ;
    And, strange thy taste,
Of all the varied scenes that met thine eye—
Of all the spots for building 'neath the sky—
    To choose this waste.

Did fortune try thee ? was thy little purse
Perchance run low, and thou, afraid of worse,
    Felt here secure ?
Ah, no ! thou need'st not gold, thou happy one !
Thou know'st it not. Of all God's creatures, man
    Alone is poor !

What was it, then ? some mystic turn of thought,
Caught under German eaves, and hither brought,
    Marring thine eye
For the world's loveliness, till thou art grown
A sober thing that dost but mope and moan
    Not knowing why ?

Nay, if thy mind be sound, I need not ask,
Since here I see thee working at thy task
    With wing and beak.
A well-laid scheme doth that small head contain,
At which thou work'st, brave bird, with might and main,
    Nor more need'st seek.

In truth, I rather take it thou hast got
By instinct wise much sense about thy lot,
    And hast small care
Whether an Eden or a desert be
Thy home so thou remain'st alive, and free
    To skim the air.

God speed thee, pretty bird ; may thy small nest
With little ones all in good time be blest.
    I love thee much ;
For well thou managest that life of thine,
While I ! Oh, ask not what I do with mine !
    Would I were such !

The Desert.

CHAPTER XIII.

JEFFREY carried Mrs. Carlyle's sad verses with him to the
'glades' of Richmond, to muse upon them, and fret over
his helplessness.   To him his cousin's situation had no re-
lieving feature, for he believed that Carlyle was entered
on a course which would end only less ruinously than Irving's—that he was sacrificing his own prospects, as well
as his wife's happiness, to arrogant illusions.   The fact
was not as Jeffrey saw it.   Carlyle was a knight errant,
on the noblest quest which can animate a man.   He was
on the right road, though it was a hard one; but the lot
of the poor lady who was dragged along at his bridle-rein
to be the humble minister of his necessities was scarcely
less tragic.   One comfort she had—he had recovered her
pony for her, and she could occasionally ride with him.
His mother came now and then to Craigenputtock to stay
for a few days; or when a bit of work was done they
would themselves drive over to Scotsbrig.   So far as Carlyle himself was concerned, his letters give an unusually
pleasant impression of his existing condition.

To Mrs. Carlyle, Scotsbrig.

Craigenputtock : June 29, 1832.

My dear Mother,—You shall have a short note from me, though
my task should stand half done all night.   Peter Austin I expect
will take you this on Monday, and tell you all about our last peat-
leading, and what not ; but I imagine you will not dislike a word
under my own hand also.

Thank Jean for her letter : it gave us great relief to know that you were getting into your natural way again; that the rest were all in theirs. Let us hope this good state of matters still holds. As for yourself, I think you must go and have a plunge in the Solway this fine weather. When I come down next I will try to keep an eye on the moon, bring the clatch with me, and roll you along therein myself. I too want much to be bathed.

We are all going on as you saw us, or better. Jane is a little out-of-sorts these two or three days, but in general seems clearly improving. The boy has cleaned the garden, which looks well now, and is at this moment slashing like a Waterloo hero among the nettle and dock hosts over the paling. I hope they will not smother him up, but that his little arm and blunt hook will cut a way through them. Betty has got 'Noolly' (the cow) back again, little improved in temper, she says. Soft grass will soften her.

As for myself, I am doing my utmost, and seeing, as you counselled, not 'to make it too high.' In spite of 'the Taylors' applauses' I find myself but a handless workman too often, and can only get on by a dead struggle. This thing, I calculate, will be over in two weeks, and so the stone rolled from my heart again— for a little. I mean to run over and ask what you are doing shortly after; most probably I will write first, by Notman.[1] For the rest, I am well enough, and cannot complain while *busy*. I go riding every fair morning, sometimes as early as six, and enjoy this blessed June weather, oftenest on the Galloway side, the road being open and good now. My beast is wholly satisfactory: learns fast to *ride*, is already a good canterer, tame, quiet, and biddable as ever horse was. The boy has had it in the cart, too, and finds no difficulty in handling it. So, dear mother, on *that* head set your heart at rest.

No 'Examiner' came this week. I have charged Alick to send you over the 'Courier' by Peter. The following week you will find either *it* or something at the post office at the usual time. Any way there are no news of moment. The poor old King has been hit (by a solitary blackguard) with a stone. Wellington was peppered with 'mud and dead cats' along the whole length of London. I am sad for him, yet cannot but laugh to think of the business : the cast-metal man riding slowly five long miles, all the way like a pillar of *glass !* Every beast, you see, has its burden; every dog its day.

Now, dear mother, you see I must finish. My brotherly love to

---

[1] The carrier.

them all. Take care of yourself, and let me find you well. All good be with you all, now and ever!

Your affectionate son,
T. CARLYLE.

To John Carlyle, Naples.

Craigenputtock : July 2, 1832.

We are all well, and where we were. Our mother was here with us for a fortnight not quite three weeks ago, and I took her down in the gig, by Alick's, too, in whose house and farm [1] we found all prosperous. He was making a gate when we came up to the brae, but soon threw down his axes in a delight to see us. It is thought he has not changed for the worse, and may do well in the Water of Milk, which he looks like doing, for there is a great improvement in him, and increase not only of gravity, but of earnest sense and courage. His little girl is a queer, gleg, crowing creature, whom he takes much delight in. Jamie, too, and the sisters are doing well, and seem to go on judiciously enough together, a proper enough spirit seeming to pervade all of them. Our good mother is very serious, almost sad (as she well may be), yet not unhealthy, not altogether heavy of heart. She has her trust on what cannot die.

Such much for Annandale, where you see there are, as our mother piously says, many mercies still allotted to us.

As to Craigenputtock, it is, as formerly, the scene of scribble-scribbling. Jane is in a weakly state still, but I think clearly gathering strength. Her life beside me constantly writing here is but a dull one ; however, she seems to desire no other ; has, in many things, pronounced the word *Entsagen*, and looks with a brave if with no joyful heart into the present and the future. She manages all things—poultry, flowers, bread-loaves ; keeps a house still like a bandbox, then reads, or works (as at present) on some translation from Goethe. I tell her many times there is *much* for her to do if she were trained to it : her whole sex to deliver from the bondage of frivolity, dollhood, and imbecility, into the freedom of valour and womanhood. Our piano is quite out of tune, and little better than a stocking-frame ; this is an evil not remediable just yet, so we must want music. We have a boy servant named McWhir, a brisk, wise little fellow, who can scour knives, weed carrot beds, yoke gigs, trim saddle-horses, go errands, and

[1] New farm to which Alick Carlyle had removed, called Catlinns.

cart coals—a very factotum of a boy—at the rate of one sovereign per *semestre*. He brings the horses round every favourable morning (Alick and Jamie got *me* a noble gray mare at Longtown), and Jane and I go off riding, for which we have now *two* roads, the Glaister Hill one being remade and smoothed, and a bridge just about built over the Orr. Our weather in these mornings would hardly do discredit to Italy itself. Furthermore, a huge stack of the blackest peats was built up for us last week. McWhir has cleaned the garden, full of roses now, has hewn down innumerable nettle and dock weeds in the '-new wood,' where some of the trees are quite high, and is busy this day weeding the 'hedge' and the walk. We have had no visits but one of a day from John Welsh of Liverpool, who seemed happy and fished in the Orr. I have work enough; respect more than I deserve; am not without *thoughts* from time to time; and so *we* play our part. Of my writings this is the list: one often mentioned on *Samuel Johnson*, which you will one day read with a little pleasure; a *Trauerrede*, also often mentioned, on the Death of Goethe, printed in Bulwer's Magazine, never yet paid for, or seen by me in print; a speculative-radical discussion of some 'Corn-Law Rhymes' (bold enough, yet with an innocent smile on its countenance), of which I corrected the proof (twenty-four pages) the week before last for Napier; finally, this thing I am now at the thirtieth page of, on *Goethe's Works*, a *barocque* incongruous concern, which I am principally anxious to get *done* with. James Fraser is again willing to employ me (though at that double rate), the people having praised *Johnson*. With the editorial world, in these mad times, I stand at present on quite tolerable footing. I mean to be in Edinburgh some time before very long, and keep matters going. Here, too, let me mention that I am at no loss for money myself, and have safely received your remittance of 100*l.*, and written to Alick that I will bring it down with me next time, or send it sooner; to Jeffrey I will write a fit message on the same subject to-morrow.[1] All friends were touched with a kind of *wae* joy to see, as I said, 'the colour of Jack's money,' after so many misventures and foiled struggles. Poor Jack will be himself again, in spite of all that, and make the world stand about, stiff as it is, and make a little (straight) pathkin for him. Fear it not: you are already free of

[1] John Carlyle had received money from Jeffrey besides the advances which he had received from his brother. He was now diligently paying all his debts.

debt, and in that the miserablest of all millstones is rolled from off you. I too expect to pay the Advocate his money (perhaps along with yours) : then I too shall owe no man anything. Anti-gigmanism is the fixed unalterable Athanasian Creed of this house : Jane is almost stronger in it (and in Anti-fine-ladyism) than myself. So while the fingers will wag, and the head and heart are uncracked, why should we care ? The world is a thing that a man must learn to despise, and even to neglect, before he can learn to reverence it, and work in it, and for it.

Of external persons or news we hear or see little. Mrs. Strachey sent an apologetic little letter to Jane the other week. She was just leaving Shooter's Hill, and about settling in Devonshire, I think at Torquay. She is earnest, sad, but not broken or dispirited. From John Mill I had a kind sheet of news and speculations. Mrs. Austin wrote lately that Goethe's last words were, *Macht die Fensterladen auf, damit ich mehr Licht bekomme !* Glorious man ! Happy man ! I never think of him but with reverence and pride. Jeremy Bentham is dead, and made his body be lectured over in some of their anatomical schools—by Southwood Smith, I think. You have likely seen this in the papers ; also that Sir Walter Scott lies struck with apoplexy, deprived of consciousness, and expected inevitably to die, at an hotel in Jermyn Street ! He has a son and daughter there too ; and dies in an inn. I could almost cry for it. Oh all-devouring Time ! Oh unfathomable Eternity ! Edward Irving is out of his chapel, and seems to be preaching often in the fields. He has rented Owen's huge, ugly bazaar (they say) in Gray's Inn Road, at seven guineas a week, and lectures there every morning. Owen the Atheist, and Irving the Gift-of-Tongues-ist, time about : it is a mad world. Who our poor friend's audience are I hear not. It is said many even of his women have given in. Some of his adherents seem to come before the police occasionally when they gather crowds on the street. His father, worthy old Gavin, was taken away, a few days ago, from sight of these perversities. Electioneering goes on here, in which I take no interest, more than in a better or worse terrier-fight. Reform-bill-ing is the universal business, not mine. . . .

I wholly understand your internal contentions at this period— the struggling, *Verwerfen*, and *Aufnehmen* that you have. It is a heavy burden on the shoulders of every true man, specially at this epoch of the world. It is by action, however, that we learn and attain certainty. The time for this with you is coming ; be ready for it. You have my deepest sympathy in these spiritual trials ; nevertheless I see them to be *necessary*. Not till now have you decidedly looked to me as if you were about becoming *a man*, and finding a manful basis for yourself. I have better hope than ever that it will turn for good. Keep up your heart, my dear brother ; show yourself a valiant man, worthy of the name you bear (for you too bear the name of a *brave man*), worthy of yourself. Trust in *me ;* love me. God forever bless you !

Your affectionate

T. CARLYLE.

So passed the summer. The Goethe paper (which did not please him : ' the time not having come to speak properly about Goethe') being finished and despatched, Carlyle took up Diderot. Diderot's works, five and twenty large volumes of them, were to be read through before he could put pen to paper. He could read with extraordinary perseverance from nine in the morning till ten at night without intermission save for his meals and his pipes. The twelfth of August brought the grouse shooting and young Welsh relations with guns, who drove him out of his house, and sent him on a few days' riding tour about the country. On returning he at once let the shooting of Craigenputtock, that he might be troubled with such visitors no more. A small domestic catastrophe followed, the maid-servant having misconducted herself and having to be sent away at an hour's notice. Her place could not be immediately filled, and all the work fell on Mrs. Carlyle. ' Oh mother, mother ! ' exclaimed Carlyle in telling her the story, ' what trouble the Devil does give us ; how busy he is wheresoever men are ! I could not have fancied this unhappy, shameless, heartless creature would have proved herself so ; but she was long known for a person that did not *speak the truth*, and of such (as I have often remarked) there never comes good.'

Meanwhile ' he stuck,' as he said, ' like a burr to his reading, and managed a volume every lawful day (week day). On Sabbath he read to his assembled household (his wife, the maid, and the stable-boy) in the Book of Genesis.' And so the time wore on.

To John Carlyle, Naples.

Craigenputtock : August 31, 1832.

Your letters, I see, are all opened and re-sealed again before they arrive ; but it makes little difference, since such is the will of the Potentates, poor fellows. We have no Carbonari secrets to treat of, and are quite willing to let any biped or quadruped reign in Italy, or out of it, so long as he can.

All is well here in its old course. My article works are all published, and away from me. The Goethe, which was the last of them, went off in a printed shape to Catlinns on Wednesday. It is a poor, fragmentary thing ; some of it was put into Teufelsdröckh's mouth, and I had a letter from London since asking where Teufelsdröckh's great work (' Die Kleider ') was to be fallen in with ! Did I say that the ' Corn-law Rhymes ' was printed without the slightest mutilation ? So far well ! I have now written to Napier to pay me for it, and with the proceeds mean forthwith to clear scores with the 'Advocate,' and sign myself *Nemini Debens.* This is one fruit which springs from my labours ; and why should I calculate on any other ? There are two little translations of mine off to Fraser—the ' Mährchen,' with a Commentary ; a shorter piece named ' Novelle.' F. is very complaisant with me ; whether he accept or reject these trifles is left with himself. My next task is a very tedious one, an essay on *Diderot ;* as a preliminary for which I have twenty-five octavo volumes to read, and only some eight of them done yet. It will serve me till the end of September, and be worth next to nothing when done. I have engaged for it, and must accomplish it. For the rest, be under no fear lest I overwork myself. Alas ! quite the other danger is to be dreaded. I do not neglect walking or riding (as, for instance, this morning). Besides, the air here is quite specially bracing and good. I have had a kind of fixed persuasion of late that I was one day to get quite well again, or nearly so—some day, that is, between this and the Greek kalends. Indeed, on the whole, I am full of a sentiment which I name ' desperate hope,' and have long been getting fuller. We shall see what will come of it. Meanwhile, in my imprisonment here, whether for life or not, I have bethought me that I ought to get infinitely more *reading* than I have now means of, and *will* get it one way or other, though the Dumfries libraries I have been prying into the rules and state of as yet yield nothing. A very large mass of magazines, reviews, and such like, I have consumed like smoke within the last month, gaining, I think, no knowledge except of the *no*-knowledge of the writing world. Books produce a strange effect on me here : I swallow them with such unpausing impetuosity from early morning to late night, and get altogether filled and intoxicated with them. A little talk were wholesome dissipation for me, but it is not to be had, and one can do without it. My Janekin, if not a great speaker, is the best of listeners, and what she does say is in general real speech and not clatter.

On Monday, the 13th of this month, apprehending with reason an inroad of grouse-killers, I fled about six in the morning (as it had been previously arranged) into Galloway. I breakfasted with Skirving of Croys, rode through Castle Douglas with its withered ' Reform Jubilee' triumphal arch (most villages have had such), and about two o'clock was in the parlour of Kirk Christ. The Churches were in high spirits to see me ; I remembered with a kind of shudder that it was *nine* years since you and I went thither on my last previous visit. The old people are hardly changed, look healthy and prosperous ; all was trim about them, flourishing crops, and the hope of harvest just about to begin realising itself. Great change in the younger parties : two female infants become rather interesting young ladies ; John, whom I remembered in bib and tucker, shot up to six feet and more, a talking, prompt, rather promising young man, intended for the factor line. I could not but reflect, as I have done more than once of late, how small a proportion of mere *intellect* will serve a man's turn if all the rest be right. John Church, as I said, promises well ; James, of Calcutta, is doing admirably well ; and their heads are both of the smallest. Church was full of Herculaneum, and will question you strictly when he gets you. Poor Donaldson, the schoolmaster, my old comrade in Kirkcaldy, has had to put away his wife for the sin of drunkenness, and was a saddish kind of sight to me. I called on old Gordon ; terrified him much, but found him a very worthy and sensible man. Finally, on Thursday morning I departed for Girthon, and by rough ways and over deep rivers reached home that evening about six. Galloway was beautiful, all green and orange under the clear mellow sky. I had glanced into a peopled country, seen old friends, and not wholly wasted my time.

From Annandale I hear good news and nothing else three days ago. They are all well; our mother rather better than usual. Jamie had begun his harvest; the crops excellent, the weather rather damp.

Alick gets the ' Courier ' newspaper from us weekly; our mother the 'Examiner,' of which she is exceedingly fond. In respect of this latter your punctuality is now and then desiderated; Tom Holcroft, who sends it to us, misses about one in the month, and I suppose cannot help it. I have just written to Mill, inquiring whether he can form no other arrangement for us. Holcroft has never written, and I hear not a word about him or Badams or any one *von diesem Geschlechte.* Neither has the 'noble lady' ever written, though she was written to months ago. Perhaps I should rather honour her for this omission or forbearance; Jane and I had evidently become hateful to all that diabolic household, and on our side quite satisfied, not to say sated, of it. Nevertheless the noble lady, quick as a lynx to see this, stood by us faithfully and acted with friendliest regard and very reverence to the very last. Now perhaps she thinks such effort superfluous, and so do we. Her feeling, we know, is kindly, and *can* be translated into no action of importance. Poor old Montagu seemed wearied out and failing. Badams used to say he would not last long. Procter is an innocent kind of body, but not undeserving the name our little lady here used to give him, 'that dud.' A more entire *dud* it would perhaps be difficult to find in the poetical or periodical world. Mrs. P. is honest, keen, and shallow. God mend them and us! we can do them ' neither ill na' good.'

My British news are now nearly written. I need not trouble you with Reform Bill rejoicings—and then, alas! with the electioneerings. It is here that the Reform Bill comes to the test. Set the angel Gabriel to elect a Parliament: how shall he succeed when there is none to elect? However, a new generation will rise —and then. The 'Advocate' I find is at Edinburgh canvassing, and will succeed though the whole country (that had much hope in him) have been disappointed. They say he will be made a judge when any vacancy occurs and will be set free of politics. It were a happy change.

Of Edward Irving I hear nothing except through the newspapers. Last week it was said they had taken a large house (now used as an exhibition establishment) in Newman Street, Oxford Street, and were to put a gallery in it, and were to preach and shriek there. He has published three papers in 'Fraser' on his Tongues. I read the last yesternight, and really wondered over it. He says he cannot believe that God whom they had so prayed to, &c., would *cheat* them. Neither can I. Oh, my poor friend Irving, to what base uses may we come!

But you have enough of this. I must now turn for a moment to Naples.

We have every reason to be satisfied with the accounts you send us. All seems moving as it ought, or nearly so. If you be spared to come back to us, you will have means of settling yourself where you see fittest; above all, you will have *inward* means. We shall find you, I can well perceive, a new man in many things. All right; only do not *turn yourself inwards.* Man may doubt as he will, but the great fact remains: *He is here,* and 'not to ask questions, but to do work.' *Kein Grübeln! N'écoute toi! Cor ne edito!* Do not come back from Italy as if you had been living in a well; speak with all people; no mortal but has something to tell could you once get him to speak TRUTH. Continue to mind your duties; to write in your journal; to *see* and to *do* with utmost possible freedom. I write these things in the shape of *precept,* but I know they might as well be put down like commendations and encouragements, for you already practise and in great part accomplish them. Do it more and more. I am glad you like Naples, and find it strange and notable. Had I the Oriental wishing carpet I were soon beside you noting it too. Gell has proved a little worse than I expected—not much worse. Do you speak Italian perfectly? As for the English—once knowing them to be nonentities, you do right to heed them no more; their whole secret is already understood. Not so with Italians. Even nonentities and *simulacra* (who, as Fichte said, *gar nicht existiren*) of the human sort are worth studying till you see how they are painted and made up. But in any case you are not without society. Your own Countess can tell you innumerable things. You see there what multitudes are so anxious to see—an epitome of English fashionable life; and both for theory and practice can learn much from it. Tell me more about the inside of your household —what you talk of, what you read, what you do. Describe all your 'household epochs' till I can figure them. Did you ever see Thorvaldsen at Rome? Have you met any Italian of a literary cast? any of a *thinking* character, literary or not? Is there any 'Count Menso' now in Naples (Milton's friend and Tasso's)? Is

the blood of St. January now in existence ? Did you see it there ?
Where does Carlo Botta live, the historian ? What of Manzoni ?
Or are all these Lombards and unknown in your country ? I
could ask questions without end. Finally, dear Jack, be of good
heart, for better things are in store for thee. There is a task for
every mortal in this world of the Almighty's ; for thee there is one
greater than for most. Let us stand to our work full of ' desperate hope.' There is on the whole nothing to be afraid of. ' He
that has looked death in the face will start at no shadows.' Come
home to us when the time arrives—to us that love you. Many
hearts will give you welcome, and rejoice to see you in the way of
well-doing. Our dear mother you must consider, much against
her will, wishing and meaning to say many things but unable.
So for the rest you know the affection of them all. Jane will not
send compliments—scarcely even kind regards. ' She meant to
write the whole letter herself, but did not know there was such a
hurry, and now I have done it.' Patience ! there is a good time
coming. The good wifie is clearly very much improved in health
(though troubled with a little cold for the last week) ; and im-
putes her cure to no medicine so much as to an invaluable *three-
fold* (trefoil) which grows in the bogs here, and makes most excellent bitter infusion. Our old mother also is to have some of it.
I, too, have tried it, and find it a praiseworthy pharmacy.

Adieu.   T. C.

P.S.—Cholera is spreading ; is at Carlisle, at Ayr, at Glasgow ;
has hardly yet been in our county—at least, only as imported.
It is all over Cumberland. ' Four carriers, one of them from
Thornhill, breakfasted together at Glasgow, and *all* died on the
way home.' The Thornhill one did, we know. It has gone back
to Sunderland and Newcastle. Medical men can do *nothing*, except frighten those that are frightable. The mortality, after all,
is no wise so quick as in typhus form ; is seen every year ; but men
are natural blockheads, and *common* death is not death.

Extracts from Note Book.

August 8.—I cannot understand *Morals*. Our current Moral
Law (even that of philosophers) affronts me with all manner of
perplexities. *Punishment* neither is nor can be in proportion to
fault ; for the commonest of all examples take the case of an erring woman.

And then how strange is the influence of what we call *honour :* when our fellow men are once come to be asked for their vote, how strangely do they alter every thing! Where are the limits of conscience and honour? what relation (even for the anti-gig-man) do the two mutually bear? Moral *force* and moral *correctness*—how shall the litigation be settled between these? Ought there to *be* any unpardonable offence? Ought the judge in any case to say irrevocably, *Be thou outcast* (as proud fathers have done to erring daughters for instance)? The world has declared, Yes. Neither is there wanting some ground for it. Necessity rules our existence : Man should step in and be as stern as Necessity, and *take the word out of its mouth.* Perhaps ; yet not with clear certainty. This is 'the Place of Hope.' Should man's mind have sudden boundless transitions of that sort ; have *vaporific points*, and *freezing points*, or should it not? *Weiss nicht.* It is all confused to me : seems to be all refounding itself. Happily the practical is no wise dubious.

Toleration, too, is miserably mistaken; means for most part only indifference and contempt : *Verachtung, ja Nichtachtung.* What is bad *is* a thing to be the sooner the better *abolished.* Whether this imply *hatred* or not will depend on circumstances. Not toleration, therefore, but the quickest possible abolition : that were our rule. A wicked hatred, in abolishing, *substitutes* new badness (as bad or worse). The pure, *praiseworthy*, useful Hatred were that which abolished and did not substitute.[1]

I am getting very weary of the 'Nature of the Time,' 'Progress

---

[1] This sentence did not please Carlyle or adequately express his meaning. Suppose we put it in this way. A set of people are living in a village which threatens to fall about their ears. The thatch is rotting, the foundations sinking, the walls cracking. Is the village to be pulled down, and are the people to be left houseless? The shelter is bad; but still it is some shelter— better than none—and likely to serve till something sounder can be provided. If it be doing no harm otherwise, this would be clearly the rule. But suppose the village to be breeding the plague by generating poisonous vapours. Then clearly the people will be better off with no roof over them but the sky. Substitute for the village, Paganism, Romanism, or any other lingering creed which eager persons are impatient to be rid of. Is Romanism morally poisonous? Knox and Cromwell answered clearly, Yes ; and with good reason, and so did not tolerate it. We, with or without good reason, have found it no longer poisonous, and so do tolerate. Both may be right. In our toleration there is no indifference or contempt. In the intolerance of Cromwell there was a hatred of the intensest kind—hatred of evil in its concrete form.

of the Species,' and all that business. The Time is here; men should use it, not talk about it: while they talk and lay not hold, it is gone and returns not.

Great is self-denial! Practice it where thou needest it. Life goes all to ravels and tatters where that enters not. The old monks meant very wisely: hit thou the just medium.

Thou complainest that enjoyments are withheld from thee, and thereby (thou caring nothing for *enjoyment* for its own sake) thy *culture* and experiences are in many ways obstructed. Be consistent: cultivate thyself in the want of enjoyment: gather quite peculiar experiences therein.

August 11.—A strange force of what I call 'desperate hope' is gathering in me: I feel a kind of defiant assurance that much shall yet be well with me, the rather as I care little *whether or not.*

It is true: evil must always continue: yet not this evil and that evil. *The* thing convicted of falsehood *must* be forthwith cast out: the Radical is a believer, of the gross, heathen sort; yet our only believer in these times.

Politics confuse me—what my duties are therein? As yet I have *stood apart*, and till quite new aspects of the matter turn up, shall continue to do so. The battle is not between Tory and Radical (that is but like other battles); but between believer and unbeliever.

Am inclined to consider myself a most sorry knave; but must cease *considering* and begin to work, whether at —— (?) or at Diderot? At the latter in any case *to-day;* and herewith enough.

> Oh! life turmoil—to-day—to-morrow
>   Unfathomed thing thou wert and art:
> In sight, in blindness, joy and sorrow
>   The wondrous Thomas plays his part.
>
> Awhile behold him flesh-clothed *spirit*,
>   He reaps and sows the allotted hours,
> Would much bequeath, did much inherit,
>   Oh! help the helpless, heavenly powers.

Seneca was born to be of the Church of England. He is the father of all that work in sentimentality, and, by fine speaking and decent behaviour, study to serve God and Mammon, to stand well with philosophy and not ill with Nero. His *force* had mostly oozed out of him, or 'corrupted itself into *benevolence*, virtue, sensibility.' Oh! the everlasting clatter about virtue! virtue! In the Devil's name be virtuous, and no more about it! Seneca could have been a Bishop Heber; Dr. Channing, too, and that set, have some kindred with him. He was, and they are, better than nothing, *very greatly* better. *Sey gerade, sey verträglich.*

September 3.—Beautiful autumn days! I am reading Diderot, with intent to write on him; not at all in a very wholesome state of mind or body, but must put up with it, the thing needs to be *done.*

I thank Heaven I have still a boundless appetite for reading. I have thoughts of lying buried alive here for many years, forgetting all stuff about 'reputation,' success, and so forth, and resolutely setting myself to gain insight, by the only method not shut out from me—that of books. Two articles (of fifty pages) in the year will keep me living; employment in that kind is open enough. For the rest, I really find almost that I do *best* when *forgotten* of men, and nothing above or around me but the imperishable Heaven. It never wholly seems to me that I am to die in this wilderness: a feeling is always dimly with me that I am to be called out of it, and have work fit for me before I depart, the rather as I can do *either way.* Let not solitude, let not silence and unparticipating isolation make a savage of thee—these, too, have their advantages.

On Saturday (September 15), being summoned to Dumfries as a juryman, and my whole duty consisting in answering 'Here' when my name was called, I ran out to the Bank, got my draft from Cochrane (for 'Goethe') converted into cash, added to it what otherwise I had, and paid the Lord Advocate 103*l.* 10*s.*, my own whole debt, and John's (43*l.* 10*s.*, which had been already sent me for that end); a short, grateful letter accompanied the banker's cheque, and the whole would reach its destination at latest last Monday morning. I now once more owe no man any money, have 5*l.* in my possession still, and a matter of 50*l.* or 60*l.* due to me. Be thankful!

I must to Edinburgh in winter; the solitude here, generally very irksome, is threatening to get injurious, to get intolerable. Work, work! and gather a few pounds to take thee.

Opinions of the article, 'Goethe,' Cochrane writes, are all 'eminently unfavourable.' The 'eminently' he has inserted on second thoughts by means of a *caret*. He is a wondrous man to see editing, that Cochrane; what one might call an *Editing Pig*, as there are learned pigs, &c. He is very punctual in *paying*, and indeed generally; that is his only merit. Use him sharply, almost contemptuously, and he remains civil, and does better than most. Bibliopoly, bibliopoesy, in all their branches, are sick, sick, hastening to death and new *genesis*. Enough! *Ach gar zu viel.*

Great meaning that lies in *irrevocability*, as in 'eternal creeds,' 'eternal forms of government,' also in final irreversible engagements we make (marriage, for one). Worth considering this. The proper element of belief, and therefore of concentrated action. On a thing that were seen to be *temporary* (finite and not infinite), who is there that would spend and be spent?

Sir Walter Scott died nine days ago. Goethe at the spring equinox, Scott at the autumn one. A gifted spirit then is wanting from among men. Perhaps he died in good time, so far as his own reputation is concerned. He understood what *history* meant; this was his chief intellectual merit. As a thinker, not feeble— strong, rather, and healthy, yet limited, almost mean and *kleinstädtisch*. I never spoke with Scott (had once some small epistolary intercourse with him on the part of Goethe, in which he behaved not very courteously, I thought), have a hundred times seen him, from of old, writing in the Courts, or hobbling with stout speed along the streets of Edinburgh; a large man, pale, shaggy face, fine, deep-browed grey eyes, an expression of strong homely intelligence, of humour and good humour, and, perhaps (in later years among the wrinkles), of sadness or weariness. A solid, well-built, effectual mind; the merits of which, after all this delirious exaggeration is done, and the reaction thereof is also done, will not be forgotten. He has played his part, and left *none like* or second to him. *Plaudite!*

In the middle of October, the Diderot article being finished, the Carlyles made an expedition into Annandale. They stayed for a day or two at Templand. Carlyle, 'having nothing better to do,' rode over, with Dr. Russell, of Thornhill, to Morton Castle, 'a respectable old ruin, which looked sternly expressive, striking enough, in the pale October evening.' The castle had belonged to the Randolphs, and had been uninhabited for two centuries. The court was then a cattlefold. In the distance they saw the remains of the old Church of Kilbride, where Dr. Russell told Carlyle, 'there still lay open and loose on the wall a circular piece of iron framing, once used for supporting the baptismal ewer, and protected for 350 years by a superstitious feeling alone.' Leaving Templand, they drove round by Loch Ettrick, Kirkmichael, and Lockerby, stopping to visit Alex. Carlyle in his new farm, and thence to Scotsbrig. Here the inscription was to be fixed on old Mr. Carlyle's grave in Ecclefechan churchyard. It was the last light of dusk when they arrived at the spot where Carlyle himself is now lying. 'Gloomy empire of TIME!' he wrote, after looking at it. 'How all had changed, changed; nothing stood still, but some old tombs with their cross-stones, which I remembered from boyhood. Their strange *süss-schauerliche* effect on me! Our house where we had all *lived* was within stone cast; but this, too, knew us no more again at all for ever.'

After ten days they returned to Craigenputtock, bringing 'sister Jane' with them, who was followed afterwards by the mother. The winter they meditated spending in Edinburgh. The following pleasant letter to John Carlyle was written a day or two before they started on this tour.

To John Carlyle, Rome.

Craigenputtock: October 17, 1832.

I finished my 'composition' the day before yesterday. Am bound for Annandale in the end of the week; and so here we are. I will not seal this till I have seen our mother, for I have *heard* nothing of them in a positive shape for many weeks.

There is little or nothing to be written of transactions, when the change of weather and of nervous sensibility are almost our only events. You can picture out Puttock, and how I sit here (in the library), with a blazing fire of peats and coals, careless of the damp, surly elements, having dulness only to struggle with. We keep a Famulus to go errands, yoke the gig, curry the cattle, and so forth; who proves very useful to us. Jane is sitting in the dining-room; reads, sews, rules her household, where cow, hens, human menials, garden crop, all things animate and inanimate, need looking to. She is not quite so brisk as she was, and the trefoil [1] has long been discontinued. However, she is certainly far better than while in London, and, on the whole, continuing to gather strength. The grey mare about six weeks ago kicked her harness to pieces with us, down at John McKnight's, without the slightest provocation, but did *us* no damage; I even brought the dame home on her back. However, such conduct was not to be dreamt of; so we despatched the animal to Alick, to make ready for the 'rood fair,' who, as we since vaguely learn (for they have not even informed us of this), has sold her to Jamie, that he, in carts and plough-harness, may teach her 'another road to the well.' With unexampled dexterity, having procured an awl and thread from Dumfries, I mended the old harness again (indiscernibly to the naked eye); and now little Harry draws us, and makes no bones of the matter, being in good heart and well provided with fodder, both long and short: that is the way we manage. All is tight and sufficient round us, and need not be in disorder: we want for nothing in the way of earthly proviant, and have many reasons to be content and diligent. Recreation we have none; a walk, a ride, on some occasions a combined *drive* for health's sake alone. Miss Whigham (of Allanton) called here the other day, and this is simply our only call since we came from London! Poor William Carson,[2] indeed, bounces up about once in the month to tea; but he is nigh distracted and one cannot count on him. I tried the schoolmaster, but he is a poor rawboned Grampus, whom I lent a book to, but could get no more good of. I have tried some of the peasants, but them also without fruit. In short, mortal communion is not to be had for us here. What, then, but do without it? Peter Austin (of Carstamon—Castra Montium—we, too, have had our Romans) is very useful to us; a decent, punctual man, the shrewdest of these parts. On the whole, I do not think I shall ever get anything better than a cheap and very peculiar *lodging* here; no home, I

[1] The supposed tonic made of the sorrel which grew freely in the Craigenputtock woods.

[2] A young neighbour.

imagine, has been appointed. For whom *is* such appointed ? The most have not even lodgings except by sufferance. The Advocate acknowledges his debt cleared ; it is the only thing we have heard of him for a great while. I imagine our relationship is a good deal cooled, and may now be visibly to him, as it has long been visibly to me, a rather fruitless one. His world is not our world : he dwells in the glitter of saloon chandeliers, walking in the ' vain show ' of parliamenteering and gigmanity, which also he feels to be vain ; we, in the whirlwind and wild piping battle of fate, which, nevertheless, by God's grace, we feel to be not vain and a show, but true and a reality. Thus may each without disadvantage go his several ways. If Jeffrey's well-being ever lay in my reach how gladly would I increase it ! But I hope better things for him ; though he is evidently declining in the world's grace, and knows as well as the world that his political career has proved a nonentity. Often have I lamented to think that so genial a nature had been (by the *Zeitgeist* who works such misery) turned into that frosty, unfruitful course. But, as George Rae said, ' D—n you, be wae for yoursel',' so there we leave it. On that busy day I got the proof sheets of that Fraser concern, *The Tale by Goethe*, which is his leading item for this month, but has not got hither yet. It is not a bad thing ; the commentary cost me but a day, and does well enough. The produce belongs to my little dame to buy pins for her ; she got it as present long ago at the *Hill*, and reckoned it unavailable. Fraser applied for a paper on ' Walter Scott :' I declined, having a great aversion to that obituary kind of work—so undertaker-like ; but I said I might perhaps do it, afterwards. This thing I have been cobbling together last is a long paper on 'Diderot,' for Cochrane. I had an immense reading, to little purpose otherwise, and am very glad to have it all behind me. And now, after a few days' sight of friends, I must back hither into the wold, and dig a little more.

We are not for Edinburgh till six weeks hence, so there is time to do something previously. I shall have funds enough : there is this thing ; Napier, too, owes me above 60*l.*, some of it for nine or ten months, and seems to be shy of paying. I shall see better what he means in Edinburgh ; his ' Review,' except for Macaulay (who as yet has only sung old songs of Liberalism and the like, with a new windpipe) is the utterest ' dry rubbish shot here ;' yet by a kind of fatality it may linger on who knows how long, and perhaps Naso does not think my *moisture* would improve it. *A la bonne* *heure!* There are plenty of able editors zealous enough to employ me; this is all the fame (*Fama Diva!*) I fall in with, or need; so that when you come home, Doctor, there will be a considerable volume for you to read, and I, in the interim, have lived thereby. I do not mean to work much at Edinburgh for a while, but to *ask* and *look;* that makes me the busier at present. It is three years I have been absent, and several things will be changed.

Your offer, dear Jack, is kind, brotherly, suitable; neither shall you be forbid to pay your 'debts,' and much more (if you come to have the means, and we both prove worthy); but in the meanwhile it were madness to reap corn not yet in the ear (or kill the goose for her golden eggs, if you like that figure better); your great outlook at present is to get yourself set up in medical practice, for which end all the money you can possibly save will be essential. I look to see you a faithful doctor, *real,* not an imaginary worker in that fold whereto God's endowment has qualified and appointed you. The rest I say honestly is within the merest trifle of indifferent to me. How *long* (were there nothing more in it) will it last? Walter Scott is now poorer than I am; has left all his *wages* behind. If he spoke the truth it was well for him; if not, not well.

Adieu, dear brother; adieu

T. CARLYLE.

Jeffrey's relations with Carlyle might be cooling. To his cousin his affection was as warm as ever, though they seemed to enjoy tormenting each other. He had been long silent, finding a correspondence which could not help Mrs. Carlyle exceedingly painful. He had been busy getting himself returned for Edinburgh; but something more than this—impatience, provocation, and conscious inability to do any good—had stopped his pen. Now, however, he heard that the Carlyles were actually coming to Edinburgh, and the news brought a letter from him of warm anticipation.

The journey, which had been arranged for the beginning of December, was delayed by the illness of Mrs. Carlyle's grandfather, her mother's father, old Mr. Welsh of Templand, which ended in death. Mrs. Carlyle went

down to assist in nursing him, leaving her husband alone
with his mother at Craigenputtock, himself busy in charge
of the household economies, which his mother, either out
of respect for her daughter-in-law, or in fear of her, declined to meddle with. He had to congratulate himself
that the establishment was not on fire; nevertheless, he
wrote that his 'coadjutor's return would bring blessings
with it.' The illness, however, ended fatally, and she
could not come back to him till it was over.

To John Carlyle, Rome.

Craigenputtock: December 2, 1832.

Mrs. Welsh, I told you in my last letter, was not well; we had
driven over the moors out of Annandale, and seen her as we past,
apparently in a rather better state. But scarcely had sister Jane
after a week got conveyed home again, and our mother got up
hither, on pressing invitation, to see us, when a letter came from
Templand with intelligence that poor old grandfather was much
worse, and Mrs. Welsh, throwing by all her own ailments, had
started up to watch over him; whereupon my Jane thought it
right to set off without delay, and so left my mother and me by
ourselves here. It is needless to fill your sheet with long accounts of comings and goings, of agitations, sorrowings, and con-
fusions; enough to inform you that the old man now lies no more
on a sick bed, but in his last home beside his loved ones in the
churchyard of Crawford, where we laid him on Friday gone a
week. He had the gentlest death, and had numbered fourscore
years. Fond remembrances, and a mild long-anticipated sorrow
attended him. Man issues from eternity; walks in a 'Time Element' encompassed by eternity, and again in eternity disappears.
Fearful and wonderful! This only we know, that God is above it,
that God made it, and rules it for good. What change of life this
may produce for Mrs. Welsh we have not understood yet. Most
probably she will retain the home at Templand, and give up the
ground and farming establishment. Such at least were her wisest
plan. But Jane and I hastened off on the Saturday to relieve my
mother, who was watching here in total loneliness, agitated too
with change of servants and so forth.

For the rest receive thankfully the assurance that all continues

well. The cholera, of which I wrote to you,[1] is gone, taking about
500 souls with it, which from a population of 13,000, was, in the
space of some four weeks, rather an alarming proportion. The terror of the adjacent people, which was excessive and indeed dis-
graceful, has hardly yet subsided. Happily the pest does not
spread ; a few cases occurred in the Galloway villages, elsewhere
none, or hardly any, and so it went its way as mysteriously as it
had come. Nobody connected much with us has been taken, many
as were exposed. Death, however, in other shapes, is as of old
busy. James Thomson of Cleughside is gone lately. . . . Old
Wull Nay is dead ; his poor old wife (they say) bitterly lamented,
and 'hung by the hearse,' which, however, could not stay. . . . A
son of Davie Corrie, married about a year ago, is also dead. What
is this whole earth but a kind of Golgotha, a scene of Death-Life,
where inexorable *Time* is producing all and devouring all ? Happily there is a Heaven round it ; otherwise for me it were not in-
habitable. Courage ! courage !

Uns zu verewigen sind wir ja da.

On Wednesday I got your letter at Dumfries ; called also at the
bank, and found 135*l.* ready, for which I took a bank receipt that
shall be ready for you on your home-coming. I do not need the
money at present, and you will need it ; therefore, much as I rejoice in the spirit you display, let it *dabey bleiben* till we see how
times turn. You may by possibility become a moneyed man ; I
never. The relation between us in any case is already settled.

Alick is grown more collected, has lost none of his energy, nor
on occasion his biting satire, which however his wife is happily
too thick-skinned to feel. They will struggle on I think, and not
be defeated. Jamie too goes along satisfactorily, a shrewd sort of
fellow with much gaiety, who sometimes in his laughter-loving
moods reminds me slightly of you. No two of the house have such
a heart-relish for the ludicrous, though we all like it. Our good
mother is in tolerable health and heart. She improved much with
us here the first two weeks, but fell off again for want of exercise
and excitement. She read here about the persecutions of the
Scotch Church, and in some of Knox's writings I had ; not even
disdaining 'Fraser's Magazine,' or the *Reviews.* She is still very
zealous, and predicts black times (with us) for the world. It seemed

---

[1] As being at Dumfries.

to her that Lady Clare would be much amazed with your descriptions of Scotch life, and might learn much from it. From Almack's to Ecclefechan is a wide interval, yet strange things come together. Strictly speaking the wretched Ecclefechan existence is the more tolerable of the two, for in it there is a pre-ordination of Destiny, and something *done*, namely muslin woven, and savage bipeds boarded and bedded. Alas! the hand of the Devil lies heavy on all men. But days quite saturated with *Antigigmanism* are surely coming, and from these better will arise. The completest, profoundest of all past and present Antigigmen was Jesus Christ. Let us think of this, for much follows from it. Better times are coming, surely coming. Cast *thou* thy bread on the wild, agitated waters, thou wilt find it after many days. That is enough.

At Edinburgh I expect books, some conversation with reasonable, earnest, or even with unreasonable, baseless men; on the whole some guidance, economical if not spiritual. Sir William Hamilton is one I hope to get a little good of; of others, too, whom hitherto I have not personally known. Of my own acceptance with all manner of persons I have reason to speak with thankfulness, indeed with astonishment. It is little man can do for man, but of that little I am no wise destitute. In any case we will live in our own hired house, on our own earned money, and see what the world can show us. I get more earnest, graver, not unhappier, every day. The whole Creation seems more and more Divine to me, the Natural more and more Supernatural. Out of Goethe, who is my near neighbour, so to speak, there is no writing that *speaks* to me (*mir anspricht*) like the Hebrew Scriptures, though they lie far remote. Earnestness of soul was never shown as there. *Ernst is das Leben;* and even to the last, soul resembles soul. Here, however, speaking of Goethe, I must tell you that last week, as our mother and I were passing Sandywell, a little parcel was handed in which proved to be from Eckermann, at Weimar. It made me glad and sad. There was a medal in it, struck since the poet's death. Ottilie had sent it me. Then a gilt cream-coloured essay on Goethe's *Practische Wirksamkeit* by one F. von Müller, a Weimar *Kunstfreund* and intimate of deceased's, with an inscription on it by him. Finally the third *Heft* of the sixth volume of 'Kunst und Alterthum,' which had partly been in preparation, and now posthumously produced itself; to me a touching kind of sight. Eckermann wrote a very kind letter, explaining how busy he was with reducting the fifteenth volume of *Nachgelassenen Schriften*, the titles of all which he gave me. There is a volume of 'Dichtung und Wahrheid,' and the completion of 'Faust.' These are the most remarkable. I have read Müller's essay, which is sensible enough—several good things also are in the *Heft*, towards the last page of which I came upon these words (by Müller, speaking of Goethe) : 'Among the younger British, Bulwer and Carlyle very especially attract him. The beautiful pure disposition of the last, with his calm, delicate perceptiveness, raises Goethe's recognition of him to the warmest regard : ' [1] This of *liebevollste Zuneigung* was extremely precious to me. Alas ! *und das Alles ist hin*. Ottilie promises to write, but I think *not*.

And now, dear Jack, before closing let us cast a glance towards Rome. Your two last letters are very descriptive of your household ways, and give us all much satisfaction. We can figure you far better than before. Continue to send the like. I wish you were well settled for the winter. There seems nothing else to be wished at present. I can understand your relation to your patient to be a delicate one ; but you appear to have good insight into it, and to be of the most promising temper. ' *Geradheit, Urtheil und Verträglichkeit.*' I miss none of these three ; they make in all cases a noble mixture. Be of good cheer, *in omne paratus*, you will return home to us a much more productive kind of character than you were ; learned, equipped in *many* ways, with all that is worthy in your character developed into action, or much nearer development. Be diligent in business, fervent in spirit. What is all our life, and all its ill-success or good success, that we should fear it ? An eternity is already around us. Time (wherein is the disease we call Life), will soon be done, and then ! Let us have an eye on that city that *hath* foundations.

God ever bless you, dear brother,
T. CARLYLE.

A letter follows from Mrs. Austin :—

To Mrs. Carlyle, Craigenputtock.

26 Park Road, London : December 25, 1832.

Dearest Friend,—Writing to you, which ought from all natural causes to be one of my greatest and dearest pleasures, is become

[1] ' Unter den jüngern Britten ziehen Bulwer und Carlyle ihn ganz vorzüglich an, und das schöne reine Naturell des letztern, seine ruhige zartsinnige Auffassungsgabe steigern Goethe's Anerkennung bis zur liebevollsten Zuneigung.'

a sort of dread and pain and oppression. I feel as if I had no means of saying anything because I have so much to say; because I would fain tell you how I love you and your husband; how I look to you as objects that would console and refresh and elevate one to think of; how I want your sympathy and approbation, and sometimes comfort; because I have endless facts to tell and thoughts to communicate, requisitions to ask—and then—to write thus seems mocking myself and you. A quire of such sheets as these would not hold *all* I should like to write. But my business is not to do as I like; and you and he will not think the worse of me for my self-denial. You may have seen somewhere or other that an early and long toil of mine is finished; a selection from the Old Testament. If I knew how I should send you a copy, just that you might see that I *work!* Mr. Carlyle will think *that* worth praise, though there be many defects in the *how*. Also look, if by any chance the New Monthly Magazine comes in your way, for an article entitled ' On the recent attempts to revolutionise Germany.' I translated from a journal P. Pücklers sent me, with commendation. Other Germans admire it. I excite horror among my Radical friends for not believing that all salvation comes of certain organic forms of government; and, as I tell Mrs. Jeffrey, am that monster made up ' of all we Whigs hate,' a Radical and an Absolutist.

Meantime Falk goes on. Falk *eigentlich* has long been done; but matter keeps congregating around him. Frau von Goethe sent me by Henry Reeve, ' Goethe in seiner practischen Wirksamkeit,' by Von Müller, Kanzler of Weimar. She sent it ' with her best love,' and with the assurance that *He* was just about to write to me when he died—that one of the last things he read was my translation, with which he kindly said he was much pleased. You will be able to estimate the value I set upon this faint shadow of a communication with him.

How I wish Mr. Carlyle may like—in any degree—what I have done. And then you, like a loyal wife as you are, will like it too. And yet it is nothing but compilation and translation—mere drudgery. Well, dearest friend, there are men enough and women enough to dogmatise, and to invent, and to teach and preach all things, Political Economy included. I can write nothing, and teach nothing; but if I can interpret and illustrate, it is something; and I have the advantage of remaining, what a remnant of womanly superstition about me makes me think best for us—a woman. These are 'auld world notions.' You know that word in my vocabulary excludes no particle of strength, courage, or activity. But *a well-chosen field* is the thing. What say you?

My husband is tolerably; working or standing against the stream of washy violence which inundates us all. What is better, and what the practical many dream not of, he is ever daily and hourly converting, purifying, elevating—himself; for which small business your reformers of crowds have little time and less taste.

Lucy grows a tall, fair girl. At least, people call her handsome. She is, at any rate, intelligent and simple, and strong, and not like the children of the '*upper classes.*' Mrs. Bulwer told me that her little girl of four said, in answer to some question about her little cousins, 'I suppose they have seen by the papers that I go to school.' Here is 'diffusion of knowledge' with a vengeance, and matter for the excellent Carlyle to moralise upon, 'auf seine Art und Weise.' Would I were there to hear. Henry Reeve is at Munich, and greatly attached to Schelling, who is quite fatherly to him.

And now God bless you. New years or old make no great difference in my wishes for you, which will outlast a year and I trust a world. Write to me, my dear friend, and believe that my affection and deep esteem are not the feebler for my want of time to tell of them.

Yours,
S. Austin.

CHAPTER XIV.

A.D. 1833. ÆT. 38.

Extracts from Journal.

Edinburgh, January 12, 1833.—Arrived here on Monday night last. Nasty fog; ghastly kind of light and silence in Dalveen Pass; the wearisome, dreaming-awake kind of day I always have in state coaches. Mill's letter awaiting me here. Village-like impression of Edinburgh after London. People are all kind; I languid, bilious, not very open to kindness. Dr. Irving advises immediate application for a certain Glasgow Astronomy Professorship. I shall hardly trouble myself with it. Deeply impressed with the transiency of time; more and more careless about all that time can give or take away. Could undertake to teach astronomy, as soon as most things, by way of honest day-labour: not otherwise, for I have no zeal now that way. To *teach* any of the things I am interested in were for the present impossible; all is unfixed, nothing has yet grown; at best, is but growing. Thus, too, the futility of founding universities at this time: the only university you can advantageously found were a public library. This is *never* out of season; therefore not now, when all else in that kind is.

Have long been almost idle; have long been out of free communion with myself. Must *suffer* more before I can begin thinking. Will try to write: but what? but when? On the whole, what a wretched thing is all fame! A renown of the highest sort endures, say, for two thousand years. And then? Why, then, a fathomless *eternity* swallows it. *Work* for eternity: not the meagre rhetorical eternity of the periodical critics, but for the real eternity, wherein dwelleth the Divine! Alas! all here is so dark. Keep firm in thy eye what light thou hast.

Daily and hourly the world natural grows more of a world magical to me: this is as it should be. Daily, too, I see that there is no true poetry but in *reality*. Wilt thou ever be a poetkin? *Schwerlich:* no matter.

'I have long been almost idle.' The dark mood was back in Carlyle, and these words explain it. When idle he was miserable; when miserable he made all about him miserable. At such times he was 'gey ill to live wi'' indeed.

Sick of Craigenputtock, sick of solitude, sick with thoughts of many kinds for which he could as yet find no proper utterance, Carlyle had gone to Edinburgh to find books and hear the sound of human voices. Books he found in the Advocates' Library, books in plenty upon every subject; on the one subject, especially, which had now hold of his imagination. The French Revolution had long interested him, as illustrating signally his own conclusions on the Divine government of the world. Since he had written upon Diderot, that tremendous convulsion had risen before him more and more vividly as a portent which it was necessary for him to understand. He had read Thiers' history lately.[1] Mill, who had been a careful student of the Revolution, furnished him with memoirs, pamphlets, and newspapers. But these only increased his thirst.

In the Advocates' Library at Edinburgh he was able to look round his subject, and examine it before and after; to look especially to scattered spiritual and personal phenomena; to look into Mirabeau's life, and Danton's, and Madame Roland's; among side pictures to observe Cagliostro's history, and as growing out of it the melodrama of 'The Diamond Necklace.' All this Carlyle devoured with voracity, and the winter so spent in Edinburgh was of immeasurable moment to him. Under other aspects the place was unfortunately less agreeable than he had expected to find it. In his choice of a future residence he had been hesitating between London and Edinburgh. In

[1] Carlyle once gave me a characteristic criticism of Thiers. It was brief. 'Dig where you will,' he said, 'you come to water.'

his choice of a subject on which to write he had been
doubting between 'The French Revolution' and 'John
Knox and the Scotch Reformation.' On both these points
a few weeks' experience of the modern Athens decided
him. Edinburgh society was not to his mind. He discerned, probably, not for the first time in human history,
that a prophet is not readily acknowledged in his own
country. No circle of disciples gathered round him as
they had done in Ampton Street. His lodgings proved
inconvenient, and even worse. Neither he nor his wife
could sleep for the watchman telling the hours in the
street. When they moved into a back room they were
disturbed by noises overhead. A woman, it appeared, of
the worst character, was nightly entertaining her friends
there. They could do with little money in Craigenputtock; life in Edinburgh, even on humble terms, was expensive. Napier was remiss in his payments for the articles in the 'Edinburgh Review.' He was generally six
months in arrear. He paid only after repeated dunning,
and then on a scale of growing illiberality. These, however, were minor evils, and might have been endured.
They had gone up with light hearts, in evident hope that
they would find Edinburgh an agreeable change from the
moors. Carlyle himself thought that, with his increasing
reputation, his own country would now, perhaps, do something for him. His first letter to his brother, after his arrival, was written in his usual spirits.

By Heaven's grace, he said, I nowise want merchants of a sort
for my wares; and can still, even in these days, live. So long as
that is granted, what more is there to ask? All gigmanity is of
the Devil, devilish : let us rather be thankful if we are shut out
even from the temptation thereto. It is not want of money or
money's worth that I could ever complain of : nay, often too it
seems to me as if I did *best* when no *praise* was given me, and I
stood alone between the two eternities with my feet on the rock.
But what I mourn over is the too frequent obscuration of faith

within me; the kind of exile I must live in from all classes of
articulate speaking men; the dimness that reigns over all my practical sphere; the etc., etc., for there is no end to man's complaining. One thing I have as good as ascertained : that Craigenputtock cannot for ever be my place of abode ; that it is at present,
and actually, one of the worst abodes for me in the whole wide
world. One day I will quit it, either quietly or like a *muir-break;*
for I feel well there are things in me to be told which may cause
the ears that hear them to tingle ! *Alles mit Mäss und Regel!* As
yet I decide on nothing ; will no wise desert the whinstone stronghold till I better see some road from it. I could live again in
Edinburgh, perhaps still more willingly in London, had I means.
My good wife is ready for all things, so we wait what the days
bring forth. Perhaps the future may be kinder to us both ; but
is not the present kind ? Full of work to do ? Write me all things,
my dear brother, and fear not that you shall ever want my sympathy. Keep diligent in business, fervent in spirit, serving God ;
that is the sum of all wisdom.

For the first week or two Edinburgh itself was not disagreeable. ‘The transition was singular from the bare
solitary moors to crowded streets and the concourse of
men.’ The streets themselves were ‘orderly and airy.’
‘The reek of Auld Reekie herself was the clearness of
mountain tops compared to the horrible vapours of London.’ Friends came about them, Jeffrey, Sir William
Hamilton, Harry Inglis, and many more, all kind and
courteous ; but their way of thinking was not Carlyle's
way of thinking, ‘the things they were running the race
for were no prizes for him,’ and ‘he felt a stranger among
them.’ ‘When he gave voice’ ‘they stared at him.’
‘When they had the word,’ he said, ‘he listened with a
sigh or a smile.’ [1] Then came another disappointment. A
Professorship at Glasgow was vacant. Jeffrey, as Lord
Advocate, had the appointment, or a power of recommending which would be as emphatic as a *congé d'élire.* Carlyle gave Jeffrey a hint about it, but Jeffrey left for Lon-

[1] Gibbon's expression.

don directly after, and Carlyle instinctively felt that he was not to have it. ' My own private impression,' he said, ' is that I shall never get any promotion in this world, and happy shall I be if Providence enable me only to stand my own friend. That is, or should be, all the prayer I offer to Heaven.'

Extracts from Journal.

February 1, 1833.—Have been exploring on all hands the foolish history of the Quack Cagliostro. Have read several books about him, searching far and wide after him ; learned, I ought to admit, almost nothing. Shall I study this enigma, then write my solution or no-solution.

Am quite bewildered, *dérouté,* know not whither to address the little energy I have : sick, too, and on the whole solitary, though with men enough about me. Sir William Hamilton, the one that approaches nearest being earnest : he, too, does not attain earnestness, and his faculty is not of the instructive kind. ' Help thyself ; heaven will help thee ! '

The Advocate is gone : to join the new Reformed Parliament, where may he prosper ! Our relation is done, all but the outward shell of it, which may stick there as long as it can. *Respectability* and Fate-warfare march not long on one road. All is whiggery here, which means 'I will believe whatsoever I shall be forced to believe.' In this country, as in France, the main movement will come from the capital. Perhaps it may be sooner than one expects. The pressure of economical difficulty is rapidly augmenting ; misery of that and all kinds is prevalent enough here ; everything wears an uneasy, decaying aspect, yet far short of what strikes one in London. A sorrowful, poor, unproductive struggle, which nevertheless this Age was fated and bound to undertake. On with it then.

Wilson I have not seen. Is he afflicted with my Radicalism ? Is he simply too lazy to call on me, or indisposed to take the trouble of etiquette upon him, for object so little momentous ? Shall I stand on etiquette then ? It is of small consequence, though perhaps the issue will be that we stand not only apart but divided, which I have no wish to do. Moir has been here ; in all senses a *neat* man, in none a strong one. Great stupidity reigns here I think ; but what then ? Grow thou wiser ! Brewster has lost his canvass for Leslie's Professorship and is about entering the English Church, they say, being promised a living. 'Once a noble soap bell, now a drop of sour suds.' Such is the history of many men.

The bitter old Hebrew implacability of that couplet—

> On those that do me hate
> I my desire shall see.

One day they will be even *as I wish them!* Envy no man, for such, sooner or later, will be his hard fortune. Nay, in any case does he not at last die! One of my best moods (many are too *bad*) is that of sincere pity for all breathing men. Oftenest it is a sincere indifference. Yesterday it seemed to me death was actually a cheerful looking thing : such a boundless *Possibility;* no longer hampered by the so strait limits of this world's time and space. Oh for faith! Truly the greatest 'God announcing miracle' always is faith, and now more than ever. I often look on my mother (nearly the only genuine Believer I know of) with a kind of sacred admiration. Know the worth of Belief. Alas! canst thou acquire none?

That the Supernatural differs not from the Natural is a great Truth, which the last century (especially in France) has been engaged in demonstrating. The Philosophers went far wrong, however, in this, that instead of raising the natural to the supernatural, they strove to sink the supernatural to the natural. The gist of my whole way of thought is to do not the latter but the *former*. I feel it to be the epitome of much good for this and following generations in my hands and in those of innumerable stronger ones. *Belief*, said one the other night, has done immense evil : witness Knipperdolling and the Anabaptists, etc. 'True,' rejoined I, with vehemence, almost with fury (Proh pudor!), 'true belief has done some evil in the world; but it has done all the good that was ever done in it; from the time when Moses saw the Burning Bush and *believed* it to be God appointing him deliverer of His people, down to the last act of belief that you and I executed. Good never came from aught else.'

To John Carlyle.

Edinburgh : February 10.

I have not been idle during the last month though not employed in the way I most approve of. Since the article Diderot, written in October, I have never put pen to paper till last week, when I bégan a piece for Fraser to be entitled 'Cagliostro.' I had found some books about that quack here : it will take me about three weeks and do well enough as a *parergon.* A new fluctuation has come over my mode of publication lately : so that the things most at heart with me must lie in abeyance for some time. It begins to be presumable that the 'Edinburgh Review' can no longer be my vehicle, for this reason, were there no others, that Napier is among the worst of *payers.* What the poor man means I know not ; most likely he is in utter *want of cash :* but at any rate he needs to be twice dunned before money will come from him ; and at present owes me some 30*l.*, for which a third dunning will be requisite. This, then, simply will not do ; I will look elsewhere, take new measures, as indeed solidity or permanence of any kind in authorship is at this time not to be looked for. Your foundation is like that of a man supporting himself in bog-lakes on floating sheaves or sods. The massiest will sink in a minute or two, and you must look out for new. Fraser, whose magazine I call the *mud* one (in contradistinction to Tait's, or the Sahara-sand one), is very fond of me, and at bottom an honest creature. Tait also would be glad to employ me, as poor Cochrane is. . . . On the whole we shall find means. . . . Meanwhile I have been reading violently, about the Scotch Kirk, in Knox, and others ; about the French Revolution, in Thiers, which Mill sent me ; about the Diamond Necklace, the Greek Revolt, and what not. I read with the appetite of one long starved ; am oftenest of all in the Advocates' Library, and dig, not without result, there. My head is never empty ; neither is my heart, though the contents of both are by times *rugged* enough. They must even be elaborated, made smooth and sweet. I could write whole volumes, were there any outlet : and will (if God spare me) both write them and find an outlet. These books, I fancy, will be one of our main conquests in Edinburgh. As to the men here, they are beautiful to look upon after mere black-faced sheep ; yet not persons of whom instruction or special edification in any way is to be expected. From a Highlander you once for all *cannot* get breeches. Sir William Hamilton is almost the only *earnest* character I find in this city : we take somewhat to each other ; meet sometimes with mutual satisfaction, always with good-will.

George Moir has got a house in Northumberland Street, a wife, too, and infants ; is become a Conservative, settled everywhere into *dilettante ;* not very happy, I think ; dry, civil, and seems to feel *unheimlich* in my company. *Aus dem wird Nichts.* Weir has become a Radical spouter, and they say is gone or going to Glasgow to start as 'able Editor.' Did I tell you, by the way, that London 'Spectator' Douglas had come to Dumfries in that capacity, and was weekly emitting a Radical 'Dumfries Times' there? A company of malcontent writers and others had made a joint-stock for that end; it is feared unsuccessfully. John Gordon is true as steel to his old loves; otherwise a rather somnolent man; we see him pretty often. He has got appointed College Clerk (or some such thing), and has now 300*l.* a year and is happy enough. Mitchell is quiet, in very poor health, yet cheerful, hopeful even, a respectable schoolmaster now and henceforth. I saw a large *didactic* company at dinner with him yesterday (for nothing else would satisfy him), and astonished them I fear with my exposition of belief and Radicalism, as compared with opinion and Whiggism. There was an 'old stager,' a Doctor Brown, travelling tutor college lecturer, statist, geologist, spiritual scratcher, and scraper in all senses: a cold, sharp, hard, unmalleable 'logic chopper' good to behold—at rare intervals. There was also an advocate, Semple, an overfoaming Kantist, the best-natured and liveliest of all small men; a very bottle of champagne (or soda water) uncorked: we did well enough.

The Advocate came jigging up to us very often, but is now gone to London. He asked kindly for you, and desired to be kindly remembered to his 'old friend the Doctor.' I dined with him once (Jane could not go). Napier (besides his being 'for ever in the small debt court!') is a man of wooden structure limited in all ways. I do not dislike him, but feel I can get no good of him. Wilson, who is said to be grown far quieter in his habits, has only come athwart me once. He, too, lion as he is, cannot look at me as I look at him with *free* regard, but eyes me from behind veils, doubtful of some mischance from me, political or other. I suppose I shall see little of him, and at bottom need not care.

As to our special *Befinden*, we are quite peaceable, content, for the present; though both of us have a dirty under-foot kind of catarrh for the last three weeks, whereby Jane in particular suffers considerable—vexation, rather than pain. Otherwise she is at least not worse. We go out not often, yet oftener than we wish; have society enough; the best the ground yields: the time for returning to Puttock will *too* soon be here. I have not abated in my dislike for that residence, in my conviction that it is no longer good for me. Of solitude I have really had enough. You would be surprised, I am much surprised myself, at the wondrous figure I often make when I rejoin my fellow creatures. The talent of conversation, though I generally talk enough and to spare, has, as it were, quite forsaken me. In place of skilful, adroit fencing and parrying, as was fit and usual, I appear like a wild, monstrous Orson amongst the people, and (especially if bilious) smash everything to pieces. The very sound of my voice has got something savage-prophetic. I am as a John Baptist girt about with a leathern girdle, and whose food is locusts and wild honey. One must civilise; it is really quite essential. Here, too, as in all things, practice alone can teach. However, we will wait and watch, and do nothing rashly. Time and chance happen unto all men.

When you return to London you must see Mill; he is growing quite a believer, *mystisch gesinnt*, yet with all his old utilitarian logic quite alive in him; a remarkable sort of man, faithful, one of the faithfullest (yet with so much calmness) in these parts.

Carlyle, it will have been observed, had for some time spoken cheerfully of his wife, as not well, but as better than she had been. He observed nothing, as through his life he never did observe anything, about her which called away his attention from his work and from what was round him. A characteristic postscript in her own hand gives a sadly different picture of her condition.

My dear John,—If I kept my word no better in my daily walk and conversation than I do in this matter of writing, I should deserve to be forthwith drummed out of creation, but I beg you to believe my failure here an exception to the general rule.

In truth, I am always so sick now and so heartless that I cannot apply myself to any mental effort without a push from necessity; and as I get the benefit of your letters to Carlyle and see how faithfully he pays you back, I always persuade myself when the time comes that there is no call on me to strike into the correspondence. But I assure you my silence has nothing to do with indifference. I watch your *thun und lassen* with true and sisterly interest, and rejoice with my husband to see you in so hopeful a course. Everyone gets the start of poor me. Indeed, for the last year I have not made an inch of way, but have sate whimpering on a milestone lamenting over the roughness of the road. If you would come home and set my 'interior' to rights, it would wonderfully facilitate the problem of living. But perhaps it is best for me that it should not be made easier.

Edinburgh society pleased less the longer the Carlyles stayed. The fault partially, perhaps, was in Carlyle's own spiritual palate, which neither that nor anything was likely to please.

As for the people here (he tells his mother at the beginning of March), they are very kind, and would give us three dinners for one that we can eat; otherwise, I must admit them to be rather a barren set of men. The spirit of Mammon rules all their world— Whig, Tory, Radical. All are alike of the earth, earthy. They look upon me as a strong, well-intending, utterly misguided man, who must needs run his head against posts. They are very right. I shall never make any fortune in the world; unless it were that highest of all conceivable fortunes, the fortune to do, in some smallest degree, my All-wise Taskmaster's bidding here. May He, of His great grace, enable me! I offer up no other prayer. Are not my days numbered: a span's thrift in the sea of eternity? Fool is he who would speak lies or act lies, for the better or worse that can befall him for that least of little whiles. I say, therefore, lie away worthy brethren, lie to all lengths, be promoted to all lengths; but as for me and my house we will not lie at all. Again I say, God enable us! and so there it rests. Ought not my father's and my mother's son to speak even so?

A few days later he writes to his brother Alick.

Edinburgh continues one of the dullest and poorest, and, on the whole, paltriest of places for me. I cannot remember that I have heard one sentence with true meaning in it uttered since I came hither. The very power of thought seems to have forsaken this Athenian city; at least, a more entirely shallow, barren, unfruitful, and trivial set of persons than those I meet with, never, that I remember, came across my bodily vision. One has no right to be angry with them; poor fellows; far from it! Yet does it remain evident that 'Carlyle is wasting his considerable talents on impossibilities, and can never do any good'? Time will show. For the present, poor man, he is quite fixed to try. . . . At any rate, there are some good books here that one can borrow and read; kindly disposed human creatures, too, who, though they cannot without a shudder see one spit in the Devil's face so, yet wish one well, almost love one.

To Mill also he had written a letter full of discontent, and looking, in the absence of comfort in Edinburgh society about him, for sympathy from his friend. But Mill rather needed comfort for himself than was in a situation to console others. He, like many others, had expected that the Reform Bill would bring the Millennium, and the Millennium was as far off as ever.

To his mother, whatever his humour, Carlyle wrote regularly. To her, more than even to his brother, he showed his real heart. She was never satisfied without knowing the smallest incidents of his life and occupation; and he, on his part, was on the watch for opportunities to give her pleasure. He had sent her from Edinburgh a copy of 'Thomas à Kempis,' with an introduction by Chalmers. The introduction he considered 'wholly, or in great part, a *dud*.' Of the book itself he says : 'None, I believe, except the Bible, has been so universally read and loved by Christians of all tongues and sects. It gives me pleasure to think that the Christian heart of my good mother may also derive nourishment and strengthening from what has already nourished and strengthened so many.' In Edinburgh he described himself as at home, yet not at home; unable to gather out of the place or its inhabitants the sustenance which he had looked for.

To Mrs. Carlyle, Scotsbrig.

Edinburgh : February 13, 1833.

From the first the appearance of the place, as contrasted with the boiling uproar of London, has seemed almost stagnant to us. There is no such thing as getting yourself properly *elbowed* in a 'flood of life.' The noise, too (except that of the watchman while we slept in a front room), is quite trifling and inadequate ! As for the people, they are now, as formerly, all of *one sort:* meet twenty of them in a day, they are all most probably talking of the same subject ; and that mostly an insignificant one, and handled in an insignificant way. And yet, poor fellows, how are they to be blamed? It is 'more their misfortune than their crime.' What sense is in them they no doubt honestly exhibit. Some cheering exceptions, too, one now and then falls in with ; indeed, for my own small share, I can no wise complain that honest sympathy, even love, and respect far beyond desert, is withheld from me here. This I receive with the greater clearness of appreciation, that (hardened by long custom) I had from of old *learned to do without it.* Nevertheless, that also is a mercy, and should be thankfully made use of. I think I have seen few people of note since I last wrote. I met Wilson in the street one day, and ex-changed civilities with him. He is looking a little older ; was wrapped in a cloak for cold, and undertook to come and talk at home with me, ' if I would allow him,' the very first day he had leisure. I am glad we met, since now there need be no awk-wardness or grudge between us : whether we meet a second time or not is of little or no moment. Henry Inglis has had my book reading,[1] and returns it with a most ecstatic exaggerated letter ; wherein this is comfortable, that he has seized the drift of the speculation, and can, if he pleases, lay it to heart. There are, per-haps, many such in this island whom it may profit ; so that I stand by the old resolution to print at my own risk so soon as I have 60*l.* to spare, but not till then. Meanwhile, my dear mother, I beg you again and again to take care of yourself ; especially in this wild, gusty February weather. Consider your welfare not as your own, but as that of others, to whom it is precious beyond price. I hope they are all kind, submissive, and helpful to you : it well beseems them and me. Forgive them if any of them of-fend ; for I know well no offence is intended : it is but the sinful infirmity of nature, wherein mortals should bear with one another. Oh ! ought we not to live in mutual love and unity, as a thing seemly for men, pleasing in the sight of God ! We shall so soon be parted, and *then,* Happy is he who has *forgiven much.*

From the Journal.

Friday, 15 (*March ?*).—Beautiful spring day ; the season of hope ! My scribble prospering very *ill.* Persevere, and thou wilt

---

[1] *Sartor* in MS.

improve. Sir Wm. Hamilton's supper (three nights ago) has done me mischief; will hardly go to another. Wordsworth talked of there (by Captain T. Hamilton, his neighbour). Represented verisimilarly enough as a man full of English prejudices, idle, alternately gossiping to enormous lengths, and talking, at rare intervals, high wisdom; on the whole, endeavouring to make out a plausible life of *halfness* in the Tory way, as so many on all sides do. Am to see him if I please to go thither; would go but a shortish way for that end.

The brevity of life; the frightful voracity of *Time!* This is no fancy; it is a wondrous unfathomable reality, and daily grows more wondrous to me. 'Poor is what my lord doth say;' let him to work then.

Beautiful that *I,* here and now, am alive! Beautiful to see so many incorporated spirits, all six feet high (as in the oldest heroic ages), all full of force, passion, impetuosity, mystery, as at the first. 'The young new blood!' it flows and flows; the spirit host marches unweariedly on—whither?

To Mrs. Carlyle, Scotsbrig.

March 16, 1833.

I have begun a kind of scribblement. It is for 'Fraser;' a foolish story about a certain Italian 'King of Quacks,' whom I have long been curious about, and am now going to make known to all the world—for some forty guineas, if I can get them. You will see it in time. The long piece I did on the Frenchman in summer came to be corrected very lately. It also will soon be out, and I hope will give satisfaction at Scotsbrig. I have plenty of other things to write; but should now rather lay myself out for getting books and materials. Craigenputtock is the place for writing. This same 'King of Quacks' ought to pay our expenses here and back again. I am growing little richer, yet also no poorer. The book can hardly be printed this season, but one ought to be content. I really am rather content; the rather as I do not imagine there is any completer *anti-gigman* extant in the whole world at present.

Among the new figures I have seen, none attracts me in any measure except perhaps Knox's Dr. McCrie, whom I mean (as he rather pressingly invited me) to go and call on were I a little at leisure. A broad, large, stiff-backed, stalking kind of man, dull, heavy, but intelligent and honest. We spoke a little about Scotch worthies and martyrs, and I mean to ask him more. My notion of writing a book on that subject grows rather than decays.

If I tell you that our health is very much what it was (the old doctor still coming about Jane, but professing his inability to help her much), I think there is a very copious picture of our condition here. As for you, my dear mother, Alick would persuade me that you are in the usual way, 'resigned wonderfully, and even contented. . .' He says, 'it is only after having had something to do with this world that we can learn rightly to love and reverence such a life as hers.' Be resigned, my dear mother. '*Still* trust in God.' He will not leave us nor forsake us, not in death itself, nor in aught that lies between us and death. On *our* love, moreover, count always, as on a thing yours by good right. The longer I live, the more I feel how good is your right. Let us hope then to find you well in the early days of May, if not sooner; once again in this pilgrimage to meet in peace. Might we but meet in peace where there is parting no more! This also if it be for good will be provided us. God is great. God is good.

March 26.—I have finished my paper on the 'Quack of Quacks,' but got no new one fallen to, the house being in a kind of racket for the present. Mrs. Welsh is here, and Miss Helen Welsh from Liverpool; and though, if I determined on it, I can have my own fire and room, and bolt it against all people, it seems not worth while at present, for I am better resting. I had made myself *bilious* enough with my writing, and had need to recover as I am doing.

As for my own dame, she agrees but indifferently with these wild March winds: as I fear my mother does too. The advice I will always reiterate is, take care of yourself, dear mother. Such splashing and sleeting, with bright deceitful sun-blinks, and the firm, nipping north wind, need in all ways to be guarded against.

Napier has been obliged (by dunning) to pay me my money; he has paid rather stintedly, but it will do. We are to dine with him on Friday. My *writing* for him is probably over.

Did Alick show you Irving's speech at the Annan Presbytery? I read it with a mixture of admiration and deep pain; the man is of such heroic temper, and of head so distracted. The whole matter looked to me like a horrid kind of Merry Andrew tragedy. Poor Dow, I think, will end in a madhouse: Irving will end one cannot prophesy how; he must go from wild to wilder. This is

the issue of what once appeared the highest blessing for him—
Popularity!

Lady Clare was returning to England for the summer.
John Carlyle was coming with her, and the family were
looking eagerly forward to his arrival in Annandale.

To John Carlyle, Florence.

Edinburgh : March 29, 1833.

You will find much changed in Dumfriesshire, but not the affection of those that remain for you. There will be much to tell,
much to speculate upon and devise for the time that is to come.
. . I have thought much about your future of late ; see it like
all our futures, full of obstruction : nevertheless will not cease
to hope good. It is a most ruinous chaotic time, this of ours, a
time of confusion outward and inward, of falsehood, imbecility,
destitution, desperation, unbelief ; woe to him who has within
him no light of Faith, to guide his steps through it! My main
comfort about you is to see the grand practical lesson of *Ertsagen,*[1]
impressing itself in ineffaceable devoutness on your heart ; herein,
it is well said, *eigentlich beginnt das Leben.* Whoso is a man may
in all seasons, scenes, and circumstances live like a man. Let us
take the world bravely then, and fight bravely to the end, since
nothing else has been appointed us. I have inquired with myself
often whether you should settle here, at London, or where. This
is but a pitiful place, but indeed all places are pitiful. In the
grand universal race towards ruin (economical) we are, as I judge,
almost a whole generation behind London. Nevertheless, here too
things are advancing with most rapid pace ; a few years will bring
us a long way. Universal Poverty is already here ; numerous persons, and these are the wisest, determine this season to fly over
seas, to America, Australia, anywhither where the famine is not.
Ruin economical is not far distant ; and then in regard to ruin
spiritual I should say that *it* was already triumphant among us ;
while in chaotic London there were blissful symptoms here and
there discernible of *palingenesia.* This makes the difference. In
London, amid its huge deafening hubbub of a Death-song, are to
be heard tones of a Birth-song ; while here all is putrid, scanda-

---

[1] This word, which so often occurs in Carlyle's letters, means briefly a resolution fixedly and clearly made to do without the various pleasant things—
wealth, promotion, fame, honour, and the other rewards with which the world
rewards the services which it appreciates.

lous, decadent, hypocritical, and sounds through your soul like lugubrious universal *Nænia*, chaunted by foul midnight hags. There is misanthropy and philanthropy for you expressed with poetic emphasis enough.

In sober truth, however, it might almost surprise one to consider how infinitely small a quantity, not of enlightened speech, one catches here, but even of speech at all; for the jargon that is uttered without conviction from the teeth outwards, who would name that speech? Peace be with it! There are books to be got at; air to breathe; and, lastly, a coach to carry you back moorwards when that becomes more tolerable.

Most likely I mentioned last time that I was writing a paper on *Cagliostro*. I might, perhaps with advantage, have asked you some questions about his last scene of life, your Roman St. Angelo, but I did not recollect that possibility, and now the thing is all finished off, perhaps more carefully than it deserved to be. It is for Fraser, and may perhaps suit him well enough; otherwise I value the article below a pin's price; it will do no ill, and that is the most one can say of it. I am partly minded next to set forth some small narrative about the *Diamond Necklace*, once so celebrated a business, but must wait a day or two till I have *freies Feld*. It will serve me till about the time of our departure homewards, which we date a month hence. . . . . Wilson I have met only once; I had called on him before; as he never returned it, I could not go near him again, more especially after all the blathering stuff he had uttered on the matter for years past. I still read his Magazine palaver with an affectionate interest; believe that there is nothing to be got from him. We will not quarrel, but also we shall not agree. This night Gordon invites me to meet him at supper, but I cannot resolve to go; the man is not worth an indigestion. De Quincey, who has been once seen out this winter, sent me word he would come and see me; he will do no such thing, poor little fellow; he has hardly got out of his *cessio bonorum*, and for the present (little Moir, his friend, pathetically says) 'is living on game which has spoiled on the poulterer's hands,' having made a bargain to that effect with him, and even run up a score of fifteen pounds. Sir William Hamilton I like best of any, but see little of him. I even met the 'hash' B . . . . , who has mounted a carriage now and rides prosperously. 'I saw the wicked great in power.' It was at Moir's, this rencounter, at dinner; the 'hash' somewhat reconciled to me by his presence;

I traced in him several features of my friend Cagliostro, and said honestly, Live then, enjoy thyself as subaltern quack. The devil is very busy with us all. Naso I visited in the dining way yesternight, for the first and probably last time. He affected to be extremely kind, and our party (with an American anti-slave enthusiast in it) went off quite happily; but Naso wants that first fundamental requisite of genius, I fear, common honesty. He has paid me, and shabbily, and on compulsion, that last debt of his; and now as I reckon our editorial relation may have terminated. That pecuniary defalcation of his again sorrowfully altered my scriptory method of procedure. But we cannot help it. Must even turn ourselves elsewhere.

The Reformed Parliament disappoints every one but me and the Tories. Endless jargon; no business done. I do not once a month look at the side of the world it sits on; let it go to the Devil its own way. . . . Of poor Edward Irving your Galignani will perhaps have told you enough; he came to Annan to be deposed; made a heroico-distracted speech there, Dow finishing off with a Holy Ghost shriek or two; whereupon Irving, calling on them to 'hear that,' indignantly withdrew. He says, in a letter printed in the newspapers, that he 'did purpose to tarry in those parts certain days, and publish in the towns of the coast the great name of the Lord;' which purpose 'he did accomplish,' publishing everywhere a variety of things. He was at Ecclefechan, Jean writes us; gray, toilworn, haggard, with 'an immense cravat the size of a sowing-sheet covering all his breast;' the country people are full of zeal for him; but everywhere else his very name is an offence in decent society. 'Publish in the towns of the Coast!' Oh! it is a *Pickle-herring Tragedy:* the accursedest thing one's eye could light on. As for Dow, he must surely ere long end in a madhouse. For our poor friend one knows not what to predict.

Jane has walked very strictly by old Dr. Hamilton's law, without any apparent advantage. Her complaint seems like mine, a kind of seated dyspepsia; no medicine is of avail, only regimen (when once one can find it out), free air, and, if that was possible, cheerfulness of mind. She bears up with fixed resolution, appears even to enjoy many things in Edinburgh, yet has grown no stronger of late. We must take the good and the ill together, and still hope for the better. She sends you her affection, and hopes we shall all meet at Craigenputtock once more. Be it so, if it pleases God. All things, as your faith tells you, *will* turn out for good if we ourselves prove good. Meanwhile, the only clear duty of man lies in this, and nothing else—work, work wisely, while it is called to-day. Nothing in this universe now frightens me, though yearly it grows more stupendous, more divine; and the terrestrial life appointed us more poor and brief. Eternity looks grander and kinder if Time grow meaner and more hostile. I defy Time and the spirit of Time.

Farewell, dear John.

Ever your brother,
T. Carlyle.

The account of the visit to Edinburgh began with an extract from Carlyle's Note-book. It may end with another.

March 31.

Wonderful, and alas! most pitiful alternations of belief and unbelief in me. On the whole *no* encouragement to be met with here in Edinburgh; 'all men,' says John Gordon naively, 'are quite taken up with making a livelihood.' It is taken for granted, I find, that of me nothing can be made—that I am, economically speaking, but a lost man. No great error there, perhaps; but if it is added by my friends themselves that therefore I am spiritually lost? One's ears are bewildered by the inane chatter of the people; one's heart is for hours and days overcast by the sad feeling: 'There is none then, not one, that will believe in me!' Great in this life is the communion of man with man. Meanwhile, continue to believe in *thyself*. Let the chattering of innumerable gigmen pass by thee as what it is. Wait thou on the bounties of thy unseen Taskmaster, on the hests of thy inward *Dæmon*. Sow the seed field of Time. What if thou see no fruit of it? another will. Be not weak.

Neither fear thou that this thy great message of the Natural *being* the Supernatural will wholly perish unuttered. One way or other it will and shall be uttered—write it down on paper any way; speak it from thee—so shall thy painful, destitute existence not have been in vain. Oh, in vain? Hadst thou, even thou, a message from the Eternal, and thou grudgest the travail of thy embassy? O thou of little faith!

CHAPTER XV.

THE four months' experience of Edinburgh had convinced
Carlyle that there at least could be no permanent home
for him. If driven to leave his 'castle on the moor,' it
must be for London—only London. In April he found
that he had gathered sufficient materials for his article on
the Diamond Necklace, which he could work up at Craigenputtock. At the beginning of May he was again in
Annandale on his way home, Mrs. Carlyle miserably ill,
and craving like a wounded wild animal to creep away out
of human sight. ' I left Edinburgh,' he wrote, ' with the
grieved heart customary to me on visits thither ; a wretched
infidel place ; not one man that could forward you, co-
operate with you in any useful thing. Scarcely one I could
find (except Sir William Hamilton) that could speak a sincere word. I bought several books in Edinburgh, carried
back with me materials enough for reflection ; the very
contradictions, even unjust ones, you meet with, are elements of new progress. My presence there was honoured
with many a kind civility, too ; was publicly acknowledged
by a kind of lampoon, laudative-vituperative (as it ought
to be), by one Brown, editor of a newspaper, whom I have
known at a distance as a blustering bubblyjock much given
to fabrication ; on the other hand, I relieved Professor
Wilson from the necessity of fabricating any more in my
behalf by decidedly *cutting* him the day before we left
town. I was quite wearied with the man, his deep desire
to be familiar with me, his numerous evasions to meet me,

his lies to excuse these; and so in mere Christian charity brought it to an end. My feelings to him remain, I hope, unchanged, as much as I can make them—admiration for a very superior talent, for many gleams of worth and generosity; contempt, pity for his cowardice, for his want of spiritual basis, which renders all his force a self-destructive one, properly no force at all. Thus did I finish off with Edinburgh, not in the most balsamic fashion.'

The work which Carlyle had done in the winter had more than paid his modest expenses. He was still undetermined how next to proceed, and felt a need of rest and reflection. It seemed, he said, as if 'the first act of his life was closing, the second not yet opened.' Means to go on upon were found in the hitherto unfortunate Teufelsdröckh. Unable to find an accoucheur who would introduce him to the world complete, he was to be cut in pieces and produced limb by limb in 'Fraser's Magazine.' Fraser, however, who had hitherto paid Carlyle twenty guineas a sheet for his articles (five guineas more than he paid any other contributor), had to stipulate for paying no more than twelve upon this unlucky venture. Ten sheets were to be allotted to Teufel in ten successive numbers. Thus 'Sartor Resartus' was to find its way into print at last in this and the following year, and sufficient money was provided for the Craigenputtock housekeeping for another twelve months.

The summer so begun was a useful and not unpleasant one. John Carlyle, returning from Italy, spent two months of it in his brother's house, intending at the end of them to rejoin Lady Clare and go again abroad with her. There were occasional visits to Scotsbrig. Many books were read, chiefly about the French Revolution, while from the Journal it appears that Carlyle was putting himself through a severe cross-examination, discovering, for one thing, that he was too intolerant, ' his own private discontent mingling considerably with his zeal against evildoers,' too contemptuously indifferent 'to those who were not forwarding him on his course;' wanting in courtesy, and 'given to far too much emphasis in the expression of his convictions.' It was necessary for him to ascertain what his special powers were, and what were the limits of them. 'I begin to suspect,' he wrote, 'that I have no *poetic* talent whatever, but of this, too, am no wise absolutely *sure*. It still seems as if a whole magazine of faculty lay in me all undeveloped; held in thraldom by the meanest physical and economical causes.'

One discovery came on him as a startling surprise.

'On the whole art thou not among the *vainest* of living men? At bottom among the very *vainest*? Oh, the sorry, mad ambitions that lurk in thee! God deliver me from vanity, from self-conceit, the first sin of this universe, and the last, for I think it will *never* leave us.'

Mrs. Carlyle continued ill and out of spirits, benefiting less than she had hoped from her brother-in-law's skill in medicine, yet contriving now and then to sketch in her humourous way the accidents of the moorland existence. She had an unlucky habit of dating her letters only by the day of the week, or sometimes not at all, and as those to Annandale were sent often by private hand, there is no post-mark to make good her shortcomings.

The following letter to her mother-in-law, however, is assigned by Carlyle to the summer of 1833. Written at what time it may, it will serve as a genuine picture of Craigenputtock life.

To Mrs. Carlyle, Scotsbrig.

Craigenputtock.

My dear Mother,—I am not satisfied it should be even so much as *whispered* that I have been scared from Scotsbrig by the *grate reform*, or by any other cause. Surely I have come through earthquakes enough in my time (and with an honourable, thorough bearing) to have acquired a character on that head more unimpeachable. But, to be sure, the calumny was no invention of yours, but of younger heads less eminent for charity. It was the long journey I boggled at on the last occasion, being in a despairing mood at the time with want of sleep, and dearly I rued, every hour of my husband's absence, that I had not accompanied him, when, if I must needs have been ill, I might at least have been so without molestation. Another time we will do better.

Carlyle is toiling away at the new article,[1] and though by no means content with the way he makes (when is he ever content?), still, as you used to say, 'what is down will not jump out again.' In three weeks or so it will be done and then we come. I am certainly mended since you were here; but 'deed Mrs. Carle's maist ashamed to say't,' a's still weakly and takes no unusual fatigue without suffering for it. The toil and trouble I had about Betty[2] did me great mischief, which I have scarcely yet got over; for the rest that explosion has had no unpleasant consequences. The woman I got in her stead, on an investigation of three minutes, proves to be quite as clever a servant as she was whom I investigated for the space of three half-years, and rode as I compute some hundred miles after. *Deaf* as a door nail, the present individual has nevertheless conducted herself quite satisfactorily, except that Carlyle's silk handkerchief is occasionally in requisition (oftener, I think, than there is any visible cause), wiping off particles of dust; and once, by awful oversight, a small *dead* mouse was permitted to insinuate itself into his bowl of porridge. We are not to keep her, however, because of her deafness, which in any other place, where her ears would be called into vigorous action, would make her the mere effigy of a servant. I got back the black button who was here when you came, whom I know to be ignorant as a sucking child of almost everything I require her to do, but whom I hope to find honest, diligent, good humoured, and quick in the up-take.

I had a very kind letter from Mrs. Montagu last week, reproaching me with forgetfulness of her.

We have not heard from or of Jeffrey for a very long time, but he will certainly write on Wednesday to acknowledge the repayment of his debt, which is a great load off our minds.[3]

---

[1] 'Diamond necklace.—T. C.'

[2] A misconducted maid.

[3] Carlyle's debt to Jeffrey had been paid the summer before. Either, therefore, Carlyle was mistaken in the date of this letter, and for 'Diamond Necklace' we should read Diderot; or there had been some further debt of John Carlyle's.

My mother writes in great alarm about cholera, which is at Penpont within three miles of her; three persons have died. I have been expecting nothing else, and my dread of it is not greater for its being at hand. The answer to all such terrors is simply what Carlyle said a year ago to some one who told him in London, 'Cholera is here:' 'When is death not here?'

The next letter from Mrs. Carlyle bears a clear date of its own, and was written while John Carlyle was staying at Craigenputtock. It is to Eliza Miles.

Craigenputtock: July 15, 1833.

My dear Eliza,—I well remember the fine evening last year when I received your letter. I was riding alone across our solitary moor when I met my boy returning from the post-office, and took it from him and opened it and read it on horseback, too anxious for news about you to keep it for a more convenient place. Had anyone predicted to me *then* that the good, kind, trustful letter was to lie unanswered for a whole year, I should have treated such prediction as an injurious calumny which there was not the remotest chance of my justifying! Alas! and it is actually so! For a whole year I have left my dear little friend in Ampton Street to form what theory she pleased concerning the state of my mind towards her; and finally, I suppose, to set me down for heartless and fickle, and dismiss my remembrance with a sigh; for her gentle, affectionate nature is incapable, I believe, of more indignant reproach. And yet, Eliza (it was), neither the one thing nor the other. I am capable of as strong attachment as yourself (which is saying much), and if I do not abandon myself to my attachment as you do, it is only because I am older, have had my dreams oftener brought into collision with the realities of life, and learnt from the heart-rending jarring of such collision that 'all is not gold that glitters,' and that one's only safe dependence is in oneself—I mean in the good that is in one. As little am I fickle, which I must beg you to believe on trust; since my past life, which would bear me out in the boast, is all unknown to you. What is it, then, you will ask, that makes me fail in so simple a duty of friendship as the writing of a letter? It is sometimes sheer indolence, sometimes sickness, sometimes procrastination. My first impulse, after reading your letter, was to sit down and answer it by the very next post. Then I thought I will wait the Lord Advocate's return, that he may frank it. Then troubles thickened round me : my mother's illness, my grandfather's death, gave me much fatigue of body and mind. That, again, increased to cruel height my own persevering ailments. About the new year we removed to Edinburgh, where we stayed till the beginning of May. It was a fully more unhealthy winter for me than the previous one in London. I wrote to no one ; had enough to do in striving with the tempter ever present with me in the shape of headaches, heartache, and all kinds of aches, that I might not break out into fiery indignation over my own destiny and all the earth's. Since my home coming I have improved to a wonder, and the days have passed, I scarce know how, in the pleasant hopelessness that long-continued pain sometimes leaves behind.

Nay, I must not wrong myself. I have not been quite idle. I have made a gown which would delight Mrs. Page, it looks so neat and clean ; and a bonnet, and loaves of bread innumerable. At present I am reading Italian most of the day with my medical brother-in-law, who is home at present from Rome. It was my husband who, for all his frightening you with some books, raised me from Ariosto to-day, with the chiding words that it would be altogether shameful if I let his book parcel go without that letter for Miss Miles, which I had talked of writing these six months back. . . . . How is your health ? I hope you do not go often to Dr. Fisher's, or at all. The more I see of doctors the more I hold by my old heresy that they are all 'physicians of no value.' My brother-in-law is a paragon of the class, but he is so by—in as much as possible—undoctoring himself. He told me yesterday, 'Could I give you some agreeable occupation to fill your whole mind, it would do more for you than all the medicines in existence.'

I wish I had you here to drink new milk and ride my horse.

We are at home now for the summer and autumn, most likely for the winter also. We think of France next summer, and moving in the interim were scarce worth while. Surely your father might find some one travelling to Edinburgh by sea, who would take charge of you. It is the easiest and cheapest conveyance possible.

Write to me all that you are thinking and wishing, and never doubt my kind feelings towards you.

> Your sincere friend,   JANE CARLYLE.

John Carlyle remained at Craigenputtock for a month longer, and then left it to return with Lady Clare to Italy. Carlyle saw him off in the Liverpool steamer from Annan, and went back to solitude and work. He says that he was invariably sick and miserable before he could write to any real purpose. His first attempt at the Diamond Necklace had failed, and he had laid it aside. The entries in his journal show more than usual despondency.

Extracts from Journal.

August 24.—So now all this racketing and riding has ended, and I am left here the solitariest, stranded, most helpless creature that I have been for many years. Months of suffering and painful indolence I see before me ; for in much I am *wrong*, and till it is righted, or on the way to being so, I cannot help myself. Nobody asks me to work at articles, and as need does not drive me to do it for a while, I have no call in that direction. The thing I want to write is quite other than an article. Happily (this is probably my greatest happiness), the chief desire of my mind has again become to *write* a masterpiece, let it be acknowledged as such or not acknowledged. The idea of the universe struggles dark and painful in me, which I must deliver out of me or be wretched. But, then, How ? How ? We cannot think of changing our abode at present ; indeed, had we even the necessary funds for living in London itself, what better were it ? and I in such a want, in such a mood ! *Thyself* only art to blame. Take thyself vigorously to task. Cast out the unclean thing from thee, or *go deeper and deeper hellward with it.*

For the last year my faith has lain under a most sad eclipse ; I have been a considerably worse man than before.

At this moment I write only in *treble*, of a situation, of a set of feelings that longs to express itself in the voice of thunder. Be still ! Be still !

In *all* times there is a word which, spoken to men, to the actual generation of men, would thrill their inmost soul. But the way to find that word ? The way to speak it when found ? *Opus est consulto* with a vengeance.

On the whole it is good, it is absolutely needful for one to be humbled and prostrated, and thrown among the pots from time to time. Life is a school : we are *perverse* scholars to the last and require the rod.

Above me, as I thought last night in going to sleep, is the mute *Immensity ;* Eternity is behind and before. What are all the cares of this short little Platform of existence that they should give thee Pain? But on the whole man is such a *Dualism*, and runs himself into contradiction, the *second* step he makes from the beaten road of the practical. I may lament meanwhile that (for want of symbols?) those grand verities (the reallest of the real) Infinitude, Eternity, should have so faded from the view, from the grasp, of the most earnest, and left the task of *right living* a problem harder than ever.

Have to walk down to the smithy (my dame riding) and bring up a gig : thus are the high and the low mingled. I read books enough, but they are worthless and their effect worthless. Henry's *Britain, Poor Law Commission, Paris and Histor. Scenes,* &c., &c., all these are naught or nearly so; errand 'for the gig is better work for me. At any rate it is work; so to it.'

The next entry in the Journal is in another handwriting. It is merely a name—' Ralph Waldo Emerson.'

The Carlyles were sitting alone at dinner on a Sunday afternoon at the end of August when a Dumfries carriage drove to the door, and there stepped out of it a young American then unknown to fame, but whose influence in his own country equals that of Carlyle in ours, and whose name stands connected with his wherever the English language is spoken. Emerson, the younger of the two, had just broken his Unitarian fetters, and was looking out and round him like a young eagle longing for light. He had read Carlyle's articles and had discerned with the instinct of genius that here was a voice speaking real and fiery convictions, and no longer echoes and conventionalisms. He had come to Europe to study its social and spiritual phenomena; and to the young Emerson, as to the old Goethe, the most important of them appeared to be Carlyle. He had obtained an introduction to him from John Mill, in London, armed with which he had come off to Scotland. Mill had prepared Carlyle for his possible appearance not very favourably, and perhaps recognised in after years the fallibility of his judgment. Carlyle made no such mistake. The fact itself of a young American having been so affected by his writings as to have sought him out in the Dunscore moors, was a homage of the kind which he could especially value and appreciate. The acquaintance then begun to their mutual pleasure ripened into a deep friendship, which has remained unclouded in spite of wide divergences of opinion throughout their working lives, and continues warm as ever, at the moment when I am writing these words (June 27, 1880), when the labours of both of them are over, and they wait in age and infirmity to be called away from a world to which they have given freely all that they had to give.

Emerson's visit at this moment is particularly welcome, since it gives the only sketch we have of Carlyle's life at Craigenputtock as it was seen by others.[1]

From Edinburgh, writes Emerson, I went to the Highlands, and on my return I came from Glasgow to Dumfries, and being intent on delivering a letter which I had brought from Rome,[2] inquired for Craigenputtock. It was a farm in Nithsdale, in the parish of Dunscore, sixteen miles distant. No public coach passed near it, so I took a private carriage from the inn. I found the house amid desolate heathery hills, where the lonely scholar nourished his mighty heart. Carlyle was a man from his youth, an author who did not need to hide from his readers, and as absolute a man of the world, unknown and exiled on that hill farm, as if holding on his own terms what is best in London. He was tall and gaunt, with a cliff-like brow, and holding his extraordinary powers of conversation in easy command; clinging to his northern accent with evident relish; full of lively anecdote, and with a streaming humour which floated everything he looked upon. His talk, playfully exalting the most familiar objects, put the companion at once into an acquaintance with his Lars and Lemurs, and it was very pleasant to learn what was predestined to be a pretty mythology. Few were the objects and lonely the man, 'not a person to speak to within sixteen miles except the minister of Dunscore;' so that books inevitably made his topics.

[1] *English Traits*, Emerson's Prose Works, vol. ii. p. 165.
[2] From Gustave d'Eichthel. Emerson does not mention the note from Mill. Perhaps their mutual impressions were not dissimilar.

He had names of his own for all the matters familiar to his discourse. 'Blackwood's' was the 'Sand Magazine.' Fraser's nearer approach to possibility of life was the 'Mud Magazine;' a piece of road near by, that marked some failed enterprise was 'the Grave of the last Sixpence.' When too much praise of any genius annoyed him, he professed largely to admire the talent shown by his pig. He had spent much time and contrivance in confining the poor beast to one enclosure in his pen; but pig, by great strokes of judgment, had found out how to let a board down, and had foiled him. For all that, he still thought man the most plastic little fellow in the planet, and he liked Nero's death, *Qualis artifex pereo!* better than most history. He worships a man that will manifest any truth to him. At one time he had inquired and read a good deal about America. Landor's principle was mere rebellion, and *that* he feared was the American principle. The best thing he knew of that country was that in it a man can have meat for his labour. He had read in Stewart's book that when he inquired in a New York hotel for the Boots, he had been shown across the street, and had found Mungo in his own house dining on roast turkey.

We talked of books. Plato he does not read, and he disparaged Socrates; and, when pressed, persisted in making Mirabeau a hero. Gibbon he called the splendid bridge from the old world to the new. His own reading had been multifarious. 'Tristram Shandy' was one of his first books after 'Robinson Crusoe,' and 'Robertson's America,' an early favourite. 'Rousseau's Confessions' had discovered to him that he was not a dunce; and it was now ten years since he had learned German by the advice of a man who told him he would find in that language what he wanted.

He took despairing or satirical views of literature at this moment; recounted the incredible sums paid in one year by the great booksellers for puffing. Hence it comes that no newspaper is trusted now, no books are bought, and the booksellers are on the eve of bankruptcy.

He still returned to English pauperism, the crowded country, the selfish abdication by public men of all that public persons should perform. Government should direct poor men what to do. 'Poor Irish folk come wandering over these moors; my dame,' he said, 'makes it a rule to give to every son of Adam bread to eat, and supplies his wants to the next house. But here are thousands of acres which might give them all meat, and nobody to bid these poor Irish go to the moor and till it. They burned the stacks, and so found a way to force the rich people to attend to them.'

We went out to walk over long hills, and looked at Criffel, then without his cap, and down into Wordsworth's country. There we sat down and talked of the immortality of the soul. It was not Carlyle's fault that we talked on that topic, for he has the natural disinclination of every nimble spirit to bruise itself against walls, and did not like to place himself where no step can be taken. But he was honest and true, and cognisant of the subtle links that bind ages together, and saw how every event affects all the future. ' Christ died on the tree : that built Dunscore kirk yonder ; that brought you and me together. Time has only a relative existence.'

He was already turning his eyes towards London with a scholar's appreciation. London is the heart of the world, he said, wonderful only from the mass of human beings. He liked the huge machine. Each keeps its own round. The baker's boy brings muffins to the window at a fixed hour every day, and that is all the Londoner knows or wishes to know on the subject. But it turned out good men. He named certain individuals, especially one man of letters, his friend, the best mind he knew, whom London had well served.

Emerson stayed for a night and was gone in the morning, seeking other notabilities. Carlyle liked him well. Two days later he writes to his mother :—

Three little happinesses have befallen us : first, a piano tuner, procured for five shillings and sixpence, has been here, entirely reforming the piano, so that I can hear a little music now, which does me no little good. Secondly, Major Irving of Gribton, who used at this season of the year to live and shoot at Craigenvey, came in one day to us, and after some clatter offered us a rent of five pounds for the right to shoot here, and even tabled the cash that moment, and would not pocket it again. Money easilier won never sate in my pocket ; money for delivering us from a great nuisance, for now I will tell every gunner applicant, ' I cannot, sir ; it is let.' Our third happiness was the arrival of a certain young unknown friend, named Emerson, from Boston, in the United States, who turned aside so far from his British, French, and Italian travels to see me here ! He had an introduction from Mill and a Frenchman (Baron d'Eichthal's nephew), whom John knew at Rome. Of course we could do no other than welcome him ; the rather as he seemed to be one of the most lovable creatures in himself we had ever looked on. He stayed till next day with us, and talked and heard talk to his heart's content, and left us all really sad to part with him. Jane says it is the first journey since Noah's Deluge undertaken to Craigenputtock for such a purpose. In any case we had a cheerful day from it, and ought to be thankful.

During these months, the autumn of 1833 and the beginning of the year which followed, a close correspondence was maintained between Carlyle and John Mill. Carlyle's part of it I have not seen, but on both sides the letters must have been of the deepest interest. Thinly sprinkled with information about common friends, they related almost entirely to the deepest questions which concern humanity ; and the letters of Mill are remarkable for simplicity, humility, and the most disinterested desire for truth. He had much to learn about Carlyle ; he was not quick to understand character, and was distressed to find, as their communications became more intimate, how widely their views were divided. He had been bred a utilitarian. He had been taught that virtue led necessarily to happiness, and was perplexed at Carlyle's insistance on *Entsagen* (renunciation of personal happiness) as essential to noble action. He had been surprised that Carlyle liked Emerson, who had appeared to him perhaps a visionary. Carlyle, intending to write another book, was hesitating between a life of John Knox and the French Revolution. Either subject would give him the opportunity, which he wanted, of expressing his spiritual convictions. His inclination at this moment was towards the history of his own country, and he had recommended Mill to write on the Revolution. Mill felt that it would be difficult if not impossible for him, without expressing completely his views on Christianity, which the condition of public feeling in England would not allow him to do. He spoke tenderly and reverently of the personal character of the

Founder of Christianity, and on this part of the subject he wrote as if he was confident that Carlyle agreed with him. But, below the truth of any particular religion, there lay the harder problem of the existence and providence of God, and here it seemed that Carlyle had a positive faith, while Mill had no more than a sense of probability. Carlyle admitted that so far as external evidence went, the Being of God was a supposition inadequately proved. The grounds of certainty which Carlyle found in himself, Mill, much as he desired to share Carlyle's belief, confessed that he was unable to recognise. So again with the soul. There was no proof that it perished with the body, but again there was no proof that it did not. Duty was the deepest of all realities, but the origin of duty, for all Mill could tell, might be the tendency of right action to promote the general happiness of mankind. Such general happiness doubtless could best be promoted by each person developing his own powers. Carlyle insisted that every man had a special task assigned to him, which it was his business to discover; but the question remained, by whom and how the task was assigned; and the truth might only be that men in fact were born with various qualities, and that the general good was most effectually promoted by the special cultivation of those qualities.

But I will not attempt to pursue further so interesting an exposition of Mill's views when I am forbidden to use his own language, and must express his meaning in a circuitous paraphrase. The letters themselves may perhaps be published hereafter by those to whom they belong. I have alluded to the correspondence only because it turned the balance in Carlyle's mind, sent him immediately back again to Marie Antoinette and the Diamond Necklace, and decided for him that he should himself undertake the work which was to make his name famous.

CHAPTER XVI.

WHEN John Carlyle left Craigenputtock to rejoin Lady Clare, the parting between the brothers had been exceptionally sad. The popularity with Review editors which had followed Carlyle's appearance in London was as brief as it had been sudden. His haughty tone towards them, and his theory of 'the Dogs' Carrion Cart,' as a description of the periodicals of the day, could not have recommended him to their favour. The article on Goethe was received unfavourably, Cochrane said with unqualified disapproval. 'Sartor' when it began to appear in 'Fraser' piecemeal, met a still harder judgment. No one could tell what to make of it. The writer was considered a literary maniac, and the unlucky editor was dreading the ruin of his magazine. The brothers had doubtless talked earnestly enough of the threatening prospect. John, who owed all that he had and was to his brother's care of him, and was in prosperous circumstances, was leaving that brother to loneliness and depression, and to a future on which no light was breaking anywhere. Carlyle felt more for John than for himself, and his first effort after John was gone was to comfort him.

For me and my moorland loneliness (he wrote on the 27th of August) never let it settle in your heart. I feel assured from of old that the only true enemy I have to struggle with is the unreason within myself. If I have given such things harbour within me, I must with pain cast them out again. Still, then, still! Light will arise for my outward path, too; were my inward light once clear again, and the world with all its tribulations will lie under my feet. ' Be of good cheer, I have *overcome* the world :' so said the wisest man, when what was his overcoming? Poverty, despite, forsakenness, and the near prospect of an accursed Cross. ' Be of good cheer ; I have overcome the world.' These words on the streets of Edinburgh last winter almost brought tears into my eyes. But, on the whole, quarrel not with my deliberate feeling that this wilderness is no wholesome abode for me ; that it is my *duty* to strive, with all industry, energy, and cheerful determination to change it for one less solitary. Consider also that I am far past the years for headlong changes, and will not rush out to the warfare without a plan and munitions of war. Nay, for a time my first duty must be composure ; the settling of innumerable things that are at sixes and sevens within myself.

I am writing nothing yet, but am not altogether idle. Depend upon it, I shall pass the winter here far more happily than you expect. So fear not for me, my dear brother ; continue to hope of me *that the work* given me ' to do may be done.'

Mrs. Carlyle, who was still ailing, was carried off by her mother a few days later, in the hope that change of air and relief from household work might be of use to her, and was taking a tour through the hills about Moffat. Carlyle himself was left in utter solitude at Craigenputtock. How he passed one day of it he tells in a letter, which he sent after his Goody Coadjutor, as he called her, soon after she had left him.

To Mrs. Carlyle, Moffat.

September 7.

Yesterday mornning, while the bright sun was welcoming you (I hope without headache) to the watering-place, I stirred little, yet was not wholly idle. I adjusted various small matters, wrote a long letter to poor Mrs. Swan[1]—a long one, yet the lamest utterance of my feeling on that sad matter, for I was stupid and could not even feel my feeling rightly, much less *think* it. After dinner I went to walk. Sitting with my back at the big stone in the ' Sixpence,' looking out over the void moor, I hear a little squeak of glad, unmelodious singing : and presently Midge, in red jacket

---

[1] Of Kirkcaldy. Her husband, ' Provost Swan,' who had been one of Carlyle's friends in the old days, was just dead.

with a bundle, heaves in sight, clashes back astonished into a kind of minuet, answers my questions with a '*Sur!*' and then to the repetition of it, 'How they were all at the hut?' chirps out with the strangest new old-woman's tone, 'Oh, bravely!' Poor little savage! I met her again in the way back (she had been with Nancy's gown, I suppose), and did *not* kill her with my eyes, but let her shy past me. The red Midge in that vacant wilderness might have given Wordsworth a sonnet. All day, I must remark, Nancy had been busy as a town taken by storm, and, indeed, still is, though I know not with what: most probably washing, I think; for yesterday there appeared once a barrow with something like clothes-baskets, and to-day white sheets hang triumphantly on the rope. She gets me all my necessaries quite punctually; and as fit, no questions are asked. *Notybene*, after a long effort I remembered the shelling of your peas, and told her of it. After tea, I did—what think you?—composed some beautiful doggerel on the Linn of Crichope and fair Ludovina (I hope she is fair): quite a jewel of a piece, for which, however, there is no room on this page.[1]

Of the present Saturday the grandest event might be the following: Sickish, with little work, I took my walk *before* dinner. Reaching home at the corner of the house, I met a pig apparently

[1] Room was found for it on the margin of the lettter :—

CRICHOPE LINN.

(*Loquitur genius loci.*)

Cloistered vault of living rocks,
    Here have I my darksome dwelling;
Working, sing to stones and stocks,
    Where beneath my waves go welling.

Beams flood-borne athwart me cast
    Arches see, and aisles moist gleaming;
Sounds for aye my organ blast,
    Grim cathedral, shaped in dreaming.

Once a Lake, and next a Linn,
    Still my course sinks deeper; boring
Cleft far up where rays steal in,
    That as 'Gullet' once was roaring.

For three thousand years or more
    Savage I, none praised or blamed me;
Maiden's hand unbolts my door—
    Look of loveliness hath tamed me.

in a state of distraction (grating harsh thunder, its lugs over its shoulders distractedly flow), pursued by Nancy in the same! The sow has not so much broken the gate as rent it, the side posts of it, into two, and left it hanging 'like a bundle of flails.' After dinner I, with a sublime patience, borrow 'Joseph's wimble,' and under ten thousand midge bites, with tools blunt as a wild Indian's, actually construct a brand-new, most improved gate, which you shall look upon not without admiration—if it swing so long. I sent a new message to the joiner, but do not in the least expect him. I had meant to excerpt from Bayle and such like, but the Fates, you see, had mostly ordered it *otherwise*. Night found me, like Basil Montagu, 'at my post,' namely, at my gate post, and nigh done with it. I had tea and Goody's letter, and so here we are.

But now, dear wifie, it is fit I turn a moment to thy side. Is my little Janekin getting any sleep in that unknown cabin? Is she enjoying aught, hoping aught, except the *end* of it, which *is*, and should be, one of her hopes? I shall learn 'all' on Wednesday (for she will write, as I do); and then 'all and everything.' When? I am patient as possible hitherto, and my patience will stretch if I know that you enjoy yourself, still more that your health seems to profit. Take a little amusement, dear Goody, if thou canst get it. God knows little comes to thee with me, and thou art right patient under it. But, courage, dearest! I swear better days are coming, *shall* come. The accursed, baleful cloud that has hung over my existence *must* (I feel it) dissipate, and let in the sun which shines on all. It *must*, I say. What is it but a

> Maiden mild, this level path
>   Emblem is of her bright being;
> Long through discord, darkness, scath,
>   Goes she helping, ruling, freeing.
>
> Thank her, wanderer, as thou now
>   Gazest safe through gloom so dreary:
> Rough things plain make likewise thou,
>   And of well-doing be not weary.
>
> 'Gullet' one day cleft shalt be,
>   Crichope cave have new sunk story;
> Thousand years away shall flee—
>   Flees not goodness or its glory.
>
> 'Ach Gott, wie lahm, wie krüppel-lahm!'

cloud, properly a shadow, a chimæra? Oh, Jeannie! But enough. If I am happy, art not thou, also, happy in my happiness? Hope *all* things, dearest, and be true to me still, as thou art. And so *felicissima Notte!* Sleep well, for it is now midnight, and dream of me if thou canst. With best love to mother and cousinkin,

Ever thy own husband,

T. CARLYLE.

To Mrs. Carlyle, Scotsbrig.

Craigenputtock : September 20, 1833.

My dear Mother,—Jack, as you will find, has got safe over the water, and begins his expedition as prosperously as could be desired. He goes into Germany, and then up the Rhine, towards the Swiss Alps, where that river springs, a beautiful road. Most likely he will pass through Constance, where our noble Huss testified to the death. He may tell us what he says to the 'scarlet woman,' and her abominations there! You and I shall not be with him to lecture from that text; but his own thoughts (for all that he talks so) will do it. The dumb ashes of Huss speak louder than a thousand sermons. . . . But I must tell you something of myself : for I know many a morning, my dear mother, you 'come in by me' in your rambles through the world after those precious to you. If you had eyes to see on these occasions you would find everything quite tolerable here. I have been rather *busy,* though the fruit of my work is rather inward, and has little to say for itself. I have yet hardly put pen to paper ; but foresee that there is a time coming. *All* my griefs, I can better and better see, lie in good measure at my own door : were I right in *my own heart,* nothing else would be far wrong with me. This, as you well understand, is true of every mortal, and I advise all that hear me to *believe* it, and to lay it practically to their own case. On the whole, I am promising to occupy myself more wholesomely, and to be happier here all winter than I have been of late. Be ' diligent in well-doing ; ' that is the only secret for happiness anywhere : not a universal one or infallible (so long as we continue on earth), yet far the best we have.

For the last two weeks Jane has been away from me at Moffat. I led the loneliest life, I suppose, of any human creature in the king's dominions, yet managed wonderfully, by keeping myself continually at work. I clomb to the hill top on Sabbath day for my walk and saw Burnswark, and fancied you all at the sermon close by. On Monday morning I went over to Templand, and found my bit wifie altogether *défaite*, not a whit better, but worse, of Moffat and its baths, and declaring she would not leave me so soon again in a hurry.

To John Carlyle.

October 1, 1833.

If you ask what I have performed and accomplished for myself, the answer might look rather meagre. I have not yet put pen to paper. The *new chapter* of my history as yet lies all too confused. I look round on innumerable fluctuating masses : can begin to build no edifice from them. However, my mind is not empty, which is the most intolerable state. I think occasionally with energy; I read a good deal; I wait, not without hope. What other can I do? Looking back over the last seven years, I wonder at myself; looking forward, were there not a fund of tragical in-difference in me, I could lose head. The economical outlook is so complex, the spiritual no less. Alas! the *thing* I want to do is precisely the thing I cannot do. My mind would so fain deliver itself adequately of that 'Divine idea of the world,' and only in quite inadequate approximation is such deliverance possible. I want to write what Teufelsdröckh calls a story of the *Time-Hat*, to show forth to the men of these days that they also live in the *age of miracles!* We shall see. Meanwhile, one of the subjects that engages me most is the French Revolution, which, indeed, for us is the subject of subjects. My chief errand to Paris were freer in-quiry into this.[1] One day, if this mood continues, I may have something of my own to say on it. But to stick nearer home. I have as good as engaged with myself not to go even to Scotsbrig till I have written something, with which view partly, on Satur-day last, I determined on two things I could write about (there are twenty others if one had any vehicles): the first, 'A History of the Diamond Necklace;' the next, an 'Essay on the Saint Simonians.' I even wrote off to Cochrane as diplomatically as I could, to ask whether they would suit him. Be his answer what it may,[2] I think I shall fasten upon that Necklace business (to

---

[1] Carlyle had wished to spend the winter in Paris, but was prevented by want of means.

[2] The answer was unfavourable. All editors, from this time forward, gave Carlyle a cold shoulder till the appearance of the *French Revolution*. After the first astonishment with which his articles had been received, the world generally had settled into the view taken at Edinburgh, that fine talents,

prove myself in the narrative style), and commence it (sending for books from Edinburgh) in some few days. For the rest I have books enough; your great parcel came about a fortnight ago. I have already read what Mill sent for me. Finally, yesterday no farther gone, I drove over to Barjarg,[1] in the middle of thick small rain, to get the keys of the library, which I found most handsomely left for me, so that I could seize the catalogue and some half-dozen volumes to return at discretion. It is really a very great favour; there are various important works there, reading which I am far better than at any university. For the first time in my life I have free access to some kind of book-collection. I, a book-man! One way and another we look forward to a cheerfullish kind of winter here.

I will try for Winckelmann. . . . In my heterodox heart there is yearly growing up the strangest, crabbed, one-sided persuasion, that *art* is but a reminiscence now: that for us in these days prophecy (well understood), not poetry, is the thing wanted. How can we *sing* and *paint* when we do not yet *believe* and *see?* There is some considerable truth in this: how much I have not yet

which no one had denied him, were being hopelessly thrown away—that what he had to say was extravagant nonsense. Whigs, Tories, and Radicals were for once agreed. He was, in real truth, a Bohemian, whose hand was against every man, and every man's hand, but too naturally, was against him, and the battle was sadly unequal. If Carlyle had possessed the peculiar musical quality which makes the form of poetry, his thoughts would have swept into popularity as rapidly and as widely as Byron's. But his verse was wooden. Rhymes and metre were to him no wings on which to soar to the empyrean. Happy for him in the end that it was so. Poetry in these days is read for pleasure. It is not taken to heart as practical truth. Carlyle's mission was that of a prophet and teacher—and a prophet's lessons can only be driven home by prose.

[1] A large country house ten miles from Craigenputtock, the library of which had been placed at Carlyle's service. Scotland had grown curious about him, however cold or hostile ; and the oddest questions were asked respecting his identity and history. Henry Inglis, an Edinburgh friend, writes to Mrs. Carlyle : 'Swift, I think it is, who says, "Truly you may know a great man by the crowd of blockheads who press round and endeavour to obstruct his path." A blockhead of my acquaintance (I have an extensive acquaintance amongst them) chose to ask me the other day whether the Carlyle who screams hebdomadally in the church in Carruthers Close was *our* Carlyle. I consider such a remark almost equal to receiving the hand of fellowship from Goethe. It is nearly the same thing to be the disclaimed or the misunderstood of an Ass, and the acknowledged of a Prophet.' The Barjarg acknowledgment of Carlyle's merits was a kind more honourable to its owner.

fixed. Now, what, under such point of view, is all existing art and study of art? What was the great Goethe himself? The greatest of contemporary men; who, however, is not to have any followers, and should not have any.

Extracts from Journal.

October 28.—No man in modern times, perhaps no man in any time, ever came through more confusion with less imputation against him than Lafayette. None can accuse him of variableness; he has seen the world change like a conjuror's pasteboard world; *he* stands there unchanged as a stone-pillar in the midst of it. Does this prove him a great man, a good man? Nowise—perhaps only a limited man.

The difference between Socrates and Jesus Christ! The great Conscious; the immeasurably great Unconscious. The one cunningly manufactured; the other created, living, and life-giving. The epitome this of a grand and fundamental diversity among men. Did *any* truly great man ever go through the world without *offence;* all rounded in, so that the current moral systems could find no fault in him? Most likely, never.

Washington is another of our perfect characters; to me a most limited, uninteresting sort. The thing is not only to avoid error, but to *attain* immense masses of truth. The ultra-sensual *surrounds* the sensual and gives it meaning, as eternity does time. Do I understand this? Yes, partly, I do.

If I consider it well, there is hardly any book in the world that has sunk so deep into me as 'Reinecke Fuchs.' It co-operates with other tendencies. Perhaps my whole speculation about 'clothes' arose out of that. It now absolutely haunts me, often very painfully, and in shapes that I will not write even here.

Yet, again, how beautiful, how true, is this other: 'Man is an incarnate word.' Both these I habitually feel.

'This little life-boat of a world, with its noisy crew of a mankind,' vanishing 'like a cloud-speck from the azure of the All.' How that thought besieges me, elevating and annihilating. What is 'fame'? What is life?

All barriers are thrown down before me; but then, also, all tracks and points of support. I look hesitatingly, almost bewilderedly, into a confused sea. The necessity of caution suggests itself. Hope *diminished* burns not the less brightly, like a *star* of hope. *Que faire? Que devenir?* Cannot answer. It is not I only that must answer, but Necessity and I.

Meanwhile, this reading is like a kind of manuring compost partly, of which my mind has need. Be thankful that thou hast it, that thou hast time for applying it. In *economics* I can yet hold out for a number of months.

Friday, November 1.—What a time one loses in these winter days lighting fires! lighting candles! I am in the dining-room, which would fain smoke, for it blows a perfect storm. Twelve o'clock is at hand, and not a word down yet!

'Edinburgh Review' came last night. A smart, vigorous paper by Macaulay on Horace Walpole. Ambitious; too antithetic; the heart of the matter not struck. What will that man become? He has more force and emphasis in him than any other of my British contemporaries (coevals). Wants the root of belief, however. May fail to accomplish much. Let us hope better things.

How confused, helpless; how dispirited, impotent; how miserable am I! The world is so vast and complex; my duty in it will not in the least disclose itself. One has to shape and to be shaped. It is all a perplexed imbroglio, and you have by toil and endeavour to *shape* it. 'Nothing would ever come to me in my sleep!'

Vain to seek a 'theory of virtue;' to plague oneself with speculations about such a thing. Virtue is like health—the harmony of the whole man. Some property of it traceable in every part of the man; its complete character only in the whole man. Mark this; it is not far from the truth, and as I *think* it, nearer than as I here express it.

My mode of writing for the last two days quite the old one, and very *far from the right.* How alter it? It must be altered. Could I not write more as I do *here?* My style is like no other man's. The first sentence bewrays me. How wrong is that? Mannerism at least!

Shall I go to London and deliver a course of lectures? Shall I

endeavour to write a *Time-Hat?* Shall I write a Life of Bona-
parte? A French Revolution? The decease of bookselling perplexes me. Will *ever* a good book henceforth be paid for by the
public? Perhaps; perhaps not. Never more in general. *Que
faire?* Live and struggle. And so now to work.

The dejected tone so visible in these entries was due to
no idle speculative distress, but to the menacing aspect
which circumstances were beginning to assume. The editors and booksellers were too evidently growing shy; and
unless articles could find insertion or books be paid for, no
literary life for Carlyle would long be possible. Employment of some other kind, however humble and distasteful,
would have to be sought for and accepted. Anything,
even the meanest, would be preferable to courting popularity, and writing less than the very best that he could;
writing '*duds*,' as he called it, to please the popular taste.
An experienced publisher once said to me: 'Sir, if you
wish to write a book which will sell, consider the ladies'-
maids. Please the ladies'-maids, you please the great
reading world.' Carlyle would not, could not, write for
ladies'-maids.

The dreary monotony of the Craigenputtock life on
these terms was interrupted in November by interesting
changes in the family arrangements. The Carlyles, as
has been more than once said, were a family whose warmest affections were confined to their own circle. Jean, the
youngest sister, the 'little crow,' was about to be married
to her cousin, James Aitken who had once lived at Scotsbrig, and was now a rising tradesman in Dumfries; a
house-painter by occupation, of a superior sort, and possessed of talents in that department which with better opportunities might have raised him to eminence as an artist. 'James Aitken,' Carlyle wrote, 'is an ingenious,
clever kind of fellow, with fair prospects, no bad habit,
and perhaps *very* great skill in his craft. I saw a copied

Ruysdael of his doing which amazed me.' The 'crow' had not followed up the poetical promise of her childhood. She had educated herself into a clear, somewhat stern, well-informed and sensible woman. Hard Annandale farm-work had left her no time for more. But, like all the Carlyles, she was of a rugged, independent temper. Jean, her mother said, was outgrowing the contracted limits of the Scotsbrig household. Her marriage consequently gave satisfaction to all parties. Carlyle himself was present at the ceremony. 'A cold mutton pie of gigantic dimensions' was consumed for the breakfast; 'the stirrup-cup' was drunk, Carlyle joining, and this domestic matter was happily ended.

But Jean's marriage was not all. James Carlyle, the youngest brother, who carried on the Scotsbrig farm, had a similar scheme on foot, and had for himself fallen in love; 'nothing since Werter's time equalling the intensity of his devotion.' He, too, was eager to be married; but as this arrangement would affect his mother's position, Carlyle, as the eldest of the family, had to interfere to prevent precipitancy. All was well settled in the following spring, Carlyle making fresh sacrifices to bring it about. His brother Alick owed him more than 200*l*. This, if it could be paid, or when it could be paid, was to be added to his younger brother's fortune. His mother was either to continue at Scotsbrig, or some new home was to be found for her, which Carlyle himself thought preferable. His letter to the intending bridegroom will be read with an interest which extends beyond its immediate subject.

You have doubtless considered (he said) that such an engagement must presuppose one condition : our mother and sisters forming some other establishment also. I should not be surprised, indeed, if you had fancied that our mother and your wife might try to live together at Scotsbrig; but depend upon it, my dear brother, this will never and in no case do. The house must belong to your wife from the instant she sets foot in it; neither mother nor sister must any longer be there to contest it with her. The next question then for all of us, and for you too, is, What will my mother and the two lassies do? I have thought of it often; and though changes are always grievous, I think there are means to get a new way of life devised for our dear mother and those who yet need her guidance, and see them supported without burdening anyone. They must have, of course, a habitation of their own. With my mother's money, with the interest of the girls' money, with mine (or what was Alick's, now in your hands), which I think of adding to it, they will be able to live decently enough, I think, if we can be judicious in choosing some place for them.

In this latter 'if,' however, you yourself see that *Martinmas* is by no means the fit time; that Whitsunday, the universal term-day of the country, is the soonest they can be asked to find new quarters. Now, as your wife cannot be brought home to Scotsbrig before that time, my decided advice were that you did not wed till then. I understand what wonderful felicities young men like you expect from marriage; I know too (for it is a truth as old as the world) that such expectations hold out but for a little while. I shall rejoice much (such is my experience of the world) if in your new situation you feel *as* happy as in the old; say nothing of happier. But, in any case, do I not know that you will never (whatever happens) venture on any such solemn engagement with a direct duty to fly in the face of?—the duty, namely, of doing to your dear mother and your dear sisters *as you would wish that they should do to you.* Believe me, my dear brother, wait. Half a year for such an object is not long! If you ever repent so doing, blame me for it.

And so now, my dear James, you have it all before you, and can consider what you will do. Do nothing that is *selfish*, nothing that you cannot front the world and the world's Maker upon! May He direct you right.

Carlyle, perhaps, judged of possibilities by his own recollections. *He,* when it would have added much to his own wife's happiness, and might have shielded her entirely from the worst of her sufferings, had refused peremptorily to live with her mother, or let her live with them, except on impossible terms. He knew himself and his peremptory disposition, and in that instance was probably right. His own mother happily found such an arrangement *not* impossible. Her son married, and she did not leave her home, but lived out there her long and honoured life, and ended it under the old roof.

Carlyle himself, meanwhile, was soon back again with his 'Diamond Necklace' and his proof-sheets of 'Teufelsdröckh' at Craigenputtock, where his winter life stands pictured in his correspondence.

To John Carlyle.

Craigenputtock : November 18, 1833.

I will now record for you a little smallest section of universal history : the scene still Annandale. The Tuesday after the wedding I sate correcting the second portion of 'Teufelsdröckh' for 'Fraser's Magazine,' but towards night Alick, according to appointment, arrived with his 'little black mare' to drive me 'somewhither' next day. We after some consultation made it Annan, and saw ourselves there about one o'clock. A damp, still afternoon, quite Novemberish and pensive-making. The look of those old familiar houses, the *jow* of the old bell, went far into my heart. A struggling funeral proceeded up the street; Senhouse Nelson (now Reform Bill Provost), with Banker Scott, in such priggish clothes as he wears, and two others of the like, stood on Benson's porch stairs gazing into inanity. Annan still stood there : and I—here. Ben was from home ; his little son gone to London, the maid thought, into some hospital, some navy appointment, into she knew not what. Finally, we determined on seeking out Waugh.[1] Old Marion, as clean and dour as ever, hobblingly admitted us. There sate the Doctor, grizzle-locked (since I saw him), yellow, wrinkled, forlorn, and outcast looking, with beeswax and other tailor or botcher apparatus on a little table, the *shell* of an old coat lying dismembered on the floor ; an-

---

[1] Son of a thriving citizen of Annan, who had been Carlyle's contemporary and fellow-student at Edinburgh, a friend of Irving, at whose rooms, indeed, Carlyle first became acquainted with Irving : who, with money, connections, and supposed talents, had studied medicine, taken his degree, and was considered to have the brightest prospects, had gone into literature, among other adventures, and now, between vanity and ill-fortune, had drifted into what is here described.

other not yet so condemnable, which with his own hand he was struggling to rehabilitate ; a new cuff I saw (after he had huddled the old vestment on) evidently of his own making ; the front button holes had all exploded, a huge rent lay under one armpit, extending over the back ; the coat *demanded* mending, since turning was not to be thought of. *There* sate he ; into such last corner (with the pale winter sun looking through on him) had *Schicksal und eigne Schuld* hunted the ill-starred Waugh. For the first time I was truly *wae* for him. He talked too with such meekness, yet is still mad ; talking of 1,200*l.* to be made by a good comedy, and such like. When we came out (since the state of his coat would not allow him to come with us) Alick and I settled that at least we would assure ourselves of his having food ; Alick, therefore, got twenty shillings to take him four hundredweight of potatoes and eight stone of meal ; three-fourths of which have been already handed in (without explanation) ; the rest will follow at Candlemas. So goes it in native Annandale. A hundred times since has that picture of Waugh, botching his old coat at the cottage window, stranded and cast out from the whole occupied earth, risen in my head with manifold meaning.[1] His 'Prophecy Book' has not paid its expenses. His 'Pathology' the Longmans, very naturally, would not have. I endeavoured to convince him that literature was hopeless, doubly and trebly hopeless for him. Further advice I did not like to urge ; my sole consolation is to know that for the present he has plenty of meal and potatoes, and salt cheap. Perhaps it is likely he will fall into his mother's state, let an indolent insanity get the mastery over him, and spend his time mostly in bed. I rather traced some symptoms of that : *Gott behüte.*

Here at Craigenputtock everything is in its stillest condition. I have read many books, put through me a vast multitude of thoughts unutterable and utterable. In health we seem to improve, especially Janekin. We have realised a shower-bath at Dumfries, and erected it in the room over this ; the little dame fearlessly plunges it over her in coldest mornings. I have had it only twice. Further, of external things, know that by science I extracted the dining-room *lock*, had it repaired, and now it shuts like a Christian lock ! This is small news, yet great. In my little library are two bell-ropes (brass wire and curtain-ring), the daintiest you ever saw ; finally, the 'Segretario Ambulante' in fittest

[1] The fate of unsuccessful 'literature.'

framing hangs right behind my back (midway between the doors
and the fire) and looks *beautiful;* really the piece of art I take most
pleasure in of all my *Kunst-Vorrath.* He is a delightful fellow;
shows you literature in its simplest quite steadfast condition, below which it *cannot* sink. My own portrait was to have been
framed similarly and hung by him as counterpart, but Jane has
put in rosewood and gilding, much to my dislike, and it hangs
now on the other side of the wall (in the drawing-room), and keeps
mostly out of my sight. If you think that our piano will still act,
that one *reach* of the peat-stack is carried in, and all else in its
old state, you may fancy us all tight and right, so far as the *case*
of life goes. As to the kernel or spiritual part, there can hardly
any description be given, so much of it has not yet translated itself
into words. I am quiet; not idle, not unhappy; by God's blessing shall yet see how I can turn myself. Cochrane refuses both
my projected articles. I have nevertheless written the 'Diamond
Necklace;' at least, it is rough hewn in the drawer here, and only
these marriages have kept me from finishing it. The other article
I could not *now* have undertaken to write, the Saint Simonians, as
you may perhaps know, having very unexpectedly come to light
again, and set to giving missionary lectures of a most questionable
sort in London. Mill is not there to tell me about them, but in
Paris; so I can understand nothing of it, except that they are *not*
to be written of, being once more in the fermenting state. Cochrane and I have probably enough done; but as Wull Brown says,
'perhaps it is just as well; for I firmly intended, &c.' I believe
I must go back ere long and look at London again. In the meantime learn, study, read; consider thy ways and be wise! 'Teufelsdröckh,' as was hinted, is coming out in 'Fraser'—going 'to
pot' probably, yet not without leaving me some money, not without making me quit of him. To it again! Try it once more!
Alick was here since Saturday; came up with two sacks of old
oats for Harry; went away this morning with a load of wood, &c.
Not till Saturday last did we hear a word from the Advocate. He
now writes to Jane in the frostiest, most frightened manner; makes
honourable mention of you; to me he hardly alludes except from
a far distance. Jane will have it that he took many things to himself in the article 'Diderot,' a possible thing, which corresponds,
too, with the cessation of his letters. I love the Advocate, and
partially pity him, and will write to him in such choicest mood as
I can command at present.

My dear Mother,—I hope Notman delivered you the pills, so stupidly forgotten. The hasty scrawl that went with them would signify that we were here and little more ; I was hardly this twelvemonth in such a hurry. Since then all goes on as it was doing ; in spite of this most disastrous weather, the worst we have had for long, we indeed sit snug and defy the tempest ; but Macadom's stable-slates jingling off from time to time suggest to us what many are suffering ; some doubtless far out in the 'wide and wasteful main.' Both Jane and I go walking by *night*, if not by day, if there is a gleam of clearness. I take now and then a kind of *deck* walk to-and-fro at the foot of the avenue, in a spot where you know the wood shelters one from all winds that can blow.

We saw Jean and her man and household as we passed through Dumfries ; it was all looking right enough ; one could hope that they might do very well there. Aitken, I find, by a picture over his mantelpiece, has quite another talent for *painting* than I gave him the smallest credit for ; it is really a *surprising* piece to have been executed there. As to Jean, we have always known her as a most reasonable, clear, and resolute little creature ; of her, in all scenes and situations, good is to be anticipated. So we will wish them heartily a blessing with hope.

Ever since Alick left us I have been *writing* with all my old vehemence. This day too insisted on doing my *task*. It is about the 'Diamond Necklace,' that story you heard some hint of in Cagliostro ; we shall see what it turns to. I am in the drawing-room to-night, with my big table (and side *half* to the fire, which is hot enough) ; Jane at my back also writing; *what* she will not tell me. We have been here together these three days ; the rain had run down the vents actually in large streams and damped everything. This is what I call descriptive minuteness. Let me also say I have been reading in poor Waugh's book, and find your opinion of it verified ; it is actually ' far better than one could have expected,' and contains some interesting things. Poor Waugh ! Poor fellow—after all !

Alick's little letter (one of the smallest I ever read, but not the *emptiest*) informed us of what had been passing at Catlinns, and that you were there, he said, *well*. Have you returned from the expedition still well ? I cannot too often impress on you the danger of winter weather ; you have a tendency to apprehension for every one but yourself. Catlinns is not a good place in winter, and were Jenny not the healthiest of women, must have been very trying for *her*.

But there is another expedition, my dear mother, to which you are bound, which I hope you are getting ready for. Come up with Austin and Mary to Jean; stay with her till you rest; sending me up word *when;* on Wednesday or any other day I will come driving down and fetch you. In about a week hence, as I calculate, I shall be done with *this* scribblement, and then we can read together and talk together and walk together. Besides, this, in the horrid winter weather, is a better lodging for you than any other, and we will take better care of you—we promise. The blue room shall be dry as fire can make it; no *such* drying, except those *you* make at Scotsbrig, where on one occasion, as I remember, you spent the whole time of my visit in drying my clothes. Lastly, that when 'you come you may *come*.' Jane bids me communicate to Jamie that she wants three stone of meal, but will not take it unless he take pay for it.

And so, dear mother, this scribble must end, as others have done. To-morrow, I believe, is my eight-and-thirtieth birthday! You were then young in life: I had not yet entered it. Since then—how much! how much! They are in the land of silence (but, while we live, not of forgetfulness!) whom we once knew, and, often with thoughts too deep for words, wistfully ask of their and our Father above that we may again know. God is great: God is good! It is written 'He will wipe away all tears from every eye.' Be it as He wills: not as we wish. These things continually almost dwell with me, loved figures hovering in the background or foreground of my mind. A few years more and we too shall be with them in eternity. Meanwhile it is this *Time* that is ours: let us be busy with *it* and work, work, for the night cometh.

I send you all, young and old, my heart's blessing, and remain as ever, my dear mother, Your affectionate

T. CARLYLE.

To John Carlyle, Rome.

Craigenputtock: December 24, 1833.

My dear Brother,—The description you give us of your Roman life is copious and clear: very gratifying to us; such matter as we like best to see in your letter. For myself, however, I can discern what perhaps our good mother does not so well, that with all favourable circumstances you have need of your philosophy there.

Alas! all modes of existence need such : we are, once for all, ' in a conditional world.' Your great grievance doubtless is that properly your office gives you nothing to do. Three hundred a year with sumptuous accommodation you have, but that is all. The days have to fly over you, and you seem to remain, as it were, windbound ; little more than an article of aristocratic state so far as your own household goes. This I can well see and sympathise in. It is hard, indeed, and grating to one's love of action ; a thing *intolerable*, did it threaten to continue for ever. But you are no longer a headstrong youth, but grown a deliberate man. Accordingly I see you adjust yourself to this also, from this also gather nourishment and strength. You are *equipping* yourself (in that strange way, so it was ordered) for your life voyage : patience, and the anchor is lifted. In the meanwhile, too, you know well *no* situation imposes on us the necessity of *idleness ;* if not in one way, if not in one of a hundred ways, you will work in the hundred and first. Continue, I beg you, to be mild, and either tolerant or *silently* intolerant. Let them go their way : go thou thine. What medical practice is to be come at, eagerly take. In defect of this read your Winckelmann, or any other solid book most appropriate to the place ; converse with all manner of mortals whose knowledge, as above ignorance, can directly or indirectly teach you aught. I should prefer Romans, I think, to any such a set of English as you have ; in any case if it is a man, and not a shadow of a man, one can get some good of him. My poor ' Segretario Ambulante,' actually converting disorder into order here in a small way, and realising victual for himself, is worth a hundred mere Clothes Horses and Patent Digesters, by what glorious name soever they may call themselves, that either do nothing, or the reverse of doing, which is even lower than nothing. Patience, therefore, my dear brother ! *Ohne Hast aber ohne Rast.* Let the cooks boil, and the tailors sew, and the shovel hat emit weekly his modicum of dishwater disguised as water of life ; it is all in the course of nature : ' like the crane's hoarse jingling flight that over our heads in long-drawn shriek sends down its creaking gabble, and tempts the silent wanderer that he look aloft at them a moment. These go their way and he goes his ; so likewise shall it be with us.'

And so now for a little Dumfriesshire news. Our good mother continues in her old state of health, or rather better, as they report to me. I expect her about Wednesday week. Austin and

Mary [1] will bring her to Jean's, and then on some appointed day I
go down to fetch her with the gig. Austin can find no farm, he
told us. What arrangement he will make for the coming year is
not yet apparent. Many a time, I think, the foolish creatures,
had they known better what stuff hope is made of, might as well
have stayed where they were. But at any rate it was a change to
be made—whether to-day or to-morrow is perhaps of little moment. A kind of sadness naturally came over our mother's mind
at this new proof of terrestrial vicissitude, but withal she is quite
peaceful and resolute, having indeed a *deeper* basis than earth and
its vicissitudes to stand upon. I hardly know now another person
in the world that so entirely believes and acts on her belief.
Doubt not that all will shape itself, or be shapen, in some tolerable way. Jean, as you heard, is in her own house at Lochmaben
Gate; to all appearances doing perfectly well. Alick has got a
new son, whom he has named, or purposes naming, *Tom*, after
me. He can get along amid the black mud acres of Catlinns, but
with a continual struggle. One of his day-dreams for many a
year has been America. I have ceased to oppose it so firmly of
late; indeed, I often enough think what if I should go to America myself! Thousands and millions must yet go; it is properly
but another section of our own country, though they rebelled very
justly against George Guelph, and beat him, as they ought. We
shall do or determine nothing rashly, the rather as for the present
nothing presses.

As for Craigenputtock, it stands here in winter grimness, in
winter seclusion. Nothing could exceed the violence of the December weather we have had; trees uprooted, Macadam slates
jingling down, deluges of rain: Friday, in particular, did immense mischief to ships and edifices all over the island; such a
day as has not been seen for a quarter of a century, they say. We
nestled ourselves down here: '*better a wee bush than no bield.*'
The shortest day is now behind us; we shall look forward to a
spring which will be all the gladder. I continue to read great
quantities of books. I have also, with an effort, accomplished the
projected piece on the Diamond Necklace. It was finished this day
week; really, a queer kind of thing, of some forty and odd pages.
Jane, at first, thought we should print it at our own charges, set our
name on it, and send it out in God's name. Neither she nor I are
now so sure of this, but will consider it. My attempt was to make

[1] Carlyle's sister.

reality ideal; there is considerable significance in that notion of mine, and I have not yet seen the limits of it, nor shall till I have tried to go *as far* as it will carry me. The story of the *Diamond Necklace* is all told in that paper with the strictest fidelity, yet in a kind of *musical* way. It seems to me there is no epic possible that does not first of all ground itself on belief. What a man *does not believe* can never at bottom be of true interest to him. For the rest I remain in the completest isolation from all manner of editors. Teufelsdröckh is coming regularly out in 'Fraser's,' with what effect or non-effect I know not, consider not; and this is all I have to do with the world of letters and types. Before very long I shall most probably begin something else: at all events, go over again to the Barjarg library, and so use my time and not waste it. I have a considerable quantity and quality of things to impart to my brothers in this earth, if God see meet to keep me in it, and no editor, nor body of editors, nor, indeed, the whole world and the devil to back it out, can wholly prevent me from imparting them. Forward, then—*getrösten Muthes.*

My thirty-eighth birthday happened on the 4th last. I am fast verging towards forty, either as fool or physician. The flight of time is a world-old topic. I was much struck and consoled to see it handled quite in my own spirit in the Book of Job, as I read there lately. Oh! Jack, Jack, what unutterable things one would have to utter, had one organs. We have had some five or six letters from the Advocate: mostly unanswered yet. He asks me why I am not as cheerful a man as you? Babbles greatly about one thing and the other. They gave him a dinner at Edinburgh, listened patiently to his account of himself, pardoned him for the sake of *langsyne.* We hear now, not from himself, that some Lord Cringletie or other is about resigning, and that Jeffrey is to be made a JUDGE. It will be a happy change. Macaulay goes to India with 10,000*l.* a year. Jeffrey calls him the greatest (if I remember rightly) man in England, not excepting the Chancellor. How are we to get on without him at all? Depend upon it we shall get on better, or worse.

And now, my dear brother, leaving these extraneous things and persons, let me commend us all again to you, the absent, and therefore *best* loved. We shall not see you at our New Year's Day, but I here promise to think of you quite specially, and even drink your health (from my heart), though it were only in water, that day. Let us, as I said, be patient and peaceable. There are other new years coming, when we shall not be so far apart. Meanwhile, be strong. Remember always what you said of the rush-bush here at Puttock on the wayside : 'It stands there because the whole world could not prevent its standing;' one of the best thoughts I ever heard you utter—a really true and pregnant thought. So, too, with ourselves. Let us resist the devil, the world, and the flesh. Alas! it is ill to do; yet one should for ever endeavour. Cheer up your low heart in the midst of those Roman ruins. There is a time still young and fruitful, which belongs to *us*. Get impatient with nobody. How easy it is to *bid* you do this; yet, really, it is right and true : the thing we have to do were to abolish and abandon the worthless. If we cannot do this all at once, let us, at least, not make it worse by adding our own badness to it.

God be with you, my dear John.

BROTHER TOM.

Mrs. Carlyle writes a postscript between the lines—

My dear Brother,—I am told there is great space left for me to add anything. Say, judge with your own eyes, where. If I had known a letter was to go this week I should have been first in the field. My good intentions, always unfortunate, were frustrated last time; but Carlyle always chooses a day for writing when I am particularly engaged with household good and individual evil. God bless you, however! Some day I shall certainly repay your long, kind letter as it deserves. I continue to take your pills. The prescription is in four pieces. I am better than last winter, but 'association of ideas' is still hard on me.

CHAPTER XVII.

THE economical situation of the Carlyles at Craigenputtock grew daily more pressing. The editors gave no sign
of desiring any further articles. 'Teufelsdröckh' was
still coming out in 'Fraser;' but the public verdict upon
it was almost universally unfavourable. The 'Diamond
Necklace,' which in my opinion is the very finest illustration of Carlyle's literary power, had been refused in its
first form by the editor of the 'Foreign Quarterly.' Fevered as he was with the burning thoughts which were
consuming his very soul, which he felt instinctively, if
once expressed, would make their mark on the mind of
his country, Carlyle yet knew that his first duty was to
provide honest maintenance for himself and his wife—
somewhere and by some means; if not in England or
Scotland, then in America. His aims in this direction
were of the very humblest, not going beyond St. Paul's.
With 'food and raiment' both he and his wife could be
well content. But even for these, the supplies to be derived from literature threatened to fail, and what to do
next he knew not. In this situation he learnt from a
paragraph in a newspaper that a new Astronomy Professorship was about to be established in Edinburgh. Some
Rhetoric chair was also likely to be immediately vacant.
One or other of these, especially the first, he thought that
Jeffrey could, if he wished, procure for him. Hitherto
all attempts to enter on the established roads of life had

failed. He had little hopes that another would succeed; but he thought it to be his duty to make the attempt. He was justly conscious of his qualifications. The mathematical ability which he had shown in earlier times had been so remarkable as to have drawn the attention of Legendre. Though by the high standard by which he habitually tried himself Carlyle could speak, and did speak, of his own capabilities with mere contempt, yet he was above the affectation of pretending to believe that any really fitter candidate was likely to offer himself. 'I will this day write to Jeffrey about it,' he says in his Diary on the 11th of January. 'Any hope? Little. My care for it also not much. *Let us do what we can.* The issue not with *us.*' He cared perhaps more than he had acknowledged to himself. He allowed his imagination to rest on a possible future, where, delivered from the fiery unrest which was distracting him, he might spend the remainder of his life in the calm and calming study of the stars and their movements. It was a last effort to lay down the burden which had been laid upon him, yet not a cowardly effort—rather a wise and laudable one—undertaken as it was in submission to the Higher Will.

It failed—failed with an emphasis of which the effects can be traced in Carlyle's Reminiscences of his connection with Jeffrey. He condemns especially the tone of Jeffrey, which he thought both ungenerous and insincere. Insincere it certainly was, if Jeffrey had any real influence, for he said that he had none, and if he had already secured the appointment for his own secretary, for he said that he had not recommended his secretary. It may have been ungenerous if, as Carlyle suspected, Jeffrey had resented some remarks in the article on Diderot as directed against himself, for he endeavoured to lay the blame of unfitness for promotion upon Carlyle himself; but there is no proof at all that Carlyle's surmise was correct.

Within the last few days (Carlyle wrote to his brother) I have made a proposal for a public office, and been rejected! There is to be an Astronomical Professor and Observer in Edinburgh, and no man of the smallest likelihood to fill it. I thought what an *honest* kind of work it was; how honestly I would work at it for my bread, and harmonise it with what tended infinitely higher than bread, and so wrote to the poor Advocate with great heartiness, telling him all this. He answered me by return of post in a kind of polite fishwoman shriek; adds that my doctrines (in literature) are 'arrogant, anti-national, absurd;' and to crown the whole 'in conclusion,' that the place withal is for an old secretary of his (who has not applied to *him*), unless I can convince the electors that I am fitter; which I have not the faintest disposition to do. I have written back to the poor body, suppressing all indignation, if there were any; diffusing over all the balm of pity, and so in a handsome manner terminate the business. One has ever and anon a kind of desire to 'wash away' this correspondent of ours; yet really it were not right. I can see him even in this letter to be very thoroughly miserable, and am bound to help him, not aggravate him. His censures, too, have something flattering even in their violence—otherwise impertinent enough; he cannot tolerate me, but also he cannot despise me; and that is the sole misery. On the whole, dear Jack, I feel it very wholesome to have my vanity humbled from time to time. Would it were rooted out forever and a day! My mother said when I showed her the purport of the letter, 'He canna hinder thee of God's providence,' which also was a glorious truth.

In this severe judgment there was possibly some justice. The doubt which Jeffrey pretended to feel, whether Carlyle was equal to the duties of handling delicate instruments without injuring them, cannot have been quite sincere. The supposition that a man of supreme intellectual qualification could fail in mastering a mere mechanical operation could only have originated in irritation. Carlyle already possessed a scientific knowledge of his subject. A few days' instruction might easily have taught him the mere manual exercise. It is possible, too, that if Jeffrey had gone out of his way to represent to Airy and Herschel, with whom the choice rested, what Carlyle's qualities really were, he might have saved to a Scotch university Scotland's greatest son, who would have made the School of Astronomy at Edinburgh famous throughout Europe, and have saved Scotland the scandal of neglect of him till his fame made neglect impossible.

In fairness to Jeffrey, however, whose own name will be remembered in connection with Carlyle as his first literary friend, we must put the Lord Advocate's case in his own way. If he was mistaken, he was mistaken about Carlyle's character with all the world. Everyone in Jeffrey's high Whig circle, the Broughams and Macaulays and such like, thought of Carlyle as he did. High original genius is always ridiculed on its first appearance ; most of all by those who have won themselves the highest reputation in working on the established lines. Genius only commands recognition when it has created the taste which is to appreciate it. Carlyle acknowledged 'that no more unpromotable man than he was perhaps at present extant.'

Mrs. Carlyle had answered Jeffrey's *frosty* communication in the preceding November with a playfulness which, so far as she was concerned, had disarmed his anger with her, and he had fallen nearly back into his old tone.

Unpermitted though I am to publish Jeffrey's letters, I must, in allowing him to vindicate himself, adhere, as nearly as I can without trespassing, to his own language.

In the first week in December he had written affectionately to Mrs. Carlyle and kindly to Carlyle himself, pressing them to pay him a visit at Craigcrook. He professed and assuredly felt (for his active kindness in the past years places his sincerity above suspicion) a continued interest in Carlyle, some provocation, some admiration, and a genuine desire for his happiness. Carlyle thought that he did not please Jeffrey because he was so 'dreadfully in earnest.' The expression had in fact been used by Jeffrey ; but what really offended and estranged him was Carlyle's extraordinary arrogance—a fault of which no one who knew Carlyle, or who has ever read his letters, can possibly acquit him. He *was* superior to the people that he came in contact with. He knew that he was, and being incapable of disguise or affectation, he let it be seen in every sentence that he spoke or wrote. It was arrogance, but not the arrogance of a fool, swollen with conceit and vapour, but the arrogance of Aristotle's ' man of lofty soul,' ' who being of great merit,' knows that he is so, and chooses to be so regarded. It was not that Carlyle ever said to himself that he was wiser than others. When it came to introspection, never had anyone a lower opinion of himself; but let him be crossed in argument, let some rash person, whoever he might be, dare to contradict him, and Johnson himself was not more rude, disdainful, and imperious; and this quality in him had very naturally displeased Jeffrey, and had served to blind him, at least in some degree, to the actual greatness of Carlyle's powers. In this letter Jeffrey frankly admitted that he disliked the wrangling to which Carlyle treated him. Never having had much of a creed himself, he thought he had daily less; and having no tendency to dogmatism and no impatience of indecision, he thought zeal for creeds and anxiety about positive opinions more and more ludicrous. In fact, he regarded discussions which aimed at more than exercising the faculties and exposing intolerance very tiresome and foolish.

But for all that he invited Carlyle with genuine heartiness to come down from his mountains and join the Christmas party at Craigcrook. Carlyle professed to be a lover of his fellow-creatures. Jeffrey said he had no patience with a philanthropy that drew people into the desert and made them fly from the face of man.

The good-humoured tone of his letter, and the pleasant banter of it, ending as it did with reiterated professions of a willingness to serve Carlyle if an opportunity offered, made it natural on Carlyle's part to apply to him when an opportunity did present itself immediately after. Jeffrey's letter had been written on December 8. Three weeks later the news of the intended Astronomy Professorship reached Craigenputtock, while Carlyle was told also that Jeffrey would probably have the decisive voice in the appointment. Carlyle wrote to him at once to ask for his good word, and there came by return of post the answer which he calls the 'fishwoman's shriek,' and which it is clear that he never forgave. For some reason—for the reason, possibly, which Carlyle surmised, that he expected the situation to be given to his own secretary—Jeffrey was certainly put out by being taken thus at his word when he had volunteered to be of use.

Impatiently, and even abruptly, he told Carlyle that he had no chance of getting the Astronomy Chair, and that it would be idle for him (Jeffrey) to ask for it. The appointment was entirely out of his own sphere, and he would be laughed at if he interfered. As a matter of fact, the most promising candidate was his secretary, a gentleman who had already been nominated for the Observatory at the Cape, and wished to go through some preliminary observing work at Edinburgh. But this gentleman, he said, had not applied to him for a recommendation, but trusted to his own merits. It was matter of notoriety that no testimonial would be looked at except from persons of weight and authority in that particular branch of science, and he was perfectly certain—indeed he *knew*—that the Government would be entirely guided by their opinions. The place would be given, and it was difficult to say that it ought not to be given, according to the recommendations of Herschel, Airy, Babbage, and six or seven other men of unquestionable eminence in the astronomical department, without the least regard to unprofessional advisers. If

Carlyle could satisfy *them* that he was the fittest person for the place, he might be sure of obtaining it; if he could not, he might be equally sure that it was needless to think of it. Whether Carlyle's scientific qualifications were such that he would be able to satisfy them, Jeffrey would not pretend to judge. But he added a further reason for thinking that Carlyle had no chance of success. He had had no practice in observing, and nobody would be appointed who was not both practised and of acknowledged skill. Sir David Brewster and Lord Napier looked on this as the most important qualification of all, and would abate much scientific attainment to secure tactical dexterity and acquired habits of observation. Herschel, it was said, was of the same opinion, and they were unlikely to trust the handling of their instruments to one who had not served an apprenticeship in the mechanical parts of the business. They were already crying out about the mischief which another professor had occasioned by his awkwardness, mischief which it would cost 500*l.* and many months of work to repair. The place to be given was, in fact, essentially an observer's place, there being little expectation that a class of practical astronomy would be formed out of the students at Edinburgh. It was not to be wondered at, therefore, that this qualification was regarded as indispensable.

Had Jeffrey stopped here, Carlyle would have had no right to complain. It is probable, but after all it is not certain, that Carlyle would have made a good observer, even if the technical knowledge could have been acquired without damage to the equatorials. Carlyle, no doubt, was a person whom the electors should have been grateful for the opportunity of choosing, if they had known what his intellectual powers were; but it is not clear that they could have known, or that Jeffrey could have persuaded them if he had tried. The 'secretary' was not only qualified as an observer, but he had been already selected for a most responsible place at Capetown. Brewster could have spoken for Carlyle's knowledge of mathematics; but mathematics alone were insufficient; and in fact it is difficult to see by what reasons any conceivable board or body of men would have at that time been justified in preferring Carlyle.

But Jeffrey went beyond what was necessary in using the occasion to give Carlyle a lecture. He was very sorry, he said; but the disappointment revived and increased the regret which he had always felt, that Carlyle was without the occupation, and consequent independence, of some regular profession. The profession of *teacher* was, no doubt, a useful and noble one; but it could not be exercised unless a man had something to teach which was thought worth learning, and in a way that was thought agreeable; and neither of those conditions was fulfilled by Carlyle. Jeffrey frankly said that he could not set much value on paradoxes and exaggerations, and no man ever did more than Carlyle to obstruct the success of his doctrines by the tone in which he set them forth. It was arrogant, obscure vituperation, and carried no conviction. It might impress weak, fanciful minds, but it would only revolt calm, candid, and thoughtful persons. It might seem harsh to speak as he was doing; but he was speaking the truth, and Carlyle was being taught by experience to know that it was the truth. Never, never would he find or make the world friendly to him if he persisted in addressing it in so extravagant a tone. One thing he was glad to find, that Carlyle was growing tired of solitude. He would be on his way to amendment if he would live gently, humbly, and, if possible, gaily, with other men; let him once fairly come down from the barren and misty eminence where he had his bodily abode, and he would soon be reconciled to a no less salutary intellectual subsidence.

Disagreeable as language of this kind might be to Carlyle,

it was, after all, not unnatural from Jeffrey's point of view ; and there was still nothing in it which he was entitled to resent : certainly nothing of the ' fishwoman.' It was the language of a sensible man of the world who had long earnestly endeavoured to befriend Carlyle, and had been thwarted by peculiarities in Carlyle's conduct and character which had neutralised all his efforts. There was, in fact, very little in what Jeffrey said which Carlyle in his note-book was not often saying to and of himself. We must look further to explain the deep, ineffaceable resentment which Carlyle evidently nourished against Jeffrey for his behaviour on this occasion. The Astronomical chair was not the only situation vacant to which Carlyle believed that he might aspire. There was a Rhetoric chair—whether at Edinburgh or in London University, I am not certain. To this it appears that there had been some allusion, for Jeffrey went on to say that if he was himself the patron of that chair he would appoint Carlyle, though not without misgivings. But the University Commissioners had de-cided that the Rhetoric chair was not to be refilled unless some man of great and established reputation was willing to accept it, and such a man Jeffrey said he could not in his conscience declare Carlyle to be. Had it been Macaulay that was the candidate, then, indeed, the Commissioners would see their way. Macaulay was the greatest of living Englishmen, not excepting the great Brougham himself. But Carlyle was—Carlyle. It was melancholy and pro-voking to feel that perversions and absurdities (for as such alone he could regard Carlyle's peculiar methods and doc-trines) were heaping up obstacles against his obtaining either the public position or the general respect to which his talents and his diligence would have otherwise entitled him. As long as society remained as it was and thought as it did, there was not the least chance of his ever being admitted as a teacher into any regular seminary.

There was no occasion for Jeffrey to have written with such extreme harshness. If he felt obliged to expostulate, he might have dressed his censures in a kinder form. To Carlyle such language was doubly wounding, for he was under obligations to Jeffrey, which his pride already endured with difficulty, and the tone of condescending superiority was infinitely galling. He was conscious, too, that Jeffrey did not understand him. His extravagances, as Jeffrey considered them, were but efforts to express thoughts of immeasurable consequence. From his boyhood upwards he had struggled to use his faculties honestly for the best purposes; to consider only what was true and good, and never to be led astray by any worldly interest; and for reward every door of preferment was closed in his face, and poverty and absolute want seemed advancing to overwhelm him. If he was tried in the fire, if he bore the worst that the world could do to him and came out at last triumphant, let those who think that they would have behaved better blame Carlyle for his occasional bursts of impatience and resentment. High-toned moral lectures were the harder to bear because Goethe far off in Germany could recognise in the same qualities at which Jeffrey was railing the workings of true original genius.

Even so it is strange that Carlyle, after the victory had long been won when his trials were all over and he was standing on the highest point of literary fame, known, honoured, and admired over two continents, should have nourished still an evident grudge against the poor Lord Advocate, especially as, after the appearance of the 'French Revolution,' Jeffrey had freely and without reserve acknowledged that he had all along been wrong in his judgment of Carlyle. One expression casually let fall at the end of one of Jeffrey's letters, to which I need not do more than allude, contains a possible explanation. Jeffrey was always gentlemanlike, and it is not conceivable that he intended to affront Carlyle, but Carlyle may have taken the words to himself in a sense which they were not meant to bear; and a misunderstanding, to which self-respect would have forbidden him to refer, may have infected his recollections of a friend whom he had once cordially esteemed, and to whom both he and his brothers were under obligations which could hardly be overrated. But this is mere conjecture. It may be simply that Jeffrey had once led Carlyle to hope for his assistance in obtaining promotion in the world, and that when an opportunity seemed to offer itself, the assistance was not given.

Never any more did Carlyle seek admission into the beaten tracks of established industry. He was impatient of *harness*, and had felt all along that no official situation was fit for him, or he fit for it. He would have endeavoured loyally to do his duty in any position in which he might be placed. Never would he have accepted employment merely for its salary, going through the perfunctory forms, and reserving his best powers for other occupations. Anything which he undertook to do he would have done with all his might; but he would have carried into it the stern integrity which refused to bend to conventional exigencies. His tenure of office, whether of professor's chair or of office under government, would probably have been brief and would have come to a violent end. He never offered himself again, and in later times when a professorship might have been found for him at Edinburgh, he refused to be nominated. He called himself a Bedouin, and a Bedouin he was; a free lance owing no allegiance save to his Maker and his own conscience.

On receiving Jeffrey's letter, he adjusted himself resolutely and without complaining to the facts as they stood. He determined to make one more attempt, either at Craigenputtock or elsewhere, to conquer a place for himself, and earn an honest livelihood as an English man of letters. If that failed, he had privately made up his mind to try his fortune in America, where he had learnt from Emerson, and where he himself instinctively felt, that he might expect more favourable hearing. He was in no hurry. In all that he did he acted with a deliberate circumspection scarcely to have been looked for in so irritable a man. The words 'judicious desperation,' by which he describes the principle on which he guided his earlier life, are exactly appropriate.

Including Fraser's payments for 'Teufelsdröckh' he was possessed of about two hundred pounds, and until his brother John could repay him the sums which had been advanced for his education, he had no definite prospect of earning any more—a very serious outlook, but he did not allow it to discompose him. At any rate he had no debts; never had a debt in his life except the fifty pounds which he had borrowed from Jeffrey, and this with the Advocate's loan to his brother was now cleared off. The 'Diamond Necklace' had proved unsaleable, but he worked quietly on upon it, making additions and alterations as new books came in. He was not solitary this winter. In some respects he was worse off than if he had been solitary. With characteristic kindness he had taken charge of the young Scotchman whom he had met in London, William Glen, gifted, accomplished, with the fragments in him of a true man of genius, but with symptoms showing themselves of approaching insanity, in which after a year or two he sank into total eclipse. With Glen, half for his friend's sake, he read Homer and mathematics. Glen, who was a good scholar, taught Carlyle Greek. Carlyle taught Glen Newtonian geometry; in the intervals studying hard at French Revolution history. His inward experience lies written in his Diary.

Saturday, Jan. 11, 1834.—So long since my pen was put to paper here. The bustle, the confusion has been excessive. Above three weeks ago by writing violently I finished the 'Diamond Necklace,' a singular sort of thing which is very far from pleasing me. Scarcely was the 'Necklace' laid by when the Glens arrived, and with them the entirest earthquake. Nothing could be done, nothing so much as thought of. Archy [1] often only went off on Sunday; William not near so ill as we anticipated. I have him at geometry, which he actually learns; mean to begin reading Homer with him. Will he ever recover? We have hope and ought to endeavour.

Wednesday gone a week I went down to Dumfries and brought up my mother, who is still here reading and sewing. She is wonderfully peaceful, not unhappy; intrinsically an admirable woman whom I ought to be right thankful that I have for mother.

Letter from Mill about a new Radical Review in which my co-operation is requested. Shall be ready to give it if they have any payment to offer. Dog's-meat Bazaar which you enter muffled up, holding your nose, with 'Here, you master, able editor, or whatever your name is, take this mess of mine and sell it for me—at the old rate, you know.' This is the relation I am forced to stand in with publishers as the time now runs. May God mend it.

Magazine Fraser writes that 'Teufelsdröckh' excites the most unqualified disapprobation—*à la bonne heure*.

Feb. 9.—Nothing done yet—nothing feasible devised. Innumerable confused half-thoughts; a kind of *moulting* season with me; very disconsolate, yet tending, as I believe or would fain believe, to profit. Almost all things go by systole and diastole, even one's spiritual progress. Neglect, humiliation, all these things *are* good, if I will use them wisely. From the uttermost deeps of darkness a kind of unsubduable hope rises in me; grows stronger and stronger.

Began *Homer* two weeks ago: nearly through the first book now —like it very considerably. Simplicity, sincerity, the singleness (not quite the word) and massive repose as of an ancient picture. Indeed, all the engravings of Pompeii antiques, and such like, that I have seen grow singularly present with me as I read. A most quieting wholesome task too; will persist in it. Poor Glen is my

[1] Brother of William Glen.

very sufficient help here. Have sent for Heyne, Blackwell, and other books, as further helps. Dacier here, but nearly unproductive for me.

Read 'Beattie's Life,' by Sir Wm. Forbes (from Barjarg, where I was some days ago), *Schneidermässig*, religious 'Gigmanity,' yet lovable, pitiable, in many respects worthy. Of all literary men, Beattie, according to his deserts, was perhaps (in those times) the best rewarded; yet alas! also, at length, among the unhappiest. How much he enjoyed that is far from *thee!*—converse with minds congenial; an element not of *black cattleism*, but of refinement, plenty, and encouragement. Repine not; or, what is more to be dreaded, *rebel not*.

Feb. 13.—Reading in those larger quartos about the *Collier*. Nearly done with it now. View of the rascaldom of Paris, tragical at this distance of time (for where is now that reiving and stealing, that squeaking and jabbering—of lies?) : otherwise unprofitable. What to do with that 'Diamond Necklace' affair I wrote? must correct it in some parts which these new books have illuminated a little.

Letter from Jeffrey indicating that *he* can or will do nothing in the 'Rhetoric Professor' business had I resolved on trying him. Better to be done with all that business, and know that I have *nothing* to hope for in that quarter, or any such, and adjust myself thereto. Rebel not; be still; still and strong!

Finished the first book of *Homer* last night. Pleasantest most purely poetical reading I have had for long. Simplicity (not multiplicity), almost vacuity, yet sincerity, and the richest toned artless music. The question at present with me, *What* does he mean by his gods? In the question of *belief* some light to be sought from Homer still; he is still far from clear to me.

Bulwer's 'England and the English':

> Weightiest of harrows, what horse will ply it?
> Cheeriest of sparrows meanwhile will try it.

Intrinsically a poor creature this Bulwer; has a bustling whisking agility and restlessness which may support him in a certain degree of significance with some, but which partakes much of the nature of *levity*. Nothing truly notable can come of him or of it,

Sunday, Feb. 16.—Beautiful days; this is the third of them. Unspeakably grateful after the long loud howling deluge of a winter. Blackbirds singing this morning—had I not been so sick!

Friday, Feb. 21.—Still reading, but with indifferent effect. *Homer* still grateful—grows easier; one hundred lines have been done more than once in an evening. Was Thersites intended to have any wit, humour, or even fun in his raillery? Nothing (with my actual knowledge of Greek) comes to light but mere beggarly abuse, and miry blackguardism. When Ulysses weals his back with that bang of his sceptre, how he sinks annihilated like a cracked bug! Mark too the sugar-loaf head, bald but for down; the squint, the shoulders drawn together over his back: a perfect beauty in his kind. How free otherwise is Ulysses with his sceptre! 'Whatever man of the Δῆμος he met' he clanked him over the crown. It does not seem to me so incredible as it did, that opinion of Voss's. The 'characters' in Homer, might they not be like the pantaloon, harlequin, &c. of the Italian comedy, and sustained (what is there meant by sustaining?) by various hands? One thing is clear, and little more to *me* at present. The whole is very *old*. 'Achilles sitting weeping by the hoary beach looking out into the dark-coloured sea;' still, *einfach*, with a kind of greatness.

Mein Leben geht sehr übel: all dim, misty, squally, disheartening, at times almost heart-breaking. Nevertheless it seems to me clear that I am in a growing state: call this a *moulting season* for the mind; say I shall come out of it new coated, made young again!

Yesterday we for the first time spoke seriously of setting off for London to take up our abode there next Whitsunday. Nothing but the wretchedest, forsaken, discontented existence here, where almost your whole energy is spent in keeping yourself from flying out into exasperation. I had never much hope of foreign help: perhaps the only man I put even a shadow of dependence upon was Jeffrey; and he has, two or three weeks ago, convinced me that he will never do anything for me; that he dares not; that he cannot; that he does not wish to do it. Why not try for ourselves, while as yet we have strength left, and old age has not finally lamed us? *Andar con Dios!* Unutterable thoughts are in me, and *these* words are but faint chirpings. May God direct us and go with us! My poor mother! But once for all one must cut himself loose though his heart bleed; it is better than perennial torpor which ends in death.

March 25.—Strange days these are; again quite original days in my life. Cannot express any portion of their meaning in words; cannot even try it.

I dig the garden flower-beds, though not hoping to see them spring. It is a bodeful, *huge* feeling I have, like one to be delivered from a Bastille; and who says, delivered? or cast out?

Thousand voices speak to me from the distance out of the dim depths of the old years. I sit speechless. If I live, I *shall* speak.

Many things are sad to me : the saddest is to forsake my poor mother ; for it is kind of *forsaking,* though she, too, sees well the necessity of it. May He to whom she ever looks not forsake her!

Be still, be wise, be brave! The world is all before thee; its *pains* will soon (how very soon) be over; the *work* to be done in it will continue—through eternity. Oh, how fearful, yet how great!

So far the Diary. The letters, or portions of them, fill the interval between the notes, and wind up the story of the Carlyles' life in the Dumfriesshire highlands.

To John Carlyle, Rome.

Craigenputtock : January 21, 1834.

On Wednesday gone a fortnight I drove down to Dumfries to fetch up our mother, who had been waiting at Jean's there for several days. We got home betimes; found Archy Glen and William, the former of whom went off on the following day and left us a little more composure. My mother was wonderfully cheerful and composed. She read various things—Campan's ' Memoirs,' and such like, with great interest; sewed a little, smoked and talked, and, on the whole, was very tolerably off. Her calmness in the midst of so many vicissitudes, and now while her immediate future is still so problematical, was very gratifying to me; showed the admirable spirit she is of. It is one of the saddest possibilities now that lies before me, the losing of such a parent. One thing with another, and altogether apart from natural affection, I have seen no woman in the whole world whom I would have preferred as a mother. On the following Sunday Alick and Jamie both arrived, so that again we had a full house. They stayed till Wednesday morning, when I accompanied them as far as Stroquhan ; it had been arranged that Alick was to come next Saturday to Dumfries and meet our mother there if the day was tolerable. She and I accordingly set off; met Alick there, who had his cart, and I reyoked poor Harry and turned back again to the solitude of our moors. Our mother was wrapped to all lengths, and, having the wind favourable, I hope would not suffer much from cold.

As for our household it is much as you can fancy it. Jane continues in a tolerable, in an improving state of health, though the last five weeks of bustle have done her no good. I, when I take walking enough, get along as I was wont in that particular. Continued sickness is a miserable thing, yet one learns to brave it. . . .

What you say of periodicals is mournfully true ; yet it is true also that a man must provide food and clothes for himself as long as he honestly can. While you write down a truth you do an honest duty, were the devil himself your editor, and all fellow contributors mere incubi and foul creatures. One loses repute by it, but nothing more ; and must front that loss for a gain which is indispensable. Indeed, had I (written) the best book possible for me, I see not, such is the condition of things, where I could so much as get it printed. *Your* money, my dear boy, I will not take at this time till you are settled with it, and making more. Come home, and let us settle in London together, and front the world together, and see whether it will beat us ! Let us try it. And in the meanwhile never fear but I hold on ; now as ever it lies with myself. Mill tells me that he and Buller and a number of Radicals with money capital, and what they reckon talents, have determined on a new Radical Review, which they want me to write in. Unitarian Fox is to be editor. I calculate that it may last three years at any rate, for money is found to that length. If they pay me rightly they shall have a paper or two; if not, not. The Radicals I say always are barren as Sahara, but *not* poisonous. In my prophecy of the world they are my *enfants perdus*, whom I honestly wish well to. James Fraser writes me that ' Teufelsdröckh ' meets with the most unqualified disapproval, which is all extremely proper. His payment arrives, which is still more proper. On the whole, dear Jack, it is a contending world ; and he that is born into it must fight for his place or lose it. If we are under the *right flag*, let the world do its worst and heartily welcome.

God bless thee, dear brother! *Auf ewig.*   T. CARLYLE.

To Mrs. Carlyle, Scotsbrig.

January 28, 1834.

I wrote to poor Jeffrey, but not till any anger I felt had gone off, and given place to a kind of pity. 'Poor fellow!' I thought: 'what a miserable *fuff* thou gettest into, poor old exasperated politician! I will positively have pity on thee, and do thee a little good if I can!' In this spirit was my letter written; a short careless letter winding up the business handsomely, not ravelling it further. He is off to London to-day I fancy, to worry and be worried in that den of discord and dishonesty; actually, I doubt, to lose his last allotment of health, almost his life, if he be not soon delivered. 'He cannot hinder thee of God's providence,' is also a most precious truth: not he nor the whole world with the Devil to back it out! *This* is a fact one ought to lay seriously to heart and see into the meaning of. Did we see it rightly, what were there beneath the moon that should throw us into commotion? Except writing letters, I have not put pen to paper yet. I sent word to Mill that I *would* write two essays for his new periodical, the second of which is perhaps to be on John Knox; but I suppose there is no great hurry.

To Alexander Carlyle.

February 18, 1834.

. . . Poor Mrs. Clow it seems has been called away. She was not long left a *superfluity* in the world, but has found a home beside her old partner where there will be none to grudge her. Oh Time! Time! how it brings forth and devours! And the roaring flood of existence rushes on for ever similar, for ever changing! Already of those that we looked up to as grown men, as towers of defence and authority in our boyhood, the most are clean gone. We ourselves have stept into their position, where also we cannot linger. Unhappy they that have no footing in eternity; for here in time all is but cloud and the baseless fabric of a vision!

But to turn back to the earth; for in the earth too lies the pledge of a higher world—namely, a *duty* allotted us. Tell me, my dear brother, how you fare on that wild Knowhead, what kind of cheer you are of. The little children I imagine must be your chief blessing; and surely you are thankful for them, and will struggle with your whole strength to instruct them and protect them, and fit them for the long journey (long, for it is as long as eternity) that lies before them. Little Jane will be beginning to have many notions of things now. Train her to this as the corner-stone of all morality : to stand by the *truth; to abhor a lie as she does hell-fire.* Actually the longer I live I see the greater cause to look on falsehood with detestation, with terror, as the beginning of all else that is of the Devil. *My* poor little namesake has no knowledge of good or evil yet; but I hope he will grow to be a strong man and do his name credit. For yourself, I am glad to see you make so manful a struggle on that uncomfortable clay footing, which however you must not quite quarrel with. In the darkest weather I always predict better days. The world is God's world, and wide and fair. If they hamper us too far we will try another side of it. Meanwhile I will tell you a fault you have to guard against, and is not that the truest friendship that I can show you? Every position of man has its temptation, its evil tendency. Now yours and mine I suspect to be this : a tendency to imperiousness, to indignant self-help, and if nowise theoreti-cal, yet practical, forgetfulness and tyrannical contempt of other men. This is wrong; this is *tyranny,* I say; and we ought to guard against it. Be merciful; repress much indignation; too much of it will get vent after all. Evil destiny is nothing; let it labour us and impoverish us as it will, if it only do not lame and distort us. Alas! I feel well one cannot wholly help even this; but we ought unweariedly to endeavour.

To John Carlyle, Rome.

Craigenputtock: February 25, 1834.

We learned incidentally last week that Grace, our servant, though ' without fault to us,' and whom we with all her inertness were nothing but purposing to keep, had resolved on ' going home next summer.' The cup that had long been filling ran over with that smallest of drops. After meditating on it for a few minutes, we said to one another : ' Why not *bolt* out of all these sooty des-picabilities, of *Kerrags* and lying draggle-tails of byre-women, and peat-moss and isolation and exasperation and confusion, and go at once to London? *Gedacht, gethan!* Two days after we had a letter on the road to Mrs. Austin, to look out among the ' houses to let ' for us, and an advertisement to Mac Diarmid to try for the letting of our own. Since then, you may fancy, our heads and hearts have been full of this great enterprise, the greatest (small as it is) that I ever *knowingly* engaged in. We bring anxiously together all the experience we have gathered or got reported, look back and look forward, make the bravest resolutions, and in fine seem to see a trembling hope that we may master the enterprise (of an honest life in London); at all events, a certainty that we ought to try it. Yes, we must try it! Life here is but a kind of life-in-death, or rather, one might say, a not-being-born : one sits as in the belly of some Trojan horse, weather screened, but pining, inactive, neck and heels crushed together. Let us burst it in the name of God! Let us take such an existence as He will give us, working where work is to be found while it is called to-day. A strange shiver runs through every nerve of me when I think of taking that plunge ; yet also a kind of sacred faith, sweet after the dreary vacuity of soul I have through long seasons lived in as under an eclipsing shadow. I purpose to be *prudent,* watchful of my words, to look well about me, and with all the faculty I have pick my steps in that new arena. Thousands of sillier fellows than I flourish in it : the whole promotion I strive for is simplest food and shelter in exchange for the honestest work I can do.

We purpose for many reasons to make this a whole measure, not a half one : thus the first thing will be to give up our establishment here, to sell off all the furniture but what will equip a very modest house in the suburbs of London ; to let *this* house if we can ; if we cannot, to let it stand there and not waste more money. This Jane calls a 'burning of our ships,' which suits better with our present aims than anything else would. For indeed I feel this is as if the *last* chance I shall ever have to redeem my existence from pain and imprisonment, and make something of the faculty I have, before it be for ever hid from my eyes. No looking back then! Forward! Advance or perish! We imagine some suburban house may be got for 40*l.* Leigh Hunt talked much about a quite delightful one he had (for 'ten children' too) at Chelsea, all wainscoted, &c., for thirty guineas. With 200*l.* we fancy the *rigour of economy* may enable us to meet the year. I must work and seek work ; before sinking utterly I will make an 'a-fu' struggle.

Our dear mother has not heard of this ; for though I wrote to Alick a week ago, it was not then thought of. It will be a heavy stroke, yet not quite unanticipated, and she will brave it. My brother and she are the only ties I have to Scotland. I will tell

her that though at a greater distance we are not to be disunited.
Regular letters—frequent visits. I will say who knows but what
you and I may yet bring her up to London to pass her old days
waited on by both of us? Go whither she may, she will have her
Bible with her and her faith in God. She is the truest Christian
believer I have ever met with; nay I might almost say the only
true one.

P.S. from Mrs. Carlyle:—

My dear Brother,—Here is a new prospect opened up to us with
a vengeance! Am I frightened? Not a bit. I almost wish that
I felt more anxiety about our future; for this composure is not
courage, but *diseased indifference*. There is a sort of incrustation
about the inward me which renders it alike insensible to fear and
to hope. I suppose I am in what Glen calls the *chrysalis state* or
the *state of incubation*. Let us trust that like all other states which
have a beginning it will also have an end, and that the poor Psyche
shall at last get freed. In the meantime I do what I see to be my
duty as well as I can and wish that I could do it better. It seems
as if the problem of living would be immensely simplified to me
if I had health. It does require such an effort to keep oneself from
growing quite wicked, while that weary weaver's shuttle is plying
between my temples. Unhappy Melina, &c.! I have reason to
be thankful that I have had less sickness this winter than in the
two preceding ones, which I attribute partly to the change in my
pills. Your recipe is worn to tatters, but Glen copied it for me.
The note book you gave me is half filled with such multifarious
matter! No mortal gets a glimpse of it. I wish Carlyle would
let me begin a letter instead of ending it. He leaves me nothing
but dregs to impart. Would you recommend me to sup on porridge and beer? Carlyle takes it. We have got a dear little
canary bird which we call Chico, which sings all day long 'like—
like anything.'

So ends the last letter from Craigenputtock. 'The ships
were burnt,' two busy months being spent in burning them
—disposing of old books, old bedsteads, kitchen things, all
the rubbish of the establishment. The cows and poultry
were sold. Mrs. Carlyle's pony was sent to Scotsbrig.
Friends in London were busy looking out for houses.
Carlyle, unable to work in the confusion, grew unbearable,

naturally enough, to himself and everyone, and finally, at the beginning of May, rushed off alone, believing that house letting in London was conducted on the same rule as in Edinburgh, and that unless he could secure a home for himself at Whitsuntide he would have to wait till the year had gone round. In this hurried fashion he took his own departure, leaving his wife to pack what they did not intend to part with, and to follow at her leisure when the new habitation had been decided on. Mill had sent his warmest congratulations when he learnt that the final resolution had been taken. Carlyle, who had settled himself while house hunting at his old lodgings in Ampton Street, sent his brother John a brief account of his final leavetaking of Scotland.

To John Carlyle.

4 Ampton Street : May 18.

With regard to our dear mother, I bid you comfort yourself with the assurance that she is moderately well. She adjusts herself with the old heroism to the new circumstances ; agrees that I *must* come hither ; parts from me with the stillest face, more touching than if it had been all beteared. I said to Alick as we drove up the Purdamstown brae that morning, that I thought if I had all the mothers I ever saw to choose from I would have chosen my own. She is to have Harry,[1] and can ride very well on him, will go down awhile to sea-bathing at Mary's, and will spend the summer tolerably enough. For winter I left her the task of spinning me a plaid dressing gown, with which if she get too soon done she may spin another for you. She has books, above all her *Book*. She trusts in God, and shall not be put to shame. While she was at Craigenputtock I made her train me to two song tunes ; and we often sang them together, and tried them often again in coming down into Annandale. One of them I actually found myself humming with a strange cheerfully pathetic feeling when I first came in sight of huge smoky Babylon—

> For there's seven foresters in yon forest.
> And them I want to see, see,
> And them I want to see.

I wrote her a little note yesterday and told her this.

[1] The pony.

Thus the six years' imprisonment on the Dumfriesshire moors came to an end. To Carlyle himself they had been years of inestimable value. If we compare the essay on Jean Paul, which he wrote at Comely Bank, with the 'Diamond Necklace,' his last work at Craigenputtock, we see the leap from promise to fulfilment, from the immature energy of youth to the full intellectual strength of completed manhood. The solitude had compelled him to digest his thoughts. In 'Sartor' he had relieved his soul of its perilous secretions by throwing out of himself his personal sufferings and physical and spiritual experience. He had read omnivorously far and wide. His memory was a magazine of facts gathered over the whole surface of European literature and history. The multiplied allusions in every page of his later essays, so easy, so unlaboured, reveal the wealth which he had accumulated, and the fulness of his command over his possessions. His religious faith had gained solidity. His confidence in the soundness of his own convictions was no longer clouded with the shadow of a doubt. The 'History of the French Revolution,' the most powerful of all his works, and the only one which has the character of a work of art, was the production of the mind which he brought with him from Craigenputtock, undisturbed by the contradictions and excitements of London society and London triumphs. He had been tried in the furnace. Poverty, mortification, and disappointment had done their work upon him, and he had risen above them elevated, purified, and strengthened. Even the arrogance and self-assertion which Lord Jeffrey supposed to have been developed in him by living away from conflict with other minds, had been rather tamed than encouraged by his lonely meditations. It was rather collision with those who differed with him which fostered his imperiousness; for Carlyle rarely met with an antagonist whom he could not overbear with the torrent of his metaphors, whilst to himself his note-books show that he read many a lecture on humility.

He had laid in, too, on the moors a stock of robust health. Lamentations over indigestion and want of sleep are almost totally absent from the letters written from Craigenputtock. The simple, natural life, the wholesome air, the daily rides or drives, the poor food—milk, cream, eggs, oatmeal, the best of their kind—had restored completely the functions of a stomach never, perhaps, so far wrong as he had imagined. Carlyle had ceased to complain on this head, and in a person so extremely vocal when anything was amiss with him, silence is the best evidence that there was nothing to complain of. On the moors, as at Mainhill, at Edinburgh, or in London afterwards, he was always impatient, moody, irritable, violent. These humours were in his nature, and could no more be separated from them than his body could leap off its shadow. But, intolerable as he had found Craigenputtock in the later years of his residence there, he looked back to it afterwards as the happiest and wholesomest home that he had ever known. He could do fully twice as much work there, he said, as he could ever do afterwards in London; and many a time, when sick of fame and clatter and interruption, he longed to return to it.

To Mrs. Carlyle Cragenputtock had been a less salutary home. She might have borne the climate, and even benefited by it, if the other conditions had been less ungenial. But her life there, to begin with, had been a life of menial drudgery, unsolaced (for she could have endured and even enjoyed mere hardship) by more than an occasional word of encouragement or sympathy or compassion from her husband. To him it seemed perfectly natural that what his mother did at Scotsbrig his wife should do for him. Every household duty fell upon her, either directly, or in supplying the shortcomings of a Scotch maid-of-all-work.

She had to cook, to sew, to scour, to clean ; to gallop down alone to Dumfries if anything was wanted; to keep the house, and even on occasions to milk the cows. Miss Jewsbury has preserved many anecdotes of the Craigenputtock life, showing how hard a time her friend had of it there. Carlyle, though disposed at first to dismiss these memories as legends, yet admitted on reflection that for all there was a certain foundation. The errors, if any, can be no more than the slight alterations of form which stories naturally receive in repetition. A lady brought up in luxury has been educated into physical unfitness for so sharp a discipline. Mrs. Carlyle's bodily health never recovered from the strain of those six years. The trial to her mind and to her nervous system was still more severe. Nature had given her, along with a powerful understanding, a disposition singularly bright and buoyant. The Irving disappointment had been a blow to her ; but wounds which do not kill are cured. They leave a scar, but the pain ceases. It was long over, and if Carlyle had been a real companion to her, she would have been as happy with him as wives usually are. But he was not a companion at all. When he was busy she rarely so much as saw him, save, as he himself pathetically tells, when she would steal into his dressing-room in the morning when he was shaving, to secure that little of his society. The loneliness of Craigenputtock was dreadful to her. Her hard work, perhaps, had so far something of a blessing in it, that it was a relief from the intolerable pressure. For months together, especially after Alick Carlyle had gone, they never saw the face of guest or passing stranger. So still the moors were, that she could hear the sheep nibbling the grass a quarter of a mile off. For the many weeks when the snow was on the ground she could not stir beyond the garden, or even beyond her door. She had no great thoughts, as Carlyle had, to occupy her with the adminis-

tration of the universe. He had deranged the faith in
which she had been brought up, but he had not inoculated
her with his own ; and a dull gloom, sinking at last almost
to apathy, fell upon her spirits. She fought against it,
like a brave woman as she was. Carlyle's own views of
the prospects of men in this world were not brilliant. In
his 'Miscellanies' is a small poem, written at Craigenputtock, called ' Cui Bono ? ' giving a most unpromising sketch
of human destiny :—

Cui Bono?

What is Hope ? a smiling rainbow
    Children follow through the wet ;
'Tis not here, still yonder, yonder !
    Never urchin found it yet.

What is Life ? a thawing iceboard
    On a sea with sunny shore.
Gay we sail—it melts beneath us !
    We are sunk, and seen no more.

What is Man ? a foolish baby ;
    Vainly strives, and fights, and frets ;
Demanding all—deserving nothing !
    One small grave is what he gets.

In one of Mrs. Carlyle's note-books, I find an ' Answer '
to this, dated 1830 :—

Nay, this is Hope : a gentle dove,
    That nestles in the gentle breast,
Bringing glad tidings from above
    Of joys to come and heavenly rest.

And this is Life : ethereal fire
    Striving aloft through smothering clay ;
Mounting, flaming, higher, higher !
    Till lost in immortality.

And Man—oh ! hate not nor despise
    The fairest, lordliest work of God !
Think not He made the good and wise
    Only to sleep beneath the sod !

Carlyle himself recognised occasionally that she was not happy. Intentionally unkind it was not in his nature to be. After his mother, he loved his wife better than anyone in the world. He was only occupied, unperceiving, negligent ; and when he *did* see that anything was wrong with her, he was at once the tenderest of husbands.

In some such transient state of consciousness he wrote, on January 29, 1830 :—

The Sigh.

Oh ! sigh not so, my fond and faithful wife,
  In sad remembrance or in boding fear :
This is not life—this phantasm type of life !
  What is there to rejoice or mourn for here ?

Be it no wealth, nor fame, nor post is ours—
  Small blessedness for infinite desire ;
But has the King his wish in Windsor's towers ?
  Or but the common lot—meat, clothes, and fire ?

Lone stands our home amid the sullen moor,
  Its threshold by few friendly feet betrod ;
Yet *we* are here, we two, still true though poor :
  And this, too, is *the world*—the ' city of God ' !

O'erhangs us not the infinitude of sky,
  Where all the starry lights revolve and shine ?
Does not that universe within us lie
  And move—its Maker or itself divine ?

And we, my love, life's waking dream once done,
  Shall sleep to wondrous lands on other's breast,
And all we loved and toiled for, one by one,
  Shall join us there and, wearied, be at rest.

Then sigh not so, my fond and faithful wife,
  But striving well, have hope, be of good cheer ;
Not rest, but worthy labour, is the soul of life ;
  Not that but this is to be looked and wished for here.

If the occasional tenderness of these lines could have been formed into a habit Mrs. Carlyle might have borne Craigenputtock less impatiently, and as her bodily ailments were chiefly caused by exposure and overwork, she would probably have escaped the worst of them, because she would have thought it worth while to take care of herself.

Of the solitude and of the strange figures moving about the moor, to make the desolation more sensible, Carlyle has left a singular picture.

Old Esther, whose death came one of our early winters, was a bit of memorability in that altogether vacant scene. I forget the old woman's surname, perhaps McGeorge, but well recall her heavy lumpish figure, lame of a foot, and her honest, quiet, not stupid countenance of mixed ugliness and stoicism. She lived above a mile from us in a poor cottage of the next farm.[1] Esther had been a laird's daughter riding her palfrey at one time, but had gone to wreck father and self; a special 'misfortune' (so they delicately name it) being of Esther's producing. Misfortune in the shape ultimately of a solid tall ditcher, very good to his old mother Esther, had just before our coming perished miserably one night on the shoulder of Dunscore Hill (found dead there next morning), which had driven his poor old mother up to this thriftier hut and silent mode of living in our moorland part of the parish. She did not beg, nor had my Jeannie much to have given her of help (perhaps on occasions milk, old warm clothes, &c.), though always very sorry for her last sad bereavement of the stalwart affectionate son. I remember one frosty kind of forenoon, while walking meditative to the top of our hill, the silence was complete, all but one 'click clack' heard regularly like a far-off spondee or iambus, a great way to my right, no other sound in nature. On looking sharply, I discovered it to be old Esther on the highway, crippling along, towards our house most probably. Poor old soul! thought I. What a desolation! But you will meet a kind face too perhaps. Heaven is over all.

Not long after poor old Esther sank to bed—deathbed, as my Jane, who had a quick and sure eye in these things, well judged it would be. Sickness did not last above ten days: my poor wife

[1] 'Carson's, of Nether Craigenputtock, very stupid young brother used to come and bore me at rare intervals.—T. C.'

zealously assiduous and with a minimum of fuss and noise. I remember those few poor days full of human interest to her, and through her to me; and of a human pity not painful, but sweet and genuine. She went walking every morning, especially every night to arrange the poor bed, &c.—nothing but rudish hands, rude though kind enough, being about; the poor old woman evidently gratified by it, and heart thankful, and almost to the very end giving clear sign of that. Something pathetic in old Esther and her exit; nay, if I rightly bethink me, that 'click clack' pilgrimage had in fact been a last visit to Craigenputtock with some poor bit of crockery, some grey-lettered butter-plate, which I used to see 'as a wee *memorandum* o' me, mem, when I am gone.' 'Memorandum' was her word, and I remember the poor little platter for years after. Poor old Esther had awoke that frosty morning with the feeling that she would soon die, that the 'bonny leddy' had been 'unco guid' to her, and that there was still that 'wee bit memorandum.' Nay, I think she had, or had once had, the remains or complete ghost of a 'fine old riding habit,' once her own, which the curious had seen, but this she had judged it more polite to leave to the parish.

Enough of Craigenputtock. The scene shifts to London.

CHAPTER XVIII.

A.D. 1834. ÆT. 39.

Extracts from Journal.

London: May 24, 1834.—What a word is there! I left home on Thursday last (five days ago), and see myself still with astonishment here seeking houses. The parting with my sister Jean, who had driven down with me to Dumfries, was the first of the partings; that with my dear mother next day, with poor Mary at Annan, with my two brothers Alick and Jamie—all these things *were* to be done. Shall we meet again? Shall our meeting again be for good? God grant it. We are in his hands. This is all the comfort I have. As to my beloved and now aged mother, it is sore upon me,—so sore as I have felt nothing of the sort since boyhood. She paid her last visit at Craigenputtock the week before, and had attached me much, if I could have been more attached, by her quiet way of taking that sore trial. She studied not to sink my heart; she shed no tear at parting; and so I drove off with poor Alick in quest of new fortunes. May the Father of all, to whom she daily prays for me, be ever near her! May He, if it be his will, grant us a glad re-meeting and re union in a higher country. But no more of this. Words are worse than vain. I am here in my old lodging at Ampton Street, wearied, and without books, company, or other resource. The Umpire coach from Liverpool. Through the arch at Holloway came first in sight of huge smoky London, humming, in a kind of defiance, my mother's tune of 'Johnny O'Cox.' Find this lodging. Mrs. Austin very kind. See several houses. Disappointed in all. Kensington very dirty and confused. Sleep—sweet sleep. This day busy, with little work done; my feet all lamed, and not above one house seen that in any measure looks like fitting.

Went to Mrs. Austin, through the Park and Gardens. Find a Mrs. Jamieson—a shrewd-looking, hard-tempered, red-haired woman, whom I care little about meeting again. Look at many houses with them. Edward Irving starts up from a seat in Kensington Gardens, as I was crossing it with these two, and runs towards me. The good Edward! He looked pale, worn, unsound, very unhealthy. At the house we were going to no key could be got: no this, no that. Miss my dinner. Innkeepers can give me none. Dine with a dairyman on bread and milk beside his cows —a most interesting meal. Charge three halfpence, I having furnished bread. Gave the man sixpence, because I liked him. Will see the poor fellow again, perhaps. Hunt's [1] household in Cheyne Row, Chelsea. Nondescript! unutterable! Mrs. Hunt asleep on cushions ; four or five beautiful, strange, gipsy-looking children running about in undress, whom the lady ordered to get us tea. The eldest boy, Percy, a sallow, black-haired youth of sixteen, with a kind of dark cotton nightgown on, went whirling about like a familiar, providing everything : an indescribable dreamlike household. Am to go again to-morrow to see if there *be* any houses, and what they are. Bedtime now, and so good night, ye loved ones. My heart's blessing be with all!

Those who have studied Carlyle's writings as they ought to be studied, know that shrewd practical sense underlies always his metaphorical extravagances. In matters of business he was the most prudent of men. He had left his wife at Craigenputtock to pack up, and had plunged, himself, into the whirlpool of house-hunting. He very soon discovered that there was no hurry, and that he was not the best judge in such matters. He understood—the second best form of wisdom—that he did not understand, and forebore to come to any resolution till Mrs. Carlyle could join him. He wrote to her, giving a full account of his experiences.

The female head (he said) is not without a shrewdness of its own in these affairs. Moreover, ought not my little *coagitor* to have a vote herself in the choice of an abode which is to be *ours?* The sweet word *ours!* The blessed ordinance—let Hunt say what he will [2]—by which all things are for ever one between us and

---

[1] Leigh Hunt.

[2] Leigh Hunt advocated ' women's rights ' in marriage arrangements.

separation an impossibility. Unless you specially order it, no final arrangement shall be made till we both make it.

Carlyle had not been idle—had walked, as he said, till his feet were lamed under him. He had searched in Brompton, in Kensington, about the Regent's Park. He had seen many houses more or less desirable, more or less objectionable. For himself he inclined on the whole to one which Leigh Hunt had found for him near the river in Chelsea. Leigh Hunt lived with his singular family at No. 4 Upper Cheyne Row. About sixty yards off, about the middle of Great Cheyne Row, which runs at right angles to the other, there was a house which fixed his attention. Twice he went over it. 'It is notable,' he said, 'how at each new visit your opinion gets a little hitch the contrary way from its former tendency. Imagination has outgone the reality. I nevertheless still feel a great liking for this excellent old house. Chelsea is unfashionable: it was once the resort of the Court and great, however; hence numerous old houses in it at once cheap and excellent.'

A third inspection produced a fuller description—description of the place as it was fifty years ago, and not wholly incorrect of its present condition; for Cheyne Row has changed less than most other streets in London. The Embankment had yet forty years to wait.

The street (Carlyle wrote) runs down upon the river, which I suppose you might see by stretching out your head from the front window, at a distance of fifty yards on the left. We are called 'Cheyne Row' proper (pronounced *Chainie* Row), and are a 'genteel neighbourhood;' two old ladies on one side, unknown character on the other, but with 'pianos.' The street is flag pathed, sunk storied, iron railed, all old fashioned and tightly done up; looks out on a rank of sturdy old *pollarded* (that is, beheaded) lime trees standing there like giants in *tawtie* wigs (for the new boughs are still young); beyond this a high brick wall; backwards a garden, the size of our back one at Comely Bank, with trees, &c., in bad culture; beyond this green hayfields and tree avenues, once a bishop's pleasure grounds, an unpicturesque yet rather cheerful outlook. The house itself is eminent, antique, wainscoted to the very ceiling, and has been all new painted and repaired; broadish stair with massive balustrade (in the old style), corniced and as thick as one's thigh; floors thick as a rock, wood of them here and there worm-eaten, yet capable of cleanness, and still with thrice the strength of a modern floor. And then as to rooms, Goody! Three stories beside the sunk story, in every one of them three apartments, in depth something like forty feet in all—a front dining-room (marble chimney piece, &c.), then a back dining-room or breakfast-room, a little narrower by reason of the kitchen stairs; then out of this, and narrower still (to allow a back window, you consider) a china-room or pantry, or I know not what, all shelved and fit to hold crockery for the whole street. Such is the ground area, which of course continues to the top, and furnishes every bedroom with a dressing-room or second bedroom; on the whole a most massive roomy sufficient old house with places, for example, to hang, say, three dozen hats or cloaks on, and as many crevices and queer old presses and shelved closets (all tight and new painted in their way) as would gratify the most covetous Goody—rent, thirty-five pounds! I confess I am strongly tempted. Chelsea is a singular heterogeneous kind of spot, very dirty and confused in some places, quite beautiful in others, abounding with antiquities and the traces of great men—Sir Thomas More, Steele, Smollett, &c. Our row, which for the last three doors or so is a street, and none of the noblest, runs out upon a 'Parade' (perhaps they call it) running along the shore of the river, a broad highway with huge shady trees, boats lying moored, and a smell of shipping and tan. Battersea Bridge (of wood) a few yards off; the broad river with white-trowsered, white-shirted Cockneys dashing by like arrows in thin long canoes of boats; beyond, the green beautiful knolls of Surrey with their villages—on the whole, a most artificial, green-painted, yet lively, fresh, almost opera-looking business, such as you can fancy. Finally, Chelsea abounds more than any place in omnibi, and they take you to Coventry Street for sixpence. Revolve all this in thy fancy and judgment, my child, and see what thou canst *make* of it.

The discovery of this Chelsea house had been so gratifying that more amiable views could be taken, and more interest felt, with the other conditions of London life.

Let me now treat thee to a budget of small news (he goes on). Mill I have not yet seen again; we could make no appointment, being so unfixed as yet. Mrs. Austin had a tragical story of his having fallen *desperately in love* with some young philosophic beauty (yet with the innocence of two sucking doves), and being lost to all his friends and to himself, and what not ; but I traced nothing of this in poor Mill ; and even incline to think that what truth there is or was in his adventure may have done him good. Buller also spoke of it, but in the comic vein. Irving I have not again seen, though I have tried four times ; yesterday twice (at Bayswater), and the second time with great disappointment. He seems to be under the care of a Scotch *sick nurse* there ; was said to be 'asleep' when I called first, then gone (contrary to my appointment) when I called the second time. He rides twice a day down to that Domdaniel in Newman Street, rises at five in the morning, goes to bed at nine, is '*very weak*.' I had refused din- ner at the Austins for his sake ; it seemed to me as if I might have clutched him from perdition and death, and now we were not to meet again. My poor Edward ! *Heu, quantum mutatus!* But I will make a new trial. Heraud said to me, quite in the cursory style, 'Aaving (Irving) is dying and a—a—!' Heraud himself ('mad as a March hare,' Fraser said) lives close by Amp- ton Street, and is exceedingly *kedge* about me, anxious beyond measure for golden opinions of his God-dedicated Epic—of which I would not tell him any lie, greatly as he tempted me.

Fraser did not open freely to me, yet was opening. Literature still all a mystery ; nothing 'paying;' 'Teufelsdröckh' beyond measure unpopular ; an oldest subscriber came in to him and said, 'If there is any more of that d—d stuff I will, &c. &c.;' on the other hand, an order from America (Boston or Philadelphia) to send a copy of the magazine *so long* as there was anything of Carlyle's in it.' 'One spake up and the other spake down :' on the whole, Goody, I have a great defiance of all that. As to 'fame' and the like, in *very truth*, in this state of the public, it is a thing one is always better without ; so I really saw and felt the other night, clearly for the first time. Miss Martineau, for example, is done again ; going to America to try a new tack when she returns—so are they all, or *will* inevitably all be *done ;* extinguished and abolished ; for they are *nothing*, and were only *called* (and made to fancy themselves) something. Mrs. Austin herself seems to me in a kind of trial-state ; risen or rising to where she cannot hope to stand; where it will be well if she feels no giddiness, as indeed I really hope she will. A most excellent creature, of surveyable limits; her goodness will in all cases save her. Buller is better and went yesterday (I fancy) to ' the House.' We have had two long talks (on occasion of the franks) with great mutual delight. An intelligent, clear, honest, most kindly vivacious creature; the genialest Radical I have ever met. He throws light for me on many things, being very *ready* to speak. Mrs. Austin spoke ominously of his health, but to my seeing without much ground. Charlie, I think, will be among my little comforts here.

The Duke, now plain Mr. Jeffrey, but soon to be Lord Jeffrey, is still here for a week; he has left his address for me with Mrs. Austin. I determined to call some morning in passing, and did it on Monday. Reception anxiously cordial from all three; hurried insignificant talk from him still at the breakfast table; kindness playing over 'iron gravity' from me. I felt it to be a farewell visit, and that it should be 'hallowed in our choicest mood.' The poor Duke is so tremulous, he bade me 'good evening' at the door; immense jerking from Mrs. Jeffrey, yet many kind words and invitations back. . . . And so ends our dealing with bright Jeffreydom, once so sparkling, cheerful, now gone out into darkness—which shall not become foul candlestuff vapour, but darkness only. Empson is still alive; but I surely will not seek him. Napier, too, is here, or was; him, too, I will nowise seek or meddle with—the hungry *simulacrum*.

To Mrs. Carlyle, Scotsbrig.

4 Ampton Street, London : May 30, 1834.

My dear Mother,—How often have I thought of you since we parted, in all varieties of solemn moods, only seldom or never in a purely sad or painful one. My most constant feeling is one not without a certain sacredness : I determine to live worthily of such a mother; to know always, like her, that we are ever in our great Taskmaster's eye, with whom are the issues not of time only, which is but a short *vision*, but of eternity, which ends not and is a reality. Oh that I could keep these things for ever clear before me! my whole prayer with regard to life were gratified. But these things also should not make us gloomy or sorrowful : far from that. Have we not, as you often say, 'many mercies'? Is not the light to see that they are mercies the first and greatest of these?

Assure yourself, my dear mother, that all goes well. In regard to health, this incessant toil and even irregular living seems to agree with me. I take no drugs. I really feel fresher and stronger than I used to do among the moorlands. Moreover, I never was farther in my life from '*tining heart*,' which I know well were to 'tine all.' Not a bit of me! I walk along these tumultuous streets with nothing but a feeling of kindness, of brotherly pity, towards all. No loudest boasting of man's strikes any, the smallest, terror into me for the present; indeed how should it when no loudest boasting and threatening of the Devil himself would? He nor they '*cannot* hinder thee of God's providence.' No, they cannot. I have the clearest certainty that if work is appointed me here to do, it must and will be done, and means found for doing it. So fear nothing, my dear mother. Tom will endeavour not to disgrace you in this new position more than in others.

I have seen some book-publishing persons, some 'literary men' also. The great proportion are indubitablest *duds:* these two we must let pass, and even welcome when they meet us with kindliness. By far the sensiblest man I see is Mill, who seems almost fonder of me than ever. The class he belongs to has the farther merit of being genuine and honest so far as they go. I think it is rather with that class that I shall connect myself than with any other;[1] but still in many important respects I have to expect to find myself alone. Charles Buller is grown a very promising man, likely to do good in the world, if his health were only better, which as yet hampers him much. He evidently likes me well, as do all his household, and will be a considerable pleasure to me. I was dining there this day week. I saw various notable persons—Radical members, and such like; among whom a young, very rich man, named Sir William Molesworth, pleased me considerably. We have met since, and shall probably see much more of one another. He seems very honest: needs, or will need, guidance much, and with it may do not a little good.

I liked the frank manners of the young man; so beautiful in contrast with Scottish gigmanity. I pitied his darkness of mind, and heartily wished him well. He is, among other things, a vehement smoker of tobacco. This Molesworth is one of the main men that are to support that Radical Review of theirs with which

---

[1] 'No poison in the Radicals. If little apprehension of positive truth, no hypocrisy; no wilful taking up with falsehood.'

it seems likely that I may rather heartily connect myself, if it take a form I can do with. The rest of the reviews are sick and lean, ready for nothing, so far as I can see, but a gentle death. I also mean to write a *new book ;* and in a serious enough style, you may depend upon it. By the time we have got the flitting rightly over I shall have settled what and how it is to be. Either on the French Revolution, or on John Knox and our Scottish Kirk.

By dint of incessant industry I again got to see Edward Irving, and on Saturday last spent two hours with him. He seemed to have wonderfully recovered his health, and I trust will not perish in these delusions of his. He is still a good man, yet wofully given over to his idols, and enveloped for the present, and nigh choked, in the despicablest coil of cobwebs ever man sate in the midst of.

Mrs. Strachey I have seen some three times, but not in very advantageous circumstances. She is the same true woman she ever was, indignant at the oppressing of the poor, at the wrong and falsehood with which the earth is filled ; yet rather gently withdrawn from it, and hoping in what is beyond it than actively at war with it.

Carlyle was not long left alone. Mrs. Carlyle arrived— she came by Annan steamer and the coach from Liverpool at the beginning of June; old Mrs. Carlyle, standing with a crowd on the Annan pier, waving her handkerchief as the vessel moved away. Carlyle, as he returned from his walk to his lodgings in Ampton Street, was received by the chirping of little Chico, the canary bird ; his wife resting after her journey in bed. They had been fortunate in securing a remarkable woman, who was more a friend and a companion than a servant, to help them through their first difficulties—Bessy Barnet, the daughter of Mr. Badams's housekeeper at Birmingham, whom Carlyle had known there as a child. Badams was now dead, and this Bessy, who had remained with him to the last, now attached herself to Carlyle for the sake of her late master. The Chelsea house was seen by Mrs. Carlyle, and after some hesitation was approved ; and three days after they had taken possession of their future home, and Pickford's vans were at the door unloading the furniture from Craigenputtock.

Thirty-four years later Carlyle wrote:—

Tuesday, 10th of June, 1834, was the day of our alighting, amidst heaped furniture, in this house, where we were to continue for life. I well remember bits of the drive from Ampton Street: what damp-clouded kind of sky it was; how in crossing Belgrave Square Chico, whom *she* had brought from Craigenputtock in her lap, burst out into singing, which we all (Bessy Barnet, our romantic maid, sate with us in the old hackney coach) strove to accept as a promising omen. The business of sorting and settling with two or three good carpenters, already on the ground, was at once gone into with boundless alacrity,[1] and under such management as hers went on at a mighty rate; even the three or four days of *quasi* camp life, or gipsy life, had a kind of gay charm to us; and hour by hour we saw the confusion abating—growing into victorious order. Leigh Hunt was continually sending us notes; most probably would in person step across before bedtime, and give us an hour of the prettiest melodious discourse. In about a week, it seems to me, all was swept and garnished, fairly habitable, and continued incessantly to get itself polished, civilised, and beautiful to a degree that surprised me. I have elsewhere alluded to all that, and to my little Jeannie's conduct of it. Heroic, lovely, mournfully beautiful as in the light of eternity that little scene of time now looks to me. From birth upwards she had lived in opulence, and now for my sake had become poor—so nobly poor. No such house for beautiful thrift, quiet, spontaneous—nay, as it were, unconscious minimum of money reconciled to human comfort and dignity, have I anywhere looked upon where I have been.

[1] Carlyle's memory was perfectly accurate in what it retained. His account to his brother at the time gives fuller detail to the picture: 'A hackney coach, loaded to the roof and beyond it with luggage and the passengers, tumbled us all down here at eleven in the morning. By all I mean my dame and myself, Bessy Barnet, who had come the night before, and little Chico, the canary bird, who *multum jactatus* did nevertheless arrive living and well from Puttock, and even sang violently all the way, by sea and land, nay, struck up his lilt in the very London streets whenever he could see green leaves and feel the free air. There we sate on three trunks. I, however, with a match-box soon lit a cigar, as Bessy did a fire; and thus with a kind of cheerful solemnity we took possession by "raising reek," and even dined in an extempore fashion on a box lid covered with some accidental towel.' (To John Carlyle, June 17, 1834.)

The auspices under which the new life began, not from Chico's song only, were altogether favourable. The weather was fine; the cherries were ripening on a tree in the garden. Carlyle got his garden tools to work and repaired the borders, and set in slips of jessamine and gooseberry bushes brought from Scotland. To his mother, who was curious about the minutest details, he reported—

We lie safe at a bend of the river, away from all the great roads, have air and quiet hardly inferior to Craigenputtock, an outlook from the back windows into mere leafy regions with here and there a red high-peaked old roof looking through; and see nothing of London, except by day the summits of St. Paul's Cathedral and Westminster Abbey, and by night the gleam of the great Babylon affronting the peaceful skies. The house itself is probably the best we have ever lived in—a right old, strong, roomy brick house, built near 150 years ago, and likely to see three races of these modern fashionables fall before it comes down.

The French Revolution had been finally decided on as the subject for the next book, and was to be set about immediately; Fraser having offered, not indeed to give money for it, but to do what neither he nor any other publisher would venture for 'Sartor'—take the risk of printing it. Mill furnished volumes on the subject in 'barrowfuls.' Leigh Hunt was a pleasant immediate neighbour, and an increasing circle of Radical notabilities began to court Carlyle's society. There was money enough to last for a year at least. In a year he hoped that his book might be finished; that he might then give lectures; that either then or before some editorship might fall to him—the editorship, perhaps (for it is evident that he hoped for it), of Mill's and Molesworth's new Radical Review. Thus at the outset he was—for him—tolerably cheerful. On the 27th of June he sent a full account of things to Scotsbrig.

To Alexander Carlyle.

5 Cheyne Row, Chelsea : June 27, 1834.

The process of installation is all but terminated, and we in rather good health and spirits, and all doing well, are beginning to feel ourselves at home in our new *hadding*. We have nothing to complain of, much to be piously grateful for ; and thus, with a kind of serious cheerfulness, may gird ourselves up for a new career. As it was entered on without dishonest purposes, the issue, unless *we* change for the worse, is not to be *dreaded*, prove as it may.

One of the greatest moments of my life, I think, was when I waved my hat to you and Jamie from on board the steamboat. My two brothers, the last of my kindred I had to leave, stood *there*, and I stood *here*, already flying fast from them. I would not desecrate so solemn an hour by childish weakness. I turned my thoughts heavenward, for it is in heaven only that I find *any* basis for our poor pilgrimage on this earth. Courage, my brave brothers all ! Let us be found faithful and we shall not fail. Surely as the blue dome of heaven encircles us all, so does the providence of the Lord of Heaven. He will withhold no good thing from those that love Him ! This, as it was the ancient Psalmist's faith, let it likewise be ours. It is the Alpha and Omega, I reckon, of all possessions that can belong to man.

Neither my mother nor you will interpret these reflections of mine as if they betokened gloom of temper—but indeed rather the reverse. I hope we have left great quantities of gloom safe behind us at Puttock, and indeed hitherto have given little harbour to such a guest here. It is strange often to myself, with what a kind of not only fearlessness, but meek contempt and indifference, I can walk through the grinding press of these restless millions, ' listening,' as Teufelsdröckh says, ' to its loudest threatenings with a still smile.' I mean to work according to my strength. As to riches, fame, success, and so forth, I ask no questions. Were the work laid out for us but the kneading of a clay brick, let us, in God's name, *do it faithfully*, and look for our reward elsewhere. So, on the whole, to end moralising, let us sing—

Come, fingers five, come now be live,
And stout heart fail me not, not—

or, what is far before singing, let us do it, and go on doing it.

In respect of society we have what perfectly suffices—having indeed here the best chance. Mill comes sometimes; the Bullers were all here, paying us their first visit, Mrs. Austin, &c. There is really enough, and might easily be to spare. Things go in the strangest course in that respect here. A man becomes for some reason, or for no reason, in some way or other notable. Straightway his door from dawn to dusk is beset with idlers and loungers, and empty persons on foot and in carriages, who come to gather of his supposed fulness one five minutes of tolerable sensation; and so the poor man (most frequently it is a poor woman) sits in studied attitude all day, 'doing what he can do,' which is, alas! all too little; for gradually or suddenly the carriage and foot empty persons start some other scent and crowd elsewhither; and so the poor notable man, now fallen into midnight obscurity, sits in his studied attitude within forsaken walls, either to rise and set about some work (which were the best), or mournfully chant *Ichabod!* according to his convenience.

On the whole, as I often say, what is society? What is the help of *others* in any shape? None but *thyself* can effectually help thee, can effectually hinder thee! A man must have lived to little purpose six years in the wilderness of Puttock if he have not made this clear to himself.

Hunt and the Hunts, as you have heard, live only in the next street from us. Hunt is always ready to go and walk with me, or sit and talk with me to all lengths if I want him. He comes in once a week (when invited, for he is very modest), takes a cup of tea, and sits discoursing in his brisk, fanciful way till supper time, and then cheerfully eats a cup of porridge (to sugar only), which he praises to the skies, and vows he will make his supper of at home. He is a man of thoroughly London make, such as you could not find elsewhere, and I think about the *best* possible to be made of his sort: an airy, crotchety, most copious clever talker, with an honest undercurrent of reason too, but unfortunately not the deepest, not the most practical—or rather it is the most *un*practical ever man dealt in. His hair is grizzled, eyes black-hazel, complexion of the clearest dusky brown; a thin glimmer of a smile plays over a face of cast-iron gravity. He never laughs—can only titter, which I think indicates his worst deficiency. His house excels all you have ever read of—a *poetical Tinkerdom*, without parallel even in literature. In his family room, where are a sickly large wife and a whole shoal of well-conditioned wild children, you will find half a dozen old rickety chairs gathered from half a dozen different hucksters, and all seemingly engaged, and just pausing, in a violent *hornpipe*. On these and around them and over the dusty table and ragged carpet lie all kinds of litter—books, papers, egg-shells, scissors, and last night when I was there the torn heart of a half-quartern loaf. His own room above stairs, into which alone I strive to enter, he keeps cleaner. It has only two chairs, a bookcase, and a writing-table; yet the noble Hunt receives you in his Tinkerdom in the spirit of a king, apologises for nothing, places you in the best seat, takes a window-sill himself if there is no other, and there folding closer his loose-flowing 'muslin cloud' of a printed nightgown in which he always writes, commences the liveliest dialogue on philosophy and the prospects of man (who is to be beyond measure 'happy' yet); which again he will courteously terminate the moment you are bound to go: a most interesting, pitiable, lovable man, to be used kindly but with discretion. After all, it is perhaps rather a comfort to be near honest, friendly people—at least, an honest, friendly man of that sort. We stand sharp but mannerly for his sake and for ours, and endeavour to get and do what good we can, and avoid the evil.

To John Carlyle, Naples.

5 Cheyne Row : July 22, 1834.

We are getting along here as we can without cause of complaint. Our house and whole household, inanimate and rational, continue to yield all contentment. Bessy is a clever, clear-minded girl; lives quietly not only as a servant, but can cheer her mistress as a companion and friend. Most favourable change. Jane keeps in decidedly better health and spirits. Within doors I have all manner of scope. Out of doors, unhappily, the prospect is vague enough, yet I myself am not without fixed aim. The bookselling world, I seem to see, is all but a hopeless one for me. Periodical editors will employ me, as they have employed me, on this principle : for the sake of my name, and to help them to season a new enterprise. That once accomplished, they want little more to do with me. Amateurs enough exist that will dirty paper gratis, and puffery, and so forth, is expected to do the rest. Thus they kept a *gusting bone* in the four towns, and lent it out to give a flavour to weak soup ; otherwise hung it in the nook. I am much dissatisfied with the arrangement and little minded to continue it. Meanwhile, by Heaven's blessing, I find I can get a book printed with my name on it. I have fixed on my book, and am labouring (*ohne Hast, ohne Rast*) as yet afar off to get it ready. Did I not tell you the subject? The French Revolution. I mean to make an artistic picture of it. Alas! the subject is high and huge. *Ich zittre nur, ich stottre nur, und kann es doch nicht lassen.* Mill has lent me above a hundred books; I read continually, and the matter is dimly shaping itself in me. Much is in the Museum for me, too, in the shape of books and pamphlets. I was there a week ago seeking pictures; found none; but got a sight of Albert Dürer, and (I find) some shadow of his old—*teutschen,* deep, still soul, which was well worth the getting. This being my task till the end of the year, why should I curiously inquire what is to become of me next? 'There is aye life for a living body,' as my mother's proverb has it; also, as she reminded me 'if thou tine heart, thou tines a'.' I will do my best and calmest; then wait and ask. As yet, I find myself much cut off from practical companions and instructors; my visitors and collocutors are all of the theoretic sort, and worth comparatively little to me, but I shall gradually approach the other sort, and try to profit by them. With able editors I figure my course as terminated. Fraser cannot afford to pay me, besides seems more and more bent on Toryism and Irish reporterism, to me infinitely detestable.

With regard to neighbourhood I might say we were very quiet, even solitary, yet not oppressively so. Of visitors that merely *call* here we have absolutely none; our day is our own, and those that do come are worth something to us. Our most interesting new friend is a Mrs. Taylor, who came here for the first time yesterday, and stayed long. She is a living romance heroine, of the clearest insight, of the royalest volition, very interesting, of questionable destiny, not above twenty-five. Jane is to go and pass a day with her soon, being greatly taken with her. Allan Cunningham with his wife and daughter made us out last night. We are to dine there some day. Hunt is always at hand; but, as the modestest of men, never comes unless sent for. His theory of life and mine have already declared themselves to be from top to bottom at *variance,* which shocks him considerably; to me his talk is occasionally pleasant, is always clear and lively, but all too *foisonless,* baseless, and shallow. He has a theory that the world is, or should, and shall be, a gingerbread Lubberland, where evil (that is, pain) shall never come: a theory in very considerable favour here, which to me is pleasant as streams of unambrosial dishwater, a thing I simply *shut my mouth* against, as the shortest way. Irving I have not succeeded in seeing again, though I went up to Bayswater once and left my name. I rather think his wife will incline to secrete him from me, and may even have been capable of suppressing my card. I will try again, for his sake and my own. Mill is on the whole our best figure, yet all too narrow in shape, though of wide susceptibilities and very fond of us. He hunts me out old books, does *all* he can for me ; he is busy about the new Radical Review, and doubtless will need me there, at least as 'gusting bone.' Ought he to get me ? Not altogether for the asking perhaps, for I am wearied of that. *Voyons.* Thus, dear brother, have you a most full and artless picture of our existence here. You do not despair of us ; your sympathies are blended with hopes for us. You will make out of all this food enough for musing. Muse plentifully about us : to me, also, you continue precious. With you I am *double* strong. God be with you, dear Jack ! Jane stipulated for a paragraph, so I stop here.

P.S. by Mrs. Carlyle :—

Again only a postscript, my dear John, but I will write one time or other. I *will :* as yet I am too unsettled. In trying to write or read, above all things, I feel I am in a new position. When I look round on my floors once more laid with carpets, my chairs all in a row, &c., I flatter myself the tumult is subsided. But when I look within ! alas, I find my wits by no means in a row, but still engaged at an uproarious game of 'Change seats, the king's coming.' I read dozens of pages, and find at the end that I have not the slightest knowledge what they were about. I take out a notebook day after day and write the day of the week and month, and so return it. Pity the poor white woman. She will find herself by-and-by and communicate the news to you among the first : for I am sure you care for her, and would rejoice in her attainment of a calm, well-ordered being for her own sake. At all rates we are well out of Puttock everywhere.

These first letters from London would seem to indicate that Carlyle was tolerably 'hefted' to his new home and condition ; but the desponding mood was never long absent. Happy those to whom nature has given good animal spirits. There is no fairy gift equal to this for helping a man to fight his way, and animal spirits Carlyle never had. He had the keenest sense of the ridiculous ; but humour and sadness are inseparable properties of the same nature ; his constitutional unhopefulness soon returned upon him, and was taking deeper hold than he cared to let others see. The good effects of this change wore off in a few weeks : the old enemy was in possession again, and the entries in his diary were more desponding than even at Craigenputtock.

Saturday night (sunset), July 26, 1834.—Have written nothing here for above a month ; my state has been one of those it was almost frightful to *speak* of : an undetermined, unspeakable state. Little better yet ; but the book being open I will put down a word.

Nothing can exceed the *gravity* of my situation here. ' Do or die' seems the word ; and alas ! what to do ? I have no practical friend, no confidant, properly no companion. For five days together I sit without so much as speaking to anyone except my wife. Mood tragical, gloomy, as of one forsaken, who had nothing left him *but to get through his task and die.* No periodical editor wants me : no man will give me money for my work. Bad health, too (at least, singularly changed health), brings all manner of dispiritment. Despicablest fears of coming to absolute beggary, &c. &c. besiege me. On brighter days I cast these off into the dim distance, and see a world fearful, indeed, but grand : a task to do in it which no poverty or beggary shall hinder.

Can friends do much for one ? Conversing here I find that I get almost nothing ; the utmost, and that rarely, is honest, clear reception of what I give. Surely I go wrong to work. I question everybody too, but none, or almost none, can answer me on *any* subject. Hunt is limited, even bigoted, and seeing that I utterly dissent from him fears that I despise him ; a kindly clever man, fantastic, brilliant, shallow, of one topic, loquacious, unproductive. Mrs. A. (alas !) a 'Niagara of gossip ;' in certain of my humours fearful ! Mill is the best ; unhappily he is *speculative* merely ; can open out for me no practical road, nor even direct me where I may search after such. The Unitarian-philosophic fraternity (likely to open through Mrs. Taylor) also bodes little. Alone ! alone ! 'May we say' (my good father used to pray), 'may we say we are not alone, for the Lord is with us.' True ! true !

Keep thy heart resolute and still; look prudently out, take diligent advantage of what time and chance *will* offer (to thee as to all); toil along and fear nothing. Oh thou of little faith! Weak of faith indeed! God help me!

For about a month past, finding that no editor had need of me, that it would be imprudent to *ask* him to have need of me, and moreover that booksellers now would *print* books for nothing, I have again been *resolute* about the writing of a book, and even working in the direction of one. Subject, 'The French Revolution.' Whole boxes of books about me. Gloomy, huge, of almost boundless meaning; but obscure, dubious—all too deep for me; will and must *do my best.* Alas! gleams, too, of a work of art hover past me; as if this should be a *work of art.* Poor me!

In the midst of innumerable discouragements, all men indifferent or finding fault, let me mention two small circumstances that are comfortable. The first is a letter from some nameless Irishman in Cork to another here (Fraser read it to me without names), actually containing a *true* and one of the friendliest possible recognitions of me. One mortal then says I am *not* utterly wrong. Blessings on him for it. The second is a letter I got to-day from Emerson, of Boston in America; sincere, not baseless, of most exaggerated estimation. Precious is man to man.

It was long ago written, 'Woe to them that are at *ease* in Zion.' Such woe at least is not thine!

Tout va bien ici, le pain manque.

August 12.—Good news out of Annandale that they are all well; the like from Jack. I still lonely, how lonely! Health and with it spirits fluctuating, feeble, usually bad. At times nothing can exceed my gloom. Foolish weakling! However, so it is; light alternates with darkness; sorrow itself must be followed by cessation of sorrow: which is joy. As yet no prospect whatever. Mill, I discern, has given Fox the editorship of that new Molesworth periodical; seems rather ashamed of it—*à la bonne heure;* is it not probably better so? Trust in God and in thyself! Oh, could I but! all else were so light, so trivial! Enough now.

August 13.—Weary, dispirited, sick, forsaken, every way heavy laden! cannot tell what is to become of that 'French Revolution;' vague, boundless, without form and void—*Gott hilf mir!*

The idea of not very distant death often presents itself to me, without satisfaction, yet without much terror, much aversion—*ein verfehltes Leben?* Poor coward! At lowest I say nothing; what I suffer is, as much as may be, locked up within myself. A long lane that has *no* turning? Despair *not.*

How to keep living was the problem. The 'French Revolution,' Carlyle thought at this time, must be a mere sketch; finished and sold by the following spring if he was to escape entire bankruptcy. He had hoped more than he knew for the editorship of the new Review. It had been given to Fox, 'as the safer man.'

I can already picture to myself the Radical periodical (he wrote to his brother John), and can even prophesy its destiny. With myself it had not been so; (but) the only thing certain would have been difficulty, pain, and contradiction, which I should probably have undertaken; which I am far from breaking my heart that I have missed. Mill likes me well, and on his embarrassed face, when Fox happened to be talked of, I read both that editorship business, and also that Mill had *known* my want of it, which latter was all I desired to read. As you well say, disappointment on disappointment only simplifies one's course; your possibilities become diminished; your choice is rendered easier. In general I abate no jot of confidence in myself and in my cause. Nay, it often seems to me as if the extremity of suffering, if such were appointed me, might bring out an extremity of energy as yet unknown to myself, God grant me faith, clearness, and peaceableness of heart. I make no other prayer.

No doubt it was hard to bear. By Mill, if by no one else, Carlyle thought that he was recognised and appreciated; and Mill had preferred Fox to him. The Review fared as Carlyle expected: lived its short day as long as Molesworth's money held out, and then withered. Perhaps, as he said, 'With him it had not been so.' Yet no one who knows how such things are managed could blame Mill. To the bookselling world Carlyle's name, since the appearance of 'Sartor Resartus' in 'Fraser,' had become an abomination, and so far was Mill from really altering his own estimate of Carlyle that he offered to publish the

'Diamond Necklace' as a book at his own expense, 'that he might have the pleasure of reviewing it!' Carlyle at bottom understood that it could not have been otherwise, and that essentially it was better for him as it was. Through his own thrift and his wife's skill, the extremity of poverty never really came, and his time and faculties were left unencumbered for his own work. Even of Fox himself, whom he met at a dinner-party, he could speak kindly; not unappreciatively. The cloud lifted now and then, oftener probably than his diary would lead one to suppose. Carlyle's sense of the ridiculous—stronger than that of any contemporary man—was the complement to his dejection. In his better moments he could see and enjoy the brighter side of his position. On the 15th of August, two days after he had been meditating on his *verfehltes Leben*, he could write to his brother in a happier tone.

To John Carlyle, Naples.

5 Cheyne Row : August 15.

All of us have tolerable health, Jane generally better than before; I certainly not worse, and now more in the ancient accustomed fashion. I am diligent with the shower-bath; my pilgrimages to the Museum and on other town errands keep me in walking enough; once or twice weekly on an evening Jane and I stroll out along the bank of the river or about the College, and see white-shirted Cockneys in their green canoes, or old pensioners pensively smoking tobacco. The London street tumult has become a kind of marching music to me; I walk along following my own meditations without thinking of it. Company comes in desirable quantity, not deficient, not excessive, and there is talk enough from time to time. I myself, however, when I consider it, find the whole all too *thin*, unnutritive, unavailing. All London-born men, without exception, seem to me narrow built, considerably perverted men, rather fractions of a man. Hunt, by nature a *very* clever man, is one instance; Mill, in quite another manner, is another. These and others continue to come about me as with the cheering sound of temporary *music*, and are right welcome so. A higher co-operation will perhaps somewhere else or some time hence disclose itself.

> There was a piper had a cow,
>   And he had nought to give her ;
> He took his pipes and played a spring,
>   And bade the cow consider.

Allan Cunningham was here two nights ago : very friendly, full of Nithsdale, a pleasant *Naturmensch.* Mill gives me logical developments of *how* men act (chiefly in politics) ; Hunt, tricksy devices and crotchety whimsicalities on the same theme. *What* they act is a thing neither of them much sympathises in, much seems to know. I sometimes long greatly for Irving—for the old Irving of fifteen years ago ; nay, the poor actual gift-of-tongues Irving has seemed desirable to me. We dined with Mrs. (Platonica) Taylor and the Unitarian Fox one day. Mill was also of the party, and the husband—an obtuse, most joyous-natured man, the pink of social hospitality. Fox is a little thickset, bushy-locked man of five and forty, with bright, sympathetic, thoughtful eyes, with a tendency to pot-belly and *snuffiness.* From these hints you can construe him ; the best *Socinian philosophist* going, but not a whit more. I shall like well enough to meet the man again, but I doubt he will not me. Mrs. Taylor herself did not yield unmixed satisfaction, I think, or receive it. She affects, with a kind of sultana noble-mindedness, a certain girlish petulance, and felt that it did not wholly prosper. We walked home, however, even Jane did, all the way from the Regent's Park, and felt that we had done a duty. For me, from the Socinians as I take it, *wird nichts.*

The 'French Revolution' perplexes me much. More books on it, I find, are but a repetition of those before read ; I learn nothing, or almost nothing, further by books, yet am I as far as possible from understanding it. *Bedenklichkeiten* of all kinds environ me. To be *true* or not to be true : there is the risk. And then to be *popular,* or not to be popular ? That, too, is a question that plays most completely with the other. We shall see ; we shall try. *Par ma tête seule !*

My good Jack has now a clear view of me. We may say, in the words of the Sansculotte Deputy writing to the Convention of the Progress of Right Principles, *Tout va bien ici, le pain manque !* Jane and I often repeat this with laughter. But in truth we live very cheap here (perhaps not much above 50*l.* a-year dearer than at Puttock), and so can hold out a long while independent of chance. Utter poverty itself (if I hold fast by the faith) has no terrors for me, should it ever come.

I told you I had seen Irving. It was but yesterday in Newman Street, after four prior ineffectual attempts. William Hamilton, who was here on Saturday, told me Irving was grown worse again, and Mrs. Irving had been extremely ill; he, too, seemed to think my cards had been withheld. Much grieved at this news, I called once more on Monday: a new failure. Yesterday I went again, with an insuppressible indignation mixed with my pity; after some shying I was admitted. Poor Irving! he lay there on a sofa, begged my pardon for not rising; his wife, who also did not, and, probably, could not well rise, sate at his feet all the time I was there, miserable and haggard. Irving once lovingly ordered her away; but she lovingly excused herself, and sate still. He complains of biliousness, of pain at his right short rib; has a short, thick cough, which comes on at the smallest irritation. Poor fellow, I brought a short gleam of old Scottish laughter into his face, into his voice; and that, too, set him coughing. He said it was the Lord's will; looked weak, dispirited, partly embarrassed. He continues toiling daily, though the doctor says rest only can cure him. Is it not mournful, hyper-tragical? There are moments when I determine on sweeping in upon all tongue work and accursed choking cobwebberies, and snatching away my old best friend, to save him from death and the grave.

So passed on the first summer of Carlyle's life in London. 'The weather,' he says, 'defying it in hard, almost brimless *hat*, which was *obligato* in that time of slavery, did sometimes throw me into colic.' In the British Museum lay concealed somewhere 'a collection of French pamphlets' on the Revolution, the completest in the world, which, after six weeks' wrestle with officiality, he was obliged to find 'inaccessible' to him. Idle obstruction will put the most enduring of men now and then out of patience, and Carlyle was not enduring in such matters; but his wife was able on the first of September to send to Scotsbrig a very tolerable picture of his condition.

To Mrs. Carlyle, Scotsbrig.

Chelsea : September 1, 1834.

My dear Mother,—Could I have supposed it possible that any mortal was so stupid as not to feel disappointed in receiving a letter from *me* instead of my husband, I should have written to you very long ago. But while this humility becomes me, it is also my duty (too long neglected) to send a little adjunct to my husband's letters, just to assure you ' with my own hand' that I continue to love you amidst the hubbub of this ' noble city ' [1] just the same as in the quiet of Craigenputtock, and to cherish a grateful recollection of your many kindnesses to me ; especially of that magnanimous purpose to 'sit at my bedside' through the night preceding my departure, 'that I might be sure to sleep.' I certainly shall never forget that night, and the several preceding and following : but for the kindness and helpfulness shown me on all hands I must have traiked,[2] one would suppose. I had every reason to be thankful then to Providence and my friends, and I have had the same reason since.

All things since we came here have gone more smoothly with us than I at all anticipated. Our little household has been set up again at a quite moderate expense of money and trouble ; wherein, I cannot help thinking, with a *chastened vanity*, that the superior shiftiness and thriftiness of the Scotch character has strikingly manifested itself. The English women turn up the whites of their eyes and call on the 'good heavens' at the bare idea of enterprises which seem to me in the most ordinary course of human affairs. I told Mrs. Hunt one day I had been very busy *painting*. 'What ?' she asked ; 'is it a portrait ?' Oh no, I told her, something of more importance : a large wardrobe. She could not imagine ; she said, 'how I could have patience for such things.' And so, having no patience for them herself, what is the result ? She is every other day reduced to borrow my tumblers, my teacups ; even a cupful of porridge, a few spoonfuls of tea are begged of me, because 'Missus has got company, and happens to be out of the article ;' in plain, unadorned English, because 'missus' is the most wretched of managers, and is often at the point of not having a copper in her purse. To see how they live and waste

---

[1] Phrase of Basil Montagu's.—T. C.'
[2] ' "Traiked" means perished. Contemptuous term, applied to cattle, &c. Traik = German *dreck*.—T. C.'

here, it is a wonder the whole city does not 'bankrape [1] and go out of sicht;' flinging platefuls of what they are pleased to de-nominate 'crusts' (that is, what I consider the best of the bread) into the ashpits. I often say with honest self-congratulation, 'In Scotland we have no such thing as crusts.' On the whole, though the English ladies seem to have their wits more at their finger-ends, and have a great advantage over me in that respect, I never cease to be glad that I was born on the other side of the Tweed, and that those who are nearest and dearest to me are Scotch.

I must tell you what Carlyle will not tell of himself, that he is rapidly mending of his Craigenputtock gloom and acerbity. He is really at times a tolerably social character, and seems to be regarded with a feeling of mingled terror and love in all com-panies, which I should think the diffusion of Teufelsdröckh will tend to increase.

I have just been called away to John Macqueen, who was fol-lowed by a Jock Thomson, of Annan, whom I received in my choicest mood to make amends for Carlyle's unreadiness,[2] who was positively going to let him leave the door without asking him in, a neglect which he would have reproached himself for after.

My love to all. Tell my kind Mary to write to me; she is the only one that ever does.

Your affectionate,
JANE W. CARLYLE.

Carlyle's letter under the same cover (franked by Sir John Romilly) communicates that the writing of the 'French Revolution' was actually begun.

Of Chelsea news we have as good as none to send you, which, indeed, means intrinsically good enough news. We go on in the old fashion, adhering pretty steadily to our *work*, and looking for

---

[1] 'To "bankrape" is to "bankrupt" (used as a *verb* passive). "And then he bankrapit and gaed out of sicht." A phrase of my father's in the little sketches of Annandale biography he would sometimes give me.—T. C.'

[2] 'Macqueen and Thomson were two big graziers of respectability—Mac-queen a *native* of Craigenputtock. Thomson, from near Annan, had been a schoolfellow of mine. They had called here without very specific errand; and I confess what the letter intimates (of my silent wish to have evaded such interruption, &c.) is the exact truth.—T. C.'

our main happiness in that. This is the dull season in London, and several of our friends are fled to the country. However, we have still a fair allowance of company left us; and what is best, the company we have is none of it *bad*, or merely 'a consuming of time,' but rational and leads to something. The best news I have is that this day (September 1) I mean to begin *writing* my book; nay, had it not been for the present sheet, would already have been at it! Wish me good speed; I have meditated the business as I could, and must surely strive to do my best. With a kind of trembling hope I calculate that the enterprise may prosper with me; that the book may be at least a true one, and tend to do God's service, not the Devil's. It will keep me greatly on the stretch these winter months, but I hope to have it printed and out early in spring; what is to be done next, we shall then see. The world must be a tougher article than I have ever found it, if it altogether beats me. I have defied it, and set my trust *elsewhere*, and so it can do whatsoever is permitted and appointed it. As to our other doings and outlooks, I have written of them all at great length to Alick the other day, so that as you are likely to see his letter I need not dwell on them. I have seen Mill and various other agreeable persons since (for our company comes often in rushes), but met with no further adventure.

The close of the letter refers to economics, and to the generous contributions furnished by Scotsbrig to the Cheyne Row establishment.

The sheet is fading very fast; Jane's little note too is ready, and I have still some *business* to do. We spoke long ago about a freight of eatable goods we wanted out of Annandale at the fall of the year. As you are the punctuallest of all, I will now specify the whole to you, that you may bestir yourself, and stir up others in the proper quarter to be getting them ready. Here is the list of our wants, as I have extracted it by questions out of Jane. First, sixty pounds of butter in two equal *pigs* (the butter here is 16*d.* a pound!); secondly, a moderately-sized sweet-milk cheese; next, two smallish bacon-hams (your beef-ham was just broken into last week, and is in the best condition); next, about fifteen stone of right oatmeal (or even more, for we are to give Hunt some stones of it, and need almost a pound daily: there is not now above a stone left); and after that, as many hundredweights of potatoes as you think will keep (for the rule of it is this: we take two pounds daily, and they sell here at three halfpence, or at lowest a penny, a pound, and are seldom good): all this got ready and packed into a hogshead or two will reach us by Whitehaven, and we will see how it answers.

John Carlyle meanwhile was prospering with Lady Clare, and was in a position to return to his brother the generosity of earlier days. It was perfectly true, as Carlyle had said, that what any one of the family possessed the others were free to share with him. In September John sent home 130*l.* for his mother.[1]

To John Carlyle, Rome.

Chelsea: September 21, 1834.

Your kind letter, my dear Jack, was read over with a feeling such as it merited: it went nearer my heart than anything addressed to me for long. I am not sure that there were not *tears* in the business, but they were not sad ones. Your offers and purposes are worthy of a brother, and I were but unworthy if I met them in any mean spirit. I believe there is no other man living from whom such offers as yours were other to me than a pleasant sound which I *must disregard;* but it is not so with these; for I actually can (without damage to any good feeling in me), and will, if need be, make good use of them. We will, as you say, stand by one another; and so each of us, were all other men arranged against us, have one friend. Well that it is so. *Wohl ihm dem die Geburt den Bruder gab.* I will not speak any more about this, but keep it laid up in my mind as a thing to act by. I feel, as I once said, *double-*strong in the possession of my poor *Doil,*[2] and so I suppose we shall quarrel many times yet, and instantly agree

---

[1] Carlyle carried it to the City to be forwarded to the bank at Dumfries, and he enlarged his experiences of London on the way. 'In my perambulations,' he said, 'I came upon a strange anarchy of a place—the Stock Exchange. About a hundred men were jumping and jigging about in a dingy, contracted apartment, and yelping out all manner of sounds, which seemed to be auctioneer's offers, not without much laughter and other miscellaneous tumult. I thought of the words " trades' contentious hell"; but had no room for reflections. A rednecked official coming up with the assurance that this place was " private, sir," I departed with a " thousand pardons " and satisfaction that I *had* seen the Domdaniel. These were my discoveries in the city.'

[2] Family nickname for John Carlyle.

again, and argue and sympathise, and on the whole stand by one another through good and evil, and turn *two* fronts to the world while we are both spared in it. *Amen!* There are many wallowing in riches, splendent in dignities, who have no such possession as this. Let us be thankful for it, and approve ourselves worthy of it.

I have not yet earned sixpence since I came hither, and see not that I am advancing towards such a thing: however, I do not 'tine heart.' Indeed, that money consideration gives me wonderfully little sorrow; we can hold out a *long time* yet. It is very true also what you say, that soliciting among the bibliopoles were the *worst* policy. Indeed I have no deeper wish than that bread for me of the brownest sort were providable elsewhere than with them. We shall not cease to try. One comfortable thing is the constant conviction I have that here or nowhere is the place for me. I must swim or sink *here*. Withal, too, I feel the influences of the place on me *rebuking* much in my late ways of writing and speech: within my own heart I am led to overhaul many things, and alter or mourn for them. I might say generally that I am leading a rather painful but not unprofitable life. *At spes infracta!* I look up to the everlasting sky, and with the azure infinitude all around me cannot think that I was made in vain. These things, however, I do not well to speak of yet, or perhaps at all. The best news is that I have actually *begun* that 'French Revolution,' and after two weeks of blotching and bloring have produced—two clean pages! *Ach Gott!* But my hand is out; and I am altering my style too, and troubled about many things. Bilious, too, in these smothering, windless days. It shall be *such* a book: quite an epic poem of the Revolution: an apotheosis of Sansculottism! Seriously, when in good spirits I feel as if there were the matter of a very considerable work within me; but the task of shaping and uttering will be frightful. Here, as in so many other respects, I am alone, without models, without *limits* (this is a great want), and must—just do the best I can.

The expected provision barrels from Scotsbrig were long in arriving, and Carlyle had to quicken the family movements in the end of October by a representation of the state of things to which he and his wife were reduced. 'It will seem absurd enough to tell you,' he wrote to his mother, 'that we are in haste now after waiting so long; but the truth is, our meal has been done for a fortnight, and we have the strangest shifts for a supper. Amongst others, flour porridge, exactly shoemaker's paste, only clean; and at last have been obliged to take to some of the Scotch oatmeal sold in the shops here—very dear—fivepence a quart by measure—which though rough, is quite sound, which therefore we can thankfully use; so you need not suppose us starving. The butter too is almost always excellent (churned I believe out of milk), at the easy rate of sixteenpence a pound! In regard to provision I shall only add that the beef-ham daily plays its part at breakfast, and proves thoroughly *genuine.* The butcher came here one day to saw the bone of it, and asked with amazement whether it was pork or not. He had never heard of any ham but a bacon one, and departed from us with a new idea. N.B.—We get coffee to breakfast (at eight or nearly so), have very often mutton-chops to dinner at three, then tea at six; we have four pennyworth of cream, two pennyworth of milk daily. This is our diet, which I know you *would* rather know than not know.'

For the rest, life went on without much variety. 'Bessy Barnet' left Cheyne Row after two months, being obliged to return to her mother, and they had to find another servant among the London maids of all work. Carlyle crushed down his dispiritment; found at any rate that 'nothing like the *deep sulkiness* of Craigenputtock' troubled him in London. He felt that 'he was in the right workshop if he could but get acquainted with the tools.' 'Teufelsdröckh,' circulating in a stitched-up form, made out of the sheets of 'Fraser,' was being read, a few persons really admiring it; the generality turning up their eyes in speechless amazement. Irving had departed, having gone to Scotland, where he was reported as lying ill at Glasgow, and, to Carlyle's very deep distress, likely to die.

Among minor adventures, Carlyle was present at the burning of the Houses of Parliament. 'The crowd,' he says, 'was quiet, rather pleased than otherwise; whewed and whistled when the breeze came, as if to encourage it. "There's a flare-up for the House of Lords!" "A judgment for the Poor Law Bill!" "There go their *Hacts!*" Such exclamations seemed to be the prevailing ones: a man *sorry* I did not see anywhere.'

Horny-handed Radicalism gave Carlyle a grim satisfaction. He considered modern society so corrupt that he expected, or rather desired, an immediate end to it. But Radicalism, too, had its unfavourable aspects, especially when it showed itself in the direction of female emancipation.

Mill and one or two of his set (he said) are on the whole the reasonablest people we have. However, we see them seldom, being so far off, and Mill himself, who would be far the best of them all, is greatly occupied of late times with a set of quite opposite character, which the Austins and other friends mourn much and fear much over; Fox the Socinian, and a flight of really wretched-looking 'friends of the species,' who (in writing and deed) struggle not in favour of duty being *done*, but against duty of any sort being *required*. A singular creed this; but I can assure you a very observable one here in these days: by me deeply hated as the GLARE which is its colour (*die seine Farbe ist*) and substance likewise mainly. Jane and I often say, 'Before all mortals beware of friends of the species'! Most of these people are very indignant at marriage and the like, and frequently, indeed, are obliged to divorce their own wives, or be divorced; for though this world is already blooming (or is one day to do it) in everlasting 'happiness of the greatest number,' these people's own *houses* (I always find) are little hells of improvidence, discord, and unreason. Mill is far above all that, and I think will not sink into it; however, I do wish him fairly far from it, and though I cannot speak of it directly, would fain help him out. He is one of the best people I ever saw.

The next letter is from Mrs. Carlyle, which Carlyle interprets.

'Mournfully beautiful,' he says, 'is this letter to me; a clear little household light shining pure and brilliant in the dark obstructive places of the past. The two East Lothian friends are George Rennie the sculptor, and his pretty sister, wife of an ex-Indian ship captain.'

'Eliza Miles and the Mileses are the good people in Ampton Street with whom we lodged. Eliza, their daughter, felt quite captivated with my Jane, and seems to have vowed eternal loyalty to her almost at first sight; was for coming to be our servant at Craigenputtock; actually wrote proposing it then—a most tempting offer to us, had not the rough element and the delicate aspirant been evidently irreconcilable! She continued to visit us here at moderate intervals, wrote me, after my calamity befell, the one letter of condolence I could completely read. She was a very pretty and to us interesting specimen of the London maiden of the middle classes; refined, polite, pious, clever both of hand and mind. No gentlewoman could have a more upright, modest, affectionate, and unconsciously high demeanour. Her father had long been in a prosperous upholsterer's business, but the firm had latterly gone away. He was a very good-natured, respectable man, quietly much sympathised with in his own house. Eliza, with her devout temper, had been drawn to Edward Irving, went daily alone of her family to his chapel in those years 1831-2, and was to the last one of his most reverent disciples. She did in her soft, loyal way right well in the world; married poorly enough, but wisely, and is still living a rich man's wife and the mother of prosperous sons and daughters.

' "Buller's Radical meeting" was a meeting privately got up by Charles Buller, but ostensibly managed by others, which assembled itself largely and with emphasis at the London Tavern, to say what it thought of the first re-appearance of Peel and Co. after the Reform Bill—"first Peel Ministry," which lasted only a short time. I duly attended the meeting (never another in my life), and remembered it well. Had some interest—not much. The two thousand human figures, wedged in the huge room into one dark mass, were singular to look down upon, singular to hear their united voice coming clearly as from one heart, their fiery " Yes," their sternly bellowing " No." I could notice too what new laws there were of speaking to such a mass : no matter how intensely consentaneous your two thousand were, and how much you *agreed* with every one of them, you must likewise begin where they began, follow pretty exactly their *sequence* of thoughts, or they lost sight of your intention, and for noise of contradiction to you and to one another you could not be heard at all. That was new to me, that second thing, and little or nothing else was. In the speeches I had no interest except a phenomenal ; indeed, had to disagree throughout more or less with every part of them. Roebuck knew the art best, kept the two thousand in constant reverberation, more and more rapturous, by his adroitly correct series of commonplaces. John Crawford, much more original, lost the series, and had to sit down again ignominiously unheard. I walked briskly home much musing. Found her waiting, eager enough for any news I had.—T. C.'

To Mrs. Carlyle, Scotsbrig.

Chelsea : November 21, 1834.

My dear Mother,—Now that franks are come back into the world, one need not wait for an inspired moment to write ; if one's letter is worth nothing it costs nothing ; nor will any letter that tells you of our welfare and assures you of our continual affection be worth nothing in your eyes, however destitute of news or anything else that might make it entertaining.

The weather is grown horridly cold, and I am chiefly intent, at present, on getting my winter wardrobe into order. I have made up the old black gown, which was dyed puce for me at Dumfries, *with my own hands*. It looks twenty per cent. better than when it was new ; and I shall get no other this winter. I am now turning my pelisse. I went yesterday to a milliner to buy a bonnet. An old, very ugly lady, upwards of seventy I am sure, was bargaining about a cloak at the same place; it was a fine affair of satin and violet; but she declared repeatedly that 'it had *no air*,' and for her part she could not put on such a thing. My bonnet, I flatter myself, *has* an *air*. A little brown feather nods over the front of it, and the crown points like a sugar-loaf! The diameter of the fashionable ladies at present is about three yards; their *bustles* are the size of an ordinary sheep's fleece. The very servant girls wear bustles. Eliza Miles told me a maid of theirs went out one Sunday with *three* kitchen dusters pinned on as a substitute.

The poor Mileses are in great affliction. Mr. Miles about the time we came to London got into an excellent situation, and they were just beginning to feel independent, and look forward to a comfortable future, when one morning, about a week ago, Mr. Miles, in walking through his warerooms, was noticed to stagger, and one of the men ran and caught him as he was falling. He was carried to a public-house close by, his own house being miles off, and his wife and daughter sent for. He never spoke to them, could never be removed, but there, in the midst of confusion and riot, they sate watching him for two days, when he expired. I went up to see them so soon as I heard of their misfortune. The wife was confined to bed with inflammation in her head. Poor Eliza was up and resigned-looking, but the picture of misery. A gentleman from Mr. Irving's church was with her, saying what he could.

Mrs. Montagu has quite given us up; but we still find it possible to carry on existence. I offended her by taking in Bessy Barnet, in the teeth of her vehement admonition, and now I suppose she is again offended that I should receive a discharged servant of her daughter-in-law's. I am sorry that she should be so whimsical, for as she was my first friend in London I continue to feel a sort of tenderness for her in spite of many faults which cleave to her. But her society can quite readily be dispensed with nevertheless; we have new acquaintances always turning up, and a pretty handsome stock of old ones.

A brother and sister, the most intimate friends I ever had in East Lothian, live quite near (for London), and I have other East Lothian acquaintances. Mrs. Hunt I shall soon be quite terminated with, I foresee. She torments my life out with borrowing. She actually borrowed one of the brass fenders the other day, and

I had difficulty in getting it out of her hands; irons, glasses, tea-cups, silver spoons are in constant requisition, and when one sends for them the whole number can never be found. Is it not a shame to manage so with eight guineas a week to keep house on? It makes me very indignant to see all the waste that goes on around me, when I am needing so much care and calculation to make ends meet; when we dine out, to see as much expended on a dessert of fruit (for no use but to give people a colic) as would keep us in necessaries for two or three weeks. My present maid has a grand-uncle in town with upwards of a hundred thousand pounds, who drives his carriage and all that; at a great dinner he had he gave five pounds for a couple of pine-apples when scarce; and here is his niece working all the year through for eight, and he has never given her a farthing since she came to London.

My mother gave a good account of your looks. I hope you will go and see her again for a longer time; she was so gratified by your visit. I have just had a letter from her, most satisfactory, telling me all she knows about any of you. She gives a wonderful account of some transcendentally beautiful shawl which Jean had made her a present of. I am sure never present gave more contentment.

Carlyle is going to a Radical meeting to-night; but there is no fear of his getting into mischief. Curiosity is his only motive; and I must away to the butcher to get his dinner. I wish you may be able to read what I have written. I write with a steel pen, which is a very unpliable concern, and has almost cut into my finger. God bless you all. A kiss to Mary's new baby when you see it.

Yours affectionately,

JANE CARLYLE.

'Above a month before this date,' Carlyle adds, 'Edward Irving rode to the door one evening, came in and stayed with us some twenty minutes—the one call we ever had of him here; his farewell before setting out to ride towards Glasgow, as the doctors, helpless otherwise, had ordered. He was very friendly, calm, and affectionate; chivalrously courteous to *her*, as I remember. "Ah, yes," looking round the room, "you are like an Eve—make every place you live in beautiful." He was not sad in manner, but was at heart, as you could notice, serious, even solemn. Darkness at hand and the weather damp, he could not loiter. I saw him mount at the door; watched till he turned the first corner, close by the rector's garden door, and had vanished from us altogether. He died at Glasgow before the end of December.'

Irving was dead, and with it closed the last chapter of Jane Welsh's early romance. Much might be said of the effect of it both on Irving and on her. The characters of neither of them escaped unscathed by the passionate love which had once existed between them. But all that is gone, and concerns the world no longer. I will add only an affectionately sorrowful letter which Carlyle wrote at the time to his mother when the news from Glasgow came.

To Mrs. Carlyle, Scotsbrig.

Chelsea: December 24, 1834.

Poor Edward Irving, as you have heard, has ended his pilgrimage. I had been expecting that issue, but not so soon; the news of his death, which Fraser the bookseller (once a hearer of his) communicated quite on a sudden, struck me deeply; and the *wae* feeling of what it has all been, and what it has all ended in, kept increasing with me for the next ten days. Oh, what a wild, weltering mass of confusion is this world! how its softest flatterings are but bewitchments, and lead men down to the gates of darkness! Nothing is clearer to me than that Irving was driven half mad, and finally killed, simply by what once seemed his enviable fortune, and by the hold it took of him; killed as certainly (only a little more slowly) as if it had been a draught of sweetened arsenic! I am very sad about him: ten years ago, when I was first here, what a rushing and running; his house never empty of idle or half-earnest, wondering people, with their carriages and equipments; and *now*, alas, it is all *gone*, marched like a deceitful vision; and all is emptiness, desertion, and his place knows him no more! He was *a good man* too; that I do heartily believe; his faults, we may hope, were abundantly expiated in *this* life, and now his memory—as that of the just ought—shall be hallowed with us. One thing with another, I have not found another such man. I shall never forget these last times I saw him; I longed much to help him, to deliver him, but could not do it. My poor first friend—my first, and best! Fraser applied to me to write a word about him; which I did, and, after much hithering and thithering, I ascertain to-day that it is at last to be printed[1] (in some tolerable neighbourhood, for we discorded about that) in his magazine. I will send you a copy of it, and another for his mother, which you may deliver her yourself. Go and see the poor old forsaken widow: it will do her good, and yourself. Tell her that her son did not live for Time only, but for Eternity too; that he has fought the good fight, as we humbly trust, and is not *dead* but sleepeth. There are few women whom I pity more than poor old Mrs. Irving at this moment: few years ago all was prosperous with her: she had sons, a cheerful household; could say, *Oh, Edward, I am proud of ye:* now 'ruin's ploughshare' has passed over her, and it is all fled.

Tenderly, beautifully, Carlyle could feel for his friend. No more touching 'funeral oration' was ever uttered over a lost companion than in the brief paper of which here he spoke; and his heart at the time was heavy for himself also. He had almost lost hope. At no past period of his life does the Journal show more despondency than in this autumn and winter. He might repeat his mother's words to himself, ' tine heart, tine a'. ' But the heart was near ' tined ' for all that.

Extracts from Journal.

Monday, September 8, 1834.—Pain was not given thee merely to be miserable under; learn from it, turn it to account.

Yesterday set out to go and see Mrs. Taylor—Jane with me. Broke down in the park; *könnte nichts mehr,* being sick and weak beyond measure; sate me down in a seat looking over the green with its groups, Jane gone to make a call in the neighbourhood; Mrs. Taylor with her husband make their appearance, walking; pale she, and passionate and sad-looking: really felt a kind of interest in her.

' French Revolution ' begun, but, alas! not in the right style, not in the style that can stand. The mind has not yet grappled

---

[1] Republished in the fourth volume of Carlyle's *Miscellanies.*

with it heartily enough : must seize it, crush the secret out of it, and make or mar.

Acknowledgments of 'Teufelsdröckh' worthless to me one and all. 'Madam,' said I the other night to poor hollow Mrs. ——, ' it is a work born in darkness, destined for oblivion, and not worth wasting a word on.'

September 10.—'French Revolution' shapeless, dark, unmanageable. Know not this day, for example, on what side to attack it ; yet *must* forward. One of the things I need most is to subdue my polemics, my ill-nature.

September 27.—Walk in the evening by Millbank and the dusty, desolate shore with Jane : gloom ; rest. One day in the little garden see a huge spider kill a fly ; see it kill a second, lift something and angrily kill *it*. Consider what a world of benevolence this is ; how many forces are at work in Nature ; how multiplex, unfathomable is she.

October 1.—This morning think of the old primitive Edinburgh scheme of *engineership ;* [1] almost meditate for a moment resuming it *yet !* It were a method of gaining bread, of getting into con tact with men, my two grand wants and prayers. In general, it may be said no man ever so wanted any practical adviser, or shadow of one ; it is utterly, from of old (and even the very appearance of it), withheld from me. Sad ; not irremediable now. My isolation, my feeling of loneliness, unlimitedness (much meant by this), what tongue shall tell ? Alone, alone ! Woes too deep —woes which cannot be written even here. Patience, unwearied endeavour !

Surprised occasionally and grieved to find myself not only so disliked—suspected—but so known. Though at Puttock I saw no audience, I had one, and often (in all Whig circles) a most writhing one. *Dommage ?* Yes and no.

Didst thou ever hitherto want bread and clothes ? No. Courage, then ! But above all things, *diligence.* And so to work.

Sunday, October 5.—Calm, smoky weather. A pale sun gets the better of the vapours towards noon, the sad sinking year. See M'Culloch and speak with him. Promise to see him again. A

---

[1] After throwing up the law, Carlyle had for a few days thought of becoming an engineer.

hempen man, but *genuine* hemp. Hunt *invites* us over pressingly for the evening. Go, and sit talking; not miserable, yet with the deepest sea of misery lying in the background. 'Remote, unfriended, solitary, low.' Courage! Do not tine *heart*. On the whole, how *much* have I to learn! Let me not think myself too old to learn it.

Meanwhile here is another blessed, still day given me. Let me work wisely therein while it lasts. Oh that I could weep and pray! Does a God hear these dumb troublous aspirations of my soul? *Credamus! ut vivamus!*

November 1.—What a long-drawn wail are these foregoing pages, which I have just read! Why add another note to it at present? In general, except when writing, I never feel myself that I am *alive*. So the last week too has been a doleful one. Complain not. Struggle, thou weakling.

November 27.—It is many days since I have written aught here; days of suffering, of darkness, despondency; great, not yet too great for me. Ill-health has much to do with it, ill-success with the book has somewhat. No prospect, no definite hope nor the slightest ray of such. Stand to thy tackle! Endure! Endeavour! It must alter, and shall; but on with this present task, at any rate. That thou hast clear before thee.

Radical meeting (Buller's) at the City of London Tavern on Friday night last. Meaning of a multitude of men : their fierce *bark* (what in Annandale we call a *gollie*) primary indispensability of *lungs*. Radical Murphy, with cylindrical high head (like a water-can), pot belly, and voice like the Great Bell of Moscow. All in earnest. Can Wellington stay in? for long, may be doubted. Peel not yet heard of.

1835.—Twelve o'clock has just struck : the last hour of 1834, the first of a new year. Bells ringing (to me dolefully). A wet wind blustering. My wife in bed, very unhappily ill of a foot which the puddle of a maid scalded three weeks ago. I, after a day of fruitless toil, reading and re-reading about that Versailles 6th of October still. It is long time since I have written anything here. The future looks too black round me, the present too doleful, unfriendly. I am too sick at heart, wearied, wasted in body, to complain, even to myself. My first friend Edward Irving is dead above three weeks ago. I am friendless here, or as good as that. My book cannot get on, though I stick to it like a *bur*. Why should I say Peace, peace, when there is no peace? May God grant me strength to do or to endure aright what is appointed me in this coming, now commencing, division of time. Let me not despair—nay, I do not in general. Enough to-night, for I am *done!* Peace be to my mother and all my loved ones that yet live. What a noisy inanity in this world.

With these words I close the story of Carlyle's apprenticeship. His training was over. He was now a master in his craft, on the eve, though he did not know it, of universal recognition as an original and extraordinary man. Henceforward his life was in his works. The outward incidents of it will be related in his wife's letters and in his own explanatory notes. My part has been to follow him from the peasant's home in which he was born and nurtured to the steps of the great position which he was afterwards to occupy; to describe his trials and his struggles, and the effect of them upon his mind and disposition. He has been substantially his own biographer. But no one, especially no one of so rugged and angular a character, sees the lights and shadows precisely as others see them. When a man of letters has exercised an influence so vast over successive generations of thinkers, the world has a right to know the minutest particulars of his life; and the sovereigns of literature can no more escape from the fierce light which beats upon a throne, than the kings and ministers who have ruled the destinies of states and empires. Carlyle had no such high estimate of his own consequence. His poor fortunes he considered to be of moment to no one but himself; but he knew that the world would demand an account of him, and with characteristic unreserve he placed his journals and his correspondence in my hands with no instructions save that I should tell the truth about him, and if shadows there were, that least of all should I conceal them.

If in this part of my duty I have erred at all, I have erred in excess, not in defect. It is the nature of men to dwell on the faults of those who stand above them. They are comforted by perceiving that the person whom they have heard so much admired was but of common clay after all. The life of no man, authentically told, will ever be found free from fault. Carlyle has been seen in these volumes fighting for thirty-nine years—fighting with poverty, with dyspepsia, with intellectual temptations, with neglect or obstruction from his fellow-mortals. Their ways were not his ways. His attitude was not different only from their attitude, but was a condemnation of it, and it was not to be expected that they would look kindly on him. His existence hitherto had been a prolonged battle ; a man does not carry himself in such conflicts so wisely and warily that he can come out of them unscathed ; and Carlyle carried scars from his wounds both on his mind and on his temper. He had stood aloof from parties ; he had fought his way *alone*. He was fierce and uncompromising. To those who saw but the outside of him he appeared scornful, imperious, and arrogant. He was stern in his judgment of others. The sins of passion he could pardon, but the sins of insincerity, or half-sincerity, he could never pardon. He would not condescend to the conventional politenesses which remove the friction between man and man. He called things by their right names, and in a dialect edged with sarcasm. Thus he was often harsh when he ought to have been merciful ; he was contemptuous where he had no right to despise ; and in his estimate of motives and actions was often unjust and mistaken. He, too, who was so severe with others had weaknesses of his own of which he was unconscious in the excess of his self-confidence. He was proud—one may say

savagely proud. It was a noble determination in him that
he would depend upon himself alone; but he would not
only accept no obligation, but he resented the offer of help
to himself or to anyone belonging to him as if it had been
an insult. He never wholly pardoned Jeffrey for having
made his brother's fortune. His temper had been ungov-
ernable from his childhood; he had the irritability of a
dyspeptic man of genius; and when the Devil, as he called
it, had possession of him, those whose comfort he ought
most to have studied were the most exposed to the storm:
he who preached so wisely ' on doing the duty which lay
nearest to us,' forgot his own instructions, and made no
adequate effort to cast the Devil out. Nay, more: there
broke upon him in his late years, like a flash of lightning
from heaven, the terrible revelation that he had sacrificed
his wife's health and happiness in his absorption in his
work; that he had been oblivious of his most obvious obligations, and had been negligent, inconsiderate, and selfish. The fault was grave and the remorse agonising.
For many years after she had left him, when we passed
the spot in our walks where she was last seen alive, he
would bare his grey head in the wind and rain—his features wrung with unavailing sorrow. Let all this be acknowledged; and let those who know themselves to be
without either these sins, or others as bad as these, freely
cast stones at Carlyle.

But there is the other side of the account. In the
weightier matters of the law Carlyle's life had been without speck or flaw. From his earliest years, in the home at
Ecclefechan, at school, at college, in every incident or recorded aspect of him, we see invariably the same purity,
the same innocence of heart, and uprightness and integrity
of action. As a child, as a boy, as a man, he had been
true in word and honest and just in deed. There is no
trace, not the slightest, of levity or folly. He sought his

friends among the worthiest of his fellow-students, and to
those friends he was from the first a special object of respect and admiration. His letters, even in early youth,
were so remarkable that they were preserved as treasures
by his correspondents. In the thousands which I have
read, either written to Carlyle or written by him, I have
found no sentence of his own which he could have wished
unwritten, or, through all those trying years of incipient
manhood, a single action alluded to by others which those
most jealous of his memory need regret to read, or his biographer need desire to conceal. Which of us would not
shiver at the thought if his own life were to be exposed to
the same dreadful ordeal, and his own letters, or the letters
of others written about him, were searched through for
the sins of his youth? These, it may be said, are but
negative virtues. But his positive qualities were scarcely
less beautiful. Nowhere is a man known better than in
his own family. No disguise is possible there; and he
whom father and mother, brother and sister love, we may
be sure has deserved to be loved.

Among the many remarkable characteristics of the Carlyle household, whether at Mainhill or Scotsbrig, was the
passionate affection which existed among them and the
special love which they all felt for 'Tom.' Well might
Jeffrey say that Carlyle would not have known poverty if
he had not been himself a giver. His own habits were
Spartan in their simplicity, and from the moment when
he began to earn his small salary as an usher at Annan,
the savings of his thrift were spent in presents to his father
and mother and in helping to educate his brother. I too
can bear witness that the same generous disposition remained with him to the end. In his later years he had
an abundant income, but he never added to his own comforts or luxuries. His name was not seen on charity lists,
but he gave away every year perhaps half what he re-

ceived. I was myself in some instances employed by him
to examine into the circumstances of persons who had applied to him for help. The stern censor was in these instances the kindest of Samaritans. It was enough if a
man or woman was miserable. He did not look too curiously into the causes of it. I was astonished at the pro-
fuseness with which he often gave to persons little worthy
of his liberality.

Nor was there even in those more trying cases where
men were prospering beyond their merits any malice or
permanent ill-will. He was constitutionally atrabilious and
scornful; but the bitterness with which he would speak
of such persons was on the surface merely. 'Poor devil,'
he would say of some successful political Philistine, 'after all, if we looked into the history of him, we should
find how it all came about.' He was always sad: often
gloomy in the extreme. Men of genius rarely take cheerful views of life. They see too clearly. Dante and Isaiah
were not probably exhilarating companions; but Carlyle,
when unpossessed and in his natural humour, was gentle,
forbearing, and generous.

If his character as a man was thus nobly upright, so he
employed his time and his talents with the same high sense
of responsibility—not to make himself great, or honoured,
or admired, but as a trust committed to him for his Maker's
purposes. 'What can you say of Carlyle,' said Mr. Ruskin
to me, 'but that he was born in the clouds and struck by
the lightning?'—'struck by the lightning'—not meant for
happiness, but for other ends; a stern fate which never,
theless in the modern world, as in the ancient, is the por
tion dealt out to some individuals on whom the heavens
have been pleased to set their mark. Gifted as he knew
himself to be with unusual abilities, he might have risen
to distinction on any one of the beaten roads of life, and
have won rank and wealth for himself. He glanced at

the Church, he glanced at the Bar, but there was something working in him like the Δαίμων of Socrates, which warned him off with an imperious admonition, and insisted on being obeyed. Men who fancy that they have a 'mission' in this world are usually intoxicated by vanity, and their ambition is in the inverse ratio of their strength to give effect to it. But in Carlyle the sense of having a mission was the growth of the actual presence in him of the necessary powers. Certain associations, certain aspects of human life and duty, had forced themselves upon him as truths of immeasurable consequence which the world was forgetting. He was a *vates*, a seer. He perceived things which others did not see, and which it was his business to force them to see. He regarded himself as being charged actually and really with a message which he was to deliver to mankind, and, like other prophets, he was 'straitened' till his work was accomplished. A Goethe could speak in verse, and charm the world into listening to him by the melody of his voice. The deep undertones of Carlyle's music could not modulate themselves under rhyme and metre. For the new matter which he had to utter he had to create a new form corresponding to it. He had no pulpit from which to preach, and through literature alone had he any access to the world which he was to address. Even 'a man of letters' must live while he writes, and Carlyle had imposed conditions upon himself which might make the very keeping himself alive impossible; for his function was sacred to him, and he had laid down as a fixed rule that he would never write merely to please, never for money, that he would never write anything save when especially moved to write by an impulse from within; above all, never to set down a sentence which he did not in his heart believe to be true, and to spare no labour till his work to the last fibre was as good as he could possibly make it.

These were rare qualities in a modern writer whose bread depended on his pen, and such as might well compensate for worse faults than spleen and hasty temper. He had not starved, but he had come within measurable distance of starvation. Nature is a sharp schoolmistress, and when she is training a man of genius for a great moral purpose, she takes care by 'the constitution of things' that he shall not escape discipline. More than once better hopes had appeared to be dawning. But the sky had again clouded, and at the time of the removal to London the prospect was all but hopeless. No man is bound to fight for ever against proved impossibilities. The 'French Revolution' was to be the last effort. If this failed Carlyle had resolved to give up the game, abandon literature, buy spade and rifle and make for the backwoods of America. 'You are not fit for that either, my fine fellow,' he had sorrowfully to say to himself. Still he meant to try. America might prove a kinder friend to him than England had been, in some form or other. Worse it could not prove.

For two years the writing of that book occupied him. The materials grew on his hands, and the first volume, for the cause mentioned in the 'Reminiscences,' had to be written a second time. All the mornings he was at his desk; in the afternoons he took his solitary walks in Hyde Park, seeing the brilliant equipages and the knights and dames of fashion prancing gaily along the Row. He did not envy them. He would not have changed existences with the brightest of these fortune's favourites if the wealth of England had been poured into the scale. But he did think that his own lot was hard, so willing was he to do anything for an honest living, yet with every door closed against him. 'Not one of you,' he said to himself as he looked at them, 'could do what I am doing, and it concerns you too, if you did but know it.'

They did not know it and they have not known it. Fifty years have passed since Carlyle was writing the 'French Revolution.' The children of fashion still canter under the elms of the Park, as their fathers and mothers were cantering then, and no sounds of danger have yet been audible to flutter the Mayfair dove-cotes. 'They call me a great man now,' Carlyle said to me a few days before he died, ' but not one believes what I have told them.' But if they did not believe the prophet, they could worship the new star which was about to rise. The Annandale peasant boy was to be the wonder of the London world. He had wrought himself into a personality which all were to be compelled to admire, and in whom a few recognised, like Goethe, the advent of a new moral force the effects of which it was impossible to predict.

INDEX.

[By Arrangement with the Author.]

The Best Biography of the Greatest of the Romans.

CÆSAR: A SKETCH.

BY

JAMES ANTHONY FROUDE, M.A.

Library Edition, 8vo, Cloth, Gilt Top, $2.50.
POPULAR EDITION (from same plates), 12mo, 75 Cents.
Uniform with Popular Edition of Froude's History
of England, and Short Studies.

There is no historical writer of our time who can rival Mr. Froude in vivid delineation of character, grace and clearness of style, and elegant and solid scholarship. In his *Life of Cæsar*, all these qualities appear in their fullest perfection, resulting in a fascinating narrative which will be read with keen delight by a multitude of readers, and will enhance, if possible, Mr. Froude's brilliant reputation.

CRITICAL NOTICES.

"The book is charmingly written, and, on the whole, wisely written. There are many admirable, really noble, passages ; there are hundreds of pages which few living men could match. * * * The political life of Cæsar is explained with singular lucidity, and with what seems to us remarkable fairness. The horrible condition of Roman society under the rule of the magnates is painted with startling power and brilliance of coloring.—*Atlantic Monthly.*

"Mr. Froude's latest work, "Cæsar," is affluent of his most distinctive traits. Nothing that he has written is more brilliant, more incisive, more interesting. * * * He combines into a compact and nervous narrative all that is known of the personal, social, political, and military life of Cæsar ; and with his sketch of Cæsar, includes other brilliant sketches of the great men, his friends or rivals, who contemporaneously with him formed the principal figures in the Roman world."—*Harper's Monthly.*

"This book is a most fascinating biography, and is by far the best account of Julius Cæsar to be found in the English language."—*London Standard.*

"It is the best biography of the greatest of the Romans we have, and it is in some respects Mr. Froude's best piece of historical writing."—*Hartford Courant.*

Mr. Froude has given the public the best of all recent books on the life, character and career of Julius Cæsar."—*Phila. Eve. Bulletin.*

. *For sale by all booksellers, or will be sent prepaid, upon receipt of price, by*

CHARLES SCRIBNER'S SONS,
743 AND 745 BROADWAY, NEW YORK.

Now in process of publication, uniform with Epochs of Modern History, *each volume in 12mo size, and complete in itself.*

Epochs of Ancient History.

A series of Books narrating the HISTORY OF GREECE AND ROME, and of their relations to other Countries at Successive Epochs. Edited by the Rev. G. W. COX, M. A., Author of the "Aryan Mythology," "A History of Greece," etc., and jointly by CHARLES SANKEY, M. A., late Scholar of Queen's College, Oxford.

Volumes already issued in the "Epochs of Ancient History." Each one volume 12mo, cloth, $1.00.

The GREEKS and the PERSIANS. By the Rev. G. W. Cox, M. A., late Scholar of Trinity College, Oxford : Joint Editor of the Series. With four colored Maps.

The EARLY ROMAN EMPIRE. From the Assassination of Julius Cæsar to the Assassination of Domitian. By the Rev. W. Wolfe Capes, M. A., Reader of Ancient History in the University of Oxford. With two colored maps.

The ATHENIAN EMPIRE from the FLIGHT of XERXES to the FALL of ATHENS. By the Rev. G. W. Cox, M. A., late Scholar of Trinity College, Oxford : Joint Editor of the Series. With five Maps.

The ROMAN TRIUMVIRATES. By the Very Rev. Charles Merivale, D. D., Dean of Ely.

EARLY ROME, to its Capture by the Gauls. By Wilhelm Ihne, Author of "History of Rome." With Map.

THE AGE OF THE ANTONINES. By the Rev. W. Wolfe Capes, M. A., Reader of Ancient History in the University at Oxford.

The GRACCHI, MARIUS, and SULLA. By A. H. Beesly. With Maps.

THE RISE OF THE MACEDONIAN EMPIRE. By A. M. Curteis, M. A. 1 vol., 16mo, with maps and plans.

TROY—Its Legend, History, and Literature, with a sketch of the Topography of the Troad. By S. G. W. Benjamin. 1 vol. 16mo. With a map.

The above 9 volumes in Roxburg Style. Sold only in sets. Price, per set, $9.00.

*** *The above books for sale by all booksellers, or will be sent, post or express charges paid, upon receipt of the price by the Publishers,*

CHARLES SCRIBNER'S SONS,

743 and 745 Broadway, New York.

"These volumes contain the ripe results of the studies of men who are authorities in their respective fields."—THE NATION.

Epochs of Modern History.

Each 1 vol. 16mo., with Outline Maps. Price per volume, in cloth, $1.00.

EACH VOLUME COMPLETE IN ITSELF AND SOLD SEPARATELY.

EDITED BY EDWARD E. MORRIS, M.A.

The ERA of the PROTESTANT REVOLUTION. By F. SEEBOHM, Author of "The Oxford Reformers—Colet, Erasmus, More."

The CRUSADES. By the Rev. G. W. Cox, M.A., Author of the "History of Greece."

The THIRTY YEARS' WAR, 1618—1648. By SAMUEL RAWSON GARDINER.

The HOUSES of LANCASTER and YORK; with the CONQUEST and LOSS of FRANCE. By JAMES GAIRDNER, of the Public Record Office.

The FRENCH REVOLUTION and FIRST EMPIRE; an Historical Sketch. By WM. O'CONNOR MORRIS, with an Appendix by Hon. ANDREW D. WHITE, Prest. of Cornell University.

The AGE OF ELIZABETH. By the Rev. M. CREIGHTON, M.A.

The PURITAN REVOLUTION. By J. LANGTON SANFORD.

The FALL of the STUARTS; and WESTERN EUROPE from 1678 to 1697 By the Rev. EDWARD HALE, M.A., Assist. Master at Eton.

The EARLY PLANTAGENETS and their relation to the HISTORY of EUROPE the foundation and growth of CONSTITUTIONAL GOVERNMENT. By the R WM. STUBBS, M.A., etc., Regius Professor of Modern History in the University Oxford.

The BEGINNING of the MIDDLE AGES; CHARLES the GREAT and ALFRED; the HISTORY of ENGLAND in its connection with that of EUROPE in the NINTH CENTURY. By the Very Rev R. W. CHURCH, M.A., Dean of St. Paul's.

The AGE of ANNE. By EDWARD E. MORRIS, M.A., Editor of the Series.

The NORMAN KINGS and the FEUDAL SYSTEM. By the Rev. A H. JOHNSON, M.A. EDWARD III. By the Rev. W. WARBURTON, M.A., late Her Majesty's Senior Inspector of Schools.

FREDERICK the GREAT and the SEVEN YEARS' WAR. By F. W. LONGMAN, of Ballic College, Oxford.

The above 13 Volumes in Roxburg Style, Leather Labels and Gilt Top. Put up in a handsome Box. Sold only in Sets. Price per Set, $13.00.

∴ The above book for sale by all booksellers, or will be sent, post or express charges paid, upon receipt of the price by the publishers,

CHARLES SCRIBNER'S SONS,

743 AND 745 BROADWAY, NEW YORK

"Two as interesting and valuable books of travel as have been published in this country." NEW YORK EXPRESS.

DR. FIELD'S TRAVELS ROUND THE WORLD.

I.
FROM THE LAKES OF KILLARNEY TO THE GOLDEN HORN.

II.
FROM EGYPT TO JAPAN.

By HENRY M. FIELD, D.D., Editor of the N. Y. Evangelist

Each 1 vol. 12mo. Cloth, gilt top, uniform in sty'e, $2.

CRITICAL NOTICES.

By George Ripley, LL.D., in the New York Tribune.

Few recent travellers combine so many qualities that are adapted to command the interest and sympathy of the public. While he indulges, to its fullest extent, the characteristic American curiosity with regard to foreign lands, insisting on seeing every object of interest with his own eyes, shrinking from no peril or difficulty in pursuit of information—climbing mountains, descending mines, exploring pyramids, with no sense of satiety or weariness, he has also made a faithful study of the highest authorities on the different subjects of his narrative, thus giving solidity and depth to his descriptions, without sacrificing their facility or grace.

From the New York Observer.

The present volume comprises by far the most novel, romantic, and interesting part of the Journey [Round the World], and the story of it is told and the scenes are painted by the hand of a master of the pen. Dr. Field is a veteran traveller; he knows well what to see, and (which is still more important to the reader) he knows well what to describe and how to do it.

By Chas. Dudley Warner, in the Hartford Courant.

It is thoroughly entertaining; the reader's interest is never allowed to flag; the author carries us forward from land to land with uncommon vivacity, enlivens the way with a good humor, a careful observation, and treats all peoples with a refreshing liberality.

From Rev. Dr. R. S. Storrs.

It is indeed a charming book—full of fresh information, picturesque description, and thoughtful studies of men, countries, and civilizations.

From Prof. Roswell D. Hitchcock, D.D.

In this second volume, Dr. Field, I think, has surpassed himself in the first, and this is saying a good deal. In both volumes the editorial instinct and habit are conspicuous. Dr. Prime has said that an editor should have six senses, the sixth being "a sense of the *interesting*." Dr. Field has this to perfection. * * *

From the New York Herald.

It would be impossible by extracts to convey an adequate idea of the variety, abundance, or picturesque freshness of these sketches of travel, without copying a great part of the book.

Rev. Wm. M. Taylor, D.D., in the Christian at Work.

Dr. Field has an eye, if we may use a photographic illustration, with a great deal of collodion in it, so that he sees very clearly. He knows also how to describe just those things in the different places visited by him which an intelligent man wants to know about.

⁎ *The above books for sale by all booksellers, or will be sent, post or express charges paid, upon receipt of the price by the publishers.*

CHARLES SCRIBNER'S SONS,
743 AND 745 BROADWAY, NEW YORK

A DELIGHTFUL BOOK.

CHARLES KINGSLEY:

HIS LETTERS

AND

MEMORIES OF HIS LIFE.

EDITED BY HIS WIFE.

WITH STEEL PORTRAIT AND ILLUSTRATIONS.

ABRIDGED EDITION.

One volume 8vo. 500 Pages. Cloth, ... $2.50.

OPINIONS OF THE PRESS.

From the Chicago Tribune.

"The warm admiration of the author, which his books excite, will be confirmed by the deeper glimpses into his heart which this volume of 'Letters and Memorials' allow."

From the N. Y. Tribune.

"It will be read with far greater interest than the lives of the impossible models of perfection that fill so large a space in English and American biography."

From the Chicago Union.

"To men and women of pure minds and right aspirations, it would be hard to suggest a more entertaining volume."

From the Boston Advertiser.

"The reader is made to feel the richness and strength of his nature from his early youth, his ardor, his intense emotions, his unselfishness, his great physical vigor, his thorough manliness, his broad, splendid usefulness."

From the London Saturday Review.

"The book discharges very completely the most essential functions of a biography. It enables us to know Mr. Kingsley thoroughly well ; to appreciate his strongest motives ; to understand what he thought about himself and his performances ; and to form a tolerably complete estimate of his work."

From the British Quarterly Review.

"Mrs. Kingsley has edited these memorials of her distinguished husband with good taste and great care. . . . The book is worthy of the subject, intensely interesting alike from the wide circle of subjects it touches, and the beautiful, gifted, humane, and sympathetic spirit which it brings so near to us."

*** *The above book for sale by all booksellers, or will be sent, post or express charges paid, upon receipt of the price by the publishers,*

CHARLES SCRIBNER'S SONS,

743 AND 745 BROADWAY, NEW YORK.

"Infinite riches in a little room." —MARLOWE.

COMPLETION OF THE FIRST

BRIC-A-BRAC SERIES.

Personal Reminiscences of Famous Poets and Novelists, Wits and Humorists, Artists, Actors, Musicians, and the like.

EDITED BY

RICHARD HENRY STODDARD.

Complete in ten volumes, square 12mo. Per vol. $1.50.

The BRIC-A-BRAC SERIES has achieved for itself a success altogether exceptional in the history of publishing in this country.

OVER SIXTY THOUSAND VOLUMES

Of the first series have been sold in eighteen months. The BRIC-A-BRAC SERIES constitutes a

COMPLETE REPOSITORY OF REMINISCENCES

Of prominent men and women of this and the last century. Characteristic anecdotes of every individual of note in art, literature, the drama, politics, or society are related, and they are told by those who know how to give point to a good story.

THE SERIES COMPRISES THE FOLLOWING TEN VOLUMES:

I. CHORLEY, PLANCHÉ, and YOUNG.
II. THACKERAY and DICKENS, with fac-simile of a letter by Thackeray.
III. MÉRIMÉE, LAMARTINE, and SAND.
IV. BARHAM, HARNESS, and HODDER.
V. THE GREVILLE MEMOIRS, with Portrait of Greville.
VI. MOORE and JERDAN, with 4 Illustrations.
VII. CORNELIA KNIGHT and THOMAS RAIKES, with 4 Illustrations.
VIII. O'KEEFFE, KELLY, and TAYLOR, with 4 Illustrations.
IX. LAMB, HAZLITT, and Others, with 4 Illustrations and fac-simile of a letter by Lamb.
X. CONSTABLE and GILLIES, with 4 Illustrations.

A sixteen-page Descriptive Catalogue of the Series, containing Specimen Illustrations, sent to any address upon application.

NOW READY:

COMPLETE SETS OF THE BRIC-A-BRAC SERIES IN THE FOLLOWING STYLES:—

1. CLOTH, IN A NEAT BOX $15.00
2. HALF VELLUM, RED EDGES, in a handsome box, of an entirely new style.. 17.50
3. HALF CALF, EXTRA, in a handsome box, of an entirely new style.... 20.00

Sent, post-paid, or express charges paid, on receipt of price by the Publishers,

SCRIBNER, ARMSTRONG, & CO.

743 & 745 Broadway, New York.

" Of more value
Than stamps in gold, or sums in sealed bags."
— SHAKESPEARE.

THE SANS SOUCI SERIES

[UNIFORM WITH THE BRIC-A-BRAC SERIES.]

**Personal Reminiscences of Famous Poets and Novelists,
Wits and Humorists, Artists, Actors, Musicians,
and the like.**

EDITED BY RICHARD HENRY STODDARD.

COMPLETE IN THREE VOLUMES.

Each neat 12mo, *Illustrated*, tastefully bound in extra cloth, crimson **and black.**
Per volume, $1.50.

I.

AN ANECDOTE BIOGRAPHY

— OF —

PERCY BYSSHE SHELLEY.

COMPILED BY RICHARD HENRY STODDARD.

With Portraits of Byron and Shelley, and facsimile of a Poem by the latter

From the NEW YORK EVENING POST.

*" Mr. Stoddard has given us a new and in some respects a unique biography
of the poet . . . an essentially fresh 'Anecdote Biography' of surpassing
interest."*

II.

Haydon's Life, Letters, and Table-Talk.

With Portraits of Wordsworth, Keats,
Haydon, and Wilkie, and facsimile
of a letter by Haydon.

*" Since the appearance of the ' Greville
Memoirs' there has been no collection of
reminiscences which compares with this in
point and interest."*—N. Y. DAILY TIMES.

III.

Men and Manners One Hundred Years Ago.

Edited by HORACE E. SCUDDER.

With Four Illustrations.

*This volume comprises extremely inter-
esting reminiscences of persons distinguished in this country during the Revolu-
tionary period.*

*These works sent, post or express charges paid, upon receipt of the price, by the
Publishers.*

CHARLES SCRIBNER'S SONS,
743 AND 745 BROADWAY, NEW YORK.

The

Letters *of* Charles Dickens.

Edited by his Sister-in-Law and his Eldest Daughter.

With several Fac-simile Letters.

Three Volumes, 12mo, cloth, each, - $1.50.

Parts of this correspondence record Dickens's experiences from day to day with the minuteness of a diary, introducing the most capital anecdotes and inimitable descriptions, and the letters have naturally aroused an interest which hardly anything else could have awakened, unless it had been a posthumous work of the great novelist. Indeed, the correspondence is actually what the editors say in their preface that they have tried to make it—"another book from Charles Dickens's own hands—a portrait of himself by himself." Altogether, the letters give such a revelation of the man as nothing else could give so well, and as might make a substitute for any biography.

CRITICAL NOTICES.

"Their literary merit is great and genuine ; they are freshly and spontaneously written in English that is clear and strong and unaffected in a high degree. The picture they give of their author is striking and singularly pleasant. They bring home to the reader the full force of his personality, in all its richness and expansiveness, its indomitable energy and splendid self-consciousness, its elasticity and resolution, the irresistible authority of its union of vigor and charm ; and they heighten the reader's opinion of him as a private man and as a man of genius."—*London Athenæum.*

"No formal portrait could be half so vivid. In this book, which was never intended to be a book, we come nearer to the man as he was, than any biographer could have brought us. . . . The letters do not show us Dickens at work, but Dickens at play, relieved from the strain of facing the public, and tossing off the impressions of the moment for the sympathetic appreciation of his own inner circle. The editors say that no man ever expressed *himself* more in his letters than Charles Dickens. No man certainly ever expressed a livelier or more considerate friendship, a purer affection, or a more exhilarating sense of the ridiculous."—*Fortnightly Review.*

"Some of the new letters published within the last week from the pen of Charles Dickens are amongst the most amusing compositions in the English language. . . . They flash Dickens on you with as much vigor as if they gave you a glimpse of him in a magic-lantern."—*London Spectator.*

"That bright sparkling style, that tenderness of heart and fund of cheery humor, that odd, keen, humorous way of observing and noting things, that appreciation of and affection for hosts of friends, which we already knew to be among his most lovable traits, are to be yet once more tasted and enjoyed in these pages."—*Literary World.*

"The attractiveness of these volumes lies in their free and natural exhibition of Mr. Dickens's mind and heart. His personality saturates them."—*Congregationalist.*

"Of three things noticeable in this correspondence, one is the prevailing cheerfulness of high spirits. . . . The other two noticeable things are the great excellence flexibility and simpleness of style from the very first, and the surprising quantity of highly entertaining epistolary writing produced by this one man."—*Boston Courier.*

** For sale by all booksellers, or sent postpaid, upon receipt of price,

CHARLES SCRIBNER'S SONS,

Nos. 743 AND 745 BROADWAY, NEW YORK.

A NEW EDITION.

Books and Reading.

BY

NOAH PORTER, LL.D., President of Yale College.

*With an appendix giving valuable directions for courses of
reading, prepared by* JAMES M. HUBBARD, *late
of the Boston Public Library.*

1 vol., crown 8vo.,   -   -   - $2.00.

It would be difficult to name any American better qualified
than President Porter to give advice upon the important
question of " What to Read and How to Read." His
acquaintance with the whole range of English literature is
most thorough and exact, and his judgments are eminently
candid and mature. A safer guide, in short, in all literary
matters, it would be impossible to find.

"The great value of the book lies not in prescribing courses of reading, but in a
discussion of principles, which lie at the foundation of all valuable systematic reading."
—*The Christian Standard.*

"Young people who wish to know what to read and how to read it, or how to pursue
a particular course of reading, cannot do better than begin with this book, which is a
practical guide to the whole domain of literature, and is full of wise suggestions for the
improvement of the mind."—*Philadelphia Bulletin.*

"President Porter himself treats of all the leading departments of literature of course
with abundant knowledge, and with what is of equal importance to him, with a very
definite and serious purpose to be of service to inexperienced readers. There is no better
or more interesting book of its kind now within their reach."—*Boston Advertiser.*

"President Noah Porter's 'Books and Reading' is far the most practical and satisfactory treatise on the subject that has been published. It not only answers the questions
'What books shall I read?' and 'How shall I read them?' but it supplies a large and
well-arranged catalogue under appropriate heads, sufficient for a large family or a small
public library."—*Boston Zion's Herald.*

*** *For sale by all booksellers, or sent, post-paid, upon receipt of
price, by*

CHARLES SCRIBNER'S SONS, PUBLISHERS,
743 AND 745 BROADWAY, NEW YORK.

AUTHORIZED AMERICAN EDITIONS.

Froude's Historical Works.

THE HISTORY OF ENGLAND,

From the Fall of Woolsey to the Death of Elizabeth.

THE COMPLETE WORK IN TWELVE VOLUMES.

By JAMES ANTHONY FROUDE, M. A.

MR. FROUDE is a pictorial historian, and his skill in description and fullness of knowledge make his work abound in scenes and passages that are almost new to the general reader. We close his pages with unfeigned regret, and we bid him good speed on his noble mission of exploring the sources of English history in one of its most remarkable periods. — *British Quarterly Review.*

THE NEW LIBRARY EDITION.

Extra cloth, gilt top, and uniform in general style with the re-issue of Mommsen's Rome and Curtius's Greece. *Complete* in 12 vols. 12mo, in a box. Sold only in sets. Price per set, $18.00.

NOTE. *The old Library, Chelsea, and Popular Editions will be discontinued. A few sets and single volumes can still be supplied.*

SHORT STUDIES ON GREAT SUBJECTS.

THE NEW LIBRARY EDITION. Three vols. 12mo. Uniform in General Style with the New Library Edition of the History of England. Per vol............ $1.50

THE ENGLISH IN IRELAND
During the Eighteenth Century.

Three vols. 12mo. New Library Edition. Per vol....... $1.50

₌ *The above books for sale by all booksellers, or will be sent, post or express charges paid, upon receipt of the price by the Publishers,*

CHARLES SCRIBNER'S SONS,
743 AND 745 BROADWAY, NEW YORK.